Rick Steves

IRELAND

2011

ISBN: 978-1-59880-664-9   US $22.95

9 781598 806649

Rick Steves'

IRELAND

Rick Steves & Pat O'Connor

2011

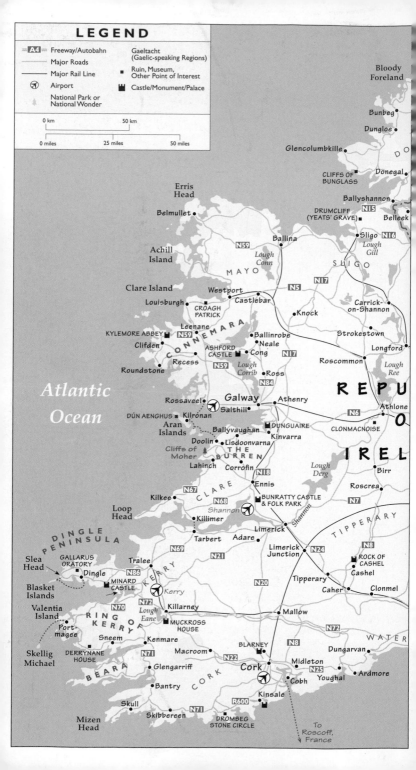

LEGEND

=**A4**= Freeway/Autobahn

Major Roads

Major Rail Line

✈ Airport

🌲 National Park or
National Wonder

■ Gaeltacht
(Gaelic-speaking Regions)

■ Ruin, Museum,
Other Point of Interest

🏰 Castle/Monument/Palace

0 km   50 km

0 miles   25 miles   50 miles

Bloody
Foreland

Bunbeg

Dungloe

Glencolumbkille

CLIFFS OF
BUNGLASS

Donegal

DO

Erris
Head

Belmullet

Ballyshannon

DRUMCLIFF
(YEATS' GRAVE)

N15

Belleek

Sligo   N16

Lough
Gill

SLIGO

Ballina

N59

Lough
Conn

MAYO

N5

N17

Carrick-
on-Shannon

Achill
Island

Clare Island

Westport

Castlebar

Knock

Strokestown

Longford

Louisburgh

CROAGH
PATRICK

Roscommon

Lough
Ree

KYLEMORE ABBEY

N59

Leenane

Ballinrobe

Neale

Clifden

C O N N E M A R A

ASHFORD
CASTLE

Cong

N17

REPU

Recess

Roundstone

N59

Lough
Corrib

Ross

N84

Athenry

N6

Athlone

O

Rossaveel

Galway

Salthill

DÚN AENGHUS

Kilrónan

Aran
Islands

Ballyvaughan

DUNGUAIRE

Kinvarra

CLONMACNOISE

IREL

Doolin

Lisdoonvarna

Cliffs of
Moher

T H E
B U R R E N

Lahinch

Corrofin

N18

Lough
Derg

Birr

Atlantic
Ocean

C L A R E

Ennis

Roscrea

Kilkee

N67

N68

BUNRATTY CASTLE
& FOLK PARK

N7

Loop
Head

Shannon

Shannon

TIPPERARY

Killimer

Limerick

D I N G L E
P E N I N S U L A

Tarbert

Adare

Limerick
Junction

N24

N8

Slea
Head

GALLARUS
ORATORY

Tralee

N69

N21

Tipperary

ROCK OF
CASHEL

Cashel

Dingle

N86

MINARD
CASTLE

K E R R Y

Kerry

N20

Caher

Clonmel

Blasket
Islands

Killarney

N72

Mallow

Valentia
Island

Port-
magee

R I N G
O F
K E R R Y

Lough
Leane

MUCKROSS
HOUSE

N72

WATER

Skellig
Michael

DERRYNANE
HOUSE

Sneem

N70

Kenmare

Macroom

N22

BLARNEY

N8

Dungarvan

B E A R A

Glengarriff

N71

Cork

Midleton

N25

Ardmore

Bantry

C O R K

✈

Youghal

Skull

Skibbereen

N71

Kinsale

Cobh

Mizen
Head

DROMBEG
STONE CIRCLE

R600

To
Roscoff,
France

SIGHTS

1. Abbey Theatre
2. Book of Kells & Trinity Old Library
3. Chester Beatty Library
4. Christ Church Cathedral
5. Dublin Castle
6. Dublin City Hall
7. Dublin Writers' Museum
8. Dublinia
9. Duke Pub (Literary Pub Crawl)
10. Garden of Remembrance
11. General Post Office
12. Gogarty's Pub (Musical Pub Crawl)
13. To Guinness Storehouse & Kilmainham Gaol
14. Ha' Penny Bridge
15. Hugh Lane Gallery
16. James Joyce Cultural Centre
17. Merrion Square
18. National Gallery
19. National Library
20. National Museum: Archaeology & History
21. To National Museum: Decorative Arts & History
22. Number 29 Georgian House
23. Old Jameson Distillery & Smithfield Village
24. St. Patrick's Cathedral
25. St. Stephen's Green

Transportation:

26. To Airport & M1 to Belfast
27. Busaras Central Bus Station
28. Connolly Station
29. To Heuston Station

LEGEND

- Pedestrian-Friendly Area
- Popular Shopping Area
- DART Commuter Rail Line
- T - Red Line LUAS Tram with stops
- T - Green Line LUAS Tram with stops
- Landmark or Point of Interest
- Tourist Information

| 0 | 250 m |
| 0 | 250 yds |

Dublin

To Croke Park Stadium & GAA Museum

To Howth

N. GREAT GEORGE'S ST.
W. RUTLAND

SUMMERHILL

SEAN MACDERMOTT LOWER

RAILWAY ST.

BUCKINGHAM

16 JAMES JOYCE CULTURAL CENTRE

GATE THEATRE

CATHAL BRUGHA ST.

GARDINER ST. LOWER

MABBOT LN.

CORPORATION ST.

FOLEY ST.

Connolly

28 CONNOLLY STATION

LOWER SHERIFF ST.

PARNELL STATUE

O'CONNELL UPPER

GRESHAM HOTEL

FATHER MATTHEW STATUE

ST. MARY'S PRO-CATHEDRAL

TALBOT ST.

MARLBOROUGH ST.

TALBOT PL.

STORE ST.

AMIENS ST.

George's Dock

To The Point

INNER DOCK

MILLENNIUM SPIRE

MOORE LN.

EARL ST.

BUSARAS CENTRAL BUS STATION 27

MEMORIAL RD.

Busaras

ST. GEORGE'S DOCK

MAYOR ST.

To O₂ Theatre & Car Ferry Terminal

GENERAL POST OFFICE 11

O'CONNELL STREET LOWER

PRINCE'S ST. NORTH

ABBEY ST. LOWER

IFSC

CUSTOM HOUSE QUAY

LARKIN STATUE

ST. MIDDLE

ABBEY ST.

Abbey

1 ABBEY THEATRE

CUSTOM HOUSE

FAMINE STATUES

NORTH WALL QUAY

O'CONNELL STATUE

EDEN QUAY

Liffey

BACHELORS WALK

O'CONNELL BRIDGE

BURGH QUAY

GEORGE'S QUAY

CITY QUAY

ASTON QUAY

D'OLIER ST.

POOLBEG ST.

TARA ST.

MOSS ST.

PRINCES ST.

TARA STREET STATION

GLOUCESTER ST.

ST. EAST

WESTMORELAND ST.

TOWNSEND ST.

LOMBARD ST. EAST

LWR SANDWITH ST.

12

FLEET ST.

ANGLESEA ST.

BAR

BANK OF IRELAND

COLLEGE

PEARSE ST.

MARKS LN.

SOUTH CUMBERLAND ST.

PEARSE STREET STATION

To Dun Laoghaire

CAMPANILE

MAIN ENTRANCE

GREEN

POST

ST. ANDREW ST.

MOLLY MALONE STATUE

2 BOOK OF KELLS

TRINITY COLLEGE

NASSAU ST.

ENTRANCE

LEINSTER ST. S.

LINCOLN PL.

FENIAN ST.

BOYNE ST.

UPPER SANDWITH ST.

CLARE ST.

GRAFTON ST.

CLARENDON ST.

DUKE ST.

9

DAWSON ST.

SOUTH FREDERICK ST.

SETANTA PL.

KILDARE ST.

NATIONAL LIBRARY 19

NATIONAL GALLERY 18

OSCAR WILDE STATUE

MERRION SQUARE NORTH

To Ballsbridge & US Embassy

ANNE ST. S.

MOLESWORTH ST.

DENZILLE LN.

ST. ANN'S

NATIONAL MUSEUM: ARCHAEOLOGY & HISTORY 20

Merrion Square 17

St. Stephen's Green

GOV'T. BLDGS.

WEST MERRION SQUARE SOUTH

MERRION SQUARE EAST

FUSILIERS' ARCH

ST. STEPHEN'S GREEN NORTH

MERRION ST.

FITZWILLIAM LN.

FITZWILLIAM ST.

YEATS STATUE

St. Stephen's Green

FAMINE VICTIMS' MEMORIAL

LOWER BAGGOT ST.

22 #29 GEORGIAN HOUSE

25

EAST

SOUTH

To National Concert Hall

To Dun Laoghaire & Wicklow Mountains

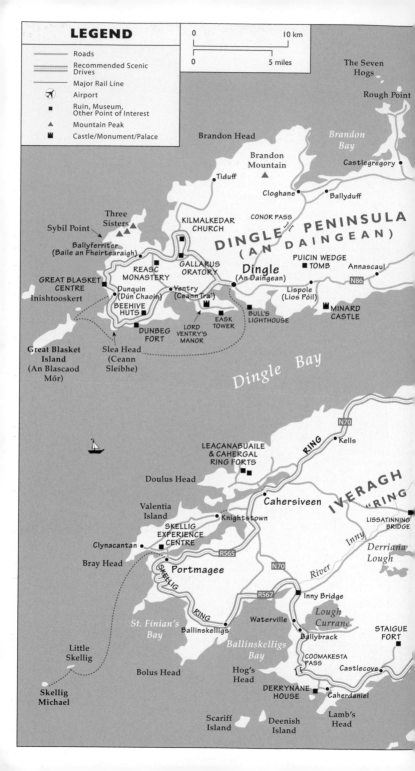

LEGEND

Roads	
Recommended Scenic Drives	
Major Rail Line	
✈	Airport
■	Ruin, Museum, Other Point of Interest
▲	Mountain Peak
♜	Castle/Monument/Palace

0   10 km
0   5 miles

The Seven Hogs

Rough Point

Brandon Head

Brandon Bay

Brandon Mountain ▲

Castlegregory

Tiduff

Cloghane

Ballyduff

CONOR PASS

DINGLE PENINSULA (AN DAINGEAN)

Three Sisters

Sybil Point

Ballyferriter (Baile an Fheirtearaigh)

KILMALKEDAR CHURCH

GALLARUS ORATORY

Dingle (An Daingean)

PUICIN WEDGE TOMB

Annascaul

N86

REASC MONASTERY

Ventry (Ceann Trá)

Lispole (Lios Póil)

GREAT BLASKET CENTRE

Inishtooskert

Dunquin (Dún Chaoin)

BEEHIVE HUTS

BULL'S LIGHTHOUSE

MINARD CASTLE

DUNBEG FORT

LORD VENTRY'S MANOR

EASK TOWER

Great Blasket Island (An Blascaod Mór)

Slea Head (Ceann Sleibhe)

Dingle Bay

N70

RING

Kells

LEACANABUAILE & CAHERGAL RING FORTS

IVERAGH

"RING"

Doulus Head

Cahersiveen

LISSATINNING BRIDGE

Valentia Island

Knightstown

Inny

Derriana Lough

SKELLIG EXPERIENCE CENTRE

Clynacantan

R565

N70

River

Bray Head

SKELLIG

Portmagee

R567

Inny Bridge

RING

Lough Currane

STAIGUE FORT

Little Skellig

St. Finian's Bay

Ballinskelligs

Waterville

Bolus Head

Ballinskelligs Bay

Ballybrack

COOMAKESTA PASS

Castlecove

Hog's Head

DERRYNANE HOUSE

Caherdaniel

Skellig Michael

Scariff Island

Deenish Island

Lamb's Head

Dingle & "Ring of Kerry" Peninsulas

CONTENTS

Ireland

You probably won't find the proverbial pot of gold in Ireland, but you will find plenty of treasure, starting with the engaging and feisty Irish people.

Belly up to the bar in a neighborhood pub and engage a local in conversation. Want to really get to know the Irish? Ask for directions. It's almost always a rich experience, and a fast way to connect with locals. Nearby friends often chime in with additional tidbits that may or may not be useful, and soon it's a communal chitchat session.

That legendary Irish "gift of gab" has its roots in the ancient Celtic culture. With no written language, the Celts passed their history, laws, and folklore verbally from generation to generation. Even today, most transactions come with an ample side-helping of friendly banter. As an Irishman once joked, "How can I know what I think until I hear what I say?"

The Irish love their proverbs and revere their past. According to an old Irish adage, "When God made time, he made a lot of it." Irish history stretches back thousands of years, yet it is as close as the mist-shrouded ruins around the next bend of a country road. Ireland is dusted with undisturbed prehistoric stone circles, burial mounds, standing stones, and table-like dolmens...some older than the pyramids, and all speckled with moss. While much of Europe has buried older cultures under new, Ireland still reveals its cultural bedrock, dating back to the time when our ancestors finally stopped hunting and gathering and began to build to last. It's a place to connect with your roots, even if you're not Irish.

Though a relatively small island, Ireland has had a disproportionately large impact on the rest of the world. Geographically isolated in the damp attic of Dark Age Europe, Christian Irish monks tended the flickering flame of literacy, then bravely reintroduced it to the barbaric Continent. Ireland later turned out some of modern literature's greatest authors. In the 1800s, great waves of Irish

fled famine and colonial oppression, seeking new opportunities abroad and making their mark in the US, Canada, and Australia. And although peace now prevails in Northern Ireland, its conflict long held the world's attention, with its volatile mix of religion and politics.

About the size of the state of Maine, the island of Ireland has a population roughly equal to that of Detroit or Boston.

Politically, the Irish people are split between the Republic of Ireland to the south (with 4.3 million people and four-fifths of the land) and Northern Ireland (with 1.7 million people). Northern Ireland is a country of the United

Kingdom—like Scotland or Wales—while the Republic is an independent nation with its own seat at the UN...stuck alphabetically between Iraq and Israel.

The island is further quartered into four provinces (Leinster, Munster, Connaught, and Ulster) and 32 counties (26 in the Republic and 6 in the North), each with its own identity and regional pride.

This 300-mile-long, saucer-shaped island, ringed with some of Europe's most scenic coastal cliffs, is only 150 miles across at its widest point—no matter where you go in Ireland, you're never more than 75 miles from the sea. Despite being as far north as Newfoundland, Ireland has a mild maritime climate, thanks to the Gulf Stream—

snowfall is rare and temporary here. Rainfall, on the other hand, ranges from over 100 inches a year in soggy, boggy Connemara to about 30 inches a year in Dublin. Any time of year, bring rain gear. As Ireland's own Oscar Wilde once quipped, "There is no bad weather...only inappropriate clothing."

Republic of Ireland

Forget everything you learned from ads for Lucky Charms cereal or Irish Spring soap, and immerse yourself in authentic Ireland.

Passionate, poetic, and pugnacious...the Irish have confounded others throughout time. Queen Elizabeth I, as tough a British monarch as has ever graced the throne, once famously hissed in frustration that the Irish "were all Blarney" as she negotiated with the highly evasive Irish lord of Blarney Castle. An exasperated Sigmund Freud said, "The Irish are the only race whose insanities can not be cured by psychoanalysis." And the Irish inspired the English poet G. K. Chesterton to write:

The great Gaels of Ireland
The lord hath made them mad
For all their wars are merry
And all their songs are sad.

The Irish seem born with a love of music. At social gatherings, everyone's ready to sing his or her "party piece." Performances are judged less by skill than by uninhibited sincerity or showmanship. Nearly every Irish household has some kind of musical instrument on a shelf or in a closet. And live music is a weekly (if not nightly) draw at most town pubs worth their salt. Pub music ranges from traditional instrumentals (jigs and reels) to ballads (songs of tragic love lost or heroic deeds done) to contemporary sing-along strummers. It's worth staying until the wee hours for the magical moment when a rare *shan nos* (Gaelic for "old style") lament is sung to a hushed and attentive pub crowd.

Part of the fun of traveling in Ireland is getting an ear for how locals express themselves in English (sort of)—from the surprised distant relative who is "gobsmacked" (astounded) by your appearance, to the businessman in the pub who complains that the weak economy is utterly "banjaxed" (messed up).

You're most likely to hear the Irish Gaelic language (similar to but different from Scottish Gaelic, and—more distantly—Welsh) spoken in the Gaeltacht, the government-subsidized cultural preserve found mostly in far western coastal regions. But less than 5 percent of the Irish are fluent in Gaelic, and school kids—who must pass rigorous exams to graduate—agonize over its complex grammar.

The Republic of Ireland tilts toward the US—both geographically and economically. Every Irish family seems to have a brother, niece, cousin, or uncle in America. About 50 million people claim Irish descent in North America alone. Irish immigrants brought with them to the US the first political organization for the downtrodden: the "green machine" grassroots voting blocks that came to dominate big-city politics in Boston, New York, and Chicago. To cozy up to these valuable votes, every politician wanted to be seen marching in the parade on St. Patrick's Day. Today, St. Patrick's Day is the most widely celebrated national feast day in the English-speaking world, and a particularly raucous four-day festival in Dublin.

During the "Celtic Tiger" boom years (1995-2007), American corporations saw big advantages in locating here, making Ireland an economic beachhead on European turf. Ireland's "Silicon Bog" is home to such big names as IBM, Intel, Microsoft, Apple, and Google. Ireland's recent economic success (a bit tarnished now

due to the global recession) is the model that new Eastern European EU nations hope to emulate. The Irish are also big pharmaceutical producers: More Viagra is made in Ireland than in any other country...though the proudly virile Irish males claim it's all for export.

Other famous exports from the Republic of Ireland include rock and contemporary music (U2, Thin Lizzy, the Corrs, Sinéad O'Connor, Enya, The Swell Season—Glen Hansard and Markéta Irglová), traditional Irish music (the Chieftains, Dubliners), opera (the Irish tenors and John McCormack), dance (Riverdance), trivia *(Guinness Book of World Records)*, crystal (Waterford), beer (Guinness), festivals (Halloween has Celtic roots), maritime disasters (*Titanic* and *Lusitania*), British military heroes (the Duke of Wellington), authors (Jonathan Swift, W. B. Yeats, James Joyce, George Bernard Shaw, Samuel Beckett, Oscar Wilde, and Frank McCourt), and actors (Colin Farrell, Richard Harris, Barry Fitzgerald, Gabriel Byrne, and Maureen O'Hara).

Until recently Ireland was one of the most ethnically homogenous nations on earth, but the Celtic Tiger economy changed all that, attracting thousands of Eastern Europeans (mostly Poles), Africans (mostly Nigerians), and South Americans (mostly Brazilians). The 2006 census found that 10 percent of Ireland's population had been born elsewhere.

That cultural exchange may have something to do with Ireland's appealing cuisine. At one time known only for its poor imitation of bad British food, today's Irish cuisine has gone global. Expatriate chefs have come home with newly refined tastes, and immigrants have added a world of new flavors. Modern Irish cuisine is skillfully prepared with fresh local ingredients. Irish beef, lamb, and dairy products are among the EU's best. And there's a wealth of trout and salmon streams and a rich ocean of fish and shellfish choices right offshore. While fish and potatoes remain staples, potatoes are often replaced with rice or pasta in many dishes.

Travelers on a budget will invariably encounter the Holy Trinity of pub grub: Irish stew, chicken curry, and fish-and-chips. Popular beer choices are Guinness (a dark porter), Smithwicks (a reddish ale), and Harp (a golden lager). The most common spirit is triple-distilled Irish whiskey.

Sports in the Republic are dominated by the Gaelic Athletic Association (GAA), which operates Irish hurling and football (not to be confused with soccer) leagues. Each county fields a team of skilled amateur players. The weekend sports heroes of each county are not professional players, but otherwise regular guys during the workweek—teachers, truck drivers, bakers, and the like. Horse racing and dog racing appeal to those enjoying a wager. And it's hard to go 20 miles in Ireland without running into a golf course.

Most Irish claim to be Catholic, and shrines to the Virgin

Mary still grace rural roadsides. But church attendance has decreased dramatically over the past 25 years, due in part to child-abuse scandals at parochial schools. If not for the influx of newly arriving devout Catholic Poles, attendance would be even lower. Yet the shamrock—used by St. Patrick to explain the concept of the Holy Trinity—remains the most recognizable symbol of Ireland. And the resilient Irish people maintain an unsinkable and optimistic belief in the future.

Northern Ireland

Northern Ireland is an underrated and often overlooked region that usually surprises visitors with its friendliness.

An interesting hybrid of Irish and Scottish cultures, Northern Ireland is only 17 miles from Scotland at its closest point. The accents you'll hear in the North are distinctly different from their Republican counterparts.

Northern Ireland is part of the United Kingdom and occupies six of the nine counties of the ancient Irish province of Ulster. It's small enough to have one phone book for the entire province (about the same population as Phoenix). Its coast boasts the alligator-skin volcanic geology of the Giant's Causeway and the lush Glens of Antrim, while its interior is dominated by rolling hills of pastoral serenity and Lough Neagh, the UK's biggest lake.

The people of the North generally fall into two categories: those who feel they're British (Unionists) and those who feel they're Irish (Nationalists). Those born in the North can choose which of the two passports they want. The Troubles—the decades-long conflict between Unionists and Nationalists—were always more about nationality than religion.

Thanks to those who have actively sought peace, the ugly ruptures of the past are healing. Both paramilitary camps have set aside their arms, and Northern Ireland is now statistically the second-safest place in the world (after Japan).

The industrious people of Northern Ireland have a legendary work ethic. When they emigrated to the US, they became known as the

Scotch-Irish and played a crucial role in our nation's founding. They were signers of our Declaration of Independence, a dozen of our presidents, and the ancestors of Davy Crockett and Mark Twain. They have a proclivity for making things

that go. They've produced far-reaching inventions like Dunlop's first inflatable tire. The Shorts aircraft factory (in Belfast) built the Wright Brothers' first six aircraft for commercial sale and the world's first vertical take-off jet. The *Titanic* was the only flop of Northern Ireland's otherwise successful shipbuilding industry. The once-futuristic DeLorean sports car was made in Belfast.

Notable people from Northern Ireland include musicians Van Morrison and James Galway, and actors Liam Neeson and Kenneth Branagh. The North also produced Christian intellectual and writer C. S. Lewis, Victorian physicist Lord Kelvin, and soccer-star playboy George Best—who once famously remarked, "I spent most of my money on liquor and women...and the rest I wasted."

The Northern Irish have a good sense of humor and a long memory. Commercial pilots joke to their arriving passengers to set their watches to local time: 1690 (the date of the famous Battle of the Boyne).

About half of the people in Northern Ireland attend church weekly—significantly more than in the Republic (30 percent) or the rest of the UK (15 percent). Only in Northern Ireland can a union between a Christian man and woman of the same ethnicity and nationality be considered a "mixed marriage."

Like in the Republic, sports are big in the North. In addition to football and hurling, you'll also find some sports up North that are rare in the Republic—such as motorcycle racing and cricket. With close ties to Scotland, many Northern Irish fans follow the exploits of the soccer teams from Glasgow—but which team you root for betrays which side of the tracks you come from. Those who cheer for Glasgow Celtic are likely Nationalist Catholic; those waving banners for the Glasgow Rangers are likely Unionist Protestant. Luckily, sports with no sectarian history are now being introduced, such as the Belfast Giants ice hockey team—a hit with both communities.

Northern Ireland has inextricable ties with the Republic. The town of Armagh, in central Northern Ireland, is the seat of both the Protestant and Catholic Archbishops of all Ireland (Republic and North). People from both countries cross the border on a daily basis to shop; there are no crossing restrictions along the 225-mile border. Dublin businessmen from the Republic have invested large sums in the rejuvenation of Belfast's once-derelict Titanic Quarter in the North. And vacationers from the North often head over to the Republic's County Donegal for midsummer holidays. The president of the Republic, Mary McAleese, was born in Belfast. The fact remains, however, that more citizens of the Republic have been to London than have visited the northern end of their own island.

No matter which side of the border you visit, today's Ireland is cosmopolitan, vibrant, business-savvy, and impressively globalized. The caricatures of tweed-clad bogtrotters and AK-47-armed terrorists have faded. But the seductive scenery and culture as old as the stones remain. The Irish people have a worldwide reputation as talkative, athletic, musical, moody romantics with a quick laugh and a ready smile. Come join them.

INTRODUCTION

Flung onto the foggy fringe of the Atlantic pond like a mossy millstone, Ireland drips with mystery, drawing you in for a closer look and then surprising you. An old farmer cuts turf from the bog, while his son staffs the tech helpline for an international software firm. Buy them both a pint in a pub that's whirling with playful conversation and exhilarating traditional music. Pious, earthy, witty, brooding, proud, and unpretentious, Irish culture is an intoxicating potion to sip or slurp—as the mood strikes you.

This book breaks Ireland into its best big-city, small-town, and rural destinations. It gives you all the information and opinions necessary to wring the maximum value out of your limited time and money in each of these locations. Experiencing Irish culture, people, and natural wonders economically and hassle-free has been my goal for three decades of traveling, tour guiding, and travel writing. With this new edition, I pass on to you the lessons I've learned, updated for your trip in 2011.

The destinations covered in this book are balanced to include the most exciting big cities and great-to-be-alive-in small towns. Note that this book covers the highlights of the entire island, including Northern Ireland. While you'll find the predictable biggies—such as the Book of Kells, the Newgrange tomb (at Brú na Bóinne), and the Cliffs of Moher—I've also mixed in a healthy dose of Back Door intimacy (rope-bridge hikes, holy wells, and pubs with traditional Irish music). This book is selective. On a short trip, visiting both the monastic ruins of Glendalough and Clonmacnoise is redundant; I cover only the best—Glendalough. There are plenty of great manor-house gardens; again, I recommend just the top one—the Gardens of Powerscourt.

The best is, of course, only my opinion. But after spending more than half of my adult life exploring and researching Europe,

Map Legend

⅛ View Point	✈ Airport		) (	Tunnel
↑ Entry Arrow	ⓣ Taxi Stand		———	Pedestrian Zone
⊖ Tourist Info	⊤ Tram Stop		-------	Railway
WC Restroom	ⓑ Bus Stop		....	Ferry/Boat Route
♜ Castle	ⓟ Parking		⊢——⊣	Tram
⌂ Church	)(Mtn. Pass		�	Stairs
▪ Statue/Point of Interest	⬚ Park		- - - - -	Walk/Tour Route
			-----------	Trail

Use this legend to help you navigate the maps in this book.

I've developed a sixth sense for what touches the traveler's imagination. The places featured in this book will give anyone the "gift of gab."

About This Book

Rick Steves' Ireland 2011 is a personal tour guide in your pocket. Better yet, it's actually two tour guides in your pocket: The co-author of this guidebook is Pat O'Connor. As you can tell from the lad's name, Pat has long had a travel passion for the Emerald Isle. He's the Ireland specialist and senior Ireland tour guide at my company, Rick Steves' Europe Through the Back Door. Together, Pat and I keep this book up-to-date and accurate (though for simplicity, from this point "we" will shed our respective egos and become "I").

This book is organized by destination. Each of these destinations is a mini-vacation on its own, filled with exciting sights, strollable towns, homey affordable places to stay, and memorable places to eat. In the following chapters, you'll find these sections:

Planning Your Time suggests a schedule, with thoughts on how best to use your limited time.

Orientation includes specifics on public transportation, helpful hints, local tour options, easy-to-read maps, and tourist information.

Sights describes the top attractions and includes their cost and hours.

Self-Guided Walks take you through interesting neighborhoods, with a personal tour guide in hand.

Sleeping describes my favorite hotels, from good-value deals

Key to This Book

Updates

This book is updated every year, but things change. For the latest, visit www.ricksteves.com/update, and for a valuable list of reports and experiences—good and bad—from fellow travelers, check www.ricksteves.com/feedback.

Abbreviations and Times

I use the following symbols and abbreviations in this book:

Sights are rated:

▲▲▲	**Don't miss**
▲▲	**Try hard to see**
▲	**Worthwhile if you can make it**
No rating	**Worth knowing about**

Tourist information offices are abbreviated as **TI,** and bathrooms are **WC**s. To categorize accommodations, I use a **Sleep Code** (described on page 24).

Like Europe, this book uses the **24-hour clock.** It's the same through 12:00 noon, then keep going: 13:00, 14:00, and so on. For anything over 12, subtract 12 and add p.m. (14:00 is 2:00 p.m.).

When giving **opening times,** I include both peak season and off-season hours if they differ. So, if a museum is listed as "May-Oct daily 9:00-16:00," it should be open from 9 a.m. until 4 p.m. from the first day of May until the last day of October (but expect exceptions).

For **transit** or **tour departures,** I first list the frequency, then the duration. So, a train connection listed as "2/hour, 1.5 hours" departs twice each hour, and the journey lasts an hour and a half.

to cushy splurges.

Eating serves up a range of options, from inexpensive pubs to fancy restaurants.

Connections outlines your options for traveling to destinations by train, bus, and plane, plus route tips for drivers.

Ireland: Past and Present gives you a quick overview of Irish history, a look at contemporary Ireland, a taste of the Irish language, and an Irish-Yankee vocabulary list.

The **appendix** is a traveler's tool kit, with telephone tips, useful phone numbers, transportation basics (on trains, buses, car rentals, driving, and flights), recommended books and films, a festival list, climate chart, handy packing checklist, and a hotel reservation form.

Browse through this book and select your favorite sights. Then have a great trip! Traveling like a temporary local, you'll get the absolute most out of every mile, minute, and dollar. I'm happy that you'll be visiting the places I know and love, and meeting my favorite Irish people.

Planning

This section will help you get started on planning your trip—with advice on trip costs, when to go, and what you should know before you take off.

Travel Smart

Your trip to Ireland is like a complex play—easier to follow and really appreciate on a second viewing. While no one does the same trip twice to gain that advantage, reading this book in its entirety before your trip accomplishes much the same thing.

Design an itinerary that enables you to visit sights at the best possible times. Note holidays, specifics on sights, and days when sights are closed. If you're using public transportation, read up on the tips for trains and buses (see pages 446 and 451 in the appendix). If you're renting a car, study my driving tips and the examples of road signs (see page 452).

Mix intense and relaxed periods in your itinerary. To maximize rootedness, minimize one-night stands. It's worth a long drive after dinner to be settled into a town for two nights. B&Bs are also more likely to give a good price to someone staying more than one night. Every trip (and every traveler) needs at least a few slack days (for picnics, laundry, people-watching, and so on). Pace yourself. Assume you will return.

Reread this book as you travel, and visit local TIs. Upon arrival in a new town, lay the groundwork for a smooth departure; write down (or print out from an online source) the schedule for the train or bus you'll take when you depart. Drivers can study the best driving route to their next destination.

Get online at Internet cafés or at your hotel, and buy a phone card or carry a mobile phone: You can get tourist information, learn the latest on sights (special events, English tour schedules, etc.), book tickets and tours, make reservations, reconfirm hotels, research transportation connections, check weather, and keep in touch with your loved ones.

Connect with the culture. Set up your own quest for the best pub, traditional music, ruined castle, or ring fort. Be open to unexpected experiences. Slow down to appreciate the sincerity of your Irish hosts. Ask questions—most locals are eager to point you in their idea of the right direction. Keep a notepad in your pocket for organizing your thoughts. Wear your money belt, and figure out how to estimate prices in dollars. Those who expect to travel smart, do.

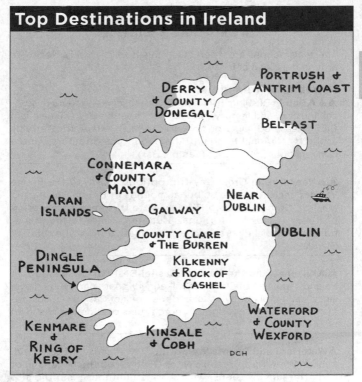

Top Destinations in Ireland

PORTRUSH &
ANTRIM COAST

DERRY
& COUNTY
DONEGAL

BELFAST

CONNEMARA
& COUNTY
MAYO

NEAR
DUBLIN

ARAN
ISLANDS

GALWAY

DUBLIN

COUNTY CLARE
& THE BURREN

DINGLE
PENINSULA

KILKENNY
& ROCK OF
CASHEL

KENMARE
&
RING OF
KERRY

KINSALE
& COBH

WATERFORD
& COUNTY
WEXFORD

DCH

Trip Costs

Five components make up your total trip cost: airfare, surface transportation, room and board, sightseeing and entertainment, and shopping and miscellany.

Airfare: A basic round-trip flight from the US to Dublin costs $900 to $1,300—including taxes and fuel charges—depending on what city you fly from and when (cheaper in winter). If your travels take you beyond Ireland, consider saving time and money in Europe by flying "open jaw" (into one city and out of another; for example, into Dublin and out of Paris).

Surface Transportation: For a three-week whirlwind trip of all my recommended Irish destinations, allow $300 per person for public transportation (trains and buses), or $900 per person (based on two people sharing) for a three-week car rental, parking, gas, and insurance. Car rentals are cheapest when arranged from the US. Because Ireland's train system has gaps, you'll likely save money by simply buying train and bus tickets as you go, rather than buying a railpass. For more on public transportation and car rental, see "Transportation" in the appendix.

Room and Board: You can thrive in Ireland on $125 a day

Ireland at a Glance

These attractions are listed (as in this book) roughly clockwise around the island of Ireland.

Republic of Ireland

▲▲▲Dublin Bustling Irish capital, with fascinating tours (historical, musical, and literary), passionate rebel history (Kilmainham Gaol), treasured Dark Age gospels (Book of Kells), intricate Celtic artifacts (National Museum: Archaeology and History), and a rambunctious pub district (Temple Bar).

▲▲Near Dublin Great day-trip options: North to the Boyne Valley's ancient pre-Celtic burial mounds of Brú na Bóinne and majestic Norman castle of Trim, west to the green horse-racing pastures of the Irish National Stud, and south to the graceful Gardens of Powerscourt and evocative monastic ruins of Glendalough.

▲▲Kilkenny and the Rock of Cashel Best two destinations in Ireland's interior: the town of Kilkenny with its narrow medieval lanes, cathedrals, and castle; and the Rock of Cashel with its dramatic hilltop hodgepodge of church ruins overlooking the Plain of Tipperary.

▲Waterford and County Wexford Gritty historic port town with famous Waterford Crystal Visitor Centre, and the hinterland of early Norman invasions, with a huge lighthouse and the JFK ancestral farm.

▲▲Kinsale and Cobh County Cork's two quaint harbor towns: Gourmet capital Kinsale guarded by squat Charles Fort, and emigration hub Cobh—the *Titanic's* last stop.

▲▲Kenmare and the Ring of Kerry Colorful, tidy town and ideal base for side-stepping the throngs flocking to drive Ireland's most-famous scenic loop route.

▲▲▲Dingle Peninsula My favorite fishing village (a traditional Irish-music pub paradise), which serves as a launchpad for the gorgeous Slea Head loop drive (or bike ride), featuring a wealth of Celtic and early Christian sites.

▲▲**County Clare and the Burren** Ireland's rugged western fringe, with the take-your-breath-away Cliffs of Moher, stone landscape of the Burren, cozy trad music crossroads of Doolin, and handy Shannon Airport access from friendly Ennis.

▲**Galway** Energetic university city with thriving pedestrian street scene, great people-watching pubs, and the west coast's best base from which to reach the Burren, Aran Islands, and Connemara.

▲▲▲**Aran Islands** Three windswept, treeless limestone islands in the Atlantic, laced with a maze of angular rock walls, crowned by Iron Age ring forts, and inhabited by sparse villages of hardy fisher-folk.

▲▲**Connemara and County Mayo** Lushly green and hilly Irish outback of cottages, lakes, and holy peaks, dotted with photogenic settlements such as Cong, Kylemore Abbey, and leafy, riverside Westport.

Northern Ireland
▲**Belfast** No-nonsense industrial revolution metropolis, with stirring sectarian political murals, grandly domed City Hall, sprawling Ulster Folk and Transport Museum, and the charming nearby Victorian seaside retreat of Bangor.

▲▲**Portrush and the Antrim Coast** Unpretentious beach resort of arcades and amusement park rides, a stone's throw from the geologic wonderland of the Giant's Causeway, dramatic cliff-edge ruins of Dunluce Castle, and exhilarating Carrick-a-Rede Rope Bridge.

▲**Derry and County Donegal** Seventeenth-century English settlement ringed by stout town walls—infamous as the powder keg that ignited Ireland's tragic modern "Troubles"—with an insightful city history museum and access to the rugged beauty of Donegal.

per person for room and board (allow less for villages and more for Dublin). A $125-per-day budget allows an average of $20 for lunch, $30 for dinner, $5 for snacks or a Guinness, and $70 for lodging (based on two people splitting a $140 double room that includes breakfast). That's doable, particularly outside Dublin, and it's easy for many travelers to come in under budget. Students and tightwads eat and sleep for $60 a day ($30 for a bed in a hostel, $30 a day for meals—mostly picnics—and snacks).

Sightseeing and Entertainment: In cities, figure about $10-15 per major sight (e.g., the Book of Kells at Dublin's Trinity College-$14), $5 for minor ones (climbing church towers), $15-20 for guided walks, $40-45 for day-trip bus tours, and up to $80 for splurge experiences (such as the Dunguaire Castle medieval banquet or a flight to the Aran Islands).

An overall average of $25 a day for sightseeing and entertainment works for most people. Don't skimp here. After all, this category is the driving force behind your trip—you came to sightsee, enjoy, and experience Ireland. Two sightseeing passes—the Heritage Card and the Heritage Ireland Touring Guide—can help you economize and simplify your sightseeing (see "Sightseeing Passes," page 20).

Shopping and Miscellany: Figure roughly $2 per postcard, tea, or ice cream cone, and $5 per pint of beer. Shopping can vary in cost from nearly nothing to a small fortune. Good budget travelers find that this category has little to do with assembling a trip full of lifelong and wonderful memories.

Sightseeing Priorities

Depending on the length of your trip, here are my recommended priorities:

3 days:	Dublin
5 days, add:	Dingle Peninsula
7 days, add:	Galway, a day in Belfast
9 days, add:	County Clare/Burren
11 days, add:	Northern Ireland's Antrim Coast
15 days, add:	Aran Islands, Wicklow Mountains, Kilkenny
19 days, add:	Kinsale, Waterford, Valley of the Boyne
23 days, add:	Ring of Kerry, Connemara, Derry, Donegal

(This includes virtually everything on the "Ireland's Best Three-Week Trip by Car" map and itinerary on page 10.)

When to Go

July and August are peak season—my favorite time—with long days, the best weather, and the busiest schedule of tourist fun. Summer crowds don't go up as dramatically in Ireland as they do in much of Europe. Still, travel during "shoulder season" (May,

Major Holidays and Weekends

Popular places are even busier on weekends, especially sunny weekends, which are sufficient cause for an impromptu holiday in this soggy corner of Europe. Three-day weekends can make towns, trains, buses, roads, and hotels even more crowded. Book your accommodations well in advance if you'll be traveling during busy times.

In 2011, expect crowds during these holiday periods: New Year's Day; St. Patrick's Day (March 17, celebrated March 12-17 in Dublin); Good Friday through Easter Monday (April 22-25); Christmas; and December 26. In addition, Ireland recognizes these UK and Ireland-only Bank Holiday Mondays, which close banks and bring crowds for the long weekend: May 2 and 30, June 6, August 1 and 29, and October 31. In Belfast in Northern Ireland, some businesses close for the week leading up to the controversial July 12th Orangemen marches (see page 324).

Reserve in advance for Dublin for any weekend, for Galway during its many peak-season events (listed on page 278), and for Dingle throughout July and August. For more information, check the list of holidays and festivals near the end of the appendix.

early June, Sept, and early Oct) is easier and a bit less expensive. Shoulder-season travelers get minimal crowds, decent weather, the full range of sights and tourist fun spots, and the ability to grab a room almost whenever and wherever they like—often at a flexible price. Winter travelers find absolutely no crowds and soft room prices, but shorter sightseeing hours. Some attractions are open only on weekends or are closed entirely in the winter (Nov-Feb). The weather can be cold and dreary, and nightfall draws the shades on sightseeing well before dinnertime. While Ireland's rural charm falls with the leaves, city sightseeing is fine in the winter.

Plan for rain no matter when you go. Just keep traveling and take full advantage of "bright spells." The weather can change several times in a day, but rarely is it extreme. Bring a jacket and dress in layers. Daily averages throughout the year range between 42°F and 70°F. Temperatures below 32°F cause headlines, and days that break 80°F—while increasing in recent years—are still rare. For more information, see the climate chart in the appendix.

While sunshine may be rare, summer days are very long. Dublin is as far north as Edmonton, Canada, and Portrush is as far north as Ketchikan on the Alaskan panhandle. The mid-summer sun is up from 4:30 until 22:30. It's not uncommon to have a gray day, eat dinner, and enjoy hours of sunshine afterward.

Ireland's Best Three-Week Trip by Car

Day	Plan	Sleep in
1	Fly into Dublin, rent car, Glendalough	Kilkenny
2	Kilkenny with side-trip to Cashel	Kilkenny
3	Waterford	Waterford
4	Explore Wexford	Waterford
5	Cobh	Kinsale
6	Kinsale	Kinsale
7	Muckross House and Farms	Kenmare
8	Ring of Kerry	Dingle
9	Dingle Peninsula loop	Dingle
10	Blaskets, Dingle town (laundry and rest)	Dingle
11	Cliffs of Moher, Burren, Dunguaire Castle banquet	Galway
12	Galway	Galway
13	Aran Islands	Aran Islands
14	Tour Connemara and County Mayo	Westport
15	Drive to Northern Ireland	Derry
16	Side-trip to Donegal	Derry
17	Explore Derry, then drive to Portrush	Portrush
18	Explore Antrim Coast	Portrush
19	Belfast	Belfast
20	Drive to Valley of the Boyne sights, return car	Dublin
21	Dublin	Dublin
22	Dublin	Dublin
23	Fly home	

While this three-week itinerary (stretched to 23 days by using weekends at each end) is aggressive and designed to be done by car, most of it can be done by train and bus. For three weeks without a car, spend your first three nights in Dublin, using buses and taxis. Cut back on the recommended sights with the most frustrating public transportation (Ring of Kerry, the Burren, Valley of the Boyne, Connemara, and Counties Mayo, Wexford,

Know Before You Go

Your trip is more likely to go smoothly if you plan ahead. Check this list of things to arrange while you're still at home.

You need a **passport**—but no visa or shots—to travel in Ireland. You may be denied entry into certain European countries if your passport is due to expire within three to six months of your ticketed date of return. Get it renewed if you'll be cutting it close. It can take up to six weeks to get or renew a passport (for more and Donegal). You can book day tours by bus for some of these areas at local tourist offices. For at least two people traveling together, taxis—though expensive—can work in a pinch if bus schedules don't fit your plans (i.e., Cork to Kinsale). If you have time for only one idyllic peninsula on your trip, I'd suggest the Dingle Peninsula over the Ring of Kerry (for specifics, see sidebar on page 198).

on passports, see www.travel.state.gov). Pack a photocopy of your passport in your luggage in case the original is lost or stolen.

Book your rooms well in advance if you'll be traveling during peak season and any major **holidays** (see sidebar). If you're picking up a car at Dublin Airport, consider a gentler **small-town start** in Kilkenny or Trim, and let Dublin be the finale, when you're rested and ready to tackle the city.

Call your **debit- and credit-card companies** to let them know the countries you'll be visiting, to ask about fees, and more (see page 15).

Do your homework if you want to buy **travel insurance.** Compare the cost of the insurance to the likelihood of your using it and your potential loss if something goes wrong. For more information, see www.ricksteves.com/insurance.

If you're bringing an MP3 player, you can download free information from **Rick Steves Audio Europe,** featuring hours of travel interviews and more (at www.ricksteves.com and on iTunes; for details, see page 462).

If you're planning on **renting a car** in Ireland, you'll need your driver's license. An International Driving Permit is recommended (see page 452).

Because **airline carry-on restrictions** are always changing, visit the Transportation Security Administration's website (www .tsa.gov/travelers) for an up-to-date list of what you can bring on the plane with you...and what you have to check. If you're flying into Dublin from London, note that you may only be allowed one carry-on (no extras like a purse or backpack); check with your airline or at the British transportation website (www.dft.gov.uk).

Practicalities

Emergency and Medical Help: In Ireland, dial 999 for police or medical emergencies. If you get sick, do as the Irish do and go to a pharmacist for advice. Or ask at your hotel for help—they'll know the nearest medical and emergency services.

Lost or Stolen Passport: To replace a passport, you'll need to go in person to a US embassy (see page 444). While not required, having a backup form of ID—ideally a photocopy of your passport and driver's license—speeds up a replacement. For more info, see www.ricksteves.com/help.

Time Zones: Like Great Britain, Ireland is one hour earlier than most of continental Europe. Ireland is also generally five/ eight hours ahead of the East/West Coasts of the US; the exceptions are the beginning and end of Daylight Saving Time: Ireland and Europe "spring forward" the last Sunday in March (two weeks after most of North America) and "fall back" the last Sunday in October (one week before North America). For a handy online time converter, try www.timeanddate.com/worldclock.

Business Hours: In Ireland, most stores are open Monday through Saturday from roughly 10:00 to 17:30, with a late night on Wednesday or Thursday (until 19:00 or 20:00), depending on the neighborhood. Sundays have the same pros and cons as they do for travelers in the US (special events, limited hours, banks and many shops closed, limited public transportation, no rush hours, street markets are lively with shoppers). Saturdays are virtually weekdays with earlier closing hours and no rush hour (though transportation connections can be less frequent than on weekdays).

Watt's Up? Ireland's electrical system is different from North America's in two ways: the shape of the plug (three square prongs—not the two round prongs used in continental Europe) and the voltage of the current (220 volts, instead of 110 volts). For your North American plug to work in Ireland, you'll need an adapter, sold inexpensively at travel stores in the US. As for the voltage, newer electronics or travel appliances (such as hair dryers, laptops, and battery chargers) automatically convert the voltage— if you see a range of voltages printed on the item or its plug (such as "110-220"), it'll work in Ireland and Europe. Otherwise, you can buy a converter separately in the US (about $20), though these tend to be heavy and unreliable, and get really hot when in use. For small appliances that don't automatically convert voltage, I suggest going without or buying a cheap replacement in Ireland. Low-cost hair dryers and other small appliances are sold at Dunnes and Tesco stores in bigger cities (ask your hotelier for the closest branch).

Discounts: Discounts (called "concessions" in Ireland) aren't listed in this book. However, many Irish sights offer discounts for seniors (loosely defined as those who are retired or willing to call themselves a senior), youths (ages 8-18), groups of 10 or more, families, and students with proper identification cards (www.isic.org). Always ask. Some discounts are available only for EU citizens.

News: Americans keep in touch via the *International Herald Tribune* (published almost daily throughout Europe and online at www.iht.com). Other newsy sites are http://news.bbc.co.uk and www.europeantimes.com. Every Tuesday, the European editions of *Time* and *Newsweek* hit the stands with articles of particular interest to travelers in Europe. Sports addicts can get their daily fix online at www.espn.com or from *USA Today*. Many hotels have CNN or BBC News television channels.

Money

This section offers advice on how to pay for purchases on your trip (including getting cash from ATMs and paying with plastic), dealing with lost or stolen cards, VAT (sales tax) refunds, and tipping.

What to Bring

Bring both a credit card and a debit card. You'll use the debit card at cash machines (ATMs) to withdraw euros or pounds for most purchases, and the credit card to pay for larger items. Some travelers carry a third card as a backup, in case one gets demagnetized or eaten by a temperamental machine.

As an emergency backup, bring several hundred dollars in hard cash (in easy-to-exchange $20 bills). Avoid using currency exchange booths (lousy rates and/or outrageous fees); if you have foreign currency to exchange, take it to a bank. Don't use traveler's checks—they're a waste of time (long waits at slow banks) and a waste of money in fees.

Cash

Cash is just as desirable in Ireland as it is at home. Small businesses (hotels, restaurants, and shops) prefer that you pay your bills with cash. Some vendors will charge you extra for using a credit card, and some won't take credit cards at all.

Throughout Europe, ATMs are the standard way for travelers to get cash. To withdraw money from an ATM, you'll need a debit card (ideally with a Visa or MasterCard logo for maximum usability), plus a PIN code. Know your PIN code in numbers, because there are only numbers—no letters—on European keypads. You could use a credit card for ATM transactions, but it's generally more expensive (because it's considered a "cash advance" rather than a "withdrawal"). For security, it's best to shield the keypad when entering your PIN at the ATM.

When using an ATM, taking out large sums of money can reduce the number of per-transaction bank fees you'll pay. If the machine refuses your request, try again and select a smaller amount (some cash machines limit the amount you can withdraw—don't take it personally). If that doesn't work, try a different machine.

Most ATMs in Ireland are located outside of a bank. Try to use the ATM when the branch is open; if your card is eaten by a machine, you can immediately go inside for help. If the ATM dispenses big bills, try to break them at a bank or larger store, because it's easier to pay for purchases at small businesses using smaller bills.

Even in mist-kissed Ireland, you'll need to keep your cash safe. Use a money belt—a pouch with a strap that you buckle around your waist like a belt and wear under your clothes. Pickpockets target tourists. A money belt provides peace of mind, allowing you to carry lots of cash safely. Don't waste time every few days tracking down a cash machine—withdraw a week's worth of money, stuff it in your money belt, and travel!

Credit and Debit Cards

Visa and MasterCard are more commonly accepted than American Express. While you can use either a credit card or a debit card for most transactions, using a credit card offers a greater degree of fraud protection (since debit cards draw funds directly from your account).

Just like at home, credit and debit cards are accepted by larger hotels, restaurants, and shops. I typically use my debit card to withdraw cash from ATMs and my credit card only in a few specific situations: to book hotel reservations by phone, to make major purchases (such as car rentals, plane tickets, and long hotel stays), and to pay for things near the end of my trip (to avoid another visit to the ATM).

Ask Your Credit- or Debit-Card Company: Before your trip, contact the company that issued your debit or credit cards.

• Confirm your card will work overseas, and alert them that you'll be using it in Europe; otherwise, they may deny transactions if they perceive unusual spending patterns.

• Ask for the specifics on transaction **fees.** When you use your credit or debit card—either for purchases or ATM withdrawals—you'll often be charged additional "international transaction" fees of up to 3 percent (1 percent is normal) plus $5 per transaction. If your fees are too high, consider getting a card just for your trip: Capital One (www.capitalone.com) and most credit unions have low-to-no international fees.

• If you plan to withdraw cash from ATMs, confirm your daily **withdrawal limit** (€300 is usually the maximum). Some travelers prefer a high limit that allows them to take out more cash at each ATM stop, while others prefer to set a lower limit in case their card is stolen.

• Ask for your credit card's **PIN** in case you encounter Europe's "chip-and-PIN" system.

Chip and PIN: If your card is declined for a purchase in Europe, it may be because of chip and PIN, which requires cardholders to punch in a PIN instead of signing a receipt. Much of Europe, including Ireland, Great Britain, France, the Netherlands, and Scandinavia, is adopting this system. Chip and PIN is used by some merchants and also at automated payment machines—such as those at train stations, parking garages, luggage lockers, and self-serve pumps at gas stations. If you're prompted to enter your PIN (but don't know it), ask if the cashier can print a receipt for you to sign instead, or just pay cash. If you're dealing with an automated machine that won't take your card, look for a cashier nearby who can make your card work. The easiest solution is to carry sufficient cash.

Dynamic Currency Conversion: If merchants offer to convert your purchase price into dollars (called dynamic currency

Exchange Rates

I've priced things throughout this book in the local currencies. The Republic of Ireland uses the euro currency. Northern Ireland, which is part of the United Kingdom, has retained its traditional currency, the British pound sterling. Border towns in the North might take euros, but at a lousy exchange rate. (To get the latest rates and print a cheat sheet, see www.oanda.com).

1 euro (€1) = about $1.25
1 British pound (£1) = about $1.60

Republic of Ireland: To convert prices in euros to dollars, add about 25 percent: €20 = about $25, €50 = about $65. Like dollars, one euro (€) is broken down into 100 cents. You'll find coins ranging from 1 cent to 2 euros and bills ranging from 5 euros to 500 euros.

Northern Ireland: To convert prices in pounds to dollars, add 60 percent: £20 = about $32, £50 = about $80. The British pound sterling (£), also called a "quid," is broken into 100 pence (p). Pence means "cents." You'll find coins ranging from 1p to £2 and bills from £5 to £50.

Northern Ireland issues its own currency, which is worth the same as an English pound. If you're traveling on to Great Britain, note that English and Northern Ireland's Ulster pounds are technically interchangeable in both regions, although Ulster pounds are "undesirable" in Britain. Banks in either region will convert your Ulster pounds into English pounds at no charge. Don't worry about the coins, which are accepted throughout Great Britain and Northern Ireland.

conversion, or DCC), refuse this "service." You'll pay even more in fees for the expensive convenience of seeing your charge in dollars.

Damage Control for Lost Cards

If you lose your credit, debit, or ATM card, you can stop people from using it by reporting the loss immediately to the respective global customer-assistance centers. Call these 24-hour US numbers collect: Visa (410/581-9994), MasterCard (636/722-7111), and American Express (623/492-8427).

At a minimum, you'll need to know the name of the financial institution that issued you the card, along with the type of card (classic, platinum, etc.). Providing the following information will allow for a quicker cancellation of your missing card: full card number, whether you are the primary or secondary cardholder, the card-holder's name exactly as printed on the card, billing address, home phone number, circumstances of the loss or theft, and identification verification (your birth date, your mother's maiden name, or your Social Security number—memorize this, don't carry a copy). If you are the secondary cardholder, you'll also need to provide the primary cardholder's identification-verification details. You can generally receive a temporary card within two or three business days.

If you promptly report your card lost or stolen, you typically won't be responsible for any unauthorized transactions on your account, although many banks charge a liability fee of $50.

Tipping

Tipping in Ireland isn't as automatic and generous as it is in the US, but for special service, tips are appreciated, if not expected. As in the US, the proper amount depends on your resources, tipping philosophy, and the circumstance, but some general guidelines apply.

Restaurants: At a pub or restaurant with waitstaff, check the menu or your bill to see if the service is included; if not, tip about 10 percent. At pubs where you order at the counter, you don't have to tip.

Taxis: To tip the cabbie, round up. For a typical ride, throw in an extra euro or so (for a €9 fare, give €10); for a long ride, round to the nearest €10 (for a €56 fare, give €60). If the cabbie hauls your bags and zips you to the airport to help you catch your flight, you might want to toss in a little more. But if you feel like you're being driven in circles or otherwise ripped off, skip the tip.

Special Services: It's thoughtful to tip a euro to someone who shows you a special sight and who is paid in no other way. Tour guides at public sights sometimes hold out their hands for tips (€1-2) after they give their spiel. If I've already paid for the tour, I don't tip extra unless they've really impressed me. At hotels, if you let porters carry your luggage, it's polite to give them a euro per bag (another reason to pack light). I don't tip the maid, but if you do, you can leave a euro per overnight at the end of your stay.

In general, if someone in the service industry does a super job for you, a small tip (the equivalent of a euro or two) is appropriate...but not required.

When in doubt, ask. If you're not sure whether (or how much) to tip for a service, ask your hotelier or the TI; they'll fill you in on how it's done on their turf.

Getting a VAT Refund

Wrapped into the purchase price of your Irish souvenirs is a Value-Added Tax (VAT) of about 21 percent. You're entitled to get most of that tax back if you purchase more than €175 (about $220) worth of goods at a store that participates in the VAT-refund scheme. Getting your refund is usually straightforward and, if you buy a substantial amount of souvenirs, well worth the hassle. If you're lucky, the merchant will subtract the tax when you make your purchase. (This is more likely to occur if the store ships the goods to your home.) Otherwise, you'll need to:

Get the paperwork. Have the merchant completely fill out the necessary refund document, called a "Tax-Free Shopping Cheque." You'll have to present your passport at the store.

Get your stamp at the border or airport. Process your cheque(s) at your last stop in the EU (e.g., at the airport) with the customs agent who deals with VAT refunds. It's best to keep your purchases in your carry-on for viewing, but if they're too large or dangerous (such as knives) to carry on, track down the proper customs agent to inspect them before you check your bag. You're not supposed to use your purchased goods before you leave. If you show up at customs wearing your new Irish sweater, officials might look the other way—or deny you a refund.

Collect your refund. You'll need to return your stamped document to the retailer or its representative. Many merchants work with a service, such as Global Refund (www.globalrefund.com) or Premier Tax Free (www.premiertaxfree.com), which have offices at major airports, ports, or border crossings. These services, which extract a 4 percent fee, can refund your money immediately in your currency of choice or credit your card (within two billing cycles). If the retailer handles VAT refunds directly, it's up to you to contact the merchant for your refund. Or you can mail the documents from your point of departure (using a stamped, addressed envelope you've prepared or one that's been provided by the merchant). You'll then have to wait—it could take months.

Customs for American Shoppers

You are allowed to take home $800 worth of items per person duty-free, once every 30 days. The next $1,000 is taxed at a flat 3 percent. After that, you pay the individual item's duty rate. You can also bring in duty-free a liter of alcohol (slightly more than a standard-size bottle of wine; you must be at least 21), 200 cigarettes, and up to 100 non-Cuban cigars.

As for food, you can take home vacuum-packed cheeses; dried herbs, spices, or mushrooms; and canned fruits or vegetables, including jams and vegetable spreads. Baked goods, candy, chocolate, oil, vinegar, mustard, and honey are OK. Fresh fruits or vegetables (even that banana from your airplane breakfast) are not permitted. Meats are generally not allowed. Just because a duty-free shop in an airport sells a food product doesn't mean it will automatically pass US customs. Be prepared to lose your investment.

Note that you'll need to carefully pack any bottles of wine, jam, honey, oil, and other liquid-containing items in your checked luggage, due to the three-ounce limit on liquids in carry-on baggage. To check customs rules and duty rates before you go, visit www.cbp.gov, and click on "Travel," then "Know Before You Go."

Sightseeing

Sightseeing can be hard work. Use these tips to make your visits to Ireland's finest sights meaningful, fun, efficient, and painless.

Plan Ahead

Set up an itinerary that allows you to fit in all your must-see sights. Most sights keep stable hours, but you can easily confirm the latest by checking their website or asking the local TI.

Don't put off visiting a must-see sight—you never know when a place will close unexpectedly for a holiday, strike, or restoration. On holidays (see list on page 464), expect shorter hours or closures.

When possible, visit major sights first thing (when your energy is best), and save other activities for the afternoon. Hit a sight's highlights first, then see the rest if you have the stamina and time.

Going at the right time helps avoid crowds. This book offers tips on specific sights. Try visiting very early, at lunch, or very late. Evening visits are usually peaceful, with fewer crowds.

Study up. To get the most out of the self-guided walks and sight descriptions in this book, read them before you visit.

At Sights

Here's what you can typically expect: Some important sights may have metal detectors or conduct bag searches that will slow your entry, while others may require you to check daypacks and coats. They'll be kept safely. If you have something you can't bear to part with, stash it in a pocket or purse. To avoid checking a small backpack, carry it under your arm like a purse as you enter. From a guard's point of view, a backpack is generally a problem while a purse is not.

Flash photography is sometimes banned, but taking photos without a flash is usually OK. Look for signs or ask. Flashes damage oil paintings and distract others in the room. Even without a flash, a handheld camera will take a decent picture (or buy postcards or posters at the museum bookstore). If photos are permitted, video cameras are generally OK, too.

Museums may have special exhibits in addition to their

permanent collection. Some exhibits are included in the entry price; others come at an extra cost (which you may have to pay even if you don't want to see the exhibit).

Many sights rent audioguides, which generally offer dry-but-useful recorded descriptions in English (about €5; sometimes included with admission). If you bring along your own pair of headphones and a Y-jack, you can sometimes share one audioguide with your travel partner and save money. Guided tours are most likely to occur during peak season; these range widely in quality and cost around €4.

Expect changes—artwork can be on tour, on loan, out sick, or shifted at the whim of the curator. To adapt, pick up any available free floor plans as you enter. Ask the museum staff if you can't find a particular piece.

Important sights often have an on-site café or cafeteria (usually a good place to rest and have a snack or light meal). The WCs at many sights are free and nearly always clean.

Many places sell postcards and guidebooks that highlight their attractions. Before you leave, scan the postcards and thumb through the biggest guidebook (or skim its index) to be sure you haven't overlooked something that you'd like to see.

Most sights stop admitting people 30-60 minutes before closing time, and some rooms close early (generally about 45 minutes before the actual closing time). Guards usher people out, so don't save the best for last.

Every sight or museum offers more than what is covered in this book. Use the information in this book as an introduction—not the final word.

Sightseeing Passes

Ireland offers two different passes (each covering a different set of sights) that can save you money. The first is smart for anyone, and the second works best for two people traveling together. Twosomes who love to sightsee should get both passes.

The **Heritage Card** gets you into 96 historical monuments, gardens, and parks maintained by the OPW (Office of Public Works) in the Republic of Ireland. It will pay off if you plan on visiting half a dozen or more included sights over the course of your trip (€21, seniors age 60 and older-€16, students-€8, families-€55, cov-

ers entry to all Heritage sights for one year, comes with handy map and list of sights' hours and prices, purchase at any Heritage sight or Dublin's tourist information office on Suffolk Street, cash only, tel. 01/605-7700 or 01/647-6592, fax 01/661-6764, www.heritage ireland.ie, heritagecard@opw.ie). People traveling by car are most likely to get their money's worth out of the card.

Without the Heritage Card, your costs will add up fast, and you'll waste time in line. Adult entry prices range from €1.60 to €10.30. An energetic sightseer with three weeks in Ireland will probably pay to see nearly all 20 of the following sights (covered in this book): Dublin Castle-€4.50, Kilmainham Gaol-€6 (Dublin), Brú na Bóinne (Knowth and Newgrange tombs and Visitors Centre)-€11, Hill of Tara-€3, Old Mellifont Abbey-€3, Battle of the Boyne-€4, Trim Castle-€4 (Valley of the Boyne), Glendalough Visitors Centre-€3 (Wicklow Mountains), Kilkenny Castle-€6 (Kilkenny), Rock of Cashel-€6 (Cashel), Reginald's Tower-€3 (Waterford), Charles Fort-€4, Desmond Castle-€3 (Kinsale), Muckross House-€7 (near Killarney), Derrynane House-€3 (Ring of Kerry), Garnish Island Gardens-€4 (near Kenmare), Great Blasket Centre-€4 (near Dingle), Ennis Friary-€3 (Ennis), Dún Aenghus-€3 (Inishmore, Aran Islands), and Glenveagh Castle and National Park-€5 (Donegal). This totals €90; a pass saves you nearly €70 (about $85) per person over paying individual entrance fees. It also moves you through ticket lines quicker. Note that scheduled tours given by OPW guides at any of these sites are included in the price of admission—regardless of whether you have the Heritage Card—and that the card covers no sights in Northern Ireland.

Ambitious travelers covering more ground should seriously consider the **Heritage Island Explorer Touring Guide** (€7), which

does not overlap with the above Heritage sights and gives a variety of discounts (usually 2-for-1 discounts, but occasionally 20 percent off) at 87 sights in both the Republic and Northern Ireland. This is a great no-brainer deal for two people traveling together—you just need to buy one Touring Guide, so you'll save the cost of the guide after only a couple of stops. (Solo travelers might have to go to half a dozen sights before the discounts recoup the initial €7.) At some sites that already have free admission, you'll get 10 percent off on purchases at their shop or café (for example,

at the National Museum in Dublin). You can buy the guide at TIs and participating sights, but study the full list of sights first (tel. 01/205-4998, fax 01/284-4845, www.heritageisland.com). Discounted sights mentioned in this guidebook include: Trinity College Library (Book of Kells), Christ Church Cathedral, St. Patrick's Cathedral, Dublin City Hall, Dublinia, Hugh Lane

INTRODUCTION

Gallery, Old Jameson Distillery, Guinness Storehouse, Number Twenty-Nine Georgian House (all aforementioned sights in Dublin), Power & Glory (Trim), Irish National Stud (Kildare), Gardens of Powerscourt (Enniskerry), Avondale House (Wicklow Mountains), Bru Boru Cultural Centre (Cashel), *Dunbrody* Famine Ship (New Ross), Waterford Crystal Visitor Centre (Waterford), Old Midleton Distillery (Midleton), Blarney Castle (County Cork), Kerry County Museum (Tralee), Burren Centre (Kilfenora), Caherconnell Ring Fort (Burren), Aillwee Cave (Burren), Atlantic Edge exhibit (Cliffs of Moher), Clare Museum (Ennis), Kylemore Abbey (Letterfrack), Strokestown Park National Famine Museum (Strokestown), Mount Stewart House and Gardens, Somme Heritage Centre (near Bangor), Tower Museum (Derry), and Belleek Pottery Visitors Centre (Belleek).

Sleeping

I favor accommodations (and restaurants) handy to your sight-seeing activities. Rather than list hotels scattered throughout a city, I choose two or three favorite neighborhoods and recommend the best accommodations values in each, from $25 bunk beds to fancy-for-my-book $250 doubles. Outside of Dublin you can expect to find good doubles for $100-150, including tax and a cooked breakfast.

I look for places that are friendly; clean; a good value; located in a central, safe, quiet neighborhood; and not mentioned in other guidebooks. I'm more impressed by a handy location and a fun-loving philosophy than hair dryers and shoeshine machines. For tips on making reservations, see page 30.

I've described my recommended accommodations using a Sleep Code (described later in this section). Prices listed are for one-night stays in peak season, include a hearty breakfast (unless otherwise noted), and assume you're booking direct and not through a TI. You should find prices listed in this book to be good through 2011 (except for major holidays and festivals—see page 464).

Given the economic downturn, hoteliers are willing and eager to make a deal. I'd suggest emailing several hotels to ask for their best price. Comparison-shop and make your choice. As you look over the listings, you'll notice that some hotels promise special prices to my readers who book direct (without using a room-finding service or hotel-booking website, which take a commission). To get these rates, mention this book when you reserve, then show the book upon arrival.

In general, prices can soften up if you do any of the following: offer to pay cash, stay at least three nights, or mention this book.

Lodging Vouchers

Many US travel agents sell vouchers for lodging in Ireland. In essence, you're paying ahead of time for your lodging, with the assurance that you'll be staying in B&Bs and guesthouses that live up to certain standards. I don't recommend buying into these, since your choices will be limited to only the places in Ireland that accept vouchers. Sure, there are hundreds in the program to choose from. But in this guidebook, I list any place that offers a good value—a useful location, nice hosts, and a comfortable and clean room—regardless of what club they do or don't belong to. Lots of great B&Bs choose not to participate in the voucher program because they have to pay to be part of it, slicing into their already thin profit. And many Irish B&B owners lament the long wait they endure between the date a traveler stays with them and the date the voucher company reimburses them. In short, skip it. The voucher program is just another middleman between you and the innkeeper.

You can also try asking for a cheaper room or a discount, or offer to skip breakfast. To save money off-season, consider arriving without a reservation and dropping in at the last minute.

When establishing prices, confirm if the charge is per person or per room (if a price is too good to be true, it's probably per person). Because many places in Ireland charge per person, small groups often pay the same for a single and a double as they would for a triple. Note: In this book, room prices are listed per room, not per person.

The Republic of Ireland and Northern Ireland have banned smoking in the workplace (pubs, offices, taxicabs, etc.), but some hotels still have a floor or two of rooms where guests are allowed to smoke. If you don't want a room that a smoker might have occupied before you, let the hotelier know when you make your reservation. About 90 percent of my recommended B&Bs prohibit smoking. While some places allow smoking in the sleeping rooms, breakfast rooms are nearly always smoke-free.

Many places listed have three floors of rooms and steep stairs; expect good exercise and be happy you packed light. Elevators are rare except in the larger hotels. If you're concerned about stairs, call and ask about ground-floor rooms or pay for a hotel with a lift (elevator).

Be careful of the terminology: An "en suite" room has a bathroom (toilet and shower/tub) inside the room; a room with a "private bathroom" can mean that the bathroom is all yours, but it's across the hall; and a "standard" room has access to a bathroom that's shared with other rooms and down the hall. Figuring there's

Sleep Code

(€1 = about $1.25, country code: 353)

To help you easily sort through my listings, I've divided the rooms into three categories based on the price for a standard double room with bath:

> **$$$** Higher Priced
> **$$** Moderately Priced
> **$** Lower Priced

I always rate hostels as $, whether or not they have double rooms, because they have the cheapest beds in town.

Prices can change without notice; verify the hotel's current rates online or by email. For other updates, see www.ricksteves.com/update.

To give maximum information in a minimum of space, I use the following code to describe the accommodations. Prices are listed per room, not per person. When a price range is given for a type of room (such as double rooms listing for €100-150), it means the price fluctuates with the season, size of room, or length of stay.

S = Single room, or price for one person in a double.

D = Double or twin room. (I specify double- and twin-bed rooms only if they are priced differently, or if a place has only one or the other. When reserving, you should specify.)

T = Three-person room (often a double bed with a single).

Q = Four-person room (adding an extra child's bed to a T is usually cheaper).

b = Private bathroom with toilet and shower or tub.

s = Private shower or tub only. (The toilet is down the hall.)

According to this code, a couple staying at a "Db-€100" hotel would pay a total of €100 (about $125) per night for a room with a private bathroom. Unless otherwise noted, credit cards are accepted and breakfast is included.

If I mention "Internet access" in a listing, there's a public terminal in the lobby for guests to use. If I include "Wi-Fi," you can generally access it in your room (usually for free), but only if you have your own laptop.

little difference between "en suite" and "private" rooms, some places charge the same for both. If you want your own bathroom inside the room, request "en suite."

If money's tight, ask for a standard room. You'll almost always have a sink in your room. And, as more rooms go "en suite," the hallway bathroom is shared with fewer standard rooms.

"Twin" means two single beds, and "double" means one

double bed. If you'll take either one, let them know, or you might be needlessly turned away. Most hotels offer family deals, which means that parents with young children can easily get a room with an extra child's bed or a discount for larger rooms. Call to negotiate the price. Teenagers are generally charged as adults. Kids under five sleep almost free.

Note that to be called a "hotel," a place technically must have certain amenities, including a 24-hour reception (though this rule is loosely applied). A place called "townhouse" or "house" is like a big B&B or a small family-run hotel—with fewer amenities but more character than a "hotel." TVs are standard in rooms.

Ireland has a rating system for hotels and B&Bs. These stars and shamrocks are supposed to imply quality, but I find that they mean only that the place sporting symbols is paying dues to the tourist board. Rating systems often have little to do with value.

Hoteliers and B&B hosts can be a great help and source of advice. Most know their city well, and can assist you with everything from public transit and airport connections to finding a good restaurant, the nearest Internet café, or launderette.

Even at the best places, mechanical breakdowns occur: air-conditioning malfunctions, sinks leak, hot water turns cold, and toilets gurgle and smell. Report your concerns clearly and calmly at the front desk. For more complicated problems, don't expect instant results.

If you suspect night noise will be a problem, ask for a quiet room in the back or on an upper floor. To guard against theft in your room, keep valuables out of sight. Some rooms come with a safe, and others have safes at the front desk. Use them if you're concerned.

Checkout can pose problems if surprise charges pop up on your bill. If you settle up your bill the day before you leave, you'll have time to discuss and address any points of contention (before 19:00, when the night shift usually arrives).

If you're traveling beyond my recommended destinations, you'll find accommodations where you need them. Any town with tourists has a TI that books rooms or can give you a list and point you in the right direction. In the absence of a TI, ask people on the street or in pubs and restaurants for help. The Republic of Ireland also has a nationwide room-booking phone number; within Ireland, dial 1-800-363-626 (Mon-Sat 9:00-20:00, closed Sun).

Types of Accommodations
B&Bs

Compared to hotels, bed-and-breakfast places give you double the cultural intimacy for half the price. While you may lose some of the conveniences of a hotel—such as lounges, in-room phones, frequent bed-sheet changes, and being able to pay with a credit card—I happily make the trade-off for the lower rates and personal touches. If you have a reasonable but limited budget, skip hotels and go the B&B way. In 2011, you'll generally pay €40-60 (about $56-84) per person for a double room in a B&B in Ireland. Prices include a big cooked breakfast. The amount of coziness, teddies, tea, and biscuits tossed in varies tremendously.

B&Bs range from large guesthouses with 15-20 rooms to small homes renting out a spare bedroom, but they typically have six rooms or fewer. The philosophy of the management determines the character of a place more than its size and facilities offered. Avoid places run as a business by absentee owners. My top listings are run by people who enjoy welcoming the world to their breakfast table.

Book direct. If you buy the lodging vouchers sold by many US travel agents (see sidebar), you'll pay more. If you have a local TI book a room for you, it'll take a 10 percent commission from the B&B and may charge you up to €5. But if you book direct, the B&B gets it all, and you'll have a better chance of getting a discount. I have negotiated special prices with this book (often for payment in cash).

B&Bs come with their own etiquette and quirks. Keep in mind that B&B owners are at the whim of their guests—if you're getting up early, so are they; and if you check in late, they'll wait up for you. It's polite to call ahead to confirm your reservation the day before and give them a rough estimate of your arrival time. This allows them to plan their day and run errands before or after you arrive...and also allows them to give you specific directions for driving or walking to their place.

A few tips: B&B proprietors are selective as to whom they invite in for the night. At some B&Bs, children are not welcome. Risky-looking people (two or more single men are often assumed to be troublemakers) find many places suddenly full. If you'll be staying for more than one night, you are a "desirable." In popular

weekend-getaway spots, you're unlikely to find a place to take you for Saturday night only. If my listings are full, ask for guidance. (Mentioning this book can help.) Owners usually work together and can call up an ally to land you a bed.

Laundry

If you're not planning to wash your clothes in the sink in your room, it's a good idea to plan ahead for when you'll need to do laundry. Figure on an average of about €10 per load (up to €12 for smaller towns with only one launderette).

Most launderettes in Ireland are drop-off rather than self-serve. Drop-off operations are a smarter use of your valuable travel time. The €5 you might save plugging coins into a self-serve washer/dryer is not worth the two or three hours you'll waste when you could be out enjoying a local sight.

Drop your load off first thing in the morning, and pick it up late that afternoon (washed, dried, and kind-of folded). If you wait until too late in the morning to drop it off, they might not be able to get it done for you by closing time that day (be sure to confirm closing time when you drop it off). Note that most places are closed on Sunday; waiting to pick up your load until Monday morning may cramp your plans. When I know I might be distracted by sightseeing, I set my alarm watch to go off late in the afternoon to remind me to pick up my laundry.

If you've packed only basic, practical wash-and-wear clothes, you have nothing to fear from an Irish launderette. If you're traveling with your favorite silk kimono, don't tempt fate—it might come back leprechaun-size.

B&Bs serve a hearty "Irish fry" breakfast (for more about B&B breakfasts, see "Eating," later in this chapter). You'll quickly figure out which parts of the "fry" you do and don't like. B&B owners prefer to know this up front, rather than serve you the whole shebang and have to throw out uneaten food. Because your B&B owner is also the cook, there's usually a quite limited time span when breakfast is served (typically about an hour, starting at about 8:00). It's an unwritten rule that guests shouldn't show up at the very end of the breakfast period and expect a full cooked breakfast—instead, if you're running late, aim to arrive at least 10 minutes before breakfast ends. If you do arrive at the last minute (or if you need to leave before breakfast is served), most B&B hosts are happy to let you help yourself to cereal, fruit, and coffee; ask politely if it's possible.

B&Bs are not hotels: If you want to ruin your relationship with your hostess, treat her like a hotel clerk. Americans often assume they'll get new towels each day. The Irish don't, and neither will you. Hang them up to dry and reuse. And pack a washcloth (many Irish B&B's don't provide them).

In almost every B&B, you'll encounter unusual bathroom fixtures. The "pump toilet" has a flushing handle that doesn't kick in unless you push it just right: too hard or too soft, and it won't go. Be decisive but not ruthless. There's also the "dial-a-shower," an electronic box under the showerhead where you'll turn a dial to select the heat of the water, and (sometimes with a separate dial or button) turn on or shut off the flow of water. Virtually all rooms have sinks.

Some B&Bs stock rooms with a hot-water pot, cups, tea bags, and coffee packets (if you prefer decaf, buy a jar at a grocery, and dump it into a baggie for easy packing). Electrical outlets sometimes come with switches on the outlet to turn the current on or off; if your electrical appliance isn't working, flip the switch.

Most B&Bs come with thin walls and doors. This can make for a noisy night, especially with people walking down the hall to use the bathroom. If you're a light sleeper, bring earplugs. And please be quiet in the halls and in your rooms (talk softly, and keep the TV volume low)...those of us getting up early will thank you for it.

Your B&B bedroom might not include a phone. In the mobile-phone age, street phone booths can be few and far between. Some B&B owners will allow you to use their phone, but understandably they don't want to pay for long-distance charges. If you must use their phone, show them your international calling card (see page 439) and keep the call short (5-10 minutes max). If you plan to stay in B&Bs and make frequent calls, consider buying an Irish mobile phone (see page 442). And if you're bringing your laptop, look for places with Wi-Fi (noted in my hotel listings). Ask your host about using this service, as some rooms might have better reception than others.

A few B&B owners are also pet owners. And, while pets are rarely allowed into guest rooms, and B&B proprietors are typically very tidy, those with pet allergies might be bothered. I've tried to list which B&Bs have pets, but if you're allergic, ask about pets when you reserve.

Remember that you'll likely need to pay cash for your room. Think ahead so you have enough cash to pay up when you check out.

Big, Cheap, Modern Hotels

Hotel chains—popular with budget tour groups—offer predictably comfortable, no-frills accommodations at reasonable prices. These hotels are popping up in big cities in Ireland. They can be located near the train station, in the city center, on major arterials, and outside the city center. What you lose in charm, you gain in savings. I can't stress this enough: Check online for the cheapest deals. And be sure to go through the actual hotel's website rather than an online middleman.

These hotels are ideal for families, offering simple, clean, and modern rooms for up to four people (two adults/two children) for €100-150, depending on the location. Note that couples or families (up to four) pay the same price for a room. Most rooms have a double bed, single bed, five-foot trundle bed, private shower, WC, and TV. Hotels usually have an attached restaurant, good security, an elevator, and a 24-hour staffed reception desk. Of course, they're as cozy as a Motel 6, but many travelers love them. You can book online (be sure to check their websites for deals) or over the phone with a credit card, then pay when you check in. When you check out, just drop off the key, Lee.

The biggies are Jurys Inn (call their hotels directly or book online at www.jurysinns.com), Comfort/Quality Inns (Republic of Ireland tel. 1-800-500-600, Northern Ireland tel. 0800-444-444, US tel. 877-424-6423, www.choicehotels.com), and Travelodge (also has freeway locations for tired drivers, reservation center in Britain tel. 08700-850-950, www.travelodge.co.uk).

Hostels

Ireland has hundreds of hostels of all shapes and sizes. Choose your hostel selectively. Hostels can be historic castles or depressing tenements, serene and comfy or overrun by noisy school groups.

You'll pay an average of €30 for a dorm bed, €2 for sheets, and €3 for breakfast. People of any age are welcome, if they don't mind dorm-style accommodations (usually in rooms of four to eight beds) and meeting other travelers. Cheap meals are sometimes offered, and kitchen facilities may be available.

There are two basic types of hostels: official and independent. Unfortunately, many of the official hostels (overseen by Hostelling International) have become overpriced, and in general, I no longer recommend them. But many of the independent hostels are more fun, easygoing, and cheaper. Hostels of Europe (www.hostelseurope.com) and Hostels.com have good listings. Ireland's Independent Holiday Hostels (www.hostels-ireland.com) is a network of independent hostels, requiring no membership and welcoming all ages. All IHH hostels are approved by the Irish Tourist Board.

Self-Catering Cottages and Apartments

Travelers wanting to slow down and base themselves in one place for extended periods can rent a cottage or an apartment (sometimes called "flats" in Ireland). This type of lodging varies greatly, but almost always includes a kitchen and living room. The owners discourage short stays, and usually require a minimum one-week rental, plus a deposit.

I focus on short-term-stay sleeping recommendations in this

book (B&Bs, guesthouses, and hotels), rather than self-catering options. But if a B&B I've listed also offers a worthwhile self-catering option nearby, I'll mention it.

A variety of organizations specialize in this longer-term alternative. Your most reliable source for places that live up to certain standards is the Irish Tourist Board (for online info, try www .tourismireland.com).

Phoning

To call Ireland from the US or Canada, you'll need to know that the country code for the Republic of Ireland is 353, and for Northern Ireland, it's 044. To call from the US or Canada to the Republic of Ireland, dial 011-353-local number (drop the initial 0 from the local number). To call Northern Ireland, dial 011-44-28 (28 is Northern Ireland's area code without its initial 0), then the local number. For more tips on calling, see page 438.

Making Reservations

Given the quality of the places I've found for this book, I recommend that you reserve your rooms in advance, particularly if you'll be traveling during peak season. Book several weeks ahead, or as soon as you've pinned down your travel dates. Note that some national holidays jam things up and merit your making reservations far in advance (see "Major Holidays and Weekends" sidebar on page 9). Just like at home, holidays that fall on a Monday, Thursday, or Friday can turn the weekend into a long holiday, so book the entire weekend in advance.

Requesting a Reservation: To reserve, contact hotels directly by email, phone, or fax. Email is the clearest and most economical way to make a reservation. Or you can go straight to the hotel website; many have secure online reservation forms and can instantly inform you of availability and any special deals. But be sure you use the hotel's official site and not a booking agency's site—otherwise you may pay higher rates than you should. If phoning from the US, be mindful of time zones (see page 12).

The hotelier wants to know these key pieces of information (also included in the sample request form in the appendix):
- number and type of rooms
- number of nights
- date of arrival
- date of departure
- any special needs (e.g., bathroom in the room or down the hall, twin beds vs. double bed, air-conditioning, quiet, view, ground floor, etc.)

When you request a room, use the European style for writing dates: day/month/year. For example, for a two-night stay in

July I would request "2 nights, arrive 16/07/11, depart 18/07/11." (Consider in advance how long you'll stay; don't just assume that you can tack on extra days once you arrive.) Mention any discounts offered—for Rick Steves readers or otherwise—when you make the reservation.

If you don't get a reply to your email or fax, it usually means the hotel is already fully booked (but you can try sending the message again, or call to follow up).

Confirming a Reservation: If the hotel's response includes its room availability and rates, it's not a confirmation. You must tell them that you want that room at the given rate. Most hoteliers will request your credit-card number for a one-night deposit to hold the room. While you can email your credit-card information (I do), it's safer to share that confidential info via phone call, fax, two successive emails, or secure online reservation form (if the hotel has one on its website).

Canceling a Reservation: If you must cancel your reservation, it's courteous to do so with as much advance notice as possible—at least three days. Simply make a quick phone call or send an email. Family-run hotels and B&Bs lose money if they turn away customers while holding a room for someone who doesn't show up. Understandably, many hotels bill no-shows for one night.

Hotels in larger cities such as Dublin sometimes have strict cancellation policies. For example, you might lose a deposit if you cancel within two weeks of your reserved stay, or you might be billed for the entire visit if you leave early. Internet deals may require prepayment, with no refunds for cancellations. If concerned, ask about cancellation policies before you book.

If canceling via email, request confirmation that your cancellation was received to avoid being accidentally billed.

Reconfirm Your Reservation: Always call to reconfirm your room reservation a day or two in advance from the road. Smaller hotels and B&Bs appreciate knowing your time of arrival. If you'll be arriving after 17:00, be sure to let your hotelier know. On the small chance that a hotel loses track of your reservation, bring along a hard copy of their emailed or faxed confirmation. Don't have the TI reconfirm rooms for you; they'll take a commission.

Reserving Rooms as You Travel: You can make reservations as you travel, calling hotels or B&Bs a few days to a week before your visit. If everything's full, don't despair. Call a day or two in advance and fill in a cancellation. If you'd rather travel without any reservations at all, you'll have greater success snaring rooms if you arrive at your destination early in the day. When you anticipate crowds (weekends are worse), call hotels at about 9:00 or 10:00 on the day you plan to arrive, when the hotel clerk knows who'll be checking out and just which rooms will be available.

Eating

Dennis Leary once quipped, "Irish food isn't cuisine...it's penance." Ireland has long been labeled the "land of potatoes," but times have changed. You'll find modern-day Irish cuisine delicious and varied, from vegetables, meat, and dairy products to fresh- and saltwater fish. Try the local specialties wherever you happen to be eating.

The traditional breakfast, the "Irish Fry" (known in the North as the "Ulster Fry"), is a hearty way to start the day—with juice, tea or coffee, cereal, eggs, bacon, sausage, a grilled tomato, sautéed mushrooms, and optional black pudding (made from pigs' blood). Toast is served with butter and marmalade. This meal tides many travelers over until dinner. But there's nothing un-Irish about skipping the "fry"—few locals actually start their day with this heavy traditional breakfast. You can simply skip the heavier fare and enjoy the cereal, juice, toast, and tea.

Picnicking saves time and money. Try boxes of orange juice (pure, by the liter), fresh bread (especially Irish soda bread), tasty Cashel blue cheese, meat, a tube of mustard, local-eatin' apples, bananas, small tomatoes, a small tub of yogurt (it's drinkable), rice crackers, gorp or nuts, plain digestive biscuits (the chocolate-covered ones melt), and any local specialties. At open-air markets and supermarkets, you can get produce in small quantities. Supermarkets often have good deli sections, packaged sandwiches, and sometimes salad bars. I often munch a relaxed "meal on wheels" in a car, train, or bus to save 30 precious minutes for sight-seeing.

At classier restaurants, look for "early-bird specials," allowing you to eat well and affordably, but early (about 17:30-19:00, last order by 19:00). At a sit-down place with table service, tip about 10 percent—unless the service charge is already listed on the bill (for details, see page 17).

Pub Grub and Beer

Pubs are a basic part of the Irish social scene, and, whether you're a teetotaler or a beer-guzzler, they should be a part of your travel here. "Pub" is short for "public house." It's an extended living room where, if you don't mind the stickiness, you can feel the pulse of Ireland.

Smart travelers use pubs to eat, drink, get out of the rain, watch the latest sporting event, and make new friends. Unfortunately, many city pubs have been afflicted with an excess of brass, ferns, and video games. The most traditional atmospheric pubs are in the countryside and smaller towns.

Pub grub gets better every year—it's Ireland's best eating value. For about $15-20, you'll get a basic hot lunch or dinner in friendly surroundings. Pubs that are attached to restaurants, advertise their food, and are crowded with locals are more likely to have fresh food and a chef than to be the kind of pub that sells only lousy microwaved snacks.

Pub menus consist of a hearty assortment of traditional dishes, such as Irish stew (mutton with mashed potatoes, onions, carrots, and herbs), soups and chowders, coddle (bacon, pork sausages, potatoes, and onions stewed in layers), fish-and-chips, collar and cabbage (boiled bacon coated in bread crumbs and brown sugar, then baked and served with cabbage), boxty (potato pancake filled with fish, meat, or vegetables), and champ (potato mashed with milk and onions). Irish bread nicely rounds out a meal. In coastal areas, a lot of seafood is available, such as mackerel, mussels, and Atlantic salmon. There's seldom table service in Irish pubs. Order drinks and meals at the bar. Pay as you order, and don't tip.

I recommend certain pubs, and your B&B host is usually up-to-date on the best neighborhood pub grub. Ask for advice (but adjust for nepotism and cronyism, which run rampant).

When you say "a beer, please" in an Irish pub, you'll get a pint of Guinness (the black beauty with the blonde head). If you want a small beer, ask for a glass or a half-pint. Never rush your bartender when he's pouring a Guinness. It takes time—almost sacred time.

The Irish take great pride in their beer. At pubs, long hand pulls are used to draw the traditional, rich-flavored "real ales" up

from the cellar. These are the connoisseur's favorites: They're fermented naturally, vary from sweet to bitter, and often have a hoppy or nutty flavor. Experiment with obscure local microbrews. Short hand pulls at the bar mean colder, fizzier, mass-produced, and less interesting keg beers. Stout is dark and more bitter, like Guinness. If you think you don't like Guinness,

try it in Ireland. It doesn't travel well and is better in its homeland. Murphy's is a very good Guinness-like stout, but a bit smoother and milder. For a cold, refreshing, basic, American-style beer, ask for a lager, such as Harp. Ale drinkers swear by Smithwick's (I know I do). Caffrey's is a satisfying cross between stout and ale.

INTRODUCTION

Try the draft cider (sweet or dry)...carefully. Teetotalers can order a soft drink.

Pubs are generally open daily from 11:00 to 23:30 and Sunday from noon to 22:30. Children are served food and soft drinks in pubs (sometimes in a courtyard or the restaurant section). You'll often see signs behind the bar asking that children vacate the premises by 20:00. You must be 18 to order a beer, and the Gardí (police) are cracking down hard on pubs that don't enforce this.

You're a guest on your first night; after that, you're a regular. A wise Irishman once said, "It never rains in a pub." The relaxed, informal atmosphere feels like a refuge from daily cares. Women traveling alone need not worry—you'll become part of the pub family in no time.

Craic (crack), Irish for "fun" or "a good laugh," is the sport that accompanies drinking in a pub. People are there to talk. To

encourage conversation, stand or sit at the bar, not at a table.

The Irish government passed a law making all pubs in the Republic smoke-free. Smokers take their pints outside, turning alleys into covered smoking patios. An incredulous Irishman responded to the law by saying, "What will they do next? Ban drinking in pubs? We'll never get to heaven if we don't die."

It's a tradition to buy your table a round, and then for each person to reciprocate. If an Irishman buys you a drink, thank him by saying, "Go raibh maith agat" (guh rov mah UG-ut). Offer him a toast in Irish—"Slainte" (SLAWN-chuh), the equivalent of "cheers." A good excuse for a conversation is to ask to be taught a few words of Gaelic.

Traditional Irish Music

Traditional music is alive and popular in pubs throughout Ireland. "Sessions" (musical evenings) may be planned and advertised or impromptu. Traditionally, musicians just congregate and play for the love of it. There will generally be a fiddle, a flute or tin whistle, a guitar, a *bodhrán* (goatskin drum), and maybe an accordion or mandolin. Things usually get going at about 21:30 (but note that Irish punctuality is unpredictable). Last call for drinks is at about 23:30.

The music often comes in sets of three songs. The wind and string instruments embellish melody lines with lots of tight orna-mentation. Whoever happens to be leading determines the next song only as the song the group is playing is about to be finished. If he wants to pass on the decision, it's done with eye contact and a nod. A *ceilidh* (KAY-lee) is an evening of music and dance...an Irish hoedown.

Percussion generally stays in the background. The *bodhrán* (BO-run) is played with a small, two-headed club. The performer's hand stretches the skin to change the tone and pitch. You'll sometimes be lucky enough to hear a set of bones crisply played. These are two cow ribs (boiled and dried) that are rattled in one hand like spoons or castanets, substituting for the sound of dancing shoes in olden days.

Watch closely if a piper is playing. The Irish version of bagpipes, the *uilleann* (ILL-in) pipes are played by inflating the airbag (under the left elbow) with a bellows (under the right elbow) rather than with a mouthpiece like the Scottish Highland bagpipes. *Uilleann* is Gaelic for "elbow," and the sound is more melodic, with a wider range than the Highland pipes. The piper fingers his chanter like a flute to create individual notes, and uses the heel of his right hand to play chords on one of three regulator pipes. It takes amazing coordination to play this instrument well, and the sound can be haunting.

Occasionally, the fast-paced music will stop and one person will sing a lament. Called *sean nos* (Gaelic for "old style"), this slightly nasal vocal style may be a remnant of the ancient story-telling tradition of the bards whose influence died out when Gaelic culture waned 400 years ago. This is the one time when the entire pub will stop to listen as sad lyrics fill the room. Stories—often of love lost, emigration to a faraway land, or a heroic rebel death struggling against English rule—are always heartfelt. Spend a lament studying the faces in the crowd.

A session can be magical or lifeless. If the chemistry is right, it's one of the great Irish experiences. The music churns intensely while members of the group casually enjoy exploring each other's musical style. The drummer dodges the fiddler's playful bow. Sipping their pints, they skillfully maintain a faint but steady buzz. The floor on the musicians' platform is stomped paint-free, and barmaids scurry artfully through the commotion, gathering towers of empty, cream-crusted glasses. Make yourself right at home, "playing the boot" (tapping your foot) under the table in time with the music. Talk to your neighbor. Locals often have an almost evangelical interest in explaining the music.

INTRODUCTION

How Was Your Trip?

Were your travels fun, smooth, and meaningful? If you'd like to share your tips, concerns, and discoveries, please fill out the survey at www.ricksteves.com/feedback. I value your feedback. Thanks in advance—it helps a lot.

Traveling as a Temporary Local

We travel all the way to Europe to enjoy differences—to become temporary locals. You'll experience frustrations. Certain truths that we find "God-given" or "self-evident," such as cold beer, ice in drinks, bottomless cups of coffee, hot showers, and bigger being better, are suddenly not so true. One of the benefits of travel is the eye-opening realization that there are logical, civil, and even better alternatives.

The Irish generally like Americans. But if there is a negative aspect to their image of us, it's that we are loud, aggressive, impolite, rich, superficially friendly, and a bit naive.

While the Irish look bemusedly at some of our Yankee excesses—and worriedly at others—they nearly always afford us individual travelers all the warmth we deserve. Judging from all the happy feedback I receive from travelers who have used this book, it's safe to assume you'll enjoy a great, affordable vacation—with the finesse of an independent, experienced traveler.

Thanks, and have a grand holiday!

Back Door Travel Philosophy
From *Rick Steves' Europe Through the Back Door*

Travel is intensified living—maximum thrills per minute and one of the last great sources of legal adventure. Travel is freedom. It's recess, and we need it.

Experiencing the real Europe requires catching it by surprise, going casual..."Through the Back Door."

Affording travel is a matter of priorities. (Make do with the old car.) You can travel—simply, safely, and comfortably—anywhere in Europe for $120 a day plus transportation costs. In many ways, spending more money only builds a thicker wall between you and what you came to see. Europe is a cultural carnival, and, time after time, you'll find that its best acts are free and the best seats are the cheap ones.

A tight budget forces you to travel close to the ground, meeting and communicating with the people, not relying on service with a purchased smile. Never sacrifice sleep, nutrition, safety, or cleanliness in the name of budget. Simply enjoy the local-style alternatives to expensive hotels and restaurants.

Connecting with people carbonates your experience. Extroverts have more fun. If your trip is low on magic moments, kick yourself and make things happen. If you don't enjoy a place, maybe you don't know enough about it. Seek the truth. Recognize tourist traps. Give a culture the benefit of your open mind. See things as different but not better or worse. Any culture has much to share.

Of course, travel, like the world, is a series of hills and valleys. Be fanatically positive and militantly optimistic. If something's not to your liking, change your liking.

Travel can make you a happier American, as well as a citizen of the world. Our Earth is home to six and a half billion equally important people. It's humbling to travel and find that people don't have the "American Dream"—they have their own dreams. Europeans like us, but, with all due respect, they wouldn't trade passports.

Thoughtful travel engages us with the world. In tough economic times, it reminds us what is truly important. By broadening perspectives, travel teaches new ways to measure quality of life.

Globe-trotting destroys ethnocentricity, helping us understand and appreciate different cultures. Rather than fear the diversity on this planet, celebrate it. Among your most prized souvenirs will be the strands of different cultures you choose to knit into your own character. The world is a cultural yarn shop, and Back Door travelers are weaving the ultimate tapestry. Join in!

REPUBLIC OF IRELAND

REPUBLIC OF IRELAND

 The Republic of Ireland has existed since 1922, but its inhabitants proudly claim their nation to be the only modern independent state to sprout from purely Celtic roots (sprinkled with a few Vikings and shipwrecked Spanish Armada sailors for seasoning). The Romans never bothered to come over and organize the wild Irish. Through the persuasive and culturally enlightened approach of early missionaries such as St. Patrick, Ireland may also be the only country to have initially converted to Christianity without bloodshed. Irish culture absorbed the influences of Viking raiders and Norman soldiers of fortune, eventually enduring the 750-year shadow of English occupation.

Just a few decades ago, Ireland was an isolated agricultural economic backwater that had largely missed out on the Industrial Revolution. Things began to turn around when Ireland joined the European Community (precursor to the EU) in 1973. The Irish government instituted farsighted tax laws, including a corporate tax rate of only 12.5 percent (compared to 35 percent in the US) to entice foreign corporations to set up shop here.

Today, the Republic attracts expatriates returning to Ireland and new foreign investment. As the only officially English-speaking country to have adopted the euro currency, Ireland makes an efficient base from which to access the European marketplace. More than 35 percent of the Irish population is under 25 years old, leading many high-tech and pharmaceutical firms to locate here, taking advantage of this young, well-educated labor force. And for the first time, Ireland has become a destination for immigrants, who've come mostly from the Third World and the newer EU members. Eastern Europeans (especially Poles) come in search of higher pay...a reversal from the days when Irish fled to start new lives abroad.

Other aspects of modern life are making inroads in traditional Ireland. In 2003, shops began charging customers for plastic sacks for carrying goods (in 2010, the surcharge was €0.22), which has cut down on litter. In 2004, smoking was banned in all Irish pubs. Some pubkeepers grumble about lost business, but the air

Republic of Ireland

has cleared. And you can't drive too far without running into road construction, as the newly affluent Irish try to cope with more cars crowding their streets. New motorways are making travel between bigger cities faster, but the country is still laced with plenty of humble country lanes perfect for getting scenically lost.

The vast majority of Irish people speak English, but you'll encounter Irish Gaelic if you venture to the western Irish fringe. The Irish love of conversation shines through wherever you go. The warm welcome you'll receive has its roots in ancient Celtic laws of hospitality toward stranded strangers.

All that conversation is helped along by the nebulous concept of Irish time, which never seems to be in short supply. Small shops have opening times posted as "9:00ish until 5:00ish." The local bus usually makes a stop at "10:30ish." A healthy disdain for being a slave to the clock seems to be part of being Ir-ish.

At first glance, Ireland's landscape seems unspectacular, with few mountains higher than 3,000 feet and an interior consisting of grazing pastures and peat bogs. But its seductive beauty

REPUBLIC OF IRELAND

Republic of Ireland Almanac

Official Name: The Republic of Ireland (aka just "Ireland" or, in Irish, Éire).

Population: Ireland's 4.3 million people (same as Kentucky) are of Celtic stock. They speak English, though Irish (Gaelic) is spoken in pockets along the country's west coast. Nearly nine in ten are nominally Catholic, though only one in three attends church.

Latitude and Longitude: 53°N and 8°W. The latitude is equivalent to Alberta, Canada.

Area: With 27,000 square miles—half the size of New York State—it occupies the southern 80 percent of the island of Ireland. The country is small enough that radio broadcasts manage to cover traffic snarls nationwide, rather than city-wide.

Geography: The isle is mostly flat, ringed by a hilly coastline. The climate is moderate, with cloudy skies about every other day.

Biggest Cities: The capital of Dublin (1.5 million) is the only big city; one in three Irish live in the greater Dublin area. Cork has 180,000 people, while Limerick and Galway have about 75,000 apiece.

Economy: The Gross Domestic Product is $177 billion (similar to Alabama's), and the GDP per capita is $42,200—one of Europe's highest, and 20 percent more than Britain's. Major moneymakers include tourism and exports (especially to the US and UK) of machines, medicine, Guinness, glassware, crystalware, and software. Traditional agriculture (potatoes and other root vegetables) is fading fast, but dairy still does well.

Government: The elected president, Mary McAleese, appoints the prime minister (Brian Cowen), who is nominated by Parliament. The Parliament consists of the 60-seat Senate, chosen by an electoral college, and the House of Representatives, with 166 seats apportioned after the people vote for a party. Major parties include Fianna Fail, Fine Gael, and Sinn Fein, the political arm of the (fading) Irish Republican Army. Ireland is divided into 26 administrative counties—including Kerry, Clare, Cork, Limerick, and so on.

Flag: The Republic of Ireland's flag is made of three vertical bands of green, white, and orange.

The Average Irish: A typical Irish person is 5'6", 35 years old, has 1.85 kids, and will live to be 78. Every day, he or she drinks four cups of tea and spends $5 on alcohol.

slowly grows on you. The gentle rainfall, called "soft weather" by the locals, really does create 40 shades of green—and quite a few rainbows as well. Ancient, moss-covered ring forts crouch in lush valleys, while stone-strewn monastic ruins and lone castle turrets brave the wind on nearby hilltops. Charming fishing villages dot the coast near rugged, wave-battered cliffs. Slow down to contemplate the checkerboard patterns created by the rock walls outlining the many fields. Examine the colorful small-town shop fronts that proudly state the name of the proprietor.

The resilient Irish character was born of dark humor, historical reverence, and an optimistic, "we'll get 'em next time" rebel spirit. Though the influence of the Catholic Church is less apparent these days, it still plays a major part in Irish life. The national radio and TV station, RTE, pauses for 30 seconds at noon and at 18:00 to broadcast the chimes of the Angelus bells. The Irish say that if you're phoning heaven, it's a long-distance call from the rest of the world, but a local call from Ireland.

DUBLIN

With reminders of its stirring history and rich culture on every corner, Ireland's capital and largest city is a sightseer's delight. Dublin holds its own above its weight class in arts, entertainment, food, and fun. Dublin's fair city will have you humming, "Cockles and mussels, alive, alive-O."

Founded as a Viking trading settlement in the ninth century, Dublin grew to be a center of wealth and commerce, second only to London in the British Empire. Dublin, the seat of English rule in Ireland for 750 years, was the heart of a "civilized" Anglo-Irish area (eastern Ireland) known as "the Pale." Anything "beyond the Pale" was considered uncultured and almost barbaric...purely Irish.

The Golden Age of English Dublin was the 18th century. The British Empire was on a roll, and the city was right there with it. Largely rebuilt during this Georgian era, Dublin—even with its tattered edges—became an elegant and cultured capital.

Those glory days left a lasting imprint on the city. Squares and boulevards built in the Georgian style give the city an air of grandeur (Georgian is British for Neoclassical...named for the period when four consecutive King Georges occupied the British throne). The National Museum, the National Gallery, and many government buildings are in the Georgian section of town. Few buildings (notably Christ Church and St. Patrick's cathedrals) survive from before this Georgian period.

But nationalism—and a realization of the importance of human rights—would forever change Dublin. The American and French revolutions inspired Irish intellectuals to buck British rule, and life in Dublin was never quite the same after the Rebellion of 1798. In 1801, the Act of Union with Britain resulted in the loss of Ireland's parliament (no need for two with the dominant one in London). As the Irish members of parliament moved to Westminster, the movers and shakers of the Anglo-Irish aristocracy followed suit, and Dublin slowly began to decay.

Throughout the 19th century, as Ireland endured the Great Potato Famine and saw the beginnings of the modern struggle for independence, Dublin was treated—and felt—more like a British colony than a partner. The tension culminated in the Easter Uprising of 1916, followed a few years later by independence from Britain, and Ireland's civil war. With many of its grand streets left in ruins, Dublin emerged as the capital of the British Empire's only former colony in Europe.

While bullet-pocked buildings and dramatic statues keep memories of Ireland's struggle for independence alive, the city is looking ahead to a brighter future. Dubliners are energetic and helpful, while visitors enjoy a big-town cultural scene wrapped in a small-town smile.

Planning Your Time

On a three-week trip through Ireland, Dublin deserves three nights and two days. Be aware that some important sights close on Mondays. Consider this ambitious sightseeing plan:

Day 1:

10:15	Follow the Trinity College guided walk.
11:00	Visit the Book of Kells and Old Library ahead of midday crowds.
12:00	Browse Grafton Street, have lunch there or picnic on Merrion Square.
13:30	See Number Twenty-Nine Georgian House (closed Mon).
15:00	Head to the National Museum: Archaeology and History branch (also closed Mon).
17:00	Return to hotel, rest, have dinner—eat well for less during early-bird specials.
19:30	Go for an evening guided pub tour (musical or literary).
22:00	Drop in on Irish music in the Temple Bar area.

Day 2:

10:00	Take the Dublin Castle tour.
11:30	Hop on one of the hop-on, hop-off buses, jumping off to see the Guinness Storehouse and Kilmainham Gaol (bring a sandwich to munch in transit on the

open-top bus, or stop off to picnic in one of Dublin's green squares).

15:00   Leave the bus at Parnell Square, visit the Garden of Remembrance, and stroll down to O'Connell Bridge, sightseeing and shopping as you like along the way.

Evening   Catch a play, concert, or Comhaltas traditional music in Dun Laoghaire.

With More Time: Dublin, while relatively small, can keep you busily sightseeing for days without even leaving the center of town. And with all its music, theater, and after-hour tours—not to mention the lively pub scene—evenings are just as fun.

Orientation to Dublin

(area code: 01)

Greater Dublin sprawls with a million and a half people—a third of the country's population. But the center of tourist interest is a tight triangle between O'Connell Bridge, St. Stephen's Green, and Christ Church Cathedral. Within this triangle you'll find Trinity College (Book of Kells), Grafton Street (top pedestrian shopping zone), Temple Bar (trendy and touristy nightlife center), Dublin Castle, and the hub of most city tours and buses. The only major

sights outside this easy-to-walk triangle are the Kilmainham Gaol, the Guinness Storehouse, and the National Museum: Decorative Arts and History branch (all west of the center).

The River Liffey cuts the town in two. Focus on the southern half, where most of your sightseeing will take place. Dublin's wide main drag, O'Connell Street, starts north of the river at the Parnell monument and runs south, down to the central O'Connell Bridge. After crossing the bridge, it continues south as the major city axis past Trinity College and through pedestrian-only Grafton Street to St. Stephen's Green. Get used to the fact that many long Dublin streets change their names every few blocks. A prime example of this are the numerously named Quays (pronounced "keys"), which run east-west along the Liffey River.

The suburban port of Dun Laoghaire (dun LEERY) lies south of Dublin, 25 minutes away by DART commuter train. Travelers connecting by ferry to Holyhead in Wales—or those just looking for a mellow town to sleep in outside of urban Dublin—can easily home-base here. Another option is the northern suburb of Howth, also 25 minutes away on the DART and closer to the air-

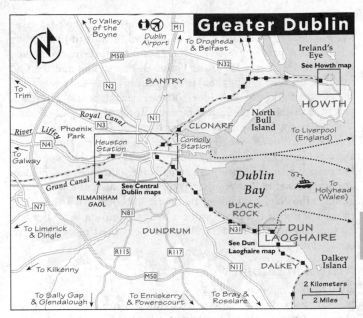

Greater Dublin

Within the map: To Valley of the Boyne · Dublin Airport · M1 · To Drogheda & Belfast · M50 · N32 · Ireland's Eye · See Howth map · To Trim · N2 · SANTRY · N1 · HOWTH · Royal Canal · N3 · CLONARF · North Bull Island · To Liverpool (England) · River Liffey · Phoenix Park · Heuston Station · Connolly Station · N4 · To Galway · Dublin Bay · Grand Canal · See Central Dublin maps · KILMAINHAM GAOL · N7 · N81 · BLACK-ROCK · To Holyhead (Wales) · To Limerick & Dingle · DUNDRUM · N31 · DUN LAOGHAIRE · See Dun Laoghaire map · R115 · R117 · Dalkey Island · To Kilkenny · N11 · DALKEY · M50 · To Sally Gap & Glendalough · To Enniskerry & Powerscourt · To Bray & Rosslare · 2 Kilometers · 2 Miles

DUBLIN

port. Room prices are about a third cheaper in Dun Laoghaire or Howth than in downtown Dublin.

Tourist Information

Dublin's main tourist information office (TI) is a thriving hub of ticket and info desks filling an old church (Mon-Sat June-Sept 9:00-17:30, Oct-May 9:30-17:30; Sun 10:30-15:00 year-round; a block off Grafton Street on Suffolk Street, tel. 01/850-230-330 or 01/605-7700, www.visitdublin.com). It has a bus-info desk, sandwich bar, more maps and books than you'll ever need, and racks advertising the busy entertainment scene. You can buy tickets to many theater and concert events here. It's also a good place to pick up brochures for destinations throughout Ireland. There's another TI at the airport (daily 8:00-22:00) and one at the Dun Laoghaire ferry terminal (Mon-Sat 9:30-12:45 & 14:00-17:30, closed Sun). A smaller satellite TI is halfway down the east side of O'Connell Street (Mon-Sat 9:00-17:00, closed Sun).

Pick up the TI's *The Guide*, which includes a decent city map (free). Inside is a minimal schedule of happenings in town. The excellent *Collins Illustrated Discovering Dublin Map* (€8 at TIs and newsstands) is the ultimate city map, listing just about everything of interest, along with helpful opinions and tidbits of Dublin history.

Dublin Pass: This sightseeing pass is a good deal only if you like to visit lots of sights quickly (€35/1 day, €55/2 days, €65/3 days, €95/6 days, sold at TIs, www.dublinpass.ie). The pass saves a few minutes, when you'd otherwise need to wait in line to buy a ticket. It covers 31 museums, churches, literature-related sights, and expensive stops such as the Guinness Storehouse and the Old Jameson Distillery, plus the Aircoach airport bus—one-way from the airport to the city only (doesn't cover Airlink buses). However, the pass doesn't include the famous Book of Kells at Trinity College or any bus tours or walking tours, and some of the sights it claims to "cover"—such as the National Gallery, the Chester Beatty Library, and the National Museum's Archaeology and Decorative Arts branches—are actually free (although passholders get other benefits that regular visitors won't, such as a free glossy guide at the National Gallery that normally costs €5). The booklet that comes with the pass can be a handy planning tool. But the bottom line is that most travelers won't get their money's worth out of this pass.

Arrival in Dublin
By Train
Dublin has two train stations. **Heuston Station,** on the west end of town, serves west and southwest Ireland (30-minute walk from O'Connell Bridge; take taxi or bus #90—see below). **Connolly Station,** which serves the north, northwest, and Rosslare, is closer to the center (10-minute walk from O'Connell Bridge). Each station has ATMs, but only Heuston has lockers (small lockers-€4/day, large-€6/day, 7-day maximum).

The two train stations are connected by the red line of the LUAS commuter train (see "Getting Around Dublin" on page 51) and by bus. Bus #90 runs along the river, linking both train stations, the bus station, and the city center (€1, 6/hour).

To reach Heuston Station from the city center, catch bus #90 on the south side of the river; to get to Connolly Station and Busaras Central Bus Station from the city center, catch #90 on the north side of the river.

By Bus
Bus Éireann, Ireland's national bus company, uses the **Busaras** (Bu-SAUR-us...like a dinosaur) **Central Bus Station** next to Connolly Station (10-minute walk or short ride on bus #90—described above—to the city center).

By Plane
The airport has ATMs, change bureaus, car-rental agencies, baggage check, a café, and a supermarket at the parking lot (tel. 01/814-1111, www.dublinairport.ie).

Getting Between the Airport and Downtown by Bus: You

have two main choices: Airlink (double-decker green bus) or Aircoach (single-deck blue bus). Both pick up on the street directly in front of airport arrivals at ground level. Consider buying a €13.30 **Rambler** city-bus pass at the airport TI (see "Getting Around Dublin" on page 51), which covers the Airlink bus into town—but read the following description first to make sure Airlink is the best choice for your trip.

Airlink: Airlink buses #747 and #748 are the handiest and cost the same (€6, pay driver, 3/hour, 35-45 minutes, tel. 01/873-4222, www.dublinbus.ie). **Bus #747** connects the airport to O'Connell Street, then Busaras Central Bus Station (a block from Connolly Station); this bus is best for reaching my recommended hotels near Parnell Square (north of the city center). **Bus #748** connects the airport to Connolly Station, the Tara Street DART station (handy connections to Dun Laoghaire), Aston Quay (near O'Connell Bridge), Wood Quay (near Christ Church Cathedral), and finally to Heuston Station. Bus #748 is better for hotels in the city center—ask the driver which stop is closest to your hotel.

Aircoach: To reach recommended hotels near St. Stephen's Green (south of the city center), the Aircoach is best (€7, covered by Dublin Pass, 3/hour, runs 5:00-23:30; pay driver and confirm best stop for your hotel, tel. 01/844-7118, www.aircoach.ie).

City Bus: The cheapest (and slowest) way from the airport to downtown Dublin is by city bus; buses marked #16A, #41, #41A, and #41B go to O'Connell Street (€2.20, exact change required, no change given, 4/hour, 55 minutes).

Getting Between the Airport and Suburbs: The best way to get to Dun Laoghaire is to take the Aircoach bus (€8, hourly, 50 minutes, tel. 01/844-7118, www.aircoach.ie). Otherwise, take Airlink bus #748 to Tara Street Station and transfer onto the DART light rail system (€8 for Airlink/DART combo-ticket). For Dun Laoghaire, take DART direction: Bray; for Howth, take DART direction: Howth.

Taxis from the airport into Dublin cost about €35; to Dun Laoghaire, about €50; to Howth, about €25.

By Ferry
Irish Ferries dock at the mouth of the River Liffey (at Dublin Docklands, near the town center), while the **Stena Line** docks at Dun Laoghaire (easy DART train connections into Dublin, 4/hour, 25 minutes). For more information, see "Dublin Connections" on page 96.

By Car
Trust me: You don't want to drive in downtown Dublin. Cars are unnecessary for sightseeing in town, parking is expensive (about

Go with the E-flow

To eliminate traffic snarls, the M-50 ring road's coin-operated tollbooths have been replaced with an automated tolling surveillance system that records the license plate numbers of cars that pass through. This means you'll need an E-flow pass to cover the €3 toll per trip on this outer belt. If you go through without a pass, you have until 20:00 the following evening to pay the toll, or you'll arrive home to discover a hefty fine tacked onto the credit card you used to rent the car.

Most car-rental companies take care of this charge for you: Your car likely already comes with an E-flow pass, and the rental company will automatically charge your credit card €3 for each M-50 journey. However, to avoid potential duplicate charges, ask when you pick up your car at the airport to confirm that it has an E-flow. If it does not, you can buy a pass at an airport newsstand (ask to be directed to the nearest shop selling them). The shop clerk will ask to see your rental-car registration number (marked on your keys) to input into the system.

Once you have the pass, simply carry it with you (no need to display it in the car). For pass details, see www.eflow.ie.

€30/day), and traffic will get your fighting Irish up. Save your car-rental days for cross-country travel between smaller towns and see this energetic city by taxi, bus, or on foot. If you have a car, sleep out in the suburbs (Dun Laoghaire or Howth), and ask your inn-keeper about the best places to park.

Drivers renting a car at Dublin Airport, but not staying in Dun Laoghaire or Howth, can bypass the worst of the big-city traffic by making use of the M-50 ring road to whisk themselves south or west. Ask your car-rental company about an E-flow pass before using the motorway (see sidebar).

Helpful Hints

High Costs: Despite the busted Celtic Tiger economic boom (1995-2007—R.I.P.), Ireland is still one of the EU's most expensive countries. Restaurants and lodging—other than hostels—are more expensive the closer you get to the touristy Temple Bar district (see cheaper options under "Sleeping in Dublin" on page 85). A pint of beer in a Temple Bar pub costs almost €6 (a sobering thought).

Pickpockets: Irish destinations, especially Dublin, are not immune to this scourge. Wear a money belt or risk spending a couple of days of your cherished vacation in bureaucratic purgatory (on the phone canceling credit cards—see page 16—and at the embassy waiting for a replacement passport—

see below). Wasting vacation time this way is like paying to wait in line at the DMV.

Tourist Victim Support Service: This service can be helpful if you run into any problems (Mon-Sat 10:00-18:00, Sun 12:00-18:00, tel. 01/478-5295, www.itas.ie).

US Embassy: It's on 42 Elgin Road in the Ballsbridge neighborhood (Mon-Tue and Thu-Fri 8:30-11:30 for passport concerns, closed Wed and Sat-Sun, tel. 01/668-7122 or 01/668-8777, http://dublin.usembassy.gov).

Festivals: Book ahead during festivals and for any weekend. St. Patrick's Day is a five-day extravaganza in Dublin (March 17-20 in 2011, www.stpatricksday.ie). June 16 is Bloomsday, dedicated to the Irish author James Joyce and featuring the Messenger Bike Rally (www.jamesjoyce.ie). On rugby weekends (about four per year), during the all-Ireland Gaelic football and hurling finals (Sundays in September), and during summer rock concerts, hotels raise their prices and are packed.

Internet Access: Internet cafés have sprung up on nearly every street. **Viva Internet** is close to Christ Church Cathedral (Mon-Thu 10:00-22:00, Fri 10:30-22:00, Sat-Sun 12:00-22:00, Lord Edward Street near City Hall, tel. 01/672-4725). **Emailinternet** is central (daily 9:00-21:00, 6 Grafton Street, easy-to-miss door is directly opposite AIB Bank, tel. 01/677-8298, www.emailinternet.ie). **Global Internet Café** is north of the River Liffey (Mon-Fri 8:00-23:00, Sat 9:00-23:00, Sun 10:00-23:00, 8 Lower O'Connell Street, tel. 01/878-0295).

Laundry: Patrick Street Launderette, a block southwest of Jurys Inn Christ Church on Patrick Street, is full-service only. Allow four hours and about €10 for a load (Mon-Fri 9:00-20:00, Sat 9:00-18:00, closed Sun, tel. 01/473-1779). The **All-American Launderette** offers self- and full-service options (Mon-Sat 8:30-19:00, Sun 10:00-18:00, 40 South Great George's Street, tel. 01/677-2779).

Car Rental: For Dublin car-rental information, see page 445.

Getting Around Dublin

You'll do most of Dublin on foot, though when you need public transportation, you'll find it readily available and easy to use.

By Bus: Buses are cheap and cover the city thoroughly. Most lines start at the four quays, or piers, that are nearest to O'Connell Bridge. If you're away from the center, nearly any bus takes you back downtown. Some bus stops are "request only" stops: Be alert to the bus numbers (above the windshield) of approaching buses. When you see your bus coming, extend your arm straight out, palm outward, to flag it down. Tell the driver where you're going, and he'll ask for €1.15-2.20 depending on the number of stops.

Bring change or lose any excess. Bus #90 connects the bus and train stations (see "Arrival in Dublin—By Train" on page 48).

The bus office at 59 Upper O'Connell Street has free bus-route maps and sells two different city-bus passes (Mon 8:30-17:30, Tue-Fri 9:00-17:30, Sat 9:00-14:00, closed Sun, tel. 01/873-4222, www.dublinbus.ie). The three-day **Rambler pass** costs €13.30 and covers the Airlink airport bus (but not Aircoach buses or DART trains). The one-day **Short Hop pass,** which costs €10.20, includes DART trains (but not Airlink or Aircoach buses). Passes are also sold at each TI, and at newsstands and markets citywide (mostly Centra, Mace, Spar, and Londis).

By DART (Train): Speedy commuter trains run along the coast, connecting Dublin with Dun Laoghaire's ferry terminal, Howth's harbor, and recommended B&Bs. Think of the DART line as a giant "C" that serves coastal suburbs from Bray in the south to Howth in the north (€2.30, €4.20 round-trips valid the same day only, Eurailpass valid but you'll use up a valuable flexi-day, tel. 01/703-3504, www.irishrail.ie/home). For more information, see "Getting to Dun Laoghaire" on page 99 and "Getting to Howth" on page 105.

By LUAS (Light Rail): The city's light-rail system has two main lines (red and green) that serve inland suburbs. The more useful line for travelers is the red line, connecting the Heuston and Connolly train stations (a 15-minute ride apart) at either edge of the Central 1 Zone. In between, the Busaras Central Bus Station, Smithfield, and Museum stops can be handy (€1.50, 6/hour, runs 5:30-24:30, tel. 1-800-300-604, www.luas.ie). Check the 15-foot-high pillars at each boarding platform that display the time and destination of the next LUAS train. Make sure you're on the right platform for the direction you want to go.

By Taxi: Taxis are everywhere and easy to hail (cheaper for 3-4 people). Cabbies are honest, plentiful, friendly, and good sources of information (€5 minimum 8:00-20:00, €6 minimum 20:00-8:00, figure about €10 for most crosstown rides, €40/hour for guided joyride). If you call to arrange a pickup (e.g., from your hotel), they'll tack on a €2 fee.

Tours in Dublin

While Dublin's physical treasures are lackluster by European standards, the city has a fine story to tell and people with a natural knack for telling it. It's a good town for walking tours, and the competition is fierce. Dublin is noisy; if you can't hear the guide, move in closer. Pamphlets touting creative walks are posted all over town. Choices include medieval walks, literary walks, Georgian Dublin walks, traditional music pub crawls, and even a rock-and-stroll walk tracing the careers of contemporary Irish bands. Taking an evening walk is a great way to meet other travelers. The Dublin TI also offers series of free, good-quality "iWalks" for travelers with iPods or other MP3 players (download with maps at www.visitdublin.com).

For help finding the departure points of the following recommended tours, see the map on page 62.

By Foot

▲▲**Historical Walking Tour**—This is your best introductory walk. A group of hardworking history graduates—many of whom claim to have done more than just kiss the Blarney Stone—enliven Dublin's basic historic strip (Trinity College, Old Parliament House, Dublin Castle, and Christ Church Cathedral). You'll get the story of their city, from its Viking origins to the present. Guides speak at length about the roots of Ireland's struggle with Britain. As you listen to your guide, you'll stand in front of buildings that aren't much to look at, but are lots to talk about (May-Sept daily at 11:00 and 15:00, April and Oct daily at 11:00, Nov-March Fri-Sun only at 11:00). All walks last two hours and cost €12 (but get the €10 "student" discount rate with this book in 2011, free for kids under 14, departs from front gate of Trinity College, private tours available, mobile 087-688-9412 or 087-830-3523, www.historical insights.ie).

▲▲▲**Traditional Irish Musical Pub Crawl**—This impressive and entertaining tour visits the upstairs rooms of three pubs;

there, you'll listen to two musicians talk about, play, and sing traditional Irish music. While having only two musicians makes the music a bit thin (Irish music aficionados will say you're better off just finding a good session), the evening—though touristy—is not gimmicky. It's an education in traditional Irish music. The musicians, who also demonstrate a few instruments, clearly enjoy introducing rookies to their art and are very good at it. In the summer, this popular tour frequently sells out—reserve ahead (€12, €1 discount with this book in 2011, beer extra, allow 2.5 hours, April-Oct daily at 19:30, Nov-March Thu-Sat only, maximum 50 tourists, meet upstairs at Gogarty's Pub at the corner of Fleet and Anglesea in the Temple Bar area, tel. 01/475-3313, www.musical pubcrawl.com).

▲**Dublin Literary Pub Crawl**—Two actors take 40 or so tourists on a walk, stopping at four pubs. Their clever banter introduces

DUBLIN

Dublin

To Trim
via N-3

NEW CABRA RD.

OLD CABRA RD.

BLACKHORSE AVE.

ANNAMOETRE

N. CIRCULAR RD.

PHIBSBOROUGH RD.

NORTH RD.

PRUSSIA ST.

AUGHRIM ST.

MANOR ST.

GRANGEGORMAN

ZOO

ZOO RD.

CHESTERFIELD AVE.

INFIRMARY RD.

Phoenix
Park

NATIONAL MUSEUM
DECORATIVE ARTS &
HISTORY
(COLLINS BARRACKS)

SMITH-
FIELD

OLD JAMESON
DISTILLERY

WELLINGTON
OBELISK

WELLINGTON RD.

CONYNGHAM RD.

Museum

Smith-
field

S. CIRCULAR RD.

River Liffey

HEUSTON
STATION

WOLFE TONE QUAY

VICTORIA QUAY

FOUR
COURTS

To Galway
via N-4

ST. JOHN'S RD. W.

MILITARY RD.

GUINNESS
BREWERY
PROPERTY

CON COLBERT RD.

IRISH MUSEUM
OF MODERN ART

INCHICORE RD.

KILMAINHAM LN.

PROSPECT TERR.

GUINNESS
STOREHOUSE

MEATH ST.

KILMAINHAM
GAOL

James's

UPPER BASIN ST.

BELLEVIEW ST.

LUAS TRAM
GREEN LINE

S. CIRCULAR RD.

MARROWBONE LN.

CORK ST.

Rialto

Fatima

SUIR RD.

Suir Road

REUBEN ST.

DOLPHIN'S BARN ST.

CLANBRASSIL ST.

To
Tallaght

DOLPHIN RD.

MOURNE RD.

CRUMLIN RD.

S. CIRCULAR RD.

Grand

PARNELL RD.

Canal

200 Meters
200 Yards

the novice to the high *craic* of James Joyce, Seán O'Casey, and
W. B. Yeats. The two-hour tour is punctuated with 20-minute
pub breaks (free time). While the beer lubricates the social fun,
it dilutes the content of the evening. This is an easygoing excuse
to drink beer in busy pubs, hook up with other travelers, and get
a dose of Irish witty lit. But if you want straight lit and drama,
find a real performance—there are many throughout the summer, such as the lunchtime hour at the Dublin Writers' Museum,

described on page 76 (€13, €1 discount with this book in hand in 2011, April-Oct daily at 19:30, Nov-March Thu-Sun at 19:30; you can normally just show up, but call ahead July-Aug when it can fill up; meet upstairs in the Duke Pub—off Grafton on Duke Street, tel. 01/670-5602, mobile 087-263-0270, www.dublinpubcrawl .com). Connoisseurs of Irish pubs will want to buy the excellent *Dublin Literary Pub Crawl* guidebook by pub-crawl founder Colm Quilligan.

Dublin at a Glance

▲▲▲**Traditional Irish Musical Pub Crawl** A fascinating, practical, and enjoyable primer on traditional Irish music. **Hours:** April-Oct daily at 19:30, Nov-March Thu-Sat only. See page 53.

▲▲▲**National Museum: Archaeology and History** Interesting collection of Irish treasures from the Stone Age to today. **Hours:** Tue-Sat 10:00-17:00, Sun 14:00-17:00, closed Mon. See page 61.

▲▲▲**Kilmainham Gaol** Historic jail used by the British as a political prison—today a museum that tells a moving story of the suffering of the Irish people. **Hours:** Daily 9:30-18:00. See page 78.

▲▲**Historical Walking Tour** Your best introduction to Dublin. **Hours:** May-Sept daily at 11:00 and 15:00, April and Oct daily at 11:00, Nov-March Fri-Sun only at 11:00. See page 53.

▲▲**Trinity College Tour** Ireland's most famous school, best visited with a 30-minute tour led by one of its students. **Hours:** May-Sept daily 10:15-15:40, Feb-April and Oct-Nov Sat-Sun only, no tours Dec-Jan; weather permitting. See page 59.

▲▲**Book of Kells in the Trinity Old Library** An exquisite illuminated manuscript, the most important piece of art from the Dark Ages. **Hours:** May-Sept daily 9:30-16:30; Oct-April Mon-Sat 9:30-16:30, Sun 12:00-16:30. See page 59.

▲▲**Number Twenty-Nine Georgian House** Restored 18th-century house; tours provide an intimate glimpse of middle-class Georgian life. **Hours:** Tue-Sat 10:00-17:00, Sun 12:00-17:00, closed Mon. See page 64.

▲▲**Grafton Street** The city's liveliest pedestrian shopping mall. **Hours:** Always open. See page 64.

▲▲**Dublin Castle** The city's historic 700-year-old castle, featuring ornate English state apartments, tourable only with a guide. **Hours:** Mon-Sat 10:00-16:45, Sun 14:00-16:45. See page 65.

▲▲**Chester Beatty Library** American expatriate's eclectic yet sumptuous collection of literary and religious treasures from

Islam, the Orient, and medieval Europe. **Hours:** May-Sept Mon-Fri 10:00-17:00, Sat 11:00-17:00, Sun 13:00-17:00; Oct-April Tue-Fri 10:00-17:00, Sat 11:00-17:00, Sun 13:00-17:00, closed Mon. See page 65.

▲▲**Temple Bar** Dublin's trendiest neighborhood, with shops, cafés, theaters, galleries, pubs, and restaurants—a great spot for live traditional music. **Hours:** Always open. See page 68.

▲▲**O'Connell Bridge** Landmark bridge spanning the River Liffey at the center of Dublin. **Hours:** Always open. See page 69.

▲▲**O'Connell Street** Dublin's grandest promenade and main drag, packed with history and ideal for a stroll. **Hours:** Always open. See page 71.

▲**National Gallery** Fine collection of top Irish painters and European masters. **Hours:** Mon-Sat 9:30-17:30, Thu until 20:30, Sun 12:00-17:30. See page 61.

▲**Merrion Square** Enjoyable and inviting park with a fun statue of Oscar Wilde. **Hours:** Always open. See page 64.

▲**St. Stephen's Green** Relaxing park surrounded by fine Georgian buildings. **Hours:** Always open. See page 64.

▲**National Museum: Decorative Arts and History** Shows off Irish dress, furniture, silver, and weaponry with a special focus on the 1916 rebellion, fight for independence, and civil war. **Hours:** Tue-Sat 10:00-17:00, Sun 14:00-17:00, closed Mon. See page 80.

▲**Guinness Storehouse** The home of Ireland's national beer, with a museum of beer-making, a gallery of clever ads, and the spectacular Gravity Bar with panoramic city views. **Hours:** Daily 9:30-17:00, July-Aug until 19:00. See page 79.

▲**Gaelic Athletic Association Museum** High-tech museum of traditional Gaelic sports such as hurling and Irish football. **Hours:** July-Aug Mon-Sun 9:30-18:00; Sept-June Mon-Sat 9:30-17:00, Sun 12:00-17:00. On game Sundays, it's open only to ticket-holders. See page 80.

DUBLIN

1916 Rebellion Walks—This two-hour walking tour breathes gritty life into the most turbulent year in modern Irish history, when idealistic Irish rebels launched the Easter Uprising—eventually leading to independence from Britain. Guide Lorcan Collins has written a guidebook called *The Easter Rising*—worth seeking out—and is passionate about his walks (€12, €2 discount with this book in 2011, daily March-Oct Mon-Sat at 11:30, Sun at 13:00, no tours Nov-mid-March, depart from International Bar at 23 Wicklow Street, mobile 086-858-3847, www.1916rising.com).

Pat Liddy Walking Tours—Trained by one of Dublin's top historians, these guides take small groups on enthusiastic and informal two-hour walks of various neighborhoods. Each tour has a different focus, such as Viking, Medieval, Macabre, Georgian Dublin, Guinness, and famous Dublin writers (€5-12, depends on tour—see website; daily May-Oct at 10:00, 12:00, and 14:30; meet in front of TI on Suffolk Street, tel. 081/820-5205 or 087/905-2480, www.walkingtours.ie).

Rebel Tours of Dublin—These 1.5-hour walks focus on revolutionary events in Dublin from 1913 to 1923 as Ireland shed British rule. Strongly opinionated, these guides view history through the lens of Irish Republicanism (€5, departs Mon-Sat at 11:30 from Sinn Fein Bookshop at 58 Parnell Square, tel. 01/814-8542, www.sinnfeinbookshop.com).

By Bus (on Land and Water)

▲Hop-on, Hop-off Bus Tours—Two companies (Dublin City Tour and City Sightseeing) offer hop-on, hop-off bus tours of Dublin, doing virtually identical 1.5-hour circuits. You can get on or off at your choice of about 20 stops (4/hour, daily 9:30-17:00, ticket valid for 24 hours). Buses are mostly topless, with live running commentaries. This type of tour, which runs in many European cit-

ies but isn't always well executed, is made-to-order for Dublin, and buses run so frequently that they make your sightseeing super-efficient. Both companies go to the Guinness Storehouse and Kilmainham Gaol (although the Dublin City Tour bus stops a few blocks from the Gaol). Buy your ticket on board. Each company's map, free with your ticket, details various discounts that you'll get at Dublin's sights (such as the Guinness Storehouse, Viking Splash tour, Old Jameson Distillery, Dublin Writers' Museum, Dublinia, Christ Church Cathedral, and others). **Dublin City Tour** (green buses) drivers provide fun and quirky narration (€16, tel. 01/873-4222, www.dublinsightseeing.ie). **City Sightseeing** (red buses) come with both a guide and a driver, rather than a driver who guides (€16, tel. 01/872-9010, www.irishcitytours.com).

▲**Viking Splash Tours**—If you'd like to ride in a WWII amphibious vehicle—driven by a Viking-costumed guide who's as liable to spout history as he is to growl—this is for you. The tour starts with a group roar from the Viking within us all. At first, the guide talks as if he were a Viking ("When we came here in 841..."), but soon the patriot emerges as he tags Irish history onto the sights you pass. Near the end of the 1.25-hour tour (punctuated by occasional group roars at passersby), you don a life jacket for a slow spin up and down a boring canal. Although it's covered, the boat is breezy—dress appropriately. Kids who expect a Viking splash may feel like they've been trapped in a classroom, but historians will enjoy the talk more than the gimmick (€20, Feb-Nov daily 10:00-16:00, none Dec-Jan, departs about hourly from the north side of St. Stephen's Green opposite Dawson Street, ticket office at 64-65 Patrick Street, tel. 01/707-6000, www.vikingsplash.com).

Sights in Dublin

South of the River Liffey

Trinity College

Founded in 1592 by Queen Elizabeth I to establish a Protestant way of thinking about God, Trinity has long been Ireland's most prestigious college. Originally the student body was limited to rich Protestant males. Women were admitted in 1903, and Catholics—though allowed entrance by the school much earlier—were only given formal permission by the Catholic Church to study at Trinity in the 1970s. Today, half of Trinity's 12,500 students are women, and 70 percent are culturally Catholic (although only about 20 percent of Irish youth are churchgoing).

▲▲**Trinity College Tour**—Trinity students organize and lead 30-minute **tours** of their campus (look just inside the gate for

posted departure times and a ticket-seller on a stool). You'll get a rundown of the mostly Georgian architecture; a peek at student life past and present; and the enjoyable company of your guide, a witty Irish college kid (€10, includes €9 fee to see Book of Kells, where the tour leaves you; May-Sept daily 10:15-15:40, Feb-April and Oct-Nov Sat-Sun only, no tours Dec-Jan, departs roughly every 30 minutes, weather permitting).

▲▲**Book of Kells in the Trinity Old Library**— The only Trinity campus interior welcoming tourists is the Old Library (just follow the signs), with its precious Book of Kells. Written on vellum (calfskin) in the late eighth century—by Irish monks on the island of Iona, Scotland—this enthusiastically decorated copy of the four Gospels was taken safely inland to the Irish monastery at Kells in A.D. 806 after a series of Viking raids. Arguably the finest piece of art from what is generally called the Dark Ages, the Book of Kells shows that monastic life in this far fringe of Europe was far from dark.

The first-class "Turning Darkness into Light" **exhibit,** with a one-way route, puts the 680-page illuminated manuscript in its historical and cultural context, preparing you to see the original book and other precious manuscripts in the treasury. Make a point to spend time in the exhibit (before reaching the actual Book of Kells). Especially interesting are the five-minute video clips show-

ing the exacting care that went into tran-scribing the monk-uscripts and the ancient art of bookbinding. Two screens (on opposite walls of the exhibition room) silently demon-strate the monks' labors of love.

The manuscript has been bound into four separate volumes, and at any given time, two of the four gospels are on display in the **treasury.** The crowd around the one glass case that displays the treasures can be off-putting, but hold your own and get up close. You'll see four richly decorated, 1,200-year-old pages—two text and two decorated cover

pages. The library treasury also displays two other books—likely the Book of Armagh (A.D. 807) and the Book of Durrow (A.D. 680)—neither of which can be checked out.

Next, a stairway leads upstairs to the 200-foot-long main chamber of the Old Library (from 1732), stacked to its towering ceiling with 200,000 of the library's oldest books. Here, you'll find one of a dozen surviving original copies of the **Proclamation of the Irish Republic.** Patrick Pearse read these words outside the General Post Office on April 24, 1916, starting the Easter Uprising that led to Irish independence. Read the entire thing...imagining it was yours. Notice the inclusive opening phrase and the seven signatories (each of whom was executed).

Another national icon is nearby: the 15th-century **Brian Boru harp,** the oldest surviving Irish harp (its name is misleading—the Irish High King Brian Boru died 400 years before the harp was created). The Irish love of music is so intense that Ireland is the only nation with a musical instrument as its national symbol. You'll see this harp's likeness everywhere, including on the back of all Irish euro coins and government documents. The harp's inspirational effect on the Gaelic culture was so strong that Queen Elizabeth I, who tried to eradicate the Gaelic culture during her reign (1558-1603), ordered Irish harpists to be hung wherever found and their instruments smashed.

Cost and Hours: €9, included in €10 Trinity College tour—see earlier; May-Sept daily 9:30-16:30; Oct-April Mon-Sat 9:30-16:30, Sun 12:00-16:30; tel. 01/896-2320. A long line often snakes out of the building. Minimize your wait by avoiding the midday crunch (roughly 11:00-14:30). For more on the Book of Kells, see page 423 in the Ireland: Past and Present chapter.

Museums South of Trinity College

▲▲▲**National Museum: Archaeology and History**—Showing off the treasures of Ireland from the Stone Age to modern times, this branch of the National Museum is itself a national treasure. Under one dome, it's wonderfully digestible. Ireland's Bronze Age gold fills the center. Up four steps, a prehistoric Ireland exhibit rings the gold. In a corner (behind a 2,000-year-old body), you'll find the treasury, with the museum's most famous pieces (brooches, chalices, and other examples of Celtic metalwork). The collection's superstar is the gold, enamel, and amber eighth-century Tara Brooch. The best Viking artifacts in town are upstairs with the medieval collection. If you'll be visiting Cong (in Connemara, near Galway—see page 304), seek out the original Cross of Cong.

Cost and Hours: Free, Tue-Sat 10:00-17:00, Sun 14:00-17:00, closed Mon, good café, between Trinity College and St. Stephen's Green on Kildare Street, tel. 01/677-7444—call in morning for sporadic tour schedule, www.museum.ie. For background information, read "Irish Art" on page 421.

Nearby: As you exit the museum, glance over at **Leinster House,** next door (guarded and safely distant from the street). It was once the Duke of Leinster's town residence. Today, it houses the Irish Dail and Seanad (parliament and senate), which meet here 90 days of each year.

▲**National Gallery**—This museum has Ireland's best collection of European masters: Vermeer, Caravaggio, Monet, and Picasso. It also features a hall that displays the work of top Irish painters, including Jack Yeats (the brother of the famous poet). It's impressive—although not nearly as extensive as national galleries in London or Paris. Study the floor-plan flier and take advantage

South Dublin

Tour Departure Points
1 Historical Walking Tour
2 Musical Pub Crawl
3 Literary Pub Crawl
4 1916 Rebellion Walks
5 Pat Liddy Walking Tours
6 Viking Splash Tours
7 Trinity College Tour

150 Meters
150 Yards

of the free audioguide. Be sure to walk the series of rooms on the ground floor devoted to Irish painting and get to know artists you may never have heard of before. Visit the National Portrait Gallery on the mezzanine level for an insight into the great personalities of Ireland. You'll find Caravaggio and Vermeer on the top floor. In his *Taking of Christ*, Caravaggio, master of the chiaroscuro style, makes dramatic use of light and shadow for emphasis. Vermeer's *Lady Writing a Letter with her Maid*, one of only 35 known works by the Dutch artist, shows his trademark focus on life's quiet moments.

Cost and Hours: Free, Mon-Sat 9:30-17:30, Thu until 20:30, Sun 12:00-17:30, Merrion Square West, tel. 01/661-5133, www .nationalgallery.ie.

Tours: The museum offers free audioguide tours (donations accepted) and free 45-minute guided tours (Sat at 14:00, Sun at 13:00 and 14:00).

National Library—Literature holds a lofty place in the Irish psyche. To feel the fire-and-ice pulse of Ireland's most famous literary greats, visit the annually changing exhibits in the library basement. The exhibits flesh out the very human passions of these writers, with samples of handwritten manuscripts and surprisingly interesting mini-documentaries of the times they lived in. Upstairs, you can get help making use of the library records to trace your genealogy (free, Mon-Wed 9:30-21:00, Thu-Fri 9:30-17:00, Sat 9:30-13:00, closed Sun, tel. 01/603-0277, 2-3 Kildare Street, www.nli.ie).

Merrion Square and Nearby

▲**Merrion Square**—Laid out in 1762, this square is ringed by elegant Georgian houses decorated with fine doors—a Dublin trademark. (If you're inspired by the ornate knobs and knockers, there's a shop by that name on nearby Nassau Street.) The park, once the exclusive domain of the residents, is now a delightful public escape. More inviting than St. Stephen's Green, it's ideal for a picnic. To learn what "snogging" is, walk through the park on a sunny day, when it's full of smooching lovers. Oscar Wilde, lounging wittily on a boulder on the corner nearest the town center and surrounded by his clever quotes, provides a fun photo op (see photo on page 76).

▲▲**Number Twenty-Nine Georgian House**—The carefully restored house at Number 29 Lower Fitzwilliam Street gives an intimate glimpse of middle-class Georgian life (which seems pretty high-class). From the sidewalk, descend the stairs to the basement-level entrance (corner of Lower Fitzwilliam and Lower Mount Streets, opposite southern corner of Merrion Square). Start with an interesting 15-minute video (you're welcome to bring in a cup of coffee from the café) before joining your guide, who takes you on a fascinating 35-minute walk through this 1790 Dublin home (€6, tours leave regularly, Tue-Sat 10:00-17:00, Sun 12:00-17:00, closed Mon, tel. 01/702-6165, www.esb.ie/no29).

Grafton Street and St. Stephen's Green

▲▲**Grafton Street**—Once filled with noisy traffic, today's Grafton Street is Dublin's liveliest pedestrian shopping mall. A 10-minute stroll past street musicians takes you from Trinity College to St. Stephen's Green (and makes you wonder why some American merchants are so terrified of a car-free street). Walking south from Trinity College, you'll pass a buxom statue of "sweet" Molly Malone (also known as "the tart with the cart"). Next, you'll pass two venerable department stores: the Irish Brown Thomas and the English Marks & Spencer. Johnson's Court alley leads to the Powerscourt Townhouse Shopping Centre, which tastefully fills a converted Georgian mansion. The huge, glass-covered St. Stephen's Green Shopping Centre and the peaceful green itself mark the top of Grafton Street. For fun, gather a pile of coins and walk the street, putting each human statue into action with a donation. Consider stopping at the recommended Bewley's Café for coffee with a second-floor view of the action.

▲**St. Stephen's Green**—This city park was originally a medieval commons, complete with gory public executions. It was enclosed in 1664 and gradually surrounded with fine Georgian buildings. Today, it provides 22 acres of grassy refuge for Dubliners. At the northwest corner (near the end of Grafton Street) you'll be confronted by a looming marble arch erected to honor British officers killed during the Boer War. Locals nicknamed it "Traitor's Arch," as most Irish sympathized with the underdog Boers. On a sunny afternoon, this open space is a wonderful world apart from the big city. When marveling at the elegance of Georgian Dublin, remember that during the Georgian period (when the American colonies were fighting King George), Dublin was the second-most important city in the British Empire. Area big shots knew that any money wrung from the local populace not spent in Dublin would end up in London. Since it was "use it or lose it," they used it—with gusto—to beautify their city.

Dublin Castle and Nearby

▲▲**Dublin Castle**—Built on the spot of the first Viking fortress, this castle was the seat of English rule in Ireland for 700 years.

 Located where the Poddle and Liffey rivers came together, making a black pool (*dubh linn* in Irish), Dublin Castle was the official residence of the viceroy who implemented the will of the British royalty. In this stirring setting, the Brits handed power over to Michael Collins and the Irish in 1922. Today, it's used for fancy state and charity functions.

Standing in the courtyard, you can imagine the ugliness of the British-Irish situation. Notice the statue of justice above the gate—pointedly without her blindfold and admiring her sword. As Dubliners say, "There she stands, above her station, with her face to the palace and her arse to the nation." The fancy interior is viewable only with a 45-minute tour, which offers a fairly boring room-by-room walk through the lavish state apartments of this most English of Irish palaces. The tour finishes with a look at the foundations of the Norman tower and the best remaining chunk of the 13th-century town wall.

Cost and Hours: €4.50, buy tickets in courtyard under portico opposite clock tower, required tours depart 2/hour, Mon-Sat 10:00-16:45, Sun 14:00-16:45, tel. 01/677-7129, www.dublincastle.ie.

▲▲**Chester Beatty Library**—Chester Beatty was a rich American mining engineer who retired to Ireland in 1950, later becoming its first honorary citizen. He left his priceless and eclectic collection to his adopted homeland as a public charitable trust.

Today, Ireland has put a modern glass roof over the parade ground separating two old army barracks and filled it with Beatty's treasures. It's a small collection, delightfully displayed and described. The top floor focuses on the world's great religions (strong on Islam and Christianity) with displays on dervish whirls, calligraphy in Islam, and early Asian Christian manuscripts. The bottom floor is all about the written word, with topics including etching, medieval bookbinding, and fine old manuscripts.

As you wander, you'll see books carved out of jade, ornate snuff bottles, rhino-horn cups, and even the oldest surviving copy of St. Paul's letter to the Romans (A.D. 180). Other highlights include a graceful Burmese book written on palm leaves—bound together to unfold like an accordion—and a densely ornamental sunburst motif from a 500-year-old Iranian Quran.

Cost and Hours: Free; May-Sept Mon-Fri 10:00-17:00, Sat 11:00-17:00, Sun 13:00-17:00; Oct-April Tue-Fri 10:00-17:00, Sat 11:00-17:00, Sun 13:00-17:00, closed Mon; coffee shop, tel. 01/407-0750, www.cbl.ie). You'll find the library behind Dublin Castle (follow the signs).

Dublin City Hall—The first Georgian building in this very Georgian city stands proudly overlooking Dame Street, in front of the gate to Dublin Castle. Built in 1779 as the Royal Exchange, it introduced the Georgian style (then very popular in Britain and on the Continent) to Ireland. Step inside (it's free) to feel the prosperity and confidence of Dublin in her 18th-century glory days. In 1852, it became the City Hall. Under the grand rotunda, a cycle of heroic paintings tells the city's history. (The mosaics on the floor convey such homilies as "Obedience makes the happiest citizenry.")

Pay your respects to the 18-foot-tall statue of Daniel O'Connell, the great orator and liberator who, in 1829, won emancipation for Catholics in Ireland from the much-despised Protestants over in London. The body of modern Irish rebel leader Michael Collins lay in state here after his assassination in 1922. The greeter sits like the Maytag repairman at the information desk, eager to give you more information. Downstairs is the excellent *Story of the Capital* exhibition, which has storyboards and video clips of Dublin's history.

Cost and Hours: €4, free audioguide, coffee shop, Mon-Sat 10:00-17:00, closed Sun, tel. 01/222-2204, www.dublincity.ie.

Dublin's Cathedrals and Nearby

Because of Dublin's English past (particularly Henry VIII's Reformation, which led to the dissolution of the Catholic monasteries in 1539—in Ireland as well as England), neither of its top two churches is Catholic. Christ Church Cathedral and nearby St. Patrick's Cathedral are both Church of Ireland (Anglican). In the late 19th century, the cathedrals underwent extensive restoration. The rich Guinness brewery family forked out the dough to try to make St. Patrick's Cathedral outshine Christ Church—whose patrons were the equally rich, rival Jameson family of distillery fame. However, in Catholic Ireland, these Anglican sights feel hollow, and they're more famous than visit-worthy.

Christ Church Cathedral—Occupying the same site as the first wooden church built on this spot by King Sitric in Viking times (c. 1040), the present structure dates from a mix of periods: Norman and Gothic, but mostly Victorian Neo-Gothic (1870s restoration work). Inside you'll find the reputed tomb of the Norman warlord Strongbow, who led the thin edge of the English military wedge that eventually dominated Ireland for centuries. This oldest building in Dublin has an unusually large underground crypt, containing stocks, statues, and the cathedral's silver.

Cost and Hours: €6 donation to church includes downstairs crypt silver exhibition, €11 combo-ticket includes Dublinia, daily 9:45-16:15, free brochure with self-guided tour.

Evensong: A 45-minute evensong service is sung regularly several times a week (Wed-Thu at 18:00, Sat at 17:00, Sun at 15:30; less regularly during the summer).

▲Dublinia—This exhibit, which highlights Dublin's Viking and medieval past, is a hit with youngsters. Beefed up during a 2010 renovation, the exhibits are laid out on three floors. The ground floor focuses on Viking Dublin, explaining life aboard a Viking ship and inside a Viking house. Viking traders introduced urban life and commerce to Ireland—but kids will be most interested in gawking at their gory weaponry.

The next floor up reveals medieval Dublin's day-to-day life in medieval times, from chivalrous knights and damsels in town fairs to the brutal ravages of the Plague. The huge scale model of medieval Dublin is especially well done. The top floor's "History Hunters" section is devoted to how the puzzles of modern archaeology and science shed light on Dublin's history. From this floor you can climb a couple of flights of stairs into the tower for so-so views of Dublin, or exit across an enclosed stone bridge to adjacent Christ Church Cathedral.

Cost and Hours: €6.95, €11 combo-ticket includes Christ Church Cathedral—saving you €1.95, daily March-Sept 10:00-17:00, Oct-Feb 11:00-16:30, last entry 45 minutes before closing, top-floor coffee shop open in summer, across from Christ Church Cathedral, tel. 01/679-4611, www.dublinia.ie.

St. Patrick's Cathedral—The first church here was built on the site where St. Patrick baptized local pagan converts. The core of the Gothic structure you see today was built in the 13th century. After the Reformation, it passed into the hands of the Anglican

Church. A century later, Oliver Cromwell's puritanical Calvinist troops—who considered the Anglicans to be little more than Catholics without a pope—stabled their horses here as a sign of disrespect.

Jonathan Swift (author of *Gulliver's Travels*) was dean of the Cathedral in the 18th century. His grave is located near the front door (on the right side of the nave). Check out the large wooden Door of Reconciliation hanging in the north transept, with the rough hole in the middle. This was the Chapter House door through which two feuding, sword-bearing 15th-century nobles shook hands..."chancing their arms" and giving us that expression of trust.

Cost and Hours: €5.50 donation to church; Mon-Sat 9:00-17:00, Sun 12:30-14:30, last entry one hour before closing.

Evensong: Mon-Fri at 17:45, Sun at 15:15, none Wed July-Aug.

▲▲Temple Bar

Three hundred years ago, this was the city waterfront, where tall sailing ships offloaded their goods (a "bar" was a loading dock along the river, and the Temples were a dominant merchant family). Eventually, the city grew eastward, reclaiming tidal mudflats, to create the docklands of modern Dublin. Once a thriving Georgian center of craftsmen and merchants, this neighborhood fell on hard times in the 19th century. Ensuing low rents attracted students and artists, giving the area a bohemian flair. With government tax incentives and lots of development money, the Temple Bar district has now become a thriving cultural (and beer-drinking) hot spot. This much-promoted center—with trendy shops, cafés, theaters, galleries, pubs with live music, and restaurants—feels like the heart of the city. It's Dublin's "Left Bank," and like in Paris, it's on the south shore of the river. It fills the cobbled streets between Dame Street and the River Liffey.

Temple Bar is an absolute spectacle in the evening, when it bursts with revelers. The noise, rude crowds of foreigners, and inflated prices have driven most Dubliners away. But even if you're just gawking, don't miss the opportunity to wander through this human circus. Summer weekend nights can be a real zoo. Women in funky hats, part of loud "hen" (bachelorette) parties, promenade down the main drag as drunken dudes shout from pub doorways to get their attention. Be aware that a pint of beer here is €6—about €1 more than at less-glitzy pubs just a couple of blocks away (north of the River Liffey or south of Dame Street).

Temple Bar Square, just off Temple Bar Street (near Ha' Penny Bridge), is the epicenter of activity. It hosts free street theater and a Saturday book market, and has handy ATMs. On busy weekends, people-watching here is a contact sport. You're bound to meet some characters.

Irish music fans find great CDs at **Claddagh Records** (Cecilia Street, just around the corner from Luigi Malone's, Mon-Sat 11:30-17:30, closed Sun). Unlike big, glitzy chain stores, this is a little hole-in-the-wall shop staffed by informed folks who love turning visitors on to Irish tunes. Grab a couple of CDs for your drive through the Irish countryside. Farther west and somewhat hidden is **Meeting House Square,** with a lively organic-produce market (Sat 10:00-18:00). Bordering the square is the **Irish Film Institute** (main entry on Eustace Street), which shows a variety of art-house flicks. A bohemian crowd relaxes in its bar/café, awaiting the next film (6 Eustace Street, box office daily 13:30-21:00, tel. 01/679-5744, www.irishfilm.ie).

Rather than follow particular pub or restaurant recommendations (mine are listed later, under "Eating in Dublin"), venture down a few side lanes off the main drag to see what looks good. The pedestrian-only **Ha' Penny Bridge,** named for the halfpence toll people used to pay to cross it, leads from Temple Bar over the River Liffey to the opposite bank and more sights. If the rowdy Temple Bar scene gets too much, cross over to the north bank of the River Liffey on the Millennium Pedestrian Bridge (next bridge west of the Ha' Penny Bridge), where you'll find a mellower, more cosmopolitan choice of restaurants with outdoor seating in the Millennium Walk district.

North of the River Liffey
▲▲O'Connell Bridge

This bridge spans the River Liffey, which has historically divided the wealthy, cultivated south side of town from the poorer, cruder north side. While there's plenty of culture north of the river, even today "the north" is considered rougher and less safe. Dubliners joke that north-side residents are known as "the accused," while residents on the south side are addressed as "your honor."

From the bridge, look upriver (west) as far upstream as you can see. On the left in the distance, the **big concrete building**—considered an eyesore by locals—houses the city planning commission, which, ironically, is in charge of making sure new buildings

North Dublin

1 Daniel O'Connell Statue
2 Abbey Theatre
3 James Larkin Statue
4 Millennium Spire
5 General Post Office
6 Moore Street Market
7 St. Mary's Pro-Cathedral
8 Father Matthew Statue
9 Gresham Hotel
10 Charles Stewart Parnell Monument
11 Gate Theatre
12 Garden of Remembrance
13 Dublin Writers' Museum
14 James Joyce Cultural Centre
15 The Hugh Lane Gallery & Francis Bacon Studio

Accommodations & Services
16 Jurys Inn Custom House
17 The Townhouse
18 Jurys Inn Parnell Street
19 Belvedere Hotel
20 Charles Stewart Hotel
21 Internet Café

are built in good taste. It squats on the still-buried precious artifacts of the first Viking settlement, established in Dublin in the ninth century.

Across the river stands the **Four Courts**—the Supreme Court building. It was shelled and burned in 1922, during the tragic civil war that followed Irish independence. The national archives office burned, and irreplaceable birth records were lost, making it more difficult today for those with Irish roots to trace their ancestry. The closest bridge upstream—the elegant iron **Ha' Penny Bridge** (see photo on previous page)—leads left, into the Temple Bar nightlife district. Just beyond that old-fashioned, 19th-century bridge is Dublin's pedestrian **Millennium Bridge,** inaugurated in 2000. (Note that buses leave from O'Connell Bridge—specifically Aston Quay—for the Guinness Storehouse and Kilmainham Gaol.)

Turn 180 degrees and look downstream to see the tall **Liberty Hall** union headquarters—for now, the tallest building in the Republic (16 stories tall, some say in honor of the 1916 Easter Uprising)—and lots of cranes. Modern Dublin is developing downstream. The Irish (forever clever tax fiddlers) have subsidized and revitalized this formerly dreary quarter with great success. A short walk downstream along the north bank leads to a powerful series of gaunt statues memorializing the Great Potato Famine of 1845-1849.

▲▲O'Connell Street Stroll

Dublin's grandest street leads from O'Connell Bridge through the heart of north Dublin. Since the 1740s, it has been a 45-yard-wide promenade, and ever since the first O'Connell Bridge connected it to the Trinity side of town in 1794, it's been Dublin's main drag. (However, it was only named O'Connell after independence was won in 1922.) These days, the city has made the street more pedestrian-friendly. Though lined with fast-food and souvenir shops, O'Connell Street echoes with history.

• *Take the following stroll along the wide, tree-lined median strip, which is less crowded than either sidewalk, and closer to the statues I mention here. Start at the base of the street, near O'Connell Bridge.*

Modern Ireland's Turbulent Birth: A Timeline

Imagine if our American patriot ancestors had fought both our Revolutionary War and our Civil War over a span of seven chaotic years...and then appreciate the remarkable resilience of the Irish people. Here's a summary of what happened when.

1916: A nationalist militia called the Volunteers (led by **Patrick Pearse**) and the socialist Irish Citizen Army (led by **James Connolly**) join forces in the **Easter Uprising,** but they fail to end 750 years of British rule. The uprising is unpopular with most Irish, who are unhappy with the destruction in Dublin and preoccupied with the "Great War" on the Continent. But when 16 rebel leaders (including Pearse and Connolly) are executed, Irish public opinion reverses as sympathy grows for the martyrs and the cause of Irish Independence.

Two important rebel leaders escape execution. New York-born **Eamon de Valera** is spared because of his American passport (the British don't want to anger their potential ally in World War I). **Michael Collins,** a low-ranking rebel officer who fought in the uprising at the General Post Office, refines urban guerrilla-warfare strategies in prison, then blossoms after his release as the rebels' military and intelligence leader in the power vacuum that followed the executions.

1918: World War I ends, and a general election is held in Ireland. Outside of Ulster, the nationalist **Sinn Fein** party wins 73 out of 79 seats in Parliament. Only 4 out of 32 counties vote to maintain the Union with Britain (all 4 are in Ulster, part of which would become Northern Ireland). Rather than take their seats in London, Sinn Fein representatives abstain from participating in a government they see as foreign occupiers.

1919: On January 19, the abstaining Sinn Fein members set up a rebel government in Dublin called Dail Eireann. On the same day, the first shots of

Statues and Monuments: O'Connell Street is lined with statues celebrating great figures in Ireland's fight for independence. At the base of the street stands **Daniel O'Connell** (1775-1847), known as "the Liberator" for founding the Catholic Association and demanding Irish Catholic rights in the British Parliament.

Walk a block east down Abbey Street to find the famous **Abbey Theatre**—rebuilt after a fire into a nondescript, modern building. It's still the much-loved home of the Irish National Theatre.

the **Irish War of Independence** are fired as rebels begin ambushing police barracks, which are seen as an extension of British rule. De Valera is elected by the Dail to lead the rebels, with Collins as his deputy. Collins' web of spies infiltrate British intelligence at Dublin Castle. The Volunteers rename themselves the **Irish Republican Army;** meanwhile the British beef up their military presence in Ireland by sending in tough WWI vets, the Black & Tans. A bloody and very personal war ensues.

1921: Having lived through the slaughter of World War I, the British tire of the extended bloodshed in Ireland and begin negotiations with the rebels. De Valera leads rebel negotiations, but then entrusts them to Collins (a clever politician, De Valera sees that whoever signs a treaty will be blamed for its compromises). Understanding the tricky position he's been placed in, Collins signs the **Anglo-Irish Treaty** in December, lamenting that in doing so he has signed his "own death warrant."

The Dail narrowly ratifies the treaty (64 to 57), but Collins' followers are unable to convince De Valera's supporters that the compromises are a stepping stone to later full independence. De Valera and his anti-treaty disciples resign in protest. **Arthur Griffith,** founder of Sinn Fein, assumes the presidential post.

In June, the anti-treaty forces, holed up in the Four Courts building, are fired upon by Collins and his pro-treaty forces—thus igniting the **Irish Civil War.** The British want the treaty to stand and even supply Collins with cannons, meanwhile threatening to re-enter Ireland if the anti-treaty forces aren't put down.

1922: In August, Griffith dies of stress-induced illness, and Collins is assassinated 10 days later. Nevertheless, the pro-treaty forces prevail, as they are backed by popular opinion and better (British-supplied) military equipment.

1923: In April, the remaining IRA forces dump (or stash) their arms, ending the civil war...but many of their bitter vets vow to carry on the fight. De Valera distances himself from the IRA and becomes the dominant Irish political leader for the next 40 years.

The statue of **James Larkin** (see next page) honors the founder of the Irish Transport Workers' Union. The one monument that didn't wave an Irish flag—a tall column crowned by a statue of the British hero of Trafalgar, Admiral Horatio Nelson—was blown up in 1966...the IRA's contribution to the local celebration of the Easter Uprising's 50th anniversary.

This spot is now occupied by the 390-foot-tall, stainless steel **Millennium Spire** that was finally completed in 2003. While it trumpets rejuvenation on that side of the river, it's a memorial to nothing and has no real meaning. Dubious Dubliners call it the tallest waste of €5 million in all of Europe. Its nickname? Take your pick: the Stiletto in the Ghetto, the Stiffy on the Liffey, the Pole in the Hole, the Poker near the Croker (after the nearby Croke Park), or the Spike in the Dike.

• *On your left is the...*

General Post Office: This is not just any P.O. It was from here that Patrick Pearse read the Proclamation of Irish Independence in 1916, kicking off the Easter Uprising. The

G.P.O. building itself—a kind of Irish Alamo—was the rebel headquarters and scene of a five-day bloody siege that followed the proclamation. Its pillars remain pockmarked with bullet holes (open for business and sightseers Mon-Sat 8:00-20:00, closed Sun).

• *Turn left (west) past the post office, down people-filled Henry Street (residents' favorite shopping lane), then wander to the right into the nearby...*

Moore Street Market: Many of its merchants have staffed the same stalls for more than 30 years. Start a conversation. It's a great workaday scene. You'll see lots of mums with strollers—a reminder that Ireland is one of Europe's youngest countries, with more than 35 percent of the population under the age of 25 (Mon-Sat 8:00-18:00, closed Sun).

• *Back on O'Connell Street, return to the median strip and continue your walk. A block east (right) of O'Connell, down Cathedral Street, is...*

St. Mary's Pro-Cathedral: Although this is Dublin's leading Catholic church, it rather curiously isn't a "cathedral." The pope declared Christ Church to be a cathedral in the 12th century—and later, St. Patrick's. (The Vatican has chosen to stubbornly ignore the fact that Christ Church and St. Patrick's haven't been Catholic for centuries.) Completed in 1821, this church is done in the style of a Greek temple.

• *Continuing up O'Connell Street, you'll find a statue of...*

Father Matthew: A leader of the temperance movement of the 1830s, some historians claim Father Matthew was responsible for enough Irish peasants staying sober to enable Daniel O'Connell to organize them into a political force. (Perhaps studying this example, the USSR was careful to keep the price of vodka affordable.)

Charles Stewart Parnell
(1846-1891)

Parnell, who led the Irish movement for Home Rule in the 1880s, served time in Kilmainham Gaol. A Cambridge-educated Protestant of landed-gentry stock and a member of Parliament, he had a vision of a modern and free Irish nation filled mostly with Catholics but not set up as a religious state. Despite his privileged birth, Parnell gained the love of the Irish people—who remembered their grandparents' harsh evictions during the famine—through his tireless work on land reforms to secure fair rents and land tenure. Momentum seemed to be on his side. With the British prime minister of the time, William Gladstone, in favor of a similar form of Home Rule, it looked as if all of Ireland was ripe for independence, as a Commonwealth nation similar to Canada or Australia. Then a sex scandal broke around Parnell and his mistress, the wife of another Parliament member. The press, egged on by the powerful Catholic bishops (who didn't want a secular, free Irish state), battered away at the scandal until finally Parnell was driven from office. Sadly, after that, Ireland became mired in the Troubles of the 20th century: an awkward independence (1921) featuring a divided island, a bloody civil war, and sectarian violence ever since. Wracked with exhaustion and only in his mid-40s, Parnell is thought to have died of a broken heart.

Nearby, the fancy **Gresham Hotel** is a good place for an elegant tea or beer. In an earlier era, this was where the beautiful people would alight during visits to Dublin. In the 1960s, Richard Burton and Liz Taylor stayed here while he was filming *The Spy Who Came in from the Cold*. (In those days, parts of Dublin were drab enough to pass for an inaccessible Eastern Bloc city.)

• *Standing boldly at the top of O'Connell Street is a monument to...*

Charles Stewart Parnell: The names of the four ancient provinces of Ireland and all 32 Irish counties (North *and* South, since this was erected before Irish independence) ring the monument, honoring Charles Stewart Parnell, the member of Parliament who nearly won Home Rule for Ireland in the late 1800s. (A sex scandal cost Parnell the support of the Church, which let the air out of the movement for a free Ireland.)

• *Continue straight up Parnell Square East. At the **Gate Theatre** (on the left), Orson Welles and James Mason had their professional acting debuts.*

Dublin's Literary Life

Dublin in the 1700s, grown rich from a lucrative cloth trade, was one of Europe's most cultured and sophisticated cities.

The buildings were decorated in the Georgian style still visible today, and the city's Protestant elite shuttled between here and London, bridging the Anglo-Irish cultural gap. Jonathan Swift (1667-1745), the great satirical writer, was also dean of St. Patrick's Cathedral (1713-1745) and one of the city's eminent citizens. Then, around the turn of the 20th century, Dublin produced some of the world's great modern writers: Oscar Wilde (1854-1900), William Butler Yeats (1865-1939), and James Joyce (1882-1941), to name just a few. For more on Irish literature, see page 425.

One block up on the left is the...

Garden of Remembrance: Honoring the victims of the

1916 Uprising, the park was dedicated in 1966 on the 50th anniversary of the revolt that ultimately led to Irish independence. The bottom of the cross-shaped pool is a mosaic of Celtic weapons, symbolic of how the early Irish would proclaim peace by throwing their weapons into a lake or river. The Irish flag flies above the park: green for Catholics, orange for Protestants, and white for the hope that they can live together in peace (free, daily 8:30-18:00).

• *On the uphill side, across the street, is a splendidly restored Georgian mansion, housing the...*

Dublin Writers' Museum: No other country so small has produced such a wealth of literature (see page 425). As interesting to fans of Irish literature as it is boring to those who aren't, this three-room museum features the lives and works of Dublin's great writers (€7.50, includes helpful audioguide, ask about €11.50 combo-ticket with James Joyce Museum in Dun Laoghaire; Mon-Sat 10:00-17:00, Sun 11:00-17:00, June-Aug Mon-Fri until 18:00; coffee shop, 18 Parnell Square North, tel. 01/872-2077, www.writersmuseum.com). For an easy, affordable, and enjoyable literary performance in summer, consider "The Writers Entertain," a one-man show (€13, June-Aug daily at 13:10, 50 minutes, upstairs in a fine reading room).

With hometown wits such as Swift, Yeats, Joyce, Wilde, and Shaw, Dublin has a checklist of residences and memorials to see. Aficionados of James Joyce's work may want to hike two blocks east to visit the **James Joyce Cultural Centre** (€5; June-Aug Tue-Sat 10:00-17:00, Sun 12:00-17:00, closed Mon; Sept-May closed Sun-Mon; 35 North Great George's Street, tel. 01/878-8547). There's more Joyce memorabilia in Dun Laoghaire at the **James Joyce Museum** (see page 102).

• *Next door to the Dublin Writers' Museum is...*

The Hugh Lane Gallery: In a grand Neoclassical build-ing, this has a fine, bite-size selection of Pre-Raphaelite, French Impressionist, and 19th- and 20th-century Irish paintings (free, Tue-Thu 10:00-18:00, Fri-Sat 10:00-17:00, Sun 11:00-17:00, closed Mon, tel. 01/222-5564, www.hughlane.ie). Sir Hugh went down on the *Lusitania* in 1915; due to an unclear will, his collection is shared by this gallery and the National Gallery in London. Check out their free classical concerts (Sundays at noon).

Tucked in the back of the gallery is the **Francis Bacon Studio,** reconstructed here in its original (messy) state from its London location at the time of the artist's death in 1992. Born in Dublin and inspired by Pablo Picasso, Bacon's shocking paint-ings reflected his belief that "chaos breeds energy." This compact space contains touch-screen terminals, display cases of personal items, and a few unfinished works. The 10-minute film interview of Bacon may fascinate like-minded viewers...and disquiet others (free, same hours as rest of gallery).

• *Your walk is over. Here on the north end of town, it's convenient to visit the Gaelic Athletic Association Museum at Croke Park Stadium (described on page 80, a 20-minute walk or short taxi ride away). Otherwise, hop on your skateboard and zip back to the river.*

Dublin's Smithfield Village

This neighborhood is worth a look for the Old Jameson Distillery whiskey tour and Dublin's most authentic traditional-music pub. The two sights are clustered together, two blocks northwest of the Four Courts—the Supreme Court building. The area is dominated by a long modern square that still fulfills its original function as a horse market (first Sat mornings of the month, great for people-watching). The **Fresh Market,** near the top of the square, is a handy grocery stop for urban picnic fixings (Mon-Sat 7:00-22:00, Sun 8:00-22:00).

Old Jameson Distillery—Whiskey fans enjoy visiting the old distillery. You get a 10-minute video, a 20-minute tour, and a free shot in the pub. Unfortunately, the "distillery" feels fake and put together for tourists. The Bushmills tour in Northern Ireland (in a working factory, see page 366) and the Midleton tour near Cork (in the huge original factory, page 179) are better experiences. If you do take this tour, volunteer energetically when offered the chance: This will get you a coveted seat at the whiskey taste-test table at the tour's end (€13.50, daily 9:30-18:30, last tour at 17:15, Bow Street, tel. 01/807-2355). Jameson also offers "Irish Nights"—a splurge dinner-and-dance shindig with all the trimmings (€62.50, April-Oct Thu-Sat at 19:00; includes guided tour, cocktail, and four-course meal; book ahead, tel. 01/807-2355, www.jamesonwhiskey .com/ojd).

Cobblestones Pub—Hiding in a derelict-looking building at the top of the square, this pub offers Dublin's least glitzy and most rewarding traditional-music venue. The candlelit walls, covered with photos of honored trad musicians, set the tone. Music is revered here, as reflected in the understated sign: "Listening area, please respect musicians" (daily 17:00-23:45, trad-music sessions Mon-Wed at 21:30, Thu-Sat at 17:00, at north end of square, 100 yards from Old Jameson Distillery's brick chimney tower, tel. 01/872-1799).

Outer Dublin

The Kilmainham Gaol and the Guinness Storehouse are located to the west of the old center and can be combined in one visit (linked by a 20-minute walk or a 5-minute taxi ride).

▲▲▲**Kilmainham Gaol (Jail)**—Opened in 1796 as both the Dublin County Jail and a debtors' prison, it was considered a model in its day. In reality, this jail was frequently used by the British as a political prison. Many of those who fought for Irish indepen-dence were held or executed here, including leaders of the rebellions of 1798, 1803, 1848, 1867, and 1916. National heroes Robert Emmett and Charles Stewart Parnell each did time here. The last prisoner to be held here was Eamon de Valera, who later became president of Ireland. He was released on July 16, 1924, the day Kilmainham was finally shut down. The buildings, virtually in ruins, were restored in the 1960s. Today, it's a shrine to the Nathan Hales of Ireland.

Start your visit with a one-hour guided **tour** (2/hour, includes 15-minute prison-history slide show in the prison chapel—spend waiting time in museum). It's touching to tour the cells and places of execution—hearing tales of terrible colonialism and heroic patriotism—alongside Irish schoolkids who know these names well. The museum is an excellent exhibit on Victorian prison life and Ireland's fight for independence. Don't miss the museum's dimly lit Last Words 1916 hall upstairs, which displays the stirring final letters that patriots sent to loved ones hours before facing the firing squad.

Cost and Hours: €6, daily 9:30-18:00, last entry 1.5 hours before closing, tel. 01/453-5984. The humble cafeteria serves little more than sandwiches.

Connecting the Gaol and Guinness Storehouse: To get from Aston Quay or the Guinness Storehouse to Kilmainham Gaol, you can take a taxi, or catch bus #51B, #78A, or #79. Another option is to take one of the hop-on, hop-off buses (see page 58): City Sightseeing stops right at Kilmainham Gaol, while Dublin City Tour stops 200 yards away, in front of the modern art museum in Kilmainham hospital. Both tours stop at the Guinness Storehouse.

To catch the city bus from the jail to the Guinness Storehouse, leave the prison and take three rights—crossing no streets—to the bus stop, and hop bus #51B or #78A.

▲**Guinness Storehouse**—A visit to the Guinness Storehouse is, for many, a pilgrimage. Arthur Guinness began brewing the famous stout here in 1759. By 1868, it was the biggest brewery in the world. Today, the sprawling brewery fills several city blocks. Around the world, Guinness brews more than 10 million pints a day. The home of Ireland's national beer welcomes visitors, for a price, with a sprawling modern museum, but there are no tours of the actual working brewery. The museum fills the old fermentation plant that was used from 1902 through 1988, and then reopened in 2000 as a huge,

shrine-like place. Step into the middle of the ground floor and look up. A tall, beer-glass-shaped glass atrium—14 million pints big—leads past four floors of exhibitions and cafés to the skylight. Then look down at Arthur's original 9,000-year lease, enshrined under glass in the floor...at £45 per year, it's been quite a bargain. Atop the building, the **Gravity Bar** provides visitors with a commanding 360-degree view of Dublin—with vistas all the way to the sea—and a free beer.

The actual exhibit makes brewing seem more grandiose than it is and treats Arthur like the god of human happiness. Highlights are the cooperage (with 1954 film clips showing the master wood-keg-makers plying their now virtually extinct trade), a display of the brewery's clever ads, and the Gravity Bar, which really is spectacular.

Cost and Hours: €13.50, includes a €5 pint; €1 off with your hop-on, hop-off bus ticket or 10 percent discount when booked online; daily 9:30-17:00, July-Aug until 19:00; enter on Bellevue Street, bus #78A from Aston Quay near O'Connell Bridge, or bus #123 from Dame Street and O'Connell Street; tel. 01/408-4800, www.guinness-storehouse.com. Both hop-on, hop-off bus tours stop here.

▲**National Museum: Decorative Arts and History**—This branch of the National Museum, which occupies the huge, 18th-century stone Collins Barracks in west Dublin, displays Irish dress, furniture, weapons, silver, and other domestic baubles from the past 700 years. History buffs will linger longest in the "Soldiers & Chiefs" exhibit, which covers the Irish at war both at home and abroad since 1500 (including the American Civil War). The sober finale is the "Understanding 1916" room, offering Ireland's best coverage of its painful "Terrible Beauty" national birth. Guns, personal letters, and death masks help illustrate the 1916 Easter Uprising, War of Independence against Britain, and Ireland's civil war. Croppies Acre, the large park between the museum and the river, was the site of Dublin's largest soup kitchen during the Great Potato Famine in 1845-1849.

Cost and Hours: Free, Tue-Sat 10:00-17:00, Sun 14:00-17:00, closed Mon, good café; on north side of the River Liffey in Collins Barracks on Benburb Street, roughly across the river from Guinness Storehouse, easy to reach by LUAS—get off at Museum stop; tel. 01/648-6453, www.museum.ie. Call ahead for sporadic tour times.

▲**Gaelic Athletic Association Museum**—The GAA was founded in 1884 as an expression of an Irish cultural awakening (see sidebar). It was created to foster the development of Gaelic sports, specifically Gaelic football and hurling, and to ban English sports such as cricket and rugby. The GAA played an important part in the fight for independence. This museum, at 82,000-seat Croke Park Stadium in east Dublin (a 20-minute walk northeast of Parnell Square), offers a high-tech, interactive introduction to Ireland's favorite games. Relive the greatest moments in hurling and Irish-football history. Then get involved: Pick up a stick and try hurling, kick a football, and test your speed and balance. A 15-minute film (played on request) gives you a "Sunday at the stadium" experience.

Cost and Hours: €6; July-Aug daily 9:30-18:00; Sept-June Mon-Sat 9:30-17:00, Sun 12:00-17:00; on game Sundays the museum is open to ticket-holders only; located under the stands at

Ireland's Gaelic Athletic Association

The GAA has long been a powerhouse in Ireland. Ireland's national pastimes of Gaelic football and hurling pack stadiums all over the country. When 80,000 people—paying at least €20 to €30 each—stuff Dublin's Croke Park Stadium and you consider that all the athletes are strictly amateur, you might wonder, "Where does all the money go?"

Ireland has a long tradition of using the revenue generated by these huge events to promote Gaelic athletics and Gaelic cultural events throughout the country in a grassroots and neighborhood way. So, while the players (many of whom are schoolteachers whose jobs allow for evenings and summers free) participate only for the glory of their various counties, the money generated is funding children's leagues, school coaches, small-town athletic facilities, and traditional arts, music, and dance—as well as the building and maintenance of giant stadiums such as Croke Park (which claims to be the third-largest stadium in Europe).

In America, sports are often considered to be a form of entertainment. But in Ireland, sports have a deeper emotional connection. Gaelic sports are a heartfelt expression of Irish identity. There was a time when the Irish were not allowed to be members of the GAA if they also belonged to a cricket club (a British game). In 1921, during the War of Independence, Michael Collins (leader of the early IRA, who practically invented urban guerrilla warfare) orchestrated the simultaneous assassination of a dozen British intelligence agents around Dublin in a single morning. The Black & Tans retaliated immediately. As grizzled British WWI veterans, clad in black police coats and tan surplus army pants, they had been sent to Ireland to stamp out the rebels. Knowing Croke Park would be full of Irish Nationalists, they entered the packed stadium during a Gaelic football match and fired into the stands, killing 13 spectators as well as a Tipperary player. It was Ireland's first Bloody Sunday, a tragedy repeated 51 years later in Derry.

Today Croke Park's "Hill 16" grandstands are built on rubble dumped here after the 1916 Uprising...literally sacred ground. And the Hogan stands are named after the murdered player from Tipperary.

Croke Park Stadium—enter from St. Joseph's Avenue off Clonliffe Road; tel. 01/819-2323, www.crokepark.ie/gaa-museum. The €15, one-hour museum-plus-stadium-tour option is worth it only for rabid fans who yearn to know which locker room is considered the unlucky one.

Hurling or Gaelic Football at Croke Park Stadium—Actually seeing a match here, surrounded by incredibly spirited Irish fans, is a fun experience. Hurling is like airborne hockey with no injury time-outs. Gaelic football is like a rugged form of soccer; you can carry the ball, but must bounce or kick it every three steps. Matches are held most Saturday or Sunday afternoons in summer (May-Aug), culminating in the hugely popular all-Ireland finals on Sunday afternoons in September. Tickets are available at the stadium except during the finals (€15-55, box office open Mon-Fri 9:30-13:00 & 14:15-17:30, tel. 01/836-3222, www.gaa.ie). Choose a county to support, buy something colorful to wear or wave, scream yourself hoarse, and you'll be a temporary local.

Greyhound Racing—For an interesting, lowbrow look at Dublin life, consider going to the dog races and doing a little gambling. Your best bets are Wednesday, Thursday, and Saturday at Shelbourne Park; and Monday, Tuesday, and Friday at Harold's Cross Racetrack (€10, races start at 20:00, tel. 01/497-1081, www.igb.ie).

Shopping in Dublin

Shops are open roughly Monday-Saturday 9:00-18:00 and until 20:00 on Thursday. They have shorter hours on Sunday (if they're open at all). Good shopping areas include:

• **Grafton Street,** with its neighboring streets and arcades (such as the fun Great George's Arcade between Great George's and Drury Streets), and nearby shopping centers (Powerscourt Townhouse and St. Stephen's Green). Francis Street creaks with antiques.

• **Henry Street,** home to Dublin's top department stores (pedestrian-only, off O'Connell Street).

• **Nassau Street,** lining Trinity College, with the popular Kilkenny department store, the Irish Music store, and lots of touristy shops.

• **Dundrum Town Mall,** a vast suburban shopping mall (no tourists). The LUAS light rail goes directly there from St. Stephen's Green.

• **Temple Bar,** worth a browse any day for its art, jewelry, New Age paraphernalia, books, music (try Claddagh Records—see page 69), and gift shops. On Saturdays at Temple Bar's Meeting House Square, it's food in the morning (from 9:00) and books in the afternoon (until 18:00).

• **Millennium Walk,** a trendy lane stretching two blocks north from the River Liffey to Abbey Street. It's filled with hip restaurants, shops, and coffee bars. It's easy to miss—look for the south entry at the pedestrian Millennium Bridge, or the north entry at Jervis Street LUAS stop.

• **Street markets,** such as Moore Street (produce, noise, and lots of local color, Mon-Sat 8:00-18:00, closed Sun, near General Post Office), and St. Michan Street (fish, Tue-Sat 7:00-15:00, closed Sun-Mon, behind Four Courts building).

Entertainment in Dublin

Ireland has produced some of the finest writers in both English and Irish, and Dublin houses some of Europe's finest theaters. Though the city was the site of the first performance of Handel's *Messiah* (1742), these days Dublin is famous for its rock bands (U2, Thin Lizzy, Sinéad O'Connor, and Live Aid founder Bob Geldof's band the Boomtown Rats all started here).

Abbey Theatre is Ireland's national theater, founded by W. B. Yeats in 1904 to preserve Irish culture during British rule (€20-40, generally nightly at 19:30, Sat matinees, 26 Lower Abbey Street, tel. 01/878-7222, www.abbeytheatre.ie). **Gate Theatre** does foreign plays as well as Irish classics (Cavendish Row, tel. 01/874-4045, www.gatetheatre.ie). The **Gaiety Theatre** offers a wide range of quality productions (King Street South, tel. 01/677-1717, www.gaietytheatre.com). Street theater takes the stage in Temple Bar on summer evenings. Browse the listings and fliers at the TI.

O$_2$ Theatre, once a railway terminus (easy LUAS access), is now sponsored by a hip phone company. Residents call it by its geographic nickname: The Point. It's considered the country's top live-music venue (East Link Bridge, tel. 01/676-6170 or 01/676-6154, www.theO2.ie).

At the **National Concert Hall,** the National Symphony Orchestra performs most Friday evenings (€20-40, off St. Stephen's Green at Earlsfort Terrace, tel. 01/417-0000, www.nch.ie).

Pub Action: Folk music fills Dublin's pubs, and street entertainers ply their trade in the midst of the party people in Temple Bar and among shoppers on Grafton Street. The Temple Bar area in particular thrives with music—traditional, jazz, and pop. Although it's pricier than the rest of Dublin, it really is the most comfortable and fun place for tourists and locals (who come here to watch the tourists). For locations, see the "Dublin Restaurants" map on page 92.

Gogarty's Pub has top-notch sessions downstairs daily at 14:00 and upstairs nightly from 21:00 (at corner of Fleet and Anglesea, tel. 01/671-1822). Use this pub as a kickoff for your Temple Bar evening. It's also where the Traditional Irish Musical Pub Crawl starts (see page 53).

A 10-minute hike up the river west of Temple Bar takes you to a twosome with a local and less-touristy ambience. **The Brazen Head,** which lays claim to being the oldest pub in Dublin, is a hit for an early dinner and late live music (nightly from 21:30), with atmospheric rooms and a courtyard perfect for balmy evenings. They also host "Food, Folk, and Fairies" evenings. For €44, you get a hearty four-course meal punctuated by solid Irish history interwoven with more nebulous fairy tales (May-Oct Tue-Sat 19:00-22:00, near Christ Church Cathedral at 20 Bridge Street, pub tel. 01/677-9549, show tel. 01/492-2543, www.irishfolktours .com). **O'Shea's Merchant Pub,** just across the street, is encrusted in memories and filled with locals taking a break from the grind. They have live traditional music nightly at 21:30 (the front half is a restaurant, the magic is in the back half—enter on Bridge Street, tel. 01/679-3797).

At **Palace Pub,** climb upstairs to a cozy room that is a favorite for traditional-music sessions (at east end of Temple Bar, where Fleet Street hits Westmoreland Street, 21 Fleet Street).

Porterhouse has an inviting and varied menu, Dublin's best selection of microbrews, and live music. You won't find Guinness here, just tasty homebrews. You can check their music schedule online (€12-15 entrées, corner of Essex Street East and Parliament Street, tel. 01/671-5715, www.porterhousebrewco.com/livetemple bar.html).

Pubs at two locations of the **Arlington Hotel** host Irish music and dinner shows. At either place, you'll be entertained by an Irish Rovers-type band singing ballads and a dance troupe scuffing up the floorboards to the delight of tour groups (€30, shows nightly 21:00-23:00, dinner reservations required, www.arlington hoteltemplebar.com). The Arlington Hotel O'Connell Bridge is north of the River Liffey at 23 Bachelors Walk, just off the north end of the bridge (tel. 01/804-9100). The Arlington Hotel Temple

Bar is south of the river at the corner of Lord Edward Street and Exchange Street Upper, roughly opposite City Hall (tel. 01/670-8777). Make sure you know at which location you're booking reservations.

To sample truly traditional Irish song and dance, consider heading to **Comhaltas Ceoltoiri Éireann** in nearby Dun Laoghaire (see page 102).

Pub Crawls: For guided pub crawls (focusing on either Irish literature or music), see page 53.

Sleeping in Dublin

Dublin is popular, loud, and expensive. Rooms can be tight. Book ahead for weekends any time of year, particularly in summer and during rugby weekends. On Sundays in September, fans converge on Dublin from all over the country for the all-Ireland finals in Gaelic football and hurling. In summer, occasional big rock concerts can make rooms hard to find. Prices are often discounted on weeknights (Mon-Thu) and from November through February. Check for specials on hotel websites.

Big and practical places (both cheap and moderate) are most central near Christ Church Cathedral, on the edge of Temple Bar. For classy, older Dublin accommodations, you'll stay a bit farther out (southeast of St. Stephen's Green). If you're on a tight budget (or a light sleeper), get a room in quiet Dun Laoghaire (page 103) or small-town Howth (page 108), where rooms are roughly a third cheaper. Both are an easy 25-minute DART train ride into the city.

DUBLIN

Sleep Code

(€1 = about $1.25, country code: 353, area code: 01)
S = Single, **D** = Double/Twin, **T** = Triple, **Q** = Quad, **b** = bathroom, **s** = shower only. Breakfast is included and credit cards are accepted unless otherwise noted.

To help you easily sort through these listings, I've divided the rooms into three categories, based on the price for a standard double room with bath:

$$$ Higher Priced—Most rooms €145 or more.
$$ Moderately Priced—Most rooms between €85-145.
$ Lower Priced—Most rooms €85 or less.

Prices can change without notice; verify the hotel's current rates online or by email. For other updates, see www .ricksteves.com/update.

Dublin Accommodations

1. Jurys Inn Christ Church
2. Harding Hotel
3. Kinlay House
4. Four Courts Hostel
5. Trinity Lodge
6. Trinity College Accomm. Office
7. Grafton Capital Hotel
8. Albany House
9. Fitzwilliam Townhouse
10. To Baggot Court Town House, Number 31 & Mespil Hotel
11. Avalon House Hostel
12. To Schoolhouse Hotel & Roxford Lodge Hotel
13. Internet Cafés (2)
14. Launderettes (2)

South of the River Liffey
Near Christ Church Cathedral

These hotels face Christ Church Cathedral, a 5-minute walk from the best evening scene (at Temple Bar), and 10 minutes from the sightseeing center (Trinity College and Grafton Street). The cheap hostels in this neighborhood have some double rooms. Full Irish breakfasts, which cost €10-15 at the hotels, are half that price at the many small cafés nearby; try the **Queen of Tarts** or **Chorus Café** (see listings under "Eating in Dublin," later).

   $$$ Jurys Inn Christ Church, one of three Jurys Inns in downtown Dublin, is central and offers business-class comfort in all of its 182 identical rooms. This no-nonsense, American-style hotel chain has a winning keep-it-simple-and-affordable formula. If ye olde is getting old (and you don't mind big tour groups), these are a good option (€99-130 Sun-Thu; €140-160 Fri-Sat for one, two, or three adults or two adults and two kids; breakfast-€10). Its four floors are strictly non-smoking. Request a room far from the noisy elevator (book long in advance for weekends, check website for discounts, parking-€15/day, Christ Church Place, tel. 01/454-0000, fax 01/454-0012, US tel. 800-423-6953, www.jurysinns .com, jurysinnchristchurch@jurysinns.com). The other Jurys Inns, described later, are near Connolly Station and Parnell Square.

$$ Harding Hotel is a hardworking, hardwood place with 55 earth-tone rooms that get stuffy on rare hot days (Sb-€55-70; Db-€70-97 Sun-Thu, or €99-120 Fri-Sat; extra bed-€25, breakfast-€7.50; Rick Steves' readers get 10 percent discount in 2011 if booking by email, phone, fax, or the hotel's official site; on weekends, request a quiet upper-floor room away from the fun but noisy ground-floor pub; in Copper Alley across the street from Christ Church Cathedral, tel. 01/679-6500, fax 01/679-6504, www.hardinghotel.ie, info@hardinghotel.ie).

$ Kinlay House, around the corner from Harding Hotel, is the backpackers' choice—definitely the place to go for cheap beds, a central location, and an all-ages-welcome atmosphere. This huge, red-brick, 19th-century Victorian building has 200 metal, prison-style beds in spartan, non-smoking rooms. There are singles, doubles, and four- to six-bed coed dorms (good for families), as well as a few giant dorms. It fills up most days. Call well in advance, especially for singles, doubles, and summer weekends (D-€50-78, Db-€60-84, dorm beds-€12-30, includes continental breakfast, free Internet access and Wi-Fi, free 10-minute international phone call, kitchen access, launderette-€8, left luggage-€1/day, travel desk, TV lounge, small lockers-€1/day, lots of stairs, Christ Church, 2-12 Lord Edward Street, tel. 01/679-6644, fax 01/679-7437, www.kinlaydublin.ie, info@kinlaydublin.ie).

$ Four Courts Hostel is a 236-bed hostel beautifully located immediately across the river from the Four Courts. It's within a five-minute walk of Christ Church Cathedral and Temple Bar. Bare and institutional (as hostels typically are), it's also spacious and well-run, with a focus on security and efficiency (dorm beds-€13-30, S-€45, Sb-€55, bunk D-€68, bunk Db-€70, includes small breakfast, non-smoking, elevator, Internet access and Wi-Fi, free 10-minute international phone call, game room, laundry service, some parking-€10/day, left luggage room, 15-17 Merchant's Quay, bus #748 from airport, bus #90 from Connolly Station or Busaras Central Bus Station, tel. 01/672-5839, fax 01/672-5862, www.fourcourtshostel.com, info@fourcourtshostel.com).

Trinity College Area

You can't get more central than Trinity College; these two listings offer a good value for what you're spending.

$$$ Trinity Lodge offers fine quiet lodging in 23 rooms split between two Georgian townhouses on either side of Frederick Street South, just south of Trinity College (Sb-€90-140, Db-€89-165, Tb-€129-225, Qb-€150-250, 12 South Frederick Street, tel. 01/617-0900, fax 01/617-0999, www.trinitylodge.com, trinitylodge@eircom.net).

$$ Trinity College turns its 800 student-housing rooms on campus into no-frills, affordable accommodations in the city center each summer. Look for the easy-to-miss Accommodations Office (open Mon-Fri 9:00-12:45 & 14:00-17:00) inside the huge courtyard, 50 yards down the wall on the left from the main entry arch (mid-May-Sept, S-€60, Sb-€72, D-€89, Db-€125, Tb-€210, Qb-€240, all rooms have up to 3 twin beds, includes continental breakfast, cooked breakfast-€4 extra, tel. 01/896-1177, fax 01/671-1267, www.tcd.ie/accommodation/visitors, reservations@tcd.ie).

Near St. Stephen's Green

Dublin is filled with worn-yet-comfy townhouses. Albany House, Fitzwilliam Townhouse, and Baggot Court Town House offer dependable, basic lodging.

$$$ Grafton Capital Hotel has a good central location and fine rooms. The popular downstairs pub is noisy on weekend nights, so light sleepers should request a room facing the back (Db-€89-169, Tb-€119-199, breakfast-€15, three non-smoking floors, 2 blocks west of St. Stephen's Green on Lower Stephen's Street, tel. 01/648-1100, fax 01/648-1122, www.capital-hotels.com, info@graftoncapital-hotel.com).

$$ Albany House's 43 restful rooms come with high ceilings, Georgian elegance, and some street noise—request a quieter room at the back (Sb-€80-110, Db-€120-140, Tb-€140-170, Una promises 10 percent off when booking direct by phone or email with this book in 2011, non-smoking, just one block south of St. Stephen's Green at 84 Harcourt Street, tel. 01/475-1092, fax 01/475-1093, www.albanyhousedublin.com, albany@indigo.ie).

$$ Fitzwilliam Townhouse rents 14 good-value rooms in a Georgian townhouse near St. Stephen's Green (Sb-€59-89, Db-€69-129, Tb-€89-149, Qb-€99-159, breakfast-€6.50-9.50, all non-smoking, 41 Upper Fitzwilliam Street, tel. 01/662-5155, fax 01/676-7488, www.fitzwilliamtownhouse.com, info@fitzwilliamtownhouse.com).

$$ Baggot Court Town House, with the same owners as the Fitzwilliam (above), has 16 nice rooms a block farther from St. Stephen's Green (Sb-€55-105, Db-€65-139, Tb-€89-149, non-smoking, free parking, 92 Lower Baggot Street, tel. 01/661-2819, fax 01/661-0253, www.baggotcourt.com, reservations@baggotcourt.com).

$ Avalon House Hostel, near Grafton Street, rents 281 simple, clean backpacker beds in refurbished rooms (dorm beds-€14-26, S-€32-36, Sb-€37-41, twin D-€50-68, twin Db-€60-78, includes continental breakfast, elevator, free Internet access and Wi-Fi, launderette, kitchen, lockers-€1/day, helpful staff, a few minutes off Grafton Street at 55 Aungier Street, tel. 01/475-0001, fax 01/475-0303, www.avalon-house.ie, info@avalon-house.ie).

Away from the Center, Southeast of St. Stephen's Green

The listings that follow are unique places (except for the business-class Mespil Hotel), and charge accordingly. If you're going to break the bank, do it here.

$$$ **Number 31** is a hidden gem reached via gritty little Leeson Close (a lane off Lower Leeson Street). Its understated elegance is top-notch, with 6 rooms in a former coach house and 15 rooms in an adjacent Georgian house; the two buildings are connected by a quiet little garden. Guests appreciate the special touches (such as a sunken living room) and tasty breakfasts served in a classy glass atrium (Sb-€100-140, Db-€180-220, Tb-€240-280, Qb-€280-340, all non-smoking, Wi-Fi, free parking, 31 Leeson Close, tel. 01/676-5011, fax 01/676-2929, www.number31 .ie, info@number31.ie).

$$$ **The Schoolhouse Hotel** taught as many as 300 students in its heyday (1861-1969) and was in the middle of the street fight of the 1916 Easter Uprising. Now it's a serene hideout with 31 pristine rooms and a fine restaurant (Sb-€89-169, Db-€99-179, book early, 2-8 Northumberland Road, tel. 01/667-5014, fax 01/667-5015, www.schoolhousehotel.com, reservations@schoolhousehotel .com).

$$$ **Mespil Hotel** is a huge, modern, business-class hotel renting 255 identical three-star rooms (most with a double and single bed, phone, TV, and voicemail) at a good price with all the comforts. This place is a cut above Jurys Inn (Sb, Db, or Tb-€79-195, breakfast-€10, elevator, non-smoking floors, Wi-Fi, apartments for weeklong stays, 10-minute walk southeast of St. Stephen's Green or bus #10, 50-60 Mespil Road, tel. 01/488-4600, fax 01/667-1244, www.mespilhotel.com, mespil@leehotels.com).

$$ **Roxford Lodge Hotel** is a memorable splurge. In a quiet residential neighborhood a 20-minute walk from Trinity College, it has 20 tastefully decorated rooms awash with Jacuzzis and saunas. The €150-200 executive suite is honeymoon-worthy (Sb-€85-95, Db-€95-140, Tb-€100-150, Qb-€110-170, breakfast-€12, secure free parking, 46 Northumberland Road, tel. 01/668-8572, fax 01/668-8158, www.roxfordlodge.ie, reservations@roxfordlodge.ie).

North of the River Liffey
Near Connolly Station

This once-tattered neighborhood (like much of the north side) is now in full rejuvenation mode. To locate these hotels, see the map on page 70.

$$$ **Jurys Inn Custom House,** on Custom House Quay, offers the same value as the other Jurys Inns in Dublin, but it's less central. Its 239 rooms border the financial district, a 10-minute riverside hike from O'Connell Bridge. Of the three Jurys Inns in town, this one is most likely to have rooms available (Db-€79-140 Sun-Thu, or €120-160 Fri-Sat, breakfast-€13, tel. 01/854-1500, fax 01/829-0400, US tel. 800-423-6953, www.jurysinns.com, jurys inncustomhouse@jurysinns.com).

$$ The Townhouse, with 81 small, stylish rooms (some with pleasant views into a central garden courtyard), hides behind a brick Georgian facade one block north of the Customs House (Sb-€60-70, Db-€80-120, Tb-€120-144, Internet access and Wi-Fi; small first-come, first-served parking lot; 47-48 Lower Gardiner Street, tel. 01/878-8808, fax 01/878-8787, www.townhouseof dublin.com, info@townhouseofdublin.com).

Near Parnell Square

A swanky neighborhood 200 years ago, this is now workaday Dublin with a steady urban hum. To locate these hotels, see the map on page 70.

$$$ Jurys Inn Parnell Street, built in 2006 as part of the steady gentrification of Dublin's north side, has 253 predictably soulless but good-value rooms. It's a block from the north end of O'Connell Street and the cluster of museums on Parnell Square (Db-€79-140 Sun-Thu, or €139-160 Fri-Sat, breakfast-€10.50, tel. 01/878-4900, fax 01/878-4999, www.jurysinns.com, jurysinn parnellst@jurysinns.com).

$$ Belvedere Hotel has 92 plain-vanilla rooms that are short on character but long on dependable, modern comforts (Db-€69-99 Sun-Thu, or €89-129 Fri-Sat, cheaper if booked online, Great Denmark Street, tel. 01/873-7700, fax 01/873-7776, www .belvederehotel.ie, reservations@belvederehotel.ie).

$ Charles Stewart Hotel, big and basic, offers 54 forgettable rooms. But it's in a great location for a good price (Sb-€45-59, Db-€50-79, Tb-€75-89, Qb-€95-109, frequent midweek discounts, includes cooked breakfast, ask for a quieter room in the back, just beyond top end of O'Connell Street at 5-6 Parnell Square East, tel. 01/878-0350, fax 01/878-1387, www.charlesstewart.ie, info @charlesstewart.ie).

Eating in Dublin

It's easy to find fine, creative eateries all over town. While you can get decent pub grub for €12-15 on just about any corner, consider saving that for the countryside. There's just no pressing reason to eat Irish in cosmopolitan Dublin. In fact, going local these days is the same as going ethnic. The city's good restaurants are packed from 20:00 on, especially on weekends. Eating early (18:00-19:00) saves time and money, as many better places offer an early-bird special. Many restaurants serve free jugs of ice water with a smile.

Quick and Easy near Grafton Street

Cornucopia is a small, earth-mama-with-class, proudly veg-etarian, self-serve place two blocks off Grafton. It's friendly and

Dublin Restaurants

1 Cornucopia
2 O'Neill's Pub
3 The Duke Pub
4 Davy Burns Pub
5 Bewley's Café & Theatre
6 Wagamama Noodle Bar
7 Juice
8 Yamamori

9 Dunne's (Grocery)
10 Marks & Spencer (Grocery)
11 The Church
12 The Epicurean Food Hall
13 Spar Market
14 Queen of Tarts
15 Chorus Café
16 Le Caprice & Trocadero

youthful, with hearty €12 lunches and €15 dinner specials (Mon-Wed 8:30-21:00, Thu-Sat 8:30-22:30, Sun 12:00-19:00, 19 Wicklow Street, tel. 01/677-7583).

O'Neill's Pub is a venerable, dark, and tangled retreat offering good grub, including dependable €12-15 carvery lunches. It's very central, located across from the main TI (daily 12:00-22:00, Suffolk Street, tel. 01/679-3656).

⑰	Boulevard Café	㉔	Copper Alley Bistro
⑱	Eden	㉕	Gogarty's Pub
⑲	Il Baccaro	㉖	The Brazen Head Pub
⑳	Gallagher's Boxty House	㉗	O'Shea's Merchant Pub
㉑	Bad Ass Café	㉘	Palace Pub
㉒	Luigi Malone's	㉙	Porterhouse
㉓	The Shack	㉚	Arlington Hotel Pubs (2)

Two pubs on Duke Street—**The Duke** and **Davy Burns**—serve reliable pub lunches. (The nearby Cathach Rare Books shop, at 10 Duke Street, displays a rare edition of *Ulysses* inscribed by Joyce, among other treasures, in its window.)

Bewley's Café is an old-time favorite, offering light meals from €10 and full meals from €12-15. Sit on the ground floor among Art Deco lamps and windows by stained-glass artist Harry Clarke, or head upstairs to the bright atrium decorated by art students (self-service Mon-Sat 8:00-22:00, Sun 9:00-22:00, 78 Grafton Street, tel. 01/672-7720). For a taste of witty Irish lunch theater, check out **Bewley's Café Theatre** upstairs; you can catch a fun hour-long performance while having a lunch of soup and brown bread for €15 (Mon-Sat at 13:00 during a play's run—doors open at 12:45, closed Sun, booking info tel. 086-878-4001, www.bewleyscafe theatre.com).

Wagamama Noodle Bar, like its popular sisters in Britain, is a pan-Asian slurp-a-thon with great and healthy noodle and rice dishes (€12-17) served at long communal tables by energetic waiters (daily 12:00-23:00, no reservations, often a line but it moves quickly, South King Street, underneath St. Stephen's Green Shopping Centre, tel. 01/478-2152).

South Great George's Street is lined with hardworking little eateries. **Juice** keeps vegetarians happy (daily 12:00-22:00, 73 South Great George's Street, tel. 01/475-7856).

Yamamori is a plain, mellow, and modern Japanese place serving seas of sushi and noodles (€12 lunches daily 12:30-17:30, €16-20 dinners nightly 17:30-23:00, 71 South Great George's Street, tel. 01/475-5001).

Supermarkets: **Dunnes,** on South Great George's Street, is your one-stop shop for assembling a picnic meal (Mon-Sat 8:30-19:00, Sun 11:00-19:00, across from Yamamori). They have another outlet in the basement of the St. Stephen's Green Shopping Centre. **Marks & Spencer** department store has a fancy grocery store in the basement, with fine take-away sandwiches and salads (Mon-Fri 9:00-20:00, Thu until 21:00, Sat 8:30-19:00, Sun 12:00-18:30, Grafton Street).

Hip and Fun in North Dublin

The Church is a trendy café/bar/restaurant/club/beer garden housed in the former St. Mary's Church. The choir balcony has a huge pipe organ and a refined menu; the ground floor nave is dominated by a long bar and pub grub; and a disco thumps like hell in the bunker-like basement. On warm summer nights, the outdoor terrace is packed. Eating here is as much about the scene as the cuisine (daily 17:00-23:00, €25 four-course early-bird special before 19:00, reservations smart Fri and Sat nights, corner of St. Mary's and Jervis Streets, tel. 01/828-0102).

The Epicurean Food Hall offers a fun selection of food stalls with big and splittable portions. It's a hit with locals—and visitors—needing to eat cheaply (100 yards north of the Ha' Penny Bridge on Lower Liffey Street).

Fast and Cheap near Christ Church Cathedral

Many of Dublin's late-night grocery stores sell cheap salads, microwaved meat pies, and made-to-order sandwiches (such as **Spar Market,** open 24 hours a day, off the top of Dame Street on Parliament Street). A €10 picnic dinner brought back to the hotel might be a good option after a busy day of sightseeing.

Queen of Tarts does yummy breakfasts, fruit salads, sandwiches, and wonderful pastries with quiet streetside seating. Get yours to go, and enjoy a picnic with a Georgian view in one of Dublin's grassy squares (€6-8 breakfasts, €8-12 lunches, Mon-Fri 8:00-19:00, Sat-Sun 9:00-19:00, hidden beside Kinlay House on Cow's Lane, tel. 01/670-7499).

Chorus Café is a friendly little hole-in-the-wall diner, perfect for breakfast, lunch, or dinner with a newspaper (€8 breakfasts, €10 lunches, €12-18 dinners, Mon-Fri 8:30-22:00, Sat 9:30-22:00, closed Sun, Fishamble Street, next door to the site of the first performance of Handel's *Messiah*, tel. 01/616-7088).

Dining at Classy Restaurants and Cafés

These three stylish restaurants serve well-presented food at fair prices. They're located within a block of each other, just south of Temple Bar and Dame Street, near the main TI.

Le Caprice is a fine, relaxing Italian place, with a good wine selection and a friendly staff (€15 pastas, €22-29 meals, Tue-Sun 17:00-22:30, closed Mon, 12 St. Andrew Street, tel. 01/679-4050). Consider their two-course early-bird special if your plans allow for an early dinner (€18, finish by 20:15).

Trocadero, across the street, serves beefy European cuisine to Dubliners interested in a slow, romantic meal. The dressy, red-velvet interior is draped with photos of local actors. Come early or make a reservation—it's a favorite with theatergoers (€19-30 meals, Mon-Sat 17:00-24:00, closed Sun, 4 St. Andrew Street, tel. 01/677-5545). The three-course pre-theater special is a fine value at €25 (17:00-19:00, leave by 19:45).

Boulevard Café is mod, trendy, and likeable, dishing up Mediterranean cuisine that's heavy on the Italian. Their salads, pasta, and sandwiches run about €9-15, and three-course lunch specials are €16 (Mon-Sat 10:00-18:00). Dinners cost about €17-24 (Mon-Sat 12:00-24:00, closed Sun, 27 Exchequer Street, smart to reserve for dinner, tel. 01/679-2131).

In Temple Bar

Eden is a classy refuge serving a variety of contemporary Irish dishes in an airy space with a pleasant outdoor terrace (€20-29 dishes, Mon-Sat 12:30-15:00 & 17:00-22:00, Sun 12:00-16:00 & 18:00-21:30; on Meeting House Square, a half-block off the busy tourist thoroughfare; tel. 01/670-5372). They offer a three-course pre-theater menu for €27 (Sun-Thu only before 19:00).

Il Baccaro, a cozy Italian wine tavern with an arched brick ceiling, is tucked in a quiet corner of Meeting House Square (€13-18 pasta dinners, daily 17:30-22:30, lunches Sat 12:00-16:00 only, closed Sun, tel. 01/671-4597).

Gallagher's Boxty House is touristy and traditional—a good, basic value with creaky floorboards and old Dublin ambience. Its specialty is the boxty, the generally bland-tasting Irish potato pancake filled and rolled with various meats, veggies, and sauces. The "Gaelic Boxty" is the liveliest (€15-25, daily 10:00-22:30, also serves stews and corned beef, 20 Temple Bar, reservations wise, tel. 01/677-2762).

Bad Ass Café is a grunge diner—where Sinéad O'Connor was once a waitress—serving cowboy/Mex/veggie/pizzas to old and new hippies. No need to dress up (€10 lunch specials, €15-18 dinners, daily 11:30-23:00, kids' specials, 9 Crown Alley, just off Meeting House Square, tel. 01/671-2596).

Luigi Malone's, with its fun atmosphere and varied menu of pizza, ribs, pasta, sandwiches, and fajitas, is just the place to take your high-school date (€15-26 dishes, Mon-Sat 12:00-22:00, Sun 13:00-21:30, corner of Cecilia and Fownes streets, tel. 01/679-2723).

The Shack, while a bit touristy, has a reputation for good quality. It serves traditional Irish, chicken, seafood, and steak dishes (€16-25 entrées, €19 three-course early-bird special offered 17:00-19:00, open daily 12:00-22:00, in the center of Temple Bar, 24 East Essex Street, tel. 01/679-0043).

Copper Alley Bistro, a bit farther from the Temple Bar chaos and more reasonably priced, serves dependable comfort-food lunches and dinners (daily 12:00-21:00, corner of Fishamble and Lord Edward streets, just opposite Christ Church Cathedral, tel. 01/679-6500).

Dublin Connections

Note that trains and buses generally run less frequently on Sundays.

By Train from Dublin's Heuston Station to: Tralee (every two hours, 5/day on Sun, most change in Mallow but one direct evening train, 4 hours), **Ennis** (7/day, 3-3.75 hours), **Galway** (8/day, 2.5-3 hours). Train info: recorded timetable tel. 01/805-4222, www.irishrail.ie.

By Train from Dublin's Connolly Station to: Rosslare (3-4/day, 3 hours), **Portrush** (7/day, 2/day Sun, 5 hours, transfer in Belfast or Coleraine). The **Dublin-Belfast train** connects the two

Irish capitals in two hours at 90 mph on one continuous, welded rail (8/day Mon-Sat, 5/day Sun, €36 "day return" tickets, check online for special deals, can cost more Fri-Sun, tel. 01/836-3333). Train info: tel. 01/836-6222. Northern Ireland train info: tel. 048/9089-9400.

To Dun Laoghaire: See "Getting to Dun Laoghaire" on page 99.

By Bus to: Belfast (hourly, most via Dublin Airport, 2.75-3 hours), **Trim** (almost hourly, 1.25-1.75 hours), **Ennis** (hourly, 5 hours), **Galway** (hourly, 3.25 hours; faster on CityLink; hourly, 2.5 hours, tel. 890-280-808, www.citylink.ie), **Limerick** (hourly, 3.75 hours), **Tralee** (8/day, 6 hours), **Dingle** (4/day, 8-9 hours, transfer at Limerick and Tralee). Bus info: tel. 01/836-6111, www.bus eireann.ie.

Dublin Airport: The airport is well-connected to the city center seven miles away; for transportation options into the city, see "Arrival in Dublin" on page 48. Airport info: tel. 01/814-1111, www.dublinairport.ie. Airlines are listed below and in the appendix. To sleep at Dublin Airport, a safe bet is the **$$ Radisson SAS Hotel** (Db-€79-109, best prices if booked online, tel. 01/844-6000, http://hotels.radissonsas.com).

Connecting Ireland and Britain

Spend a few minutes online researching your transportation options across the Irish Sea. Most airline and ferry companies routinely offer discounts (often as much as €10) for tickets purchased from their websites. Before sorting out rail/ferry prices with individual companies, try **www.sailrail.co.uk,** which deals with several companies and has fares low enough to compete with cheap airlines.

If you're going directly to London, flying is your best bet. Check **Ryanair** first (1.5 hours, Irish tel. 081-830-3030, www.ryanair.com). Other options include **British Airways** (Irish tel. 1-890-626-747, US tel. 800-247-9297, www.ba.com), **Aer Lingus** (tel. 081-836-5000, www.aerlingus.com), and **bmi** (Irish tel. 01/407-3036, US tel. 800-788-0555, www.flybmi.com). To get the lowest fares, ask about round-trip ticket prices and book months in advance (though Ryanair offers deals nearly all the time).

Dublin and Liverpool: Sea-Cat has ferries for car and foot passengers (weekly via the Isle of Man, 4 hours, €43 one-way for foot passengers, tel. 800-805-055, www.steam-packet.com). Check in one to two hours before the sailing time—call to confirm details.

Dublin and Holyhead: Irish Ferries sails between Dublin and Holyhead in North Wales. The dock is a mile east of O'Connell Bridge (4/day: 2 slow, 2 fast; slow boats—3.5 hours, €30 one-way walk-on fare; fast boats—2 hours, €35; Dublin tel. 0818-300-400, Holyhead tel. 08705-329-129, www.irishferries.com).

Dun Laoghaire and Holyhead: Stena Line sails a huge catamaran between Dun Laoghaire (near Dublin) and Holyhead in North Wales (3/day: 2 slow, 1 fast; slow boats—3.25 hours, fast boat—2 hours, €30 one-way walk-on fare, €4 extra if paying with credit card, reserve by phone—they book up long in advance on summer weekends, Dun Laoghaire tel. 01/204-7777, recorded info tel. 01/204-7799, can book online at www.stenaline.com).

Ferries to France

With the glut of discount airlines that have sprung up over the past decade (see page 459), it makes little sense to waste your valuable time on a 20-hour-plus ferry ride when you could fly to France in less than 3 hours. Aer Arann connects far-flung western Irish towns to the continent via Dublin or London (www.aerarann .com).

But if the nostalgia of a long, slow ferry ride and the risk of rough seas appeal to you, look into Irish Ferries, which connects Ireland (Rosslare) with France (Cherbourg and Roscoff) every other day (less frequently Jan-March). While Cherbourg has the quickest connection to Paris, your overall time between Ireland and Paris is about the same (20-25 hours) regardless of which port is used on the day you sail. One-way fares range from €59 to €69 and are cheapest if booked online. Eurailpass-holders get 30 percent off. In both directions, departures are generally between 15:30 and 16:00 and arrive late the next morning.

While passengers can nearly always get on, reservations are wise in summer and easy by phone. If you anticipate a crowded departure, you can reserve a seat for €15. Cabins (2 beds) go for €69-99. The easiest way to get a bed (except during summer) is from the information desk upon boarding. The cafeteria serves bad food at reasonable prices. Upon arrival in France, buses and taxis connect you to your Paris-bound train (Irish Ferries: Dublin tel. 0818-300-400, www.irishferries.com, info@irishferries.com).

Dun Laoghaire and Howth

Dun Laoghaire (dun LEERY) and Howth (rhymes with "growth") are two peas in a pod, dangling from opposite ends of Dublin Bay's crescent-shaped shoreline. They offer quieter, cheaper lodging alternatives to Dublin. Both offer easy DART light rail access to the city center, just a 25-minute ride away. Each houses its only worthwhile sightseeing options in pillbox martello (masonry) towers. And they were each once home to famous Irish writers: James Joyce in Dun Laoghaire and W. B. Yeats in Howth. The fundamental difference between the two is that Dun Laoghaire (south of Dublin) has the ferry port to Wales, while Howth (north of Dublin) is closer to the airport.

DUBLIN

Dun Laoghaire

Dun Laoghaire is seven miles south of Dublin. This snoozy suburb, with the ferry terminal for Wales and easy connections to

downtown Dublin, is a great small-town base for exploring the big city.

The Dun Laoghaire harbor was strategic enough to merit a line of martello towers, built to defend against an expected Napoleonic invasion (one tower now houses the James Joyce Museum). By the mid-19th century, its massive breakwaters were completed, protecting a huge harbor. Ships sailed regularly from here to Wales (60 miles away), and the first train line in Ireland connected the terminal with Dublin.

Getting to Dun Laoghaire

Buses run between Dublin and Dun Laoghaire, but the **DART** commuter train is much faster and not subject to Dublin traffic delays (4/hour, 25 minutes, runs Mon-Sat about 6:00-23:30, Sun from 9:00, €2.30 one-way, €4.20 round-trips are good same day only, 3-day pass-€11.40, Eurailpass valid but uses a flexi-day, tel. 01/703-3504, www.irishrail.ie). If you're coming from Dublin, catch a DART train marked "Bray" and get off at the Sandycove/Glasthule or Dun Laoghaire stop, depending on which B&B you choose. If you're leaving Dun Laoghaire, catch a train marked "Howth" to get to Dublin. Get off at the central Tara Street Station if you want to sightsee in Dublin; or, for train connections north (or the Airlink bus to the airport), ride it one stop farther to Connolly Station.

The **Aircoach bus** goes to and from the Dublin Airport via the Port Tunnel. You can catch it at either the Town Hall in Dun Laoghaire or opposite St. Joseph's Church in nearby Glasthule (€8, departs Dun Laoghaire starting at 4:00 and from the airport's short-term parking lot starting at 5:00 until 23:00, hourly, 50 minutes, tel. 01/844-7118, www.aircoach.ie).

The **taxi** fare from Dun Laoghaire to central Dublin is about €35; to the airport, about €50. Try ABC Taxi service (tel. 01/285-5444). With DART access into Dublin, and cheap or sometimes free parking, Dun Laoghaire is ideal for those with **cars** (which can cost more than €30/day to park in Dublin).

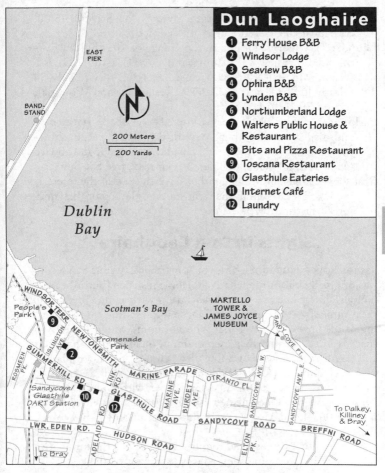

Dun Laoghaire

1. Ferry House B&B
2. Windsor Lodge
3. Seaview B&B
4. Ophira B&B
5. Lynden B&B
6. Northumberland Lodge
7. Walters Public House & Restaurant
8. Bits and Pizza Restaurant
9. Toscana Restaurant
10. Glasthule Eateries
11. Internet Café
12. Laundry

Orientation to Dun Laoghaire

A busy transportation hub, Dun Laoghaire has a coastline defined by its nearly mile-long breakwaters—reaching like two muscular arms into the Irish Sea. The breakwaters are popular for strollers, bikers, bird-watchers, and fishermen.

Tourist Information: The TI is in the ferry terminal (Mon-Sat 10:00-12:45 & 14:00-18:00, closed Sun).

Helpful Hints

Internet Access: U-surf.ie provides a fast connection (€4/hour, Mon-Sat 9:00-23:00, Sun 11:00-23:00, 88B Lower George's Street, tel. 01/231-1186).

Post Office: It's on Lower George's Street (Mon-Fri 9:00-18:00, Sat 9:00-13:00, closed Sun).

Laundry: Try **Jeeves,** located in the village of Glasthule, a five-minute downhill walk from Sandycove/Glasthule DART station (Mon-Sat 8:30-18:00, closed Sun, full-service only, 34 Glasthule Road, next to Daniel's Restaurant and Wine Bar, tel. 01/230-1120).

Parking: If you don't have free parking at your B&B, try the pay-and-display street-parking system. Buy a ticket at machines spaced along the street, and display it on your dashboard (Mon-Fri 8:00-19:00, €1/hour, 3-hour max, free Sat-Sun).

Best Views: Hike out to the lighthouse, at the end of the interesting East Pier; or climb the tight stairs to the top of the James Joyce Museum/tower.

Sights in Dun Laoghaire

James Joyce Museum—This squat martello tower at Sandycove was originally built to repel a Napoleonic invasion, but it became famous chiefly because of its association with James Joyce. The great author lived here briefly and made it the setting for the opening of his novel *Ulysses*. Today, the museum's round exhibition space is filled with literary memorabilia, including photographs and rare first editions. For a fine view, climb the claustrophobic, two-story spiral stairwell sealed inside the thick wall to reach the rooftop gun mount (€6, €11.50 combo-ticket with Dublin Writers' Museum, March-Oct Tue-Sat 10:00-13:00 & 14:00-17:00, Sun 14:00-18:00, closed Mon, open by appointment only Nov-Feb, tel. 01/280-9265).

The sandy little cove and rounded rocks beside the tower are a safe and clean swimming spot, a favorite for kids of all ages.

Entertainment in Dun Laoghaire

For an evening of pure Irish music, song, and dance, check out the **Comhaltas Ceoltoiri Éireann,** an association working to preserve this slice of Irish culture. It got started in the 1950s when Elvis and company threatened to steal the musical heart of the new generation. Judging by the pop status of traditional Irish music these days, Comhaltas accomplished its mission. Their Seisiun evening is a stage show mixing traditional music, song, and dance (€10, July-Aug Mon-Thu at 21:00, followed by informal music session at 22:30). On Fridays all year long, they have a *ceilidh* (KAY-lee), where everyone does set dances. This style, the forerunner of square dancing, evolved from the French Quadrille dances of 200 years ago, with two couples making up a set (€10 includes friendly point-ers, 21:30-24:30). At 21:00 on Tuesdays and Wednesdays (free) and Saturdays (€3), there are informal sessions by the fireside. All musicians are welcome. Performances are held at the Cuturlann na Éireann center at 32 Belgrave Square in Monkstown (near the Seapoint DART stop, or take bus #7 from Dun Laoghaire, tel. 01/280-0295, www.comhaltas.ie). Their bar is free to enter (no cover charge) and often filled with music.

Sleeping in Dun Laoghaire

(€1 = about $1.25, country code: 353, area code: 01)

In Dun Laoghaire, near Sandycove DART Station

These listings are within a couple of blocks of the Sandycove/ Glasthule DART station and a 10-minute walk to the Dun Laoghaire DART station/ferry landing.

$ **Ferry House B&B,** with four high-ceilinged rooms, is a family-friendly place on a dead-end street (Sb-€45-60, Db-€65-75, Tb-€90-100, Qb-€110, €5 discount with cash and direct booking, non-smoking, 15 Clarinda Park North just off Clarinda Park West, tel. 01/280-8301, www.ferryhousedublin.com, ferry_house @hotmail.com, Eamon and Pauline).

$ **Windsor Lodge** rents four fresh, inviting rooms on a quiet street a block off the harbor and a block from the DART station (Db-€50-70, Tb-€90, cash only, non-smoking, 3 Islington Avenue, tel. 01/284-6952, mobile 086/844-6646, www.windsorlodge.ie, windsorlodgedublin@gmail.com, Mary O'Farrell).

$ **Seaview B&B,** a modern house run by Mrs. Kane, has three big, cheery rooms and a welcoming guests' lounge with a bright and friendly feeling (S-€35, Db-€70 with this book in 2011, cash only, non-smoking, just above Rosmeen Gardens at 2 Granite Hall, tel. & fax 01/280-9105, www.seaviewbedandbreakfast.com, seaviewbedandbreakfast@hotmail.com).

Near the Dun Laoghaire DART Station

$$ **Ophira B&B** is a historic house with four comfortably creaky rooms run by active diver, hiker, and biker John O'Connor (Sb-€40-55, Db-€55-80, Tb-€85-110, Qb-€100-140, non-smoking, Wi-Fi, parking available, 10 Corrig Avenue, tel. 01/280-0997, www.ophira.ie, info@ophira.ie).

$ **Lynden B&B,** with a classy 150-year-old interior hiding behind a somber front, rents four big rooms (S-€39-44, D-€55-60, Db-€65-70, cash only, past Mulgrave Street to 2 Mulgrave Terrace, tel. 01/280-6404, fax 01/230-2258, www.lyndenbandb .com, lynden@iol.ie, Maria Gavin).

$ Northumberland Lodge has four big, airy rooms (S-€35-40, Sb-€45, D-€60, Db-€65, cash only, TV lounge, 36 Northumberland Avenue, tel. 01/280-3262, mobile 086-102-9287, cora .northumberland@hotmail.com, Mrs. Howard).

Eating in Dun Laoghaire

If staying in Dun Laoghaire, I'd definitely eat here rather than in Dublin.

George's Street, Dun Laoghaire's main drag three blocks inland, has plenty of eateries and pubs, many with live music. **Walters Public House and Restaurant** is a bright, modern place above a pub, offering good food to a dressy crowd. The multi-terraced back patio of the pub is great for a drink on a warm evening (€16-26 meals, €8-14 pub meals, daily 17:30-22:00, 68 Upper George's Street, tel. 01/280-7442). A good bet for families is the kid-friendly **Bits and Pizza** (daily 12:00-22:00, off George's Street at 15 Patrick Street, tel. 01/284-2411).

Toscana, on the waterfront, is a popular little cubbyhole, serving hearty Italian dishes and pizza. Its prime location makes it easy to incorporate into your evening stroll. Reserve for dinner (€11-24 meals, daily 12:00-22:00, 5 Windsor Terrace, tel. 01/230-0890).

Glasthule (called simply "the village" locally, just down the street from the Sandycove/Glasthule DART station) has an array of fun, hardworking little restaurants. The big **Eagle House pub** dishes up great Indian food and hearty €10-19 pub meals in a wonderful atmosphere; it's a super local joint for a late drink (Mon-Sat 12:30-21:30, Sun 12:30-19:30, tel. 01/280-4740). The nearby **Daniel's Restaurant and Wine Bar** is less atmospheric, but it's also good (€18-24 meals, Tue-Sun 18:00-22:30, closed Mon, 34 Glasthule Road, tel. 01/284-1027). **Centra Market** is right next door and has your picnic makings (daily 7:00-23:00, Glasthule Road).

Howth

Eight miles north of Dublin, Howth rests on a teardrop-shaped peninsula that pokes the Irish Sea. Its active harbor teems with fishing boats bringing in the daily catch. Weary Dubliners come here for refreshing coastal cliff walks near the city.

Located at the north terminus of the DART light rail line, Howth makes a good place for travelers to settle in, with easy connections to Dublin for sightseeing.

Howth was once an important gateway to Dublin. Near the neck of the peninsula is the suburb of Clontarf, where Irish High King Brian Boru defeated the last concerted Viking attack in 1014. Eight hundred years later, a squat martello tower was built on a bluff above Howth's harbor to defend it from a Napoleonic invasion that never came. The harbor then grew as a port for shipping from Liverpool and Wales. It was eventually eclipsed by Dun Laoghaire, which was first to gain rail access. Irish rebels smuggled German-supplied guns into Ireland via Howth in 1914, making the 1916 Easter Uprising possible. These days this hamlet is so sleepy, it didn't open a TI until 2009.

Getting to Howth

The **DART** light rail system zaps travelers between Howth and the city twice as fast as the bus and sans traffic (4/hour, 25 minutes, runs Mon-Sat about 6:00-23:30, Sun from 9:00, €2.30 one-way, €4.20 round-trips good same day only, 3-day pass-€11.40, Eurailpass valid but uses a flexi-day, tel. 01/703-3504, www.irish rail.ie). If you're coming from Dublin, catch a DART train marked "Howth" (not *Howth Junction, Malahide*, or *Drogheda*) and ride it to the end of the line—passing through Howth Junction en route. All trains departing Howth head straight to Dublin's Connolly Station, then continue on to Tara and Pierce stations.

If you choose to go by **bus,** #31 or #31B link Dublin's Eden Quay and the well-marked bus stop on Howth's harborfront (1 hour, €2). A **taxi** from the airport takes about 20 minutes and costs about €25. Try Executive Cabs (tel. 01/839-6020). With easy DART access into Dublin and plentiful parking, Howth is a good option for those with **cars** (which can cost more than €30/day to park in Dublin).

Orientation to Howth

Howth perches on the north shore of the peninsula, clustered along a quarter-mile harborfront promenade that stretches from the DART station (in the west) to the martello tower on the bluff (in the east). Its two stony piers clutch like crab claws at the Irish Sea. The West Pier has the fishing action and TI, while the East Pier extends to a stubby 200-year-old lighthouse and views of a rugged nearby island, Ireland's Eye. Abbey Street extends south, uphill from the harbor near the base of the martello tower bluff, becoming Main Street with most of the shops and pubs, along with the post office (Mon-Fri 9:00-13:00 & 14:15-18:00, Sat

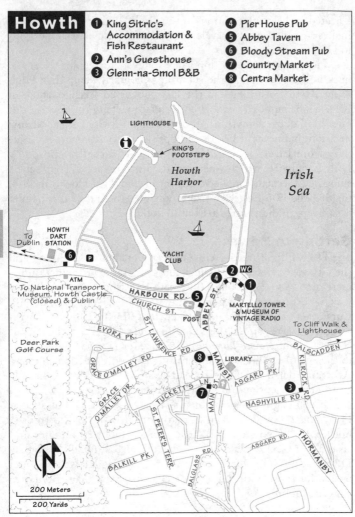

Howth

1 King Sitric's Accommodation & Fish Restaurant
2 Ann's Guesthouse
3 Glenn-na-Smol B&B
4 Pier House Pub
5 Abbey Tavern
6 Bloody Stream Pub
7 Country Market
8 Centra Market

LIGHTHOUSE

KING'S FOOTSTEPS

Howth Harbor

Irish Sea

To Dublin

HOWTH DART STATION

6

P

ATM

To National Transport Museum, Howth Castle (closed) & Dublin

YACHT CLUB

P

HARBOUR RD.

CHURCH ST.

POST

2 WC

4

1

5

ABBEY ST.

MARTELLO TOWER & MUSEUM OF VINTAGE RADIO

To Cliff Walk & Lighthouse

EVORA PK.

ST. LAWRENCE RD.

Deer Park Golf Course

GRACE O'MALLEY RD.

GRACE O'MALLEY DR.

8

7

MAIN ST.

LIBRARY

ASGARD PK.

BALSCADDEN

KILROCK RD.

3

NASHVILLE RD.

TUCKETT'S LN.

ST. PETER'S TERR.

BALKILL PK.

BALGLASS RD.

ASGARD RD.

THORMANBY

N

200 Meters
200 Yards

DUBLIN

9:00-13:00, closed Sun) and library (free Internet access, only one terminal, Mon and Wed 14:00-20:30, Tue and Thu-Sat 10:00-13:00 & 14:00-17:00, closed Sun). Ulster Bank has the only ATM in town, across the street from the DART station and to the left of the Gem Newsstand.

Tourist Information

The TI is at the far end of the West Pier, on the ground floor of the Aqua Building (May-Oct daily 9:30-17:00, shorter hours off-season, 1 West Pier, tel. 01/839-6955, www.howthismagic.com). If the TI is closed, another good info source is your innkeeper.

Sights in Howth

Other than coastal walks, sightseeing here pales in comparison to Dublin. Nearby Howth Castle is privately owned and cannot be toured.

Museum of Vintage Radio—The three-story martello tower on the bluff overlooking the East Pier is the only sight in Howth worth a glance. Curator Pat Herbert has spent almost 50 years acquiring his collection of lovingly preserved radios, phonographs, and even a hurdy-gurdy (a crank-action musical oddity)—all of which still work. Check out the WWII-era radio disguised as a picture frame, which was used by the resistance in occupied France (€5, May-Oct daily 11:00-16:00, Nov-April Sat-Sun only 11:00-16:00, entry up driveway off Abbey Street, www.ei0mar.org).

Before leaving the compact bluff, catch the views of the harbor and the nearby island of Ireland's Eye. Spot the distant martello tower on the island's west end and the white guano coating its eastern side, courtesy of a colony of gannets.

National Transport Museum—Housed in a large shed on the castle grounds, this is a dusty waste of time unless you find rapture in old trams and buses (€3, June-Aug Mon-Fri 10:00-17:00, Sat-Sun 14:00-17:00, Sept-May by appointment only, tel. 01/848-0831).

St. Mary's Abbey—Looming above Abbey Street, the current ruins date from the early 1400s. Before that, a church built by Norse King Sitric in 1042 stood at this site. The entrance to the ruins is on Church Street, above the abbey grounds.

East and West Piers—The piers make for mellow strolls after a meal. Poke your head into the various fishmonger shops along the West Pier to see the day's catch. At the end of the pier (on the leeward side), you'll find the footsteps of King George IV carved into the stone after his 1821 visit. The East Pier is a quiet jetty barbed with a squat lighthouse and the closest views of Ireland's Eye. If you want to get even closer to the island, book a boat excursion (€15 round-trip, daily in summer on demand from 10:00-18:00, call for off-season trips, tel. 086/845-9154, www.islandferries.net).

Hiking Trails—Trails above the eastern cliffs of the peninsula offer enjoyable, breezy exercise. For a scenic three-hour round-trip, walk past the East Pier and martello tower, following Balscadden Road uphill. You'll soon pass Balscadden House, where writer W. B. Yeats spent part of his youth (watch for plaque on left). Where the road dead-ends, you'll find the well-marked trailhead. The trail is easy to follow, and soon you'll be walking south around the craggy coastline to grand views of the Bailey Lighthouse on the southeast rim of the peninsula. The gate to the lighthouse grounds is always locked, so enjoy the view from afar before retracing your steps back to Howth.

Sleeping in Howth

(€1 = about $1.25, country code: 353, area code: 01)

$$$ King Sitric's Accommodation is Howth's best lodging option and has a fine harborfront seafood restaurant (described below). It fills the old harbormaster's house with eight well-kept rooms and a friendly staff (Sb-€110-145, Db-€150-205, Tb-€190-245, discounts for 2-night stay, online deals, non-smoking, East Pier below mar-tello tower, tel. 01/832-5235, fax 01/839-2442, www.kingsitric.ie, info@kingsitric.ie, Aidan and Joan MacManus).

$$ Ann's Guesthouse, next door to King Sitric's, sports four bright, airy rooms on its top floor—two with skylight views of the harbor (Sb/Db-€80, 5 East Pier, tel. 01/832-3197, www.annsof howth.com, annsofhowth@eircom.net, Jon Cooke).

$ Glenn-na-Smol B&B is a homey house with six unpre-tentious rooms in a quiet setting, a 10-minute walk uphill along the coast behind the martello tower (Sb-€45, Db-€70, Tb-€95, Qb-€100, cash only, Wi-Fi, parking, corner of Nashville Road & Kilrock Road, tel. 01/832-2936, rickards@indigo.ie, Sean and Kitty Rickard).

Eating in Howth

King Sitric's Fish Restaurant, one of the area's most famous seafood experiences, serves Irish versions of French classics in a dining room (upstairs) with harbor views. Chef Aidan MacManus rises early each morning to select the best of the day's catch on the pier, to be enjoyed that evening by happy customers (€22-30 meals, Mon and Wed-Sat 18:30-22:00, Sun 13:00-19:00, closed Tue, res-ervations smart, tel. 01/832-5235, www.kingsitric.ie).

For pub grub, try the **Pier House Pub** on the waterfront (trad-music sessions Sat at 21:30 and Sun at 13:00, 4 East Pier, tel. 01/839-6344). Farther up the hill you'll find the **Abbey Tavern** on Abbey Street (occasional trad music and dance, call for schedule, tel. 01/839-0307 or 01/832-2006) and the **Bloody Stream Pub** in front of the DART station (tel. 01/839-5076). The **Country Market** sells picnic supplies, and its cheap and friendly upstairs tea room offers lunch (Mon-Sat 7:00-19:00, Sun 7:00-17:00, Main Street). The **Centra Market** is a block closer to the waterfront (daily 7:00-22:00, Main Street).

NEAR DUBLIN

Brú na Bóinne • Trim • Glendalough •
Wicklow Mountains • Irish National Stud

Not far from urban Dublin, the stony skeletons of evocative ruins sprout from the lush Irish countryside. The story of Irish history is told by ancient burial mounds, early Christian monastic settlements, huge Norman castles, and pampered estate gardens. In gentler inland terrain, the Irish love of equestrian sport is nurtured in grassy pastures ruled by spirited thoroughbreds. These sights are separated into three regions: north of Dublin (the Valley of the Boyne, including Brú na Bóinne and the town of Trim), south of Dublin (Glendalough and the Wicklow Mountains), and west of Dublin (the Irish National Stud).

North of Dublin: The Valley of the Boyne

The peaceful, green Valley of the Boyne, just 30 miles north of Dublin, has an impressive concentration of historical and spiritual sights: The enigmatic burial mounds at Brú na Bóinne are older than the Egyptian pyramids. At the Hill of Tara (seat of the high kings of Celtic Ireland), St. Patrick preached his most persuasive sermon. The valley also contains the first Vatican-endorsed monastery in Ireland and several of the country's finest high crosses. You'll see Trim's 13th-century castle—Ireland's biggest—built by Norman invaders, and you can wander the site of the historic

Valley of the Boyne

Battle of the Boyne (1690), in which the Protestants turned the tide against the Catholics and imposed British rule until the 20th century.

Planning Your Time

Of these sights, only Brú na Bóinne is worth ▲▲▲ (and deserves a good three hours). The others, while relatively meager physically, are powerfully evocative to anyone interested in Irish history and culture. Without a car, I'd visit only Brú na Bóinne, taking the shuttle bus from Dublin (see "Getting There" on page 112).

The region is a joy by car, because all of the described sights are within a 30-minute drive of each other. If you eat your Weetabix and get an early start, you could do the entire region in a day. Though the sights are on tiny roads, they're well-marked with brown, tourist-friendly road signs. You'll navigate best using an Ordnance Survey atlas.

As you plan your Ireland itinerary, if you're flying into or out of Dublin, and want to avoid the intensity and expense of that big city, consider using Trim as an overnight base (45-minute drive from airport; accommodations listed on page 118) and tour these sights from there.

Tours of the Valley of the Boyne

If you lack a car and like tours, consider one of these round-trip excursions from Dublin.

Mary Gibbon's Tours visits the Brú na Bóinne (including inside the Newgrange tomb), the Hill of Tara, and the Hill of Slane in a six-hour trip (€38, Mon-Fri only, 9:30 pickup at Mespil Hotel at 50-60 Mespil Road, 10:15 pickup at Dublin TI on Suffolk Street, 10:25 pickup at Royal Dublin Hotel on O'Connell Street, home by 16:30, book direct rather than through TI, tel. 086/355-1355, www.newgrangetours.com, info@newgrangetours.com).

Over the Top Tours leaves Dublin at 9:00 and returns by 17:30, with stops at the Hill of Tara, the Hill of Slane (free time for lunch), Fourknocks (prehistoric tombs, less famous than Brú na Bóinne), and the monasteries of Monasterboice and Old Mellifont Abbey (€29, daily, 9:00 pickup at Dublin TI on Suffolk Street, 9:20 pickup at Royal Dublin Hotel on O'Connell Street, 14-seat minibus, reservations required, hold seat by leaving credit-card number, Ireland toll-free tel. 1-800-424-252, Dublin tel. 01/860-0404, www.overthetoptours.com, info@overthetoptours.com).

Brú na Bóinne

The famous archaeological site properly known as Brú na Bóinne—"dwelling place of the Boyne"—is also commonly referred to as "Newgrange" (actually one of the tombs). The well-organized site, worth ▲▲▲, centers on a state-of-the-art museum. Visitors are given appointments for shuttle buses that ferry small groups five minutes away to one of two 5,000-year-old passage tombs where a guide gives a 30-minute tour. **Newgrange** is more famous, and allows you inside. **Knowth** (rhymes with "south") opened more recently and is more extensive, but you can't go inside the tomb. At the turnstile, you'll buy a ticket to one or both sights, and be given bus departure times (if you plan to see both sights, note that buses depart 1.5 hours apart). Newgrange sells out first, and it comes with a longer wait. If you opt for Knowth, be sure to see the museum's replica of the Newgrange passage entrance (where a short tour and winter solstice light-show demo often occur upon request); the replica is connected to the video room. Each site is different enough and worthwhile, but for many, seeing just one is adequate. For information on the prehistoric art, see page 421.

Newgrange is one single mound and the more restored of the Brú na Bóinne sites. Dating from 3200 B.C., it's 500 years older than the pyramids at Giza. While we know nothing of the builders, it most certainly was a sacred spot dealing with some kind of Sun God ritual. During the tour, you'll squeeze down a narrow

passageway to a cross-shaped central chamber, located under a 20-foot-high igloo-type
stone dome. Bones and ashes were placed
here under 200,000 tons of stone and dirt to
wait for a special moment. As the sun rose on
the shortest day of the year (winter solstice,
Dec 21), a ray of light crept slowly down the
60-foot-long passageway. For 17 minutes, it lit
the center of the sacred chamber. Perhaps this
was the moment when the souls of the dead
were transported to the afterlife, via that mysterious ray of life-giving and life-taking light.

Knowth (the second Brú na Bóinne site)
is a necropolis of several grassy mounds around one 85-yard-wide
grand tomb. The big mound, covering 1.5 acres, has two passages
aligned so that on the spring and fall equinoxes, rays from the
rising and setting sun shine down the passageways to the center
chamber. Neither of the passages is open to the public, but when
you visit a room cut into the mound—designed to expose the
interior construction layers—you get a glimpse down one of the
passages. The Knowth site thrived from 3000 to 2000 B.C., with
mysterious burial rituals and sun-tracking ceremonies to please the
gods and ensure the regular progression of seasons for crops. The
site then evolved into the domain of fairies and myths for the next
2,000 years, and became an Iron Age fortress in the early centuries
after Christ. Around A.D. 1000, it was an all-Ireland political center, and, later, a Norman fortress was built atop the mound. You'll
see plenty of mysteriously carved stones and new-feeling grassy
mounds that you can look down on from atop the grand tomb.

Cost and Hours: Allow an hour for the excellent museum
and an hour for each of the tombs you visit. The museum in the
Brú na Bóinne Visitors Centre is included in the following prices:
Newgrange-€6, Knowth-€5. The site is open May-Sept daily 9:00-
18:00, slightly shorter hours off-season. Newgrange is open year-
round, while Knowth is open April-Oct only. Tel. 041/988-0300.

Crowd-Beating Tips: Visits are limited, and on busy summer
days those arriving in the afternoon may not get a spot (no reservations possible). In peak season, try to arrive by 9:30 to avoid a wait
caused by big tour-bus day-trip crowds from Dublin. Generally
upon arrival you'll get a bus departure time for one or both of the
passage-tomb sites (the last shuttle bus leaves 1.75 hours before
closing). Spend your wait visiting the museum, watching the great
seven-minute video, and munching lunch in the cheery cafeteria.
You can't drive directly to the actual passage tombs.

Getting There: To reach the Brú na Bóinne Visitors Centre
from Dublin by **car,** drive north on N-1 to Drogheda, where signs

direct you to the center.

If you don't have a car and you're not taking a tour, hop on the **Newgrange shuttle bus** that runs from Dublin directly to the Visitors Centre (€17 round-trip, 45 minutes, must book in advance, departs at 8:45 and 11:15 from TI on Suffolk Street and at 9:00 and 11:30 from Royal Dublin Hotel on O'Connell Street, return trips depart at 13:00 and 16:00 from the Visitors Centre, run by Over the Top Tours, book by calling 01/860-0405 or 1-800-424-252).

More Sights in the Valley of the Boyne

▲▲Battle of the Boyne Site

One of Europe's lesser-known battlegrounds (but huge in Irish history), this is the pastoral riverside site of the pivotal battle in which the Protestant British broke Catholic resistance, establishing Protestant rule over all Ireland and Britain.

It was here in 1690 that Protestant King William III, with his English/Irish/Dutch/Danish/French Huguenot army, defeated his father-in-law—who was also his uncle—Catholic King James II and his Irish/French army. King William's forces, on the north side of the Boyne, managed to fight their way across the river, and by the end of the day, King James was fleeing south in full retreat. He soon left Ireland, but his forces fought on until their final defeat a year later. James the Second (called "James da Turd" by those who scorn his lack of courage and leadership) never returned, and he died a bitter ex-monarch in France. King William of Orange's victory, on the other hand, is still celebrated in Northern Ireland every July 12, with controversial marches by Unionist "Orangemen."

The 50,000 soldiers who fought here made this the largest battle ever to take place in the British Isles. Yet it was only a side skirmish in an even larger continental confrontation pitting France's King Louis XIV against the "Grand Alliance" of nations threatened by France's dominant military and frequent incursions into neighboring lands.

Louis ruled by divine right, answerable only to God—and James modeled himself after Louis. Even the Pope (who could control neither Louis nor James and was equally disturbed by Catholic France's aggressions) backed Protestant King William against Catholic King James—just one example of the pretzel logic that was the European mind-set at the time.

NEAR DUBLIN

The site of the Battle of the Boyne was bought in 1997 by the Irish Office of Public Works, part of the Republic's governmental efforts to honor a place sacred to Unionists in Northern Ireland—despite the fact that the battle's outcome ensured Catholic subordination to the Protestant minority for the next 230 years.

The Visitors Centre is housed in a mansion built on the battlefield 50 years after the conflict. The exhibits do a good job illustrating the international nature of the battle and its place in the wider context of European political power struggles. The highlight is a huge battleground model with laser lights that move troops around the terrain, showing the battle's ebb and flow on that bloody day. A separate 15-minute film (shown in the former stable house) runs continuously and does a fine job of fleshing out the battle.

The Saturday and Sunday afternoon "Living History" demonstrations in summer are a treat for history buffs, with guides clad in 17th-century garb as they explain musket loading and firing (at 11:00, 13:00, and 15:00), as well as cavalry combat (at 12:00 and 14:00).

Cost and Hours: €4, daily May-Sept 10:00-18:00, March-April 9:30-17:30, Oct-Feb 9:00-17:00, tea room/cafeteria, tel. 041/980-9950, www.battleoftheboyne.ie.

▲Hill of Tara

This was the most important center of political and religious power in pre-Christian Ireland. While aerial views show plenty of mysterious circles and lines, wandering with the sheep among the well-worn ditches and hills leaves you with more to feel than to see. Visits are made meaningful by an excellent 20-minute video presentation and the caring 20-minute guided walk that follows (always available upon request and entirely worthwhile).

You'll see the Mound of Hostages (a Bronze Age passage grave, c. 2500 B.C.), a couple of ancient sacred stones, a war memorial, and vast views over the Emerald Isle. While ancient Ireland was a pig pile of minor chieftain-kings scrambling for power, the high king of Tara was king of the mountain. It was at this ancient stockade that St. Patrick directly challenged the king's authority. When confronted by the high king, Patrick convincingly explained the Holy Trinity using a shamrock: three petals with one stem. He won the right to preach Christianity throughout Ireland, and the country had a new national symbol.

This now-desolate hill was also the scene of great modern events. In 1798, passionate young Irish rebels chose Tara for its defensible position, but were routed by better organized (and more sober) British troops. (The cunning British commander had sent three cartloads of whiskey along the nearby road earlier in the day, knowing the rebels would intercept it.) In 1843, the great orator and champion of Irish liberty Daniel O'Connell gathered 500,000 Irish peasants on this hill for his greatest "monster meeting"—a peaceful show of force demanding the repeal of the Act of Union with Britain (kind of the Woodstock of its day). In a bizarre final twist, a small group of British Israelites—who believed they were one of the lost tribes of Israel, ending up in Britain—spent 1899 to 1901 recklessly digging up parts of the hill in a misguided search for the Ark of the Covenant.

Stand on the Hill of Tara. Think of the history it's seen, and survey Ireland. It's understandable why this "meeting place of heroes" continues to hold a powerful place in the Irish psyche.

Cost and Hours: €3, includes video and 20-minute guided walk, mid-May-mid-Sept daily 10:00-18:00, last tour at 17:00; otherwise, access to site is free but visitors center is closed; tel. 046/902-5903. Wear good walking shoes because the ground is uneven and often wet.

Old Mellifont Abbey

This Cistercian abbey (the first in Ireland) was established by French monks who came to the country in 1142 to bring the Irish monks more in line with Rome. (Even the abbey's architecture was unusual, marking the first time in Ireland that a formal, European-style monastic layout was used.) Cistercians lived isolated rural lives; lay monks worked the land, allowing the more educated monks to devote all their energy to prayer. After Henry VIII dissolved the abbey in 1539, centuries of locals used it as a handy quarry. Consequently, little survives beyond the octagonal lavabo, where the monks would ceremonially wash their hands before entering the refectory to eat. The lavabo gives a sense of the abbey's former grandeur. The excellent 45-minute tours, available upon request and included in your admission, give meaning to the site.

Cost and Hours: €3, May-Sept daily 10:00-18:00, last entry 17:00, no tours Oct-April when site is free and you can explore on your own, tel. 041/982-6459.

Monasterboice

This ruined monastery is visit-worthy for its round tower and its ornately carved high crosses—two of the best such crosses in Ireland. In the Dark Ages, these crosses, illustrated from top to bottom with Bible stories, gave monks a teaching tool as they preached to the illiterate masses. Imagine the crosses in their heyday, when they were brightly painted (before years of wind and rain weathered the paint away). Today, Monasterboice is basically an old graveyard.

The 18-foot-tall Cross of Murdock (Muiredach's Cross, A.D.

923, named after an abbot) is considered the best high cross in Ireland. The circle—which characterizes the Irish high cross—could represent the perfection of God. Or, to help ease pagans into Christianity, it may represent the sun, which was worshipped in pre-Christian Celtic society. Whatever its symbolic purpose, its practical function was to support the weight of the crossbeam.

Face the cross (with the round tower in the background) and study the carved sandstone. The center panel shows the Last

Judgment, with Christ under a dove, symbolizing the Holy Spirit. Those going to heaven are on Christ's right, and the damned are being ushered away by a pitchfork-wielding devil on his left. Working down, you'll see the Archangel Michael weighing souls, as the Devil tugs demonically at the scales; the adoration of the three—or four—Magi; Moses striking the rock to bring forth water; scenes from the life of David; and, finally, Adam, Eve, and the apple next to Cain slaying Abel. Imagine these carvings with their original, colorful paint jobs. Check out the plaque at the base of the nearby tree, which further explains the carvings on the cross.

Find the even-taller cross nearest the tower. It seems the top section was broken off and buried for a period, protecting it from weathering. The bottom part remained standing, enduring the erosive effect of Irish weather that smeared the once-crisp features.

The door to the round tower was originally 15-20 feet above the ground (accessible by ladder). After centuries of burials, the ground level has risen.

Cost and Hours: Free and always open.

Trim

The sleepy, workaday town of Trim, straddling the River Boyne, is marked by the towering ruins of Trim Castle. Trim feels littered with mighty ruins that seem to say, "This little town was big-time…700 years ago." The tall Yellow Steeple (over the river from the castle) is all that remains of the 14th-century Augustinian Abbey of St. Mary. A pleasant half-mile walk back toward Dublin takes you to the sprawling ruins of Saints Peter and Paul Cathedral (from 1206), once the largest Gothic church in Ireland. Across the 15th-century Norman bridge from the cathedral are the 13th-century ruins of the Hospital of St. John the Baptist.

If you're flying into or out of Dublin Airport and don't want to deal with big-city Dublin, Trim is a perfect alternative—an easy

45-minute, 30-mile drive away. You can rent a car at the airport and make Trim your first overnight base (getting used to driving on the other side of the road in easier country traffic), or spend your last night here before returning your car at the airport. Either way, you don't need or want a car in Dublin (where parking is expensive and sightseeing is best on foot, or by bus or taxi).

Orientation to Trim

(area code: 046)
Trim's main square is a traffic roundabout, and everything's within a block or two. Most of the shops and eateries are on or near Market Street, along with banks and a supermarket.

Tourist Information
The TI is right next to the castle entrance and includes a handy coffee shop. Drop in for a free map and take a moment to ask them about the filming of *Braveheart* (June-Aug Mon-Sat 10:00-17:00, Sun 13:00-17:00, shorter hours Sept-May, Castle Street, tel. 046/943-7227).

Helpful Hints
Internet Access: The **library** offers 30 minutes of free Internet access (Tue and Thu 10:00-20:30, Wed and Fri-10:00-13:00 & 14:00-17:00, closed Sat-Mon, High Street).

Post Office: It's tucked in the back of the **Spar Market** (Mon-Fri 9:00-17:30, Sat 9:00-13:00, closed Sun, Emmett Street).

Laundry: The launderette is located close to Market Street (Mon-Sat 9:00-13:00 & 13:30-17:30, closed Sun, Watergate Street, tel. 046/943-7176).

Parking: To park on the street or in a public lot, use the pay-and-display street-parking system. Buy a ticket at machines spaced along the street, and display it on your dashboard (Mon-Sat 9:00-18:00, €0.80/hour, 2-hour max, free Sun).

Fishing Tours: Marc O'Regan leads backcountry trout and pike fishing trips, making a splash with anglers who want to experience Ireland's bountiful lakes and rivers (tel. 046/943-1635, www.crannmor.com). O'Regan and his wife run the recommended Crannmór B&B.

Sights in Trim

▲▲**Trim Castle**—This is the biggest Norman castle in Ireland. Its mighty keep towers above a very ruined outer wall in a grassy riverside park at the edge of the sleepy town. The current castle was completed in the 1220s and served as a powerful Norman statement to the restless Irish natives. It remains an impressive sight—so impressive it was used in the 1994 filming of *Braveheart* (which was actually about Scotland's—not Ireland's—fight for freedom from the English).

The best-preserved walls ring the castle's southern perimeter and sport a barbican gate that contained two drawbridges. At the base of the castle walls, notice the cleverly angled "batter" wall—used by defenders who hurled down stones that banked off at great velocity into the attacking army.

The massive 70-foot-high central keep has 20 sides. Offering no place for invaders to hide, it was tough to attack. You can go inside only with the included tour. In a mostly hollow shell, you'll climb a series of tightly winding original staircases and modern, high catwalks, learn about life in the castle, and end at the top with great views of the walls and the countryside.

Make time to take a 15-minute walk outside, circling the castle walls and stopping at the informative plaques that show the castle from each viewpoint during its gory glory days. Night strollers are treated to views of the castle hauntingly lit in blue-green hues.

Cost and Hours: €3 for castle grounds, €4 for entrance to keep and required tour; roughly April-Oct daily 10:00-18:00, last entry 17:00; Nov-March Sat-Sun only 10:00-17:00, last entry 16:00, closed Mon-Fri; 45-minute tours run 2/hour but tour spots are limited, so call in peak season to save frustration of arriving to find nothing available; tel. 046/943-8619).

The Power & Glory—This grade-schoolish, 30-minute slideshow overview of the personalities and history of the castle is followed by an exhibit on life here in Norman times (€3, Mon-Sat 9:30-17:30, Sun 12:00-17:00, shorter hours off-season, show runs on demand, in visitors center with TI next to castle, Castle Street, tel. 046/943-7227). The show and a cup of coffee help to pass the time as you wait for your castle tour.

Sleeping in Trim

$$ Highfield House B&B, across the street from the castle and a five-minute walk from town, is a stately 180-year-old former maternity hospital, with hardwood floors and seven spacious, high-ceilinged rooms (Sb-€50-55, Db-€78-84, Tb-€99-110, non-smoking rooms, family-friendly, free Internet access and Wi-Fi; overlooks roundabout where Dublin Road hits Trim, just before

Trim

ATHBOY RD.

↑ To ❸

To Athboy & Kells

KILDALKEY RD.

KELLS RD.

SUPER-MARKET Ⓑ

RING RD.

ST. PATRICK'S CHURCH OF IRELAND

HAGGARD ST.

Ⓑ

To Navan & Brú na Bóinne

R161

SARSFIELD AVE.

ST. LOMAN'S ST.

CHURCH LN.

Ⓟ

NAVAN GATE ST.

LACKANASH RD.

❷

HIGH ST.

❾

❽

YELLOW STEEPLE

SHELL GAS STATION

❿

WATERGATE ST.

ABBEY LN.

ST. MARY'S ABBEY

SHEEP'S GATE

MARKET ST.

BRIDGE ST.

❺

Ⓟ

Ⓑ

River Boyne

200 Meters

200 Yards

POST & SPAR MARKET

Ⓟ

🏰

TRIM CASTLE

Ⓑ

❻

EMMET ST.

FINNEGAN'S WAY

CASTLE ST.

ST. PATRICK'S CATHOLIC CHURCH

NEW DUBLIN RD.

NEW HAGGARD RD.

PATRICK ST.

Ⓟ

❶

WELLINGTON COLUMN

❼

R154

To Sts. Peter & Paul Cathedral, Airport & Dublin

To ❹

To Longwood

RING RD.

R160

R159

To Enfield

NEAR DUBLIN

❶ Highfield House B&B
❷ White Lodge B&B
❸ To Crannmór Guest House & Dunderry Lodge Rest.
❹ To Tigh Catháin B&B
❺ Franzini O'Brien's Rest.

❻ Marigold Chinese Rest.
❼ Castle Arch Hotel Rest.
❽ James Griffin Pub
❾ Library (Internet Access)
❿ Launderette

castle at Maudlins Road; tel. 046/943-6386, fax 046/943-8182, www.highfieldguesthouse.com, highfieldhouseaccom@eircom.net, Geraldine and Edward Duignan).

$ White Lodge B&B, a 10-minute walk northwest of the castle, has six comfortably unpretentious rooms with an oak-and-granite lounge (Sb-€45, Db-€68, Tb-€76, Qb-€84, 10 percent discount for active-duty members of the US and Canadian armed

Sleep Code

(€1 = about $1.25, country code: 353, area code: 046)
S = Single, **D** = Double/Twin, **T** = Triple, **Q** = Quad, **b** = bathroom,
s = shower only. Credit cards are accepted and breakfast is
included unless otherwise noted.

To help you easily sort through these listings, I've divided
the rooms into two categories, based on the price for a
standard double room with bath:

$$ Higher Priced—Most rooms more than €70.
$ Lower Priced—Most rooms €70 or less.

Prices can change without notice; verify the hotel's
current rates online or by email. For other updates, see www
.ricksteves.com/update.

forces with this book, free Internet access and Wi-Fi, parking,
New Road, tel. 046/943-6549, www.whitelodgetrim.com, white
lodgetrim@eircom.net, Todd O'Loughlin). They also offer a
family-friendly, self-catering house next door.

Countryside B&Bs

These two B&Bs are in the quiet countryside about a mile outside
Trim (phone ahead for driving directions).

At **$$ Crannmór Guest House,** north of town, Anne
O'Regan decorates five rooms with cheery color schemes (Sb-€45-
55, Db-€76-80, Tb-€90, Qb-€110, Wi-Fi, Dunderry Road, tel.
046/943-1635, fax 046/943-8087, www.crannmor.com, cranmor
@eircom.net). Her professional-guide husband Marc knows all the
best fishing holes (see "Fishing Tours" on page 117).

Mrs. Keane's **$$ Tigh Catháin B&B,** southwest of town, has
four large, bright, lacy rooms with a comfy, rural feel (Db-€75-80,
Tb-€90-100, cash only, Wi-Fi, on R-160/Longwood Road, tel.
046/943-1996, mobile 086-257-7313, www.tighcathaintrim.com,
mariekeane@esatclear.ie).

Eating in Trim

A country-market town, Trim offers basic meat-and-potatoes
lunch and dinner options. Don't waste time searching for gour-
met food. The restaurants and cafés along Market Street are
friendly, wholesome, and unassuming (soup-and-sandwich delis
close at 17:30).

Franzini O'Brien's is the only place in town with a fun dinner menu and enough business to make it work. They serve pasta, steak, fish, and fajitas in a modern, candlelit ambience. Nothing's Irish except the waiters (€15-26 dishes, Mon-Sat 17:30-21:00, Sun 13:00-21:00, €20 two-course or €25 three-course early-bird dinners before 19:30, French's Lane, tel. 046/943-1002).

If you feel like having Chinese food, **Marigold** fits the bill (Mon-Sat 17:00-23:00, Sun 16:00-23:00, Emmett Street, tel. 046/943-8788).

For a tasty splurge of gourmet cooking out in the country, get driving directions to **Dunderry Lodge,** four miles north of Trim off the Dunderry Road (Mon-Sat 19:30-21:30, Sun 12:30-14:30 & 18:30-20:30, €20 early-bird dinner Mon-Fri 17:30-19:00, tel. 046/943-1671).

The **Castle Arch Hotel,** popular with locals, serves hearty pub grub at reasonable prices in its bistro (€11-14 meals, daily 12:30-21:30, tel. 046/943-1516).

For a fun pub experience, check out Trim's best watering hole, the **James Griffin** (on High Street). It's full of local characters and old-fashioned atmosphere, with live Irish music on Monday and Wednesday nights.

Groceries: **Spar Market** has everything you need to create a picnic (Mon-Fri 7:30-21:00, Sat-Sun 8:00-21:00, Emmett Street).

Trim Connections

Trim has no train station; the nearest is in Drogheda 25 miles away on the coast, but there are no bus connections to Trim from there.

Buses from Trim to **Dublin** (10/day, 1 hour) pick you up at the bus shelter next to the TI and castle entry on Castle Street. For details, see www.buseireann.ie.

South of Dublin: Glendalough and the Wicklow Mountains

The Wicklow Mountains, while only 10 miles south of Dublin, feel remote—enough so to have provided a handy refuge for opponents to English rule. Rebels who took part in the 1798 Irish uprising hid out here for years. When the frustrated British built a military road in 1800 to help flush out the rebels, the area became more accessible. Today, this same road—now R-115—takes you through the Wicklow area to Glendalough at its south end. While the valley is the darling of the Dublin day-trip tour organizers, it doesn't live up to the hype. But two blockbuster sights—Glendalough and the Gardens of Powerscourt—make a visit worth considering.

South of Dublin

To Galway

CASTLETOWN HOUSE   M4   River Liffey

Dublin

Howth • To Liverpool (England)

Dublin Bay   To Holyhead (Wales)

N7   N11

Dun Laoghaire   Dalkey

M50   N31

R114   M117   Killiney

R115

Enniskerry   M11   Bray   Irish Sea

R759   GARDENS OF POWERSCOURT   R117

R760

Sally Gap   GREAT SUGAR LOAF   Greystones

Poulaphouca Reservoir   Lough Tay   R755

Hollywood   R759   R761

R756   Lough Dan   Roundwood   N11

N81   R115

Wicklow Gap   R764

GLENDALOUGH   R758   Annamoe   R763

To Kilkennny   Upper Lake   Laragh   Wicklow

R755   R752

Rathdrum   R750

AVONDALE

R752   N11

R747

Avoca

R747

5 Kilometers
5 Miles

R747   Arklow

To Rosslare

NEAR DUBLIN

Getting Around

By car or tour, it's easy. If you lack wheels, take a tour. It's not worth the trouble on public transport.

By Car: It's a delight. Take N-11 south from Dublin toward Bray, then R-117 to Enniskerry (accommodation listed on page 124), the gateway to the Wicklow Mountains. Signs direct you to the gardens and on to Glendalough. From Glendalough, if you're heading west, you can leave the valley (and pick up the highway to the west) over the famous but dull mountain pass called the Wicklow Gap.

By Tour from Dublin: Wild Wicklow Tours covers the region with an entertaining guide packing every minute with information and *craic* (good fun conversation). With a gang of 40 packed into tight but comfortable mountain-gripping buses, the guide kicks into gear from the first pickup in Dublin. Tours cover Dublin's embassy row, Dun Laoghaire, the Bay of Dublin (with the mansions of Ireland's rich and famous), the windy military road over scenic Sally Gap, and the Glendalough monasteries (€28, €25 for students and readers with this book in 2011, daily year-round, 9:10 pickup at Dublin TI on Suffolk Street, 10:00 pickup at Dun Laoghaire TI, stop for lunch at a pub—cost not included, return through Dun Laoghaire and on to Dublin by 17:30, Dun Laoghaire-ites could stay on the bus to continue into Dublin for the evening, advance booking required, tel. 01/280-1899, www.wildwicklow.ie).

Mary Gibbon's Tours visits both Glendalough and the Gardens of Powerscourt in a six-hour trip (€38, 9:15 pickup at Dublin TI on Suffolk Street, 9:25 pickup at AIB Bank at 37-38 Upper O'Connell Street, 9:45 pickup at Mespil Hotel, home by 17:00, call ahead to reserve—especially in high season, book direct rather than through TI, tel. 086/355-1355, www.newgrangetours .com, info@newgrangetours.com).

Over the Top Tours bypasses mansions and gardens to focus on Wicklow scenery. Stops include Glendalough, the Glenmacnass waterfall, and Blessington lakes (€28, 9:20 pickup at Gresham Hotel on O'Connell Street, 9:45 pickup at TI on Suffolk Street, return by 17:30, 14-seat minibus, reservations required, hold seat by leaving credit-card number, Ireland toll-free tel. 1-800-424-252, Dublin tel. 01/860-0404, www.overthetoptours.com, info @overthetoptours.com).

NEAR DUBLIN

Sights in the Wicklow Area

▲▲Gardens of Powerscourt

A mile above the village of Enniskerry, the Gardens of Powers-
court cover several thousand acres within the 16,000-acre estate. The dreamy driveway alone is a mile long. While the mansion's interior, only partially restored after a 1974 fire, isn't much, its meticulously kept aristo-cratic gardens are Ireland's best. The house was commissioned in the 1730s by Richard Wingfield, first viscount of Powerscourt. The gardens, cre-ated during the Victorian era (1858-1875), are called "the grand finale of Europe's formal gardening tradition...

probably the last garden of its size and quality ever to be created." I'll buy that.

Upon entry, you'll get a flier laying out 40-minute and one-hour walks. The "one-hour" walk takes 30 minutes at a slow amble. With the impressive summit of the Great Sugar Loaf Mountain as a backdrop, and a fine Japanese garden, Italian garden, and goofy pet cemetery along the way, this attraction provides the scenic greenery I hoped to find in the rest of the Wicklow area. The lush movies *Barry Lyndon* and *The Count of Monte Cristo* were filmed in this well-watered aristocratic fantasy.

Cost and Hours: €8, daily 9:30-17:30 year-round, great cafeteria, tel. 01/204-6000, www.powerscourt.ie. Skip the associated waterfall (€5, 4 miles away).

Sleeping in Enniskerry: Drivers coming straight from Dublin Airport can stay overnight in Enniskerry at the nearby **$$ Brook Cottage B&B,** a quiet guesthouse that's popular with hikers. It has a rambling floor plan and sports six rooms, two friendly greyhounds, comfortable beds, and traditional breakfasts in a country setting (Sb-€50-60, Db-€80, Tb-€105, cash only, 10 percent discount for multiple-night stays, Wi-Fi; from Enniskerry clock tower go 3 kilometers up Kilgarron Hill toward Glencree, look for B&B sign on the right, follow arrow sign to end of narrow lane, and pass through green gates; tel. 01/276-6039, mobile 086-824-1687, www.enniskerry.org, brookcottagebb@eircom.net, Mary and Jeff Drexler).

▲Military Road over Sally Gap

This trip is only for those with a car. From the Gardens of Powerscourt and Enniskerry, go to Glencree, where you drive the tiny military road over Sally Gap and through the best scenery of the Wicklow Mountains. Look for the German military cemetery, built for U-boat sailors who washed ashore in World War II. Near Sally Gap, notice the peat bogs and the freshly cut peat bricks drying in the wind. Many locals are nostalgic for the "good old days," when homes were always peat-fire heated. At the Sally Gap junction, turn left, where a road winds through the vast Guinness estate. Look down on the glacial lake (Lough Tay) and the Guinness mansion (famous for jet-set parties). Nicknamed "Guinness Lake," the water looks like Ireland's favorite dark-brown stout, and the sand of the beach actually looks like the head of a Guinness beer. From here, the road meanders scenically down into the village of Roundwood and on to Glendalough.

▲▲Glendalough

The steep wooded slopes of Glendalough (GLEN-da-lock, "Valley of the Two Lakes"), at the south end of Wicklow's military road, hide Ireland's most impressive monastic settlement. Founded by St. Kevin in the sixth century, the monastery flourished (despite repeated Viking raids) throughout the Age of Saints and Scholars until the English destroyed it in 1398. Though it was finally abandoned during the Dissolution of the Monasteries in 1539, pilgrims kept coming, especially on St. Kevin's Day, June 3. (This might have something to do with the fact that a pope said seven visits to Glendalough had the same indulgence value as one visit to Rome.) While much restoration was done in the 1870s, most of the buildings date from the 10th-12th centuries.

The valley sights are split between the two lakes. The lower lake has the visitors center and the best buildings. The upper lake has scant ruins and feels like a state park, with a grassy lakeside picnic area and school groups. Walkers and hikers will enjoy a choice of nine different trails of varying lengths through the lush Wicklow countryside (longest loop takes four hours, hiking-trail maps available at visitors center).

Planning Your Time: Park for free at the Glendalough Visitors Centre. Visit the center, wander the ruins (free) around the round tower, walk the traffic-free Green Road one mile to the upper lake, and then walk back to your car. Or you can drive to the upper lake (more free parking—except July-Aug, when it's €4). If you're rushed, skip the upper lake. Summer tour-bus crowds are terrible all day on weekends and 11:00-14:00 on weekdays.

Glendalough Visitor Centre: Start your visit here (€3, daily mid-March-mid-Oct 9:30-18:00, mid-Oct-mid-March 9:30-17:00, last entry 45 minutes before closing, tel. 0404/45352). The 20-minute video provides a good thumbnail background on monastic society in medieval Ireland. While the video is more general than specific to Glendalough, the adjacent museum room features this particular monastic settlement. The model in the center of the room re-creates the fortified village of the year 1050. A browse through the interactive exhibits here shows the contribution these monks made to intellectual life in Dark Age Europe (such as illuminated manuscripts and Irish minuscule, a more compact alphabet developed in the seventh century).

From the center, a short and scenic walk along the Green Road takes you to the round tower.

The Monastic Village: Easily the best ruins of Glendalough gather around the famous 110-foot-tall round tower. Towers like this (usually 60-110 feet tall) were standard features in such settlements, functioning as bell towers, storage lofts, beacons for pilgrims, and last-resort refuges during Viking raids (though given enough warning, monks were safer hiding in the surrounding forest). The towers had a high door with a pull-up ladder—both for safety and because a door at ground level would have weakened the tower's foundation. Several ruined churches (10th-12th centuries) and a sea of grave markers complete this evocative scene. Markers give short descriptions of the ruined buildings.

In an Ireland without cities, these monastic communities were mainstays of civilization. They were remote outposts where ascetics (with a taste for scenic settings) gathered to commune with God. In the 12th century, with the arrival of grander monastic orders such as the Franciscans and the Dominicans and with the growth of cities, these monastic communities were eclipsed. Today, Ireland is dotted with the reminders of this age: illuminated manuscripts, simple churches, carved crosses, and about 100 round towers.

Upper Lake: The Green Road continues one mile farther up the valley to the Upper Lake. The oldest ruins—scant and hard to find—lie near this lake. If you want a scenic Wicklow walk, begin here.

▲Avondale House

Located in south County Wicklow (known as the Garden County), this mansion is the birthplace and lifelong home of Charles Stewart Parnell, the Nationalist politician and dynamo often called the "uncrowned King of Ireland" (see page 75).

Upon entering the opulent Georgian "big house" (built in 1777), you'll first view an informative 20-minute video on Parnell's life. Then you're set free to roam with a handout outlining each room's highlights. A fine portrait of Parnell graces the grand high-ceilinged entry hall, and a painting of his American grandfather, who manned the USS *Constitution* in the War of 1812, hangs in one room. The dining room is all class, with fine plasterwork and hardwood floors. Original furniture such as Parnell's sturdy canopied bed graces the remaining rooms, and many come with cozy fireplaces and views. The lush surrounding estate of over 500 acres, laced with pleasant walking trails, was used by the Irish Forestry Service (Coillte) to try out forestry methods.

Cost and Hours: €6.50; June Tue-Sun 12:00-16:00, closed Mon; July-Aug daily 11:30-16:30; Sept-Oct Sat-Sun 12:00-16:00, closed Mon-Fri; shorter hours off-season; café, tel. 0404/46111, www.coillteoutdoors.ie.

Getting There: A visit is best done by car, as it's too far for the Dublin day-tour buses (45 miles south of Dublin). Trains depart Dublin's Connolly station (4/day, 1.5 hours) to Rathdrum; Avondale is a short taxi ride away (1.5 miles south of town).

West of Dublin: The Irish National Stud

Ireland's famed County Kildare has long been known to offer the perfect conditions for breeding horses. Its reputation dates all the way back to the 1300s, when Norman war horses were bred here. Kildare's grasslands lie on a bedrock table of limestone, infusing the soil with just the right mix of nutrients for grazing horses. And the nearby River Tully sparkles with high levels of calcium carbonate, essential for building strong bones in the expensive thoroughbreds (some owned by Arab sheiks) raised and raced here.

In 1900, Colonel William Hall-Walker (Scottish heir to the Johnny Walker distilling fortune) bought a farm on the River Tully and began breeding a line of champion thoroughbreds. His amazing successes and bizarre methods were the talk of the sport. In 1916, the colonel donated his land and horse farm to the British government, which continued breeding horses here. The farm was eventually handed over to the Irish government, which in 1945 created the Irish National Stud Company to promote the thoroughbred industry.

Today, a tour of the grounds at the Irish National Stud gives you a fuller appreciation for the amazing horses that call this place home. Animal-lovers and horse-racing fans driving between Dublin and Galway will enjoy a couple of hours here, combining the tour with lunch (inside the decent cafeteria or at a picnic table by the parking lot) and a stroll through the gardens.

Cost and Hours: €11 includes guided tour of the Irish National Stud, plus entry to Japanese Gardens, St. Fiachra's Garden, and Horse Museum; open daily early Feb-mid-Dec 9:30 17:00, closed mid-Dec-early Feb, last entry one hour before closing, 30-minute tours run 3/day at 12:00, 14:30, and 16:00. Tel. 045/522-963, www.irish-national-stud.ie.

Getting to the Irish National Stud: From M-7, **drivers** take exit #13 and follow the signs five minutes south (don't take exit #12 for the Curragh Racecourse). **Trains** departing Dublin's Heuston station stop at Kildare town (1-3/hour, 45 minutes, www.irishrail.ie). A shuttle bus runs from Kildare's train station to the National Stud (2/hour), or you can take a taxi (about €12-15). One **bus** departs Dublin's Busaras station Monday through Saturday at 9:30, and returns from the National Stud at 15:45. On Sunday, two buses run, departing Busaras at 10:00 and 12:00, with returns at 15:00 and 17:30. Confirm this schedule at the bus station in Dublin.

Tour: The guided tour begins in the **Sun Chariot Yard** (named for the winner of the 1942 Fillies Triple Crown), surrounded by stables housing pregnant mares. A 15-minute film of a live birth runs continuously in a stall in the corner of the yard.

When Irish Horses Are Running

Every Irish town seems to have a betting shop for passionate locals who love to closely follow (and wager on) their favorite horses. A quick glance at the weekend sports sections of any Irish newspaper gives you an idea of this sport's high profile. Towns from Galway to Dingle host annual horse races that draw rabid fans from all over.

The five most prestigious Irish races take place at the **Curragh Racecourse,** just south of Kildare town (March-Oct, 1 hour west of Dublin, 10 minutes from the National Stud, www.curragh.ie). Horses have been raced here since 1741. The broad, open fields nearby are where the battle scenes in *Braveheart* were filmed (the neighboring Irish army base provided the blue-face-painted extras).

The adjacent **Foaling Unit** is where births take place. The gestation period for horses is 11 months, with 90 percent of foals born at night. (In the wild, a mare and her foal born during the day would have been vulnerable to predators as the herd moved on. Instead, horses have adapted so that foals are born at night—and are able to keep up with the herd within a few hours.) Eccentric Colonel Walker noted the position of the moon and stars at the time of each foal's birth, and sold those born under inauspicious astrological signs (regardless of their parents' stellar racing records).

From here, you'll pass a working saddle-making shop and a forge where horseshoes are still hammered out on an anvil.

At the **Stallion Boxes,** you'll learn how stargazing Colonel Walker installed skylights in the stables—allowing the heavens maximum influence over the destiny of his prized animals. A brass plaque on the door of each stall proudly states the horse's name and its racing credentials. One stall bears the simple word, "Teaser." The unlucky occupant's job is to identify mares in heat...but rarely is the frustrated stallion given the opportunity to breed.

After the tour, meander down the pleasant tree-lined **Tully Walk,** with paddocks on each side. You'll see mares and foals running free, with the occasional cow thrown in for good measure (cattle have a calming effect on rowdy horses). To ensure you come home with all your fingers, take full note of the *Horses Bite and Kick* signs. These superstar animals are bred for high spirits—and are way too feisty to pet.

Other Sights: Visitors with extra time can explore three more attractions (all included in your entry ticket). The tranquil and photogenic **Japanese Gardens** were created by the colonel to depict the trials of life (beware the "Tunnel of Ignorance"). A wander through the more extensive and natural **St. Fiachra's Garden** (the patron saint of gardening) demands more time. Equestrian buffs may want to linger among the memorabilia in the small **Horse Museum,** where you can get a grip on how many hands it takes to measure a horse.

KILKENNY
and the ROCK OF CASHEL

If you're driving from Dublin (on Ireland's east coast) to Dingle (on Ireland's west coast), the best two stops to break the long journey are Kilkenny, often called Ireland's finest medieval town, and the Rock of Cashel, a thought-provoking early Christian site crowning the Plain of Tipperary. With a few extra days, there are additional worthwhile destinations along the southeast coast, such as Waterford and County Wexford (described in the next chapter). Folks with more time can continue on the scenic southern coastal route west via Cobh, Kinsale, Kenmare, and the Ring of Kerry (covered in the Kinsale/Cobh and Kenmare/Ring of Kerry chapters).

Kilkenny

Famous as "Ireland's loveliest inland city," Kilkenny gives you a feel for salt-of-the-earth Ireland. Its castle and cathedral stand like historic bookends on either end of a higgledy-piggledy High Street of colorful shops and medieval facades. It's nicknamed the "Marble City" for its nearby quarry (actually black limestone, not marble), and you can see the white seashells fossilized within the black stone steps around town. While a small town today (fewer than 10,000 residents), Kilkenny has a big history. It used to be an important center—occasionally even the capital of Ireland in the Middle Ages.

Kilkenny is a good overnight for drivers wanting to break the

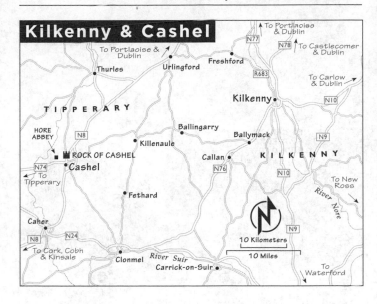

journey from Dublin to Dingle (necessary if you want to spend more time in the Wicklow area and at the Rock of Cashel). A night in Kilkenny comes with plenty of traditional folk music in the pubs (hike over the river and up John Street).

Orientation to Kilkenny

(area code: 056)

Tourist Information

The TI is a block off the bridge in the 16th-century Shee Alms poorhouse (Mon-Fri 9:30-17:30, Sat 10:00-18:00, Sun 11:00-17:00—except closed Sun in Sept-May, Rose Inn Street, tel. 056/775-1500).

Arrival in Kilkenny

The train/bus station is four blocks from John's Bridge, which marks the center of town.

If arriving by car, the **Market Yard Car Park** behind Kyteler's Inn is handy for a few hours (€1.20/hour, daily 8:00-18:00, entry off Bateman's Quay). The multistory parking garage on Ormonde Street is the best long-term bet (€1.50/hour, or get the 5-day pass for €16 if staying overnight—it allows you to come and go). Otherwise, you can use the pay-and-display meters on the street (€1.50/hour, enforced Mon-Sat 8:00-19:00).

1 Zuni Townhouse & Rest.
2 Club House Hotel
3 Butler Court
4 Berkeley House
5 Pinecrest B&B
6 Kilkenny Tourist Hostel
7 Langton's Restaurant
8 Ristorante Rinuccini
9 Pennefeather Restaurant
10 Kyteler's Inn
11 Laundry

Helpful Hints

Post Office: It's on High Street (Mon-Fri 9:00-17:30, Sat 9:00-13:00, closed Sun).

Laundry: Hennessy's is at 18 Parliament Street (Mon-Sat 9:00-17:30, closed Sun).

Walking Tour: Local guide **Pat Tynan** offers hour-long town walks that depart from the TI (€6; mid-March-Oct Mon-

Sat at 10:30, 12:15, and 15:00, Sun at 11:15 and 12:30; Nov–mid-March Sat only at 10:30, 12:15, and 15:00; mobile 087-265-1745).

Sights in Kilkenny

▲**Kilkenny Castle**—Dominating the town, this castle is a stony reminder that the Anglo-Norman Butler family controlled

Kilkenny for 500 years. The castle once had four sides, but Oliver Cromwell's army knocked down one wall when it took the castle, leaving it as the roughly "U" shape we see today.

Enter the castle gate, turn right in the courtyard, and head into the base of the turret. Here you'll find the continuously running 12-minute video explaining how the wooden fort built here by Strongbow in 1172 evolved into a 17th-century château. Then go into the main castle entrance across the courtyard from the turret to buy your entry ticket. You'll be free to walk through the castle. A pamphlet explains the exhibits, and you can also talk to stewards in important rooms.

Now restored to its Victorian splendor, the castle's highlight is the beautiful family-portrait gallery, which puts you face-to-face with the wealthy Butler family ghosts (€6, daily June–Aug 9:00-17:30, April–May and Sept 9:30-17:30, Oct–March 9:30-16:30, tel. 056/770-4100).

The **Kilkenny Design Centre,** across the street from the castle in grand old stables, is full of local crafts and offers handy cafeteria lunches upstairs (April–Dec Mon-Sat 10:00-17:30, Sun 11:00-17:30; Jan–March Mon-Sat 10:00-17:30, closed Sun; tel. 056/772-2118, www.kilkennydesign.com).

St. Canice's Cathedral—This 13th-century cathedral is early-English Gothic, rich with stained glass, medieval carvings, and floors paved in history. Check out the model of the old walled town in its 1641 heyday (€4, €6 combo-ticket with tower; June–Aug Mon-Sat 9:00-18:00, Sun 14:00-18:00; April–May and Sept Mon-Sat 10:00-13:00 & 14:00-17:00, Sun 14:00-17:00; Oct–March Mon-Sat 10:00-13:00 & 14:00-16:00, Sun 14:00-16:00; tel. 056/776-4971, www.cashel.anglican.org). The 100-foot-tall **round tower,** built as part of a long-gone pre-Norman church, recalls the need for a watchtower and refuge. The fun ladder-climb to the top affords a grand view of the countryside (€3, €6 combo-ticket with cathedral).

Rothe House—This well-preserved Tudor merchant's house expanded around interior courtyards as the prosperous family grew. The museum, which also serves as the County Kilkenny genealogy center, gives a glimpse of life here in Elizabethan times. The recently regenerated gardens at the far back were a real luxury in their time (€5; April-Oct Mon-Sat 10:30-17:00, Sun 15:00-17:00; Nov-March Mon-Sat 10:30-16:30, closed Sun; Parliament Street, tel. 056/772-2893, www.rothehouse.com).

Nightlife in Kilkenny

Kilkenny Trad Trail—Join a small group on a merry and musical pub crawl, led by two musicians eager to share their enthusiasm and knowledge of traditional music between their songs and stories (€12, June-Sept Fri-Sat at 19:00, July-Aug also Thu at 19:00, beverages extra, buy tickets after 18:30 at Bollard's Bar on St. Kieran's Street near intersection with Parliament Street, mobile 085-165-8243, www.kilkennytradtrail.net).

Theater—The Watergate Theatre houses live plays and other performances in its 300-seat space (€12-30, Parliament Street, tel. 056/776-1674, www.watergatetheatre.com).

Sleeping in Kilkenny

(area code: 056)

The first four listings are more central, clustered within a block of each other along Lower Patrick Street. The last two are at the north end of town, but still just a short walk from the action.

$$$ Zuni Townhouse, above a fashionable restaurant, has 13 boutique-chic rooms sporting colorfully angular furnishings. Ask about two-night weekend breaks and midweek specials that include a four-course dinner (Sb-€60-90, Db-€85-130, Tb-€120-200, parking in back, 26 Lower Patrick Street, tel. 056/772-3999, fax 056/775-6400, www.zuni.ie, info@zuni.ie).

$$$ Club House Hotel, originally a gentlemen's sporting club, comes with old-time Georgian elegance; a palatial, well-antlered breakfast room; and 35 large, comfy bedrooms (Sb-€50-70, Db-€100-130, 10 percent discount with this book in 2011, Lower Patrick Street, tel. 056/772-1994, fax 056/777-1920, www.clubhousehotel.com, info@clubhousehotel.com).

$$ Butler Court, across the street and uphill from the Club House Hotel, is Kilkenny's best lodging value. Ever-helpful Yvonne and John offer 10 modern rooms behind cheery yellow walls that ensure a quiet night (Sb-€60-110, Db-€90-130, Tb-€100-160, wheelchair-accessible, continental breakfast in room, Wi-Fi, 14 Lower Patrick Street, tel. 056/776-1178, fax 056/779-0767,

---

Sleep Code

(€1 = about $1.25, country code: 353)
S = Single, **D** = Double/Twin, **T** = Triple, **Q** = Quad, **b** = bathroom, **s** = shower only. All of these places include breakfast and accept credit cards.

To help you easily sort through these listings, I've divided the rooms into three categories, based on the price for a standard double room with bath:

$$$ Higher Priced—Most rooms €110 or more.
 $$ Moderately Priced—Most rooms between €80-110.
  $ Lower Priced—Most rooms €80 or less.

Prices can change without notice; verify the hotel's current rates online or by email. For other updates, see www .ricksteves.com/update.

---

www.butlercourt.com, info@butlercourt.com).

$$ Berkeley House, with 10 rooms across the street and downhill from the Club House Hotel, is small, affordable, and comfortable (Db-€80-120, Tb-€120-150, 5 Lower Patrick Street, tel. 056/776-4848, fax 056/776-4829, www.berkeleyhousekilkenny .com, info@berkeleyhousekilkenny.com).

$$ Pinecrest B&B has four nice rooms in a modern house on a quiet homey street, just a 10-minute walk from the center of town (Sb-€50-60, Db-€70-90, Tb-€105-120, cash only, parking, Bishop Meadows, just off the Freshford Road about 100 yards north of the roundabout to the New Bridge, tel. 056/776-3567, mobile 087-934-4579, pinecrestbnb@eircom.net, friendly Helen Heffernan).

$ Kilkenny Tourist Hostel, filling a fine Georgian townhouse in the town center, offers 65 cheap beds, a friendly family room, a well-equipped members' kitchen, and a wealth of local information (dorm bed-€16-17, D-€40-42, T-€60, Q-€76, cash only, Wi-Fi, laundry service-€5, 2 blocks from cathedral at 35 Parliament Street, tel. 056/776-3541, www.kilkennyhostel.ie, info @kilkennyhostel.ie).

Eating in Kilkenny

Langton's is every local's first choice, serving quality Irish dishes under a Tiffany-skylight expanse (€12-15 lunches, €16-25 dinners, daily 8:00-22:30, 69 John Street, tel. 056/776-5133).

Ristorante Rinuccini provides your classy, candlelit Italian fix (€11-16 lunches, €19-28 dinners, daily 12:00-15:00 & 17:30-22:00, €28 three-course early-bird special before 19:00, 1 The

KILKENNY & CASHEL

Parade, tel. 056/776-1575).

Zuni is a stylish splurge, offering international cuisine (daily 12:30-14:30 & 18:00-21:00, €23.50 two-course and €28.50 three-course early-bird specials before 19:30 every night but Sat, weekend reservations smart, 26 Patrick Street, tel. 056/772-3999).

Pennefeather Restaurant, above the Kilkenny Book Centre, is good for a quick, cheap, light lunch (Mon-Fri 9:00-17:30, Sat 9:00-17:00, closed Sun, 10 High Street, tel. 056/776-4063).

Kyteler's Inn serves basic pub grub in a timber-and-stone atmosphere with a heated and covered beer garden out back. Visit their fun 14th-century cellar and ask about their witch. Watch your head or risk leaving some of your DNA embedded in the low stone arches (Mon-Sat 12:00-21:00, Sun 12:00-20:00, 27 St. Kieran's Street, tel. 056/772-1064). Try a pint of Smithwick's (my favorite ale) in its hometown.

Kilkenny Connections

From Kilkenny by Train to: Dublin (5/day, 2 hours), **Waterford** (6/day, 45 minutes). For details, see www.irishrail.ie.

By Bus to: Dublin (7/day, 2.5 hours), **Waterford** (2/day, 1 hour), **Tralee** (3/day, 5.5 hours, change in Cork), **Galway** (3/day, 5 hours). For details, see www.buseireann.ie.

Rock of Cashel

Rising high above the fertile Plain of Tipperary, the Rock of Cashel—worth ▲▲▲—is one of Ireland's most historic and evocative sights. Seat of the ancient kings of Munster (c. A.D. 300-1100), this is where St. Patrick baptized King Aengus in about A.D. 450.

 Strategically located and perfect for fortification, the Rock was fought over by local clans for hundreds of years. Finally, in 1101, clever Murtagh O'Brien gave the Rock to the Church. His seemingly benevolent donation increased his influence with the Church, while preventing his rivals, the powerful McCarthy clan, from regaining possession of the Rock. As Cashel evolved into an ecclesiastical center, Iron Age ring forts and thatch dwellings gave way to the majestic stone church buildings enjoyed by visitors today.

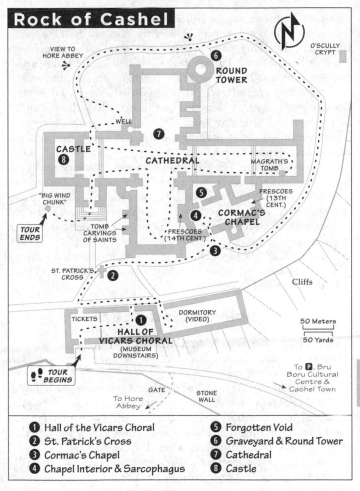

Rock of Cashel

VIEW TO HORE ABBEY

O'SCULLY CRYPT

6 ROUND TOWER

WELL

7

CASTLE

8

CATHEDRAL

MAGRATH'S TOMB

"BIG WIND CHUNK"

FRESCOES (13TH CENT.)

5

TOUR ENDS

TOMB CARVINGS OF SAINTS

4

CORMAC'S CHAPEL

FRESCOES (14TH CENT.)

3

ST. PATRICK'S CROSS

2

Cliffs

TICKETS

DORMITORY (VIDEO)

1

HALL OF VICARS CHORAL (MUSEUM DOWNSTAIRS)

50 Meters

50 Yards

TOUR BEGINS

To **P**, Bru Boru Cultural Centre & Cashel Town

GATE

STONE WALL

To Hore Abbey

1 Hall of the Vicars Choral
2 St. Patrick's Cross
3 Cormac's Chapel
4 Chapel Interior & Sarcophagus
5 Forgotten Void
6 Graveyard & Round Tower
7 Cathedral
8 Castle

KILKENNY & CASHEL

Cost and Hours: €6, families-€14, daily early June-mid-Sept 9:00-19:00, mid-March-early June and mid-Sept-mid-Oct until 17:30, mid-Oct-mid-March until 16:30, last entry 45 minutes before closing. Parking will cost you €4 (buy parking ticket at machine inside lot, display on dashboard).

Renovations: Extensive and essential restoration will keep sections of the ruins under scaffolding for the next few years (especially Cormac's Chapel).

Orientation: At the base of the Rock and next to the parking lot, you'll see WCs (none up on Rock) and the Bru Boru Cultural Centre (see page 143); you may want to visit the center to learn more about the Rock before you ascend.

It's a steep 100-yard walk up to the Rock itself. On this

200-foot-high outcrop of limestone, the first building you'll encounter is the 15th-century Hall of the Vicars Choral, housing the ticket desk, a tiny museum (with an original 12th-century high cross dedicated to St. Patrick and a few replica artifacts), and a 20-minute video (2/hour, shown in the hall's former dormitory). You'll also find a round tower, an early Christian cross, a delightful Romanesque chapel, and a ruined Gothic cathedral, all surrounded by my favorite Celtic-cross graveyard. Bring a coat—deceptively warm conditions at the parking lot may not reflect those on the high, windy, exposed Rock.

Crowd-Beating Tips: Summer crowds flock to the Rock (worst June-Aug 11:00-15:00). Try to plan your visit for early or late in the day. If you're here at a peak time, tour the Rock first and save the movie, museum, and Hall of the Vicars Choral for the end of your visit, when the tourist tide has receded. Otherwise, see the movie and museum first.

Tours: Call ahead for the tour schedule (included in entry price, 45 minutes, tel. 062/61437). Otherwise, set your own pace with the tour that I've outlined next.

Self-Guided Tour

Exploring the Rock of Cashel

• *Follow this tour counterclockwise around the Rock. To start the tour, climb the stairs opposite the ticket desk.*

❶ Hall of the Vicars Choral: This is the youngest building on the Rock (early 1400s). It housed the minor clerics appointed to sing during cathedral services. These vicars—who were granted nearby lands by the archbishop—lived comfortably here, with a large fireplace and white, lime-washed walls (to reflect light and act as a natural disinfectant). Window seats gave the blessedly literate vicars the best light to read by. The furniture is original, but the oak timber roof is a reconstruction, built to medieval specifications using wooden dowels instead of nails. The large wall tapestry, showing King Solomon with the Queen of Sheba, contains intentional errors—to remind viewers that only God can create perfection. The vicars, who formed a sort of corporate body to assist the bishop with local administration, used a special seal to authorize documents such as land leases. You can see an enlarged wooden copy of the seal (hanging above the fireplace), depicting eight vicars surrounding a seated organist. It was a good system—until some of the greedier vicars duplicated the seal for their own purposes, forcing the archbishop to curtail its use.

• *Go outside the hall and find...*

❷ St. Patrick's Cross: St. Patrick baptized King Aengus at the Rock of Cashel in about A.D. 450. Legend has it that St.

Patrick, intensely preoccupied with the holy ceremony, accidentally speared the foot of the king with his crosier staff while administering the baptismal sacrament. But the pagan king stoically held his tongue until the end of the ceremony, thinking this was part of the painful process of becoming a Christian.

This 12th-century cross, a stub of its former glory, was carved to celebrate the handing over of the Rock to the Church 650 years after St. Patrick's visit. Typical Irish high crosses use a ring around the cross' head to support its arms and to symbolize the sun (making Christianity more appealing to the sun-worshipping Celts). But instead, this cross uses the Latin design: The weight of the arms is supported by two vertical beams on each side of the main shaft, representing the two criminals who were crucified beside Christ (today only one of these supports remains).

On my first visit, 30 years ago, the original cross still stood here. But centuries of wind and rain were slowly eroding away important detail, so the cross moved into the adjacent museum and replaced by this replica.

• *Turn your back on St. Patrick's Cross, and walk about 100 feet slightly uphill along the gravel path beside the cathedral. Roughly opposite the far end of the Hall of the Vicars Choral is the entry to...*

❸ **Cormac's Chapel:** As the wild Celtic Christian church was reined in and reorganized by Rome 850 years ago, new archi-

tectural influences from continental Europe began to emerge on the remote Irish landscape. This small chapel—Ireland's first and finest Romanesque church, consecrated in 1134 by King Cormac MacCarthy—reflects this evolution. Travel in your imagination back to the 12th century, when this chapel and the tall round tower were the only stone structures on the Rock.

The "new" Romanesque style reflected the ancient Roman basilica floor plan. Its columns and rounded arches created an overall effect of massiveness and strength. Romanesque churches were like dark fortresses with thick walls, squat towers, few windows, and minimal decoration. Irish stone churches of this period (like the one at Glendalough in the Wicklow Mountains) were simple rectangular buildings with no ornate stone carving at all.

Tradition says that the chapel's easy-to-cut sandstone was quarried 12 miles away, and the blocks were passed from hand to hand back to the Rock. The two square towers resemble those in Regensburg, Germany, further suggesting that well-traveled medieval Irish monks brought back new ideas from the Continent.

• *The modern, dark-glass chapel door (always unlocked) is a recent addition to keep out nesting birds. Enter the chapel (remembering to close the door behind you) and let your eyes adjust to the low light.*

❹ **Chapel Interior:** Just inside the chapel is an empty stone **sarcophagus.** Nobody knows for sure whose body once lay here (possibly the brother of King Cormac MacCarthy). The damaged front relief is carved in the Scandinavian Urnes style. Vikings raided Ireland, intermarried with the Irish, and were melting into Irish society by the time this chapel was built. Some scholars interpret the relief design (a tangle of snakes and beasts) as a figure-eight lying on its side, looping back and forth forever, symbolizing the eternity of the afterlife.

With your back to the sarcophagus, let your eyes wander around the chapel interior. You're standing in the **nave,** lit by the three windows (partially blocked by the later cathedral) in the wall behind you. Overhead is a round vaulted ceiling with support ribs. The strong round arches support not only the heavy stone roof, but also the (unseen) second-story scriptorium chamber, where monks once carefully copied manuscripts.

The **chancel arch,** studded with fist-size heads, framed the altar (now gone). The lower heads are more grotesque, while those nearing the top become serene as they climb closer to God. The arch is off-center in relation to the nave, symbolic of Christ's head drooping to the side as he died on the cross.

Walk into the chancel and look up at the ceiling, examining the faint **frescoes,** a labor of love from 850 years ago. Frescoes are rare in Ireland because of the perpetually moist climate. (Mixing pigments into wet plaster worked better in dry climates like Italy's.) Once vividly colorful, then fading over time, these frescoes were further damaged during the Reformation. Such ornamentation was considered vain by Protestants, who piously whitewashed over them. These surviving frescoes were discovered under multiple whitewash layers during painstaking modern restoration. The rich blue color came from lapis lazuli, an expensive gemstone imported from Asia.

• *Walk through the other modern, dark-glass doorway (don't let the birds in), opposite the door you used to enter the chapel. You'll find yourself in a...*

❺ **Forgotten Void:** This enclosed space (roughly 30 feet square) was created when the newer cathedral was wedged between the older chapel and the round tower. Once the main entrance into the chapel, this forgotten doorway is crowned by a finely carved tympanum decorating the arch above it. It's perfectly preserved because the huge cathedral shielded it from the elements. The large lion (symbol of St. Mark's gospel) is being hunted by a centaur (half-man, half-horse) archer wearing a Norman helmet (essential

KILKENNY & CASHEL

conehead attire in the late Middle Ages).

As you exit the chapel (turning left), take a look at the more exposed and weathered tympanum outside, above the south entrance. The carved bloated "hippo" is actually an ox, representing Gospel author St. Luke.

• *Tiptoe through the tombstones around the east end of the cathedral to the base of the round tower.*

❻ Graveyard and Round Tower: This graveyard still takes permanent guests—but only those put on a waiting list by their ancestors in 1930. A handful of these chosen few are still alive, and once they're gone, the graveyard will be considered full. The 20-foot-tall shaft at the edge of the graveyard, marking the O'Scully family crypt, was once crowned by an elaborately carved Irish high cross—destroyed during a lightning storm in 1976.

Look out over the **Plain of Tipperary.** Called the "Golden Vale," its rich soil makes it Ireland's most prosperous farmland. In St. Patrick's time, it was covered with oak forests. A path leads to the ruined 13th-century **Hore Abbey** in the fields below (free, always open and peaceful). The abbey is named for the Cistercian monks who wore simple gray robes, roughly the same color as hoarfrost (the ice crystals that form on morning grass).

Gaze up at the **round tower,** the first stone structure built on the Rock after the Church took over in 1101. The shape of these towers is unique to Ireland. Though you might think towers like this were chiefly intended as a place to hide in case of invasion, they were instead used primarily as bell towers and lookout posts. (Enemies could smoke out anyone inside the tower, and with enough warning, monks were better off concealing themselves in the countryside.) The tower stands 92 feet tall, with walls over 3 feet thick. The doorway, which once had a rope ladder, was built high up not only for security, but also because having it at ground level would have weakened the foundation of the top-heavy structure. The interior once contained wooden floors connected by ladders, and served as safe storage for the monks' precious sacramental treasures. The tower's stability is impressive when you consider its age, the winds it has endured, and the shallowness of its foundation (only five feet under present ground level).

Continue walking around the cathedral's north transept, noticing the square holes in the exterior walls. During construction, wooden scaffolding was anchored into these holes. On your way to the cathedral entrance, in the corner where the north transept joins the nave, you'll pass a small **well**. Without this essential water source, the Rock could never have withstood a siege and would not have been as valuable to clans and clergy. In 1848, a chalice was dredged from the well, likely thrown there by fleeing medieval monks intending to survive a raid. They didn't make it. (If they had, they would have retrieved the chalice.)

• *Now enter the...*

❼ **Cathedral:** Traditionally, the choir of a church (where the clergy celebrate Mass) faces east, while the nave (where the congregation stands) stretches off to the west. Because this cathedral was squeezed between the preexisting chapel, round tower, and drinking well, the builders were forced to improvise—giving it an extra-long choir and a cramped nave.

Built between 1230 and 1290, the church's pointed arches and high, narrow windows proclaim the Gothic style of the period (and let in more light than earlier Romanesque churches). Walk under the central bell tower and look up at the rib-vaulted **ceiling**. The hole in the middle was for a rope used to ring the church bells. The wooden roof is long gone. When Lord Inchiquin (Oliver Cromwell's general) attacked the town of Cashel in 1647, hundreds of townsfolk fled to the sanctuary of this cathedral. Inchiquin packed turf around the exterior and burned the cathedral down, massacring those inside.

Ascend the terraces at the choir end of the cathedral, where the main altar once stood. Stand on the gravestones (of the 16th-century rich and famous) with your back to the open east wall (where the narrow windows have crumbled away) and look back down toward the nave. The right wall of the choir is filled with graceful Gothic windows, while the solid left wall hides Cormac's Chapel (which would have blocked any sunlight). The line of stone supports on the left wall once held the long, wooden balcony where the vicars sang. Closer to the altar, high on the same wall, is a small, rectangular window called the "leper's squint"—which

allowed unsightly lepers to view the altar during Mass without offending the congregation.

The grand **wall tomb** on the left contains the remains of archbishop Miler Magrath, the "scoundrel of Cashel," who lived to be 100. From 1570 to 1622, Magrath was the Protestant archbishop of Cashel who simultaneously profited from his previous position as Catholic bishop of Down. He married twice, had lots of kids, confiscated the ornate tomb lid here from another bishop's grave, and converted back to Catholicism on his deathbed.

• *Walk back down the nave and turn left into the south transept.*

Take a peek into the modern-roofed wooden structure against the wall on your left. It's protecting 15th-century **frescoes** of the crucifixion of Christ that were rediscovered during renovations in 2005. They're as patchy and hard to make out (and just as rare for Ireland) as the century-older frescoes in the ceiling of Cormac's Chapel. On the opposite side of this transept, in alcoves built into the wall, wonderful **carvings** of early Christian saints line the outside walls of tombs (look down at shin level).

• *Return to the nave and continue down to the far end. Exit the cathedral on the left, through the porch entrance.*

❽ **Castle:** Back outside, stand beside the huge chunk of wall debris and try to picture where it might have fit in the ruins above. This end of the cathedral was converted into an archbishop's castle in the 1400s (shortening the nave even more). Looking high into the castle's damaged top floors, you can see the bishop's residence chamber and the secret passageways that were once hidden in the thick walls. Lord Inchiquin's cannons weakened the structure during the 1647 massacre, and in 1848, a massive storm (known as "Night of the Big Wind" in Irish lore) flung the huge chunk next to you from the ruins above.

In the mid-1700s, the Anglican Church transferred cathedral status to St. John's in town, and the archbishop abandoned the drafty Rock for a more comfortable residence, leaving the ruins that you see today.

Sights near the Rock of Cashel

Bru Boru Cultural Centre—Nestled below the Rock of Cashel parking lot, next to the statue of the three blissed-out dancers, this center adds to your understanding of the Rock in its wider historical and cultural context. The highlight of the **Sounds of History Museum** downstairs is the exhibit showing the Rock's gradual evolution from ancient ring fort to grand church ruins—projected down onto a large disc that visitors gather around.

Those headed for Dingle's great traditional music scene will enjoy the surprisingly good 15-minute film introduction to Irish traditional music in the small museum theater (€5; June-Aug Mon-Sat 9:00-20:00, closed Sun; Sept-May Mon-Fri 9:00-17:00, closed Sat-Sun; cafeteria, tel. 062/61122).

KILKENNY & CASHEL

If you stay overnight in Cashel, consider taking in a performance of the Bru Boru musical dance troupe in the center's large theater (€20, €50 with dinner, mid-June-mid-Aug Tue-Sat at 21:00).

Town of Cashel—The huggable town at the base of the Rock affords a good break on the long drive from Dublin to Dingle (**TI** open mid-March-Oct daily 9:30-17:30, Nov-mid-March closed Sat-Sun, tel. 062/62511). The Heritage Centre, next door to the TI, presents a modest six-minute audio explanation of Cashel's history around a walled town model.

Sleeping in Cashel

(€1 = about $1.25, country code: 353, area code: 062)
If you spend the night in Cashel, you'll be treated to beautifully illuminated views of the ruins. The following listings are cozy, old-fashioned, and a five-minute walk from the Rock.

$$ Joy's Rockside House B&B is closest to the Rock, resting on its lower slopes. With four large, fresh rooms (all with views of the Rock), it's the best lodging value in town (Db-€80-100, Tb-€120-150, Qb-€160-200, cash only, Rock Villas Street, parking, tel. 062/63813, www.joyrockside.com, joyrocksidehouse @eircom.net, Joan and Rem Joy).

$ Rockville House, a traditional place with six fine rooms, is 100 yards from the Rock (Sb-€39, Db-€58-60, Tb-€80-85, Qb-€90, cash only, 10 Dominic Street, tel. 062/61760, Patrick Hayes).

$ Wattie's B&B has three rooms that feel lived-in and comfy (Db-€60-74, Tb-€90-110, cash only, Internet access, one wheel-chair-accessible room, parking, 14 Dominic Street, tel. 062/61923, www.wattiesbandb.ie, wattiesbandb@eircom.net, Maria Dunne).

$ Cashel Lodge is a well-kept rural oasis housed in an old stone grain warehouse behind the Rock near the Hore Abbey ruins. Its seven comfortable rooms (one a dorm with three bunks) combine unpretentious practicality with Irish country charm (dorm beds-€20-23, Db-€65-80, Tb-€75, camping spots-€10/person, breakfast-€7.50, laundry service-€10, Wi-Fi, Dundrum Road R-505, tel. 062/61003, www.cashel-lodge.com, info@cashel -lodge.com).

Eating in Cashel

Grab a soup-and-sandwich lunch at tiny **Granny's Kitchen** (next to the parking lot at the base of the Rock) or at snug **King Cormac's** (a block away, near the base of the road up to the Rock). In town, next door to the TI, **Feehan's Bar** is a convenient stop for pub grub (tel. 062/61929).

For a splurge dinner, consider the classy **Chez Hans** (€27.50 early-bird two-course fixed-price meal before 20:00 Tue-Thu or before 19:00 Fri, otherwise €25-37 entrées, Tue-Sat 18:00-22:00, closed Sun-Mon, in an old church a block below the Rock, tel. 062/61177). The same folks also run the cheaper **Chez Hans Café** up the street, serving lunch until closing (€11-17 meals, Tue-Sat 12:00-17:30, closed Sun-Mon).

Cashel Connections

Cashel has no train station; the closest one is 13 miles away in the town of Thurles.

From Cashel by Bus to: Dublin (4/day, 3 hours), **Kilkenny** (3/day, 2.5 hours), **Waterford** (6/day, 2 hours). For details, see www.buseireann.ie.

WATERFORD
and COUNTY WEXFORD

The best overnight stop in southeast Ireland is the historic Viking and Norman beach-head town of Waterford. From here, you can explore the varied sights of County Wexford. Throughout your travels here, you'll see evidence of the region's Norman roots in its high concentration of family names with old Norman (French) prefixes: De Berg, De Lacy, Devereux, Fitzgilbert, Fitzsimmons, Fitzgerald, and so on.

Sightseeing Discounts: If you plan on visiting more than one of these Waterford and Wexford sights—Waterford Crystal Visitor Centre, Waterford Museum of Treasures, Hook Head Lighthouse, *Dunbrody* Famine Ship, Irish National Heritage Park, or Old Midleton Distillery (described in the next chapter)—take advantage of **Southeast Explorer Pass** discount coupons, which offer 20 percent off each sight (ask for the coupons at the first sight you visit). The coupons do not cover the Kennedy Homestead or the National 1798 Centre.

Waterford

The oldest city in Ireland, Waterford was once more important than Dublin. Today, while tourists associate the town's name with its famous crystal, locals are quick to remind you that the crystal is named after the town, not vice versa. That said, Waterford is a plain, gray, workaday town. Pubs outnumber cafés, and freighters offload cargo at the dock. It's a dose of gritty Ireland, with fewer leprechauns per capita than other Irish destinations. Wandering the back streets, you're reminded that until a couple of generations ago, Ireland was one of the poorest countries in Western Europe.

Planning Your Time

A day is more than enough time for Waterford. Visit the Waterford Crystal Visitor Centre early or late to avoid the midday crowds. Beyond that, your best activity is the historic walk (at 11:45 or 13:45 in peak season), followed by a visit to the Waterford Museum of Treasures and Reginald's Tower. To feel the pulse of contemporary Waterford, hang out on the town's pedestrian square and stroll through its big, modern shopping mall.

Orientation to Waterford

(area code: 051)

Waterford's main drag runs along its ugly harbor, where you'll find the bus station and easy parking lots (€1.80/hour, €16 daily maximum, €5 overnight—17:00-11:00, pay at automated station before driving out of gate). All recommended accommodations and sights are within a 10-minute walk of the harbor. Both museums and the TI are on the harborfront. The stubby two-story Victorian clock tower marks the middle of the harbor. It's also the start of the pedestrian Barronstrand Street, which runs a block inland to the town square.

Tourist Information

The TI is inside the old brick granary warehouse on Merchant's Quay (July-Aug Mon-Fri 9:00-18:00, Sat 10:00-18:00, Sun 11:00-17:00; April-June and Sept-Oct Mon-Fri 9:00-18:00, Sat 10:00-18:00, closed Sun; Nov-March Mon-Sat 9:15-17:00, closed Sun; tel. 051/875-823). As with all Irish TIs, it's basically a shop with a counter where clerks tell you about places that they "endorse" (i.e., get money from).

Helpful Hints

Internet Access: Handy **Cybermart** is near the waterfront at 6 Gladstone Street (€2.50/30 minutes, Mon-Sat 9:00-21:00, closed Sun, tel. 051/873-812).

Post Office: It's on Parade Quay (Mon-Fri 9:00-17:30, Sat 9:00-13:00, closed Sun).

Laundry: **Snow White** launderette is at 61 Mayor's Walk (Mon-Sat 9:30-13:30 & 14:30-18:00, closed Sun, tel. 051/858-905).

Dinner Show: On Thursday evenings in summer, **Dooley's Hotel** hosts a musical show on the experience of Irish emigrants in America (see page 153).

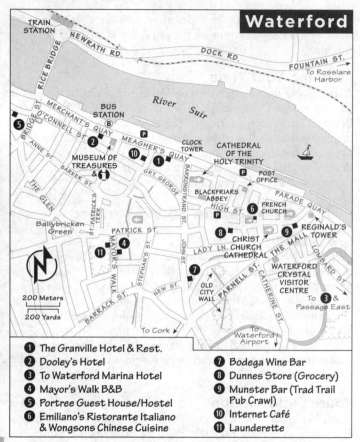

Waterford

1 The Granville Hotel & Rest.
2 Dooley's Hotel
3 To Waterford Marina Hotel
4 Mayor's Walk B&B
5 Portree Guest House/Hostel
6 Emiliano's Ristorante Italiano & Wongsons Chinese Cuisine
7 Bodega Wine Bar
8 Dunnes Store (Grocery)
9 Munster Bar (Trad Trail Pub Crawl)
10 Internet Café
11 Launderette

Taxis: Consider **Street Cabs Ltd.** (117 Parade Quay, tel. 051/877-778). **Rapid Cabs** operates local taxis (tel. 051/858-585), and **Rapid Express** offers coaches to Dublin's airport (tel. 051/872-149).

Tours of Waterford

▲▲**Waterford Historic Walking Tour**—Jack Burtchaell and his partners lead informative, hour-long, historical town walks that meet at the Waterford Museum of Treasures (behind TI) every day at 11:45 and 13:45 (just show up, pay €7 at the end, mid-March-mid-Oct only, tel. 051/873-711). The tour—really the most enjoyable thing to do in Waterford—is an entertaining walk from the TI to the Waterford Crystal Visitor Centre, giving you a good handle on the story of Waterford.

Sights in Waterford

▲▲**Waterford Crystal Visitor Centre**—With a tradition dating back to 1783, Waterford was, until recently, the largest and most respected glassworks in the world. However, the economic downturn has shattered the market for luxury items like crystal, and sadly, the big Waterford Crystal factory outside of town closed in January 2009.

The good news for crystal enthusiasts is that the company was bought by American investors, who opened a new, scaled-down factory in the town center in June 2010. While 95 percent of Waterford Crystal is now manufactured by cheaper labor in Eastern Europe and Asia, the finest glass craftsmen reside here, where they create "prestige pieces" for special-order customers.

A one-hour tour of this hardworking little factory is a joy; it's more intimate than the old, larger factory. The tour begins with a glitzy and forgettable five-minute film set to a techno-beat. But things pick up as your guide takes you into the factory to meet the craftsmen in their element. Glassblowers magically spin glowing blobs of molten glass into exquisite and recognizable shapes in minutes. A cooling-off stage allows the crystal to set. Then glass cutters deftly cradle the fragile creations against diamond-edged cutting wheels, applying exactly enough pressure to ensure that the grooves are replicated with surgical skill. You're encouraged to ask questions. It's only when they hand you an unfinished piece (with its lead-enhanced heft) that you come to appreciate the strength, touch, and hand-eye coordination glass cutters take for granted.

Afterward, visit the glittering salesroom, surrounded by hard-to-pack but easy-to-ship temptations. Take a look at the copies of famous sports trophies (they make backups of their most important commissions...just in case).

Cost and Hours: Tour—€10.50, call for times; shop free and open daily 9:00-17:00; tel. 051/332-500, www.waterford visitorcentre.com. The Visitor Centre is conveniently located on a street called The Mall, an easy two-block walk south of Reginald's Tower.

Cathedral of the Holy Trinity—In 1793, the English king granted Ireland the Irish Relief Act, which, among other things, allowed the Irish to build Catholic churches and worship publicly. With Catholic France (30 million) threatening Britain (8 million) on one side, and Ireland (6 million) stirring things up on the other, the king needed to take action to lessen Irish resentment. Allowed new freedom, the Irish built this interesting cathedral in 1796. It's Ireland's first Catholic post-Reformation church and its

Waterford's History

Arriving in 850, Vikings first established Waterford as their base for piracy. Waterford was a perfect spot for launching their ships, since it's located at the gateway to the most extensive river network in Ireland. From here, raiders could sail 50 miles into Ireland, an island with no towns, just scattered monastic settlements and small gatherings of clans—perfect for the Vikings' plan of rape, pillage, and plunder.

Later, the Vikings decided to "go legal." They turned to profiteering, setting up shop in an established trading base they named Vandrafjord, or "safe harbor"—eventually called Waterford—Ireland's first permanent town. It was from this base that the Norsemen invaded England.

In the 12th century, a deposed Irish king invited the Normans over from England, hoping to use their muscle to regain his land from a rival clan. The great warrior knight Strongbow came...and never left, beginning Ireland's long and troublesome relationship with the English. In 1170, Strongbow married the Gaelic princess Aoife in the Gothic church that once stood where Waterford's Christ Church Cathedral stands today. With this marriage, Strongbow was granted the title of King of Leinster, planting England's first roots in Ireland.

For the English, Waterford has often proved to be a tough nut to crack. During Oliver Cromwell's brutal scorched-earth campaign of 1649-1650, when his forces decimated Ireland, Waterford was the only Irish city to withstand his sieges.

only Baroque church. The building was funded by wealthy Irish wine merchants from Cádiz, Spain. Among its treasures are 10 Waterford Crystal chandeliers (free, daily 8:00-19:00).

Nearby: The cathedral faces **Barronstrand Street,** which leads from the clock tower on the harborfront to the pedestrian-friendly **town square.** The street separates the medieval town (on your left when the river is behind you) from the 18th-century city (on your right). A river once flowed here—part of the town's natural defenses just outside the old wall. The huge **shopping center** that dominates the old town was built right on top of the Viking town. In fact, the center is built over a church dating from 1150, which you can see at the bottom of the escalator (next to the kiddie rides).

▲**Reginald's Tower**—This oldest part of the oldest town in Ireland is named after Regnall, the first Viking leader of Waterford, who built a tower here in A.D. 914, and later invaded Jorvik (York, England). Dating from the late 1100s, the Norman tower you see today was once the most important corner of the town wall. The tower is supposedly Ireland's oldest intact build-

Thomas Francis Meagher
(1823-1867)

Waterford's favorite son had a short but amazing life. Born to the town's conservative mayor, Meagher joined Daniel O'Connell's nonviolent movement to repeal the Act of Union with Britain. Impatient with the slow-moving political process, Meagher joined the radical Young Irelander movement, becoming an inspiring speaker. He went to France in 1848 and returned with the first Irish tri-color flag—a gift from the French that represented the Catholics (green), the Protestants (orange), and peaceful coexistence between the two (white).

Involved in a failed uprising, Meagher was sentenced to hang, but his sentence was commuted to life in prison in Tasmania. In 1852, Meagher escaped Tasmania via an American whaling ship and sailed to New York, where he eventually became a lawyer and started an Irish newspaper. After a trip to Nicaragua (to study the feasibility of building a canal or railway across the isthmus), he returned to New York to fight in the American Civil War. Meagher was made a Union general, raised a regiment of Irish immigrants, and famously led them into battle at Antietam and Fredericksburg. After the war, he became the first governor of the Montana territory. At age 44, Thomas Francis Meagher fell off a riverboat and drowned in the Missouri River. His body was never found.

ing and its first made with mortar. Inside, you'll see a display of medieval coins, old city models, a few Viking artifacts, and a short video (€3, includes guided tour any time upon request—ask for the one-hour version, which adds a historic walk around the block to French's Church; daily Easter-Oct 10:00-18:00, Nov-Easter 10:00-17:00, last entry 30 minutes before closing, tel. 051/304-220).

The **statue** outside (in the middle of the street) is of Thomas Francis Meagher (see sidebar), whose short, hell-bent-for-leather life involved him in precarious adventures from Tasmania to Nicaragua to Montana.

▲▲**Waterford Museum of Treasures**—With the help of handheld audioguides, this museum presents a grand sweep through the history of Ireland as seen from Waterford. After an elevator ride to the top, you'll work your way down through three floors of intriguingly displayed artifacts, spiced with fiery characters such as Norman warlord Strongbow and Waterford-born action hero Thomas Francis Meagher. You'll learn why the province of Newfoundland in Canada owes over 50 percent of its population to immigrants from Waterford. The museum is housed, along with the TI, in an old stone grain warehouse where the original Waterford Crystal works once stood (€7; June-Aug Mon-Sat 9:30-18:00, Sun 11:00-18:00; Sept-May Mon-Sat 10:00-17:00, Sun 11:00-17:00; last entry one hour before closing, handy cafeteria in back, tel. 051/304-500, www.waterford treasures.ie).

In the ground-floor gift shop, you can watch **Sean Egan** create his crystal art. With 35 years of experience as a master craftsman at the former Waterford Crystal factory, he now demonstrates his fine glass-cutting skills here (free, Mon-Fri 9:00-17:00, weekends by request, tel. 051/304-500, mobile 087-123-9523, www.sean eganartglass.com).

Christ Church Cathedral—The Protestant cathedral, with 18th-century Georgian architecture, is the fourth church to stand here. Look for the exposed Gothic column six feet below today's floor level, a remnant from an earlier church where the Norman conqueror Strongbow was married (see "Waterford's History" sidebar).

Wander over to the macabre tomb of 15th-century mayor James Rice, which bears a famous epitaph: "I am what you will be, I was what you are, pray for me." To emphasize the point, he requested that his body be dug up one year after his death (1482), and his partially decomposed remains be used to model his likeness, now seen on the tomb's lid...complete with worms and frogs.

Cost and Hours: Free, €3 donation requested, daily 10:00-17:00, tours at 11:30 and 15:00.

Nightlife in Waterford

Waterford Trad Trail—Irish traditional music is played and explained by two Kilkenny-based musicians, who have a fun sense of humor and passion for the subject. They lead small groups to three venerable old pubs over the course of a couple of hours (€12, June-Aug Wed at 19:00, beverages extra, buy tickets after 18:30 at Munster Bar on Bailey's New Street behind Reginald's Tower, mobile 085-165-8243, www.kilkennytradtrail.net).

Sleep Code

(€1 = about $1.25, country code: 353, area code: 051)
S = Single, **D** = Double/Twin, **T** = Triple, **Q** = Quad, **b** = bathroom,
s = shower only. Unless otherwise noted, breakfast is included
and credit cards are accepted.

To help you easily sort through these listings, I've divided
the rooms into three categories, based on the price for a
standard double room with bath:

$$$ Higher Priced—Most rooms €120 or more.
$$ Moderately Priced—Most rooms between €70-120.
$ Lower Priced—Most rooms €70 or less.

Prices can change without notice; verify the hotel's
current rates online or by email. For other updates, see www
.ricksteves.com/update.

Sleeping in Waterford

Waterford is a working-class city. Cheap accommodations are fairly
rough; fancy accommodations are venerable old places that face the
water. Many find sleepy Ardmore, an hour southwest down the
coast, a smaller and more appealing home base (see page 178).

$$$ The Granville Hotel is Waterford's top, most historic
hotel, grandly overlooking the center of the harborfront. The place
is plush, from its Old World lounges to its extravagant rooms (Sb-
€80-90, Db-€100-160, Tb-€145-200, ask about "corporate dis-
counts," Meagher Quay, tel. 051/305-555, fax 051/305-566, www
.granville-hotel.ie, stay@granville-hotel.ie).

$$$ Dooley's Hotel, a more modern business-class place on
the harbor with 113 big, motel-style rooms, can be less expensive
(Sb-€80-129, Db-€140-198, Tb-€195-240, often discounted much
lower, Merchant's Quay, tel. 051/873-531, fax 051/870-262, www
.dooleys-hotel.ie, hotel@dooleys-hotel.ie). They also host "An
Emigrant's Tale," a song, dance, and storytelling show about Irish-
American life, at 20:45 on Thursdays (€15, €32 with dinner, May-
mid-Sept, www.anemigrantstale.net).

$$$ Waterford Marina Hotel has 81 large, comfortable
rooms and very little personality (Sb-€69-79, Db-€79-139, Wi-Fi,
Canada Street, parking, tel. 051/856-600, fax 051/856-605, www
.waterfordmarinahotel.com, info@waterfordmarinahotel.com).

$ Mayor's Walk B&B is a well-worn, grandmotherly place
that takes you right back to the 1950s. Bob and Jane Hovenden
rent four economical yet pleasant rooms (S-€28, D-€50, T-€75,

WATERFORD

cash only, Wi-Fi, 12 Mayor's Walk, tel. 051/855-427, www.mayors walk.com, mayorswalk@gmail.com).

$ Portree Guest House, just across the bridge from the train station, combines 24 basic budget rooms upstairs with 14 dorm beds in its basement hostel (Sb-€35, Db-€50, Tb-€75, Qb-€100, cash only, breakfast-€7, Wi-Fi, parking behind, Mary Street, tel. 051/874-574, fax 051/841-940, www.portreeguesthouse.ie, info @portreeguesthouse.ie).

Eating in Waterford

For something livelier than tired pub grub, consider two good restaurants (Italian and Chinese) that share a tiny street behind Reginald's Tower. They're small, popular with locals, and serve an early-bird special (two or three courses for €17-23 before 19:00): **Emiliano's Ristorante Italiano** (Tue-Sun 12:30-14:30 & 17:00-22:00, closed Mon, tel. 051/820-333) and **Wongsons Chinese Cuisine** (daily 12:30-14:30 & 17:00-22:00, tel. 051/854-866).

The relaxed **Bodega** is my favorite wine bar, run by laid-back Cormac in a warm-glow Mediterranean atmosphere (Mon-Sat 12:00-22:00, closed Sun, 54 John Street, tel. 051/844-177).

The Granville Hotel's carvery is your best €10 lunch option if you're looking for a central waterfront location (daily 12:30-14:30, otherwise good bar food daily 10:30-19:00, Meagher Quay).

Pub Grub and Music: Waterford's staple food seems to be pub grub. Several typical pubs serve dinner in the city center. For your musical entertainment, just wander around, read the notices, and follow your ears. You'll find plenty of live action on George Street, Barronstrand Street, and Broad Street.

Supermarket: **Dunnes Store** in the shopping center is your best grocery option (Mon-Wed and Sat 9:00-19:00, Thu-Fri 9:00-21:00, Sun 12:00-18:00).

Waterford Connections

From Waterford by Train to: Dublin (6/day, 2.5 hours), **Kilkenny** (6/day, 45 minutes). For details, see www.irishrail.ie.

By Bus to: Cork (almost hourly, 2.25 hours), **Kilkenny** (2/day, 1 hour), **Rosslare** (8/day, 1.5 hours), **Wexford** (8/day, 1.25 hours). Waterford bus station info: tel. 051/879-000. For details, see www .buseireann.ie.

County Wexford

The southeast corner of Ireland, peppered with pretty views and historic sites, is easily accessible to drivers as a day trip from Waterford. While most of the sights are mediocre, five worth considering are within an hour's drive of Waterford.

The dramatic Hook Head Lighthouse—capping an intriguing and remote peninsula—comes with lots of history and a great tour. The Kennedy Homestead is a pilgrimage site for Kennedy fans. The *Dunbrody* Famine Ship in New Ross gives a sense of what 50 days on a "coffin ship" with dreams of "Americay" must have been like. The Irish National Heritage Park in Wexford is a Knott's Berry Farm...circa the Stone Age. And the National 1798 Centre at Enniscorthy explains the roots of the Irish struggle for liberty.

Planning Your Time

New Ross, Enniscorthy, and Wexford are each less than 30 minutes apart, connected by fast roads. The Kennedy Homestead is a 10-minute drive from New Ross, and the lighthouse is a 45-minute trip to the end of the Hook Peninsula. All are well-signposted and easy to find. Connecting Dublin with Waterford, you could visit many of these sights in a best-of-County Wexford day en route. On a quick trip, the sights are not worth the trouble by public transit. If you'll be spending the night, Enniscorthy is a blue-collar town (with decent hotels and B&Bs) that provides a good glimpse of workaday Ireland.

If connecting Waterford to Hood Head, use the car-ferry shortcut from Passage East to Ballyhack (€8, 5-minute crossing, runs continuously, daily April-Sept 7:00-22:00, Oct-March 7:00-20:00). To reach the ferry from Waterford, take Lombard Street (near Reginald's Tower) south, and follow it all the way to Passage East (it becomes R-683).

Sights in County Wexford

▲Hook Head Lighthouse

This is the oldest operating lighthouse in Northern Europe. According to legend, St. Dubhan arrived in the fifth century and discovered the bodies of shipwrecked sailors. Dismayed, he and his followers began tending a fire on the headland to warn future

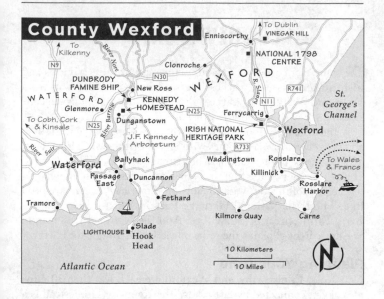

County Wexford

mariners. What you see today is essentially a structure from the 12th century, built by the Normans, who first landed five miles up the east coast (at Baginbun Head, in 1169). They established Waterford Harbor—a commercial beachhead for the rich Irish countryside they intended to conquer. This beacon assured them safe access.

Today's lighthouse is 110 feet tall and looks modern on the outside. (It was automated in 1996, and its light can be seen for 23 miles out to sea.) But it's 800 years old, built on a plan inspired by the lighthouse of Alexandria in Egypt—one of the seven wonders of the ancient world.

Since it's a working lighthouse, it can be toured only with a guide or escort. Fine 30-minute tours leave about hourly. When you're inside—seeing the lighthouse's black-stained, ribbed, vaulted ceilings and stout, 10-foot-thick walls—you can almost feel the presence of the Cistercian monks who tended this coal-burning beacon for the Normans. Climbing 115 steps through four levels rewards you with a breezy, salt-air view from the top.

Oliver Cromwell arrived here to secure the English claim to this area. He considered his two options, and declared he'd take strategic Waterford "by Hook or by Crooke." Hook is the long peninsula with the lighthouse. Crooke is a little village on the other side (just south of Passage East).

Cost and Hours: €6, March-Oct daily 9:30-17:30, tours roughly hourly depending on demand, Nov-Feb tours Sat-Sun only, last tour usually at 16:00, call to check tour times before driving out (tel. 051/397-055, www.hookheritage.ie).

Nearby: There's a decent cafeteria and a shop with fliers explaining other sights on the peninsula. Kids-at-heart can't resist climbing out on the rugged rocky tip of the windy Hook Head.

▲Kennedy Homestead

Patrick Kennedy, JFK's great-grandfather, left Ireland in 1858. Distant relatives have turned his property into a little museum/

shrine for Kennedy pilgrims. Physically, it's not much: A barn and a wing of the modern house survive from 1858. JFK dropped in by helicopter in June 1963, a few months before he was assassinated. You'll view two short videos: 5 minutes of Kennedy's visit to the farm and a 16-minute newsreel tracing the events of his 1963 trip through Ireland (both fascinating if you like Kennedy stuff).

After the videos, you're led on a 15-minute tour by Patrick Grennan, a distant Kennedy relative whose grandmother hosted the tea here for JFK. You're then free to peruse the barn, lined with Kennedy-in-Ireland memorabilia that details the history of the dynasty. While it's just a private home, anyone interested in the Kennedys will find it worth driving the treacherous, narrow lane to see.

Cost and Hours: €5; July-Aug daily 10:00-17:00; May-June and Sept Mon-Fri 11:30-16:30, closed Sat-Sun; by appointment after hours, in slow times, and Oct-April (no big deal, as it's their home); tel. 051/388-264, www.kennedyhomestead.com.

Location: It's four miles south of New Ross near Dungans-town (look for sign off R-733, long one-lane road). Don't confuse the Kennedy Homestead with the nearby JFK Arboretum—a huge park with 4,500 species of trees and a grand six-county view. It's lovely if you like trees and plants, but there's no Kennedy history.

▲▲Dunbrody Famine Ship

Permanently moored on a river in the tiny port of New Ross, this ship was built as a re-creation of similar vessels full of countless hungry Irish who sailed to America. The *Dunbrody* is a full-scale reconstruction of a 19th-century three-masted bark built in Quebec in 1845. It's typical of the trading vessels that originally sailed empty to America to pick up goods; during the famine, they found that they could

COUNTY WEXFORD

make a little money on the westward voyage. Extended families camped out for 50 days on bunk beds no bigger than a king-size mattress. Often, boats like this would arrive in America with only 50 percent of their original human cargo. Those killed by Potato Famine fever were dumped overboard, and the ships gained their morbid moniker: "coffin ships."

After a 10-minute video about the building of the vessel, you'll follow an excellent guide through the ship, encountering a couple of grumpy passengers who tell vivid tales about life aboard. Roots-seekers are welcome to peruse the computerized file of a million names of immigrants who sailed from 1846 through 1865.

Cost and Hours: €7.50, daily April-Oct 9:00-18:00, Nov-March 10:00-17:00, 45-minute tours go 2/hour, last tour leaves one hour before closing (tel. 051/425-239, www.dunbrody.com).

Location: The *Dunbrody* is in New Ross, near the Kennedy Homestead. During work hours, you'll need to feed the parking meters in the lot (€1/hour, free on Sun).

▲Irish National Heritage Park

This 35-acre wooded park, which contains an 1857 tower commemorating local boys killed in the Crimean War, features replicas of buildings from each era of Irish history. Ireland's countless ancient sights are generally unrecognizable ruins—hard to re-create in your mind. This park is intended to help out. You'll find buildings and settlements illustrating life in Ireland from the Stone Age through the 12th-century Norman Age. As a bonus, you'll see animal-skin-clad characters doing their prehistoric thing—gnawing on meat, weaving, making arrowheads, and so on.

Your visit begins with a 12-minute video, followed by a 1.5-hour tour. During 13 stops, the guide explains various stages of

Irish civilization. The highlight is a monastic settlement from the age when Europe was dark, and Ireland was "the island of saints and scholars." While you can wander around on your own, the place is a bit childish (there's nothing actually old here), and only worthwhile if you take the included tour.

Cost and Hours: €8, daily 9:30-18:30, until 17:30 in winter, last entry 1.5 hours before closing, hourly tours (tel. 053/912-0733, www.inhp.com).

Location: It's clearly signposted on the west end of Wexford—you'll hit it before entering town on the N-11 Enniscorthy road.

National 1798 Centre

Located in Enniscorthy, this museum creatively tells the story of the rise of revolutionary thinking in Ireland, which led to the ill-fated rebellion of 1798. Enniscorthy was the crucial Irish battle-ground of a populist revolution (inspired by the American and French Revolutions). The town witnessed the bloodiest days of the doomed uprising. The material is compelling for anyone intrigued by the struggles for liberty, but there's little more here than video clips of reenactments and storyboards on the walls.

Leaving the center, look east across the River Slaney, which divides Enniscorthy, and you'll see a hill with a stumpy tower on it. This is Vinegar Hill. The tower is the old windmill that once flew the green rebel flag. Drive to the top for the views that the rebels had of the surrounding British forces. The doomed rebels tried desperately to hold the high ground, with no shelter from the merciless British artillery fire.

Cost and Hours: €6; April-Oct Mon-Fri 9:30-17:00, Sat-Sun 13:00-17:00; Nov-March Mon-Fri 9:30-16:00, closed Sat-Sun; last entry one hour before closing (tel. 053/923-7596, www.1798 centre.ie).

Location: Enniscorthy is 12 miles north of Wexford town. The National 1798 Centre is the town's major sight and is well-signposted (follow the brown *Aras 98 Centre* signs).

KINSALE AND COBH

County Cork, on Ireland's south coast, is fringed with historic port towns and scenic peninsulas. The typical tour-bus route here includes Blarney Castle and Killarney—places where most tourists wear nametags. A major mistake many travelers make is allowing destinations into their itineraries simply because they're famous (from a song or as part of a relative's big-bus-tour memory). If you have the misfortune to spend the night in Killarney town, you'll understand what I mean. The town is a sprawling line of green Holiday Inns and outlet malls littered with pushy shoppers looking for three-leaf clovers.

Rather than kissing the spit-slathered Blarney Stone, spend your time in County Cork enjoying the bustling, historic maritime towns of Kinsale and Cobh.

Planning Your Time

Kinsale makes a great home base for enjoying the County Cork coast. From Kinsale, you can wade through the salty history of Cobh. Travelers approaching this region from Waterford can easily visit Ardmore and the Old Midleton Whiskey Distillery. If you're departing this region for the Ring of Kerry or Dingle, you can easily stop by Blarney Castle and Macroom en route.

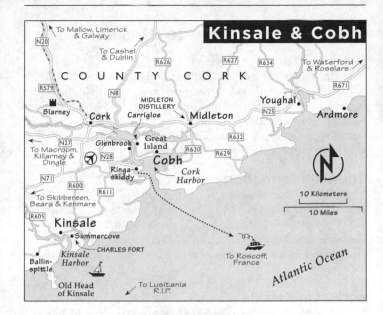

Kinsale

While nearby Cork is the biggest town in southern Ireland, Kinsale (15 miles south) is actually more historic and certainly cuter: It's delightful to visit. Thanks to the naturally sheltered bay barbed by a massive 17th-century star fort, you can submerge yourself in maritime history, from the Spanish Armada to Robinson Crusoe to the *Lusitania*. Apart from all the history, Kinsale has a laid-back Sausalito feel with a touch of wine-sipping class. Or, as a local recently told me with a wry smile, "Welcome to Happy Valley" (Eli Lilly manufactures much of its Prozac antidepressant just outside of town).

Planning Your Time

Kinsale is worth two nights and a day. The town's two tiny museums open at 10:00 and will occupy you until the 11:15 town walking tour. After lunch at the Fishy Fishy Café, head out to Charles Fort for great bay views and insights into British military life in colonial Ireland. On the way back, stop for a pint at the Bulman Bar. Finish the day with a good dinner and live music in a pub. Those on the blitz tour can give Kinsale four hours—see the fort, wander the town, and have a nice lunch—before driving on.

Orientation to Kinsale

(area code: 021)

Kinsale, because of its great natural harbor, is older than Cobh (Cork's harbor town). While the town is prettier than the actual harbor, the harbor was its reason for being. Today, Kinsale is a wealthy resort of 2,200 residents. The town's long and skinny old center is part modern marina and part pedestrian-friendly medieval town—an easy 15-minute stroll from end to end.

Tourist Information

The TI is as central as can be, at the head of the harbor across from the bus stop (July-Aug Mon-Sat 9:15-18:00, Sun 10:00-17:00; March-June and Sept-Nov Mon-Sat 9:30-17:00, closed Sun; shorter hours Dec-Feb; tel. 021/477-2234, www.kinsale.ie). It has a free town map and brochures outlining a world of activities in the vicinity.

Arrival in Kinsale

Since Kinsale doesn't have a train station, you'll arrive by **bus** (the stop is on Pier Road, 100 yards behind the TI, at the south end of town) or by **car.** Park your car and enjoy the town on foot. While Kinsale's windy medieval lanes are narrow and congested, parking is fairly easy. The most central lot is at the head of the harbor behind the TI (€2/2 hours, use pay-and-display machine, Mon-Sat 10:30-18:00, free on Sun and after 18:00). But there's a big, safe, free parking lot across the street from St. Multose Church at the top of town, a five-minute walk from most recommended hotels and restaurants. The largest lot is farthest away, a 10-minute walk east of town by the fire station. Parking on the street requires a disk (€1/hour, 2 hours maximum, use pay-and-display machine), except when it's free: before 10:30, after 18:00, or on Sundays. The outlying streets, a five-minute stroll from all the action, have wide-open parking.

Helpful Hints

Banking: The two banks in town are **Allied Irish Bank** on Pearse Street and **Bank of Ireland** on Emmett Street (both open Mon 10:00-17:00, Tue-Fri 10:00-16:00, closed Sat-Sun).

Internet Access: Your best bet is **Elasnik** (Kinsale spelled backwards), on Market Square across from the town museum (€1.50/15 minutes, €5/hour, daily 9:00-22:00, tel. 021/477-7356).

Post Office: It's on Pearse Street (Mon-Fri 9:00-17:30, Sat 9:00-13:00, closed Sun).

Laundry: Take your dirty duds to **Elite Laundry.** They'll do an average-sized load for about €10 (Mon-Fri 9:00-17:30, Sat 10:00-17:00, closed Sun, The Glen, tel. 021/477-7345).

Market: Check out the lively open-air market on Tuesdays from June through August (7:00-14:00) in the parking lot across from St. Multose Church.

Bike Rental: Mylie Murphy's rents bikes from a handy spot near the SuperValu (€10/day, Mon-Sat 9:30-18:00, closed Sun but arrangements can be made for pickup or drop-off, shorter hours in winter, tel. 021/477-2703). Paths good for biking or walking stretch around the harbor. For the best short-and-scenic route, bike past Charles Fort and two miles along the harbor to its mouth. Get other suggestions from the bike-rental shop.

Taxi: Kinsale Cabs has regular cab service and minibuses available (Market Square, tel. 021/477-2642 or 021/470-0100).

Tours in Kinsale

Don & Barry's Kinsale Historic Stroll—To understand the important role Kinsale played in Irish, English, and Spanish history, join Don Herlihy or Barry Moloney on a fascinating 1.5-hour walking tour (€6, daily April-mid-Oct at 11:15, additional early-bird tour May-Sept Mon-Sat at 9:15, no reservation necessary, meet outside TI, private tours possible, tel. 021/477-2873, www.historic strollkinsale.com). Both guides are a joy to hear as they creatively bring to life Kinsale's past, place its story in the wider sweep of history, and make the stony sights more than just buildings. They collect payment at the end, giving anyone disappointed in the talk an easy escape midway through. Don't get hijacked by imitation tours—ask for Don or Barry. This walk is Kinsale's single best attraction.

Ghost Walk Tour—This is not just any ghost tour; it's more Monty Python-style slapstick comedy than horror. Two actors (Brian and David) weave funny stunts and stories into a loose history of the town, offering an entertaining 1.25 hours of fun on Kinsale's after-dark streets (€10, May-Sept Sun-Fri at 21:00, leaves from Tap Tavern, mobile 087-948-0910). You'll spend the first 15 minutes in the back of the Tap Tavern—time to finish your drink and get to know some of the group. This tour doesn't overlap with the more serious historic town walk described above.

Kinsale

1 Blindgate House
2 Acton's Hotel
3 The Old Presbytery
4 Friar's Lodge
5 Chart House B&B
6 Cloisters B&B
7 The Anchorage B&B
8 The Olde Bakery B&B
9 San Antonio B&B
10 The Sea Gull
11 Jo's Rooms
12 Fishy Fishy Shop & Chippy
13 Fishy Fishy Café
14 Café Blue
15 Cucina Café
16 Patsy's Corner
17 Mother Hubbard's
18 Hoby's Restaurant
19 Max's Wine Bar
20 Jim Edward's Steak & Seafood
21 Cobra Tandoori
22 To Bulman Bar & Restaurant
23 The Tap Tavern (Ghost Walk)
24 An Seanachai Pub
25 Spaniard Inn
26 SuperValu Supermarket
27 Elasnik (Internet)
28 Launderette
29 Bike Rental

50 Meters
50 Yards

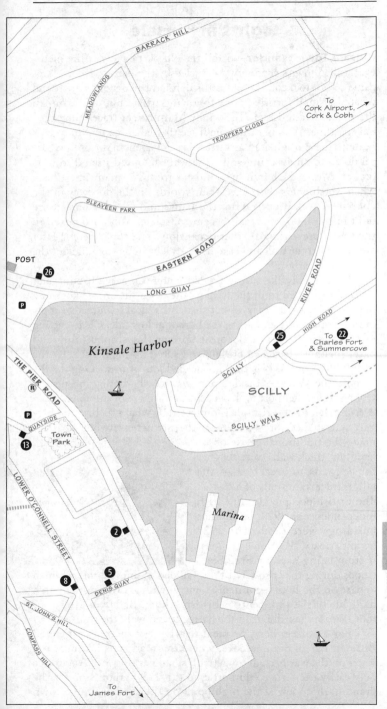

Sights in Kinsale

Kinsale Town Wander—Stroll the old part of town. The medieval walled town's economy was fueled by the harbor, where ships came to be stocked. The old walls defined the original town and created a small fortified zone following what is now O'Connell Street and Main Street. The windy Main Street traces the original coastline. Walking this, you'll see tiny lanes leading to today's harbor. These originated as piers—just wide enough to roll a barrel down to an awaiting ship. The wall detoured inland to protect St. Multose Church, which dates from Norman times (back when worshippers sharpened their swords on the doorway of the church—check it out). After the James and Charles Forts were built in the 1600s, the wall became obsolete—and also boxed in the town, preventing further expansion. The townspeople later disassembled the wall and used its ready-cut stones to build out the piers in the harbor.

What seems like part of the old center was actually built later on land reclaimed from the harbor. The town sits on the floor of a natural quarry, with easy-to-cut shale hills ideal for a ready supply of fill. Notice the mudflats in the harbor at low tide. Clear-cutting of the once-plentiful oak forest upriver (for shipbuilding and barrel-making) hastened erosion and silted up the harbor. By the early 1800s—when British ships needed lots of restocking for the Napoleonic Wars—Kinsale's port was slowly dying, and nearby Cobh's deepwater port took over the lion's share of shipping.

▲▲Charles Fort—Kinsale is protected by what was Britain's biggest star-shaped fort—a state-of-the-art defense when artillery made the traditional castle obsolete (low, thick walls were tougher for cannons to breach than the tall, thin curtain walls of a castle). The British occupied it until Irish independence in 1922. Its interior buildings were torched in 1923 by anti-treaty IRA forces to keep it from being used by Free State troops during the Irish Civil War. Guided 45-minute tours (which depart on the hour—confirm at entry) engross you in the harsh daily life of the 18th-century British soldier. Before or after your tour, peruse the exhibits in the barracks and walk the walls.

For a coffee, beer, or meal nearby, try the recommended Bulman Bar in Summercove, where the road runs low near the water on the way back to town (with small parking lot). And to see how easily the forts could bottle up this key harbor, stop for the grand harbor view at the high point on the road back into town (above Scilly, just uphill from The Spaniard pub).

Cost and Hours: €4, daily mid-March-Oct 10:00-18:00, Nov-mid-March 10:00-17:00, last entry 45 minutes before closing, a half-mile south of town in Summercove, tel. 021/477-2263.

James Fort—Older, overgrown, and filling a peaceful park, James Fort is Kinsale's other star fort, guarding the bay opposite Charles Fort. Built in the years just after the famous 1601 battle, this fort is more ruined, less interesting, and less visited than Charles Fort. Its satellite blockhouse, which sits below the fort at the water's edge opposite Summercove, controlled a strong chain that could be raised to block ships from reaching Kinsale's docks (free, always open).

Easily accessible by car or bike, it's two miles south of town along Pier Road on the west shore of the bay (cross bridge and turn left; you'll dead-end at Castle Park Marina, where you can park or leave your bike). It's up the hill behind the Dock pub. From the fort, a popular, scenic 40-minute walk goes around the James Fort Headland.

▲Desmond Castle—This 15th-century fortified urban customs house has had a long and varied history. It was the Spanish armory during Spain's 1601 occupation of Kinsale. Nicknamed "Frenchman's Prison," it served as a British prison and once housed 600 prisoners of the Napoleonic Wars (not to mention earlier American Revolutionary War prisoners captured at sea—who were treated as rebels, not prisoners, and chained to the outside of the building as a warning to any rebellion-minded Irish). In the late 1840s, it was a famine-relief center. Today, the evocative little ruin comes with a scant display of its colorful history, as well as the modest two-room Museum of Wine, highlighting Ireland's little-known connection to the international wine trade. In the Middle Ages, Kinsale was renowned for its top-quality wooden casks. Developing strong trade links with Bordeaux, local merchants traded their dependable empty casks for casks full of wine. Later, Kinsale became a "designated wine port" for tax-collection purposes.

Cost and Hours: €3, mid-April-Sept daily 10:00-18:00, last entry 17:15, tours given on request, closed Oct-mid-April, Cork Street, tel. 021/477-4855.

▲Kinsale Regional Museum—In the center of the old town, traffic circles the old town market, which later became a courthouse and is now the Regional Museum (as it's staffed by volunteers, its hours have been erratic for the past couple of years). Drop by at least to read the fun 1788 tax code for all Kinsale commercial transactions (outside at the front door). The modest museum is worth a quick visit for its fun mishmash of domestic and maritime bygones. It also gives a good perspective on the controversial

Kinsale's History

Kinsale's remarkable harbor has made this an important port since prehistoric times. The bay's 10-foot tide provided a natural shuttle service for Stone Age hunter-gatherers: They could ride it, at two miles per hour twice a day, the eight miles up and down the River Bandon. In the Bronze Age, when people discovered that it takes tin and copper to make bronze, tin came from Cornwall (in southwest England) and copper came from this part of Ireland. From 500 B.C. to A.D. 500, Kinsale was a rich trading center. The result: Lots of Stonehenge-type monuments are nearby. The best is Drombeg Stone Circle (a one-hour drive west, just off R-597 Glandore Road).

Kinsale's importance peaked during the 16th, 17th, and 18th centuries, when sailing ships ruled the waves, turning maritime countries into global powers. Kinsale was Ireland's most perfect natural harbor and the gateway to both Spain and France—potentially providing a base for either of these two powers in cutting off English shipping. Because of this, two pivotal battles were fought here in the 17th century: in 1601 against the Spanish, and in 1690 against the French. Two great forts were built to combat these threats from the Continent. England couldn't rule the waves without ruling Kinsale.

To understand the small town of Kinsale, you need to understand the big picture: In about 1500, the pope divided newly discovered lands outside of Europe between Spain and Portugal. With the Reformation breaking Rome's lock on Europe, maritime powers such as England were ignoring the pope's grant. This was important because trade with the New World and Asia brought huge wealth in spices (necessary for curing meat), gold, and silver. England threatened Spain's New World piñata, and Ireland was Catholic. Spain had an economic and a religious reason to defend the pope and Catholicism. The showdown between Spain and England for mastery of the seas (and control of all that trade) was in Ireland. The excuse: to rescue the dear Catholics of Ireland from the terrible treachery of Protestant England.

So the Irish disaster unfolded. The powerful Ulster chieftains Hugh O'Neill and Red Hugh O'Donnell and their clans had been on a roll in their battle against the English. With Spanish aid, they figured they could actually drive the English out of Ireland. In 1601, a Spanish fleet dropped off 5,000 soldiers, who established a beachhead in Kinsale. After the ships left, the Spaniards were pinned down in Kinsale by the English commander (who, breaking with martial etiquette, actually fought in the winter). In harsh winter conditions, virtually the entire Irish fighting force left the north and marched to the south coast, thinking they could liberate their Spanish allies and win freedom from England.

The numbers seemed reasonable (10,000 Englishmen versus 5,000 Spaniards as 5,000 Irish clansmen approached). The Irish attacked on Christmas Eve in 1601. But, holding the high ground around fortified and Spanish-occupied Kinsale, a relatively small force of English troops kept the Spaniards hemmed in, leaving the bulk of the English force to outnumber and rout the fighting Irish. (Today's visitors will be reminded of this crucial battle as they wander past pubs with names like "The 1601" and "The Spaniard"—see pub sign above.)

The Irish resistance was broken, and its leaders fled to Europe (the "flight of the Earls"). England made peace with Spain and began the "plantation" of mostly Scottish Protestants in Ireland (the seeds of today's Troubles in Ulster). England ruled the waves, and it ruled Ireland. The lesson: Kinsale is key. England eventually built two huge, star-shaped fortresses to ensure control of the narrow waterway, a strategy it would further develop in later fortifications built at Gibraltar and Singapore.

Kinsale's maritime history continued. Daniel Defoe used the real-life experience of Scottish privateer Alexander Selkirk, who departed from Kinsale in 1703 and was later marooned alone on a desert island, as the basis for his book *Robinson Crusoe*. (Selkirk was lucky to have been marooned when he was—his ship and all aboard later perished in a hurricane off Costa Rica.)

It was just 10 miles offshore from Old Kinsale Head that the passenger liner *Lusitania* was torpedoed by a German submarine in 1915. At the time, the liner was the fastest vessel on the seas (with a top speed of 25 knots). The primitive U-boats of the day were much slower (8 knots), giving *Lusitania*'s crew a false sense of security. Because this was the first conflict to employ submarine warfare, evasion tactics were largely untested. As the *Lusitania* sank, nearly 1,200 people were killed, sparking America's eventual entry into World War I.

Lusitania tragedy. Kinsale had maritime jurisdiction over the waters 10 miles offshore, where the luxury liner was torpedoed in 1915. Hearings were held here in the courthouse shortly afterward to investigate the causes of the disaster—which helped propel America into World War I—and to paint the German Hun as a bloodthirsty villain. Claims by Germany that the *Lusitania* was illegally carrying munitions seem to have been borne out by the huge explosion and rapid sinking of the vessel. But perhaps even more interesting, in the side room, is the boot of the 8-foot 3-inch Kinsale giant, who lived here in the late 1700s.

Cost and Hours: €2.50, Wed-Sat 10:30-17:30, Sun 14:00-17:30, closed Mon-Tue, Market Square, tel. 021/477-7930.

Sleeping in Kinsale

Kinsale is a popular place in summer for yachters and golfers (who don't flinch at paying $300 for 18 holes out on the exotic Old Head of Kinsale Golf Course). It's wise to book your room in advance. I've listed peak-season prices. These places are all within a five-minute walk of the town center.

$$$ Blindgate House, high up on the fringe of town behind St. Multose Church, offers 11 pristine rooms in fine modern comfort (Db-€110-150, Wi-Fi, tel. 021/477-7858, www.blindgatehouse.com, info@blindgatehouse.com, Maeve Coakley).

$$$ Acton's Hotel has a dependable big-hotel feel, with 73 crisp, modern rooms in a good location facing the harbor. Kids will enjoy the indoor pool (Db-€120-160, Wi-Fi, tel. 021/477-9900, fax 021/477-2231, www.actonshotelkinsale.com, res@actonshotelkinsale.com).

$$ The Old Presbytery is a fine, quiet house a block outside the commercial district, with a goofy floor plan, plush lounge, and 10 pleasant rooms. Listed in most guidebooks, it has lots of American guests. The breakfasts are a delight, the rooms are stocking-feet cozy, and Noreen McEvoy runs the place with a passion for excellence (Db-€100-110, bigger Db-€130-150, biggest Db-€150-170, family Qb-€160-180, 2 Qb suites with no breakfast-€170, 10 percent discount with cash and this book in 2011, free Internet access and Wi-Fi, private parking, 43 Cork Street, tel. 021/477-2027, www.oldpres.com, info@oldpres.com).

$$ Friar's Lodge is a recently built, shingled hotel, perched up the hill past St. John's Catholic Church. What its 18 spacious rooms lack in Old World character, they make up for in modern, dependable quality. Three modern, self-catering cottages located up the hill behind their parking lot are great for families wanting their own space (Sb-€50-80, Db-€80-130, Tb-€120-160, Qb-€150, Wi-Fi, private parking, Friar Street, tel. 021/477-7384,

Sleep Code

(€1 = about $1.25, country code: 353, area code: 021)
S = Single, **D** = Double/Twin, **T** = Triple, **Q** = Quad, **b** = bathroom,
s = shower only. Unless otherwise noted, breakfast is included
and credit cards are accepted.

To help you easily sort through these listings, I've divided
the rooms into three categories, based on the price for a
standard double room with bath:

$$$ Higher Priced—Most rooms €120 or more.
$$ Moderately Priced—Most rooms between €85-120.
$ Lower Priced—Most rooms €85 or less.

Prices can change without notice; verify the hotel's
current rates online or by email. For other updates, see www
.ricksteves.com/update.

fax 021/477-4363, www.friars-lodge.com, mtierney@indigo.ie).

$$ Chart House B&B is a luxurious Georgian home renting
a tidy little single and three grand, sumptuous doubles. It's cast-
ing distance from the harbor at the marina end of the old town,
and a level five-minute walk from fine restaurants. This quiet and
well-run place is top-end in every respect—high ceilings, chan-
deliers, and a plush living room (Sb-€45-50, Db-€90-110, deluxe
Db-€110-130, 10 percent discount with this book and when pay-
ing cash in 2011 non-smoking, Wi-Fi, parking, 6 Denis Quay, tel.
021/477-4568, fax 021/477-7907, www.charthouse-kinsale.com,
charthouse@eircom.net, Mary O'Connor).

$$ Cloisters B&B has four neat and clean rooms and a
friendly atmosphere (Sb-€35-55, Db-€70-110, Tb-€110-125, tel.
021/470-0680, www.cloisterskinsale.com, info@cloisterskinsale
.com, Mairead Ryan).

$$ The Anchorage B&B is a modern, angular stone house
on a slope overlooking town, with a fun sun patio out front and
five comfy rooms inside (Sb-€55-80, Db-€80-160, parking, tel.
021/477-3162, www.theanchoragebb.com, info@anchoragebb
.com).

$ The Olde Bakery B&B makes you feel at home, with six
quilt-bedded rooms, two friendly dogs, and a jovial breakfast at
the kitchen table cooked up by chatty Chrissie and beekeeper Tom
Quigley (D-€75-80, Db-€80-85, cash only, Wi-Fi, non-smoking,
laundry service, 56 Lower O'Connell Street, tel. 021/477-3012,
www.theoldebakerykinsale.com, oldebakery@gmail.com). Fami-
lies may want to ask about their self-catering apartment across the
street.

KINSALE & COBH

$ San Antonio B&B is a 200-year-old house with five rooms and a funky budget feel, lovingly looked after by owner Jimmie Conron. He occasionally joins other musicians who play at local pubs (Sb-€55, Db-€80, Tb-€115, cash only, tel. 021/477-2341, jimmiesan@yahoo.ie).

$ The Sea Gull, perched up the hill right next to Desmond Castle, offers six retro-homey rooms. It's run by Mrs. Mary O'Neill, who also runs The Tap Tavern down the hill (S-€45, Db-€80, Tb-€110, 10 percent discount with this book in 2011, cash only, Cork Street, tel. 021/477-2240, marytap@iol.ie).

$ Jo's Rooms is a friendly place offering eight cheap, spartan rooms in the center of town (Sb-€35-40, Db-€50-60, breakfast-€5-8 extra, cash only, Wi-Fi, completely non-smoking, small rooms with smaller double beds, 55 Main Street, tel. 021/477-2233, www.joskinsale.com, joskinsale@gmail.com).

Eating in Kinsale

Back in the 1990s, when Ireland was just getting its cuisine act together, Kinsale was the island's self-proclaimed gourmet capital.

While good restaurants are commonplace in Irish towns today, Kinsale still has an edge at mealtime. Local competition is fierce, and restaurants offer creative and tempting menus. Seafood is king. With so many options in the ever-changing scene, it's worth a short stroll to assess your options. Reservations are smart, especially if eating late or on a weekend. Restaurant connoisseurs can check the menu details of Kinsale's most famous restaurants online (www.kinsalerestaurants.com).

Lunch

The following places are good for lunch; a few offer dinner as well.

Cafés: Meals at the **Fishy Fishy Shop & Chippy** are like eating in a fish market, surrounded by the day's catch and a pristine stainless-steel kitchen. Marie and her white-aproned staff hustle wonderful steaming plates of beautifully presented seafood to eager customers (€15-20 meals, Tue-Sat 12:00-16:00 for lunch only, closed Sun-Mon, across from St. Multose Church on Guardwell Street, tel. 021/477-4453). Look at the lobster tank and ponder this: Several years ago, a soft-hearted, deep-pocketed Buddhist tourist bought up the entire day's supply of live lobster (worth more than €600) and set them free in the bay. They've refilled the tank since.

Fishy Fishy Café is bigger, with more spacious seating (indoor, balcony, and terrace). It offers the same good prices and wonderful menu with slightly longer hours, making it a great early-dinner option. Owner Martin Shanahan's cooking prowess has led him to host a weekly cooking show on Irish TV (Mon-Sat 12:00-21:00, Sun 12:00-16:30, reservations recommended, Pier Road, tel. 021/470-0415).

Other inviting cafés are **Café Blue** (open daily, at Blue Haven Hotel on Pearse Street, with lots of old-time town photos) and **Cucina Café** (closed Sun, on Market Street).

Cheap and Cheery Lunches: Try **Patsy's Corner,** packed with happy locals, or the breakfast hangout, **Mother Hubbard's.** Both are near Market Square and serve sandwiches, baguettes, or salads with coffee for under €10. Or, gather picnic supplies at the **SuperValu** supermarket (Mon-Sat 8:30-21:00, Sun 10:00-21:00, Pearse Street).

Good Dinners in the Old Center

Hoby's Restaurant, a well-established favorite for seafood and duck, offers modern cuisine in a quiet, candlelit room. It's popular with people from Cork who've come down for a romantic night out (€25 three-course dinners, Mon-Sat 18:00-22:00, closed Sun, Main Street, tel. 021/477-2200).

Several other candlelit wine-bar restaurants vie for your attention along the gently curving Main Street. **Max's Wine Bar** leads the pack, with subdued lighting and a menu that's big on quality seafood (€25 early-bird fixed-price meal before 19:30, open for lunch Wed-Sun 12:30-15:00, dinner Wed-Mon 18:30-22:30, closed Mon lunch and all day Tue, 48 Main Street, tel. 021/477-2443).

Jim Edward's Steak & Seafood keeps eaters happy in both the bar and the restaurant. Choose between the restaurant's candlelit maritime ambience (€20-30 meals, dinner only), or simpler food in the no-nonsense bar (€14-20 meals). Arrive early or wait. While cheaper and less gourmet than other Kinsale eateries, it's a high-energy place that's clearly a local family favorite for its decent steaks, seafood, and vegetables (bar daily 12:30-22:00, restaurant daily 18:00-22:00, Market Quay, tel. 021/477-2541).

Ethnic: Walk around the old-town block for a full array of inviting ethnic eateries (Thai, Chinese, and Indian). **Cobra Tandoori** is good for tasty Punjabi/Indian cuisine (€11-14 plates, daily 16:00-23:30, 69 Main Street, tel. 021/477-7911).

Fine Food near Charles Fort

Bulman Bar and Restaurant serves seafood with seasonal produce. The mussels are especially tasty; on a balmy day or evening, diners take a bucket and a beer out to the seawall. This is the only real way to eat on the water in Kinsale. The pub, strewn with fun decor and sporting a big fireplace, is also good for a coffee or beer after your visit to the fort (€14 lunches, €20-25 meals upstairs in fancy restaurant, daily 12:30-21:30, 200 yards toward Kinsale from Charles Fort in hamlet of Summercove, tel. 021/477-2131).

Nearby: Without a car (and weather permitting), enjoy Kinsale's best 45-minute stroll back into town—with great harbor views—on the Scilly Walk pedestrian trail (trailhead on left after climbing 200 yards up the steep road from Bulman Bar; look for *Scilly Walk* sign and large cement slabs that block confused cars from entering the trail).

Live Pub Music

Kinsale's pubs are packed with atmosphere and live music (though not always traditional Irish). Rather than target a certain place, simply walk the area between Guardwell, Pearse Street, and the Market Square. Pop into each pub that has live music, and then settle in your favorite. Several of the pubs wind deep into buildings. **An Seanachai** (SHAN-ah-key) means "storyteller" in Gaelic, but it's now known for its ballad music (Main Street).

Irish music purists will be rewarded if they take the five-minute taxi ride (€7 one-way) out to the **Bulman Bar** near the base of Charles Fort. This is Kinsale's best pub for traditional Irish music sessions (Wed-Sat at 21:30, Sun at 17:00, get there early to ensure a seat, see listing on page 173, tel. 021/477-2131). Otherwise, get your trad fix at the charmingly claustrophobic **Spaniard Inn,** a 10-minute walk out to the Scilly peninsula across the harbor from town. Its eye-catching golden walls fill the center of a hairpin turn on the crest of the peninsula (Wed at 21:30, you'll stand all night unless you arrive by 20:30, tel. 021/477-2436).

Kinsale Connections

Like many worthwhile corners of Ireland, Kinsale is not accessible by train. The closest train station is in Cork, 15 miles north. But buses run frequently between Kinsale (stop is on Pier Road, 100 yards behind TI, at south end of town) and Cork's bus station (9/day, 50 minutes, €7.50 one-way, €10.50 round-trip).

In **Cork,** the bus station and train station are a 10-minute walk apart. The bus station (corner of Merchant's Quay and Parnell Place) is on the south bank of the River Lee, just over the nearest bridge from the train station (north of the river on Lower Glanmire Road).

From Cork by Train to: Dublin (hourly, 2.75 hours, www.irishrail.ie).

From Cork by Bus to: Dublin (every 2 hours, 4.5 hours),

Galway (hourly, 4.25 hours), **Tralee** (hourly, 2.25 hours), **Kilkenny** (4-5/day, 2 direct, 3.5 hours). Bus info: tel. 021/450-8188 or www .buseireann.ie.

Cobh

If your ancestry is Irish, there's a good chance that this was the last Irish soil your ancestors had under their feet. Cobh (pronounced

"cove") was the major port of Irish emigration in the 19th century. Of the six million Irish who have emigrated to America, Canada, and Australia since 1815, nearly half left from Cobh.

The first steam-powered ship to make a transatlantic crossing departed from Cobh in 1838—cutting the journey time from 50 days to 18. When Queen Victoria came to Ireland for the first time in 1849, Cobh was the first Irish ground she set foot on. Giddy, the town renamed itself "Queenstown" in her honor. It was still going by that name in 1912, when the *Titanic* made its final fateful stop here before heading out on its maiden (and only) voyage. To celebrate their new independence from British royalty in 1922, locals changed the name back to its original Irish moniker: Cobh.

Orientation to Cobh

(area code: 012)
Cobh sits on a large island in Cork harbor. The town's inviting waterfront is colorful yet salty, with a playful promenade. The butcher's advertisement reads, "Always pleased to meet you and always with meat to please you." Stroll past the shops along the water. Ponder the *Lusitania* memorial on Casement Square and the modest *Titanic* memorial nearby on Pearse Square. A hike up the hill to the towering Neo-Gothic St. Colman's Cathedral rewards you with a fine view of the port.

Tourist Information: The TI is in the Old Yacht Club on the harbor (Mon-Fri 9:30-17:30, Sat-Sun 13:00-17:00, tel. 021/481-3301, www.cobhharbourchamber.ie). You can buy parking disks here or in local shops (first hour free, second hour-€1, 2-hour maximum parking anywhere in Cobh).

Post Office: It's at the back of the Centra Market (Mon-Fri 9:00-17:30, Sat 9:00-13:00, closed Sun, West Beach Street).

Cobh

To Cork
To Cuskinny East Ferry →

BISHOP STREET
PARK RD.
LAUNDRY HILL
JOHN O'CONNELL ST.
LAKE ROAD
WEST VIEW
OLD STREET
CASEMENT
100 Meters
100 Yards
WOLFE TONE ST.   ROCHE'S TERR.
ST. COLMAN'S CATHEDRAL
CATHEDRAL PL.   CHURCH ST.
HARBOUR HILL
RAHILLY ST.
SPY HILL
BURMA STEPS
Pearse Square
❺   ❻   ❹   CENTRA MARKET & POST
Casement Square   WEST BEACH   EAST BEACH
LYNCH'S QUAY
To Carrigloe & Cork
←
SPY HILL
WESTBOURNE PLACE
❷
❸
Ⓑ BUS TERMINUS
Cork Harbor
To Cork
TRAIN STATION
QUEENSTOWN STORY MUSEUM & HERITAGE CENTRE
❶

❶ Waters Edge Hotel & Restaurant
❷ Commodore Hotel
❸ Ard na Laoi B&B
❹ Taste Café
❺ Lusitania Memorial
❻ Titanic Memorial

Tours in Cobh

"Titanic Trail" Tours—Michael Martin leads one-hour walking tours of Cobh that give you unexpected insights into the tragic *Titanic* voyage, Spike Island (Ireland's Alcatraz), and Cobh's maritime history (€12.50, €9.50 if you show the 2011 edition of this book, daily at 11:00, meet at Commodore Hotel, call ahead to confirm tour times in winter, private tours available, tel. 021/481-5211 or mobile 087-276-7218, www.titanic.ie, info@titanic.ie).

Sights in Cobh

▲**The Queenstown Story**—Cobh's major sightseeing attraction, filling its harborside Victorian train station, is an earnest attempt to make the city's emigration and history interesting. The topics—the famine, Irish emigration, Australia-bound prison ships, the sinking of the *Lusitania*, and the ill-fated voyage of the *Titanic*—are interesting enough to make this museum a worthwhile stop. But the museum itself, while kid-friendly, is weak on actual historical artifacts. It reminds me of a big, interesting history picture book with the pages expanded and tacked on the wall (€7.10; May-Oct Mon-Fri 10:00-17:00, Sat-Sun 10:00-18:00; Nov-April daily 10:00-

17:00; last entry one hour before closing, tel. 021/481-3591).

Those with Irish roots to trace can use the Heritage Centre's **genealogy search service** (www.cobhheritage.com, info@cobh heritage.com).

Sleeping in Cobh

(€1 = about $1.25, country code: 353, area code: 021)
These hotels are all centrally located near the harbor, less than a five-minute walk from the Queenstown Story.

$$$ Waters Edge Hotel, located 50 yards from the Queenstown Story, has 19 bright, modern rooms and a pleasant harbor-view restaurant (Sb-€65-100, Db-€90-160, Tb-€120-180, Wi-Fi, Yacht Club Quay, tel. 021/481-5566, fax 021/481-2011, www.watersedgehotel.ie, info@watersedgehotel.ie).

$$ Commodore Hotel is a grand 150-year-old historic land-mark with 42 rooms. This place was once owned by the wealthy German Humbert family, who opened it up to *Lusitania* refu-gees after the 1915 sinking. Its high-ceilinged rooms creak with Victorian character (Sb-€57-65, Db-€114-130, Tb-€175-195, Westbourne Place, tel. 021/481-1277, fax 021/481-1672, www .commodorehotel.ie, commodorehotel@eircom.net).

$ Ard na Laoi B&B is a friendly place with five modest rooms in a great central location (Sb-€50, Db-€60-70, Tb-€90-105, 15 Westbourne Place, tel. 021/481-2742, www.ardnalaoi.ie, info@ardna laoi.ie, Michael O'Shea).

Eating in Cobh

I like the **Jacob's Ladder** restaurant in the Waters Edge Hotel. Along the waterfront, you'll find a variety of pubs serving decent grub. **Taste** is a hip little sandwich joint, a couple of doors down from the Titanic Memorial. For picnic fixings, there's the **Centra Market** (Mon-Sat 8:00-22:00, Sun 9:00-20:00, facing the water on West Beach Street).

Cobh Connections

By Car: Driving to Cobh from Cork or Waterford, leave N-25 about eight miles east of Cork, following little R-624 over a bridge, onto the Great Island, and directly into Cobh.

Kinsale to Cobh is 25 miles, takes an hour, and involves catch-ing a small ferry. Leave Kinsale north on R-600 toward Cork. Just south of Cork and its airport, go east on R-613. You will be follow-ing little *car-ferry* signs, but they ultimately take you to the wrong ferry (Ringaskiddy—to France). After you hit N-28, take R-610

KINSALE & COBH

to Monkstown and then Glenbrook, where a (poorly signposted) shuttle ferry takes you to Carrigloe on the Great Island (€5, 5 minutes, daily 7:00-22:00). Once on the island, turn right and drive two miles into Cobh. In Cobh, follow the *Heritage Centre* signs to The Queenstown Story, where you'll find easy parking at the museum (buy parking disks at nearby TI, first hour free, second hour-€1, 2-hour maximum).

By Plane: Cork Airport has become an increasingly handy entry point into (or exit point from) Ireland. Located four miles south of Cork city (on N-27/R-600 to Kinsale, a 30-minute drive away), it offers connecting flights from London Heathrow on Aer Lingus, London Stansted on Ryanair, and Belfast on Aer Arann. More distant connections can be made from Munich, Amsterdam, Paris, Warsaw, and Málaga (tel. 021/431-3131, www.corkairport .com).

To sleep near Cork Airport, consider **$$ Radisson Blu Cork Airport** (Db-€129 Mon-Thu, €110 Fri-Sun, best prices if booked online, tel. 021/494-7500, www.radissonblu.com).

More Sights in and near County Cork

These sights are convenient stops when connecting Kinsale and Cobh with Waterford (to the east) or the Ring of Kerry (to the west).

Between Waterford and Kinsale

If you're driving from Waterford (see previous chapter) to Cobh and Kinsale, you can easily visit these sights just off N-25 (listed roughly from east to west).

Ardmore

This funky little beach resort, with a famous ruined church and round tower, is a handy stop (just west of Youghal, 3 miles south of N-25 between Waterford and Cobh). A couple of buses run daily from Ardmore to Cork and to Waterford.

This humble little port town is just a line of pastel houses that appear frightened by the sea. Its beach claims (very modestly) to be "the most swimmable in Ireland."

The town's historic claim to fame: Christianity came to Ireland here first (thanks to St. Declan, who arrived in A.D. 416—15 years before St. Patrick...but with a weaker public-relations team). As if to proclaim that feat with an 800-year-old exclamation mark, one of Ireland's finest examples of a round tower stands perfectly intact, 97 feet above an evocative graveyard and a ruined church (noted for the faint remains of some early Christian carvings on its west facade). You can't get into the tower—the entrance is 14 feet off the ground.

An easy, scenic coastal loop hike (3 miles, 1 hour) leads from the parking lot of the ritzy Cliff House Hotel along the coast, eventually cutting inland and back into town (simple to follow, ask for free rudimentary map in newsstand at end of Main Street).

Sleeping in Ardmore: **$$$ Cliff House Hotel** is a died-and-gone-to-heaven splurge with 39 impeccably modern rooms, all with ocean views (Db-€170-225, Wi-Fi, tel. 024/87800, www.thecliffhousehotel.com, info@thecliffhousehotel.com).

$$ Round Tower Hotel, a sedate and traditional 12-room place, is a safe bet in town (Sb-€55-60, Db-€90-100, on R-673 leading west out of town, tel. 024/94494, rth@eircom.net).

$ Duncrone B&B has four vividly colorful rooms run by Jeanette Dunne (Sb-€45, Db-€65, Tb-€100, Wi-Fi, cash only, half-mile outside of town, up past the round tower, tel. 024/94860, www.duncronebandb.com, info@duncronebandb.com).

$ Roseville House is covered in ivy, with three pleasant rooms tended to by Pat Power (Sb-€35, Db-€60, cash only, in town 200 yards below the round tower, tel. 024/94430, mobile 087-248-7164).

Eating in Ardmore: The local favorite is **White Horses Restaurant** (Tue-Sun 11:00-22:00, closed Mon, Main Street, tel. 024/94040). For a fine lunch or dinner with cliff-perch views, check out the restaurant in the luxurious **Cliff House Hotel** (turn right at the coastal end of Main Street and drive up narrow lane to dead end, tel. 024/87800). **An Tobar,** the only pub in town, is down near the water.

▲Old Midleton Distillery

Sometime during your Ireland trip, even if you're a teetotaler, you'll want to tour a whiskey distillery. Of the three major dis-

tillery tours (this one, Jameson in Dublin, and Bushmills in Northern Ireland), the Midleton experience is the most interesting. After a 10-minute video, you'll walk with a guide through a great old 18th-century plant on a 45-minute tour; see waterwheel-powered crankshafts and a 31,000-gallon copper still—the largest of its kind in the world; and learn the story of whiskey. Predictably, you finish in a tasting room and enjoy a free, not-so-wee glass. The finale is a Scotch vs. Irish whiskey taste test. Your guide will take two volunteers for this. Don't be shy—raise your hand like an eager little student and enjoy an opportunity to taste the different brands.

Cost and Hours: Tour-€13.50, daily 10:00-18:00 year-round, last tour at 17:00, 2/hour in summer, 3/day in winter, on-site cafeteria, tel. 021/461-3594, www.jamesonwhiskey.com.

Location: It's 12 miles east of Cork in Midleton, about a mile off N-25, the main Cork-Waterford road. There's easy parking—just drive right into the distillery lot.

Between Kinsale and Killarney

If you're driving between Kinsale and the Ring of Kerry (see next chapter), you can easily visit these sights (listed from east to west).

Blarney Stone and Castle

The town of Blarney is of no importance, and the 15th-century Blarney Castle is an empty hulk (with no effort put forth to make it meaningful or interesting). It's only famous as the place of tourist pilgrimage, where busloads line up to kiss a stone on its top rampart and get "the gift of gab." The stone's origin is shrouded in myth (it was either brought back from the Holy Land by crusaders, or perhaps was part of Scotland's royal Stone of Scone). The best thing about this lame sight is the opportunity to watch a cranky man lower lemming tourists over the edge, belly up and head back, to kiss the stone while his partner snaps a photo—which will be available for purchase back at the parking lot. After a day of tour groups mindlessly climbing up here to perform this ritual, the stone is literally slathered with spit and lipstick.

The tradition goes back to the late 16th century, when Queen Elizabeth I was trying to plant loyal English settlers in Ireland to tighten her grip on the rebellious island. She demanded that the Irish clan chiefs recognize the crown, rather than the clan chiefs, as the legitimate titleholder of all lands. One of those chiefs was Cormac MacCarthy, Lord of Blarney Castle (who was supposedly loyal to the Queen). He was smart enough never to disagree with the Queen—instead, he would cleverly avoid acquiescing to her demands by sending a never-ending stream of lengthy and deceptive excuses, disguised with liberal doses of flattery (while subtly maintaining his native Gaelic loyalties). In her frustration, the Queen declared his endless words nothing but "blarney." Walking back, you'll cross a stream littered with American pennies—as if the good-luck fairy can change them into euros.

While the castle is unimpressive, the gardens are beautiful, well-kept, and picnic-worthy (if you are there anyway). There are even some hints of Ireland's pre-Christian past on the grounds; you can see dolmens beside the trail in the forested Rock Close.

Cost and Hours: €10, Mon-Sat 9:00-18:30, Sun 9:30-17:30, later in peak season, shorter hours in winter, free parking lot, helpful TI, tel. 021/438-5252, www.blarney castle.ie.

Location: It's five miles northwest of Cork, the major city in south Ireland. Looking for shopping galore? Adjacent Blarney Woolen Mills has it all (right next to the castle parking lot).

Macroom

This colorful, inviting market town is a handy stop between Cork and Killarney. The ghostly gateway of its ruined castle (once owned by the father of the William Penn who founded Pennsylvania) overlooks its entertaining main square, where you'll find plenty of parking. The 2006 Irish Civil War saga *The Wind That Shakes the Barley* was filmed in this area. Macroom makes for an excellent coffee or lunch stop midway between Cork and Killarney. The Next Door Café, next to Castle Hotel, serves a good, fast lunch.

KENMARE
and the RING OF KERRY

It's no wonder that, since Victorian times, visitors have been attracted to this dramatic chunk of Ireland. Mysterious ancient ring forts stand sentinel on mossy hillsides. A beloved Irish statesman maintained his ancestral estate here, far from 19th-century power politics. And early Christian hermit monks left a lonely imprint of their devotion, in the form of simple stone dwellings atop an isolated rock crag far from shore...a holy retreat on the edge of the then-known world.

Today, it seems like every tour bus in Ireland makes the ritual loop around the scenic Ring of Kerry, using the bustling and famous tourist town of Killarney as a springboard. I prefer to skip Killarney (useful only for its transportation connections). Instead, make the tidy town of Kenmare your home base, and use my suggestions to cleverly circle the much-loved peninsula—entirely missing the convoy of tour buses.

Kenmare

Cradled in a lush valley, this charming little town (known as Neidín, or "Little Nest," in Gaelic) hooks you right away with its rows of vividly colored shop fronts and go-for-a-stroll atmosphere. Its fresh appearance won it Ireland's "Tidy Town" award in 2000, and the nearby finger of the gentle sea feels more like a large lake (called the Kenmare River, just to confuse things). Far from the assembly-line tourism of Killarney town, Kenmare (rhymes with "chair") also makes a great launchpad for enjoying the sights along the road around the Iveragh (eev-er-AH) Peninsula—known to shamrock-lovers everywhere as the Ring of Kerry.

Planning Your Time

All you need in compact Kenmare is one night and a couple of hours to wander the town. Check out the Heritage Centre (in the back rooms of the TI) to get an overview of the region's history. Visit the Kenmare Lace and Design Centre (above TI, entry next door) to get a close look at its famously delicate lace. Hands-on access to an ancient stone circle is just a five-minute walk from the edge of town. Finish up by taking a peek inside Holy Cross Church to see the fine ceiling woodwork. Don't stay out too late in the pubs if you'd like to get an early start on the Ring of Kerry in the morning.

Orientation to Kenmare

(area code: 064)

Carefully planned Kenmare is shaped like an "X," forming two triangles. The upper (northern) triangle contains the town square

(colorful markets Wed and Fri in summer), the adjacent TI and Heritage Centre, and a cozy park. The lower (southern) triangle contains three one-way streets busy with shops, lodgings, and restaurants. Use the tall Holy Cross Church spire to get your bearings (next to the northeast parking lot, public WCs across the street).

Tourist Information

The helpful TI is on the town square (July-Aug daily 9:00-19:00; May-June and Sept Mon-Sat 9:00-18:00, Sun 10:00-18:00; closed Oct-April; tel. 064/664-1233).

Helpful Hints

Banking: Bank of Ireland faces the town square, and **Allied Irish Bank** takes up the corner of Henry and Main streets (both open Mon 10:00-17:00, Tue-Fri 10:00-16:00, closed Sat-Sun).

Internet Access: You'll find three terminals inside the front window of Murphy's Daybreak Supermarket on Main Street (€1.50/30 minutes), and another three in the post office (€2/30 minutes).

Post Office: It's located on Henry Street, at the intersection with Shelbourne Street (Mon-Fri 9:00-17:30, Sat 10:00-13:00,

Kenmare

Not to Scale

1 Lansdowne Arms Hotel
2 Sallyport House
3 Hawthorn House & Kenmare Fáilte Hostel
4 Willow Lodge
5 Whispering Pines B&B
6 Virginia's Guesthouse & Mulcahy's Wine Bar
7 Rockcrest House
8 Limestone Lodge
9 Watersedge B&B
10 To Parknasilla Hotel & Ring of Kerry Golf
11 Jam Deli
12 The Purple Heather
13 Café Mocha
14 The Lime Tree Rest.
15 Packies Restaurant
16 Horse Shoe Pub & Rest.
17 P. F. McCarthy's Pub & Rest.
18 Crowley's Pub
19 Foley's Pub
20 Supermarket
21 Launderette
22 Bike Rental
23 To River Valley Riding Stables
24 To Star Sailing (Boat Rental)

closed Sun).

Laundry: O'Shea's Cleaners and Launderette is the only option in town (Mon-Fri 8:30-17:30, Sat 9:30-17:30, closed Sun, a mile north of town on N-71 in Kenmare Business Park, tel. 064/664-1394).

Bike Rental: Finnegan's Corner rents bikes and has route maps and advice on maximizing scenery and minimizing traffic (€15/day, €20/24 hours; Mon-Sat 9:30-18:30, July-Aug until 19:00; Sun 12:00-18:00, leave ID for deposit, office in gift shop at 37 Henry Street, across from post office, tel. 064/664-1083).

Parking: The town's two largest public parking lots (free overnight) cling to the two main roads departing town to the north (otherwise free street parking is allowed for 2 hours).

Taxi: Try **Murnane Cabs** (mobile 087-236-4353) or **Kenmare Coach and Cab** (mobile 087-248-0800).

Tours in Kenmare

Finnegan's Tours—This company runs a variety of local day tours, departing from the TI at 10:00 and returning by 17:00. While this is little more than a scenic joyride, the tour guide gives a fun, anecdotal narration and generally makes three rest stops and one sightseeing stop (route depends on day: Ring of Kerry on Mon, Wed, and Fri; Ring of Beara on Tue; Glengarriff and Garnish Island on Thu; €25 for any tour, reserve a day in advance, can book private tours for small groups with enough notice, tel. 064/664-1491, mobile 087-248-0800, www.kenmarecoachandcab .com, kenmarecoachandcab@eircom.net).

Sights in Kenmare

Heritage Centre—This museum, in the back rooms of the TI, consists of a series of storyboards and a model of the planned town. A 20-minute visit here explains the nearby ancient stone circle, as well as the history of Kenmare's lacemaking fame and feisty, troublemaking nun—see the "Kenmare's History" sidebar (free, May-Oct Mon-Sat 9:00-18:00, Sun 10:00-18:00, closed Nov-April, tel. 064/664-1233).

Kenmare Lace and Design Centre—A single large room (above the TI) displays the delicate lacework that put Kenmare on the modern map. From the 1860s until World War I, the Poor Clare convent at Kenmare became the center of excellence for Irish lacemaking. Inspired by antique Venetian lace, but creating their own unique designs, nuns taught needlepoint lacemaking as a trade to girls in a region struggling to get back on its feet in the wake of

KENMARE

Kenmare's History: Axes, Xs, Nuns, and Lace

Bronze Age people (2000 B.C.), attracted to this valley for its abundant game and fishing, stashed their prized axe heads and daggers in hidden hoards. Almost 4,000 years later (in 1930), a local farmer from the O'Sullivan clan pried a bothersome boulder from one of his fields and discovered it to be a lid for a collection of rare artifacts that are now on display in the National Museum in Dublin (the "Killaha hoard"). The O'Sullivans (Gaelic for "descendants of the one-eyed") were for generations the dominant local clan, and you'll still see their name on many Kenmare shop fronts.

Oliver Cromwell's bloody Irish campaign (1649), which subdued most of Ireland, never reached Kenmare. However, Cromwell's chief surveyor, William Petty, knew good land when he saw it and took a quarter of what is now County Kerry as payment for his valuable services, marking the "lands down" on maps. His heirs, the Lansdownes, created Kenmare as a model 18th-century estate town and developed its distinctive "X" street plan. William Petty-Fitzmaurice, the first Marquis of Lansdowne and landlord of Kenmare, became the British Prime Minister who negotiated the peace that ended the American War of Independence in 1783.

Sister Margaret Cusack, aka Sister Mary Francis Clare, lived in the town from 1862 to 1881, becoming the famous Nun of Kenmare. Her controversial religious life began when she decided to become an Anglican nun after her fiancé's sudden death. Five years later, she converted to Catholicism, joined the Poor Clare order as Sister Mary Francis Clare, and moved with the order to Kenmare. She became an outspoken writer who favored women's rights and lambasted the tyranny of the landlords during the famine. She eventually took church funds and attempted to set herself up as abbess of a convent in Knock. Her renegade behavior led to her leaving the Catholic faith, converting back to Protestantism, writing an autobiography, and lecturing about the "sinister influence of the Roman Church."

After the devastation of the Great Potato Famine (1845-1849), an industrial school was founded in Kenmare to teach trades to destitute youngsters. The school, run by the Poor Clare sisters, excelled in teaching young girls the art of lacemaking. Inspired by lace created earlier in Italy, Kenmare lace caught the eye of Queen Victoria and became much coveted by Victorian society. Examples of it are now on display in the Victoria and Albert Museum (London), the Irish National Museum (Dublin), and the US National Gallery (Washington, DC).

KENMARE

the catastrophic famine. Queen Victoria commissioned five pieces of lace in 1885, and by the end of the century, tourists began visiting Kenmare on their way to Killarney just for a peek at the lace. Nora Finnegan, who runs the center, usually has a work in progress to demonstrate the complexity of fine lacemaking to visitors (free, May-mid-Oct Mon-Sat 10:15-13:00 & 14:15-17:30, closed Sun and mid-Oct-April, tel. 064/664-2636, www.kenmarelace.ie).

Ancient Stone Circle—Of the 100 stone circles that dot southwest Ireland (Counties Cork and Kerry), this is one of the biggest and most accessible (5-minute walk from TI, drop €2 into honor box when attendant away, always open). More than 3,000 years old, it may have been used both as a primitive calendar and a focal point for rituals. The circle has a diameter of 50 feet and consists of 15 stones ringing a large center boulder (probably a burial monument). Experts think this stone circle (like most) functioned as a celestial calendar—it tracked the position of the setting sun to determine the two solstices (in June and December), which mark the longest and shortest days of the year.

Getting There: From the city center, face the TI, turn left, and walk 200 yards down Market Street, passing a row of cute 18th-century houses on your right. Beyond the row of houses, veer right through an unmarked modern gate mounted in stone columns, and continue 50 yards down the paved road. You'll see the circle on your right.

Holy Cross Church—Finished in 1864, this is Kenmare's grand Catholic church. It's worth visiting to see the ornate wooden ceiling with 10 larger-than-life angels (carved in Germany's Black Forest).

Horseback Riding—River Valley Riding Stables offers day treks for all levels of experience through beautiful hill scenery in the Roughty River Valley (€20/hour, discounts for groups, open long hours, located about 7 miles east of Kenmare off R-569 near Kilgarvan, tel. 064/668-5360, rivervalleystables@hotmail.com).

Boating and Hiking—Star Sailing rents boats, gives sailing lessons, and organizes hill walks. Hop on a small two-person sailboat (€40/hour) or canoe (€25/hour), or kick around in a kayak (€25/hour). Phone ahead to reserve boats or ask about hikes (located 5 miles southwest of Kenmare on R-571 on Beara Peninsula, courtesy shuttle can pick you up in Kenmare, tel. 064/664-1222, www.staroutdoors.ie; adjacent Con's Restaurant is open daily 12:00-21:00).

Beara: The Other Peninsula

This sleepy, yet scenic, wedge of land (just south of Kenmare) deserves honorable mention as a distant third choice after the Dingle and Ring of Kerry peninsulas. But locals rave about it like we would our home sports team. If you have the luxury of two nights in Kenmare, Beara is worth considering. If you don't have a full day to spare, a memorable half-day can be spent enjoying Garnish Island and Healy Pass, skipping the rest of the peninsula.

Garnish Island is a rocky island refuge, cloaked in garden splendor, plopped down in the corner of Bantry Bay. Crowned by a stout martello tower (a bunker built to repel feared Napoleonic invasions, free to climb for views), the gardens were the creation of a rich landlord, who turned the barren 37 acres into a lushly vegetated fantasy in the early 1900s. You'll meander past Italian reflecting pools, a Grecian temple framing views of a placid bay, and a walled garden nursery clad in roses. Pine-forested trails, punctuated with rhododendrons, connect it all. Boats depart from the well-marked pier in Glengarriff, about 18 miles (30 km) south of Kenmare, for the scenic 15-minute cruise past seal-sunning rocks to the island (boat-€12 round-trip, 3/hour; gardens-€4, March-Oct daily 9:30-17:30; tea room, snacks, and WCs at island's pier; tel. 027/63116, www.harbourqueenferry.com).

A narrow, eight-mile mountain road (R-574) feels like a toboggan run as it squiggles over the peninsula's lumpy spine at **Healy Pass.** The views from the 1,000-foot summit make you marvel at the road-building skills of the famine-era workmen. The road linked the north coast (County Kerry)

Golfing—Another way to experience Ireland's 40 shades of green is to splurge on a scenic day on the links. The Kenmare Golf Club is right on the edge of town (greens fees Mon-Fri €35, Sat-Sun €45, on R-569 toward Cork, tel. 064/664-1291). Or try the Ring of Kerry Golf and Country Club (greens fees-€50, 4 miles west of town on N-70, pre-booking advisable on weekends, tel. 064/664-2000, www.ringofkerrygolf.com).

Nightlife in Kenmare

Music in Pubs

Wander the entire Kenmare town triangle and stick your head in wherever you hear something you like. Music usually starts at

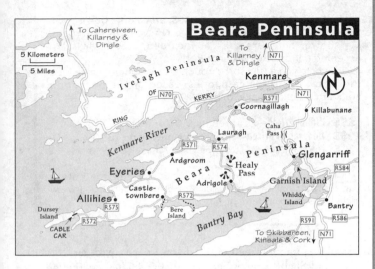

to the south coast (County Cork) to facilitate food-relief deliveries 165 years ago. The barren, rocky landscape makes it easy to spot approaching cars (remember to look up on hairpin turns). Be cooperative by pulling over at wide spots to allow safe passage, and honk to alert other cars as you approach blind, rocky curves.

The rest of the peninsula is pastoral in the middle and edged with scenic cliffs near the tip. Ireland's only cable car connects the headland with mellow Dursey Island. Castletownbere (on the south coast) is a fishing port with plenty of pubs for lunch. Allihies and Eyeries (on the north coast) are two of the most colorfully painted towns in Ireland, splattered with pastels and vivid hues.

21:30 (although some pubs have early 18:30 sessions—ask at the TI) and ranges from Irish traditional sessions to sing-along strummers. **Crowley's** is an atmospheric little shoebox of a pub with an unpretentious clientele. **Foley's** jug-stacked window invites you in for a folksy songfest. The Lansdowne Arms Hotel (described next) sponsors live traditional sessions in their **Bold Thady Quill Bar.**

Sleeping in Kenmare

$$$ Lansdowne Arms Hotel is the town's venerable grand hotel, with generous public spaces. This centrally located, 200-year-old historical landmark rents 26 large, crisp rooms (Sb-€50-85, Db-€90-150, Tb-€165-225; online discounts, most rooms

KENMARE

Sleep Code

(€1 = about $1.25, country code: 353, area code: 064)
S = Single, **D** = Double/Twin, **T** = Triple, **Q** = Quad, **b** = bathroom,
s = shower only. Breakfast is included; credit cards are
accepted unless otherwise noted.

To help you easily sort through these listings, I've divided
the rooms into three categories, based on the price for a
standard double room with bath:

$$$ **Higher Priced**—Most rooms €100 or more.
$$ **Moderately Priced**—Most rooms between €75-100.
$ **Lower Priced**—Most rooms €75 or less.

Prices can change without notice; verify the hotel's
current rates online or by email. For other updates, see www
.ricksteves.com/update.

non-smoking, music in pub until late on Fri-Sat, parking, corner
of Main and Shelbourne Streets, tel. 064/664-1368, fax 064/664-
1114, www.lansdownearms.com, info@lansdownearms.com).

$$$ Sallyport House, an elegantly quiet house with five
rooms filled with antique furniture, has been in Helen Arthur's
family for generations. Ask her to point out the foot-worn door-
step that was salvaged from the local workhouse and built into her
stone chimney (Sb-€70-110, Db-€110-140, Tb-€150-180, closed
Nov-mid-March, cash only, no kids, non-smoking, parking,
5-minute walk south of town before crossing Our Lady's Bridge,
tel. 064/664-2066, fax 064/664-2067, www.sallyporthouse.com,
port@iol.ie).

$$ Hawthorn House is a fine, modern, freestanding house
with a lounge, a warm and classy hostess, and 10 comfy rooms
sporting fine woodwork courtesy of Mr. O'Brien, who's also a
carpenter. Its quiet residential location is just a block from all the
pub and restaurant action (Db-€90-100, Tb-€120-140, Qb-€140,
may be cheaper when slow, Wi-Fi, ample parking, Shelbourne
Street, tel. 064/664-1035, www.hawthornhousekenmare.com, info
@hawthornhousekenmare.com, Mary and Noel O'Brien). Their
two modern, self-catering apartments next door work well for
those wanting to linger (weekly rentals).

$$ Willow Lodge, on the main road at the edge of town,
feels American-suburban, with a chatty and friendly hostess and
seven comfortable rooms (Sb-€60-90, Db-€90-100, Tb-€150, cash
only, non-smoking, Wi-Fi, parking, 100 yards beyond Holy Cross
Church, tel. 064/664-2301, www.willowlodgekenmare.com, wil-
lowlodgekenmare@yahoo.com, Gretta Gleeson-O'Byrne).

$$ Whispering Pines B&B rents five rooms with sincere, traditional Irish hospitality in a spacious Irish house (Sb-€60, Db-€76-84, Tb-€110, cash only, non-smoking, Wi-Fi, at the edge of town on Bell Height, tel. 064/664-1194, wpines@eircom.net, John and Mary Fitzgerald).

$$ Virginia's Guesthouse is well-kept and ideally located near the best restaurants. Its eight rooms, in an older building, are freshly renovated, roomy, and appealing (Sb-€40-70, Db-€60-90, Tb-€90-130, non-smoking, Wi-Fi, upstairs above Mulcahy's Wine Bar on Henry Street, tel. 064/664-1021, www.virginias-kenmare.com, virginias@eircom.net).

$ Rockcrest House is secluded down a quiet, leafy lane, with six large rooms and a fine front-porch view (Sb-€35-50, Db-€60-80, Tb-€90-110, cash only, non-smoking, Wi-Fi; as you pass the TI heading north out of town, take the first left after crossing the bridge; tel. 064/664-1248, www.rockcresthouse.com, dodwy@eircom.net, Marian and David O'Dwyer). Ask about their two self-catering cottage rentals.

$ Limestone Lodge stands rock-solid beside a holy well, with four comfy rooms in a quiet location. Friendly hostess Siobhan Thomas is an expert on Kenmare's famous lace (Sb-€45, Db-€70, Tb-€99, Qb-€132, cash only, all non-smoking, Wi-Fi, tel. 064/664-2231, mobile 087-757-4411, www.limestonelodgekenmare.com, info@limestonelodgekenmare.com).

$ Watersedge B&B is in a new building a mile south of town, isolated on a forested hillside and overlooking the estuary. It has four clean, colorful rooms and a kid-pleasing backyard (Sb-€45-50, Db-€64-70, Tb-€75-85, cash only, non-smoking, Wi-Fi, parking, tel. 064/664-1707, mobile 087-413-4235, www.watersedgekenmare.com, watersedgekenmare@gmail.com, Noreen O'Shea). To get here, drive south over Our Lady's Bridge, stay on the road (bearing left), look for the sign, and turn into the driveway on the right. Go a couple of hundred yards up the bumpy paved road, then—at the end of the white cinder-block wall (on left)—turn right onto the gravel lane and drive a hundred yards to the dead-end.

$ Kenmare Fáilte Hostel (fawl-chuh) maintains 40 budget beds in a well-kept, centrally located building with more charm than most hostels (dorm beds-€18 in rooms without bath, D-€44, Db-€52, T-€60, Tb-€69, Q-€76, Qb-€88, closed Nov-April, Shelbourne Street, tel. 064/664-2333, www.kenmare.eu/failtehostel, failtefinn@eircom.net).

Sleeping in Luxury out on the Ring of Kerry
$$$ Parknasilla Hotel is a 19th-century luxury hotel lost in 300 plush acres of a subtropical park overlooking the wild Atlantic Ocean. The tranquility, combined with old-fashioned service and

Victorian elegance, makes this a good stop for anyone interested in luxuriating on the Ring of Kerry. Originally an old railroad hotel for Romantic Age tourists, in recent decades it's been a ritual splurge for Irish families (Db-€159 with breakfast, higher July-Aug, croquet, 19th-century diversions, park walks, see website for details and their complex pricing scheme, tel. 064/667-5600, www.parknasillahotel.ie).

Eating in Kenmare

This friendly little town offers plenty of quality choices. If dining, make a reservation or get a table early, as many finer places book up later in the evening during the summer. Pub dinners are a good value and easier on the budget, but their kitchens close earlier than restaurants.

Lunch
Soup-and-sandwich lunch options abound. **Jam** is a handy deli that can make sandwiches or wraps to go for picnics (Mon-Sat 8:00-18:00, closed Sun, Henry Street). **The Purple Heather** has great salads and omelets (€9-15 meals, Mon-Sat 11:00-18:00, closed Sun, Henry Street, tel. 064/664-1016). **Café Mocha** is a basic €5 sandwich shop (Mon-Fri 9:00-17:30, Sat-Sun 10:00-17:00, on the town square, tel. 064/664-2133). **Murphy's Daybreak** supermarket is a good place to stock up for a Ring of Kerry picnic (Mon-Sat 8:00-22:00, Sun 8:00-21:00, Main Street).

Dinner
The Lime Tree Restaurant occupies the former Lansdowne Estate office, which gave more than 4,000 people free passage to America in the 1840s. These days, it serves delicious, locally caught seafood dishes in a modern yet cozy dining hall. It's wise to reserve ahead (€21-29 meals, April-Oct daily 18:30-21:30, closed Nov-March, Shelbourne Street, tel. 064/664-1225).

Packies is a popular bistro with a leafy, low-light interior and cottage ambience serving traditional cuisine with French influence. Their seafood gets rave reviews (€20-30 meals, Mon-Sat 18:00-22:00, closed Sun, reservations wise, Henry Street, tel. 064/664-1508).

Mulcahy's Wine Bar has a jazz-mellowed, elegant ambience and creatively presented gourmet dishes. Chef Bruce Mulcahy's "fusion cuisine" is inspired by his travels, with Indian, Japanese, and American influences, and there's always a good vegetarian entrée (€18-28 meals, daily 18:00-22:00, reservations smart, 36 Henry Street, tel. 064/664-2383, mobile 087-236-4449).

Horse Shoe Pub and Restaurant, specializing in steak and spareribs, somehow turns rustic farm-tool decor into a romantic candlelit sanctuary (€17-25 meals, Mon-Fri 12:00-15:00 & 17:00-22:00, Sat-Sun 17:00-22:00, Main Street, tel. 064/664-1553).

P. F. McCarthy's Pub and Restaurant, which feels like a sloppy saloon, serves reasonable salad or sandwich lunches and filling dinner fare. Their barbecued-ribs meal (€15) is a fine value (€14-22 meals, Mon-Sat 10:30-21:00, closed Sun, 14 Main Street, tel. 064/664-1516).

Kenmare Connections

Kenmare has no train station (the nearest is in Killarney, 20 miles away) and only a few bus connections (www.buseireann.ie). Most buses transfer in Killarney (described next).

From Kenmare by Bus to: Killarney (3/day, 45 minutes), **Tralee** (3/day, 2 hours), **Dingle** (3/day, 3 hours, change in Killarney), **Kinsale** (4/day, 4-5 hours, 2 changes), **Dublin** (3/day, 7.5 hours, change in Killarney and Limerick).

Near Kenmare

These attractions are near Kenmare, at the eastern (inland) end of the Ring of Kerry. If you're approaching the region from Kinsale and Cobh, drive through Killarney and visit Muckross House and Muckross Traditional Farms (near the lakes), as well as Kissane Sheep Farm (in the mountains), the day before you make the big Ring of Kerry loop. This plan allows you to get an early start from Kenmare and helps you avoid all the bus traffic on the Ring.

Killarney

Killarney is a household word among American tourists. And it seems to be on every big-bus tour itinerary. Springing from the bus and train station of this thriving regional center are a few colorful streets lined with tourist-friendly shops and restaurants. Killarney's suburbs sprawl with vast hotels that, except for the weather, feel more like Nebraska than Ireland. Killarney's elegant Neo-Gothic church stands tall as if to say the town existed and mattered long before tourism. But then you realize it dates from 1880...just about when Romantic Age tourism here peaked. For non-shoppers, Killarney's charm is its location at the doorstep of Killarney National Park. And for any tour organizer, it's the logical jumping-off point for excursions around the famous Ring of Kerry peninsula.

If you're traveling in the region without a car, you'll have to stop here. The Killarney bus and train stations flank the big, modern Killarney Outlet Centre mall. (In some touristy parts

KENMARE

of Ireland, like this one, every other shopping center is called an "outlet"—implying factory-direct values.) If you have a layover between connections, walk five minutes straight out from the front of the mall, and check out Killarney's shop-lined High Street and New Street. The **TI** is a 15-minute walk from the train station, on Beech Street.

Killarney Connections
From Killarney Around the Ring of Kerry: Bus Éireann drives the loop around the Ring of Kerry from Killarney—suitable for a quick peek. While it generally stops only long enough to pick up and drop off travelers en route, there is a 50-minute stop in Sneem (€23, daily July-mid-Sept, departs the Killarney bus station at 12:45 and returns to Killarney at 17:45, no reservation needed). You can catch this same bus from Tralee at 11:50, returning to Tralee by 18:45 (€25).

    By Bus to: Kenmare (3/day, 45 minutes), **Tralee** (hourly, 40 minutes), **Dingle** (5/day, 1.5-2 hours, 2 direct, 3 with change in Tralee), **Shannon Airport** (6/day, 3.5 hours), **Dublin** (every 2 hours, 6 hours, change in Limerick). The bus station has a left-luggage desk. For bus schedules, call 01/836-6111 or visit www .buseireann.ie.

    By Train to: Tralee (8/day, 30 minutes), **Cork** (every 2 hours, 1.5 hours, most with change in Mallow), **Waterford** (2/day, 3 hours), **Dublin** (every 2 hours, 6/day on Sun, 3.5 hours, 1 direct in morning, rest with change in Mallow). For train schedules, call 01/836-6222 or visit www.irishrail.ie.

    To Muckross House: There's no bus service. You can hike 30 minutes (get directions from TI), rent a bike, hire a horse buggy, or catch a cab (€12).

Muckross House
Perhaps the best Victorian stately home you'll see in the Republic of Ireland, Muckross House (built in 1843) is magnificently set at the edge of Killarney National Park, adjacent to a fascinating open-air farm museum.

    Cost and Hours: €7 for house, €7 for farms, €12 combo-ticket includes both. House open daily 9:00-17:00, July-Aug until 19:00, shorter hours in winter, last entry one hour before closing; farms open May-Sept only; tel. 064/667-0144.

    Tours: The only way to see the interior of the house is to take the 45-minute guided tour, which gives more meaning to your visit (included with admission, offered frequently throughout the day). Book your tour as soon as you arrive (they can fill up). Then enjoy a walk in the gardens until your tour begins.

    Getting There: Muckross House is conveniently located

KENMARE

for a break on the long ride from Kinsale or Cashel to Dingle or Kenmare. From Killarney, follow signs to Kenmare, where you'll find Muckross House three miles south of town. As you approach from Killarney, you'll see a small parking lot two miles before the actual parking lot. This is used by horse-and-buggy bandits to hoodwink tourists into thinking they have to pay to clip-clop to the house. Giddy-up on by to find a big, safe, and free parking lot right at the mansion.

⊃ Site Overview: This regular stop on the tour-bus circuit includes several sights in one: the mansion, a set of traditional farms that show rural life in the 1930s, a fine garden idyllically set on a lake, and an information center for the national park. The poignant juxtaposition of the magnificent mansion and the humble farmhouses illustrates in a thought-provoking way the vast gap that once separated rich and poor in Ireland.

Muckross House takes you back to the Victorian period—the 19th-century boom time, when the sun never set on the British

Empire, and the Industrial Revolution (born in England) was chugging the world into the modern age. Of course, Ireland was a colony back then, with big-shot English landlords. During the Great Potato Famine of 1845-1849, most English gentry lived very well—profiting off the export of their handsome crops to lands with greater buying power—while a third of Ireland's population starved. You can read the Muckross House lord's defense on page 43 of the fine souvenir book.

Muckross House feels lived-in (and it was, until 1933). Its fine Victorian furniture is cluttered around the fireplace under Waterford Crystal chandeliers and lots of antlers. You'll see Queen Victoria's bedroom (ground floor, since she was afraid of house fires). Though they spent a couple of years preparing for her visit in 1861, she stayed only three nights.

The house exit takes you through an **information center** for Killarney National Park, with a relaxing 15-minute video on "Ireland's premier national park," featuring lots of geology, flora, and fauna (free, shown on request).

The **garden** is a hit for those with a green thumb, and a €1.50 guide booklet makes the nature trails interesting. A bright, modern cafeteria (with indoor/outdoor seating) faces the garden. The adjacent crafts shop shows weaving and pottery-making in action.

Muckross Traditional Farms consists of six different farmhouses showing what life was like in the 1930s. Several farms come with a person ready to feed you a little home-baked bread and reminisce about the old days. The farms are strung along a mile-long road, with an old bus shuttling those who don't want to hike (free, 4/hour).

For those interested in Irish farm life from the 1920s until electricity arrived in 1955, this is a great experience—but only if you engage the attendants in conversation. Each farm is staffed by a Kerry farmer who enjoys telling tales of life on the farm in the old days. They actually remember 1955, when they first got electricity. They'd pull on their rubber Wellington boots for safety and nervously "switch it on." Poor farmers could only afford electricity with the help of money from relatives in America. They'd have one bulb hanging from the ceiling and, later, one plug for a hot pot. Every table had a Sacred Heart of Jesus shrine above it. The plug went directly below it. No one dreamed of actually heating the house with electricity. Children slept six to a bed, "three up and three down...feet in your face." You'll learn what happened when you had the only radio in the area, and how one flagstone on the mud floor was enough for the fiddler and dancer to set the beat. Probe with your questions... get personal.

From Muckross House to Kissane Sheep Farm: As you drive south on N-71, Torc Waterfall is a couple of miles past Muckross House (a 10-minute walk from the parking lot, through one of the oldest oak forests in Ireland). Driving farther, you pass Black Valley, which separates you from a ridge with the highest point in Ireland (3,600 feet). This remote valley was the last chunk of Ireland to get electricity in 1978. The scenic pullout called Ladies View is worth a stop.

Kissane Sheep Farm

Animal lovers will enjoy an hour's visit to this hardworking 3,000-acre Irish farm, perched on a scenic slope above the Black Valley. John Kissane, whose family has raised sheep here for five generations, gives hands-on demonstrations of sheep shearing. His Dutch wife Anne explains the process and invites you to touch the pile of fresh wool afterward. You can feel the lanolin, which acts as natural waterproofing for the sheep and is extracted from the wool to sell to pharmaceutical firms (the price of wool is now so low, it's not worth selling otherwise). But the highlight of any visit is the demonstration of sheepherding by the highly alert family dogs (Border and Welsh collies trained here since puppyhood). John commands the dogs from afar using an array of verbal calls and hand signals.

Cost and Hours: €7, June-Aug daily 12:00-17:00, April-May and Sept by appointment only, closed Oct-March, on N-71 between Ladies View and Moll's Gap, tel. 064/663-4791, www.kissanesheepfarm.com, adoptasheep@eircom.net. Call ahead for demo times, which change depending on farm work.

From Kissane Sheep Farm to Kenmare: Continue driving south on N-71. Going over Moll's Gap (WCs and Avoca Café beside parking lot), you'll descend into Kenmare. The rugged, bare rock on either side of the road was rounded and smoothed by the grinding action of thousands of years of glaciers. In the distance to the north (on your right) you can see the Gap of Dunloe, a perfect example of a U-shaped glacial valley notch.

Ring of Kerry

The Ring of Kerry (the Iveragh Peninsula) has been the perennial breadwinner of Irish tourism for decades now. Lassoed by a winding coastal road (the Ring), this mountainous, lake-splattered region comes with breathtaking scenery and the highest peak in Ireland. While a virtual fleet of big, tourist-laden buses circles it each day, they all stay together and seem to stop at the same handful of attractions. Therefore, if you avoid those places at rush hour, the Ring feels remarkably unspoiled and dramatically isolated. Clever motorists, armed with a good map and a reliable alarm clock, can sidestep the crowds and enjoy one of the most rewarding days in Ireland.

Planning Your Time

More than twice the size of the Dingle Peninsula (see next chapter) and backed by a muscular tourism budget that promotes every sight as a "must-see," the Iveragh Peninsula can seem overwhelming. Be selective, and don't let them pull the turf over your eyes.

By Car: You can explore the Ring (primarily on N-70) in one satisfying day. Travelers linking overnights in Kinsale and Dingle can insert a night between them in Kenmare (a good base for enjoying the best of the Ring of Kerry). If visiting Muckross House and Kissane Sheep Farm, do so in the afternoon before arriving in Kenmare, to save all of the following day for the Ring.

KENMARE

The Ring of Kerry vs. the Dingle Peninsula

If I had to choose one spot to enjoy the small-town charm of traditional Ireland, it would be Dingle and its history-laden scenic peninsula. But the Ring of Kerry—a much bigger, more famous, and more touristed peninsula just to its south—is also great to visit. If you go to Ireland and don't see the famous Ring of Kerry, your uncle Pat will never forgive you. Here's a comparison to help with your itinerary planning.

Both peninsulas come with a scenic loop drive. Dingle's is 30 miles. The Ring of Kerry is 120 miles. Both loops come with lots of megalithic wonder. Dingle's prehistory is more intimate, with numerous little evocative stony structures. The Ring of Kerry's prehistory shows itself in three massive ring forts—far bigger than anything on Dingle.

Dingle town is the perfect little Irish burg—alive with traditional music pubs, an active fishing harbor, and the sturdy cultural atmosphere of a Gaeltacht. You can easily spend three fun nights here. In comparison, Kenmare (the best base for the Ring of Kerry loop) is pleasant but forgettable. Those spending a night on the west end of the Ring of Kerry find a rustic lack of charm in Portmagee (the base for a cruise to magical Skellig Michael).

Near Dingle, the heather- and moss-covered Great Blasket Island and the excellent Great Blasket Centre offer insights into the storytelling traditions and simple lives of hardy fisherfolk who—until 57 years ago—lived just off the tip of the Dingle Peninsula. Off the tip of the Ring of Kerry, Skellig Michael—a brutally rugged and remote chunk of rock in the Atlantic, with evocative medieval stone ruins of its long-gone hermit monks—is a world-class sight. But the Skellig Experience Centre near Portmagee on the mainland is unimpressive compared to Dingle's Great Blasket Centre.

Muckross House, with its fascinating open-air farmhouse museum and beautiful lake views of Killarney National Park, is on the eastern side of the Ring of Kerry. But it's also an efficient and natural stop for those driving between Kinsale and Dingle—so you can see it regardless of which scenic peninsula drive you take.

Both regions are beyond the reach of the Irish train system and require a car or bus service to access. Both offer memorable scenery, great restaurants, warm B&B hospitality, and similar prices. The bottom line: With limited time, choose Dingle. If you have a day or two to spare, the Ring of Kerry is also a delight.

Tackling the Kinsale-to-Dingle drive plus the Ring of Kerry, all in the same day, is doable—but you add about 2.5 hours of driving beyond the actual Ring, meaning you have little time to stop and enjoy what you came here to see.

If you're considering a boat trip out to the desperately remote and evocative island of Skellig Michael, you'll need to add another day to allow for an overnight in the Portmagee area...and hope for good weather.

By Public Transportation: You have three options for seeing the Ring of Kerry without a car, none of which is as enjoyable as driving the loop yourself: minibus tour from Kenmare (see page 185); big-bus tour from Killarney (TI tel. 064/663-1633); or public bus from Killarney (see page 194).

Driving the Ring of Kerry (Made Less Scary)

On a one-day visit to the Ring, I'd leave Kenmare by 8:30 and head clockwise (against the prevailing tour-bus traffic). Allow time for stops at Staigue Ring Fort (45 minutes) and Derrynane House (1 hour), and get to Waterville before noon. To entirely miss the chain of tour buses, which slithers (like a python swallowing a pig) counterclockwise around the Ring, get to Waterville by 11:00; shortly after that, leave the main drag for the Skellig Ring (with a road that's too narrow for big buses). By the time you rejoin the main route, the python has slunk by. On the last half of the route, there are two more hour-long stops: the Skellig Experience Centre and two additional big ring forts. For a stop-by-stop description of this route, see my self-guided driving tour on page 200.

The only downside of going against all the bus traffic is that, on the narrow parts of the Ring road, buses have the right-of-

way. There are lots of scenic-view pullouts, and it will be up to you to back up to the nearest wide spot in the road to let a less-nimble bus get through a tight curve. But with an early start, you can avoid these hassles: On my last circuit, I got to Waterville by 11:00, from where I slipped happily into the bus-free Skellig Ring...and didn't have to pass a single bus all day.

Smart drivers equip themselves with a good map before driving the Ring of Kerry loop. If you don't have one already, pick up the *Complete Road Atlas of Ireland* by Ordnance Survey (€13, sold in most TIs and bookstores in Ireland). The *Fir Tree Aerial* series provides a useful map that covers both the Iveragh (Ring of Kerry) and Dingle Peninsulas, giving you a bird's-eye feel for the terrain (€8, sold in many TIs and bookstores in County Kerry).

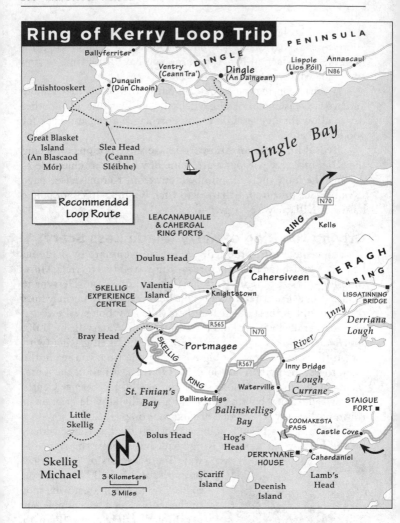

Ring of Kerry Loop Trip

DINGLE PENINSULA

Ballyferriter

Ventry (Ceann Tra')

Dunquin (Dún Chaoin)

Inishtooskert

Dingle (An Daingean)

Lispole (Lios Póil)

Annascaul

N86

Great Blasket Island (An Blascaod Mór)

Slea Head (Ceann Sléibhe)

Dingle Bay

Recommended Loop Route

LEACANABUAILE & CAHERGAL RING FORTS

N70

RING

Kells

Doulus Head

Cahersiveen

IVERAGH

SKELLIG EXPERIENCE CENTRE

Valentia Island

Knightstown

LISSATINNING BRIDGE

RING

Bray Head

R565

N70

Derriana Lough

Portmagee

SKELLIG

Inny River

R567

Inny Bridge

RING

St. Finian's Bay

Ballinskelligs

Waterville

Lough Currane

Little Skellig

Ballinskelligs Bay

STAIGUE FORT

COOMAKESTA PASS

Castle Cove

Bolus Head

Hog's Head

DERRYNANE HOUSE

Caherdaniel

Skellig Michael

N

3 Kilometers

3 Miles

Scariff Island

Deenish Island

Lamb's Head

KENMARE

The flat, inland, northeastern section of the Ring, from Killorglin to Killarney on N-72, is entirely skippable. Tank up before leaving, as gas in Kenmare is cheaper than out on the Ring.

Self-Guided Driving Tour

The Ring of Kerry

Here's a sightseeing tip sheet for my preferred clockwise route, kilometer by kilometer. If you do any exploring, you'll likely get hopelessly off, but the kilometer references still help—just do the arithmetic to figure out how far various stops are from each other. Several of these stops are explained in far greater detail later in this

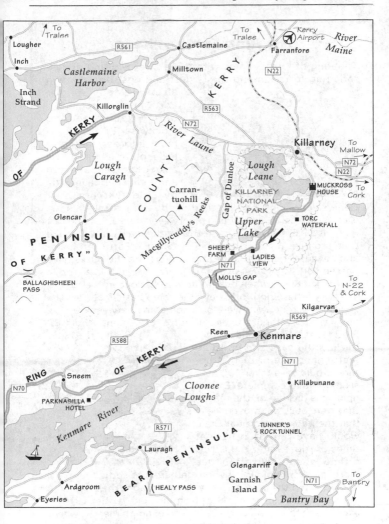

chapter, in the same order that they're listed here. To understand your options, read the rest of this chapter before you start on your tour.

0 km: Leave Kenmare.

17.6 km: On the right is Glacier Lake, with a long, smooth limestone "banister" carved by a glacier 10,000 years ago.

22.8 km: The recommended Parknasilla Hotel—a posh 19th-century hotel—is a great stop for tea and scones.

26 km: Visit the town of Sneem.

40.4 km: Turn off for the Staigue Ring Fort.

41.5 km: On the left, enjoy great views of the Beara Peninsula beyond a ruined hospital with IRA ties (it was funded in about

The Ring Forts of Kerry

The Ring of Kerry comes with three awe-inspiring prehistoric ring forts—among the largest and best-preserved in

all of Ireland. Staigue
Fort (near the beginning
of my recommended
clockwise Ring route) is
most impressive and in
a desolate setting. The
two others—Cahergal
and Leacanabuaile, side
by side just north of
Cahersiveen (closer to the end of the Ring, after Valentia
Island)—are easier to visit and plenty evocative. Each ring fort
is about a 2.5-mile (4-km) side-trip off the main drag. If you're
trying to beat the tour-bus convoy, Staigue Fort is problem-
atic because it eats up morning time before the buses have
passed you. The Cahersiveen ring forts are your last stop in
the Ring of Kerry, when bus traffic is of no concern.

All of these ring forts have the same basic features. The
circular drystone walls were built sometime between 500 B.C.
and A.D. 300 without the aid of mortar or cement. About 80
feet across, with walls 12 feet
thick at the base and up to 20
feet high, these brutish structures would have taken 100 men
six months to complete. Expert
opinion is divided on the reason
they were built, but most believe
that the people who built them
would have retreated here at
times of tribal war. As this was
a time when civilization was

morphing from nomadic hunter-gatherers to settled farmers,
herders used these forts. They likely brought their valuable
cattle inside to protect them from ancient rustlers. Other
experts see the round design as a kind of amphitheater, where
local clan chieftains would have gathered for important meetings or rituals. However, the ditch surrounding the outer walls
of Staigue Fort suggests a defensive, rather than ceremonial,
function. Without written records, we can only imagine the
part these awe-inspiring piles of finely stacked stones played
in ancient dramas.

Because this region had copper mines, southwest Ireland
has a wealth of prehistoric sights. The Bronze Age wouldn't
have been the Bronze Age without copper, which was melted
together with tin to make bronze for better weapons and
tools (2000 to 500 B.C.). The many ring forts and stone circles
reflect the affluence that the abundance of copper brought to
the region.

KENMARE

1910 by a local Englishwoman sympathetic to the Irish Republican cause). No one wants to touch these ruins today, out of fear of "kicking up a beehive."

43.5 km: Carroll's Cove has a fine beach with some of the warmest water in Ireland, grand views of Kenmare Bay, a local trailer park, and "Ireland's only beachside bar."

46.4 km: Take the turnoff for Derrynane House (Home of Daniel O'Connell).

50.4 km: Enjoy brilliant views for the next two kilometers to Coomakesta Pass.

52.4 km: The Coomakesta Pass lookout point (700-foot altitude) offers grand vistas in both directions.

54.5 km: Watch for fine views of the Skellig Islands.

56.4 km: Notice the ruins of famine villages on both sides of the road.

59.6 km: In the town of Waterville, you'll see a sculpture of Charlie Chaplin on the left. Waterville is also home to the Butler Arms Hotel—a fine stop for tea and scones in their Charlie Chaplin room (with lots of photos of the silent-film icon and his young wife frolicking as they lived well in Ireland).

65 km: After rejoining the main road and turning left, cross the small bridge that's locally famous for salmon fly-fishing. Take the first left (R-567) for the Skellig Ring loop (follow brown *Skellig Ring* signs through Ballinskelligs, and then scenically to Portmagee). At this point, you've left the big bus route.

75 km: St. Finian's Bay lies about halfway around, with a pleasant little picnic-friendly beach (but no WCs). Just before the bay is the small Skelligs Chocolate Factory (free samples and a fun visit).

80 km: Photographers and walkers will want to turn left into the driveway that advertises "Best View in County Kerry." Park and pay the €4 fee at the B&B reception. Then walk 10 minutes straight up the gravel road, where you'll be confronted by a dramatic coastal cliff that opens up onto what may indeed be the best view in County Kerry.

83 km: You reach Portmagee, a small port town and jumping-off point for boats to Skellig Islands.

83.2 km: Cross the bridge to the Skellig Experience Centre. You're now on Valentia Island, its name hinting at medieval trading connections with nearby Spain—which lies due south.

91.2 km: At the church in Knightstown, turn left for the Knightstown Heritage Museum.

93 km: Return to the main road and go through Knightstown to the tiny ferry (€5/car, runs constantly 8:00-21:00, 2-km trip).

95 km: Leaving the ferry, rejoin N-70 (the main Ring of Kerry route), turning left for the town of Cahersiveen. In Cahersiveen,

KENMARE

you can detour a few kilometers to two impressive stone ring forts, Cahergal and Leacanabuaile.

100 km: Return to N-70 at Cahersiveen and follow signs for *Glenbeigh* and *Killorglin*. Enjoy views of Dingle town (you can see the harbor and Ersk Tower) and Inch Beach.

The rest of the loop is less scenic. At Killorglin, you've seen all there is to see. From here, go either to Dingle (left) or to Kenmare/Killarney/Kinsale (right).

Sneem

Sneem is inundated by tour buses daily from 14:00 to 16:00. The rest of the day, Sneem is peaceful and laid-back. This humble town has two entertaining squares. The Irish joke, "As we're in Kerry, the square on the east side is called South Square and the one on the west is called North Square." On the first (South) square, you'll see a statue of Steve "Crusher" Casey, the local boy who reigned as world champion heavyweight wrestler (1938-1947). A sweet little peat-toned waterfall gurgles under the one-lane bridge connecting the two Sneem squares. The North Square features a memorial to former French president Charles de Gaulle's visit (he came here for two weeks of R&R during the tumultuous days in 1968 when students were revolting in Paris). Locals call it "da gallstone."

Staigue Fort

This ring fort is worth a stop on your way around the Ring (always open and free, drop €1 in the little blue donation box beside the gate). While viewing the imposing pile of stone, read "The Ring Forts of Kerry" sidebar.

Getting There: The fort is 2.5 miles (4 km) off the main N-70 road up a narrow rural access lane (look for signs just after the hamlet of Castle Cove). Honk on blind corners to warn oncoming traffic as you drive up the lane.

Derrynane House

This is the home of Daniel O'Connell, Ireland's most influential pre-independence politician, whose tireless nonviolent agitation gained equality for Catholics 180 years ago. The coastal lands of the O'Connell estate that surround Derrynane House are now a national historic park. A visit here is a window on the life of a man who not only liberated Ireland from the last oppressive anti-Catholic penal laws, but also first developed the idea of a grassroots movement—organizing on a massive scale to achieve political ends without bloodshed (see sidebar).

Daniel O'Connell
(1775-1847)

Born in Cahersiveen and elected in Ennis as the first Catholic member of the British Parliament, O'Connell was the hero of Catholic emancipation in Ireland. Educated in France at a time when the anti-Catholic penal laws limited schooling for Irish Catholics in Ireland, he witnessed the carnage of the French Revolution. Upon his return to Ireland, he saw more bloodshed during the futile Rebellion of 1798. He chose law as his profession and reluctantly killed a man who challenged him to a duel. Abhorring all this violence, O'Connell dedicated himself to peacefully gaining equal rights for Catholics in an Ireland dominated by a wealthy Protestant minority. He formed the Catholic Association with a one-penny-per-month membership fee and quickly gained a huge following (especially among the poor) with his persuasive speaking skills. Although Catholics weren't allowed to hold office, he ran for election to Parliament anyway and won a seat in 1828. His unwillingness to take the anti-Catholic Oath of Supremacy initially kept him out of Westminster, but the moral force of his victory caused the government to give in and concede Catholic emancipation the following year. Known as "the Liberator," O'Connell was making progress toward his next goal—repealing the Act of Union with Britain—when the Great Potato Famine hit in 1845. O'Connell died two years later in Genoa on his way to Rome, but his ideals lived on: His Catholic Association was the model for political organization to the Irish who later emigrated and rose within American big-city political "green machines."

Cost and Hours: €3; May-Sept daily 10:30-18:00; April and Oct Wed-Sun 10:30-17:00, closed in winter; last entry 45 minutes before closing, tel. 066/947-5113.

Getting There: Just outside the town of Derrynane, pick up a handy free map of the area from the little TI inside the brown Wave Crest market (TI open mid-March-mid-Oct daily 9:00-20:00, closed mid-Oct-mid-March, tel. 066/947-5188; market is a great place to buy picnic food). One mile after the market, take a left and follow the signs into Derrynane National Historic Park.

◉ **Self-Guided Tour:** Navigate the house's quirky floor plan with the laminated guide from the front desk. Ask about the next scheduled 20-minute audiovisual show, which fleshes out the highlights of O'Connell's turbulent life and makes the contents of the house more interesting.

In the exhibition room downstairs is a glass case containing the pistols used in O'Connell's famous duel. Beside them are his black gloves, one of which he always wore on his right hand when he went to Mass (out of remorse for the part it played in taking a man's life). The drawing room upstairs is lined with family portraits and contains his ornately carved chair with tiny harp strings and wolfhound collars made of gold. On a wall in the upstairs bedroom is a copy of O'Connell's famous speech imploring the Irish not to riot when he was arrested. The coach house (out back) shows off the enormous grand chariot that carried O'Connell through throngs of joyous Dubliners after his release from prison in 1844. He added the small chapel wing to the house in gratitude to God for his prison release.

Portmagee

Just a short row of snoozy buildings lining the bay, Portmagee is the best harbor for boat excursions out to the Skellig Islands. It's a quiet village with a handful of B&Bs, two pubs, a bakery, a market, and no ATMs. On the rough harborfront, a slate memorial to sailors lost at sea from here reads, "In the nets of God may we be gathered."

A 100-yard-long bridge connects Portmagee to gentle Valentia Island, where you'll find the Skellig Experience Centre (on the left at the Valentia end of the bridge). A public parking lot is at the Portmagee end of the bridge, with award-winning WCs (no kidding: Irish Toilet of the Year 2002 runner-up plaque proudly displayed). The first permanent transatlantic cable (for telegraph communication) was laid from Valentia Island in 1866. The tiny post office hides inside O'Connell's Market (Mon-Fri 9:00-17:30, Sat 9:00-13:00, closed Sun).

Sleeping in Portmagee

(€1 = about $1.25, country code: 353, area code: 066)

In Portmagee

$$$ **Moorings Guest House** feels like a small hotel, with 17 rooms, a pub and a fine restaurant downstairs, and the most convenient location in town, 50 yards from the end of the pier (Db-€90-140, Tb-€130-200, Qb-€170-240, tel. 066/947-7108, fax 066/947-7220, www.moorings.ie, moorings@iol.ie, Gerard and Patricia Kennedy).

$$ **Portmagee Heights B&B** is a modern, solid slate home at the edge of town, renting eight hotel-like rooms (Db-€70-80, Tb-€105-120, Wi-Fi, on the road into town, tel. 066/947-7251, www.portmageeheights.com, stay@portmageeheights.com, Monica Hussey). They also have a cool self-catering cottage across the road—great for families who want some space to themselves.

South of Portmagee, on St. Finian's Bay

$ Beach Cove B&B offers three comfortable, fresh, and lovingly decorated rooms in splendid isolation four miles south of Portmagee, over lofty Coomanaspic ridge, beside the pretty beach at St. Finian's Bay. Charming Bridie O'Connor will arrange a boat trip out to the Skelligs for you. Her adjacent cottage out back has two double rooms and a kitchen, making it ideal for families (Sb-€50-55, Db-€70, Tb-€105, tel. 066/947-9301, mobile 087-139-0224, www.stayatbeachcove.com, beachcove@eircom.net). Bridie's husband Jack is the head coach of the Kerry football team...a very important person in this part of Ireland (Kerry has won more football titles than any other Irish county).

Eating in Portmagee

These options all line the waterfront (between the pier and the bridge to Valentia Island).

The Moorings is an expensive restaurant with great seafood caught literally just outside its front door (€18-24 dinners, Tue-Sun 18:00-22:00, closed Mon, reservations smart, tel. 066/947-7108).

The **Bridge Bar,** next door, does traditional pub grub but stops serving food a bit early. Call ahead to check on their traditional music and dance schedule (€12-18 meals, daily 10:00-20:30, live music Fri and Sun nights, tel. 066/947-7108).

The **Fisherman's Bar** is less pretentious, with more locals and cheaper prices (€11-19 meals, daily 10:00-21:00, tel. 066/947-7103).

Picnic Supplies: **O'Connell's Market** is the only grocery (Mon-Sat 9:00-20:00, Sun 9:30-15:30). **Skellig Mist Bakery** can make basic lunch sandwiches to take on Skellig boat excursions (daily 9:00-17:30, tel. 066/947-7250).

Valentia Island

These two sights are on Valentia Island, across the bridge from Portmagee.

Skellig Experience Centre

Whether or not you're actually sailing to Skellig Michael (see page 209), this little center (with crude exhibits and a fine 20-minute film) explains it well—both the story of the monks and the natural environment (€5, daily July-Aug 10:00-19:00, until 18:00 in spring and fall, closed mid-Nov-mid-March, last entry one hour before closing, call ahead outside of peak season as hours may vary, on Valentia Island beside bridge linking it to Portmagee, tel. 066/947-6306, www.skelligexperience.com).

The Skellig Experience Centre arranges two-hour **boat trips,**

Communication in Ireland: Tetrapods to Lindbergh

Many Irish paleontologists believe the first fish slithered out of the water here on four stubby legs 385 million years ago, onto what would become the Isle of Saints and Scholars. Over time, those tetrapods evolved. Irish scribes—living in remote outposts like the Skellig Islands just off this coast—kept literate life alive in Europe through the darkest depths of the so-called

Dark Ages. In fact, in about the year 800, Charlemagne imported monks from this part of Ireland to be his scribes. Evolution, literacy, communication. Just more than a thousand years later, in the mid-19th century, Paul Julius Reuter—who provided a financial news service in Europe—couldn't get his pigeons to fly across the Atlantic. So he relied on ships coming from America to drop a news capsule overboard as they rounded this southwest corner of Ireland. His boys would wait in their little boats with nets to "get the scoop." They say Europe learned of Lincoln's assassination (1865) from a capsule tossed over a boat here. The first permanent cables were laid across the Atlantic from here to Newfoundland, giving the two hemispheres telegraphic communication. Queen Victoria got to be the first to send a message—greeting American president James Buchanan in 1858. The cable broke more than once, but was finally permanently secured in 1866. Marconi achieved the first wireless transatlantic communication from this corner of Ireland to America in 1901. Today, driving under the 21st-century mobile-phone and satellite tower crowning a hilltop above Valentia Island while gazing out at the Skellig Islands, a traveler marvels at the progress in communication—and the part this remote corner of Ireland played in it.

circling both Skellig Michael and Little Skellig (without actually bringing people ashore)—ideal for those who want a close look without the stair climb and vertigo that go with a visit to the island (€27.50, sailing daily about 14:45 and returning by 17:00, weather permitting, depart from Valentia Island pier 50 yards below the Skellig Experience Centre).

Knightstown Heritage Museum

The humble Valentia schoolhouse, built in 1861, houses an equally humble but interesting little museum highlighting the quirky things of historic interest on Valentia Island. You'll see a 19th-

KENMARE

century schoolroom and learn about tetrapods (those first fish to climb onto land—which locals claim happened here). You'll also follow the long story of the expensive, frustrating, and heroic battle to lay telegraph cable across the Atlantic, which finally succeeded in 1866 when the largest ship in the world connected this tiny island of Valentia with Newfoundland. This project was the initiative of the Atlantic Telegraph Company, which later became Western Union. These local stories are told with intimate black-and-white photos and typewritten pages (€3.50, April-Sept Mon-Sat 12:00-17:00, Sun 14:00-17:00, closed Oct-March, tel. 066/947-6411). If you are interested in those tetrapods, the actual "first footprints" are a 15-minute drive from here, on a rugged bit of rocky shoreline, a 10-minute hike below a parking lot (free, always viewable, get details locally).

Cahergal and Leacanabuaile Ring Forts

Crowning bluffs in farm country, four kilometers (2.5 miles) off the main road at Cahersiveen, these two windy and desolate forts are each different and worth a look. You'll hike a few hundred yards from the tiny parking lot (free, always open, no museum). Just beyond the Cahersiveen town church at the tourist office, turn left, cross the narrow bridge, turn left again, and follow signs for ancient forts—you'll see the huge stone structures in the distance. For details, see "The Ring Forts of Kerry" sidebar, earlier in this chapter.

Skellig Michael

A trip to this jagged, isolated pyramid—the Holy Grail of Irish monastic island settlements—rates as a truly memorable ▲▲▲

experience. After visiting Skellig Michael a hundred years ago, Nobel Prize-winning Irish author George Bernard Shaw called it "the most fantastic and impossible rock in the world."

Rising seven miles offshore, the Skelligs (Gaelic for "splinter") are two gigantic slate-and-sandstone rocks crouched aggressively on the ocean horizon. The larger of the two, Skellig Michael, is more than 700 feet tall and a mile around, with a tiny cluster of abandoned beehive huts clinging near its summit like stubborn barnacles. The smaller of the two, Little Skellig, is home to a huge colony of gannets (like large, graceful seagulls with six-foot wingspans), protected by law from visitors setting foot onshore.

Skellig Michael (dedicated to the archangel) was first inhabited by sixth-century Christian monks. Inspired by earlier hermit monks in the Egyptian desert, they sought the purity of isolation to get closer to God. Neither Viking raids nor winter storms could dislodge them, as they patiently built a half-dozen small, stone, igloo-like dwellings and a couple of tiny oratories. Their remote cliff-terrace perch is still connected to the sea 600 feet below by an amazing series of rock stairs. Viking Olav Trygvasson, who later became King of Norway and introduced Christianity to his country, was baptized here in 956.

Chiseling the most rudimentary life out of solid rock, the monks lived a harsh, lonely, disciplined existence for more than 500 years. They collected rainwater in cisterns and lived off fish and birds. To supplement their meager existence, they gathered bird eggs and feathers to trade with passing boats for cereals, candles, and animal hides (used for clothing and for copying scripture). They finally moved their holy community ashore to Ballinskelligs in the early 1100s.

Since you'll have only 2.5 hours to explore the island, begin by climbing the seemingly unending series of stone stairs to the monastic ruins (600 vertical feet of uneven steps with no handrails). Save most of your photographing for the way down. Those who linger too long below risk missing the enlightening 20-minute free talk among the beehive huts, given by guides who camp on the island from April through October. Afterward, poke your head into some of the huts and try to imagine the dark, damp, and devoted life of a monk here more than 1,000 years ago. After rambling through the ruins, you can give in to photo frenzy as you wander back down the stairs.

The two lighthouses on the far side of the island are now automated, and access to them has been blocked off. There are no WCs or modern shelters of any kind on Skellig Michael.

If you visit between late April and early August, you'll be surrounded by fearless rainbow-beaked puffins, which nest here in underground burrows. Their bizarre swallowed cooing sounds like a distant chainsaw. These portly little birds live off fish, and divers have reported seeing them 20 feet underwater in pursuit of their prey.

Your return boat journey usually includes a pass near Little Skellig, which looms like an iceberg with a white coat of guano—courtesy of the 20,000 gannets that circle overhead like feathered confetti. These large birds suddenly morph into sleek darts when pursuing a fish, piercing the water from more than 100 feet above. You're also likely to get a glimpse of gray seals lazing on rocks near the water's edge.

Getting to Skellig Michael: To book a boat trip from Portmagee, contact **Murphy Sea Cruise** (€40, April-Oct, office across from O'Connell's Market, tel. 066/947-7156, mobile 087-234-2168 or 087-645-1909, www.esatclear.ie/~skelligsrock, murphy seacruise@esatclear.ie), **Joe Roddy** (tel. 066/947-4268, mobile 087-284-4460, www.skelligstrips.com), **Brendan Casey** (tel. 066/947-2437, mobile 087-228-7519), or **Des Lavelle** (tel. 066/947-6124, mobile 087-237-1017).

Warning: Landing on Skellig Michael is highly weather-dependent. If the seas are too choppy, the boats cannot safely drop people at the concrete island pier (it's a bit like jumping off a trampoline onto an ice rink). Excursions are scheduled to run daily from Easter to late September, but experienced boat captains say they are able to bring visitors ashore roughly five days out of seven in an average summer week.

Your best bet is to reserve a room near Portmagee or St. Finian's Bay that fits your itinerary. Then call a few days in advance to make a boat reservation. Keep your fingers crossed for good weather. Contact the boat operator on the morning of departure to get the final word. If the seas are too rough, he can tell from Portmagee and will make a decision that morning whether or not to go (rather than taking passengers halfway out, then aborting).

Boat trips normally depart Portmagee at 10:00 (depending on tides), sail for an hour, leave you on the island from roughly 11:00 until 13:30, and get you back into Portmagee by 14:30 (with plenty of time to drive on to Dingle). There is a total fleet of 15 small boats (from Portmagee, Ballinskelligs, Waterville, and Valentia Island) that have permits to land on Skellig Michael. Each boat can carry a dozen passengers. This limits the number of daily visitors and minimizes the impact on the sensitive island ecosystem.

Bring your camera, a sandwich lunch (easy to buy at the recommended Skellig Mist Bakery in Portmagee), water, sunscreen, rain gear, and comfortable hiking shoes for rocky terrain.

KENMARE

DINGLE PENINSULA

Dingle Town • Dingle Peninsula Loop Trip •
Blasket Islands • Tralee

The Dingle Peninsula, the westernmost tip of Ireland (and Europe, for that matter), offers just the right mix of far-and-away beauty, isolated walks and bike rides, and ancient archaeological wonders—all within convenient reach of its main town. Dingle town is just large enough to have all the necessary tourist services and a steady nocturnal beat of Irish folk music.

Although crowded in summer, it still feels like the fish and the farm really matter in Dingle. Twenty-five fishing boats sail from here, tractor tracks dirty the main drag, and a faint whiff of peat fills the nighttime streets.

For over 30 years, my Irish dreams have been set here on this sparse but lush peninsula, where locals are fond of saying, "The next

parish over is Boston." There's a feeling of closeness to the land in Dingle. When I asked a local if he was born here, he thought for a second and said, "No, it was about six miles down the road." When I told him where I was from, a faraway smile filled his eyes, and he looked out to sea and sighed, "Ah, the shores of Americy." I asked his friend if he'd lived here all his life. He said, "Not yet."

Dingle feels so traditionally Irish because it's part of the Gaeltacht, a region where the government subsidizes the survival of the Irish language and culture. While English is always there, the signs, menus, and songs come in Gaelic. Children carry hurling sticks to class, and even the local preschool brags "ALL Gaelic."

DINGLE PENINSULA

Dingle Peninsula

Atlantic Ocean

3 Kilometers
3 Miles

The Seven Hogs

Rough Point

Brandon Bay

Brandon Head

Mt. Brandon

Castlegregory

See Dingle Peninsula Loop Trip map

Tiduff

Cloghane   Ballyduff

CONOR PASS

Three Sisters

D I N G L E   P E N I N S U L A
(A N   D A I N G E A N)

Sybil Point

GALLARUS ORATORY

Ballyferriter
(Baile an Fheirtearaigh)

Dingle
(An Daingean)

PUICIN WEDGE TOMB

Lispole
(Lios Póil)

Annascaul

N86

Ventry
(Ceann Tra')

Inishtooskert

MINARD CASTLE

Dunquin
(Dún Chaoin)

Slea Head
(Ceann Sléibhe)

Great Blasket Island
(An Blascaod Mór)

Dingle Bay

Dingle Town

Of the peninsula's 10,000 residents, 1,500 live in Dingle town (An Daingean). Its few streets, lined with ramshackle but gaily painted shops and pubs, run up from a rain-stung harbor always busy with fishing boats and leisure sailboats. Traditionally, the buildings were drab gray or whitewashed. Thirty-five years ago, Ireland's "tidy town" competition prompted everyone to paint their buildings in playful pastels.

It's a peaceful town. The courthouse (1832) is open one hour a month. The judge does his best to wrap up business within a half hour. During the day, you'll see teenagers—already working on ruddy beer-glow cheeks—roll kegs up the streets and into the pubs in preparation for another night of music and *craic* (fun conversation and atmosphere).

Planning Your Time

For the shortest visit, give Dingle two nights and a day. It takes six hours to get there from Dublin, Galway, or the boat dock in Rosslare. By spending two nights, you'll feel more like a local on your second evening in the pubs. You'll need the better part of a day to explore the 30-mile loop around the peninsula by bike, car, or tour bus (following my "Dingle Peninsula Loop Trip" in this chapter). To do any serious walking or relaxing, you'll need two or three days. It's not uncommon to find Americans slowing way, way down in Dingle.

Dingle's season peaks in July and August and really dies off-season. If you're traveling during the summer months, it's wise to reserve your B&B in advance. I've generally listed hours for the tourist season (April-Sept). Hours may be longer in July and August, and most places cut way back or shut down entirely from October to March.

Orientation to Dingle

(area code: 066)

Dingle—extremely comfortable on foot—hangs on a medieval grid of streets between the harborfront (where the bus to Tralee stops) and Main Street (three blocks inland). Nothing in town is more than a 10-minute walk away. Street numbers are used only when more than one place is run by a family of the same name. Most locals know most locals, and people on the street are fine sources of information. Remember, locals love their soda bread, and tourism provides the butter. You'll find a warm and sincere welcome.

Tourist Information

The TI has a staff who know the town, but not enough about the rest of the peninsula (July-Aug Mon-Sat 9:00-18:00, Sun 10:00-17:00, less off-season, on Strand Street by the water, tel. 066/915-1188). For more knowledgeable help, drop by the Mountain Man shop on Strand Street (see page 218), or talk to your B&B host.

Arrival in Dingle

By Bus: Dingle has no bus station and only one bus stop, on the waterfront behind the SuperValu supermarket. Bus Éireann does day trips to Dingle from Tralee (see "Day Trips from Tralee" on page 252).

By Car: Drivers choose two roads into town: the easy southern route or the much more dramatic, scenic, and treacherous Conor Pass (see "Dingle Route Tips for Drivers" at the end of this chapter). It's 30 miles from Tralee either way. If you're not staying overnight (i.e., parking at your B&B), use the waterfront parking lot extending west from the TI (€1/hour, pay at meter in lot and display on dashboard, daily 8:00-18:00).

By Plane: Kerry Airport, halfway between Tralee and Killarney, is a one-hour drive from Dingle (4 flights/day to Dublin). Without a car, take a taxi to Tralee (€25), then hop a bus to Dingle from there. For more on this airport, see the end of this chapter.

Dingle Area

1 Kilometer
1 Mile
(Approx. Scale)

To Tralee via Conor Pass

To Gallarus Oratory

Dingle Town
(An Daingean)

R559   OCEAN-WORLD   R569

To Ventry
(Ceann Tra) &
Slea Head
(Ceann Sléibhe)

N86

Dingle Harbor

To Inch & Killarney

R559

FOLLY LIGHTHOUSE

LORD VENTRY'S MANOR

To Great Blasket Island

EASK TOWER

FUNGIE

Dingle   Bay

Helpful Hints

Before You Go: Check the local website for a list of festivals and events (www.dingle-peninsula.ie).

Crowds: Crowds trample Dingle's charm throughout July and August. The absolute craziest times are during the Dingle Races (second weekend in Aug), Dingle Regatta (third weekend in Aug), and the Blessing of the Boats (end of Aug and

Dingle or An Daingean?

There's been a controversy lately over the name of this town and peninsula. Being a Gaeltacht, the entire region gets subsidies from the government (which supports the survival of the traditional Irish culture and language). A precondition of this financial support is that towns use their Irish (Gaelic) name. But Dingle (which is An Daingean in Irish—pronounced "on DANG-un") has voted down this dictate from Dublin. Dingle has become so wealthy from the tourist trade that it sees its famous name as a trademark, and doesn't want to become "the cute tourist town with the unpronounceable name formerly known as Dingle." Therefore, while many road signs identify the town only as "An Daingean," local businesses, all tourist information, and nearly all people—locals and tourists alike—still refer to it as Dingle.

For the sake of clarity, in this book I'll follow the local convention: Dingle instead of "An Daingean," Great Blasket Island instead of "An Blascaod Mór," and so on. But for ease of navigation, I'll also include the place's Irish name in parentheses. For a list of these bilingual place names, see "All Roads Lead to An Daingean" on page 236.

beginning of Sept). The first Mondays in May, June, and August are Bank Holidays, giving Ireland's workers three-day weekends—and ample time to fill up Dingle. The town's metabolism (prices, schedules, activities) rises and falls with the tourist crowds, so October through April is sleepy.

Money: Two banks in town, both on Main Street, offer the same rates (Mon 10:00-17:00, Tue-Fri 10:00-16:00, closed Sat-Sun) and have cash machines. The TI happily changes cash and traveler's checks at mediocre rates. Expect to use cash (rather than credit cards) to pay for most peninsula activities.

Internet Access: Dingle has three places to get online (the first two charge about €4/hour and are open daily 10:00-21:00, and the third is free): **Dingle Internet Café** (on Main Street), **The Old Forge Internet Café** (at Holy Ground), and the old **library** (Green Street, Mon-Sat 10:00-17:00, Thu until 20:00, closed Sun). The library's three free terminals are usually busy, but you can drop by and reserve a one-hour slot anytime.

Post Office: It's off Main Street, down the lane behind the Centra grocery (Mon-Fri 9:00-17:30, Sat 9:00-13:00, closed Sun).

Laundry: There is no self-service laundry in Dingle. **Dingle Cleaners** is convenient (€12 for up to 14 pounds, Mon-Sat 9:00-18:00, closed Sun, beside Moran's Market and gas station, tel. 066/915-0680, run by Ciaran—pronounced KEER-un).

Bike Rental: Bike-rental shops abound, renting 18-speed hybrids for about €15 per day. Try **Paddy's Bike Hire** (€15/day or €18/24 hours, includes helmet, daily 9:00-19:00, directly across Dykegate from An Café Liteartha, tel. 066/915-2311) or the **Mountain Man** (no helmets). If you're biking the peninsula, get a bike with skinny street tires, not slow and fat mountain-bike tires. Plan on leaving €20, plus a driver's license or passport, as a security deposit.

Taxi: Try Diarmuid Begley (mobile 087-250-4767), Sean with S.O.L. Cabs in Dingle (mobile 087-660-2323), or Tom Kearney out in Dunquin (mobile 087-933-2264).

Dingle Activities: The **Mountain Man,** a hiking shop run by local guide Adrian Curran, is a clearinghouse for information on hiking, biking, horseback riding, sea kayaking, climbing, peninsula tours, and trips to the Blasket Islands (the shop is the Dingle town contact for the Dunquin-Blasket Islands boats and shuttle-bus rides to the harbor—see "Blasket Islands" on page 248). Give them a call a few days ahead of time to see which guided, scenic, mountain day-hikes are scheduled (daily July-mid-Sept 9:00-21:00, mid-Sept-June 9:00-18:00, just off harbor at Strand Street, tel. 066/915-2400, www.the mountainmanshop.com).

Dingle Hill Walking Club: This informal, visitor-friendly hiking group is a great way to connect with fun, active locals (free, Sun at 10:00, meets in front of SuperValu, www.dinglehill walkingclub.com).

Travel Agency: Maurice O'Connor at **Galvin's Travel Agency** can book plane tickets, as well as boat rides to France (Mon-Fri 9:30-18:00, Sat 9:30-14:00, closed Sun, John Street, tel. 066/915-1409).

Farmers Market: On most Fridays from 10:00 to 14:00, farmers gather to sell their fresh produce and homemade marmalade (across the street from SuperValu).

Self-Guided Walk

▲Dingle Introductory Historical Walk

This quick 10-stop circle through town gives you a once-over-lightly overview and good orientation.

Start at the **"old roundabout"** (next to O'Flaherty's Pub, not the "new roundabout" by the hospital), which replaced the big bridge over the town river in the 1980s. Step out on the tiny pedestrian bridge (toward the bay) with the black wrought-iron railing. This was the original train line coming into Dingle (the westernmost train station in all of Europe from 1891 to 1953). The train once picked up fish here; its operators boasted that the cargo

Dingle's History

The wet sod of Dingle is soaked with medieval history. In the dimmest depths of the Dark Ages, peace-loving, book-ish monks fled the chaos of the Continent and its barbarian raids. They sailed to the drizzly fringe of the known world—places like Dingle. These monks kept literacy alive in Europe. Charlemagne, who ruled much of Europe in the year 800, imported Irish monks to be his scribes.

It was from this peninsula that the semi-mythical explorer-monk, St. Brendan, is said to have set sail in the sixth century in search of a legendary western paradise. Some think he beat Columbus to North America by almost a thousand years (see "The Voyage of St. Brendan" sidebar on page 224).

Dingle was a busy seaport in the late Middle Ages. Dingle and Tralee (covered later in this chapter) were the only walled towns in Kerry. Castles stood at the low and high ends of Dingle's Main Street, protecting the Normans from the angry and dispossessed Irish outside. Dingle was a gateway to northern Spain—a three-day sail due south. Many 14th- and 15th-century pilgrims left from Dingle for the revered Spanish church in Santiago de Compostela, thought to house the bones of St. James.

In Dingle's medieval heyday, locals traded cowhides for wine. When Dingle's position as a trading center waned, the town faded in importance. In the 19th century, it was a linen-weaving center. Until 1970, fishing dominated, and the only visitors were scholars and students of old Irish ways. In 1970, the movie *Ryan's Daughter* introduced the world to Dingle. The trickle of Dingle fans has grown to a flood as word of its musical, historical, gastronomical, and scenic charms—not to mention its friendly dolphin—has spread.

would be in London markets within 24 hours. The tracks ran right along the harborfront. All the land beyond the old buildings you see today has been reclaimed from the sea. As you look inland, the building on the left with the slate siding was the typical design for 19th-century weather-proofing. The radio tower marks the police station.

Cross the roundabout and walk 20 yards along the river up "The Mall" to the two stubby redbrick **pillars** that mark the entry to the police station. These pillars are all that remain of the 19th-century British Constabulary, which afforded a kind of Green Zone for British troops when they tried to subdue the local insurgents here. It was burned in the Civil War. The present building dates from 1938.

The big white **crucifix** across the street is a memorial to heroes who died in the 1916 Uprising. Note that it says in the people's language, "For honor and glory of Ireland, 1916 to 19." The date is unfinished until Ireland is united and free. Except for one hunger striker, the names listed are of patriots executed by the English.

At the *Russels B&B* sign, take 15 paces up the driveway to see an old stone etched with a cross sitting atop the fence. This marks the place of a **Celtic holy well,** indicating this was a sacred spot for people here 2,000 years ago. Across the street, enjoy the fine landscaping work of Jim from the Captain's House B&B.

Just beyond Jim's riverside garden (opposite the monastery) is another much-honored spot: the distribution center for **Guinness.** From this warehouse, pubs throughout the peninsula are stocked with beer. The wooden kegs have been replaced by what locals fondly call "iron lungs."

Farther up and across the street is the 19th-century **court-house.** Once a symbol of British oppression, today it's a laid-back place where, on the last Friday of each month, the roving County Kerry judge drops by to adjudicate cases (mostly domestic disputes and drunken disorderliness).

The next intersection is the "Small Bridge." Continuing straight takes you to the scenic Conor Pass. Turn left into the commercial heart of the town, up **Main Street.** The old stage-coach from Tralee ended at Dingle's first hotel, Benners (with its Georgian facade and door surviving). Across the street is St. James' Church. Since the 13th century, a church has stood here (just inside the medieval wall). Today, it's Anglican on Sundays, and filled with great traditional music several nights a week (schedule on gate; also see "Folk Concerts" on page 227). Farther uphill on the Benners side, a storefront is plastered with newspaper clippings dealing with the contentious An Daingean/Dingle name issue.

At the first intersection, take a left on Green Street. Pop into the beautiful, modern St. Mary Church. The convent behind it shows off its delightful **Díseart windows** (described later, under "Sights in Dingle"). Wander in the backyard to check out the tranquil nuns' cemetery, with its white-painted iron crosses huddling peacefully together under a big copper beech tree. Just past the church, the driveway to the priest's home leads past the "Trinity Tree," a three-part tree trunk carved by a Chilean (well-described by a panel).

Green Street leads past lots of inviting boutiques, estate agents (showing the high price of houses here), and the library. The **library,** a gift from the Carnegie Foundation, has a shelf of tourist-information books and a small exhibit (in the foyer and upstairs) about local patriot Thomas Ashe and the Blasket Island writers. The best historic photos you'll find in town decorate the library's walls with images of 19th-century Dingle. Green Street continues to the Strand, where a right takes you to the harbor.

The **harbor** was built on land reclaimed (with imported Dutch expertise) in 1992. The string of old stone shops facing the harbor was the loading station for the narrow-gauge railway that hauled the fish from Dingle to Tralee until 1953. Walk out to the end of the breakwater—newly paved and illuminated at night. The Eask Tower on the distant hill is a marker that was built in 1847 during the famine as a make-work project. In pre-radar days, it helped ships locate Dingle's hidden harbor. The fancy manor house (now a school) across the harbor was built in the 18th century by Lord Ventry, a big-shot landlord. Near the dolphin statue, you'll find an office that serves as a clearinghouse for the various boat excursions.

Sights in Dingle

▲▲**The Harry Clark Windows of Díseart**—Just behind Dingle's St. Mary Church stands St. Joseph's Convent and Díseart (dee-SHART), containing a beautiful Neo-Gothic chapel built in 1884. The sisters of this order, who came to Dingle in 1829 to educate local girls, worked heroically during the famine. During Mass in the chapel, the Mother Superior would sit in the covered stall in the rear, while the sisters—filling the carved stalls— chanted in response.

The chapel was graced in 1922 with 12 windows—the work of Ireland's top stained-glass man, Harry Clark. Long appreciated only by the sisters, these special windows—showing six scenes from the life of Christ—are now open to the public. The convent has become a center for sharing Christian Celtic culture and spirituality.

Enjoy a quick orientation by the attendant followed by a 15-minute recorded narration explaining the chapel and its windows. The scenes (clockwise from the back entrance) are: the visit of the Magi, the Baptism of Jesus, "Let the little children come to me," the Sermon on the Mount, the Agony in the Garden, and Jesus appearing to Mary Magdalene. Each face is lively and animated in the imaginative, devout, medieval, and fun-loving style of Harry Clark, whom locals talk about as if he's the kid next door.

Cost and Hours: €3.50, May-Sept Mon-Sat 9:00-17:00, closed Sun, shorter hours off-season, tel. 066/915-2476, www .diseart.ie.

▲**Fungie**—In 1983, a dolphin moved into Dingle Harbor and became a local celebrity. Fungie (FOON-ghee, with a hard *g*) is now the darling of the town's tourist trade and one reason you'll find so many tour buses parked along the harbor. With a close look at Fungie as bait, tour boats are thriving. Hardy little boats motor 7 to 40 passengers out to the mouth of the harbor, where they troll around looking for Fungie. You're virtually assured of

seeing the dolphin, but you don't pay unless you do (€16, kids-€8, one-hour trips depart 11:00-17:00 depending on demand, behind TI at Dolphin Trips office, tel. 066/915-2626). To actually swim with Fungie, rent wetsuits at Brosnan's B&B (Cooleen Street, tel. 066/915-1146 or 087-273-4970) and catch the early-morning 8:00-10:00 trip (€50 includes boat trip and wetsuit—unless you've packed your own). As Fungie is getting on in years, locals admit that he doesn't come up as often as he used to.

▲**Oceanworld**—This aquarium offers a little peninsula history, 300 different species of fish in thoughtfully described tanks, and the easiest way to see Fungie the dolphin...on video. Walk through the tunnel while fish swim overhead. You'll see local fish as well as a colorful Amazon collection. The aquarium's mission is to teach, and you're welcome to ask questions. The petting pool is fun. Splashing attracts the rays, which are unplugged (€12, families-€35, daily 10:00-18:00, July-Aug Sat-Sun until 19:00, shorter hours off-season, cafeteria, just past harbor on west edge of town, tel. 066/915-2111, www.dingle-oceanworld.ie).

▲**Short Harbor Walk from Dingle**—For an easy stroll along the harbor out of town (and a chance to see Fungie, 1.5 hours round-trip), head east from the roundabout past the Esso station. Just after Bambury's B&B, take a right, following signs to Skelligs Hotel, and go left at the Irish Coast Guard station on the bay. At the beach, climb the steps over the wall and follow the seashore path to the mouth of Dingle Harbor (marked by a tower—some 19th-century fat cat's folly). Ten minutes beyond that is a lighthouse. This is Fungie's neighborhood. If you see tourist boats out, you're likely to see the dolphin. The trail continues to a dramatic cliff.

▲**Bike and Hike to Eask Tower**—Here's a good compromise for those wanting more exercise than the mellow harbor walk (above), but less sweat than biking the entire 30-mile Slea Head loop (described on page 238). Rent a bike in town and pedal west past the aquarium, going left at the roundabout that takes you over the bridge onto R-559 towards Slea Head. After about two miles (3 km), turn left at the brown sign to *Holden's Leather Workshop.* A narrow lane leads another two miles (3 km) to a hut on the right marked *Eask Tower* (the tower looms on the bare hill above). Pay the €2 trail fee at the hut and hike straight up the hill. Pace yourself on this steep trail. You'll zigzag around sheep and tiptoe over their droppings. You'll also need to climb a couple of waist-high metal-rung gates. After 45 minutes, you'll reach the stone signal tower on the crown of the hill and enjoy fantastic views of Dingle town (to the north) and Dingle Bay with the Iveragh Peninsula (to the south).

Horseback Riding—Dingle Horse Riding takes out beginners (€30/hr for a trail ride) and experienced riders on two-hour (€60),

four-hour (€95), and six-hour (€130) excursions (readers of this book get a 10 percent discount in 2011, call ahead to book, follow Main Street out of Dingle, turn right at sign, tel. 066/915-2199, www.dinglehorseriding .com). **Long's Horseriding Centre** is farther out on the peninsula just past Ventry (look for sign on right)—an easy stop for bikers or drivers doing the Slea Head loop (€30-40/hr, a variety of rides for all levels, short rides often depart at 9:00, call to book a trip, tel. 066/915-9034, mobile 087-225-0286, www.longsriding.com). In either case, beach rides are only for advanced riders, and all horses come with English-style saddles (no horns to hang on to).

Dingle World of Leisure—This is a health club for adults and a good rainy-day option for kids, offering bowling, arcade games, a swimming pool, and a children's indoor playground (daily July-Sept 11:00-21:00, Oct-June 11:00-20:00, just off John Street, tel. 066/915-0660, www.dwol.eu).

Dingle Pitch & Putt—With 18 wildly scenic holes (ranging from 30-70 yards in length) overlooking the harbor on a lush green point a 10-minute walk out of town, this is a delight (€7 includes gear, April-Oct daily 10:00-19:00, closed Nov-March, over bridge take first left and follow signs, Milltown, tel. 066/915-2020).

Golf—Located out west, near the tip of the Dingle Peninsula in the town of Ballyferriter (Baile an Fheirtearaigh, 9 miles from Dingle town), Ceann Sibéal/Dingle Links offers a round of golf in a hard-to-beat setting (€45 greens fees, open daily, tel. 066/915-6255, www.dinglelinks.com).

The Voyage of St. Brendan

It has long been part of Irish lore that St. Brendan the Navigator (A.D. 484-577) and 12 followers sailed from the southwest of Ireland to the "Land of Promise" (what is now North America) in a *currach*—a wood-frame boat covered with ox hide and tar. According to a 10th-century monk who poetically wrote of the journey, St. Brendan and his crew encountered a paradise of birds, were attacked by a whale, and suffered the smoke of a smelly island in the north before finally reaching their Land of Promise.

The legend and its precisely described locations still fascinate modern readers. A British scholar of navigation, Tim Severin, re-created the entire journey from 1976 to 1977. He and his crew set out from Brendan Creek in County Kerry in a *currach*. The prevailing winds blew them to the Hebrides, the Faeroe Islands, Iceland, and finally to Newfoundland. While this didn't successfully prove that St. Brendan sailed to North America, it did prove that he could have.

According to his 10th-century biographer, "St. Brendan sailed from the Land of Promise home to Ireland. And from that time on, Brendan acted as if he did not belong to this world at all. His mind and his joy were in the delight of heaven."

East of Dingle Town

▲**Minard Castle**—Three miles southwest of the town of Annascaul (Abhainn an Scail), off the Lispole (Lios Póil) Road,

is the largest fortress on the peninsula. Built by the Knights of Kerry in 1551, Minard Castle was destroyed by Cromwell's troops in about 1650. With its corners undermined by Cromwellian explosives, it looks ready to split—it's no longer safe to enter this teetering ruin.

From the outside, look for the faint scallop in the doorway, the symbol of St. James. Medieval pilgrims would stop here before making a seafaring pilgrimage from Dingle to St. James' tomb at Santiago de Compostela in northern Spain. Imagine the floor plan of the castle: ground floor for animals and storage; main floor with fireplace; then living-quarters floor; and, on top, the defensive level.

The setting is dramatic, with the Ring of Kerry across the way and Storm Beach below. The beach is notable for its sandstone boulders that fell from the nearby cliffs. Grinding against each other in the wave and tidal action, the boulders eroded into cigar-shaped rocks. Pre-Christian Celts would carry them off and carve them into ogham stones to mark clan boundaries (for more on ogham stones, see page 247).

Next to the fortress, look for the "fairy fort," an Iron Age fort from about 500 B.C. Locals thought it unlucky to pluck stones from these ring forts, so they remain undisturbed, overgrown with greenery, all across Ireland.

▲**Puicin Wedge Tomb**—While pretty obscure, this is worth the trouble for its evocative setting. Above the hamlet of Lispole (Lios Póil) in Doonties, park your car and hike 10 minutes up a ridge. At the summit is a pile of rocks made into a little room with one of the finest views on the peninsula. Beyond the Ring of Kerry you may just make out the jagged Skellig Michael, noted for its sixth-century monastic settlement (see previous chapter).

Inch Strand—This four-mile sandy beach, shaped like a half-moon, was made famous by the movie *Ryan's Daughter*. It's rated a "Blue Flag" beach for its clean water and safe swimming (usually has a lifeguard in summer).

Shopping in Dingle

Dingle is a petri dish of capitalism, with boutiques and charming shops popping up all the time to meet the rising demand of all the tourists and its newly affluent residents. Shoppers enjoy plenty of options, as many fine Dingle shops show off local craftsman-ship. The **West Kerry Craft Guild**—a co-op selling the work of 14 local artists—is a delight, even if you're just browsing. The prices here are good, since you're buying directly from the art-ists (daily June-Aug 10:00-18:00, Sept-May 11:00-17:00, 18 Main Street, tel. 066/915-2976). **Dingle Crystal,** on Green Street with a cozy little café, features Sean Daly and his Waterford-trained crystal-cutting skills. Sean prides himself on his deeper, sharper design cuts (daily 10:00-19:00 in summer, shorter hours off-season; ask about crystal-cutting demonstrations in their workshop just outside town; tel. 066/915-1550, www.dinglecrystal.ie). **Lisbeth Mulcahy Weaver,** filled with traditional but stylish woven wear, is also the Dingle sales outlet of the well-known potter from out on Slea Head (Mon-Fri 9:30-18:00, Sat 10:00-18:00, Sun 12:00-17:00, Green Street, tel. 066/915-1688).

Music Shops: Danlann Gallery sells musical instruments and woodcrafts (daily 10:00-18:00 in summer, "flexible" on week-ends, shorter hours off-season, owner makes violins, Green Street). **Siopa Ceoil** is a grand little music shop enthusiastically run by Michael Herlihy, who offers quick-and-dirty *bodhrán* (traditional drum) lessons for free and sells advance tickets to the St. James Church concert (€12, see "Folk Concerts" on page 227). Michael and his omni-pleasant partner Katrina are virtual encyclopedias of Irish music knowledge (Mon-Sat 9:30-19:00, Sun 14:00-19:00, shorter hours off-season, Main Street, tel. 066/915-2618, www .siopaceoil.ie).

Nightlife in Dingle

▲▲▲Music in Dingle Pubs

Traditional pub music is Dingle town's best experience. Even if you're not into pubs, take a nap and then give these a whirl. Dingle is renowned among traditional musicians as a place to get work ("€40 a day, tax-free, plus drink"). The town has piles of pubs. There's music every night and rarely a cover charge. The scene is a decent mix of locals, Americans, and Germans. Music normally starts at about 21:30, and the last call for drinks is at "half eleven" (23:30), sometimes later on weekends. For a seat near the music, arrive early. If the place is chockablock with people, power in and find breathing room in the back. By midnight, the door is usually closed and the chairs are stacked. For more information, see "Traditional Irish Music" on page 34 in the Introduction. For locations of the following pubs, see the map on page 234.

While two pubs, the **Small Bridge Bar** (An Droichead Beag) and **O'Flaherty's,** are the most famous for their good beer and folk music, make a point to wander the town and follow your ear. Smaller pubs may feel a bit foreboding to a tourist, but rest assured that people—locals as well as travelers—are out for the *craic*. Irish culture is very accessible in the pubs; they're like highly interactive museums waiting to be explored. But if you sit at a table, you'll be left alone. Stand or sit at

the bar and you'll be engulfed in conversation with new friends. Have a glass in an empty, no-name pub and chat up the publican. Pubs are no longer smoky, but can be stuffy and hot, so leave your coat at home. The more offbeat pubs are more likely to erupt into leprechaun karaoke.

Pub Crawl: The best pub crawl start is along Holyground Street to **O'Flaherty's.** Quietly intense owner Fergus O'Flaherty, a fixture since my first visit to Dingle, sings and plays a half-dozen different instruments during nightly traditional-music sessions. His domain has a high ceiling and is dripping in old-time photos and town memorabilia—it's touristy but lots of fun. Moving up Strand Street, find lively **Murphy's,** offering ballads and traditional music nightly. A few doors farther down, **John Benny**

Moriarty's has dependably good traditional-music sessions, with John himself joining in on accordion when he's not pouring pints.

Then head up Green Street. **Dick Mack,** across from the church, is nicknamed "the last pew." Until recently, this was a tiny leather shop by day, expanding into a pub at night. Today, Dick Mack keeps the old leather-shop ambience but sells only drinks, with several rooms, a fine snug (private booth, originally designed to allow women to drink discreetly), reliably good beer, and strangely fascinating ambience. Notice the Hollywood-type stars on the sidewalk outside, recalling famous visitors. The pub was established in 1899 by Dick Mack (who was the master of the westernmost train station in Europe), whose mission was to provide "liquid replenishment" to travelers. The grandson of the original Dick Mack runs the place today. A painting in the window shows Dick Mack II with the local gang.

Green Street climbs to Main Street, where two more Dick Mack-type places are filled with locals deep in conversation (but no music): **Foxy John's** (a hardware shop by day) and **O Currain's** (across the street, a small clothing shop by day).

A bit higher up Main Street is **McCarthy's Pub,** a smoke-stained relic. It's less touristy and has occasional traditional-music sessions on its little stage. Wander down Main Street. The **Dingle Pub** is well established as *the* place for jaunty, shanty-type folk singing rather than the churning traditional beat of an Irish folk session. At the bottom of Main Street, **Small Bridge Bar** offers live music nightly. It's popular for good reason. While the tourists gather around the music, poke around the back and do an end run around the wall, which leads to a window nook that is actually closest to the musicians.

After Hours: The pubs close at about midnight. That's when people who are just warming up head up the Conor Pass Road to the **Hillgrove Lounge** (€5 cover, only place open after pub hours). Some like to hang out at **Rob Roy's,** munching a bag of greasy curry-cheese fries and watching the late-night migration. It's quite a scene.

Off-Season: From October through April, the bands play on, though at fewer pubs: Small Bridge Bar (live music nightly), John Benny Moriarty's (Mon, Wed, Thu), McCarthy's (Fri, Sat), and Murphy's (Sat).

Other Nightlife

▲▲**Folk Concerts**—Top local musicians offer a quality evening of live, acoustic, traditional Irish music in the fine little St. James' Church on Main Street (€12 advance purchase, €15 at the door; Mon, Wed, and Fri at 19:30, May-Sept only; mobile 087-284-9656; see sign on church gate or drop by the TI, Murphy's Ice

Cream shop, or Siopa Ceoil music shop for details or to book a ticket). If you're not a night owl (music in pubs doesn't begin until 21:30) or prefer not to be packed into a pub with the distractions of conversation, then this is your best opportunity to hear Irish traditional music in a more controlled environment. Keep in mind that in this setting, many of the musicians find flash photography to be an irritating distraction.

Blue Zone Jazz and Pizza Bar—Climb the stairs to enter a totally different nightlife zone—the only real mellow ambience in town, where Patrick Juillet brings a splash of French attitude to Dingle. A wonderful gourmet chef, he applies his cooking genius to pizzas (Tue-Sun 17:00-24:00, Fri-Sat until 1:00 in the morning, closed Mon, no cover, lots of live music, Green Street, tel. 066/915-0303). Warning: Patrick is very political.

Cinema—Dingle's great little theater is The Phoenix on Dykegate. Its film club (50-60 locals) meets here Tuesdays year-round at 20:30 for coffee and cookies, followed by a film at 21:00 (€8 for film, anyone is welcome). The leader runs it almost like a religion, with a sermon on the film before he rolls it. The regular film schedule for the week is posted on the door.

Sleeping in Dingle

In or near the Town Center

$$$ Greenmount House sits among chilly palm trees in the countryside at the top of town. A five-minute hike up from the town center, this guest house commands a fine view of the bay and mountains. John and Mary Curran run one of Ireland's best B&Bs, with two fine rooms (Db-€110), three superb rooms (Db-€140), and seven sprawling suites (Db-€170) in a modern building with lavish public areas and breakfast in a solarium (reserve in advance, most rooms at ground level, Wi-Fi, parking, top of John Street, tel. 066/915-1414, fax 066/915-1974, www.greenmount house.ie, info@greenmounthouse.ie). Seek out the hot tub in their back garden cabin.

$$$ Bambury's Guesthouse, big and modern with views of grazing sheep and the harbor, rents 12 airy, comfy rooms (Sb-€80, Db-€100-120, Tb-€150, less off-season, family deals, Wi-Fi; coming in from Tralee it's on your left on Mail Road, 2 blocks before Esso station; tel. 066/915-1244, fax 066/915-1786, www .bamburysguesthouse.com, info@bamburysguesthouse.com).

$$$ Barr Na Sráide Inn, central and hotel-like, has 26 comfortable rooms (Sb-€35-55, Db-€70-110, Tb-€100-150, family deals, Wi-Fi, self-service laundry, bar, parking, past McCarthy's pub, Upper Main Street, tel. 066/915-1331, fax 066/915-1446, www.barrnasraide.ie, barrnasraide@eircom.net).

Sleep Code

(€1 = about $1.25, country code: 353, area code: 066)
S = Single, **D** = Double/Twin, **T** = Triple, **Q** = Quad, **b** = bathroom, **s** = shower only. Prices vary with the season, with winter cheap and August tops. Breakfast is included unless otherwise noted. Many places only accept cash.

To help you easily sort through these listings, I've divided the rooms into three categories, based on the price for a standard double room with bath:

$$$ Higher Priced—Most rooms €100 or more.
  $$ Moderately Priced—Most rooms between €60-100.
    $ Lower Priced—Most rooms €60 or less.

Prices can change without notice; verify the hotel's current rates online or by email. For other updates, see www .ricksteves.com/update.

$$$ Benners Hotel was the only hotel in town a hundred years ago. It stands bewildered by the modern world on Main Street, with sprawling public spaces and 52 abundant, overpriced rooms (Db-€200 July-Aug, €140-160 May-June and Sept, €120 Oct-April, discounts on website, tel. 066/915 1638, fax 066/915 1412, www.dinglebenners.com, info@dinglebenners.com).

$$ Captain's House B&B is a shipshape place in the town center, fit for an admiral, with eight classy rooms, peat-fire lounges, a stay-a-while garden, and a magnificent breakfast in the conservatory. Mary, whose mother ran a guest house before Dingle was discovered, loves her work and is very good at it (Sb-€60, Db-€90-100, two great suites-€100-110, The Mall, tel. 066/915-1531, captigheircom.net, Jim and Mary Milhench).

$$ Alpine Guest House looks like a Monopoly hotel, and is fittingly comfortable and efficient. Its 14 spacious, bright, and fresh rooms come with wonderful views of sheep and the harbor, a cozy lounge, a great breakfast, and friendly owners (Sb-€45-65, Db-€70-110, Tb-€90-130, Qb-€130, less off-season, 10 percent discount with this book through 2011, strictly non-smoking, Wi-Fi, easy parking, Mail Road, tel. 066/915-1250, fax 066/915-1966, www.alpineguesthouse.com, alpinedingle@eircom.net, Paul). Driving into town from Tralee, you'll see this a block uphill from the Dingle roundabout and Esso station.

$$ Kelliher's Ballyegan House is a big, plain building on the edge of town, with six comfortable rooms and great harbor views (Db-€75, Tb-€110, cash only, non-smoking, parking, Upper John Street, tel. 066/915-1702, Hannah and James Kelliher).

To Gallarus Oratory, Ballyferriter & Slea Head

R559

200 Meters
200 Yards

THE WOOD

OCEANWORLD

To Eask Tower & Slea Head

Dingle

Harbor

FUNGIE

1 Greenmount House
2 Bambury's Guesthouse
3 Barr Na Sráide Inn
4 Benners Hotel
5 Captain's House B&B
6 Alpine Guest House
7 Kelliher's Ballyegan House
8 O'Neill's B&B
9 Eileen Collins Kirrary B&B & Sciuird Arch. Tours
10 Sraíd Eoin House & Galvin's Travel Agency

11 Heaton's Guesthouse & The Shore View Rest.
12 Castlewood House
13 Milltown House
14 Milestone House
15 Tower View B&B
16 Harbour Nights B&B

$$ O'Neill's B&B is homey and friendly, with six decent rooms on a quiet street at the top of town (Db-€70-80, family deals, cash only, strictly non-smoking, Wi-Fi, parking, John Street, tel. 066/915-1639, www.oneillsbedandbreakfast.com, info @oneillsbedandbreakfast.com, Mary O'Neill).

$$ Eileen Collins Kirrary B&B, which takes up a quiet corner in the town center, is run by the same Collins family that does archaeological tours of the peninsula (see "Sciuird Archaeology Tours" under "Tours of Dingle Peninsula" on page 247). They offer five fine rooms, great prices, a large garden, and a homey friendliness (Db-€70-76, cash only, tel. 066/915-1606, Kirrary House just off The Mall on Avondale Road, collinskirrary@eircom.net, Eileen Collins). They also rent a cozy, family-friendly, self-catering cottage that sleeps five people. A couple of hundred yards high up behind town, it has Dingle's best view.

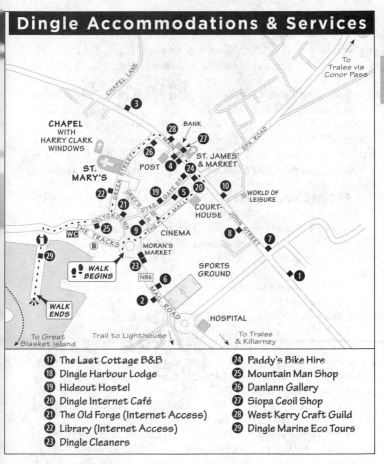

Dingle Accommodations & Services

17 The Last Cottage B&B
18 Dingle Harbour Lodge
19 Hideout Hostel
20 Dingle Internet Café
21 The Old Forge (Internet Access)
22 Library (Internet Access)
23 Dingle Cleaners
24 Paddy's Bike Hire
25 Mountain Man Shop
26 Danlann Gallery
27 Siopa Ceoil Shop
28 West Kerry Craft Guild
29 Dingle Marine Eco Tours

$$ Sraíd Eoin House offers four pleasant, top-floor rooms above Galvin's Travel Agency (Db-€70-80, Tb-€90-110, Qb-€100-120, 10 percent discount with cash and this book in 2011, Wi-Fi, John Street, tel. 066/915-1409, fax 066/915-2156, www.sraideoin bnb.com, sraideoinhouse@hotmail.com, friendly Kathleen and Maurice O'Connor).

Beyond the Pier

These accommodations are a 10-minute walk from Dingle's town center. They tend to be quieter, since they are farther from the late-night pub scene.

$$$ Heaton's Guesthouse, big, peaceful, and American in its comforts, is on the water just west of town at the end of Dingle Bay—a five-minute walk past Oceanworld on The Wood. The 16 thoughtfully appointed rooms come with all the amenities. Guests rave about the dinners in their restaurant, The Shore View—see page 235 (Db-€78-130, suite Db-€118-170, less off-season, creative breakfasts, parking, The Wood, tel. 066/915-2288, fax 066/915-2324, www.heatonsdingle.com, heatons@iol.ie, Cameron and Nuala Heaton).

$$$ Castlewood House is a palatial refuge with 12 tasteful rooms and unique furnishings. The breakfast room and patio have a wonderful view of Dingle Harbor (Sb-€70-120, Db-€98-170, Tb-€130-195, 5 percent discount with this year's edition of this book in hand, parking, The Wood, tel. 066/915-2788, www.castle wooddingle.com, info@castlewooddingle.com, Brian and Helen Heaton).

$$$ Milltown House is a plush four-star guest house with 10 rooms on a large estate across the estuary from town. It comes with grand harbor views, perfect peace, scrumptious breakfasts, and enough charm to keep Robert Mitchum happy, as he called it home during the filming of *Ryan's Daughter* (Db-€120-170, occasional discounts when slow, non-smoking, plush public spaces, memorable conservatory for breakfast with a view, tel. 066/915-1372, fax 066/915-1095, www.milltownhousedingle.com, info @milltownhousedingle.com, Mark and Anne Kerry).

$$ Milestone House, a 15-minute walk out of town, has six warmly decorated rooms, great views of Dingle Harbor, an ancient boundary stone in the front yard, and wonderful breakfasts. Friendly Barbara and Michael Carroll are brimming with sightseeing tips (Sb-€55, Db-€70-80, Tb-€110-120, Qb-€130-150, cash only, Wi-Fi, parking, tel. & fax 066/915-1831, www.mile stonedingle.com, milestonedingle@eircom.net).

$$ Tower View B&B is a big, bright-yellow modern home just outside of town on a lovely wooded lot. This kid-friendly mini-farm, with pettable animals, rents eight fine rooms (Sb-€50-60, Db-€70-80, Tb-€100-120, Qb-€120-140, Wi-Fi, just past the roundabout on the west side of town on High Road, tel. 066/915-2990, www.towerviewdingle.com, info@towerviewdingle.com, Mary and Robbie Griffin).

$$ Harbour Nights B&B weaves together a line of old row houses to create a 14-room guest house. Facing the harbor, it's run by a youthful couple (Sb-€50, Db-€80, Tb-€105-120, free Internet access in guest lounge overlooking bay, Wi-Fi, just past the aquarium on The Wood, tel. 066/915-2499, mobile 087-686-8190, www .harbournightsguesthouse.com, info@dinglebandb.com, Seán and Kathleen).

$ The Last Cottage B&B is a good budget bet, with three old-fashioned rooms in a 1909 Council House on the harbor at the far edge of town. This time warp—almost like a museum—is modest, unpretentious, and comfortably cluttered (D-€60-65, The

Wood, tel. 066/915-1469, www.dinglelastcottage.page.tl, dingle
lastcottage@gmail.com, Elvis fan Margaret Holderied).

Hostels and Dorms

$$ Dingle Harbour Lodge is a big, modern hotel on the edge
of town. You have the feeling of being a guest in a comfy hotel—
including a fancy hotel-style breakfast—without the fancy prices
(€19/person in 8-bed dorm room, Db-€65-90, Tb-€90-120, break-
fast-€8, family rooms, Wi-Fi, up a long driveway off The Wood
past the aquarium, tel. & fax 066/915-1577, www.dingleharbour
lodge.com, harbourlodge@eircom.net).

$ Hideout Hostel is friendly and central, just across the lane
from the movie theater. Michael (MEE-hall) grew up on this
street and manages a relaxed, fun atmosphere while screening out
loud stag/hen-party gangs (€18/person in 4-bed dorm room, addi-
tional nights-€15/person, Db-€50; these rates good only with 2011
edition of this book; family room available, includes continental
breakfast, all non-smoking, Wi-Fi, Dykegate Street, tel. 066/915-
0559, www.thehideouthostel.com, info@thehideouthostel.com).

Eating in Dingle

The Only Cheap Meal in Dingle: Picnic

The **SuperValu** supermarket/department store, at the base of
town, has everything and stays open late (Mon-Sat 8:00-21:00,
Sun 8:00-19:00, daily until 22:00 in July-Aug). Smaller groceries,
such as **Centra** on Main Street (Mon-Sat 8:00-21:00, Sun 8:00-
18:00), are scattered throughout the town. Consider a grand-view
picnic out on the end of the newer pier (as you face the harbor, it's
the pleasure-boat pier on your right). There are picnic tables on the
harbor side of the roundabout and benches along the busy harbor-
front. The Chinese eatery on Green Street does take-away.

Dining in Dingle

All of these restaurants are good, but I've listed them in the order
of my personal preference.

Chart House Restaurant serves contemporary cuisine in a
sleek, well-varnished dining room. Settle back into the shipshape,
lantern-lit, harborside ambience. The menu is shaped by what's
fresh and seasonal. The chef, who has a Tuscan connection and a
passion for South African wines, is committed to always offering
a good vegetarian entrée (€20-30 dinners, June-Sept daily 18:30-
22:00, Oct-May closed Tue, at roundabout at base of town, reser-
vations wise, tel. 066/915-2255, Jim McCarthy).

Out of the Blue Seafood-Only Restaurant is the locals'
choice for just plain great fresh fish. The interior is bright and

DINGLE PENINSULA

Dingle Restaurants & Pubs

To Gallarus Oratory, Ballyferriter & Slea Head

CHAPEL IN.

To Tralee via Conor Pass

N

200 Meters
200 Yards

CHAPEL WITH HARRY CLARK WINDOWS

ST. JAMES' & MARKET

BANK

GREEN ST.

POST

ST. MARY'S

To Eask Tower, Slea Head & ↑

THE WOOD STRAND

P

WC

THE TRACKS

B

GREY'S LN.

HOLYGROUND

GATE ST.

THE MALL

DYKE

COURT-HOUSE

CINEMA

JOHN ST.

MORAN'S MARKET

N86

SPORTS GROUND

Dingle Harbor

FUNGIE

To Great Blasket Island

MAIL RD.

HOSPITAL

To Tralee & Killarney

Trail to Lighthouse

❶ Chart House Restaurant
❷ Out of the Blue Restaurant
❸ The Global Village Restaurant
❹ James G. Ashe Pub & Rest.
❺ Fenton's Restaurant
❻ The Old Smokehouse
❼ The Half Door
❽ To The Shore View Rest.
❾ John Benny Moriarty's
❿ An Canteen Restaurant
⓫ Murphy's Pub
⓬ Goat Street Café
⓭ Tir Na Ri Chinese Restaurant
⓮ An Café Liteartha
⓯ Small Bridge Bar
⓰ O'Flaherty's Pub
⓱ Dick Mack Pub
⓲ Foxy John's Pub
⓳ O Currain's Pub
⓴ McCarthy's Pub
㉑ The Dingle Pub
㉒ Blue Zone Jazz & Pizza Bar
㉓ SuperValu Supermarket

elegantly simple. The menu—not printed, but on a chalkboard—is dictated by what the fishermen caught that morning. If they're closed, you know there's been a storm and the fishermen couldn't go out. The €12-17 lunches and heartier €21-30 dinners are artfully presented, with a touch of nouveau cuisine and certainly no chips (daily 12:30-15:00 & 18:30-21:30, closed Wed and after a storm, some outdoor picnic-table seating, reservations smart, just past the TI, facing the harbor on The Waterside, tel. 066/915-0811).

At **The Global Village Restaurant,** Martin Bealin concocts his favorite dishes, with inspiration gleaned from his travels around the world. He has a passion for making things from scratch and giving dishes a creative twist. No chips, no deep-fat-fried anything. It's an eclectic, healthy, fresh seafood-eaters' place (€25-30 dinners, good salads, early-bird special 17:30-19:00, open June-Sept Wed-Mon 17:30-22:00, closed Tue and through the winter, top of Main Street, tel. 066/915-2325, mobile 087-917-5920).

James G. Ashe Pub and Restaurant, an old-fashioned joint, is popular with locals for its nicely presented, top-quality, traditional Irish food and seafood at good prices. Try their beef-and-Guinness stew (€15-25 dinners, Mon-Sat 17:00-21:30, closed Sun, Main Street, tel. 066/915-0989).

Fenton's is good for seafood meals with a memorable apple-and-berry-crumble dessert (€23-30 main courses, €26 two-course and €30 three-course early-bird specials before 19:00, open Tue-Sun 18:00-21:30, closed Mon, reservations smart, on Green Street down the hill below the church, tel. 066/915-2172, mobile 087-248-2487). They have a delightful garden section out back.

The Old Smokehouse, serving happy locals in a rustic woody setting, offers good meals for a bit less money, with fresh Dingle Bay fish and fresh vegetables (€16-25 dinner plates, daily 18:00-21:30, corner of Main Street and The Mall, tel. 066/915-1061).

The Half Door is one of Dingle's long-established top-notch restaurants at the top of the town (on John Street), satisfying diners with €30-40 meals and hearty portions. While elegant, the dining room feels a bit congested (Mon-Sat 12:30-14:00 & 18:00-21:30, closed Sun, €29 early-bird three-course meal served 17:30-18:30, reservations smart, tel. 066/915-1600).

The Shore View, in Heaton's Guesthouse, serves classic seafood, lamb, and beef dishes with a modern twist and great bay views (€21-28 dinners, Mon-Sat 18:00-21:30, closed Sun, The Wood, tel. 066/915-2288).

Inexpensive Dingle Dinners

While the top-end restaurants are charging €20-30, you can eat well for €12-16 in Dingle's pubs and ethnic eateries. Fancy restaurants serve early-bird specials from 17:30 to 19:00. Many "cheap and cheery" lunch places close at 18:00. Most pubs stop serving food at about 21:00 (to make room for their beer-drinkers). Anyone will serve tap water for free. Here are some ideas:

John Benny Moriarty's is a waterfront pub dishing up traditional Irish fare with a relatively cozy interior. John, the proprietor, hopes people will come here for dinner, and stay for a drink and to enjoy his nightly live music (€12-16 hearty dinner plates, food daily 12:30-21:30, music after 21:30, The Pier).

An Canteen hides out across from the cinema, offering genuine local cooking made with fresh seasonal produce, served up in

All Roads Lead to An Daingean

The western half of the Dingle Peninsula is part of the Gaeltacht, where locals speak the Irish (Gaelic) language. In

an effort to ward off English-language encroachment, all place names on road signs were controversially changed to Irish-only in the spring of 2005. For ease of understanding, I've used the English names in this book, but you'll need this listing to navigate the peninsula's signs.

Though the signs are changing, old habits die hard: Many businesses in Dingle town are keeping easy-to-pronounce "Dingle" in their names (to make things simpler for tourists), and most locals—both here and elsewhere in Ireland—still refer to this region as Dingle.

As you travel along Slea Head Drive (known as Ceann Sléibhe in Irish), you can refer to this cheat sheet of the most useful destination names. Remember that there's a complete translation of all Irish place names in the Gazetteer section at the back of the *Complete Road Atlas of Ireland* by Ordnance Survey (€13).

English Name	Irish (Gaelic) Name	Pronounced
Dingle	*An Daingean*	on DANG-un
Ventry	*Ceann Tra'*	k'yown (rhymes with crown) thraw
Slea Head	*Ceann Sléibhe*	k'yown SHLAY-veh
Dunquin	*Dún Chaoin*	doon qween
Blasket Islands	*Na Blascaodai*	nuh BLAS-kud-ee
Great Blasket Island	*An Blascaod Mór*	on BLAS-kade moor
Ballyferriter	*Baile an Fheirtearaigh*	BALL-yuh on ERR-ter-ig
Reasc Monastery	*Mainistir Riaisc*	MON-ish-ter REE-isk
Gallarus	*Gallaras*	GAHL-russ
Kilmalkedar	*Cill Mhaoil-cheadair*	kill moyle-KAY-dir
Annascaul	*Abhainn an Scáil*	ow'en on skahl
Lispole	*Lios Póil*	leesh pohl
Tralee	*Tra' Li*	traw lee

an unpretentious atmosphere, for great prices (€12-19 meals, Thu-Tue 12:00-21:00, closed Wed, Dykegate Lane, tel. 087/965-6997).

Murphy's Pub is a favorite for good, sloppy pub grub with an extensive and kid-friendly menu and lots of fries (€12-15 plates, daily 12:00-21:00, at 21:00 the restaurant makes way for beer and music, The Strand, tel. 066/915-1450).

Goat Street Café is a good-natured, lunch-only cubbyhole away from the action, with dependable pasta and fish plates (€10-16 lunches, Mon-Sat 10:00-16:00, closed Sun, at top of town where Main Street becomes Goat Street, tel. 066/915-2770, mobile 086-826-4118).

Tir Na Ri Chinese Restaurant serves what you'd expect in a relatively plush ambience (€12-16 plates, Mon-Fri 12:30-14:30 & 17:00-23:00, Sat-Sun 17:00-23:00, also take-away, Green Street, tel. 066/915-0803).

An Café Liteartha, a likeable simple eatery hidden behind an inviting bookstore, serves tasty soup and sandwiches to a good-natured crowd of Gaelic speakers (daily 10:00-18:00, Dykegate Street, tel. 066/915-2204).

Dingle Connections

Tralee (Tra' Li), 30 miles from Dingle, is the region's transportation hub (with the nearest train station to Dingle). All bus trips make connections in Tralee.

From Dingle by Bus to: Galway (5/day, 6.5 hours), **Dublin** (4/day, 8-9 hours, transfer in Tralee and Limerick), **Rosslare** (2/day, 9 hours), **Tralee** (5/day, 1.25 hours, €12 one-way, €19 round-trip); fewer departures on Sundays. Most bus trips out of Dingle require at least one or two (easy) transfers. Remember, buses stop on the waterfront behind the SuperValu (bus info tel. 01/836-6111 or Tralee station at 066/712-3566, Tralee train info tel. 066/712-3522). For more information, see "Tralee Connections" at the end of this chapter.

Dingle Peninsula Loop Trip

A sight worth ▲▲▲, the Dingle Peninsula loop trip is about 30 miles (47 km) long and must be driven in a clockwise direction. It's easy by car, or it's a demanding four hours by bike—if you don't stop. Cyclists should plan on an early start (preferably by 9:00) to allow for enough sightseeing and lunch/rest time.

While you can take the basic guided tour of the peninsula (see "Tours of Dingle Peninsula" on page 247), the self-guided tour that follows makes it unnecessary. A fancy map is also not necessary with my instructions. I've provided distances to help locate points of interest. Just like Ireland's speed-limit signs, Ireland's car speedometers and odometers have gone metric in recent years. I've given distances below in kilometers so you can follow along with your rental-car odometer. Most Irish odometers give distances to tenths of a kilometer.

If you're driving, check your odometer at Oceanworld, as you leave Dingle (ideally, reset your odometer to zero—most likely you can do this by holding down the button next to it). Even if you get off track or are biking, you can subtract the kilometers listed below to figure out distances between points. To get the most out of your circle trip, read through this entire section before departing. Then go step-by-step (staying on R-559 and following the brown *Ceann Sleibhe/Slea Head Drive* signs). Roads are very congested mid-July to late August.

The Dingle Peninsula is 10 miles wide and runs 40 miles from Tralee to Slea Head. The top of its mountainous spine is Mount Brandon—at 3,130 feet, the second-tallest mountain in Ireland (after a nearby peak above Killarney that's almost 500 feet higher). While only tiny villages lie west of Dingle town, the peninsula is home to 500,000 sheep.

Self-Guided Tour

Leave Dingle town west along the waterfront (0.0 km at Oceanworld). Driving out of town, on the left you'll see a row of humble "two up and two down" flats from a 1908 affordable housing government initiative. Today, even these little places would cost more than €250,000.

0.5 km: There's an eight-foot tide here. The seaweed was used to make formerly worthless land arable. (Seaweed is a natu-

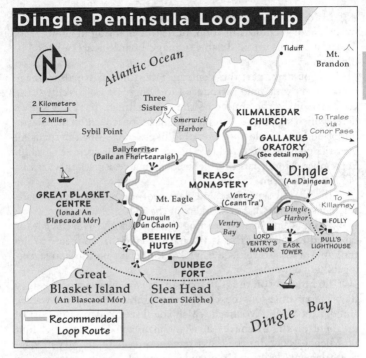

ral source of potash—it's organic farming, before it was trendy.) Across the Milltown River estuary, the fancy Milltown House B&B (with flags) was Robert Mitchum's home for a year during the filming of *Ryan's Daughter*. (Behind that is an extremely scenic pitch & putt range—described on page 223.) Look for the narrow mouth of this blind harbor (where Fungie the dolphin frolics) and the Ring of Kerry beyond that. Dingle Bay is so hidden that ships needed the Eask Tower (built as a famine-relief project in 1847 on the hill across the bay from town) to find its mouth.

0.7 km: At the roundabout, turn left over the bridge. The hardware-store building on the right was a corn-grinding mill in the 18th century. You'll pass the junction where you'll complete this loop trip later.

1.3 km: The Milestone B&B is named for the stone pillar (*gallaun* in Gaelic) in its front yard. This may have been a prehistoric grave or a boundary marker between two tribes. The stone goes down as far as it sticks up. The peninsula, literally an open-air museum, is dotted with more than 2,000 such monuments dating from the Neolithic Age (4000 B.C.) through early-Christian times. Another stone pillar stands in the field across the street, in the direction of the yellow manor house of Lord Ventry (in the distance). Its function today: cow scratcher.

Lord Ventry, whose family came to Dingle as post-Cromwellian War landlords in 1666, built this mansion in about 1750. Today it houses an all-Irish-language boarding school for 140 high-school girls.

As you drive past the Ventry estate, you'll pass palms, magnolias, and exotic flora introduced to Dingle by Lord Ventry. The Gulf Stream is the source of the mild climate (it rarely snows here), which supports subtropical plants. Consequently, fuchsias—imported from Chile and spreading like weeds—line the roads all over the peninsula and redden the countryside from June through September. More than 100 inches of rain a year gives this area its "40 shades of green."

The old red-sandstone and slate-roof cottages along the roadside housed Ventry estate workers in the 1840s.

3 km: A brown sign reading *Holden's Leather Workshop* leads up a road to the left. This is the narrow lane that connects to the trail up to Eask Tower (see page 222 for details on this active hiking/biking option).

4.6 km: Stay off the "soft margin" as you enjoy views of Ventry Bay, its four-mile-long beach (to your right as you face the water), and distant Skellig Michael, which you'll see all along this part of the route. Skellig Michael—an island jutting up like France's Mont St. Michel—contains the rocky remains of a sixth-century monastic settlement (described in previous chapter). Next to it is a smaller island, Little Skellig—a breeding ground for gannets (seagull-like birds with six-foot wingspans). In 1866, the first transatlantic cable was laid from nearby Valentia Island to Canada's Newfoundland (see sidebar on page 208). It was in use until 1965. Mount Eagle (1,660 feet), rising across the bay, marks the end of Ireland.

In the town of Ventry—or Ceann Tra'—Gaelic is the first language. Ventry is little more than a bungalow holiday village today. Urban Irish families love to come here in the summer to immerse their kids in the traditional culture and wild nature. A large hall at the edge of the village is used as a classroom where big-city students come on field trips to learn the Gaelic language. Just past the town, a lane leads left to a fine beach and mobile-home vacation community. An information board explains the history, geology, and bird life of this bay. The humble trailer park has no running water or electricity. Locals like it for its economy and proximity to the beach. From here, a lane also leads inland to Long's Horseriding Centre (described on page 223).

5.2 km: The bamboo-like rushes on either side of the road are the kind used to make the local thatched roofs. Thatching, which nearly died out because of the fire danger, is more popular now that anti-flame treatments are available. It's not the cheap roofing alternative, however, as it's expensive to pay the few quali-

Currach Boats

A *currach* is the traditional fishing boat of the west coast of Ireland—lightweight and easy to haul. In your Dingle travels,

you'll see a few actual *currach* boats—generally retired and stacked where visitors can finger them and ponder the simpler age when they were a key part of the economy. They were easy to make: Cover a wooden frame with canvas (originally cowhide) and paint with tar—presto. When transporting sheep, farmers would lash each sheep's pointy little hooves together and place it carefully upside-down in the *currach*—so it wouldn't puncture the frail little craft's canvas skin.

fied craftsman thatchers that remain in Ireland. Black-and-white magpies fly.

8.6 km: The Irish football (GAA) star Páidí Ó Sé (Paddy O'Shea) is a household name in Ireland. He won eight all-Ireland football titles for Kerry as a player. He then trained the Kerry team for many years, and he now runs the pub on the left (also notice the tiny grocery on the right; easy beach access from here).

9.2 km: The plain blue cottage hiding in the trees 100 yards off the road on the left (view through the white gate, harder to see in summer when foliage is thickest) was kept cozy by Tom Cruise and Nicole Kidman during the filming of *Far and Away*. Just beyond are fine views of the harbor and Dingle's stone tower.

10.7 km: *Taisteal go Mall* means "go slowly"; there's a red-colored, two-room school-house on the right (20 students, two teachers). During the summer, it's used for Gaelic courses for kids from the big cities. On the left is the small Celtic and Prehistoric Museum, a quirky private collection of prehistoric artifacts col-

lected by a retired busker named Harris (€4, family-€12, daily 10:00-17:30, tel. 066/915-9191).

11.1 km: The circular mound (that looks like an elevated hedge) on the right is a late-Stone Age ring fort. In 500 B.C., it was a petty Celtic chieftain's headquarters, a stone-and-earth stockade filled with little thatch dwellings. These survived untouched through the centuries because of superstitious beliefs that they were "fairy forts." While this site is unexcavated, recent digging has shown that people have lived on this peninsula since well before 4000 B.C.

11.7 km: Look ahead up Mount Eagle at the patchwork of stone-fenced fields.

12.5 km: Dunbeg Fort, a series of defensive ramparts and ditches around a central *clochan*, is open to tourists—though it's ready to fall into the sea. There are no carvings to be seen, but the small *(beg)* fort *(dun)* is dramatic (€3, daily 9:00-19:00, May-Aug until 20:00, descriptive handout, includes 10-minute video shown in the modern stone house across the street, giving a bigger picture of the prehistory of the peninsula). Forts like this are the most important relics left from Ireland's Iron Age (500 B.C.-A.D. 500).

Along the road, you'll see a new stone-roofed house built to blend in with the landscape and the region's ancient rock-slab architecture (A.D. 2000). It's the Stone House, which had been, on and off, a restaurant. A traditional *currach* boat is permanently dry-docked in the parking lot.

12.6 km: Roughly 50 yards up the hill is a thatched cottage abandoned by a family named Kavanaugh 150 years ago, during the famine. With a few rusty and chipped old artifacts and good descriptions, it provides an evocative peek into the simple lifestyles of the area in the 19th century (€3, family-€10, May-Oct daily 9:30-18:00, closed Nov-April, tel. 066/915-6241 or 087/762-2617).

13.4 km: A group of beehive huts, or *clochans*, is a short walk uphill (€2, daily 9:30-19:00, WC). These mysterious stone igloos, which cluster together within a circular wall, are a better sight than the similar group of beehive huts a mile down the road. Look over the water for more Skellig views.

Farther on, you'll ford a stream. There has never been a bridge here; this bit of road—nicknamed the "upside-down bridge"—was designed as a ford.

14.9 km: Pull off to the left at this second group of beehive huts. Look downhill at the rocky field—in the movie *Far and Away*, that's where Lord Ventry evicted (read: torched) peasants from their cottages. Even without Hollywood, this is a bleak and godforsaken land. Look above at the patches of land slowly made into farmland by the inhabitants of this westernmost piece of Europe. Rocks were cleared and piled into fences. Sand and seaweed were laid on the clay, and in time it was good for grass. The created land, if at all tillable, was generally used for growing potatoes; otherwise, it was only good for grazing. Much has fallen out of use now. Look across the bay at the Ring of Kerry in the distance, and ahead at the Blasket Islands (Na Blascaodai).

16.1 km: At Slea Head (Ceann Sleibhe)—marked by a crucifix, a pullout, and great views of the Blasket Islands (described later in this chapter)—you turn the corner on this tour. On stormy days, the waves are "racing in like white horses."

16.9 km: Pull into the little parking lot (at *Dun Chaoin* sign) to view the Blasket Islands and Dunmore Head (the westernmost

point in Europe) and to review the roadside map (which traces your route) posted in the parking lot. The scattered village of Dunquin (Dun Chaoin) has many ruined rock homes abandoned during the famine. Some are fixed up, as this is a popular place these days for summer homes. You can see more good examples of land reclamation, patch by patch, climbing up the hillside. Mount Eagle was the first bit of land that Charles Lindbergh saw after crossing the Atlantic on his way to Paris in 1927. Villagers here were as excited as he was—they had never seen anything so big in the air. About a kilometer down a road on the left, a plaque celebrates the 30th anniversary of the filming of *Ryan's Daughter*. From here, a trail leads down to a wild beach.

19.3 km: The Blasket Islands' residents had no church or cemetery on the island. This was their cemetery. The famous Blascaod storyteller Peig Sayers (1873-1958) is buried in the center. At the next intersection, drive down the little lane that leads left (100 yards) to a small stone marker (hiding in the grass on the left) commemorating the 1588 shipwreck of the *Santa María de la Rosa* of the Spanish Armada. Below that is the often-tempestuous Dunquin Harbor, from where the Blasket Islands ferry departs. Island-farmers—who on a calm day could row across in 30 min-

utes—would dock here and hike 12 miles into Dingle to sell their produce.

19.4 km: Back on the main road, follow signs to the *Ionad An Blascaod Mór* (Great Blasket Centre). You'll pass a village school from 1914 (its two teachers still teach 18 students, grades one through six).

22.3 km: Leave the Slea Head Road, turning left for the Great Blasket Centre (provides a worthwhile introduction to Blasket Islands—see page 248; also has a good cafeteria).

23.1 km: Back at the turnoff, head left (sign to *Louis Mulcahy Pottery*).

23.2 km: *Ryan's Daughter* film buffs will take a left turn here (a gravel lane) to visit the schoolhouse built for crucial scenes in that movie. Drive down the lane a couple of hundred yards and park at the dead end. Walk the trail another hundred yards (through a couple of kissing gates) and you'll see the schoolhouse below, ringed by a low stone wall. Never intended to be a permanent structure, it's the only building still standing from that outdoor movie set of 40 years ago—and it's falling apart, too. But the lonely setting is memorable.

24.5 km: Passing land that was never reclaimed, think of the work it took to pick out the stones, pile them into fences, and bring up sand and seaweed to nourish the clay and make soil for growing potatoes. Look over the water to the island aptly named the "Sleeping Giant"—see his hand resting happily on his beer belly.

24.9 km: Grab the scenic pull-out. The view is spectacular. Ahead, on the right, study the top fields, untouched since the planting of 1845, when the potatoes didn't grow, but rotted in the ground. The faint vertical ridges of the potato beds can still be seen—a reminder of the famine (easier to see a bit later). Before the famine, 40,000 people lived on this peninsula. After the famine, the population was so small that there was never again a need to farm so high up. Today, only 10,000 live on the peninsula.

The lousy farmland on both sides of the straight stretch of road was stripped of seven feet of peat (turf) in the 19th century. While the land here provided a lot of warmth back then...it provides no food today.

30 km: The town of Ballyferriter (Baile an Fheirtearaigh), established by a Norman family in the 12th century, is the largest on this side of Dingle. The pubs serve grub, and the old schoolhouse is a museum. Its modest exhibits provide the best coverage of this very historic peninsula (€2.50, May-Sept daily 10:00-17:30, closed Oct-April, tel. 066/915-6333, www.westkerrymuseum .com). The early-Christian cross in front of the schoolhouse looks real. Tap it...it's fiberglass—a prop from the *Ryan's Daughter* bus-stop scenes.

31.4 km: At the T-junction, signs direct you left to *An Daingean* (Dingle, 11 km). Go left, via *Gallaras* (and still following *Ceann Sleibhe/Slea Head Drive*). Take a right over the bridge, following signs to *Gallaras*.

32 km: Just beyond the bridge, you'll pass the Tigh Bhric market, pub, and microbrewery (great pub-grub lunches, tel. 066/915-6325). Five yards before the sign to *Mainistir Riaise* (Reasc Monastery), detour right up the lane. After 0.3 km (up the unsigned turnout on your right), you'll find the scant remains of the walled Reasc Monastery (dating from the 6th-12th centuries, free, always open). The inner wall divided the community into sections for prayer and business (cottage industries helped support the monastery). In 1975, only the stone pillar was visible, as the entire site was buried. The layer of black tar paper marks where the original rocks stop and the excavators' reconstruction begins. The stone pillar is Celtic (c. 500 B.C.). When the Christians arrived in the fifth century, they didn't throw out the Celtic society. Instead, they carved a Maltese-type cross over the Celtic scrollwork. The square building was an oratory (church—you'll see an intact oratory at the next stop). The round buildings would have been *clochan*s— those stone igloo-type dwellings. One of the cottage industries operated by the monastery was a double-duty kiln. Just outside the wall (opposite the oratory, past the duplex *clochan,* at the bottom end), find a stone hole with a passage facing the southwest wind. This was the kiln—fanned by the wind, it was used for cooking and drying grain. Locals would bring their grain to be dried and ground, and the monks would keep a 10 percent tithe. With the arrival of the Normans in the 12th century, these small religious communities were replaced by relatively big-time state and church governments.

32.8 km: Return to the main road, and continue to the right.

34.6 km: At the big hotel (Smerwick Harbor), turn left following the sign to *Gallaras* (Gallarus Oratory).

35.6 km: At the big building (with *camping* sign), make a hard

Gallarus Oratory Area

VISITORS CENTER
VIDEO
GALLARUS ORATORY
PAY PARKING LOT
WC
BIG BLDG.
R-559
PATH
FREE PARKING LOT
TO DINGLE VIA MURREAGH (AN MHUIRÍOCH) & KILMALKEDAR CHURCH
NARROW LANE
R-559
TO DINGLE
APPROX. 1/4 MILE
TO BALLYFERRITER (BAILE AN FHEIRTÉARAIGH) & SLEA HEAD
DCH

right up the long lane bordered by hedges. To park for free near the Gallarus Oratory, continue along this lane for a quarter-mile, where you'll find a five-car parking lot—which occasionally fills up (be prepared to cooperate with other drivers exiting this small lot). From the free parking lot, a sign points you up the path leading you to the oratory (about 150 yards away).

If, however, you don't mind paying €3 to park, veer left just at the start of the hedge-lined

DINGLE PENINSULA

lane into a large paved parking lot. Nearby is a small visitors center with a coffee shop, WC, and video theater. I prefer to park for free in the small lot (especially since it's closer to the oratory), but many will appreciate the large lot, handy WC, and informative 17-minute video overview of the Dingle Peninsula's historic sights (daily May-Sept 9:00-20:00, Oct-April 9:00-19:00, tel. 066/915-5333). This visitors center is the business initiative of a man who simply owns the adjacent land—not the oratory. If you park in his lot, you'll have to pay the fee, even if you skip the facilities and walk up the public lane.

The Gallarus Oratory, built about 1,300 years ago, is one of Ireland's best-preserved early-Christian churches. Shaped like an upturned boat, its finely fitted drystone walls are still waterproof. Lower your head (notice how thick the walls are), walk inside, and give your eyes a moment to adjust to the low light. A simple, small arched window offers scant daylight to the opposite wall, where the altar would have stood. Picture the interior lit by candles during medieval monastic services. It would have been tough to fit more than about a dozen monks inside (especially if they decided to do jumping jacks). Notice the holes once used to secure covering at the door, and the fine alternating stonework on the corners.

From the oratory, return to the main road and continue, following the brown *Ceann Sleibhe/Slea Head Drive* sign. If instead you continue up the narrow lane from the free parking lot, you'll end up on R-559 (a shortcut to Dingle that misses the Kilmalkedar Church ruins).

37.7 km: Bear right at the fork and immediately take a right at the next fork. Here you leave the Slea Head Drive and head for Dingle (10 km away).

39.5 km: The ruined church of Kilmalkedar (Cill Mhaoil-cheadair, on the left) was the Norman center of worship for this end of the peninsula. It was built when England replaced the old monastic settlements in an attempt to centralize their rule. The 12th-century Irish Romanesque church is surrounded by a densely populated graveyard (which has risen noticeably above the surrounding fields over the centuries). In front of the church, you'll find the oldest medieval tombs, a stately early-Christian cross (substantially buried by the rising graveyard and therefore oddly proportioned), and a much older ogham stone. This stone, which had already stood here 900 years when the church was built, is notched with the mysterious Morse code-type ogham script used from the third to seventh centuries. It marked a grave, indicating this was a pre-Christian holy spot. The hole was drilled through the top of the stone centuries ago as a place where people would come to seal a deal—standing on the graves of their ancestors and in front of the house of God, they'd "swear to God" by touching thumbs through this stone. You can still use this to renew your marriage vows (free, B.Y.O. spouse). The church fell into ruin during the Reformation. As Catholic worship went underground until the early 19th century, Kilmalkedar was never rebuilt.

40.2 km: Continue uphill, overlooking the water. You'll pass another "fairy fort" (Ciher Dorgan) on the right dating back to 1000 B.C. (free, go through the rusty "kissing gate"). The bay stretched out below you is Smerwick Harbor. In 1580 a force of 600 Italian and Spanish troops (sent by the pope to aid a rebellion against the Protestant English) surrendered at this bay to the English. All 600 were massacred by the English forces, which included Sir Walter Raleigh.

41.7 km: At the crest of the hill, enjoy a three-mile-long coast back into Dingle town (sighting, as old-time mariners did, on the Eask Tower).

46.3 km: *Tog Bog E* means "take it easy." At the T-junction, turn left. Then turn right at the roundabout.

47.5 km: You're back in Dingle town. Well done.

Tours of Dingle Peninsula

▲▲**Sciuird Archaeology Tours**—Sciuird (SCEW-erd, Irish for "excursion") tours are offered by a father-son team with Dingle history—and a knack for sharing it—in their blood. Tim Collins, a retired Dingle police officer, and his son Michael give serious 2.5-hour minibus tours (€20, departing at 10:30 and 14:00,

depending upon demand). Drop by the Eileen Collins Kirrary B&B (at Dykegate and Grey's Lane), or call 066/915-1606 to put your name on the list. Call early. Tours fill quickly in summer. Off-season (Oct-April), you may have to call back to see if the necessary six people have signed up to make a 14-seat bus worth taking out. Skipping the folk legends, your guide will show you the high-lights while driving down tiny farm roads (the Gaelic word for road literally means "cow path"), over hedges, and up ridges to hidden Celtic forts, mysterious stone tombs, and forgotten castles with sweeping seaside views. The running commentary gives an intimate peek into the history of Dingle, and their sound system allows you to hear clearly, no matter where you sit. Dress for the weather. In a gale storm with horizontal winds, Tim kept telling me, "You'll survive it."

More Minibus Tours—Moran's Tour, which does a quickie minibus tour around the peninsula, offers meager narration and a short stop at the Gallarus Oratory (€20 to Slea Head, normally May-Sept at 10:00 and 14:00 from Dingle TI, 2.5 hours; Moran's is at Esso station at roundabout, tel. 066/915-1155, mobile 087-275-3333). There are usually enough seats, though it's best to book a day ahead. But if no one shows up, consider a private Moran taxi trip around the peninsula (€90 for 4 people, cabbie narrates 2.5-hour ride).

Dingle Marine Activity Centre Cruises—Dingle Marine Eco Tours offers a two-hour birds-and-rocks boat tour of the penin-sula. The guided tour sails either east toward Minard Castle or west toward the Blasket Islands (€35, runs April-Sept only, departs at 16:00 weather permitting, office around corner from TI, mobile 086-285-8802).

Blasket Islands

This rugged group of six islands (Na Blascaodai) off the tip of Dingle Peninsula seems particularly close to the soul of Ireland. The population of Great Blasket Island (An Blascaod Mór), home to as

many as 160 people, dwindled until the government moved the last handful of residents to the mainland in 1953. Life here was hard. Each family had a cow, a few sheep, and a plot of potatoes. They cut their peat from the high ridge and harvested fish from the sea. There was no priest, pub, or doctor. Because they were not entirely dependent upon the potato, they survived the famine rela-tively unscathed. These people formed the most traditional Irish community of the 20th century—the symbol of ancient Gaelic culture.

A special closeness to an island—combined with a knack for vivid storytelling—is inspirational. From this primitive but proud fishing/farming community came three writers of international repute whose Gaelic work—basically tales of life on Great Blasket Island—is translated into many languages. You'll find *Peig* (by Peig Sayers), *Twenty Years A-Growing* (Maurice O'Sullivan), and *The Islander* (Thomas O'Crohan) in shops everywhere.

The island's café and hostel have closed down, and today Great Blasket is little more than a ghost town overrun with rabbits on a peaceful, grassy, three-mile-long poem.

Getting to the Blasket Islands

From Dunquin (Dun Chaoin): The 40-passenger Blasket Islands ferry runs hourly from Dunquin, at the tip of Dingle Peninsula; in summer, it goes every hour between 10:30 and 14:30, depending on weather and demand (€25 round-trip, April-Sept, no boats Oct-March, ferry tel. 066/915-6422, 066/915-1344, or 087/231-6131, www.blasketisland.com). There's also a scenic two-hour Blasket Island Eco Tour circuit cruise from Dunquin Harbor, which departs at 14:30 (€30, April-Sept only, same phone numbers). Or you can combine the Eco Tour with a stop for time on the island (€40, call for schedule). Dunquin has a fine hostel (tel. 066/915-6121).

From Dingle Town (An Daingean): In summer, two boats run between Dingle town and the Blasket Islands. The ride (which may include a quick look at Fungie the dolphin) traces the spectacular coastline all the way to Slea Head. The boats (*Lady Breda* and *Grievous Angel*) offer similar services from Dingle town and operate when there's enough demand. These boats also do three-hour eco-tours for those interested in puffins, dolphins, and seals. The tricky landing at Great Blasket Island's primitive little boat ramp makes getting off a challenge, and landing virtually impossible in a storm (€30 same-day round-trip; departs from the marina pier in Dingle at 12:30 and 14:30; includes 45-minute ride with 3 hours to explore island, call Mary to confirm sailing times of either boat—or for more details on the eco-tours—at tel. 066/915-1344 or mobile 087-672-6100).

▲▲Great Blasket Centre (Ionad An Blascaod Mór)

Note that this sight isn't on the Blasket Islands, but on the mainland facing the islands. It's an essential stop before visiting the islands—or a good place to learn about them without making the crossing (fits neatly with my recommended "Dingle Peninsula Loop Trip," earlier).

This state-of-the-art Blascaod and Gaelic heritage center gives visitors the best look possible at the language, literature, and way of life of Blasket Islanders. The building's award-winning design mixes interpretation and the surrounding countryside. Its spine, a sloping village lane, leads to an almost sacred view of the actual island. Don't miss the exceptional 20-minute video (shows on the half hour), then hear the sounds, read the poems, browse through old photos, and gaze out the big windows at those rugged islands... and imagine. Even if you never got past limericks, the poetry of these people—so pure and close to each other and nature—will have you dipping your pen into the cry of the birds.

Cost and Hours: €4, Easter-Oct daily 10:00-18:00, closed Nov-Easter, fine cafeteria, well signposted on the Slea Head Drive near Dunquin/Dun Chaoin, tel. 066/915-6444.

Tralee

While Killarney is the tour-bus capital of County Kerry, Tralee (Tra' Li) is its true leading city. Except for the tourist complex around the TI and during a few festivals, Tralee feels like a bustling Irish town. A little outdoor market combusts on The Square (Thu-Sat).

The famous Rose of Tralee International Festival, usually held in mid-August, is a celebration of arts and music, culminating in the election of the Rose of Tralee—the most beautiful woman at the festival. While the rose garden in the Castle Gardens surrounding the TI is in bloom from summer through October, Tralee's finest roses are going about their lives year-round in the busy streets of this workaday town.

Orientation to Tralee

(area code: 066)

For the tourist, the heart of Tralee is Ashe Memorial Hall, housing the TI and the Kerry County Museum, located near the rose garden and surrounded by the city park. Beyond the park is the Aqua Dome, looking like a flying saucer that landed on earth.

Tourist Information

The TI is hidden under the east end of Ashe Memorial Hall—facing the front entry, it's around to your left on the ground floor (TI open July-Aug Mon-Sat 9:00-18:00, Sun 10:00-18:00; May-June and Sept Mon-Sat 9:15-18:00, closed Sun; Oct-April Mon-Sat 9:15-17:00, closed Sun; also closed Sat in Jan-Feb, tel. 066/712-1288).

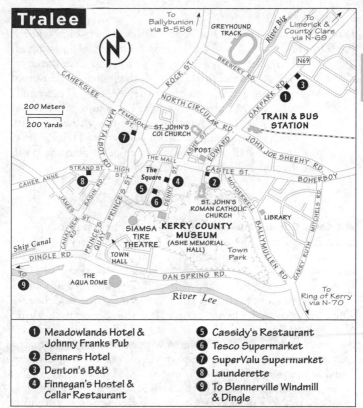

1 Meadowlands Hotel &
   Johnny Franks Pub
2 Benners Hotel
3 Denton's B&B
4 Finnegan's Hostel &
   Cellar Restaurant
5 Cassidy's Restaurant
6 Tesco Supermarket
7 SuperValu Supermarket
8 Launderette
9 To Blennerville Windmill
   & Dingle

Arrival in Tralee

From the train and bus stations (located across the parking lot from each other), Ashe Memorial Hall is a 10-minute walk through the center of town. Exit the station right, take a near-immediate left on Edward Street, then turn right on Castle Street and left on Denny. The hall is at the end of Denny. Drivers should knock around the town center until they find a sign to the TI. Parking on the street requires a disk (€1.20/hr, sold at TI and newsstands—have them date it for you—or from exact-change pay-and-display machines on the street, monitored Mon-Sat 8:30-18:30).

Helpful Hints

Post Office: It's on Edward Street (Mon-Fri 9:00-17:30, Sat 9:00-13:00, closed Sun).

Laundry: Kerin's launderette on Strand Street charges €12 for an average load (Mon-Sat 9:00-18:00, closed Sun, 103 Strand Street).

Taxis: Try **Speedy Cab** (tel. 066/712-7411) or **Behan Cab** (tel.

066/712-6296).

Day Trips from Tralee: For those without their own wheels, **Dingle** town is a rushed day trip from Tralee in summer. Bus Éireann departs from the Tralee bus and train station at 11:30, putting you in Dingle at 12:45; the last bus returns from Dingle at 17:30, getting you back to Tralee at 18:45 (June-mid-Sept only). You can also take a blitz bus tour of the **Ring of Kerry:** Bus Éireann departs the Tralee bus station at 11:50, drives the N-70 ring route, and gets you back to Tralee at 18:45 (runs late June-early Sept, stops only to pick up and drop off, also with connections from Killarney).

Sights in Tralee

▲▲**Kerry County Museum**—This is easily the best place to learn about life in Kerry. The museum has three parts: Kerry slide show, museum, and medieval-town walk. Get in the mood by relaxing for 10 minutes through the Enya-style continuous slide show of Kerry's spectacular scenery, then wander through 7,000 years of Kerry history in the museum (well-described, no need for free headphones). The Irish joke that when a particularly stupid guy moved from Cork to Kerry, he raised the average IQ in both counties—but this museum is pretty well done. It starts with good background on the archaeological sites of Dingle, progresses through Viking artifacts found in the area, and goes right up to a video showing highlights of the Kerry football team (a fun look at Irish football, which is more like rugby than soccer). Good coverage is given to adventurous Annascaul native Tom Crean, who survived three Antarctic expeditions with Scott and Shackleton. The lame finale is a stroll back in time on a re-creation of Tralee's circa-1450 Main Street (€8; May-Oct daily 9:30-17:30; Nov-April Tue-Sat 9:30-17:00, closed Sun-Mon; tel. 066/712-7777, www.kerrymuseum.ie). Before leaving, horticulture enthusiasts will want to ramble through the rose garden in the adjacent park.

Blennerville Windmill—On the edge of Tralee, just off the Dingle road, spins a restored mill originally built in 1800. Its eight-minute video tells the story of the windmill, which ground grain to feed Britain as that country steamed into the Industrial Age (€5 gets you a one-room emigration exhibit, the video, and a peek at the spartan interior of the working windmill; April-Oct daily 10:00-18:00, closed Nov-March; tel. 066/712-1064).

In the 19th century, Blennerville was a major port for America-bound emigrants. It was also the home port where the *Jeannie Johnston* was built. This modern-day replica of a 19th-century ship is now touring major Irish ports, explaining the Irish emigrant experience (most often docked in Dublin on the River Liffey).

Siamsa Tíre Theatre—The National Folk Theatre of Ireland, Siamsa Tíre (shee-EM-sah TEE-rah), stages two-hour dance and theater performances based on Gaelic folk traditions. The songs are in Irish (€25; June-Aug Mon-Sat at 8:30, no shows Sun; April-May and Sept Mon-Thu and Sat at 20:30, no shows Fri or Sun; closed Oct-March; next to Kerry County Museum building in park, tel. 066/712-3055, www.siamsatire.com, siamsaboxoffice @eircom.net).

Swimming—The Aqua Dome is a modern-yet-fortified swim-center—the largest indoor water world in Ireland—at the Dingle end of town, near Ashe Memorial Hall. Families enjoy the huge slide, wave pool, and other wet amusements (adults-€15, kids-€12, locker-€1, bring your own towels, July-Aug Mon-Fri 10:00-22:00, Sat-Sun 11:00-20:00, shorter hours off-season, tel. 066/712-8899 or 066/712-9150).

Music and Other Distractions—Tralee has several fine pubs within a few blocks of each other (on Castle Street and Rock Street) offering live traditional music most evenings. There's greyhound racing (Fri-Sat year-round plus Tue in summer, 19:30-22:00, ten 30-second races, one every 15 minutes, 10-minute walk from station or town center, tel. 066/718-0008). Entry to the track costs €10—plus what you lose gambling. At just about any time of day, you can drop into a betting office to check out the local gambling scene.

Sleeping in Tralee

(€1 = about $1.25, country code: 353, area code: 066)
Benners Hotel and Finnegan's accommodations are central. Meadowlands and Denton's B&B are next door to each other, a 10-minute walk north from the train station on Oakpark Road (or a €4 cab ride).

$$$ Meadowlands is a classy 58-room hotel with a bar that serves great pub meals. If you want to splurge in Tralee, do it here (Sb-€85-125, Db-€170-210, suites-€250-300, parking, Oakpark Road, tel. 066/718-0444, fax 066/718-0964, www.meadowlands hotel.com, info@meadowlandshotel.com).

$$ Benners Hotel has 45 predictable-quality rooms in the center of town. They charge by the room, making triples and family quads a good deal (April-Sept Sb-€49-69, Db-€59-79, Tb-€79-109, Qb-€110-150, a bit more on festival or holiday dates, cheaper off-season rates, breakfast-€9, downstairs nightclub noise until late Fri-Sat, some parking, Upper Castle Street, tel. 066/712-1877, www.bennershoteltralee.com, info@bennershoteltralee.com).

$$ Denton's B&B is a tidy, modern house with four comfy rooms hosted by enthusiastic Eileen Doherty (Sb-€40-45, Db-€60-70, Tb-€90-105, cash only, Wi-Fi, private parking, on busy Oakpark Road before it becomes N-69, tel. 066/712-7637, mobile 087-687-7341, www.dentontralee.com, dentonbandb@gmail.com).

$ Finnegan's Hostel, in a stately Georgian house, is a block from the TI at 17 Denny Street (€17 beds in 4-, 6-, 8-, or 10-bed dorms, Sb-€25-30, Db-€40-50, tel. 066/712-7610, www.finnegans hostel.com, finneganshostel@eircom.net).

Eating in Tralee

Cassidy's is consistently good (€16-24 dinners, €22.50 early-bird deal before 19:00, open Tue-Sun 17:00-22:00, closed Mon, a block off The Square, 16 Abbey Street, tel. 066/712-8833). Or try candlelit **Finnegan's Cellar** (€15-24 dinners, daily 17:30-22:30, 17 Denny Street, tel. 066/718-1400). **Johnny Franks Pub** at the Meadowlands Hotel serves the best pub grub in town (daily 12:30-21:00, Oakpark Road, tel. 066/718-0444). Shop for a picnic at **Tesco,** the big grocery off The Square (Mon-Sat 8:00-22:00, Sun 10:00-20:00), or at **SuperValu** on Rock Street (Mon-Sat 8:00-22:00, Sun 8:00-19:00).

Tralee Connections

Day-trippers can usually store bags for €2.50 per day at the train station (ask at ticket window, hours vary depending on staffing and train schedule).

From Tralee by Train to: Dublin (every 2 hours, 6/day on Sun, 1 direct in morning, otherwise change in Mallow, 4 hours). Train info: tel. 066/712-3522.

By Bus to: Dingle (4/day, less off-season and on Sun, 75 minutes, €12 one-way, €19 round-trip), **Galway** (8/day, 4.5 hours), **Limerick** (9/day, 2 hours), **Doolin/Cliffs of Moher** (2/day, 5 hours), **Ennis** (8/day, 3.25 hours, change in Limerick), **Rosslare** (3/day, 6 hours), **Shannon** (9/day, 2.5 hours), **Dublin** (8/day, 6 hours). Tralee's bus station is across the parking lot from the train station. Bus info: tel. 066/716-4700.

Car Rental: Duggan's Garage Practical Car Hire rents Fiat Puntos (€100/48 hours, includes everything but gas, must be at least 23 years old, 2 blocks from train station on Ashe Street, tel. 066/712-1124, fax 066/712-7527).

Kerry Airport

Kerry Airport is a 20-minute drive from Tralee and 45-minute drive from Dingle. It's located just off the main N-22 road, halfway between Killarney and Tralee. It has a half-dozen handy rental-car outlets and an ATM. You can connect to the airport via taxi (€25 from Tralee, €75 from Dingle) or bus (4/day to Dingle via Tralee). It offers connecting flights from **Dublin** and **Manchester** on Aer Arann (about 4/day, www.aer arann.com), **London Stansted** on Ryanair (www.ryanair.com), and even **Hahn, Germany** (near Frankfurt) on Ryanair. Airport info: tel. 066/976-4644, www.kerryairport.ie.

Dingle Route Tips for Drivers

From Tralee to Dingle: Drivers choose between the narrow, but very exciting, Conor Pass road; or the faster, easier, but still narrow N-86 through Lougher and Annascaul (Abhainn an Scail). On a clear day, Conor Pass comes with incredible views over Tralee Bay and Brandon Bay. On the north slope, pull out at the waterfall. From here, there's a fun five-minute scramble to a dramatic little glacier-created lake. Pause also at the summit viewpoint to look down on Dingle town and harbor. While in Kerry, listen to Radio Kerry FM 97. To practice your Gaelic, tune in to FM 94.4.

   Between Tralee and Galway/Burren/Doolin: The Killimer-Tarbert ferry connection allows those heading north for the Cliffs of Moher (or south for Dingle) to avoid the 80-mile detour around the Shannon River. If you're going straight to Galway, the inland Limerick route is faster. But the ferry route is more scenic and direct to the Cliffs of Moher and the Burren (hourly, 20 minutes, €18/carload, April-Sept departs Mon-Sat on the half hour 7:30-21:30 going north and on the hour 7:00-21:00 going south, on Sun the first departures are 9:30 going north and 9:00 going south, Oct-March last departures at 19:00, no need to reserve, tel. 065/905-3124, www.shannonferries.com).

COUNTY CLARE
AND THE BURREN

Ennis • Cliffs of Moher • Doolin • Lisdoonvarna •
The Burren • Ballyvaughan • Kinvarra

Those connecting Dingle in the south with Galway in the north can entertain themselves along the way by joyriding through the fascinating landscape and tidy villages of County Clare. Ennis, the county's major city, is a workaday Irish place with a medieval history and a market bustle—ideal for anyone tired of the tourist crowds. Overlooking the Atlantic, the dramatic Cliffs of Moher offer tenderfeet a thrilling hike. The Burren is a unique, windblown limestone wasteland that hides an abundance of flora, fauna, caves, and history. For your evening entertainment, you can join a tour-bus group in a castle for a medieval banquet in Kinvarra or meet up with traditional Irish music enthusiasts from around Europe for tin-whistling in Doolin.

Planning Your Time

A **car** is the best way to experience County Clare and the Burren. The region can be an enjoyable daylong drive-through or a destination in itself. None of the sights has to take much time. But do get out and walk a bit.

If driving from Dingle to Galway, I'd recommend the following day plan. Rather than the main road via Limerick, drive north from Tralee via Listowel to catch the Tarbert-Killimer car ferry (avoiding Limerick traffic and the 80-mile/1.5-hour end-run drive around the Shannon estuary; see "Dingle Route Tips for Drivers" at the end of the Dingle

County Clare & the Burren

chapter). From Killimer, drive north on N-67 via Kilkee and Milltown Malbay. The little surfer-and-golfer village of Lahinch makes a good lunch stop. Then drive the coastal route to the Cliffs of Moher for an hour break. The scenic drive through the Burren, with a couple of stops and a tour of the caves, takes about two hours. There's a 17:30 medieval banquet at Dunguaire Castle near Kinvarra (just 30 minutes south of Galway, described at the end of this chapter).

By **train** or **bus,** your gateways to this region are Ennis from the south and Galway from the north. In 2010, a new rail line was finished, connecting Limerick (via Ennis) and Galway for the first time in decades—a big plus for those staying in Ennis and relying on public transport. But linking the smaller sights within County Clare and the Burren by bus is still difficult: Book a tour instead (see "Bus Tours of the Burren," next).

Tips: Visit an ATM in Ennis, Galway, or Lahinch before you enter this region (there are no ATMs in Doolin, Lisdoonvarna, Kilfenora, or Ballyvaughan). Skip the **Bunratty Castle and Folk Park.** I'd leave this most commercial and least lively of all European open-air folk museums to the jet-lagged, big-bus American tour groups (located just a potty stop from the Shannon Airport, past Limerick on the road to Ennis).

Bus Tours of the Burren

From Galway: The **Burren Wild Tour** departs from Galway and combines an interactive walking tour of the Burren with a visit to the Cliffs of Moher. Their motto, "Don't be nuts, get off the bus," distinguishes their active hiking focus from other, more sedate tour outfits (€25, departs Galway TI at 10:00, returns by 17:30, tel. 087/877-9565 or 087/259-0160, www.burrenwalks.com).

Three other Galway-based companies—**Lally Tours, O'Neachtain Tours,** and **Galway Tour Company**—run standard all-day tours of nearby regions (€25, occasional discounts if booked online). Their tours of the Burren do a loop south of Galway, covering Kinvarra, Aillwee Cave, Poulnabrone Dolmen, and the Cliffs of Moher. Tours go most days from about 10:00 to 17:30 (departing from Kinlay House on Merchant's Road in Galway; call to confirm exact itinerary: Lally tel. 091/562-905, www.lallytours.com; O'Neachtain tel. 091/553-188, www.ontours.biz; Galway Tour Company tel. 091/566-566, www.galwaytourcompany.com). All three companies also offer day tours of Connemara, with discounts if you book two separate day tours. Drivers take cash only; to pay with a credit card, book at Galway's TI.

From Ennis: Barratt Tours runs tours of the Burren and Cliffs of Moher (see "Helpful Hints," next page).

County Clare

Ennis

This bustling market town (pop. 20,000), the main town of County Clare, provides those relying on public transit with a handy transportation hub (good connections to Limerick, Dublin, and Galway). Ennis is less than 15 miles from Shannon Airport and makes a good first- or last-night base in Ireland for travelers not locked into Dublin flights. It also offers a chance to wander around an Irish town that is not reliant upon the tourist dollar (though not shunning it either).

The center of Ennis is a tangle of contorted streets. Use the steeple of Saints Peter and Paul Cathedral and the Daniel O'Connell monument column (at either end of the main shopping drag, O'Connell Street) as landmarks.

Orientation to Ennis

Tourist Information

The TI is just off O'Connell Street Square (July-Aug daily 9:30-17:30; March-June and Sept-Dec Mon-Sat 9:30-17:00, closed Sun; Jan-Feb Mon-Fri 9:30-17:00, closed Sat-Sun; tel. 065/682-8366).

Arrival in Ennis

By Car: If you're not spending the night (i.e., stowing your car at your B&B), parking is best in one of several pay-and-display lots (€1.20/hour, Mon-Sat 9:30-17:30, free at night and on Sun, pay at meter in lot and display ticket on dashboard, usually 3-hour maximum though some lots allow 8 hours for €3.60).

By Train or Bus: The train and bus station is located southeast of town, a 15-minute walk from the town center (O'Connell Square). To reach town, exit the station parking lot and turn left on Station Road, passing through a roundabout and past the recommended Grey Gables B&B. Turn right after the recommended Old Ground Hotel onto O'Connell Street.

By Plane: Shannon Airport is about 13 miles south of Ennis. For information, see "Shannon Airport" on page 263.

Helpful Hints

Post Office: It's on Bank Place (Mon-Fri 9:00-13:00 & 14:00-17:30, Sat 9:00-13:00, closed Sun).

Laundry: Fergus launderette is opposite the Parnell Street parking lot (Mon-Sat 8:30-18:00, closed Sun, tel. 065/682-3122).

Walking Tours: Walking tours of Ennis depart from the TI and last 1.5 hours (€8, May-Oct Mon-Tue and Thu-Sat at 11:00, no tours Wed or Sun, mobile 087-648-3714, www.enniswalking tours.com).

Bus Tours: Barratt Tours operates day tours by bus, departing the TI at 11:00 and returning by 18:00. On Thursday they offer a €35 Lough Corrib cruise/Galway city tour. Most other days they run a €30 Cliffs of Moher/Burren trip (call for schedule, tel. 061/384-700, mobile 087-237-5986, www.4tours.biz).

Sights in Ennis

Clare Museum—This worthwhile museum, housed in the large TI building, has eclectic displays about ancient ax heads, submarine development, and local boys who made good—from 10th-century High King Brian Boru to 20th-century statesman Eamon de Valera (free, June-Sept Tue-Sat 9:30-17:00, closed Sun-Mon, tel. 065/682-3382, www.clarelibrary.ie).

Ennis

1 Old Ground Hotel &
  Poet's Corner Pub
2 Temple Gate Hotel
3 Grey Gables B&B
4 To Stonehaven B&B
5 Primavera
  Ristorante
6 Numero Uno
  Pizzeria
7 Cruise's Pub
8 Quinn's Pub
9 Kelly's Pub
10 To Ceol na hInse
   Show
11 Launderette

Ennis Friary—After closing in 2010 for restoration, this sight should be open for your visit in 2011. The Franciscan monks arrived here in the 13th century, and the town grew up around their friary (like a monastery). Today, it's still worth a look, with some fine limestone carvings in its ruined walls (€3, sometimes includes tour—depends on staffing, April-Sept daily 10:00-17:30, closed Oct-March, tel. 065/682-9100). Ask the guide to fully explain the crucifixion symbolism in the 15th-century *Ecce Homo* carving.

Glór Irish Music Centre—The town's modern theater center (*glór* is Irish for "sound") connects you with Irish culture. It's worth considering for traditional music, dance, or storytelling performances (€12-25, year-round usually at 20:00, 5-minute walk behind

TI, Friar's Walk, ticket office open Mon-Sat 10:00-15:00, Thu-Fri until 20:00, closed Sun, tel. 065/684-3103, www.glor.ie).

Ceol na hInse—This original stage show, housed in the local Cois na hAbhna Hall, is a fine way to spend an evening. Like other ongoing Comhaltas-sponsored cultural productions (see page 102 in the Dublin chapter), it's a celebration of Irish performing arts. The show is split in two parts. The first features great Irish music, song, and dance. After the break, you're invited to kick up your heels and take the floor as the dancers teach some famous Irish set dances. Phone ahead to see if a *ceilidh* is scheduled on off nights (€10, mid-June-mid-August Wed and Fri at 8:30, on N-18 Galway road on edge of town, tel. 065/682-4276, www.coisnahabhna.ie).

Traditional Music—Live music begins in the pubs at about 21:30. The best is **Cruise's** on Abbey Street, with music nightly year-round and good food (bar is cheaper than restaurant, tel. 065/682-8963). Other pubs offering traditional music—but only on Saturdays—are **Quinn's** on Lower Market Street (tel. 065/682-8148) and the rough-and-tumble **Kelly's** on Carmody Street, at the intersection with Drumbiggle Road (tel. 065/682-8155). The **Old Ground Hotel** hosts live music year-round in its pub (Thu-Sun, open to anyone); although tour groups stay at the hotel, the pub is low-key and feels real, not staged.

Sleeping in Ennis

The first two listings are fancy hotels that you'll share with tour groups; the last two are B&Bs.

$$$ Old Ground Hotel is a stately, ivy-covered 18th-century manse with 105 rooms and a family feel. Pan Am clipper pilots stayed here during the early days of transatlantic seaplane flights (Sb-€80-110, Db-€100-150, suite-€170-210, rates vary with season, 2-night weekend stays include a dinner, Wi-Fi, a few blocks from station at intersection of Station Road and O'Connell Street, tel. 065/682-8127, fax 065/682-8112, www.flynnhotels.com/Old _Ground_Hotel, reservations@oldgroundhotel.ie).

$$$ Temple Gate Hotel is more modern and less personal (Db-€70-140, suites-€150-190, rates lower off-season, Wi-Fi, all non-smoking, O'Connell Street Square, in courtyard with TI, tel. 065/682-3300, fax 065/682-3322, www.templegatehotel.com, info@templegatehotel.com).

$$ Grey Gables B&B has 10 tastefully decorated rooms (Sb-€38-50, Db-€75, Tb-€105, Qb-€125, cash only, Wi-Fi, wheelchair access, parking, on Station Road a block toward town center from train station, tel. 065/682-4487, www.bed-n-breakfast-ireland .com, marykeane.ennis@eircom.net, Mary Keane).

Sleep Code

(€1 = about $1.25, country code: 353, area code: 065)
S = Single, D = Double/Twin, T = Triple, Q = Quad, b = bathroom,
s = shower only. Breakfast is included and credit cards are
accepted unless otherwise noted.

To help you easily sort through these listings, I've divided
the rooms into three categories, based on the price for a standard double room with bath:

$$$ **Higher Priced**—Most rooms €75 or more.
  $$ **Moderately Priced**—Most rooms between €50-75.
    $ **Lower Priced**—Most rooms €50 or less.

Prices can change without notice; verify the hotel's
current rates online or by email. For other updates, see www
.ricksteves.com/update.

$$ Stonehaven B&B is a kid-friendly place with three com-
fortable rooms (Sb-€50-55, Db-€65-75, Tb-€85-90, cash only,
Wi-Fi, 10-minute walk from town on N-68 Kilrush Road, tel.
065/684-1775, www.stonehavenclare.com, keatingem@gmail.com,
Marie Keatinge).

Eating in Ennis

Primavera Ristorante is my pick for a satisfying Italian dinner,
cheerful atmosphere, and central location (€16-22 meals, Mon-Thu
11:00-21:30, Fri-Sat 11:00-23:00, Sun 13:00-21:30, 7 High Street,
tel. 65/684-5323).

The **Old Ground Hotel** serves up hearty meals in its Poet's
Corner pub (€10-13 lunches, €15-22 dinners, daily 12:00-21:00).

Find basic **pub grub** at one of the places mentioned earlier,
under "Traditional Music."

For an easy pub-free place for dinner, try the simple **Numero
Uno Pizzeria** (Mon-Sat 12:00-23:30, Sun 15:00-23:00, on Old
Barrack Street off Market Place, tel. 065/684-1740).

Ennis Connections

From Ennis by Train to: Galway (5/day, 1.25 hours), **Limerick** (9/
day, 40 minutes), **Dublin** (8/day, 3.25-4.25 hours). Train info: tel.
065/684-0444, www.irishrail.ie.

By Bus to: Galway (hourly, 1.25 hours), **Dublin** (hourly, 4.5
hours), **Rosslare** (5/day, 5.5-9 hours), **Limerick** (hourly, 1 hour),
Lisdoonvarna (5/day, 1.25-2.75 hours), **Ballyvaughan** (5/day,

1.75-2.75 hours), **Tralee** (9/day, 3.25 hours, change in Limerick), **Doolin** (3/day direct, 1.5 hours). Bus info: tel. 065/682-4177, www .buseireann.ie.

Shannon Airport

This is the major airport in western Ireland and comes with far less stress than Dublin's overcrowded counterpart. It has direct flights to **Dublin** (2/day, 45 minutes, Aer Lingus, www.aerlingus.ie) and **London** (7/day, 1.5 hours, Ryanair, www.ryanair.com). The airport has a **TI** (daily June-Sept 6:30-19:30, Oct-May 6:30-17:30, tel. 061/471-664, airport tel. 061/471-444, www.shannonairport.ie).

From Shannon Airport by Bus to: Ennis (14/day, 30 minutes), **Galway** (hourly, 1.75 hours), and **Limerick** (hourly, 30-50 minutes, can continue to Tralee—2 hours more, and Dingle—4/day, another 2 hours; bus tel. 061/313-333, www.buseireann.ie). Citylink also runs cheap and fast bus service to **Galway** (3/day, 1.25 hrs, bus tel. 091/564-163, www.citylink.ie).

Sleeping near Shannon Airport: If you want to stay at the airport, consider **$$$ Park Inn Shannon Airport** (Db-€99-149, less off-season, best prices if you book online, tel. 061/471-122, www .shannon.parkinn.ie).

Cliffs of Moher

A visit to the Cliffs of Moher (pronounced "more")—a ▲▲▲ sight—is one of Ireland's great natural thrills. For five miles, the

dramatic cliffs soar as high as 650 feet above the Atlantic.

Cost: There's an €8-per-car "facilities charge"—basically a parking fee—although access to the cliffs is still technically free. Be careful: Many people try to avoid the facilities charge by parking illegally on the narrow, shoulder-less road, and then walking to the cliffs (a risk not worth the euros they save). It's €5 more for the Atlantic Edge exhibit, and €2 to climb O'Brien's Tower.

Hours: May-Sept daily 9:00-18:00, closed Oct-April.

Tours: Guided tours run up to three times a day in the summer (ask at visitors center for details).

Information: You'll find a TI in the visitors center, a stonework hobbit-hole building tucked into the grassy knoll across the street from the parking lot (tel. 065/708-6141 or 065/708-1171, www.cliffsofmoher.ie).

Getting There: The Cliffs of Moher are located on R-478, south of Doolin. If you're without wheels, you can get here by bus from Galway (7/day in summer, some with change in Ennis, 2 hours, €15 round-trip, www.buseireann.ie). Or—to see (but not visit) the cliffs—you can take a boat from Doolin (described later).

⊙ Self-Guided Tour: Start in the **visitors center**, built in a concentric-circle layout with local stone. Upstairs is the Long Dock restaurant (which serves coffee and substantial cafeteria-style meals until 19:00); a photo diorama showing aerial views of the cliffs and underwater photos of local marine life; and the toilets, where you can enjoy a huge panoramic photo of the cliffs on the stall doors as you wait in line. Downstairs is a small café, a gift shop, and the new Atlantic Edge exhibit.

The **Atlantic Edge exhibit** focuses mainly on natural and geological history, native bird and marine life, and virtual interactive exhibits aimed at children (often occupied by adults). You may even learn why the cliffs are always windy. A small theater with an IMAX-style screen shows *The Ledge*, a film following a gannet who's a Jonathan Livingston Seagull wannabe, as he flies along the cliffs and then dives underwater, encountering puffins, seals, and even a humpback whale along the way.

After leaving the visitors center, walk 200 yards to the **cliff** edge and along the wall of the local Liscannor slate. Notice the squiggles made by worms, eels, and snails long ago when the slate was still mud on the seafloor.

After years of easy public access to the cliffs, numerous fatal accidents have prompted the hiring of "rangers," who are there ostensibly to answer your questions and lead guided tours, but whose main purpose is to keep people from getting too close to the cliff edge (wind gusts can be sudden, strong, and fatal).

O'Brien's Tower, built in 1835, marks the highest point of the cliffs (but isn't worth the fee to climb). Hike five minutes up to the tower and look to the north (your right). In the distance, on windy days, the Aran Islands can be seen wearing their white necklace of surf.

Nearby: Before leaving the area, drivers can take 10 minutes to check out the **holy well** of St. Bridget, located beside the tall column about a half-mile (1 km) south of the cliffs on the main road to Liscannor. In the short hall leading into the hillside spring, you'll find a treasure of personal and religious memorabilia left behind by devoted visitors seeking cures and blessings. The simple gray column outside was a folly erected 150 years ago by a local landlord with money and ego to burn.

ST BRIDGET'S WELL

Cruises from Doolin: To get a different perspective of the cliffs (looking up instead of down), you can cruise along their base. **Cliffs of Moher Cruises** makes the one-hour voyage past sea stacks and crag-perching birds. Boats depart from the pier in Doolin (same dock as Aran Islands boat, €15, runs daily April-Oct, 3/day, weather and tides permitting, call or go online for sailing schedule and to reserve, tel. 065/707-5949, mobile 087-245-3239, www.mohercruises.com). They also operate day-trip cruises from Doolin to Inisheer (the closest Aran Island), then along the base of the Cliffs of Moher and back to Doolin. You'll have more than three hours to explore Inisheer and eat lunch before sailing for the cliffs (€25, May-Sept, departs at 10:00, back in Doolin by 16:00).

Doolin

This town is a strange phenomenon. Many music-lovers go directly from Paris or Munich to Doolin, on the tourist map for its traditional music. A few years ago, this was a mecca for Irish musicians, who came together here to jam before a few lucky aficionados. But now the crowds and the foreigners have overwhelmed the musicians, and the quality of music is not as reliable. I prefer Dingle's richer music scene. Still, as Irish and European fans crowd the pubs, the *bodhrán* beat goes on.

Doolin has plenty of accommodations and a Greek-island-without-the-sun ambience. The "town" is just a few homes and shops strung out along a valley road from the tiny harbor. Residents generally divide the town into an Upper Village and Lower Village. The Lower Village is the closest thing to a commercial center.

Doolin Activity Lodge offers a handy grab-bag of services, including accommodations (see later); an Internet café (€3/30 minutes, daily 8:00-22:00, 4 terminals); a launderette (drop-off only, pick up clothes in 6 hours, no self-service, same hours as café); and bike rental (€10/day, daily 8:00-22:00, shorter hours off-season, leave passport or credit-card number as deposit). The staff can also recommend horseback riding, hiking, and fishing options.

Sights in Doolin

Traditional Music—Doolin is famous for three pubs, all featuring Irish folk music: Nearest the harbor, in the Lower Village, is **Gus O'Connor's Pub** (tel. 065/707-4168). A mile farther up the road, the Upper Village—straddling a bridge—is home to two other destination pubs: **McGann's** (tel. 065/707-4133) and **McDermott's** (tel. 065/707-4328). Music starts in the pubs between 21:30 and 22:00, finishing at about midnight. Get there before 21:00 if you want a place to sit, or pop in later and plan on standing. The *craic* is fine regardless. Pubs serve decent dinners before the music starts. (**Dial-A-Cab** is a handy service for folks without wheels wanting to link a night of fun in Doolin with a bed in Lisdoonvarna; mobile 086-812-7049 or 087-290-2060.)

Hike or Cruise to the Cliffs of Moher—From Doolin, you can hike or bike (rentals in town) up Burren Way for three miles to the Cliffs of Moher. (Get advice locally on the trail condition and safety.) Doolin also offers boat cruises along the Cliffs of Moher (see previous page).

Sleeping in Doolin

(€1 = about $1.25, country code: 353, area code: 065)

$$ **Harbour View B&B** is a fine modern house with six rooms, overlooking the valley a mile from the Doolin fiddles. Kathy Normoyle keeps the place immaculate, and serves home-baked bread from her mom's house out back (Sb-€45-55, Db-€70-76, Tb-€90, includes fine breakfast, Wi-Fi, on main road halfway between Lisdoonvarna and Cliffs of Moher, next to Aranview gas station, tel. 065/707-4154, www.harbourviewdoolin.com, clarebb @eircom.net).

$$ **Doolin Activity Lodge** is a modern compound of four stone buildings with 21 bright, airy, good-value rooms (Sb-€40-60, Db-€70-80, Tb-€105-120, Qb-€140-160, located halfway between Upper and Lower Villages, tel. 065/707-4888, fax 065/707-4877, www.doolinlodge.com, info@doolinlodge.com). The lodge offers handy amenities (see earlier for details).

$$ **Half Door B&B** is the coziest place around, with five woody rooms and a pleasant sunporch. It's just a short walk from the best pubs in the Upper Village (Sb-€45-55, Db-€70-80, Tb-€100-105, cash only, all non-smoking, Wi-Fi, a keg's roll from McDermott's pub, tel. 065/707-5959, www.halfdoordoolin.com, ann@halfdoordoolin.com).

$ **Doolin Hostel,** right in Doolin's Lower Village, caters creatively to the needs of backpackers in town for the music (dorm bed-€17, Db-€40, Tb-€60, Qb-€80, continental breakfast-€2.50, Lower Village, tel. 065/707-4006, www.doolinhostel.com, josephine@doolinhostel.com).

Eating in Doolin

Restaurants in this village have a habit of opening, then closing in less than two years (too fly-by-night to list in a guidebook). It's tough to make a go of it. But Doolin's reputation for pub grub is consistently good. In the Lower Village, try **Gus O'Connor's Pub,** and in the Upper Village, give **McGann's** a spin.

Doolin Connections

From Doolin by Bus to: Galway (5/day, 1.5-2 hours), **Ennis** (4/day, 1.5-2.5 hours).

By Ferry to the Aran Islands: For the full rundown on ferries from Doolin, see page 300. In short, if you want to day-trip from Doolin, go with Cliffs of Moher Cruises, which takes you to the closest island, Inisheer (with time to explore), then back along the Cliffs of Moher (www .mohercruises.com). If you want to visit either or both of the farther islands—Inishmaan and Inishmore—plan on an overnight stop, due to the time involved. You can choose between three ferry companies (Aran Doolin Ferries, Doolin2aran Ferries, and Doolin Ferry), but note that cancellations can occur due to wind and tides.

Lisdoonvarna

This town of 1,000 was known for centuries for its spa and its matchmakers. Today, it's pretty sleepy, except for a few weeks in September and sometimes early October, during its Matchmaking Festival (www.matchmakerireland.com), which inspired the 1997 film *The Matchmaker*. The bank is only open one day a week. Still, it's more of a town than Doolin and, apart from festival time, less touristy. Lisdoonvarna has decent traditional music in its pubs. I'd stay here, rather than in Doolin, and commute.

Sleeping in Lisdoonvarna

(€1 = about $1.25, country code: 353, area code: 065)
$$ Ballinsheen House perches on a hill with five tastefully decorated rooms and a pleasant, glassed-in breakfast terrace (Sb-€42-50, Db-€64-80, Tb-€96-118, Qb-€120, Wi-Fi, parking, 5-minute walk north of town on N-67 Galway Road, tel. 065/707-4806, mobile 087-124-1872, www.ballinsheen.com, ballinsheenhouse @hotmail.com, Mary Gardiner).

   $$ Marchmont B&B rents two large, twin/family rooms and two small doubles in a fine old house (Db-€60-70, on N-67 Galway Road near main square, just past post office, tel. 065/707-4050, marchmount@eircom.net, Eileen Barrett).

   $$ St. Enda's B&B is an old-fashioned, whitewashed place, with three modest rooms. It's been run for the last 60 years by proper proprietress Mary Finn (Sb-€45-51, Db-€60-70, non-smoking, parking, 2-minute walk north of town on N-67 Galway Road, tel. 065/707-4066).

Eating in Lisdoonvarna

The **Roadside Tavern** is a favorite local hangout with filling pub grub, great atmosphere, and occasional traditional-music sessions (daily, tel. 065/707-4084, on N-67 in town behind the Spa Hotel, hard-to-miss bright red).

The Burren

Literally the "rocky place," the Burren is just that. This 10-square-mile limestone plateau, a ▲▲ sight, is so barren that a disappointed Cromwellian surveyor of the 1650s described it as "a savage land, yielding neither water enough to drown a man, nor a tree to hang him, nor soil enough to bury him." But he wasn't much of a botanist, because the Burren is a unique ecosystem, with flora that has managed to adapt since the last Ice Age, 10,000 years ago. It's also rich in prehistoric and early Christian sites. This limestone land is littered with more than 2,000 historic locations, including about 500 Iron Age stone forts. The first human inhabitants of the Burren came about 6,000 years ago,

began cutting down trees, and are partially responsible for the stark landscape we see today.

Self-Guided Driving Tour

Exploring the Burren

The drive from Kilfenora to Ballyvaughan offers the best quick swing through the historic Burren. Begin in the town of Kilfenora, five miles southeast of Lisdoonvarna, at the T-intersection where R-476 meets R-481.

Kilfenora: This town's hardworking, community-run **Burren Centre** shows an intense 12-minute video explaining the geology and botany of the region, and then ushers you into its enlightening museum exhibits (€6, daily June-Aug 9:30-17:30, mid-March-May and Sept-Oct 10:00-17:00, closed Nov-mid-March, tel. 065/708-8030, www.theburrencentre.ie). You'll also see copies of a fine eighth-century golden collar and ninth-century silver brooch (now in Dublin's National Museum).

The ruined **church** next door has a couple of 12th-century crosses, but isn't much to see. Mass is still held in the church, which claims the pope as its bishop. As the smallest and poorest diocese in Ireland, Kilfenora was almost unable to function after the Great Potato Famine, so in 1866 Pope Pius IX supported the town as best he could—by personally declaring himself its bishop.

For lunch in Kilfenora, consider the cheap and cheery **Burren Centre Tea Room** (daily 9:30-17:30, located at far back of building) or the more atmospheric **Vaughan's Pub.** If you're spending the night in County Clare, make a real effort to join the locals at the fun set-dancing get-togethers run by the Vaughans in the **Barn Pub,** adjacent to their regular pub (€5, Thu and Sun at 21:30, tel. 065/708-8004).

• *To continue from Kilfenora into the heart of the Burren, head east out of town on R-476. After about three miles, you'll come to the junction with northbound R-480. Take the sharp left turn onto R-480, and slow down to gaze up (on the left) at the ruins of...*

Leamaneh Castle: This ruined shell of a fortified house is not open to anyone these days. From the outside, you can see how the 15th-century fortified tower house (the right quarter of the

Botany of the Burren in Brief

The Burren is a story of water, rock, geological force, and time. It supports the greatest diversity of plants in Ireland. Like nowhere else, Mediterranean and Arctic wildflowers bloom side by side in the Burren. It's an orgy of cross-pollination that attracts more insects than Doolin does music-lovers—even beetles help out. Limestone, created from layers of coral, seashells, and mud, is the bedrock of the Burren. (The same formation resurfaces 10 miles or so out to sea to form the Aran Islands.)

Geologic forces in the earth's crust heaved up the land, and the glaciers swept it bare—dropping boulders as they receded. Rain, reacting naturally with the limestone to create a mild but determined acid, slowly drilled potholes into the surface. Rainwater cut through weak zones in the limestone, leaving crevices on the surface and Europe's most extensive system of caves below. Algae grew in the puddles, dried into a powder, and combined with bug parts and rabbit turds (bunnies abound in the Burren) to create a very special soil. Plants and flowers fill the cracks in the limestone. Grasses and shrubs don't do well here, and wild goats eat any trees that try to grow, giving tender little flowers a chance to enjoy the sun. Different flowers appear throughout the months, sharing space rather than competing. The flowers are best in June and July.

remaining ruin) was expanded 150 years later (the left three-quarters of the ruin). The castle evolved from a refuge into a manor, and windows were widened to allow for better views as defense became less of a priority.

• *From the castle, turn north on R–480 (direction: Ballyvaughan). After about five miles, you'll hit the start of the real barren Burren. Keep an eye out for the next stop.*

Caherconnell (Cahercommaun) Ring Fort: One of 500 or so ring forts in the area, this can be seen to the left on the crest of a hill just off the road. You can park in the gravel lot and walk up to the modest visitors center for a 15-minute film (a high-tech virtual tour) followed by a quick wander through the small fort (€5, daily July-Aug 10:30-18:00, Easter-June and Sept-

Oct 10:30-17:00, closed Nov-Easter, tel. 065/708-9999, www .burrenforts.ie).

• *The stretch from the ring fort north to Ballyvaughan offers the starkest scenery. Soon you'll see a 10-foot-high stone structure a hundred yards off the road to the right (east, toward an ugly gray metal barn). Pull over for a closer look.*

Poulnabrone Dolmen: While it looks like a stone table, this is a portal tomb. Two hundred years ago, locals called this a "druids'

altar." Four thousand years ago, it was a grave chamber in a cairn of stacked stones. Amble over for a look. (It's crowded with tour buses at midday, but it's all yours early or late.)

Wander about for some quiet time with the wildflowers and try to think like a geologist. You're walking across a former seabed, dating from 250 million years ago when Ireland was at the equator (before continental drift nudged it north). Look for fossils—the white smudges were coral. Stones embedded in the belly of an advancing glacier ground the scratches you see in the rocks. The rounded boulders came south from Connemara, carried on a giant conveyor belt of ice, then left behind when the melting glaciers retreated north.

• *As you drive away from the dolmen (continuing north), look for the 30-foot-deep sinkhole beside the road on the right (a collapsed cave).*

From here, R-480 winds slowly downhill for about four miles, eventually leaving the rocky landscape behind and entering a comparatively lush green valley. A little before Ballyvaughan, you'll see a sign pointing up a road to your right to...

Aillwee Caves: As these are touted as "Ireland's premier show caves," I couldn't resist a look. While fairly touristy and not worth the time or money if you've seen a lot of caves, they offer your easiest look at the massive system of caves that underlie the Burren. Your guide walks you 300 yards into the plain but impressive cave, giving a serious 40-minute geology lesson. During the Ice Age, underground rivers carved countless caves such as this one. Brown bears, which became extinct in Ireland a thousand years ago, found them great for hibernating. If you take the tour, you'll need a sweater: The caves are a constant 50°F (€12, €17 combo-ticket with Birds of Prey Centre—described next, open daily at 10:00, last tour at 18:30 July-Aug, otherwise 17:30, Dec-Feb call ahead for limited tours, clearly signposted just south of Ballyvaughan, tel. 065/707-7036, www.aillweecave.ie).

Just below the caves (and on the same property) is the **Burren**

Birds of Prey Centre, with caged owls, eagles, hawks, and falcons (€8, €17 combo-ticket with Aillwee Caves, same hours as caves, bird demonstrations likely at 12:00 and 15:00 but call for daily schedule, tel. 065/707-7036, www.birdofpreycentre.com).

• *The next stop is our final destination, Ballyvaughan.*

Ballyvaughan

Really just a crossroads, Ballyvaughan is the closest town to the Burren and an ideal rural oasis for those intending to really explore the region.

Shane Connolly leads in-depth, three-hour guided **walking tours** through the Burren, explaining the diverse flora, geology, history, and man's role in shaping this landscape. Wear comfortable shoes for the wet, rocky fields, and prepare to meet a proud farmer who really knows his stuff (€15, daily at 10:00 and 15:00, call to book and confirm meeting place in Ballyvaughan, tel. 065/707-7168, http://homepage.eircom.net/~burrenhillwalks).

Sleeping in Ballyvaughan: **$$$ Rusheen Lodge** feels like an oasis on the fringe of the Burren, with six luxurious rooms and three spotless suites, as well as a great breakfast (Sb-€65-70, Db-€90-100, suites-€130-190, tel. 065/707-7092, fax 065/707-7152, www.rusheenlodge.com, rusheen@iol.ie, Karen McGann).

Eating in Ballyvaughan: The local favorite is **Logues Lodge** (across from the Spar market). They specialize in roasts as well as the usual pub-grub fare (€11-20 meals, daily 12:30-21:30, tel. 065/707-7003).

Kinvarra

This tiny town, between Ballyvaughan and Galway (30 minutes from each), is waiting for something to happen in its minuscule harbor. It faces Dunguaire Castle, a four-story tower house from 1520 that stands a few yards out in the bay.

The touristy but fun **Dunguaire Castle medieval banquet** is Kinvarra's most worthy attraction (€56, or €45 if booked online, April-Oct Fri-Tue at 17:30 and sometimes at 20:45, closed

Nov-March, reservations tel. 061/360-788, castle tel. 091/637-108, www.shannonheritage.com). Warning: The company also operates banquets at Bunratty Castle (30 miles south), so be sure that you make your reservation for the correct castle.

The evening is as intimate as 55 tourists gathered under one time-stained, barrel-vaulted ceiling can be. You get a decent four-course meal with wine (or mead if you ask sweetly), served amid an entertaining evening of Irish tales and folk songs. Remember that in medieval times, it was considered polite to flirt with wenches. It's a small and multitalented cast: one harpist and three singer/actors who serve the "lords and ladies" between tunes. The high-light is the 40-minute stage show, which features songs and poems by local writers, and comes with dessert.

The castle itself can be visited by day without taking in an evening banquet (€6, daily 10:00-16:30).

Sleeping in Kinvarra: **$$ Cois Cuain B&B** is a small but stately house with a garden, overlooking the square and harbor of the most charming village setting you'll find. Mary Walsh rents three super-homey rooms for non-smokers (Db-€75, cash only, The Quay, tel. 091/637-119).

GALWAY

Galway feels like a boomtown—rare in Western Ireland. With 75,000 people, it's the county's main city, a lively university town, and the region's industrial and administrative center. As it's near the traditional regions of Connemara and the Aran Islands, it's also a gateway to these Gaelic cultural preserves.

Galway offers tourists plenty of traditional music, easy train connections to Dublin, and a convenient jumping-off point for a visit to the Aran Islands.

While Galway has a long and interesting history, its British overlords (who ruled until 1921) had little use for anything important to the Irish heritage. Consequently, precious little from old Galway survives. What does remain has the interesting disadvantage of being built in the local limestone, which, even if medieval, looks like modern stone construction. The city's quincentennial celebration in 1984 prompted a spirit of preservation.

What Galway lacks in sights it makes up for in ambience. Spend an afternoon just wandering its medieval streets, with their delightful mix of colorful facades, labyrinthine pubs, weather-resistant street musicians, and steamy eateries.

Blustery Galway heats up after dark, with fine theaters and a pub scene that attracts even Dubliners. Visitors mix with old-timers and students as the traditional music goes round and round.

If you hear a strange language on the streets and wonder where those people are from, it's Irish, and so are they.

Planning Your Time

Galway's sights are little more than pins on which to hang the old town. The joy of Galway is its street scene. You can see its sights

Galway's History

In 1234, the medieval fishing village of Galway went big time, when the Normans captured the territory from the O'Flaherty family. Making the town a base, the Normans invited in their Angle friends, built a wall (1270), and kicked out the Irish. Galway's Celtic name (Gaillimh) comes from an old Irish word, *gall,* which means "foreigner." Except for a small section in the Eyre Square Shopping Centre and a chunk at the Spanish Arch, that Norman wall is gone.

In the 14th century, 14 merchant families, or tribes, controlled Galway's commercial traffic, including the lucrative wine trade with Spain and France. These English families constantly clashed with the local Irish. Although the wall was built to "keep out the O's and the Macs," it didn't always work. A common prayer at the time was, "From the fury of the O'Flahertys, good Lord deliver us."

Galway's support of the English king helped it prosper. But with the rise of Oliver Cromwell in the 1600s, Galway paid for that prosperity. After sieges by Cromwell's troops (in 1651) and the Protestant King William of Orange (in 1691), Galway declined. It wasn't until the last half of the 20th century that it regained some of its importance and wealth.

in three hours, but without an evening in town, you've missed the best. Many spend three nights and two days: one for the town and another for a side-trip to the Burren (see previous chapter), the Aran Islands, or the Connemara region (see following chapters). Tour companies make day trips to all three regions cheap and easy.

Orientation to Galway

(area code: 091)
The center of Galway is Eyre Square. Within two blocks of the square, you'll find the TI, Aran boat offices, a tour pickup point, accommodations (from the best cheap hostel beds to fancy hotels), and the train station. The train and public bus station butt up against the Hotel Meyrick, a huge gray railroad hotel that overlooks and dominates Eyre Square. The lively old town lies between Eyre Square and the river. From Eyre Square, Williams Gate leads right through the old town (changing names several times) to Wolfe Tone Bridge. Nearly everything you'll see and do is within a few minutes' walk of this spine.

Tourist Information
The TI, located a block from the bus/train station in the ground floor of the Forster Court Hotel, has a bookshop and many

GALWAY

Galway

To Knock & Sligo via N-17

GREYHOUND TRACK

CITY HALL

COACH STATION (PRIVATE BUS TOURS)

To Galway Airport & The Burren

COLLEGE ROAD

BROWNE DOORWAY

'HOOKER' SCULPTURE

Eyre Square

EYRE SQUARE SHOPPING CENTRE

FORSTER STREET

STATION RD

PUBLIC BUS STATION

TRAIN STATION

FRENCHVILLE LANE

Lough Atalia

QUEEN STREET

VICTORIA PLACE

DOCK ROAD

LOUGH ATALIA ROAD

Bay

GALWAY

100 Meters
100 Yards

1. Park House Hotel & Internet Access
2. Skeffington Arms Hotel
3. Hotel Meyrick
4. Jurys Inn Galway
5. Kinlay House Hostel
6. Ardawn House
7. Petra House
8. Four Seasons B&B
9. Balcony House B&B
10. Asgard Guest House
11. Kirwan's Lane Creative Cuisine
12. Busker Brownes
13. McDonagh's Fish-and-Chips
14. Nimmo's Wine Bar Bistro & Ard Bia Café
15. McSwiggan's Rest. & Pub
16. Bella Roma Restaurant
17. Galway Bakery Co. (GBC)
18. Dunne's Supermarket
19. Monroe's Pub
20. Tig Coili Pub
21. Taaffe's Pub
22. The Quays Pub
23. An Pucán Pub
24. Launderette
25. Galway Walking Tours (Harbour Hotel)

booking services (daily 9:00-17:45, Sun off-season until 12:45; tel. 091/537-700, www.discoverireland.ie). Pick up the TI's free city guide with its simplified town map.

Arrival in Galway

Trains and most buses share the same station, virtually on Eyre Square (which has the nearest ATMs). The train station can store your bag (€2.50/day, Mon-Fri 8:00-18:00, closed Sat-Sun). To get from the station to the TI, go left on Station Road as you exit the station (toward Eyre Square), then turn right on Forster Street. Citylink buses from Dublin and Dublin's airport, as well as regional day-tour buses, use the coach station (a block away), next to the TI.

Drivers staying overnight at a College Road B&B can park there for free (each has a small lot in front). For daytime parking, the most central and handiest parking garage is under the recommended Jurys Inn Galway in the town center (€2.20/hour, €20/24 hours, Mon-Sat 8:00-1:00 in the morning, Sun 9:00-18:00). To park nearby for free, try across the bridge along the Claddagh Quay. Otherwise, you'll have to buy a pay-and-display ticket and put it on your dashboard (€2.60, 2-hour maximum, buy from machines on street).

Helpful Hints

Crowd Control: Expect huge crowds—and much higher prices— during the Galway Arts Festival (July 11-24 in 2011, www .galwayartsfestival.com) and Galway Oyster Festival (late Sept, www.galwayoysterfest.com). The Galway Races are heaven for lovers of horse racing and hell for everyone else (biggest race last week of July, fall races in Sept and Oct, www.galwayraces.com); prices double for food and lodging, and simple evening strolls feel like punt returns.

Markets: On Saturday, a fun market clusters around St. Nicholas' Church (all day, but best 9:00-12:00).

Internet Access: Square Eyes is located next to the Park House Hotel (€2/30 minutes, Mon-Sat 9:00-23:00, Sun 12:00-23:00, Forster Street). Several other good places cluster along High Street near Jurys Inn.

Post Office: You'll find it on Eglinton Street (Mon-Sat 9:00-17:30, closed Sun).

Laundry: Launderland is close to the recommended B&Bs on College Road (€10 drop-off, Mon-Fri 8:30-18:30, Sat 9:00-18:00, Sun 10:00-17:00, on Bothar Ui Eithir, 2-minute walk uphill from TI, tel. 091/568-393).

Tours in Galway

▲**Hop-on, Hop-off City Bus Tours**—Guided one-hour double-decker bus tours depart from the TI and Eyre Square, making nine stops, including the cathedral, Salthill, and the Spanish Arch. You can get off and explore, and hop back on later (€10, April-Sept daily 10:30-16:30, 4/day, buses usually depart every 1.5 hours from TI on Forster Street, tel. 091/524-728 or mobile 087-679-8525).

Walking Tours—**Galway Walking Tours** are led by Fiona Brennan, who takes her guests on leisurely 1.5-hour explorations of the city (€12, departs from beside the docks at the Harbour Hotel, call to arrange start time, mobile 087-290-3499, www.galway walkingtours.com, fiona@galwaywalkingtours.com). **Gore of Galway Walks** focus on the hidden history, folklore, murder, and mayhem of the "City of the Tribes" (€8, 1.5 hours, departs from TI Mon-Thu at 17:00, mobile 086-727-4888). **Galway City Walk & Talk** tours discuss architecture, culture, and historic characters of Galway's past (€10, 2 hours, daily at 10:00, departs from City Museum, mobile 087-690-1452).

Bus Tours—Several Galway-based companies offer bus tours to the Burren and Connemara. For details, see page 258 and page 302.

Sights in Galway

Medieval Galway's "Latin Quarter"

From the top of Eyre Square, Williams Gate—named for the old main gate of the Norman town wall that once stood here—is the spine of medieval Galway. While the road changes names several times (William, Shop, High, and Quay Streets), it leads generally downhill to the River Corrib, straight past the following sights.

Lynch's Castle—Now the Allied Irish Bank, Galway's best late-15th-century fortified townhouse was the home of the Lynch family—the most powerful of the town's 14 tribes—and the only one of their mansions to survive. More than 80 Lynch mayors ruled Galway in the 16th and 17th centuries.

Collegiate Church of St. Nicholas—This church, located a half-block off the main street on the right, is the finest medieval building in town (1320), and is dedicated to St. Nicholas of Myra, the patron saint of sailors. Columbus is said to have worshipped here in 1477, undoubtedly while contemplating a scary voyage. Its interior is littered with obscure town history (€3 donation for admission).

A wonderful **open-air market** surrounds the church most Saturdays year-round and also on Sundays in summer.

The Quays—This pub was once owned by "Humanity Dick," an 18th-century Member of Parliament who was the original animal-rights activist. It's worth a peek inside for its lively interior. The lane just before it leads to the...

Druid Theatre—This 100-seat theater offers top-notch contemporary Irish theater. Drop by to see if anything's playing tonight (€16-25 tickets, Chapel Lane, tel. 091/568-660, www.druid.ie).

Directly across the alley from the theater door (under the glass Revenue Building) are the foundations of Galway's oldest building. It was once the 13th-century hall of the Norman lord Richard DeBurgo.

Spanish Arch—Overlooking the River Corrib, this makes up the best remaining chunk of the old city wall. A reminder of Galway's former importance in trade, the Arch (c. 1584) is the place where Spanish ships would unload their cargo (primarily wine).

City Museum—Fragments of old Galway are kept in this modern museum, located just behind the Spanish Arch. Enjoy temporary art exhibitions by local artists and occasional live music performances. Highlights include coverage of John F. Kennedy's 1963 visit and an intact Galway "hooker" boat hanging from the ceiling (free, Mon 14:00-17:00, Tue-Sat 10:00-17:00, closed Sun; handy café with cheap lunches, tel. 091/532-460, www.galwaycity museum.ie).

River Corrib Sights—At the River Corrib, you'll find a riverside park perfect for a picnic (or get takeout from the town's best chippy, McDonagh's, located across the street). Over the river (southeast of the bridge) is the modern housing project that replaced the original Claddagh in the 1930s. **Claddagh** (CLA-dah) was a picturesque, Gaelic-speaking fishing village with a strong tradition of independence—and open sewers. This gaggle of thatched cottages functioned as an independent community with its own "king" until the early 1900s, when it was torn down for health reasons.

The old Claddagh village is gone, but the tradition of its popular ring (sold all over town) lives on. The Claddagh ring shows two hands holding a heart that wears a crown. The heart represents

Galway Legends

Because of the dearth of physical old stuff, the town milks its legends. Here are a few that you'll encounter repeatedly:

• In the 15th century, the mayor, one of the Lynch tribe, condemned his son to death for the murder of a Spaniard. When no one in town could be found to hang the popular boy, the dad—who loved justice more than he loved his son—did it himself.

• Columbus is said to have stopped in Galway in 1477. He may have been inspired by tales of the voyage of St. Brendan, the Irish monk who is thought by some (mostly Irish) to have beaten Columbus to the New World by almost a thousand years.

• On the main drag, you'll find a pub called The King's Head. It was originally given to the man who chopped off the head of King Charles I in 1649. For his safety, he settled in Galway—about as far from London as an Englishman could get back then.

GALWAY

love, the crown is loyalty, and the hands are friendship. If the ring is worn with the tip of the heart pointing toward the wrist, it signifies that the wearer is married or otherwise taken. However, if the tip of the heart points toward the fingertip, it means the wearer is available.

Look at the **monument** (just before the bridge) given to Galway by the people of Genoa, celebrating Columbus' visit here in 1477. (That acknowledgment, from a town in Italy known for its stinginess, helps to substantiate the legendary visit.) From the middle of the bridge, look up the river. The green copper dome marks the city's Cathedral of St. Nicholas (described on the next page). Down the river is a tiny harbor with a few of Galway's famous square-rigged "hooker" fishing ships tied up and on display. Called "hookers" for their hook-and-line fishing, these sturdy yet graceful boats were later used to transport turf from Connemara, until improved roads and electric heat made them obsolete. Beyond that, a huge park of reclaimed land is popular with the local kids for Irish football and hurling. From there, the promenade leads to the resort town of Salthill.

More Sights in Galway

▲**Eyre Square**—On a sunny day, grassy Eyre Square is a popular hangout. In the Middle Ages, it was a field just outside the town wall. The square is named for the mayor who gave the land to the city in 1710. While still called Eyre Square, it now contains John

F. Kennedy Park—established in memory of the Irish-American president's visit in 1963, a few months before he was assassinated. Though Kennedy is celebrated as America's first Irish-Catholic president, several US presidents were descended from Protestant Ulster stock (even President Obama is part Irish, with roots from County Offaly). Take a look at the JFK bust (near the kids' play area) that commemorates his visit.

Walk to the rust-colored "Hooker Sculpture," built in 1984 to celebrate the 500th anniversary of the incorporation of the city. The sails represent Galway's square-rigged fishing ships ("hookers") and the vessels that made Galway a trading center so long ago. The Browne Doorway, from a 1627 fortified townhouse, is a reminder of the 14 family tribes that once ruled the town (see Lynch's Castle, listed earlier, to get a feel for an intact townhouse). Each had a town castle—much like the towers that characterize the towns of Tuscany with their feuding noble families. So little survives of medieval Galway that the town makes a huge deal of any remaining window or crest. Check out the 14 colorful flags lining the western edge of the square, each one with a different tribe name.

The Eyre Square Shopping Centre—a busy, modern shopping mall (see the arcaded entry from the square)—leads to a piece of the old town wall that includes two reconstructed towers (and an antiques market).

▲▲Cathedral of St. Nicholas—Opened by American Cardinal Cushing in 1965, this is one of the last great stone churches built

in Europe. The interior is a treat—mahogany pews set on green Connemara marble floors under a Canadian cedar ceiling. The acoustically correct cedar enhances the church's fine pipe organ. Two thousand worshippers sit in the round facing the central altar. A Dublin woman carved the 14 larger-than-life Stations of the Cross. The carving above the chapel (left of entry) is from the old St. Nicholas church. Explore the modern stained glass. Find the Irish Holy Family—with Mary knitting and Jesus offering Joseph a cup of tea. The window depicting the Last Supper is particularly creative—find the 12 apostles.

Next, poke your head into the side chapel with a mosaic of Christ's resurrection (if you're standing in the nave facing the main altar, it's on the left and closest to the front). Take a closer look at the profiled face to the right of Christ—the one looking up while praying with clasped hands. It's JFK, nearly a saint in Irish eyes at the time this cathedral was built.

Church bulletins at the doorway tell of upcoming Masses and concerts (located across Salmon Weir Bridge on outskirts of town, tel. 091/563-577).

Salmon Weir Bridge—This bridge was the local "bridge of sighs." It led from the courthouse (opposite the church) to the prison (torn down to build the cathedral—unlikely in the US). Today, the bridge provides a fun view of the fishing action. Salmon run up this river most of the summer (look for them). Fishermen, who wear waders and carry walking sticks to withstand the strong current, book long in advance to get half-day appointments for a casting spot.

Canals multiplied in this city (sometimes called the "Venice of Ireland") to power more water mills.

Outer Galway

▲**Salthill**—This small resort town packs pubs, discos, a splashy water park, amusement centers, and a fairground up against a fine, mile-long beach promenade. At the **Atlantaquaria Aquarium,** which features solely Irish water life, kids can help feed the big fish at 15:00, and the small fish at 16:00 (€10.25, Mon-Fri 10:00-17:00, Sat-Sun 10:00-18:00, touch tanks, The Promenade, tel. 091/585-100, www.nationalaquarium.ie).

For beach time, a relaxing sunset stroll, late-night traditional music, or later-night disco action, Salthill hops. A handy TI next to the aquarium is open only during the lazy summer months (June-Aug daily 9:00-17:00). To get to Salthill, catch bus #1 from Eyre Square in front of the AIB bank, next to Meyrick Hotel (€1.45, runs 7:00-23:00). For accommodations in Salthill, see page 287.

Trad on the Prom—This fine traditional-music and dance troupe was started by Galway-born performers who returned home after years of touring with *Riverdance*. It's a great way to enjoy live step dancing and accomplished musicians in a fairly intimate venue (€30, May-Sept only, call for schedule, in Salthill Hotel, 30-minute walk west of town along the Salthill promenade or short ride on bus #1 from Eyre Square, tel. 091/582-860 or mobile 087-2388-489, www.tradontheprom.com).

Dog Racing—Join the locals and cheer on the greyhounds on Thursday, Friday, and Saturday evenings from 20:00 to 22:30 (€10, barking distance from my recommended B&Bs, 10-minute walk from Eyre Square, tel. 091/562-273, www.igb.ie).

Nightlife in Galway

▲Traditional Irish Music in Pubs—Galway, like Dingle and Doolin, is a mecca for good Irish music (nightly 21:30-23:30). But unlike Dingle and Doolin, this is a university town (enrollment: 12,000), and many pubs are often overrun with noisy students. Still, your chances of landing a seat close to a churning band surrounded by new Irish friends are good any evening of the year. Touristy and student pubs are found and filled along the main drag down from Eyre Square to the Spanish Arch, and across Wolfe Tone Bridge, along William Street West and Dominick Street. Across the bridge, start at **Monroe's,** with its vast, music-filled interior (trad music Sun-Mon and Wed-Thu at 21:00, set-dancing Tue at 21:00, folk/rock music Fri-Sat, Dominick Street, tel. 091/583-397, www.monroes.ie). Several other pubs within earshot also feature almost-nightly traditional music.

Pubs known for Irish music along the main drag include

Tig Coili (sessions Mon-Sat at 18:00 and 21:00, Sun at 14:00 and 21:00, intersection of Main Guard Street and High Street, tel. 091/561-294, www.tigcoili.ie), **Taaffe's** (nightly music sessions at 17:30 and 21:30, Shop Street, across from St. Nicholas Church, tel. 091/564-066), and **The Quays** (traditional music Mon-Tue at 21:30, Fri and Sun at 17:00, young scene, Quay Street, tel. 091/568-347).

An Pucán Pub, a cauldron of music and beer drinking with an older crowd—including lots of tourists—is worth a look. An Irish dance troupe called Mystic Force performs Mondays and Wednesdays at 20:30 (music nightly at 22:00, usually traditional, just off Eyre Square on Forster Street, tel. 091/561-528, www.anpucan.com).

Sleeping in Galway

There are three price tiers for most beds in Galway: off-season, high season (Easter-Oct), and charge-what-you-like festivals and race weekends (see "Crowd Control" on page 278). I've listed high-season rates. B&Bs simply play the market. If you're on a tight budget, call around and see where the best prices are. All B&Bs include a full fried breakfast.

Sleep Code

(€1 = about $1.25, country code: 353, area code: 091)
S = Single, **D** = Double/Twin, **T** = Triple, **Q** = Quad, **b** = bathroom,
s = shower only. All of these places accept credit cards.

To help you easily sort through these listings, I've divided the rooms into three categories, based on the price for a standard double room with bath:

$$$ **Higher Priced**—Most rooms €120 or more.
$$ **Moderately Priced**—Most rooms between €60-120.
$ **Lower Priced**—Most rooms €60 or less.

Prices can change without notice; verify the hotel's current rates online or by email. For other updates, see www.ricksteves.com/update.

Hotels

For a fancy hotel, Park House Hotel offers the best value. For a budget hotel, go to Jurys. For cheap beds, hit the hostel.

$$$ Park House Hotel, a plush, business-class hotel, is ideally located a block from the train station and Eyre Square. Its 84 spacious rooms come with all the comforts you'd expect (Db-€109-169 is the "corporate rate" you should get most of the year, ask if there's a discount, often cheaper on Sun, elevator, great restaurant, free garage, helpful staff, Forster Street, tel. 091/564-924, www.parkhousehotel.ie, parkhousehotel@eircom.net).

$$$ Skeffington Arms Hotel, which feels more Irish than the Park House or Jurys Inn, escapes most of the tour-group scene because it has only 24 rooms. Centrally located on Eyre Square, it's recently renovated and furnished in a modern style (Db-€109-200, online discounts, Wi-Fi, pub next door, Eyre Square, tel. 091/563-173, fax 091/561-679, www.skeffington.ie, reception @skeffington.ie).

$$$ Hotel Meyrick, filled with palatial Old World elegance and 97 rooms, marks the end of the Dublin-Galway train line and the beginning of Galway. Since 1845, it has been Galway's landmark hotel...JFK stayed here in 1963 when it was the Great Southern (Db-€155-199, some discounts during slow times, best rates by booking online, at the head of Eyre Square, tel. 091/564-041, fax 091/566-704, www.hotelmeyrick.ie, reshm@monogram hotels.ie).

$$$ Jurys Inn Galway has 130 American-style rooms in a modern hotel, centrally located where the old town hits the river. The big, bright rooms have two double beds and huge modern bathrooms. You'll pay the same per room whether it's for a single, a couple, three adults, or a family of four (€99-119 Sun-Thu, €135-155 Fri-Sat, prices depend on season, breakfast-€9.50, elevator, 3 non-smoking floors, lots of tour groups, parking-€10, Quay Street, tel. 091/566-444, fax 091/568-415, US tel. 800-423-6953, www.jurysinns.com, jurysinngalway@jurysinns.com).

$ *Hostel:* **Kinlay House** is a no-nonsense place just 100 yards from the train station, with 224 beds (1-8 beds per room) in bare, clean, and simple rooms, including 15 doubles/twins. Easygoing people of any age feel welcome here, but if you want a double, book well ahead—several months in advance for weekends (dorm bed-€17-25, Sb-€48-60, Db-€60-70, Internet access and Wi-Fi, elevator, self-service kitchen, baggage storage, on Merchants Road just off Eyre Square, tel. 091/565-244, fax 091/565-245, www.kinlaygalway.ie, info@kinlaygalway.ie).

B&Bs

Drivers who follow city-center signs into Galway will pass a string of B&Bs just after the greyhound-racing stadium. On foot, the B&Bs are about a 10-minute walk from Eyre Square (from the station, walk up Forster Street, which turns into College Road). The following five places are lined up like battleships on College Road. Although there are other B&Bs on this road, my favorites are the ones where the owner lives on-site (and their pride of ownership shows).

$$ **Ardawn House** is a friendly B&B with nine comfortable rooms (Sb-€55-75, Db-€80-120, Tb-€110-150, Qb-€120-160, Wi-Fi, free parking, 31 College Road, near stadium on right, tel. 091/568-833, fax 091/563-454, www.ardawnhouse.com, ardawn@iol.ie, Mike and Breda Guilfoyle).

$$ **Petra House,** a peaceful-feeling brick building, rents six great rooms, including a family room. The owners, Joan and Frank Maher, keep everything lovingly maintained. Breakfasts are a highlight (Sb-€50-75, Db-€70-120, Tb-€120-140, Qb-€140-160, elegant sitting room, Wi-Fi, free parking, 29 College Road, tel. & fax 091/566-580, www.galway.net/pages/petra-house, petrahouse@eircom.net).

$$ **Four Seasons B&B** is well-kept, with seven inviting rooms hosted by Eddie and Helen Fitzgerald (Sb-€50-75, Db-€70-120, Tb-€120-140, Qb-€140-160, Wi-Fi, free parking, 23 College Road, tel. 091/564-078, www.fourseasonsgalway.com, info@fourseasonsgalway.com).

$$ **Balcony House B&B** rents eight pleasant rooms (Db-€70-120, Tb-€105-140, Qb-€140-160, free parking, 27 College Road, tel. 091/563-438, www.aaabalconyhouse.com, info@aaabalconyhouse.com). Teresa Coyne provides treats in your room on arrival.

$$ Asgard Guest House offers eight restful rooms and an appealing glass-atrium breakfast room (Sb-€45-60, Db-€70-90, Tb-€90-120, Qb-€140-160, free parking, 21 College Road, tel. 091/566-855, www.galwaycityguesthouse.com, info@galway cityguesthouse.com).

Near Galway, in Salthill

These two B&Bs are slightly west of the city, in Galway's equivalent of a beach town, with a fine sandy promenade for summer evening walks. (For more on Salthill, see page 283.) To reach either of these B&Bs, take bus #2 (3/hour, €1.45) from Eyre Square (picks up on the opposite side of square from the Skeffington Arms pub). For Carraig Beag, get off at the Knocknacarra stop; for Clarevilla, use the Threadneedle stop.

$$ Carraig Beag B&B, classy, friendly, and peaceful, is a big brick home on a residential street a block off the beach, just beyond the resort town of Salthill. Catherine Lydon and her husband, Paddy, rent six big, bright, fresh, and comfy rooms with a welcoming living room and a communal breakfast table (Sb-€55-80, Db-€80-100, family room-€90-120, cash only, closed Nov-March; 8-minute drive from Galway, follow the beach past Salthill, take second right after the golf course on Knocknacarra Road and go 2 blocks to 1 Burren View Heights; tel. 091/521-696, www.dirl.com /galway/salthill/carraig-beag.htm, thelydons@circom.net).

$$ Clarevilla B&B, a good, quiet choice 200 yards from the beach in a mellow residential area, has six serenely decorated, blue/ green rooms (Sb-€45-50, Db-€70-75, Tb-€90, cash only, Wi-Fi, non-smoking, closed Nov-Feb; 7-minute drive from Galway, follow the beach past Salthill, take right on Threadneedle Road just before the beach's high diving board, 200 yards up on the left next to Tennis Club at 38 Threadneedle Road; tel. 091/522-520, clare villa@yahoo.com).

Eating in Galway

This college town is filled with colorful, inexpensive eateries. People everywhere seem to be enjoying their food. Each of these places is at the bottom of the old town, within a block or two of Jurys Inn.

Kirwan's Lane Creative Cuisine, considered Galway's best restaurant, is a dressy place where reservations are required (€16-22 lunches, €24-30 dinners, daily 12:30-14:30 & 18:00-22:00, no lunch on Sun, on Kirwan's Lane a block from Jurys Inn, tel. 091/568-266).

Busker Brownes has three eateries in a sprawling spot popular for its good, cheap food. Enter on Cross Street for the restaurant and walk to the back for better seating, or enter on Kirwan's Lane for the ground-floor pub; the third section is upstairs from the pub (€11-25 meals, daily 10:30-21:30, jazz sessions Sun at 12:00 and Mon at 21:30, Cross Street and Kirwan's Lane, tel. 091/563-377).

McDonagh's Fish-and-Chips is a local favorite. It has a fast, cheap section and a classier restaurant. If you're determined to try Galway oysters, remember that they're in season from September through April only. At other times, you'll eat Pacific oysters—which doesn't make much sense to me (€10 lunch, €15-25 in restaurant, €20 two-course early-bird special served 17:00-18:45, open Mon-Sat 12:00-15:00 & 17:00-22:00, chipper open Sun 16:00-22:00 but restaurant closed, 22 Quay Street, tel. 091/565-001).

Nimmo's Wine Bar Bistro and **Ard Bia Café** peacefully coexist in an old stone warehouse behind the Spanish Arch. The upstairs is a mellow hangout with great cheese platters and wine. The candlelit ambience is great any night, even for a cup of coffee (€15-26 meals, café lunches Tue-Sat 10:30-15:30, wine-bar dinners Tue-Sun 18:00-21:30, closed Mon, Long Walk Street, tel. 091/561-114 or 091/539-897).

McSwiggan's, with a downstairs pub and upstairs restaurant, is a maze of wooden stairways, brick walls, and hidden alcoves, serving hearty traditional Irish meals (€12-18 lunches, €14-22 dinners, daily 12:00-22:30, Eyre Street, tel. 091/568-917).

Bella Roma serves friendly Italian trattoria-style meals, just a five-minute walk toward town from my College Road B&B listings (€13-23 meals, €20 three-course early-bird specials, daily 12:30-23:00, facing Bothar Ui Eithir 50 yards up from corner with Forster Street, tel. 091/561-996).

The **Galway Bakery Company (GBC)** is a popular, basic place for a quick Irish meal (€11-15 meals in ground-floor cafeteria, pricier restaurant upstairs, daily 12:00-21:00, 7 Williams Gate, near Eyre Square, tel. 091/563-087).

Supermarket: **Dunnes** is accessed through the Eyre Square Shopping Centre or around the corner at tiny Castle Street, off the pedestrian Williams Gate (Mon-Sat 9:00-19:00, Thu-Fri until 20:00, Sun 12:00-19:00, supermarket in basement). Lots of smaller grocery shops are scattered throughout town.

Near Galway, in Salthill

Lohan's Restaurant is right on the seafront promenade in Salthill (just west of the aquarium) and offers traditional Irish favorites at reasonable prices (€11-16 meals, daily 12:00-22:00, 232 Upper Salthill, tel. 091/522-696).

Outside Galway

If you have a car, consider a **Dunguaire Castle medieval banquet** in Kinvarra, a 30-minute drive south of Galway. The banquet starts at 17:30 and can be done very efficiently when you're driving into or out of Galway (B&Bs can accommodate late arrivals if you call; for details on the banquet, see the end of the previous chapter).

Galway Connections

From Galway by Train to: Dublin (8/day, 2.5-3 hours), **Limerick** (5/day, 2 hours), **Ennis** (5/day, 1.25 hours). For **Belfast, Tralee,** and **Rosslare,** you'll change in or near Dublin. Train info: tel. 091/561-444, www.irishrail.ie.

By Bus to: Ennis (hourly, 1.25 hours), **Doolin** (5/day, 1.5-2 hours), **Cliffs of Moher** (7/day in summer, some with change in Ennis, 2 hours), **Limerick** (hourly, 2.25 hours), **Rosslare** (hourly, 7.5 hours), **Shannon Airport** (hourly, 1.75 hours; also see Citylink, below), **Belfast** (hourly, 7 hours, change in Dublin), **Dublin** (hourly, 3.25 hours; also see Citylink, below). Bus info: tel. 091/562-000, www.buseireann.ie.

Citylink (tel. 091/564-164, www.citylink.ie) runs cheap and fast bus service from the coach station near the TI to **Dublin** (arriving at Bachelor's Walk, a block from Tara Street DART station; hourly, 2.5 hours), **Dublin Airport** (hourly, 3 hours), and **Shannon Airport** (3/day, 1.25 hours).

By Car: For ideas on driving from Galway to Derry or Portrush in Northern Ireland, see "Between Galway and Derry" at the end of the Connemara and County Mayo chapter, which describes sights in the Republic of Ireland. For sights on this route in Northern Ireland, see "Between Derry and Galway" on page 390.

ARAN ISLANDS

Strewn like limestone chips hammered off the jagged west coast, the three Aran Islands—Inishmore, Inishmaan, and Inisheer—confront the wild Atlantic with stubborn grit. The largest, Inishmore (9 miles by 2 miles), is by far the most populated, interesting, and visited. The landscape of all three islands is harsh: steep, rugged cliffs and windswept rocky fields divided by stone walls. During the winter, severe gales sweep the islands; because of this, most of the settlements on Inishmore are found on its more sheltered eastern side.

There's a stark beauty about these islands and the simple lives their inhabitants eke out of six inches of topsoil and a mean sea. Precious little of the land is productive. In the past, people made a precarious living here from fishing and farming. The scoured bedrock offered little in the way of soil for farming, so it was created by the islanders—the result of centuries of layering seaweed with limestone sand and animal dung. The fields are small, divided by several thousand miles of "drystone" wall (made without mortar). Most of these are built in the Aran "gap" style, in which spaces between angled upright stones are filled with smaller stones. This allows a farmer who wants to move stock to dismantle and rebuild the wall. It also allows the harsh winter winds to blow through without knocking down the wall. Nowadays, tourism boosts the local economy.

The islands are a Gaeltacht area. While the islanders speak Irish amongst themselves, they happily speak English for their visitors. Many of them have direct, personal connections with close relatives in America.

Today, the 900 people of Inishmore (literally "the big island")

greet as many as 2,000 visitors a
day. The vast majority of these are
day-trippers. They'll hop on a minibus at the dock for a 2.5-hour tour
to Dún Aenghus (the must-see Iron
Age fort), then spend an hour or
two browsing through the few shops
or sitting at a picnic table outside a
pub with a pint of Guinness.

The other islands, Inishmaan
and Inisheer, are smaller, much less
populated, and less touristy. While
extremely quiet, they do have
B&Bs, daily flights, and ferry service. For most, the big island is
quiet enough.

Planning Your Time

Most travelers visit Inishmore as a day trip by boat from Galway.
(Boats from Doolin are too slow and weather-dependent to allow
enough time for a same-day round-trip to Inishmore.) Here's a
good framework for a day trip: Leave Galway at 9:00 on the shuttle
bus to Rossaveel, where you'll catch the 10:30 boat. You'll step off
the boat in Kilronan at about 11:15. Arrange minibus transport
or rent a bike, visit Dún Aenghus, and grab a bite at a café near
the base of the Dún Aenghus fort trail. Explore the island during
low tide, and depart on the boat when high tides return between
16:00 and 18:00. You can squeeze an extra hour or two out of your
day trip by booking an early flight over and a late flight back from
Connemara Regional Airport near Rossaveel. For more details on
these options, see "Aran Islands Connections" at the end of this
chapter.

Staying Overnight: Travelers spending the night can savor
the quiet time before and after the day-trip crowds. Here's how I'd
suggest you spend your arrival day: Since most day-trippers make a
beeline straight off the boat to Dún Aenghus, head in the opposite
direction to check out the subtle charms of the less-visited eastern
end of the island. Grab a quick bite en route at the Óstán Árann
hotel, or buy a picnic at the Spar supermarket in Kilronan. Then
walk to either the ruins of tiny St. Benen's Church (easy 20-minute
hike one way from Tigh Fitz B&B) or the rugged Black Fort ruins
(rocky 45-minute scramble one way from Óstán Árann). Save Dún
Aenghus for later in the afternoon, after the midday crowds have
subsided (allow an hour at Dún Aenghus, closes at 18:00 March-
Oct, off-season at 16:00, last entry one hour before closing). Enjoy
an evening in the pubs and take a no-rush midmorning boat trip
back to the mainland the next day.

Inishmore Island: Kilronan

By far the Aran Islands' largest town, Kilronan is still just a village. Groups of backpackers wash ashore with the docking of each ferry. Minibuses, bike shops, and a few men in pony carts sop up the tourists.

Orientation to Inishmore

Your first stop on Inishmore is the town of Kilronan, huddling around the pier. There are about a dozen shops and B&Bs, about half as many restaurants, and a couple of bike-rental huts.

A few blocks inland up the high road, you'll find the best folk-music pub, a post office (Mon-Fri 9:00-13:00 & 14:00-17:30, Sat 9:00-13:00, closed Sun), and a tiny bank across from the roofless Anglican church ruins (open only on Wed 10:00-12:30 & 13:30-15:00, plus Thu June-Aug). A friendly Internet café lurks upstairs in the stony Aran Sweater Market building, across from the high cross (May-Sept daily 10:00-20:00, shorter hours in winter, €1/10 minutes, €5/hour, also shows *Man of Aran* film described under "Sights on Inishmore").

The huge Spar supermarket, two blocks inland from the harbor, seems too big for the tiny community and has the island's only ATM. If you don't have plenty of cash on you, get some here—most B&Bs and quite a few other businesses don't accept credit cards.

Tourist Information

Kilronan's TI is helpful, but don't rely on it for accommodations; the B&B owners who work with the TI are out of town and desperate (daily 10:00-17:00, July-Aug until 18:00, shorter winter hours, faces the harbor, tel. 099/61263). The TI will store bags for day-trippers for €1 per bag, and offers free maps of the island (though your ferry operator may have already given you one). This map is all the average day-tripper or leisure biker will need to navigate. But serious hikers who plan on scampering out to the island's craggy fringes will want to invest in the detailed black-and-white *Oileáin Árann* map by Tim Robinson (€11.50, sold in Kilronan TI and some bookstores in Galway). Public WCs are 100 yards beyond the TI on the harbor road.

Getting Around Inishmore

Just about anything on wheels functions as a taxi here. A trip from Kilronan to Dún Aenghus to the Seven Churches and back to Kilronan costs €10 per person in a shared minibus. Pony carts cost

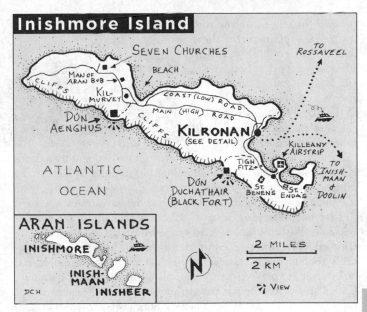

Inishmore Island

(Map labels)
SEVEN CHURCHES
TO ROSSAVEEL
MAN OF ARAN B&B
BEACH
CLIFFS
KIL-MURVEY
COAST (LOW) ROAD
DÚN AENGHUS
MAIN (HIGH) ROAD
CLIFFS
KILRONAN (SEE DETAIL)
KILLEANY AIRSTRIP
ATLANTIC OCEAN
TIGH FITZ
TO INISH-MAAN & DOOLIN
DÚN DUCHATHAIR (BLACK FORT)
ST. BENENS
ST. ENDAS
ARAN ISLANDS
INISHMORE
INISH-MAAN
INISHEER
DCH
2 MILES
2 KM
N
VIEW

about €50 for two people (€80 for 4) for a trip to Dún Aenghus and back. Biking is great, although the terrain is hilly and there are

occasional headwinds (€10/day plus €10 deposit, 30-minute ride to start of trailhead up to Dún Aenghus). Cyclists should take the high road over and the low road back—fewer hills, scenic shoreline, and, at low tide, a dozen seals basking in the sun. Keep a sharp lookout along the roads for handy, modern stone signposts (with distances in kilometers) that point the way to important sights. They're in Irish, but you'll be clued in by the small metal depictions of the sight embedded within them.

Tours on Inishmore

▲**Island Minibus Tours**—Roughly 100 vehicles roam the island, and most of them seem to be minibuses. A line of buses awaits the arrival of each ferry, offering €10, 2.5-hour island tours. Chat with a few drivers to find one who likes to talk. On my tour, I learned that 800 islanders live in 14 villages, with three elementary schools and three churches. Most islanders own a small detached field where they keep a couple of cows (sheep are too much trouble). When pressed for more information, my guide explained that there are 400 different flowers and 19 different types of bees on the island. The tour, a convenient time-saver, zips you to the end of the island for a quick stroll in the desolate fields, gives you 10 minutes to wander through the historic but visually unimpressive Seven Churches, and then drops you off for two hours at Dún Aenghus (30 minutes to hike up, 30 minutes at the fort, 20-minute hike back down, 40 minutes in café for lunch or shopping at drop-off point) before running you back to Kilronan. Ask your driver to take you back along the smaller coastal road (scenic beaches and sunbathing seals at low tide).

Guided Bike Tours—Led by Cathal Joyce, these tours are especially good for active travelers staying overnight on Inishmore, but only run if at least five people sign up. Departing from Kilronan, Cathal shows you the less traveled, more intimate, eastern end of the island with stops at St. Enda's Church, St. Benen's Church, and the Black Fort (€10, 4 hours, departs at 12:00 and 17:00, price does not include bike rental, call ahead to book and decide meeting place, mobile 087-926-9598).

Sights on Inishmore

In Kilronan

Man of Aran **Film**—This award-winning 1934 movie is a documentary about traditional island life with an all-local cast. The movie tries to re-create life in the early 1900s—when you couldn't rent bikes—and features *currach*s (canoe-like boats) in a storm, shark fishing with handheld harpoons, and farmers cultivating the fields from bare rock. It plays in the Internet café behind the Aran Sweater Market (€5, 6 showings/day).

Beyond the Town

▲▲▲**Dún Aenghus (Dun Aonghasa)**—This is the island's blockbuster sight. The stone fortress hangs spectacularly and precariously on the edge of a cliff 300 feet above the Atlantic. The crashing waves seem to say, "You've come to the end of the world." Little is known about this

2,000-year-old Celtic fort. Its concentric walls are 13 feet thick and 10 feet high. As an added defense, the fort is ringed with a commotion of spiky stones, sticking up like lances, called a *chevaux-de-frise* (literally, "Frisian horses," named for the Frisian soldiers who used pikes to stop charging cavalry). Slowly, as the cliff erodes, hunks of the fort fall into the sea. Dún Aenghus doesn't get crowded until after 11:00. I enjoyed a half-hour completely alone at 10:00 in the tourist season; if you can, get there early or late (€3, daily March-Oct 10:00-18:00, Nov-Feb 10:00-16:00, guides at the trailhead June-Aug answer questions and can sometimes give free tours up at the fort if you call ahead, 5.5 miles from Kilronan, tel. 099/61008). A small museum displays findings from recent digs and tells the story of the fort. Advice from rangers: Wear walking shoes and watch your kids closely; there's no fence between you and a crumbling 300-foot cliff overlooking the sea.

Seven Churches (Na Seacht Teampaill)—Close to the western tip of the island, this gathering of ruined chapels, monastic houses, and fragments of a high cross dates from the 8th to 11th centuries. The island is dotted with reminders that Christianity was brought to the islands in the fifth century by St. Enda, who established a monastery here. Many great monks studied under Enda. Among these "Irish apostles" who started Ireland's "Age of Saints and Scholars" (A.D. 500-900), was Columba (Colmcille in Irish), the founder of a monastery on the island of Iona in Scotland, where the Book of Kells was later written.

Kilmurvey—The island's second village sits below Dún Aenghus. With a gaggle of homes, a B&B, a great sheltered swimming beach, and a pub, this is the place for peaceful solitude (except for the folk music in the pub).

Ancient Sites near Killeany—The quiet eastern end of Inishmore offers ancient sites in evocative settings for overnight visitors with more time, or for those seeking rocky hikes devoid of crowds. First, get a good hiking map from the Kilronan TI. Then consider lunch at the Óstán Árann hotel, or assemble a picnic, to fuel up either before or after a couple of hours spent exploring these sights on foot. Ask the folks in town for directions (almost always a memorable experience in Ireland).

Closest to the road, amid the dunes one mile past the Tigh Fitz B&B and just south of the airport, is the eighth-century **St. Enda's Church** (Teaghlach Einne). Protected from wave erosion by a stubborn breakwater, it sits half-submerged in a sandy graveyard, surrounded by a sea of sawgrass and peppered with tombstones. St. Enda is said to be buried here, along with 125 other saints who flocked to Inishmore in the fifth century to learn from him.

St. Benen's Church (Teampall Bheanáin) perches high on a desolate ridge opposite the Tigh Fitz B&B. Walk up the stone-walled lane, passing a holy well and the stubby remains of a round tower. Then take another visual fix on the church's silhouette on the horizon, and zigzag up the stone terraces to the top. The 20-minute hike up from the B&B pays off with a great view. Dedicated to St. Benen, a young disciple of St. Patrick himself, this tiny (12 foot by 6 foot) 10th-century oratory is aligned north-south (instead of the usual east-west) to protect the doorway from prevailing winds.

About a five-minute walk past the Tigh Fitz B&B (heading toward the airport), you'll notice an abandoned stone pier and an adjacent, modest medieval ruin. This was **Arkin Fort,** built by Cromwell's soldiers in 1652 using cut stones taken from the round tower and the monastic ruins that once stood below St. Benen's Church. The fort was used as a prison for outlawed priests before they were sent by English authorities to the West Indies to be sold into slavery.

Hidden on a remote, ragged headland an hour's walk from Kilronan to the south side of the island, you'll find the **Black Fort** (Dún Duchathair). After Dún Aenghus, this is Inishmore's most dramatic fortification. Built on a promontory with cliffs on three sides, its defenders would have held out behind drystone ramparts, facing the island's interior attackers. Watch your step on the uneven ground, be ready to course-correct as you go, and chances are you'll have this windswept ruin all to yourself.

Entertainment on Inishmore

Pub Music—Kilronan's pubs sporadically offer music on summer nights. Nothing is regularly scheduled, so ask at your B&B or look for posted notices on the front of the Spar supermarket or post office. **Joe Watty's Pub,** on the high road 100 yards past the post office, sometimes has good Irish folk music on Wednesdays and weekends. The more central **Joe Mac's Pub** (next to the hostel) and the **American Bar** (next to the high cross at the base of the high road) are also possibilities.

Dancing—The **Halla Ronain community center** becomes a dance hall on a few Saturday nights, when from midnight to 2:00 in the morning, locals have a *ceilidh* (KAY-lee), the Irish equivalent of a hoedown. Ask at the TI to see if one is scheduled during your stay.

Kilronan

TO DÚN AENGHUS
(MAIN HIGH ROAD) & **7**

TO LOW
COAST
ROAD

200 YARDS
200 METERS

9

3

POST

12

HALLA RONAIN
COMMUNITY
CENTRE

8
6

4
11
10
2

5

13

i

1

TO
AIRPORT
(KILLEANY
ROAD)

NEW
PIER →

BOATS TO
ROSSAVEEL,
INISHMAAN & DOOLIN

ARAN ISLANDS

1 Óstán Árann Hotel & Rest.
2 The Pier House B&B & Bia Rest.
3 Clai Ban B&B
4 Tigh Catherine B&B
5 Seacrest B&B
6 Kilronan Hostel & Joe Mac's Pub
7 To Man of Aran B&B

8 Sean Cheibh Café
9 Joe Watty's Pub
10 American Bar
11 Aran Fisherman Rest. & Airport Shuttle
12 Spar Supermarket
13 Aran Sweater Market (Internet Café & Man of Aran Film)

Sleeping on Inishmore

Remember, this is a poor island. Most rooms are plain, with sparse plumbing. Only Óstán Árann and the Pier House take credit cards.

In Kilronan

$$$ Óstán Árann is Inishmore's first modern hotel, with a good restaurant and 22 large, well-furnished rooms, five with grand patio views of the harbor (Sb-€59-79, Db-€79-159, Tb-€119-199,

Sleep Code

(€1 = about $1.25, country code: 353, area code: 099)
S = Single, **D** = Double/Twin, **T** = Triple, **Q** = Quad, **b** = bathroom, **s** = shower only. Breakfast is included and most places are cash-only.

To help you easily sort through these listings, I've divided the rooms into three categories, based on the price for a standard double room with bath:

$$$ Higher Priced—Most rooms €80 or more.
  $$ Moderately Priced—Most rooms between €50-80.
   $ Lower Priced—Most rooms €50 or less.

Prices can change without notice; verify the hotel's current rates online or by email. For other updates, see www .ricksteves.com/update.

Qb-€179-259, 2- to 3-night midweek deals, Wi-Fi; 10-minute walk from pier, about 100 yards past Halla Ronain community center; tel. 099/61104, fax 099/61225, www.aranislandshotel.com, info @aranislandshotel.com).

$$$ The Pier House stands solidly 50 yards from the pier, offering 12 decent rooms, a good restaurant downstairs, and sea views from many of its rooms (Db-€70-110, tel. 099/61417, fax 099/61122, www.pierhousearan.com, pierhousearan@gmail.com).

$$ Clai Ban, the only really cheery place in town, is worth the 10-minute uphill walk from the pier. The Hernon youngsters have become avid traditional musicians (Sb-€50-70, Db-€60-70, Tb-€90-105, cash only, walk past bank out of town and down lane on left, tel. 099/61111, fax 099/61423, claibanhouse@gmail.com, Marion Hernon).

$$ Tigh Catherine is a well-kept B&B with four homey rooms overlooking the harbor (Sb-€45-50, Db-€70, cash only, on Church Road up behind the Halla Ronain community center, tel. 099/61464, mobile 087-980-9748, Catherine Mulkerrin).

$$ Seacrest B&B offers six uncluttered rooms in a central location next to the Aran Fisherman restaurant. Geraldine Faherty manages the rooms while Tom Faherty keeps the ferries afloat (Sb-€45, Db-€70, Tb-€90, cash only, non-smoking, Wi-Fi, tel. 099/61292, mobile 085-285-9777, seacrestaran@gmail.com).

Hostel: **$ Kilronan Hostel,** overlooking the harbor near the TI, is cheap but noisy above Joe Mac's Pub (€20-25 beds in 4- to 6-bed rooms, cash only, includes breakfast, free Internet access and Wi-Fi, self-service kitchen, tel. 099/61255, www.kilronan hostel.com, kilronanhostel@ireland.com).

Elsewhere on Inishmore

$$$ Man of Aran B&B, as classy as a thatched cottage can be, is in the peaceful countryside four miles outside of touristy Kilronan, toward the western end of the island. Rooms are quiet and rustic, with fireplaces. The restaurant serves €20-25 meals (with home-grown vegetables and herbs) only to overnight guests. The setting is pristine—this is where the movie of the same name was filmed more than 75 years ago (S-€55, D-€80, Db-€90, cash only, reserve well in advance; 4 miles from Kilronan, bear right 100 yards after passing Kilmurvey Beach before Dún Aenghus turnoff; tel. 099/61301, www.manofarancottage.com, manofaran@eircom.net, Maura and Joe Wolf).

Eating on Inishmore

There are few restaurants in Kilronan. The best is the modern **Óstán Árann** hotel on the south fringe of town (lunch 12:30-18:00 in the Patin Jack Bar, dinner 18:00-21:30, tel. 099/61104).

The Pier House operates the dependable **Bia Restaurant** below its guest house (€12-18 lunches, €18-25 dinners, daily 11:00-22:00, tel. 099/61811).

Otherwise, Kilronan's modest cafés dish up hearty soup, soda bread, sandwiches, and tea.

Sean Cheibh ("Old Pier"), which seems to slam out more meals than the rest of the town combined, is popular for its fish-and-chips and great clam chowder (eat in or take out, April-mid-Oct daily 11:00-19:00, closed mid-Oct-March, tel. 099/61228).

The **Spar** supermarket has all the groceries you'll need (June-Aug Mon-Sat 9:00-20:00, Sun 10:00-17:00; Sept-May Mon-Sat 9:00-18:00, closed Sun).

Aran Islands Connections

For an overview map of the region, see page 257.

By Ferry from Rossaveel: Island Ferries sails to Inishmore from Rossaveel, a port 20 miles west of Galway. The company sells tickets at the Galway TI and runs a 45-minute shuttle bus from Galway to the Rossaveel dock (3/day April-Oct, 2/day Nov-March, 40-minute crossing; coming from Galway, allow 2 hours in transit one-way including 45-minute bus ride; €25 round-trip boat cross-ing plus €7 round-trip for Galway-Rossaveel shuttle bus, WCs on board). Catch shuttle buses from Galway on Queen Street, a block behind the Kinlay House hostel (check-in 1.5 hours before sailing); shuttles return to Galway immediately after each boat arrives. Ferry schedule for April-Oct: from Rossaveel at 10:30, 13:00, and 18:30; from Inishmore at 8:15, 12:00, 16:00, and 17:00 (plus 19:30

ARAN ISLANDS

June-Aug). Island Ferries has two offices in Galway: across from Kinlay House on Merchants Road, and on Forster Street near the Park House Hotel. Tickets are also sold at the TIs in Galway and Salthill (tel. 091/568-903, after-hours tel. 091/572-273, www.aran islandferries.com).

Drivers should go straight to the ferry landing in Rossaveel, passing several ticket agencies and pay parking lots. At the boat dock, you'll find a convenient €5-per-day lot and a small office that sells tickets for Island Ferries. Check to see what's going when and for how much.

By Ferry from Doolin: Boats from Doolin to the Aran Islands can be handy, but they are often canceled or run late. Even a balmy day can be too windy (or the tide can be too low) to allow for a sailing from Doolin's crude little port. If you're traveling under tight time limits, don't risk sailing from Doolin.

While it's possible to travel from Doolin to Inishmore and back in one day, keep in mind that it's a longer trip to distant Inishmore than the other two Aran Islands (leaving less time ashore to explore this most worthwhile island before you have to turn around and sail back to Doolin). Instead, consider an overnight stay on Inishmore. (Note that parking is free beside the Doolin pier, even overnight.) If you have a car, Doolin is easy to reach; without one, it's better to get to Inishmore from Rossaveel (described earlier).

The scene at the Doolin ferry dock is a confusing mosh pit of competition. Three ferry companies have similar schedules and compete hard for your business to Inishmore. Although they all promise to get you to Inishmore in an hour, every one of my trips in the past few years has included brief stops at Inisheer and Inishmaan en route, making the actual crossing time about 1.5 hours. **Aran Doolin Ferries** has been at it longest (to Inishmore: €20 round-trip, 2/day, 1.5 hours, leaves at 10:00 and 13:00, returns at 11:30 and 16:00; to Inisheer: €15 same-day round-trip, does not include Cliffs of Moher, 2/day, 30 minutes, departs 10:00 and 13:00, returns 12:30 and 16:45; tel. 065/707-4455, www.doolinferries.com). **Doolin Ferry** offers similar schedules and prices (tel. 065/707-5555, www .doolinferry.com). **Doolin2Aran Ferries** operates essentially the same service at the same prices, and also offers a fun €25 triangular day trip from Doolin to Inisheer, the closest island, that returns to Doolin along the base of the Cliffs of Moher (departs 9:00, drops you off on Inisheer for a few hours, has you back in Doolin by 16:00, tel. 065/707-5949, mobile 087-245-3239, www.doolin2aranferries .com). **Cliffs of Moher Cruises** offers a similar Inisheer/Cliffs of Moher day trip (see "Cruises from Doolin" on page 265). No matter which company you choose, it's smart to phone a day or two ahead to confirm schedules and prices.

By Plane: Aer Arann Islands, a friendly and flexible little airline, flies daily, stopping at all three islands (3/day, up to 15/day

in peak season, €45 round-trip, groups of 4 or more pay €40 each, 10-minute flight). These flights get booked up—reserve a day or two in advance with a credit card. Their nine-seat planes take off from the Connemara Regional Airport (not the Galway airport). It's 20 slow miles west of Galway, so allow 45 minutes for the drive, plus 30 minutes to check in before the scheduled departure. A minibus shuttle—€3 one-way—runs from Kinlay House on Merchants Road in Galway an hour before each flight. The Kilronan airport on Inishmore is miniscule. A minibus shuttle travels the two miles between the airport and Kilronan (buses stop at Aran Fisherman restaurant) and costs €5 round-trip. For reservations and seat availability, contact the airline (tel. 091/593-034, fax 091/593-238, www.aer arannislands.ie, aerarann@iol.ie).

A new, sightseeing-only Aer Arann flight leaves from the same airport at 12:00 each day. You'll fly above all three Aran Islands with an extra swoop past the Cliffs of Moher (€50, 30 minutes, may not go if not enough people sign up).

ARAN ISLANDS

CONNEMARA
and **COUNTY MAYO**

If you have a car, consider spending a day exploring the wild western Irish fringe known as Connemara and straying into historic County Mayo. Gaze up at the peak of Croagh Patrick, the mountain from which St. Patrick supposedly banished the snakes from Ireland. Pass through the desolate Doo Lough valley on a road stained with tragic famine history. Bounce on a springy peat bog, and drop in at a Westport pub owned by a member of the Chieftains (a well-known traditional Irish music group). This beautiful area also claims a couple of towns—Cong and Leenane—where classic Irish movies were filmed, as well as the photogenic Kylemore Abbey.

Connemara makes a satisfying day trip by car from Galway. Without a car, you can take a tour from Galway or at least get to Westport by bus. Public transportation in this region is patchy, and some areas are not served at all. Trains connect Galway and Westport to Dublin, but not to each other.

Bus Tours of Connemara

Three Galway-based organizations—**Lally Tours, O'Neachtain Tours,** and **Galway Tour Company**—run all-day tours of nearby regions (€25). Tours of Connemara include the *Quiet Man* cottage, Kylemore Abbey, Clifden, and the "Famine Village." Galway Tour Company takes a slightly different route that includes Cong but omits the coast of Connemara. Tours go most days, heading out about 10:00 and returning at 17:30 (departing from in front of Kinlay House on Merchant's Road in Galway, call to confirm exact itinerary: Lally Tours tel. 091/562-905, www.lallytours.com; O'Neachtain Tours tel. 091/553-188, www.ontours.biz; Galway

Connemara & County Mayo Loop

Tour Company tel. 091/566-566, www.galwaytourcompany.com). All three companies also offer tours of the Burren and Cliffs of Moher, with discounts if you book two separate tours. Drivers take cash only; to pay with a credit card, book at Galway's TI.

Self-Guided Driving Tour

Connemara and Mayo Loop Trip

This tour involves a full day of driving (almost 200 miles, using Galway as your base). Start early, so your day will be less rushed. Those wanting to slow down and linger can sleep in Westport. These country roads, punctuated by blind curves and surprise bumps, are shared by trucks, tractors, cyclists, more tractors, and sheep. Drive sanely, and bring rain gear and your sense of humor. This is rural Ireland with all the trimmings.

Bring along a good map (Ordnance Survey atlases are widely sold in Ireland), and before you start, study the loop connecting these points: Galway, Cong, Westport, Louisburgh, Leenane, Kylemore Abbey, Clifden, and back to Galway.

Route Summary: Take N-84 north out of Galway. At Cross, take R-346 into Cong and R-345 back out again. At Neale, go north on R-334 and pick up N-84 again from Ballinrobe to Partry. Take R-330 from Partry to Westport. After lunch in Westport, go west on R-335 through Louisburgh and south through Doo Lough Valley all the way to Leenane. Pick up N-59 in Leenane and take it to Kylemore Abbey, continuing to Letterfrack and Connemara National Park. Continue south to Clifden, where you'll turn off onto R-341. Hug the coast through Roundstone before finding the junction with N-59 near Recess. Follow N-59 back to Galway via Maam Cross and Oughterard.

The Tour Begins

• *From Galway's Eyre Square, drive north out of town on Prospect Hill Road. Follow the signs at each roundabout in the direction of Castlebar onto N–84. You'll soon be out of Galway's suburbs and crossing miles of flat bogland laced with simple rock walls. You may notice the flags on the phone poles changing colors, from burgundy and white to green and red. These are the colors of the local hurling and football teams. You've crossed the border from County Galway into County Mayo. At Cross, take R–346 to Cong. You'll pass the grand, gray gateway of Ashford Castle (on the left) as you approach the town.*

Cong

Plan to spend an hour in Cong (1.5 hours if you include the Ashford Castle grounds). Cross the small bridge and park in front of the abbey. Drop into the **TI** across from the abbey entrance for a map (daily March-Nov 10:00-17:00, July-Aug until 18:00, closed Dec-Feb, tel. 094/954-6542). There are no banks or ATMs in Cong. Public WCs are 50 yards down the street across from the *Quiet Man* **cottage.** That's right, pilgrim, this town is where John Wayne and Maureen O'Hara made the famous John Ford film *The Quiet Man* in 1951. The cottage's modest historical exhibits (upstairs) and film props (downstairs) are really only worth it for diehard fans of the Duke (€5, mid-March-Oct daily 10:30-16:30, closed Nov-mid-March, tel. 094/954-6089). Fuel up on a cup of coffee and homemade dessert at the **Hungry Monk Café** (July-Aug daily 10:00-18:00; mid-March-June and Sept-Oct Wed-Mon 10:00-18:00, closed Tue; closed Nov-mid-March; Internet access, on Abbey Street between public WCs and TI, tel. 094/954-5842).

We're here for the ruins of **Cong Abbey** (free and always open). The abbey was built in the early 1100s, when Romanesque was going out of style and Gothic was coming in; you'll see the mixture of rounded Romanesque and pointy Gothic arch styles in the doorway. The famous Cross of Cong, which held a holy relic of what was supposedly a splinter of the True Cross, was hoisted aloft at the front of processions of Augustinian monks during High Masses in this church. This Irish art treasure is now on display in Dublin's National Museum. Rory O'Connor, the last Irish high king, died in this abbey in 1198. After O'Connor realized he could never outfight the superior Norman armies, he retreated to Cong and spent his last years here in monastic isolation.

Take a walk through the cloister and down the gravel path behind the abbey. The forested grounds are lush, and the stream

water is incredibly clear. Cong's salmon hatchery contributes to western Ireland's reputation for great fishing. The monks fished for more than sinners. They built the modest **Monks' Fishing Hut,** just over the footbridge, right on the bank so that the river flowed underneath. They lowered a net through the floor and attached a bell to the rope; whenever a fish was netted, the bell would ring.

To reach **Ashford Castle** from the abbey, face the Romanesque/Gothic main entrance and go left around the corner of the abbey, walking 15 minutes down the pleasant forested lane onto the grounds of the castle, which is hidden behind the trees. Garden-lovers happily hand over €5 to the kid hired by the castle

to patrol the bridge, just so they can stroll the lakeside paradise once owned by the Guinness beer family (stiff €5 entry fee in effect July-Aug, usually free rest of year). The renovated Victorian castle rents some of the finest rooms in all of Ireland, and casual gawkers are discouraged inside. President Reagan stayed here in 1984, and actor Pierce Brosnan chose these gardens for his wedding reception in 2001. Many scenes from *The Quiet Man* were filmed on the

castle grounds. As you stroll the grounds, contemplate the fact that "tourism" (the notion of travel solely for enjoyment) didn't exist until the Victorian Age. Before that time, travel was a chore only endured by armies, refugees, traders, emigrants, and religious pilgrims.

Cong (from *conga*, Irish for "isthmus") lies between two large lakes. Departing Cong over the same bridge on which you entered, squint down through the thick vegetation to imagine the dry canal that once existed here. Built between 1848 and 1854, this canal was a Great Potato Famine work project that stoked only appetites. The canal, complete with locks, would have linked Lough Mask to the north with Lough Corrib to the south. But the limestone bedrock proved too porous, and the canal wouldn't hold water.

• *Take R-345 out of Cong (left turn opposite the main stone gateway to the grounds of Ashford Castle). Heading north, you'll pass through the tiny hamlet of...*

Neale

About 125 years ago, a retired army captain named Boycott was hired to manage the nearby estate of Lord Erne. But the strict captain treated the tenants who worked his lands harshly, so they united to ostracize him by deserting their jobs and isolating his estate. Over time, the agitation worked, and eventually "boycotting" became a popular tactic in labor conflicts.

• *At Neale, go north on R-334, then take N-84 from Ballinrobe to Partry. At Partry, turn left off N-84 onto R-330 in the direction of Westport (the easy-to-miss turnoff is just after you pass the thatch-roofed Village Inn). In the countryside a few miles to your right is the site of the...*

Battle of Castlebar

In 1798, a French invasion force supported by locals dealt the British an embarrassing loss here. The surprised British forces were routed, and their rapid retreat is slyly remembered in Irish rebel lore as the "Castlebar races." Unfortunately for the rebels, this proved to be the last glimmer of hope for Irish victory in that uprising. The Red Coats reorganized and within weeks defeated the small force of 1,300 Frenchmen and the ill-equipped Irish rebels. The captured French soldiers were treated as prisoners of war, while the Irish rebels were executed.

• *Continue on R-330 to...*

Westport

On arrival in Westport, park along the Mall under the trees that line the canal-like river. This is a planned town, built in Georgian style in the late 1700s to support the adjacent estate of Westport House (skip it for better manors at Mount Stewart House and Muckross House). The town once thrived on the linen industry created by local Irish handlooms. But after the Act of Union with Britain in 1801, Westport was unable to compete with the industrialized British linen-makers and fell into decline. The town is still pretty and a good place for a relaxed lunch and some exploration on foot.

The **TI** is on James Street (July-Aug daily 9:00-18:00; Sept-June Mon-Fri 9:00-17:00, Sat 10:00-17:00, closed Sun; tel.

Westport

To Newport
N59
THE FAIRWAYS
KINGS HILL
PINEWOODS
DEER PARK EAST
North Wood
HORKANS HILL
THE PADDOCKS
To Castlebar, Knock & Dublin via N-5
CHURCH OF IRELAND
NEWPORT RD.
To Westport House
ST. MARY'S CRESCENT
LIBRARY
River Carrowbeg
WESTPORT HERITAGE CENTRE
ST. MARY'S CHURCH
CASTLEBAR ST.
POST
NORTH MALL
SOUTH MALL
DISTILLERY RD.
JAMES ST.
Leisure Park
THE OCTAGON
CHURCH LN.
TOWN HALL
BRIDGE ST.
WC
B
THE FAIRGREEN
To Murrisk (Coffin Ship) & Croagh Patrick
QUAY HILL
SHOP ST.
MILL ST.
To Train Station, Partry & Galway via R-330
R335
HILLSIDE RD.
HIGH ST.
CLUAIN ARD
TOBERHILL
PETER ST.
JOHN'S ROW
PROSPECT AVE.
THE ELMS
MONASTERY VIEW
100 Meters
100 Yards
N59
To Leenane
LEENANE RD.

- ❶ Clew Bay Hotel & Madden's Bistro
- ❷ Mill Times Hotel
- ❸ Boulevard Guesthouse
- ❹ Linden Hall B&B
- ❺ Abbeywood House Hostel
- ❻ J. J. O'Malleys' Pub
- ❼ O'Cee's Coffeeshop
- ❽ Stuffed Sandwich Company
- ❾ Matt Molloy's Pub
- ❿ SuperValu Supermarket
- ⓫ Laundry

CONNEMARA

098/25711). The post office is on the North Mall (Mon-Fri 9:00-17:30, Sat 9:00-13:00, closed Sun).

The **Westport Heritage Centre** gives a good overview of town history and the nearby Croagh Patrick pilgrimage tradition (€3, downstairs beneath the TI). For a short visit, free **parking** is allowed on the street for two hours; for longer stays, park at your B&B (if sleeping here), or use the pay-and-display lots (€0.60/first hour, €0.30/hour after that, pay at meter and display ticket on dashboard). **Laundry** can be dropped off early at Gills and picked up late the same day (€10/load, Mon-Fri 9:00-18:30, Sat 9:00-18:00, closed Sun, James Street, tel. 098/25819).

Sleeping in Westport: For those wanting extra time to explore,

Sleep Code

(€1 = about $1.25, country code: 353, area code: 098)
S = Single, **D** = Double/Twin, **T** = Triple, **Q** = Quad, **b** = bathroom,
s = shower only. Breakfast is included and credit cards are
accepted unless otherwise noted.

To help you easily sort through these listings, I've divided
the rooms into categories, based on the price for a standard
double room with bath:

$$$ Higher Priced—Most rooms €90 or more.
$$ Moderately Priced—Most rooms between €60-90.
$ Lower Priced—Most rooms €60 or less.

Prices can change without notice; verify the hotel's
current rates online or by email. For other updates, see www
.ricksteves.com/update.

Westport is the best place along this route to spend a night. All of
the following listings are centrally located. Prices vary quite a bit
depending on the season.

$$$ Clew Bay Hotel is a couple of doors down from the TI,
with 50 large, modern rooms decked out in cherrywood furniture
(Sb-€80-120, Db-€100-200, Tb-€150-225, Internet access, free use
of adjacent pool and fitness center, James Street, tel. 098/28088,
fax 098/25783, www.clewbayhotel.com, info@clewbayhotel.com).

$$$ Mill Times Hotel has a fresh, woody feel, with 34
comfortable rooms and convenient, free underground parking (Sb-
€50-95, Db-€90-170, Tb-€135-255, Mill Street, tel. 098/29200,
fax 098/29250, www.milltimeshotel.ie, info@milltimeshotel.ie).

$$ Boulevard Guesthouse is the best value in town. Located
right on the leafy Mall, it has six large, tasteful rooms and a
cushy lounge (Sb-€45-50, Db-€75-80, Tb-€105, Qb-€120, cash
only, discount for multiple-night stays, Wi-Fi, tel. 098/25138 or
087/284-4018, www.boulevard-guesthouse.com, info@boulevard
-guesthouse.com, Sadie and John Moran).

$$ Linden Hall B&B has an informal feel and four cozy,
colorful rooms (Sb-€30-50, Db-€60-100, Tb-€80-120, cash only,
Altamount Street, tel. 098/27005, www.lindenhallwestport.com,
lindenhall@eircom.net).

$ Abbeywood House Hostel, hidden uphill behind the
Church of Ireland, is a former monastery renting seven rooms with
views of Croagh Patrick (dorm beds-€20-24, D-€60, includes continental breakfast, kitchen, Wi-Fi, Newport Road, tel. 098/25496,
www.abbeywoodhouse.com, info@abbeywoodhouse.com).

Eating in Westport: Most of your best bets are clustered on

Bridge Street. A good choice is **J. J. O'Malleys'** pub for lunch and its upstairs restaurant for dinner (€16-25 meals, daily 17:00-22:00, Bridge Street, tel. 098/27307). **Madden's Bistro** is on the ground floor of the Clew Bay Hotel, offering contemporary casual dining (daily 12:30-21:00, James Street, tel. 098/28088). For a quick and easy lunch, try **O'Cee's Coffeeshop** (€9 cafeteria-style lunches, Mon-Sat 8:30-18:30, Sun 10:00-16:00, Shop Street, tel. 098/27000) or the **Stuffed Sandwich Company** (April-Sept Mon-Thu 10:00-18:00, Fri-Sat 9:00-20:00, Sun 11:00-18:00; Oct-March Mon-Sat 9:00-18:00, closed Sun; Bridge Street, tel. 098/27611). Irish music fans seek out **Matt Molloy's** pub (Bridge Street, tel. 098/26655). Matt Molloy isn't just the owner of the pub—he's also a flutist for the Chieftains, the group credited with much of the worldwide resurgence of interest in Irish music over the past 40 years. The **SuperValu** market has picnic fare (Mon-Sat 8:00-22:00, Sun 9:00-21:00, Shop Street).

Westport Connections: If you want to visit Westport but lack wheels, here are your options. You can take a bus to/from **Galway** (5-7/day, 1.5-2.75 hours), **Derry** (2-4/day, 4.75-5.5 hours, change in Sligo), or **Dublin** (6-7/day, 4-6 hours). For details, see www.buseireann.ie. You can also reach Dublin by train (3/day, 3.75 hours, www.irishrail.ie).

• *Leave Westport heading west on R-335. After about five miles, as you're driving along scenic Clew Bay, you'll reach a wide spot in the road called Murrisk. Stop here. In the field on your right (opposite Campbell's Pub) is the...*

CONNEMARA

Coffin Ship

This bronze ship sculpture is one of the most powerful famine memorials that you'll see in Ireland. It's a "coffin ship," like those of the 1840s that carried the sick and starving famine survivors across the ocean in hope of a new life. Unfortunately, many of the ships contracted to take the desperate immigrants were barely seaworthy, no longer fit for dependable commerce. The poor were weak from starvation and vulnerable to "famine fever," which they then spread to others in the putrid, cramped holds of these awful ships. Many who lived through the six- to eight-week journey died shortly after reaching their new country. Pause a moment to look at the silent skeletons swirling around the ship's masts. Now contemplate the fact that famine still exists in the world. And before judging the lack of effective relief intervention by the British government of that time, consider the rich world's ability to ignore similar suffering today.

• *Across the road from the coffin ship is...*

Croagh Patrick

This small mountain rises 2,500 feet above the bay. In the fifth century, St. Patrick is said to have fasted on its summit for the 40 days of Lent. It's from here that he supposedly rang his bell, driving all the snakes out of Ireland. The snakes never existed, of course, but they represent the pagan beliefs that Patrick's newly arrived Christianity replaced. Every year on the last Sunday of July, "Reek Sunday" (a "reek" is a mountain peak), 30,000 pilgrims hike three hours up the rocky trail to the summit in honor of St. Patrick. The most penitent attempt the hike barefoot (more than one comes down on a stretcher). On that Sunday, Mass is celebrated throughout the day in a modest chapel on the top.

Hikers should allow three hours to reach the top and two hours to get back down (bring plenty of water, sunscreen, and rain gear). There is a primitive WC on the summit, 30 yards below the chapel. The trail is easy to follow, but the upper half of the mountain is a steep slope of loose, shifting scree that can bang or turn exposed ankles. Both times I've climbed this, I've been glad I wore boots.

A few years ago, valuable gold deposits were discovered within Croagh Patrick. Luckily, public sentiment has kept the sacred mountain free of any commercial mining activity.

• *Continue west on R-335.*

Stretched out beside you is **Clew Bay,** peppered with numerous humpbacked islands of glacial gravel dumped by retreating glaciers at the end of the last Ice Age. A notorious 16th-century local named Grace O'Malley (dubbed the "Pirate Queen") once ruled this bay, even earning the grudging respect of Queen Elizabeth I herself with her clever exploits. John Lennon later chose Dorinish Island to found a short-lived hippie commune.

• *Passing through Louisburgh, you'll turn south to enter some of the most rugged and desolate country in Ireland.*

Doo Lough Valley

Signs of human habitation vanish from the bogland, and ghosts begin to appear beside the road. About eight miles (13 km) beyond Louisburgh, stop at the simple gray-stone cross on the left. The

Ireland's Misunderstood Nomads

When you see a small cluster of trailers at the side of an Irish road, you're looking at a dying way of life. These are

the Travellers, a nomadic throwback to the days when wandering crafts-men, musicians, and evicted unfortu-nates crowded rural Ireland. Often mis-labeled as Gypsies, they have no ethnic ties to those Eastern European nomads, but rather have an Irish heritage going back centuries.

There were once many more Travellers, who lived in tents and used horse-drawn carts as they wandered the country-side in search of work. Before the famine, when Irish hospital-ity was a given, Travellers filled a niche in Irish society. They would do odd jobs, such as repairing furniture, sweeping chimneys, and selling horses. Skilled tinsmiths, they mended pots, pans, and stills for *poitín*—Irish moonshine. (Travellers used to be called "tinkers," but they now consider this label derogatory.) Sedentary farm folk, who rarely ventured more than 20 miles from home their entire lives, depended on the roaming Travellers for news and gossip from farther-flung regions. But post-famine rural depopulation and the gradual urbanization of the countryside forced this nomadic group to adapt to an almost sedentary existence on the fringes of towns.

Today, the 30,000 remaining Travellers are outsiders, usually treated with suspicion by the traditionally conserva-tive Irish. Locals often complain that petty thefts go up when Travellers set up camp in a nearby "halting site," and that they leave garbage behind when they depart. Although most vis-ible in rural encampments, Travellers still frequent the out-door horse market at Smithfield Village in Dublin on the first Sunday of each month. The Travellers are very religious and often camp near the pilgrimage town of Knock.

Travellers tend to keep to themselves, marry young, have large families, and speak their own Gaelic-based lan-guage (called Shelta, Gammon, or Cant). Attempts to settle Travellers in government housing and integrate their chil-dren into schools have met with mixed success, as portrayed poignantly in the 1992 movie *Into the West*.

lake ahead is Doo Lough (Irish for "Black Lake"). This is the site of one of the saddest famine tales.

In the early 1800s, County Mayo's rural folk depended almost exclusively on the potato for food and were the hardest hit when the Potato Famine came in 1845. In the winter of 1849, about 600 starving Irish walked 12 miles from Louisburgh to Delphi Lodge, hoping to get food from their landlord, but they were turned away. On the walk back, almost 200 of them died along the side of this road. Today, the road still seems to echo with the despair of those hungry souls, and it inspires an annual walk that commemorates the tragedy. Archbishop Desmond Tutu made the walk in 1991, shortly before South Africa ended its apartheid system.

• *Continue south on R–335. You'll get a fine view of **Aasleagh Falls** on the left. In late May, the banks below the falls explode with lush, wild, purple rhododendron blossoms. Cross the bridge after the falls, and turn right onto N-59 toward Leenane. You'll drive along Killary Harbor, an Irish example of a fjord. This long, narrow body of water was carved by an advancing glacier.*

Leenane

This town is a good place for a break. The 1990 movie *The Field*, starring Limerick-born Richard Harris, was filmed here. Take a glance at the photos of the making of the movie on the wall of **Hamilton's Pub.** While you're there, find the old photo of the British battleships that filled Killary Harbor when King Edward VII visited a century ago. Drop into the **Leenane Cultural Centre** (on the left as you enter town) to see interesting wool-spinning and weaving demonstrations (€4, April-Oct daily 9:00-17:00, closed Nov-March, tel. 095/42337, www.sheepandwoolcentre.com).

• *As you continue west on N–59, notice the rows of blue floats in Killary Harbor. They're there to mark mussel farms growing on hanging nets in the cold seawater. As you climb out of the fjord valley about five miles past Leenane, you'll pass some good areas to get a close look at a turf cut in a peat bog.*

A Slog on the Bog

Walk a few yards onto the spongy green carpet. (Watch your step on wet days to avoid squishing into a couple of inches of water.) Find a dry spot and jump up and down to get a feel for it. Have your companion jump; you'll feel the vibrations 30 feet away.

These bogs once covered almost 20 percent of Ireland. As the climate got warmer at the end of the last Ice Age, plants began growing along the sides of the many shallow lakes and ponds. When the plants died in these waterlogged areas, there wasn't

enough oxygen for them to fully decompose. Over the centuries, the moss built up, layer after dead layer, helping to slowly fill in the lakes. During World War I, this sphagnum moss was collected to use in bandages to soak up blood (it absorbs many times its weight in fluids).

It's this wet, oxygen-starved ecosystem that has preserved ancient artifacts so well, many of which can be seen in Dublin's National Museum. Even forgotten containers of butter, churned centuries ago and buried to keep cool, have been discovered. But most bizarre are the wrinkled bog mummies that are occasionally unearthed. These human remains (sometimes close to 2,000 years old) are so incredibly intact that their eyelashes, hairstyles, and the last meal in their stomachs can be identified. They were likely sacrificial offerings to the pagan gods of Celtic times.

Since these acidic bogs contain few nutrients, unique species of carnivorous plants have adapted to life here by trapping and digesting insects. The tiny pink sundew (about two inches tall) has delicate spikes glistening with insect-attracting fluid. Take a moment to find a mossy area and look closely at the variety of tiny plants. In summer, you'll see white tufts of bog cotton growing in marshy areas.

People have been cutting, drying, and burning peat as a fuel source for more than a thousand years. The cutting usually begins in April or May, when drier weather approaches. You'll probably see stacks of "turf" piled up to dry along recent cuts. Pick up a brick and fondle it. Dried peat is surprisingly light and stiff. In central Ireland, there are even industrial peat cuts that were begun after World War II to fuel power stations. But in the past couple of decades, bogs have been recognized as a rare habitat, encouraging conservation efforts. These days, the sweet, nostalgic smell of burning peat is becoming increasingly rare.

• *Continue west on N-59. The road soon crosses a shallow lake, with a great view of Kylemore Abbey to the right. But don't stop here—you'll get a better photo from the parking lot a few hundred yards ahead. Pull into the lot and take a few minutes to enjoy the view (gate closes at 18:00).*

Kylemore Abbey

This Neo-Gothic country house was built by the wealthy English businessman Mitchell Henry in the 1860s, after he and his wife

CONNEMARA

had honeymooned in the area. Now they are both buried on the grounds. After World War I, refugee Benedictine nuns from Belgium took it over and ran it as an exclusive girls' boarding school until it closed in 2010. The best thing about the abbey is the view of it from the lakeshore. Tours inside are a letdown, so just enjoy its setting (overpriced €12 combo-ticket for abbey and gardens, daily 9:00-17:00, WCs in gift shop next to parking lot, tel. 095/41146, www.kylemoreabbey.com). The cafeteria swims with the chaos of multiple big-bus tour groups.

• *Heading west from the abbey, you'll drive less than five miles to the town of Letterfrack. Pass through the town and go left off N-59 to reach...*

Connemara National Park

This park encompasses almost 5,000 acres of wild bog and mountain scenery. The visitors center displays worthwhile exhibits of local flora and fauna, which are well-explained in the 15-minute *Man and the Landscape* film that runs every half-hour (free, mid-March-Oct daily 10:00-17:30, last admission 45 minutes before closing, tel. 095/41054, www.heritageireland.ie). Nature-lovers may want to reverse the direction of my driving loop (and skimp on sightseeing time at other stops) in order to enjoy a two-hour walking tour with a park naturalist (July-Aug Wed and Fri at 11:00, departs from visitors center). Call ahead to confirm walking tour schedules, and bring rain gear and hiking shoes.

• *If you're running short on time, you could stay on N-59 the whole way back to Galway. But I prefer to turn south off N-59 in Clifden to enjoy a scenic coastal loop on R-341.*

Coastal Connemara

The essence of scenic Connemara—rocky yet seductive—is captured in a neat little 24-mile (38-km) loop on R-341. The 12 Bens (peaks) of Connemara loom deeper inland. In the foreground, broad shelves of bare bedrock are netted with stone walls, interlocking the lumpy landscape. The ocean slaps the hardscrabble shore. Fishermen cast into their favorite little lakes, and ponies trot in windswept fields. Abandoned roofless stone cottages stand mute, their stories untold. The only settlement on this loop to speak of is Roundstone, a perfect place to stop for a cup of coffee before turning home.

• *R-341 links back up with N-59 near Recess. At the junction with N-59, turn right, and follow* Galway *signs back through Recess, Maam Cross, and Oughterard. The tour is over.*

Sights Between Galway and Derry

Travelers continuing on to Northern Ireland (or County Donegal) should get an early start. Allow a long day for the drive from Galway to Derry (or Portrush), with these interesting stops along the way. The town of Knock is right on N-17 heading north out of Galway, while Strokestown is further east in County Roscommon. Fill up your tank just before you leave the Republic, since unleaded is at least a dollar per gallon more expensive in Northern Ireland.

Knock—In 1879, locals saw the Virgin Mary, St. Joseph, and St. John appear against the south gable of this tiny town's church. Word of miraculous healings turned the trickle of pilgrims into a flood and put Knock solidly on the pilgrimage map. Today, you can visit the shrine. At the edge of the site, a small but interesting folk museum shows "evidence" of the healings, photos of a papal visit, and interesting slices of traditional life.

▲▲Strokestown Park National Famine Museum—The Great Potato Famine of 1845-1849 was the bleakest period in Irish history—so traumatic that it halved the Irish population, sent desperate Irish peasants across the globe, and crystallized Irish-nationalist hatred of British rule. The National Famine Museum fills a mansion (on the former estate of the Mahon family) in the market town of Strokestown, 60 miles northeast of Galway. Visitors can absorb the thoughtfully done exhibits explaining how three million Irish peasants survived on a surprisingly nutritious pre-famine diet of buttermilk and potatoes (12 pounds per day per average male laborer...potatoes are 80 percent water).

Major Mahon, the ill-fated landlord here during the famine, found it cheaper to fill three "coffin ships" bound for America with his evicted, starving tenants than pay the taxes for their upkeep in the local workhouse. When almost half died at sea of "famine fever," he was assassinated.

After visiting the museum, take a tour of the musty "Big House." The tours provide insights into the gulf that divided the Protestant ascendancy and their Catholic house staff. Afterward, find the servants' tunnel—connecting the kitchen to the stable—built to avoid cluttering the Mahon family's views with unsightly common laborers.

Cost and Hours: €12 for museum, house tour, and Georgian gardens; mid-March-Oct daily 11:00-17:00, closed Nov-mid-March; "Big House" tours go daily at 12:00, 14:30, and 16:00; tel. 071/963-3013, www.strokestownpark.ie).

Services: Drivers connecting Westport or Galway to either Dublin or Northern Ireland can stop here en route and grab lunch in the museum café.

CONNEMARA

NORTHERN
IRELAND

NORTHERN IRELAND

 The island of Ireland was once a colony of Great Britain. Unlike its Celtic cousins, Scotland and Wales, Ireland has always been distant from London—a distance due more to its Catholicism than the Irish Sea.

Four hundred years ago, Protestant settlers from England and Scotland were strategically "planted" in Catholic Ireland to help assimilate the island into the British economy. These settlers established their own cultural toehold on the island, while the Catholic Irish held strong to their Gaelic culture.

Over the centuries, British rule hasn't been easy. By the beginning of the 20th century, the sparse Protestant population could no longer control the entire island. When Ireland won its independence in 1921 (after a bloody guerrilla war against British rule), 26 of the island's 32 counties became the Irish Free State, ruled from Dublin with dominion status in the British Commonwealth—similar to Canada's level of sovereignty. In 1949, these 26 counties left the Commonwealth and became the Republic of Ireland, severing all political ties with Britain. Meanwhile, the six remaining northeastern counties—the only ones with a Protestant majority—chose not to join the Irish Free State, and remained part of the UK.

But embedded within these six counties—now joined as the political entity called Northern Ireland—was a large, disaffected Catholic minority who felt they'd been sold down the river by the drawing of the new international border. Their political opponents were the "Unionists"—Protestants eager to defend the union with Britain, primarily led by two groups: the long-established Orange Order and the military muscle of the newly mobilized Ulster Volunteer Force (UVF). This was countered on the Catholic side by the Irish Republican Army (IRA), which wanted all 32 of Ireland's counties to be united in one Irish nation—their political goals were "Nationalist."

In World War II, the Republic stayed neutral while the North enthusiastically supported the Allied cause—winning a spot close to London's heart. Londonderry (Derry) became an essential

Allied convoy port, while Belfast lost more than 800 civilians during two Luftwaffe bombing raids in 1940. After the war, the split between North and South seemed permanent, and Britain invested heavily in Northern Ireland to bring it solidly into the UK fold.

In the Republic of Ireland (the South), where 94 percent of the population was Catholic and only 6 percent Protestant, there was a clearly dominant majority. But in the North, at the time it was formed, Catholics were still a sizable 35 percent of the population—enough to demand attention. To maintain the status quo, Protestants considered certain forms of anti-Catholic discrimination necessary. It was this discrimination that led to the Troubles, the conflict that filled headlines from the late 1960s to the mid-1990s.

Four hundred years ago (during the Reformation), this was a fight over Protestant and Catholic religious differences. But over the last century, the conflict has been not about faith, but about politics: Will Northern Ireland stay part of the UK, or become part of the Republic of Ireland? The indigenous Irish of Northern Ireland, who generally want to unite with Ireland, happen to be Catholic. The descendants of the Scottish and English settlers, who generally want to remain part of Britain, happen to be Protestant.

Northern Ireland Almanac

Official Name: Since Northern Ireland is not an independent state, there is no official country name. Some call it Ulster, while others label it the Six Counties. Population-wise, it's the smallest country of the UK (the other three are England, Wales, and Scotland).

Population: Northern Ireland's 1.7 million people are about 45 percent Protestant (mostly Presbyterian and Anglican) and 40 percent Catholic. Another 5 percent profess different religions, and 10 percent claim no religious ties. English is far and away the chief language, though Gaelic (Irish) is also spoken in staunchly Nationalist Catholic communities.

Despite the country's genetic homogeneity, the population is highly segregated along political, religious, and cultural lines. Roughly speaking, the eastern seaboard is more Unionist, Protestant, and of English-Scottish heritage, while the south and west (bordering the Republic of Ireland) are Nationalist, Catholic, and of Irish descent. Cities are often clearly divided between neighborhoods of one group or the other. Early in life, locals learn to identify the highly symbolic (and highly charged) colors, jewelry, music, names, and vocabulary that distinguish the cultural groups.

Latitude and Longitude: 54°N and 5°W. It's as far north as parts of the Alaskan panhandle.

Area: 5,400 square miles (about the size of Connecticut), constituting a sixth of the island. Northern Ireland includes 6 of the island's traditional 32 counties.

Geography: Northern Ireland is shaped roughly like a doughnut, with the UK's largest lake in the middle (Lough Neagh, 150 square miles and a prime eel fishery). The terrain comprises gently rolling hills of green grass, rising to the 2,800-foot Slieve Donard. The weather is temperate, cloudy, moist, windy, and hard to predict.

Biggest Cities: Belfast, the capital, has 300,000 residents. Half a million people—nearly one in three Northern Irish—inhabit the greater Belfast area. Derry (called Londonderry by Unionists) has 84,000 people.

Economy: Northern Ireland's economy is more closely tied to the UK than to the Republic of Ireland. Sectarian violence has held back growth, and the economy gets subsidies from the UK and the EU. Traditional agriculture (potatoes and grain) is fading fast, though modern techniques and abundant grassland make Northern Ireland a major producer of sheep, cows, and grass seed. Modern software and communications companies are replacing old traditional manufacturing. Shipyards are rusty relics, and the linen industry is now threadbare; both are victims of cheaper labor available in Asia.

Currency: Northern Ireland uses not the euro, but the pound (£). Exchange rate: £1 = about $1.60.

Government: Northern Ireland is not a self-governing nation, but is part of the UK, ruled from London by Queen Elizabeth II and Prime Minister David Cameron, and represented in Parliament by 18 elected Members of Parliament. For 50 years (1922-1972), Northern Ireland was granted a great deal of autonomy and self-governance, known as "Home Rule." The current National Assembly (108-seat Parliament)—after an ineffective decade of political logjams—has recently begun to show signs of rejuvenation.

Politics are dominated, of course, by the ongoing debate between Unionists (who want to preserve the union with the UK) and Nationalists (who want to join the Republic of Ireland). Two high-profile and controversial figures have been at the opposite ends of this debate: the elderly firebrand Reverend Ian Paisley for the Unionists (who retired in 2008); and assassination-attack survivor Gerry Adams of Sinn Fein, the political arm of the IRA. In a hopeful development in the spring of 2007, the two allowed themselves to be photographed together across a negotiation table (a moment both had once sworn would never happen) as London returned control of the government to Belfast.

Flag: The official flag of Northern Ireland is the Union flag of the UK. But you'll also see the green, white, and orange Irish tricolor (waved by Nationalists) and the Northern Irish flag (white with a red cross and a red hand at its center), which is used by Unionists (see "The Red Hand of Ulster" on page 340).

Partly inspired by Martin Luther King Jr. and the civil rights movement in America in the 1960s—beamed into Irish living rooms by the new magic of television news—the Catholic minority in Northern Ireland began a nonviolent struggle to end discrimination, advocating for better jobs and housing. Extremists polarized issues, and demonstrations—also broadcast on TV news—became violent. Unionists were afraid that if the island became one nation, the relatively poor Republic of Ireland would drag down the comparatively affluent North, and that the high percentage of Catholics would spell repression for the Protestants. As Unionist Protestants and Nationalist Catholics clashed in 1969, the British Army entered the fray. Their role, initially a peacekeeping one, gradually evolved into acting as muscle for the Unionist government. In 1972, a watershed year, more than 500 people died as combatants moved from petrol bombs to guns, and a new, more violent IRA emerged. In that 30-year (1968-1998) chapter of the struggle for an independent and united Ireland, more than 3,000 people were killed.

A 1985 agreement granted Dublin a consulting role in the Northern Ireland government. Unionists bucked this idea, and violence escalated. That same year, Belfast City Hall draped a huge, defiant banner under its dome, proclaiming, *Belfast Says No.*

In 1994, the banner came down. In the 1990s—with Ireland's membership in the EU, the growth of its economy, and the weakening of the Catholic Church's influence—the consequences of a united Ireland became slightly less threatening to the Unionists. Also in 1994, the IRA declared a cease-fire, and the Protestant Ulster Volunteer Force (UVF) followed suit.

The Nationalists wanted British troops out of Northern Ireland, while the Unionists demanded that the IRA turn in its arms. Optimists hailed the signing of a breakthrough peace plan in 1998, called the "Good Friday Accord" by Nationalists, or the "Belfast Agreement" by Unionists. This led to the release of prisoners on both sides in 2000—a highly emotional event.

Recently, additional progress has taken place on both fronts. The IRA finally "verifiably put their arms beyond use" in 2005, and backed the political peace process. In 2009, most Loyalist paramilitary groups did the same. Meanwhile, British Army surveillance towers were dismantled in 2006, and the army formally ended its 38-year-long Operation Banner campaign in 2007.

In 2010, the peace process was jolted forward by a surprisingly forthright apology offered by British Prime Minister David Cameron, who expressed regret for the British Army's offenses on Bloody Sunday (described on page 379). The apology was prompted by the Saville Report—the results of an investigation conducted by the UK government as part of the Good Friday Accord. It found that the 1972 shootings of Nationalist civil-rights marchers on Bloody Sunday by British soldiers was "unjustified" and the victims innocent (to the intense relief of the victims' families, who had fought since 1972 to clear their loved ones' names).

Major hurdles to a lasting peace persist, but the downtown checkpoints are history, and the "bomb-damage clearance sales" are over. And today, more tourists than ever are venturing north to Belfast and Derry.

Terminology

Ulster (one of Ireland's four ancient provinces) consists of nine counties in the northern part of the island of Ireland. Six of these make up Northern Ireland (pronounced "Norn Iron" by locals), while three counties remain part of the Republic.

Unionists—and the more hard-line, working-class **Loyalists**—want the North to remain in the UK. The **Ulster Unionist Party (UUP),** the political party representing moderate Unionist views, is currently led by Sir Reg Empey (after being headed for years by Nobel Peace Prize co-winner David Trimble). The **Democratic Unionist Party (DUP),** led by Peter Robinson (protégé of the recently retired Reverend Ian Paisley), takes a harder stance in defense of Unionism. The **Ulster Volunteer Force (UVF),** the **Ulster Freedom Fighters (UFF),** and the **Ulster Defense Association (UDA)** are the Loyalist paramilitary organizations mentioned most frequently in newspapers and on spray-painted walls.

Nationalists—and the more hard-line, working-class **Republicans**—want a united and independent Ireland ruled by Dublin. The **Social Democratic Labor Party (SDLP),** founded by Nobel Peace Prize co-winner John Hume and currently led by Mark Durkan, is the moderate political party representing Nationalist views. **Sinn Fein** (shin fayn), led by Gerry Adams, takes a harder stance in defense of Nationalism. The **Irish Republican Army (IRA)** is the Nationalist paramilitary organization (linked with Sinn Fein) mentioned most often in the press and in graffiti.

To gain more insight into the complexity of the Troubles, see the University of Ulster's informative and evenhanded Conflict Archive at http://cain.ulst.ac.uk/index.html.

Safety

A generation ago, Northern Ireland was a sadly contorted corner of the world. On my first visit, I remember thinking that even the name of this region sounded painful ("Ulster" sounded to me like a combination of "ulcer" and "blister").

Today tourists in Northern Ireland are no longer considered courageous (or reckless). When locals spot you with a map and a lost look on your face, they're likely to ask, "Wot yer lookin fer?" in their distinctive Northern accent. They're not suspicious of you, but rather trying to help you find your way. You're safer in Belfast than in any other UK city—and far safer than in most major US cities. You have to look for trouble to find it here. Just don't seek out spit-and-sawdust pubs in working-class Protestant neighborhoods as a place to sing Catholic songs.

Tourists notice the tension mainly during the "marching season" (Easter-Aug, peaking in early July). July 12—"the Twelfth"—is traditionally the most confrontational day of the year in the North, when proud Protestant Unionist Orangemen march to celebrate their Britishness and their separate identity from the Republic of Ireland (often through staunchly Nationalist Catholic neighborhoods). Lay low if you stumble onto any big Orange parades.

Northern Ireland Is a Different Country

The border is almost invisible. But when you leave the Republic of Ireland and enter Northern Ireland, you *are* crossing an international border. Although you don't have to flash your passport, you do change stamps, phone cards, and money. Gas is more expensive in Northern Ireland than in the Republic (so fill up before crossing the border). However, groceries are 20 percent cheaper. These price differences create a lively daily shopping trade for those living near the border.

You won't use euros here; Northern Ireland issues its own Ulster pound, which, like the Scottish pound, is interchangeable with the English pound (€1 = about £0.85; £1 = about $1.60). Some establishments near the border may take your euros, but at a lousy exchange rate. So keep any euros for your return to the Republic, and get pounds from an ATM inside Northern Ireland instead. And if you're heading to Britain next, it's best to change your Ulster pounds into English ones (free at any bank in Northern Ireland, England, Wales, or Scotland).

BELFAST

Seventeenth-century Belfast was just a village. With the influx, or "plantation," of English and (more often) Scottish settlers, the character of the place changed. After the Scots and English were brought in—and the native Irish were subjugated—Belfast boomed, spurred by the success of the local linen, rope-making, and shipbuilding industries. The Industrial Revolution took root with a vengeance. While the rest of Ireland remained rural and agricultural, Belfast earned its nickname ("Old Smoke") during the time when many of the brick buildings that you'll see today were built. The year 1888 marked the birth of modern Belfast. After Queen Victoria granted city status to this boomtown of 300,000, its citizens built the city's centerpiece, City Hall.

Belfast is the birthplace of the *Titanic* (and many other ships that didn't sink). Two huge, mustard-colored cranes (once the biggest in the world, nicknamed Samson and Goliath) rise like skyscrapers above the harbor. They stand idle now but serve as a reminder of this town's former shipbuilding might.

Today, investments from south of the border—the Republic of Ireland—are injecting quiet optimism into the dejected shipyards where the *Titanic* was built, developing the historic Titanic Quarter. Cranes are building condos along the rejuvenated Lagan riverfront.

It feels like a new morning in Belfast. It's hard to believe that the bright and bustling pedestrian center was once a subdued, traffic-free security zone. Now there's no hint of security checks, once a tiresome daily routine. These days, both Catholics and Protestants are rooting for the Belfast Giants ice hockey team, one of many reasons to live together peacefully.

Still, it's a fragile peace and a tenuous hope. Mean-spirited murals, hateful bonfires built a month before they're actually burned, and pubs with security gates are reminders that the island is split—and 800,000 Protestant Unionists in the North prefer it that way.

Planning Your Time

Big Belfast is thin on sights. For most, one day of sightseeing is plenty.

Day Trip from Dublin: On the handy, two-hour Dublin-Belfast train (cheap €36 "day return" tickets; can cost more Fri-Sun, substantial discounts for booking online), you could make Belfast a day trip:

7:35	Catch the early-morning train from Dublin (arriving in Belfast at 9:45)
11:00	City Hall tour (Mon-Fri; later on Sat, none on Sun), browse the pedestrian zone, lunch, ride a shared black taxi up Falls Road
15:00	Side-trip to the Ulster Folk and Transport Museum in nearby Cultra
Evening	Return to Dublin (last train Mon-Sat departs Belfast at 20:10 and arrives in Dublin at 22:15)

Sunday's trains depart later and return earlier, compressing your already limited time here (first train departs Dublin at 10:00 and arrives in Belfast at 12:15; last train departs Belfast at 19:00 and pulls into Dublin at 21:05). Confirm train times at local stations. Note that the TI offers the Historic Belfast Walk at 14:00 on Wednesday, Friday, and Saturday, as well as summer Sundays (June-Sept). On Friday and Saturday, St. George's Market bustles in the morning. On Saturday, the only tours of City Hall are at 14:00 and 15:00. There are no tours on Sunday.

Staying Overnight: Belfast makes a pleasant overnight stop, with plenty of cheap hostels, reasonable B&Bs, weekend hotel deals (Fri-Sun), and a resort neighborhood full of B&Bs 30 minutes away in Bangor.

Two Days in Belfast: On the first day, follow my day-trip itinerary described earlier. For your second day, take the Living History bus tour in the morning, then visit Carrickfergus Castle in the afternoon.

Two Days in Small-Town Northern Ireland: From Dublin (via Belfast), take the train to Portrush; allow two nights and a day to tour the Causeway Coast (castle, whiskey distilleries, Giant's Causeway, resort fun), then follow the Belfast-in-a-day plan described earlier. With a third day, add Derry.

Coming from Scotland: With good ferry connections (from Stranraer or Troon in Scotland, or Liverpool in England; see

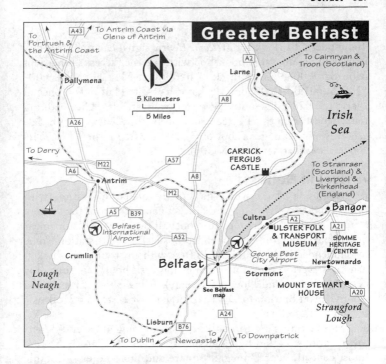

"Belfast Connections," later), it's easy to begin your exploration of the Emerald Isle in Belfast, then head south to Dublin and the Republic.

Orientation to Belfast

(area code: 028)

For the first-time visitor in town for a quick look, Belfast is pretty simple. Locate these four useful landmarks on your map, and use them to navigate as you stroll the town (listed from north to south): Albert Clock Tower, City Hall, Shaftesbury Square, and Queen's University.

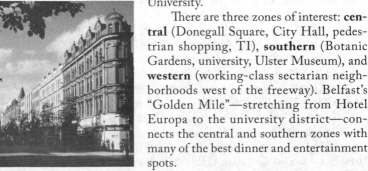

There are three zones of interest: **central** (Donegall Square, City Hall, pedestrian shopping, TI), **southern** (Botanic Gardens, university, Ulster Museum), and **western** (working-class sectarian neighborhoods west of the freeway). Belfast's "Golden Mile"—stretching from Hotel Europa to the university district—connects the central and southern zones with many of the best dinner and entertainment spots.

Tourist Information

The modern TI (look for *Welcome Centre* signs) has fine, free city maps and an enjoyable bookshop with Internet access (June-Sept Mon-Sat 9:00-19:00, Sun 11:00-16:00; Oct-May Mon-Sat 9:00-17:30, Sun 11:00-16:00; one block north of City Hall at 47 Donegall Place, tel. 028/9024-6609, www.gotobelfast.com). City walking tours depart from the TI (see "Tours in Belfast," later). For the latest on evening fun, get a copy of *What About* free at the TI or *That's Entertainment* at newsstands (50p).

Arrival in Belfast

Arriving by fast train, you'll go directly to Central Station (with ATMs and free city maps at the ticket counter). From the station, a free Centrelink bus loops to Donegall Square, with stops near Shaftesbury Square (recommended hostels), the bus station (some recommended hotels), and the TI (free with any train or bus ticket, 4/hour, never on Sun; during morning rush hour, bus runs only between station and Donegall Square). Allow about £5 for a taxi from Central Station to Donegall Square, or £7 to my B&B listings in south Belfast.

Slower trains arc through Belfast, stopping at several downtown stations, including Central Station, Great Victoria Station (most central, near Donegall Square and most hotels), Botanic Station (close to the university, Botanic Gardens, and some recommended hostels), and Adelaide (near several recommended B&Bs). It's easy and cheap to connect stations by train (£1).

Helpful Hints

US Consulate: It's at Danesfort House (Mon-Fri 8:30-17:00, closed Sat-Sun, 233 Stranmillis Road, www.usembassy.org.uk).

Market: On Friday and Saturday mornings (roughly until 14:00), **St. George's Market** is a commotion of clothes, produce, and seafood (at corner of Oxford and East Bridge Streets, five blocks east of Donegall Square, tel. 028/9043-5704).

Shopping Mall: Victoria Square is a glitzy American-style mall. Its huge glass dome reflects Belfast's economic rejuvenation. For fine city views, ride the free elevator to the observation platform high up inside the dome (Mon-Tue 9:00-19:00, Wed-Fri 9:00-21:00, Sat 9:00-18:00, Sun 13:00-18:00; 3 blocks east of City Hall—bordered by Chichester, Victoria, Ann, and Montgomery streets; www.victoriasquare.com).

Phone Tips: To call the Republic of Ireland from Northern Ireland, dial 00-353, then the area code without its initial 0, then the local number. To call Northern Ireland from the Republic of Ireland, dial 048, then the local eight-digit number.

Internet Access: Located near the Belfast International City

Hostel, **Revelations Internet Café** is at 27 Shaftesbury Square (see map on page 343; £4.50/hour, Mon-Fri 8:00-22:00, Sat 10:00-18:00, Sun 11:00-19:00, tel. 028/9032-0337).

Post Office: The main post office, with lots of fun postcards, is at the intersection of High and Bridge Streets (Mon-Fri 9:00-17:30, Sat 9:00-12:30, closed Sun, 3 long blocks north of Donegall Square). Another branch is located closer to my accommodations listings on University Road, across from the Ulster Museum (same hours as above).

Laundry: Globe Launderers is at 37-39 Botanic Avenue (£5 self-serve, £7.50 drop-off service, Mon-Fri 8:00-21:00, Sat 8:00-18:00, Sun 12:00-18:00, tel. 028/9024-3956). For the B&B neighborhood south of town, the closest is **Whistle Laundry** (£7.50 drop-off service, Mon-Fri 8:30-18:00, Sat 9:00-17:30, closed Sun, 160 Lisburn Road, at intersection with Eglantine Avenue, tel. 028/9038-1297). For locations, see the map on page 343.

Bike Rental: McConvey Cycles is south of the city center at 183 Ormeau Road (£15/24 hours, Mon-Sat 9:00-18:00, Thu until 20:00, closed Sun, tel. 028/9033-0322, www.mcconveycycles .com).

Queen's University Student Union: Located directly across University Road from the red-brick University building, the Student Union is just as handy for tourists as it is for college students. Inside you'll find an ATM (at end of main hall, on the right), WCs, a pharmacy, a mini-market, and Wi-Fi. Grab a quick and cheap £4 sandwich and coffee at **Clement's Coffee Shop** (Mon-Fri 8:30-22:30, Sat 9:00-22:00, closed Sun).

Getting Around Belfast

If you line up your sightseeing logically, you can do most of the town on foot. On wheels, you have several options.

By Train or Bus: Ask about iLink smartcards, which give individuals one day of unlimited train and bus travel. The Zone 1 card (£6.50) covers the city center and George Best Belfast City Airport. The handy Zone 2 card (£10.50) includes Cultra (Ulster Folk and Transport Museum), Bangor, and Carrickfergus Castle. Zone 3 (£16.50) gets you anywhere in Northern Ireland, including Belfast International Airport. You can purchase additional iLink days to top up your card (£5 for Zone 1, £9 for Zone 2, £15 for Zone 3). For those lingering in the North, one-week cards offer even better deals. Buy your iLink card at any train station in the city. If you're only traveling to one destination—Carrickfergus Castle, Cultra, or Bangor—a "day return" ticket is cheaper than two one-way tickets.

Buses go from Donegall Square East to Malone Road and my recommended B&Bs (#8B or #8C, 3/hour, £1.60, all-day pass costs £3.50 before 9:30 and £2.70 after).

For information on trains and buses in Belfast, contact Translink (tel. 028/9066-6630, www.translink.co.uk).

By Taxi: Taxis are reasonable and should be considered. Rather than use their meters, many cabs charge a flat £5 rate for any ride up to two miles. It's £2 per mile after that. Ride a shared cab if you're going up Falls Road (explained later, under "Sights in Belfast").

Tours in Belfast

▲**Walking Tours**—The **Historic Belfast Walk** takes you through the historic core of town (£6, 1.5 hours; departs from TI at 14:00 on Wed, Fri, and Sat; June-Sept also on Sun; confirm tour times with TI, book in advance, tel. 028/9024-6609).

Mixing drinks and history, **Historical Pub Tours of Belfast** offers two-hour walking tours that start at the Crown Dining Room pub and end six pubs later (£6; May-Oct Thu at 19:00, Sat at 16:00; book in advance, meet at pub above Crown Liquor Saloon at 46 Great Victoria Street across from Hotel Europa, tel. 028/9268-3665, www.belfastpubtours.com).

Coiste Irish Political Tours leads extended, three-hour walks along the Falls Road to explain the history of the neighborhood from an intensely Republican perspective. Led by former IRA prisoners, you'll visit murals, gardens of remembrance, peace walls, and community centers in this rejuvenating section of gritty Belfast. Tours meet beside the Divis Tower (the 20-story apartment house at the east end of the Divis Road near the A-12 Westlink motorway overpass) and end at the Milltown Cemetery (£8, Mon-Sat at 11:00, Sun at 14:00, tel. 028/9020-0770, www.coiste.ie, Seamus Kelley).

▲**Big Bus Tours**—**City Sightseeing's** Living History Tour is the best introduction to the city's recent and complicated political and social history. You'll cruise the Catholic and Protestant working-class neighborhoods as well as the dramatically situated Stormont Parliament building, with a commentary explaining the political murals and places of interest—mostly dealing with the Troubles of the last 40 years. You see things from the bus and get out only for photos (£12.50, 1.5 hours, daily on the hour 10:00-16:30, fewer tours in winter—call first; departs from High Street, 2 blocks west of Albert Clock Tower; pay cash at kiosk or on bus, or book by phone with credit card, tel. 028/9045-9035, www.city-sightseeing.com).

Minibus Tours—**McComb's** Giant's Causeway Tour visits Carrickfergus Castle, the Giant's Causeway, Dunluce Castle, Carrick-a-Rede Rope Bridge, and Old Bushmills Distillery (£20, doesn't include distillery admission, daily 9:45-18:45 depending on demand, book through and depart from Belfast International City Hostel—see page 344). McComb's Causeway Express Tour zips you straight to the Giant's Causeway, giving you 2.5 hours there, and Carrick-a-Rede Rope Bridge, where you have 1.25 hours to explore (£15, daily April-Oct, departs at 9:00, returns to Belfast at 16:00). They also have private guides (book in advance, tel. 028/9031-5333, www.minicoachni.co.uk).

Titanic Tours Belfast is run by former TV reporter Susie Millar, who is the great-granddaughter of a crew member on the

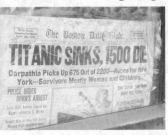

fateful cruise. It's operated as a minivan tour (seats five) that picks up and drops off at your hotel. She spends half a day driving you around the major *Titanic* sights in Belfast, explaining them as you go. This is by far Belfast's most intimate glimpse of the *Titanic*'s tragic history (ask her about her great-grandfather's departing two-penny promise). She is also available for longer, customized tours (£30, tel. 028/9065-9971, mobile 078-5271-6655, www.titanictours-belfast.co.uk, info@titanictours -belfast.co.uk).

Boat Tours—The Lagan Boat Company shows you shipyards on a 1.25-hour **Titanic Tour** cruise, narrated by a member of the Belfast Titanic Society. The tour shows off the fruits of the city's £800 million investment in its harbor, including a weir built to control the tides and stabilize the depth of the harbor (it doubles as a free pedestrian bridge over the River Lagan). The heart of the tour is a lazy harbor cruise past rusty dry-dock gates, brought alive by the guide's proud commentary and passed-around historical photos (£10; daily sailings at 12:30, 14:00, and 15:30; fewer off-season, tel. 028/9033-0844, mobile 077-1891-0423, www.laganboatcompany .com). Tours depart from the Lagan Pedestrian Bridge and Weir on Donegall Quay. The quay is located just past the leaning Albert Clock Tower, a five-minute walk from the TI.

Local Guide—**Ken Harper** has a vast knowledge of Belfast and does insightful tours from his taxi, focusing on both Catholic and Protestant neighborhoods, *Titanic*-related sights, and Belfast's favorite sons—author C. S. Lewis, musician Van Morrison, and soccer star/playboy George Best. He's also available for custom tours, which he calls "Pick Ken's Brain" (£30 minimum or

BELFAST

£10/person, 1.25 hours, tel. 028/9074-2711, mobile 0771-175-7178, www.harpertaxitours.com, kenharper2004@hotmail.com).

Sights in Belfast

Most sights of interest are located in three areas: the Catholic and Protestant neighborhoods to the west of the city center, central Belfast, and south Belfast.

Catholic and Protestant Neighborhoods

It will be a happy day when the sectarian neighborhoods of Belfast have nothing to be sectarian about. For a look at three of the original home bases of the Troubles, explore the working-class neighborhoods of Catholic Falls Road and Protestant Shankill Road (west of the Westlink motorway), or Protestant Sandy Row (south of the Westlink motorway).

Murals (found only in sectarian areas) are a memorable part of any visit to Belfast. But with more peaceful times, the character of these murals is changing. The Re-Imaging Communities Program has spent £3 million in government money to replace aggressive murals with positive ones. Paramilitary themes are gradually being covered over with images of pride in each neighborhood's culture. The *Titanic* was built primarily by proud Protestant Ulster stock and is now seen more often in their neighborhood murals—reflecting their industrious work ethic. Over in the Catholic neighborhoods, you'll see more murals depicting mythological heroes from the days before the English came.

You can get tours of Falls Road or Shankill Road (see next listings), but rarely are both combined in one tour. Ken Harper is one of a new breed of Belfast taxi drivers who will give you an insightful private tour of both (see "Local Guide," previous page).

▲▲**Falls Road (Catholic)**—At the intersection of Castle and King Streets, you'll find the Castle Junction Car Park. On the ground floor of this nine-story parking garage, a passenger terminal (entrance on King Street) connects travelers with old black cabs—and the only Irish-language signs in downtown Belfast. These shared black cabs efficiently shuttle residents from outlying neighborhoods up and down Falls Road and to the city center. This service orig-

inated more than 40 years ago at the beginning of the Troubles, when locals would hijack city buses and use them as barricades in the street fighting. When bus service was discontinued, local paramilitary groups established the shared taxi service. Although the buses are now running again, these cab rides are still a great value for their drivers' commentary.

Any cab goes up Falls Road, past Sinn Fein headquarters and lots of murals, to the Milltown Cemetery (£5, sit in front and talk to the cabbie). Hop in and out. Easy-to-flag-down cabs run every minute or so in each direction on Falls Road.

Forty trained cabbies do one-hour tours (minimum £30, £10/person for 1.5 hours, £20/additional hour, cheap for a small group of up to 6 riders, tel. 028/9031-5777 or mobile 078-9271-6660, www.taxitrax.com).

The Sinn Fein office and bookstore are near the bottom of Falls Road. The **bookstore** is worth a look. Page through books featuring color photos of the political murals that decorated these buildings. Money raised here supports the families of deceased IRA members.

A sad, corrugated structure called the **Peace Wall** runs a block or so north of Falls Road (along Cupar Way), separating the Catholics from the Protestants in the Shankill Road area. This is just one of 17 such walls in Belfast.

At the **Milltown Cemetery**, walk past all the Gaelic crosses down to the far right-hand corner (closest to the highway), where the IRA Roll of Honor is set apart from the thousands of other graves by little green railings. They are treated like fallen soldiers. Notice the memorial to Bobby Sands and nine other hunger strikers. They starved themselves to death in the nearby Maze prison in 1981, protesting for political prisoner status as opposed to terrorist criminal treatment. The prison closed in the fall of 2000.

Shankill Road and Sandy Row (Protestant)—You can ride a shared black cab through the Protestant Shankill Road area (£30 for 1-2 people, £40 for 3-6 people, 1 hour, tel. 028/9032-8775). They depart from North Street near the intersection with Millfield Road; it's not well-marked, but watch where the cabs circle and pick up locals on the south side of the street.

An easier (and cheaper) way to get a dose of the Unionist side is to walk Sandy Row. From Hotel Europa, walk a block down

Glengall Street, then turn left for a 10-minute walk along a working-class Protestant street. A stop in the Unionist memorabilia shop, a pub, or one of the many cheap eateries here may give you an opportunity to talk to a local. You'll see murals filled with Unionist symbolism. The mural of William of Orange's victory over the Catholic King James II (Battle of the Boyne, 1690) thrills Unionist hearts.

Central Belfast

▲▲**City Hall**—This grand structure's 173-foot-tall copper dome dominates the town center. Built between 1898 and 1906, with its statue of Queen Victoria scowling down Belfast's

main drag and the Union Jack flapping behind her, the City Hall is a stirring sight. In the garden, you'll find memorials to the *Titanic* and the landing of the US Expeditionary Force in 1942—the first American troops to arrive in Europe en route to Berlin.

Take the worthwhile and free 45-minute tour (Mon-Fri at 11:00, 14:00, and 15:00; Sat at 14:00 and 15:00, no tours on Sun, entrance on north side of building behind Queen Victoria statue, call to check schedule and to reserve, tel. 028/9032-0202, www.belfastcity.gov.uk/cityhall). The tour gives you a rundown on city government and an explanation of the decor that makes this an Ulster political hall of fame. Queen Victoria and King Edward VII look down on city council meetings. The 1613 original charter of Belfast granted by James I is on display. Its Great Hall—bombed by the Germans in 1941—looks as great as it did the day it was made.

If you can't manage a tour, at least step inside to admire the marble swirl staircase and the view up into the dome. A handy Bobbin coffee shop is also inside.

Linen Hall Library—Across the street from City Hall, the 200-year-old Linen Hall Library welcomes guests (notice the red hand above the former front door facing Donegall Square North; for more on its meaning, see the sidebar on page 340). Described as "Ulster's attic," the library takes pride in being a neutral space where anyone trying to make sense of the sectarian conflict can view the Troubled Images, a historical collection of engrossing political posters. It has a fine hardbound ambience, a coffee shop, and a royal newspaper reading room (free, Mon-Fri 9:30-17:30, Sat

Central Belfast

Legend:

1. Hotel Europa
2. Jurys Inn
3. Granada Travelodge
4. The Morning Star Pub & Rest.
5. Kelly's Cellars
6. Crown Liquor Saloon & Dining Room
7. Merchant Hotel & The Cloth Ear Pub
8. Taps Wine Bar
9. Marks & Spencer
10. Tesco Supermarket
11. Falls Road Taxi Garage
12. Shankill Road Taxi Queue

9:30-16:00, closed Sun, entrance on Fountain Street, 17 Donegall Square North, tel. 028/9032-1707, www.linenhall.com).

Golden Mile—This is the overstated nickname of Belfast's liveliest dining and entertainment district, which stretches from the Opera House (Great Victoria Street) to the university (University Road).

The **Grand Opera House,** originally built in 1895, bombed and rebuilt in 1991, and bombed and rebuilt again in 1993, is extravagantly Victorian and *the* place to take in a concert, play, or opera (£4 guided tours on Sun only at 11:00, 12:00, and 13:00; ticket office open Mon-Fri 9:00-20:00, Sat 10:00-20:00, closed Sun; ticket office to right of main front door on Great Victoria Street, tel. 028/9024-1919, www.goh.co.uk). The recommended **Hotel Europa,** next door, while considered the most-bombed hotel in the world, feels pretty casual but is expensive to stay in.

Across the street is the museum-like **Crown Liquor Saloon.**

Built in 1849, it's now a part of the National Trust. A wander through its mahogany, glass, and marble interior is a trip back into the day of Queen Victoria, although the privacy provided by the snugs—booths—allows for un-Victorian behavior (Mon-Sat 11:30-24:00, Sun 12:30-23:00, consider a lunch stop—see listing under "Eating in Belfast," later). Upstairs, the Crown Dining Room serves pub grub, is decorated with historic photos, and is the starting point for a pub walk (listed earlier, under "Tours in Belfast").

The Odyssey—This huge millennium-project complex offers a food pavilion, bowling alley, and **W5 science center** with stimulating, interactive exhibits for youngsters. Where else can a kid play a harp with laser-light strings? The name W5 stands for who, what, when, where, and why (£7.50, kids-£5.50, Mon-Thu 10:00-17:00, Fri-Sat 10:00-18:00, Sun 12:00-18:00, tel. 028/9046-7700, www.w5online.co.uk). There's also a 12-screen cinema and a 10,000-seat arena where the Belfast Giants professional ice hockey team skates from September to April (2 Queen's Quay, 10-minute walk north of Central Station, tel. 028/9045-1055, www.theodyssey.co.uk).

South Belfast

▲Ulster Museum—While mediocre by European standards, this is Belfast's one major museum. Recently renovated and completed in 2010, it offers an earnest and occasionally thought-provoking look at a cross-section of local artifacts.

The four-floor museum is free and pretty painless. Ride the elevator to the top floor and follow the spiraling exhibits downhill through various zones. The top floor is dedicated to rotating art exhibits, the next floor down covers local nature, and the one below that focuses on history. The ground floor contains coverage of the modern Troubles, along with a coffee shop and gift shop.

The Art Zone displays a beautifully crafted Belleek vase and a you-gotta-be-kidding-me Victorian silver-gilt toilet seat. In the Nature Zone, audiovisuals trace how the Ice Age affected the local landscape. The delicately worded History Zone gives an interesting British slant (such as the implication that the Potato Famine of 1845-1849 was caused by the Irish population doubling in 40 years—without a mention of various English contributions to the suffering). After a peek at a pretty good mummy, top things off with the *Girona* treasure. Soggy bits of gold, silver, leather, and wood were salvaged from the Spanish Armada's shipwrecked *Girona*, lost off the Antrim Coast north of Belfast in 1588.

BELFAST

Cost and Hours: Free, Tue-Sun 10:00-17:00, closed Mon, in Botanic Gardens on Stranmillis Road, south of downtown, tel. 028/9044-0000, www.nmni.com.

▲**Botanic Gardens**—This is the backyard of Queen's University, and on a sunny day, you couldn't imagine a more relaxing park setting. On a cold day, step into the Tropical Ravine for a jungle of heat and humidity. Take a quick walk through the Palm House, reminiscent of the one in London's Kew Gardens but smaller (free, Mon-Fri 10:00-12:00 & 13:00-17:00, Sat-Sun 13:00-17:00, shorter hours in winter; gardens open daily 8:00 until dusk, tel. 028/9031-4762, www.belfastcity.gov.uk/parks). The Ulster Museum is on the garden's grounds.

Near Belfast

▲▲**Ulster Folk and Transport Museum**—This 180-acre, two-museum complex straddles the road and rail at Cultra, midway between Bangor and Belfast (eight miles east of town).

The **Folk Museum,** an open-air collection of 34 reconstructed buildings from all over the nine counties of Ulster, showcases the region's traditional lifestyles. After wandering through the old-town site (church, print shop, schoolhouse, humble Belfast row house, silent movie theater, and so on), you'll head off into the country to nip into cottages, farmhouses, and mills. Most houses are warmed by a wonderful peat fire and a friendly attendant. It can be dull or vibrant, depending upon when you visit and your ability to chat with the attendants. Drop a peat brick on the fire.

The **Transport Museum** (downhill, over the road from the folk section) consists of three buildings. Start at the bottom and trace the evolution of transportation from 7,500 years ago—when people first decided to load an ox—to the first vertical take-off jet. The lowest building holds an intriguing section on the sinking of the Belfast-made *Titanic.* Nearby are exhibits on the Belfast-based Shorts aircraft company, which partnered with the Wright Brothers to manufacture the first commercially available aircraft in 1909. Two other buildings cover the history of bikes, cars, and trains. The car section rumbles from the first car in Ireland (an 1898 Benz) through the "Cortina Culture" of the 1960s to the local adventures of controversial John DeLorean and a 1981 model of his car.

The Red Hand of Ulster

All over Belfast, you'll notice a curious symbol: a red hand facing you as if swearing a pledge or telling you to halt. You'll spot it faded above the Linen Hall Library door, in the wrought-iron fences of the Merchant Hotel, on old-fashioned clothes wringers (in the Ulster Folk and Transport Museum at Cultra), above the front door of a bank in Bangor, in the shape of a flowerbed at Mount Stewart House, in Loyalist paramilitary murals, on shield emblems in the gates of Republican memorials, and even on the flag of Northern Ireland (the white flag with the red cross of St. George). It's known as the Red Hand of Ulster—and it seems to pop up everywhere. Although it's more often associated with Unionist traditions, it's one of the few emblems used by both communities in Northern Ireland.

Nationalists display the red-hand-on-a-yellow-shield as a symbol of the ancient province of Ulster. It was the official crest of the once-dominant O'Neill clan (who fought tooth and nail against English rule) and today signifies resistance to British rule in these communities.

But you'll more often see the red hand in Unionist areas. They see it as a potent symbol of the political entity of Northern Ireland. The Ulster Volunteer Force chose it for their symbol in 1913 and embedded it in the center of the Northern Irish flag upon partition of the island in 1921. You'll often see the red hand clenched as a fist in Loyalist murals.

The origin of the red hand comes from a mythological tale of two rival clans that raced by boat to claim a far shore. The first clan leader to touch the shore would win it for his people. Everyone aboard both vessels strained mightily at their oars, near exhaustion as they approached the shore. Finally, in desperation, the chieftain leader of the slower boat whipped out his sword and lopped off his right hand...which he then flung onto the shore, thus winning the coveted land. Moral of the story? The fearless folk of Ulster will do *whatever* it takes to get the job done.

Cost and Hours: £6 for Folk Museum, £6 for Transport Museum, £7.50 combo-ticket for both, £20 for families; March-Sept Tue-Sun 10:00-17:00, closed Mon; Oct-Feb Tue-Fri 10:00-16:00, Sat-Sun 11:00-16:00, closed Mon. Check the schedule for the day's special events. Tel. 028/9042-8428, www.nmni.com. Allow three hours for your visit, and expect lots of walking. Those with a car can drive from one section to the next.

Getting There: From Belfast, you can reach Cultra by taxi (£12), bus #502 (2/hour, 30 minutes from Laganside Bus Centre), or train (£4.80 round-trip, 2/hour, 15 minutes, from any Belfast train station or from Bangor). Trains and buses stop right in the park, but train service is more dependable. Public-transport schedules are skimpy on Saturday and Sunday.

Carrickfergus Castle—Built during the Norman invasion of the late 1100s, this historic castle stands sentry on the shore of Belfast

Lough. William of Orange landed here in 1690, when he began his Irish campaign against deposed King James II. In 1778, the American privateer ship *Ranger* (first ever to fly the stars-and-stripes flag), under the command of John Paul Jones, defeated the more heavily armed HMS *Drake* just offshore. These days the castle feels a bit sanitized and geared for kids, but it's an easy excursion if you're seeking a castle experience near the city.

Cost and Hours: £3; April-Sept Mon-Sat 10:00-18:00, Sun 12:00-18:00; Oct-March Mon-Sat 10:00-16:00, Sun 14:00-16:00; last entry 30 minutes before closing, tel. 028/9335-1273.

Getting There: It's a 20-minute train ride from Belfast (on the line to Larne, £3.70 round-trip). If arriving by train, turn left as you exit the train station and walk straight downhill for five minutes—all the way to the waterfront—passing under the arch of the old town wall en route. You'll find the castle on your right.

Sleeping in Belfast

Belfast is more of a business town than a tourist town, so business-class room rates are lower or soft on weekends (best prices booked from their websites).

In Central Belfast

To locate these hotels, see the map on page 337.

$$$ Hotel Europa is Belfast's landmark hotel—fancy, comfortable, and central—with four stars and good weekend rates. Modern yet elegant, this place was Bill Clinton's choice when he visited (Db-£90-120 plus £16 breakfast, President Clinton's suite-£400, 8 non-smoking floors, Great Victoria Street, tel. 028/9027-1066, fax 028/9032-7800, www.hastingshotels.com, res@eur .hastingshotels.com).

$$ Jurys Inn, an American-style place that rents 190 identical modern rooms, is perfectly located two blocks from City Hall (up

Sleep Code

(£1 = about $1.60; country code: 44, area code: 028)
To call Belfast from the Republic of Ireland, dial 048 before
the local 8-digit number.
S = Single, **D** = Double/Twin, **T** = Triple, **Q** = Quad, **b** = bathroom,
s = shower only. Unless otherwise noted, breakfast is included
and credit cards are accepted.

To help you easily sort through these listings, I've divided
the rooms into three categories, based on the price for a
double room with bath:

$$$ Higher Priced—Most rooms £90 or more.
$$ Moderately Priced—Most rooms between £60-90.
$ Lower Priced—Most rooms £60 or less.

Prices can change without notice; verify the hotel's
current rates online or by email. For other updates, see www
.ricksteves.com/update.

to 3 adults or 2 adults and 2 kids for £59-110, price varies based on
season and weekend rates, breakfast-£10 extra/person, all non-
smoking, Fisherwick Place, tel. 028/9053-3500, fax 028/9053-3511,
www.jurysinns.com, jurysinnbelfast@jurysinns.com).

$$ Granada Travelodge, quiet and extremely central, is a
basic Jurys-style business hotel with 90 cookie-cutter rooms that
are high on value but low on character (Db-£59-109, a block from
Hotel Europa and City Hall at 15 Brunswick Street, reservations
toll tel. 087-0191-1687, fax 028/9023-2999, www.travelodge.ie).

South of Queen's University

Many of Belfast's best budget beds cluster in a comfortable, leafy
neighborhood of row houses just south of Queen's University (near
the Ulster Museum). Two train stations (Botanic and Adelaide)
are nearby, and buses (£1.60) zip down Malone Road every 20
minutes. Any bus on Malone Road goes to Donegall Square East.
Taxis take you downtown for about £5 (your host can call one).

$$$ Malone Lodge Hotel, by far the classiest listing in this
neighborhood, provides slick, business-class comfort in 93 spa-
cious rooms on a quiet street (Db-£85-150, superior Db-£120-175,
weekend deals, elevator, Wi-Fi, restaurant, 60 Eglantine Avenue,
tel. 028/9038-8000, fax 028/9038-8088, www.malonelodgehotel
.com, info@malonelodgehotel.com).

$$$ Wellington Park Hotel is a dependable but overpriced
chain-style hotel with 75 rooms. It's predictable but in a good
location (Db-£132 weekdays, Db-£105 weekends, Wi-Fi, park-

South Belfast

UNIONIST
PROTESTANT
MURALS

To Dublin
via M-1

Central Belfast

Shaftesbury
Square

POST

Botanic
Station

City
Hospital
Station

CITY
HOSPITAL

100 Meters

100 Yards

Botanic
Gardens

PALM
HOUSE

QUEEN'S
UNIVERSITY

ULSTER
MUSEUM

River Lagan

POST

To ④

1 Malone Lodge Hotel
2 Wellington Park Hotel
3 Camera Guest House
4 To Malone Guest House
   & Elms Village
5 Windermere Guest House
6 Belfast Holiday Inn Express
7 Benedicts Hotel
8 Ibis Belfast Queens Quarter
9 Belfast International
   City Hostel

10 Cayenne Restaurant
11 Maggie May's Restaurant
12 Bishop's Fish-and-Chips
13 Villa Italia Restaurant
14 The Barking Dog
15 Internet Café
16 Globe Launderers
17 Whistle Laundry
18 Queen's University
   Student Union

ing, 21 Malone Road, tel. 028/9038-1111, fax 028/9066-5410, www .wellingtonparkhotel.com, info@wellingtonparkhotel.com).

$$ Camera Guest House rents 10 smoke-free rooms and has an airy, hardwood feeling throughout (S-£34, Sb-£48, Ds-£56, Db-£62, family room-£78, 44 Wellington Park, tel. 028/9066-0026, www.cameraguesthouse.com, camera_gh@hotmail.com, Bronagh and Peter).

$$ Malone Guest House is a crisp, stand-alone Victorian house fronting the busy Malone Road. It's homey and well-run by Geraldine Quinn, who rents 13 prim rooms (Sb-£35-50, Db-£60-65, Tb-£70-80, Wi-Fi, 79 Malone Road, at intersection with Adelaide Park and bus stop, tel. 028/9066-9565, www.malone guesthousebelfast.co.uk, maloneguesthousebelfast@yahoo.co.uk).

$ Windermere Guest House has 11 rooms, including several small-but-pleasant singles, in a large Victorian house (S-£31, Sb-£42, D-£56, Db-£60, T-£70, cash only, 60 Wellington Park, tel. 028/9066-2693, www.windermereguesthouse.co.uk, windermereguesthouse@ntlworld.com).

$ Elms Village, a huge Queen's University dorm complex, rents 100 basic, institutional rooms (singles only) to travelers during summer break (mid-June-early-Sept only, Sb-£43, includes breakfast, cheaper for students, coin-op laundry, self-serve kitchen; reception building is 50 yards down entry street, marked *Elms Village* on low brick wall, 78 Malone Road; tel. 028/9097-4525, fax 028/9097-4524, www.stayatqueens.com, accommodation@qub.ac.uk).

Between Queen's University and Shaftesbury Square

$$ Belfast Holiday Inn Express is a 10-minute walk east of Queen's University. Even though it's not as central as other hotels, its 114 recently refurbished rooms offer a good value (Db-£69-79, better deals online, kids free, includes breakfast, all non-smoking, elevator, by Botanic Station at 106A University Street, tel. 028/9031-1909, fax 028/9031-1910, www.exhi-belfast.com, mail @exhi-belfast.com).

$$ Benedicts Hotel, with a local feel, has 32 rooms in a good location at the northern fringe of the Queen's University district. Its popular bar is a maze of polished wood and can be loud on weekend nights (Sb-£50-70, Db-£69-80, elevator, 7-21 Bradbury Place, tel. 028/9059-1999, fax 028/9059-1990, www.benedicts hotel.co.uk, info@benedictshotel.co.uk).

$ Ibis Belfast Queens Quarter recently opened, with 56 practical rooms that are conveniently located. Part of a major European hotel chain, it's a great deal if you're not looking for cozy character (Db-£55-60, better deals online, £7 breakfast, all non-smoking, elevator, a block north of Queen's University at 75 University Street, tel. 028/9033-3366, fax 028/9033-3399, www .ibishotel.com).

$ Belfast International City Hostel is big, creatively run, and provides the best value among Belfast's hostels. It has 200 beds in single and double rooms along with dorms, and is located near Botanic Station, in the heart of the lively university district. Features include free lockers, elevator, baggage storage, pay Internet access and Wi-Fi, kitchen, self-serve laundry (£3.50), a cheap breakfast-only cafeteria, 24-hour reception, and no curfew (bed in 6-bed dorm-£10, bed in quad-£12, S-£22, D-£28-31, Db-£37, 22-32 Donegall Road, tel. 028/9031-5435, fax 028/9043-9699, www.hini.org.uk, info@hini.org.uk). Paul, the manager of the hostel, is a veritable TI, with a passion for his work. The hostel is the starting point for **McComb's** minibus tours (described earlier, under "Tours in Belfast").

Eating in Belfast

Downtown

If it's £12 pub grub you want, consider these drinking holes with varied atmospheres.

The Morning Star is woody and elegant (£9-15 restaurant dinners upstairs, £5 buffet Mon-Sat 12:00-16:00, open daily 12:00-21:00, Thu-Sat until 22:00, down alley just off High Street at 17 Pottinger's Entry, roughly opposite the post office, tel. 028/9023-5986).

Kelly's Cellars—once a rebel hangout (see plaque above door)—still has a very Irish feel. It's 300 years old and hard to find, but worth it (Mon-Sat 11:30-24:30, Sun 13:00-23:30, live traditional music nightly at 21:30 and Sat at 16:30, 32 Bank Street, 100 yards behind Tesco supermarket, access via alley on left side when facing Tesco, tel. 028/9024-6058).

Crown Liquor Saloon, a recommended stop along the Golden Mile (described earlier, under "Sights in Belfast"), is small and antique. Its mesmerizing mishmash of mosaics and shareable snugs—booths—are topped with a smoky tin ceiling (Mon-Sat lunch only 11:30-15:00, Sun 12:00-17:00, 46 Great Victoria Street, across from Hotel Europa, tel. 028/9024-3187). The **Crown Dining Room** upstairs offers dependable £9-13 meals (Mon-Sat 12:00-21:00, Sun 16:00-21:00, tel. 028/9024-3187, use entry on Amelia Street when the Crown Liquor Saloon is closed).

Supermarkets: **Marks & Spencer** has a coffee shop serving skinny lattes and a supermarket in its basement (Mon-Fri 9:00-19:00, Thu until 21:00, Sat 8:30-18:00, Sun 13:00-18:00, WCs on second floor, Donegall Place, a block north of Donegall Square). **Tesco,** another supermarket, is a block north of Marks & Spencer and two blocks north of Donegall Square (Mon-Sat 8:00-19:00, Thu until 21:00, Sun 13:00-18:00, Royal Avenue and Bank Street). Picnic on the City Hall lawn.

On Waring Street, in the Cathedral Quarter

I like the cluster of culture surrounding the Cotton Court section of Waring Street. It's about a 10-minute walk northeast of the City Hall.

Check out the lobby of **Merchant Hotel** (a grand former bank) for a glimpse of crushed-velvet Victorian splendor under an opulent dome, and consider indulging Belfast's best afternoon tea splurge. Don't show up in shorts and sneakers (£17.50 tea, daily 12:00-17:00, 35-39 Waring Street, tel. 028/9023-4888).

Taps Wine Bar is a whiff of Mediterranean warmth in a cold brick city. Try a cheerful tapas or paella meal washed down with sangria (May-Sept daily 12:00-22:00, Oct-April closed Sun-Mon, 42 Waring Street, tel. 028/9031-1414).

The Cloth Ear is a friendly modern bar serving better-than-average pub grub that comes from the kitchen of the posh Merchant Hotel next door. Irish music sessions are a Sunday afternoon tradition starting at 15:00 (Mon-Sat 12:00-21:00, Sun 13:00-19:00, 33 Waring Street, tel. 028/9026-2719).

Near Shaftesbury Square and Botanic Station

Nearby Queen's University gives this neighborhood an energetic feel, with a mixed bag of dining options ranging from cosmopolitan to deep-fried.

Cayenne is a trendy-yet-friendly restaurant refuge hiding behind Belfast's most understated exterior. It's your best bet for gourmet food—innovative global cuisine—without a snobby attitude. Owner Paul Rankin stars in the *Ready Steady Cook* TV show on BBC (£15-22 meals, £16 three-course lunch; great early-bird dinner specials before 18:45: £14.50 for two courses or £17.50 for three courses; open daily for dinner 17:00-late, also open for lunch Thu-Fri 12:00-14:15 and Sun 12:00-16:00; reservations smart on weekends; Shaftesbury Square at 7 Ascot House—look for plain, gray, blocky slab front; tel. 028/9033-1532).

Maggie May's serves hearty, simple, cheap £8-12 meals (Mon-Sat 8:00-22:30, Sun 10:00-22:30, one block south of Botanic Station at 50 Botanic Avenue, tel. 028/9032-2662).

Bishop's is the locals' choice for fish-and-chips (daily 12:00-23:30, pasta and veggie options, classier side has table service, just south of Shaftesbury Square at Bradbury Place, tel. 028/9043-9070).

Villa Italia packs in crowds hungry for linguini and *bistecca*. With its checkered tablecloths and a wood-beamed ceiling draped with grape leaves, it's a little bit of Italy in Belfast (£9-15 meals, Mon-Fri 17:00-23:00, Sat-Sun 16:00-23:00, 39 University Road, 3 long blocks south of Shaftesbury Square, at intersection with University Street, tel. 028/9032-8356).

South of Queen's University

The Barking Dog is closest to my cluster of B&B listings in this area. It's a hip grill serving tasty beefy burgers, duck, scallops, and other filling fare. If the weather's fine, the outdoor tree-shaded front tables are ideal for people-watching (£6-9 lunches, £10-15 dinners, Mon-Sat 12:00-15:30 & 17:30-22:00, Sun 12:00-21:00, near corner of Eglantine Avenue at 33-35 Malone Road, tel. 028/9066-1885).

Belfast Connections

For updated schedules and prices for both trains and buses in Northern Ireland, check with Translink (tel. 028/9066-6630, www.translink.co.uk). Consider a Zone 3 iLink smartcard, good for all-day train and bus use in Northern Ireland (see page 329). Service is less frequent on Sundays.

From Belfast by Train to: Dublin (8/day, 5/day Sun, 2 hours), **Derry** (9/day, 2.5 hours), **Larne** (hourly, 1 hour), **Portrush** (11/day, 5/day Sun, 2 hours, transfer in Coleraine).

By Bus to: Portrush (12/day, 2 hours, £8, scenic-coast route, 2.5 hours), **Derry** (20/day, 1.75 hours), **Dublin** (hourly, most via Dublin Airport, 2.75-3 hours), **Glasgow** (3/day, 5.75 hours), **Edinburgh** (3/day, 7 hours). The Europa Bus Centre is behind Hotel Europa (Ulsterbus tel. 028/9033-7003 for destinations in Scotland and England).

By Plane: Belfast has two airports. George Best Belfast City Airport (www.belfastcityairport.com) is a five-minute taxi ride from town (near the docks), while Belfast International Airport (www.belfastairport.com) is 18 miles west of town, connected by buses from the Europa Bus Centre behind the Europa Hotel. There are cheap flights to **Glasgow,** Scotland, on easyJet (www.easyjet.com) and Flybe (www.flybe.com); and flights to **London**'s Heathrow Airport on bmi (www.flybmi.com).

By Bus to Dublin Airport: Aircoach buses depart from Jurys Inn Hotel in Belfast (hourly, 6:30-20:30, 2.5 hours, £15 one-way, www.aircoach.ie).

By Ferry to Scotland: There are a number of options, ports, and companies. You can sail between Belfast and **Stranraer** on the Stena Line ferry (4-6/day, 2-3.25 hours, £25, tel. 028/9074-7747, www.stena line.co.uk).

P&O Ferry (toll tel. 0870-2424-777, www.poirishsea.com) goes from **Larne** (20 miles north of Belfast, hourly trains, 1-hour trip, TI tel. 028/2826-0088) to **Cairnryan** (10/day, 1 hour) or to **Troon** (2/day, 2 hours).

By Ferry to England: You can sail from Belfast to **Birkenhead** (10 minutes from Liverpool) on DFDS Seaways (formerly Norfolkline; daily at 10:30 and 22:30, 8 hours, fares can include meals and a cabin, toll tel. 0871-230-0330, www.norfolkline -ferries.co.uk).

Bangor

To stay in a laid-back seaside hometown—with more comfort per pound—sleep 30 minutes east of Belfast in Bangor (BANG-grr).

It's a handy alternative for travelers who find Belfast booked up by occasional conventions and conferences. Formerly a Victorian resort and Belfast seaside escape, Bangor now has a sleepy and almost residential feeling. But with elegant old homes facing its spruced-up harbor and the lack of even a hint of big-city Belfast, Bangor has appeal. The harbor is a 10-minute walk from the train station.

To visit two worthwhile sights near Bangor—the Somme Heritage Centre and Mount Stewart House—consider renting a car for the day from Enterprise in Bangor (10 Enterprise Road, tel. 028/9146-1616, www.enterprise.com). Cars can also be rented from nearby George Best Belfast City Airport, a 15-minute train trip from Bangor.

Getting There

Catch the train from Belfast Central to Bangor (2/hour, 30 minutes, go to the end of the line—don't get off at Bangor West). Before 9:30, it costs £4.90 one-way (but after 9:30, it's only £5 round-trip). Consider stopping en route at Cultra (Ulster Folk and Transport Museum; see page 339). The journey gives you a good close-up look at the giant Belfast harbor cranes.

If day-tripping into Belfast from Bangor, get off at Belfast Central (free shuttle bus to the town center, 4/hour, none on Sun), or stay on until Botanic Station for the Ulster Museum, the Golden Mile, and Sandy Row.

Orientation to Bangor

Bangor's **TI** is on the harborfront at 34 Quay Street (Mon-Fri 9:00-17:00, Sat 10:00-16:00, Sun 13:00-17:00 except closed Sun Sept-April, tel. 028/9127-0069, www.northdowntourism.com). You'll find **Speediwash Launderette** at 96 Abbey Street, a couple of blocks south of the train station (Mon-Fri 9:00-18:00, Sat 9:00-17:00, closed Sun, tel. 028/9127-0074). You can get free Internet access at the **library** on Hamilton Road (30-minute limit).

Bangor

① Hargreaves House
② Shelleven House
③ Bramble Lodge
④ Boat House Rest.
⑤ Coyles Restaurant
⑥ Rioja Bistro
⑦ Café Brazilla
⑧ Jamaica Inn
⑨ Launderette
⑩ Library (Internet Access)

Sights in Bangor

For sightseeing, your time is better spent in Belfast. But if you have time to burn in Bangor, enjoy a walk next to the water on the **Coastal Path** leading west out of town from the marina.

For a shorter walk with views of the marina, head to the end of the **North Pier,** where you'll find a mosaic honoring the D-Day fleet that rendezvoused offshore in 1944, far from Nazi reconnaissance aircraft. Keep an eye out in the marina for Rose the seal.

You can glean some local Viking history at the **North Down Museum,** behind the Town Hall on the grassy grounds uphill and opposite the train station (free, Tue-Sat 10:00-16:30, Sun 14:00-16:30, closed Mon, tel. 028/9127-1200).

BELFAST

Sleeping in Bangor

(£1 = about $1.60, country code: 44, area code: 028)

Visitors arriving in Bangor (by train) come down Main Street to reach the harbor marina. You'll find my first listing to the right, along the waterfront east of the marina on Seacliff Road. The other two listings are to the left, just uphill and west of the marina.

$$ Hargreaves House, a homey Victorian waterfront refuge, is Bangor's best value and has three cozy rooms (S-£45, Sb-£50, Db-£65, large Db-£85, non-smoking, 78 Seacliff Road, 10 percent discount with cash and 2-night stay—only with 2011 edition of this book in hand upon arrival, online discounts, Wi-Fi, 15-minute walk from train station but worth it, tel. 028/9146-4071, mobile 079-8058-5047, www.hargreaveshouse.com, info@hargreaves house.com, Pauline Mendez).

$$ Shelleven House is an old-fashioned, well-kept place with 11 prim rooms on the quiet corner of Princetown Road and Tennyson Avenue (Sb-£37-45, Db-£70-80, Tb-£85, all non-smoking, Wi-Fi, 61 Princetown Road, tel. 028/9127-1777, www .shellevenhouse.com, shellevenhouse@aol.com).

$ Bramble Lodge is closest to the train station (10-minute walk), offering three inviting rooms (Sb-£35-40, Db-£60, non-smoking, 1 Bryansburn Road, tel. 028/9145-7924, jacquihanna _bramblelodge@yahoo.co.uk).

Eating in Bangor

Habitually late diners should be aware that most restaurants in town close at 21:00 and stop seating at about 20:30.

The **Boat House** is a stout stone structure hiding the finest dining experience in Bangor. It's run by two Dutch brothers who specialize in some of the freshest fish dishes in Northern Ireland. Their £18 early-bird two-course meal or £21.50 three-course special, offered before 19:30, are great values (Mon-Sat 12:00-21:00, Sun 12:00-20:00, reserve ahead, on Sea Cliff Road opposite the TI, tel. 028/9146-9253).

Coyles has two floors of fun. Upstairs is a classy, jazzy restaurant serving £13-18 dinners (Tue-Sun 17:00-21:00, closed Mon), while downstairs is a comfy bar with dependable pub grub (daily 12:00-15:00 & 17:00-21:00, 44 High Street, tel. 028/9127-0362).

Rioja does Mediterranean bistro dishes served by an easygoing staff (Tue-Sat 17:00-21:00, lunches Fri-Sat 12:00-14:00, closed Sun-Mon, 119 High Street, tel. 028/9147-0774).

Café Brazilia, a popular locals hangout at lunch, is across from the stubby clock tower (Mon-Fri 8:30-20:30, Sat 8:30-16:30, closed Sun, 13 Bridge Street, tel. 028/9127-2763).

The **Jamaica Inn** offers pleasant pub grub with a breezy waterfront porch (food served from about 12:00-21:00, 10-minute walk east of the TI on Seacliff Road, 188 Seacliff Road, tel. 028/9147-1610).

Near Bangor

The eastern fringe of Northern Ireland is populated mostly by people who consider themselves true-blue British citizens with a history of loyalty to the crown that goes back more than 400 years. Two sights within reach by car from Bangor highlight this area's firm roots in British culture: the Somme Heritage Centre and Mount Stewart House.

Getting There

Patchy bus service (bus #6) can be used to reach these sights from Bangor (check schedule with Bangor TI first). I'd rent a car instead. Enterprise rent-a-car has a handy outlet in Bangor (10 Enterprise Road, tel. 028/9146-1616). Cars can also be rented from nearby George Best Belfast City Airport (described on page 347), which is only 15 minutes by train from Bangor or 10 minutes from Belfast Central train station. Since the airport is east of Belfast, your drive to these rural sights skips the headache of urban Belfast. Call ahead to confirm sight opening hours.

Sights near Bangor

Somme Heritage Centre

World War I's trench warfare was a meat grinder. More British soldiers died in the last year of the war than in all of World War II. Northern Ireland's men were not spared—especially during the bloody Battle of the Somme in France in July 1916. Among the Allied forces was the British Army's 36th Ulster Division, which drew heavily from this loyal heartland of Northern Ireland. Working-class soldiers and aristocrat officers alike hoped that their sacrifice in Britain's cause would prove their loyalty—and ensure that Ireland would remain British after the war (a Home Rule bill passed just before the war suggested the opposite would be the case). The 36th Ulster Division suffered brutal losses at the Battle of the Somme—of the 760 men recruited from the Shankill Road area in Belfast, only 10 percent survived.

Exhibits portray the battle experience through a mix of military artifacts, photos, historical newsreels, and life-size figures posed in trench warfare re-creations. To access the majority of the exhibits, it's essential to take the one-hour guided tour (leaving hourly, on the hour). Visiting this place is a moving experience, but it can only hint at the horrific conditions endured by these soldiers.

Cost and Hours: £5; July-Aug Mon-Fri 10:00-17:00, Sat-Sun 12:00-17:00; April-June and Sept Mon-Thu 10:00-16:00, Sat 12:00-16:00, closed Fri and Sun; Oct-March Mon-Thu 10:00-16:00, closed Fri-Sun; 233 Bangor Road, 3 miles south of Bangor just off A-21, tel. 028/9182-3214, www.irishsoldier.org. A coffee shop is located at the center.

Mount Stewart House

No manor house in Ireland better illuminates the affluent lifestyle of the Protestant ascendancy than this lush estate. After the defeat

of James II (the last Catholic king of England) at the Battle of the Boyne in 1690, the Protestant monarchy was in control—and the privileged status of landowners of the same faith was assured. In the 1700s, Ireland's Catholic rebellion seemed finally to be squashed, so Anglican landlords felt safe flaunting their wealth in manor houses surrounded by utterly perfect gardens. The Mount Stewart House in particular was designed to dazzle.

Hourly tours give you a glimpse of the cushy life led by the Marquess of Londonderry and his heirs over the past three centuries. The main entry hall is a stunner, with a black-and-white checkerboard tile floor, marble columns, classical statues, and pink walls supporting a balcony with a domed ceiling and a fine chandelier. In the dining room, you'll see the original seats occupied by the rears of European heads of state, brought back from the Congress of Vienna after Napoleon's 1815 defeat. A huge painting of Hambletonian, a prize-winning racehorse, hangs above the grand staircase, dwarfing a portrait of the Duke of Wellington in a hall nearby. The heroic duke (worried that his Irish birth would be seen as lower class by British blue-bloods) once quipped, "Just because one is born in a stable does not make him a horse."

Afterwards, wander the expansive manicured gardens. The fantasy life of parasol-toting, upper-crust Victorian society seems to ooze from every viewpoint. Fanciful sculptures of extinct dodo birds and monkeys holding vases on their heads set off predictably classic Italian and Spanish sections. An Irish harp has been trimmed out of a hedge a few feet from a flowerbed shaped like the Red Hand of Ulster. Swans glide serenely among the lily pads on a small lake.

Cost and Hours: £7.40 for house and gardens, £5.60 gardens only; July-Aug daily 12:00-18:00; May-June and Sept Wed-Mon 13:00-18:00, closed Tue; April and Oct Thu-Sun 12:00-18:00, closed Mon-Wed; March Sat-Sun 12:00-18:00, closed weekdays; closed Nov-Feb; 8 miles south of Bangor, just off A-20 beside Strangford Lough, tel. 028/4278-8387, www.nationaltrust.org.uk.

PORTRUSH
and the ANTRIM COAST

The Antrim Coast—the north of Northern Ireland—is one of the most interesting and scenic coastlines in Ireland. Portrush, at the end of the train line, is an ideal base for exploring the highlights of the Antrim Coast. Within a few miles of the train terminal, you can visit evocative castle ruins, tour the world's oldest whiskey distillery, risk your life on a bouncy rope bridge, and hike along the famous Giant's Causeway.

Planning Your Time

You need a full day to explore the Antrim Coast, so allow two nights in Portrush. An ideal day could lace together Dunluce Castle, Old Bushmills Distillery, and the Giant's Causeway, followed by nine holes on the Portrush pitch-and-putt course.

Getting Around the Antrim Coast

By Bus: In July and August, a couple of all-day bus passes are available to help you get around the region economically. The better option is the £5 **Bushmills Open Topper,** connecting Portrush, Old Bushmills Distillery, and the Giant's Causeway every two hours. The £5 **Causeway Rambler**—which links Old Bushmills Distillery, the Giant's Causeway, and the Carrick-a-Rede Rope Bridge hourly—is less convenient because it doesn't include Portrush in its circuit (to get from Portrush to Bushmills, take an £8 taxi; those who want to see the rope bridge, along with the other sights, could consider getting both bus passes). For either pass, pick up a schedule at the TI and buy the ticket from the driver (in Portrush, the Bushmills Open Topper bus stops at Dunluce Avenue, next to public WC, a 2-minute walk from TI). For more info, call Translink (tel. 028/9066-6630, www.translink.co.uk).

By Bus Tour: If you're based in Belfast, you can visit sights on the Antrim Coast with a **McComb's** tour (see page 333). Those based in Derry can get to the Giant's Causeway on a **Top Tours** tour (see page 374).

By Car: Distances are short and parking is easy. Don't miss the treacherous-yet-scenic coastal route down to the Glens of Antrim.

By Taxi: Groups (up to four) go reasonably by taxi, which costs about £10 from Portrush to the Giant's Causeway. Try Andy Brown's Taxi (tel. 028/7082-2223), Hugh's Taxi (mobile 077-0298-6110), or North West Taxi (tel. 028/7082-4446).

Portrush

Homey Portrush used to be known as "the Brighton of the North." It first became a resort in the late 1800s as railroads expanded to offer the new middle class a weekend by the shore. Victorian society believed that swimming in salt water would cure many common ailments.

This is County Antrim, the Bible Belt of Northern Ireland. When a large supermarket chain decided to stay open on Sundays, a local reverend called for a boycott of the store for not honoring the Sabbath. His words were taken seriously enough to rate an article in the newspaper.

While it's seen its best days, Portrush retains the atmosphere and architecture of a genteel seaside resort. Its peninsula is filled with family-oriented amusements, fun eateries, and B&Bs. Summertime fun-seekers promenade along the tiny harbor and tumble down to the sandy beaches, which extend in sweeping white crescents on either side.

Superficially, Portrush has the appearance of any small British seaside resort, but its history and large population of young people (students from the University of Ulster at Coleraine) give the town a little more personality. Along with the usual arcade amusements, there are nightclubs, restaurants, summer theater (July-Aug) in the town hall, and convivial pubs that attract customers all the way from Belfast.

Orientation to Portrush

(area code: 028)

Portrush's pleasant and easily walkable town center features sea views in every direction. On one side are the harbor and most of the restaurants, and on the other are Victorian townhouses and vast, salty views. The tip of the peninsula is filled with tennis courts, lawn-bowling greens, putting greens, and a park.

The town is busy with students during the school year. July and August are beach-resort boom time. June and September are laid-back and lazy. Families pack Portrush on Saturdays, and revelers from Belfast crowd its hotels on Saturday nights.

Tourist Information

The TI, more generous and helpful than those in the Republic, is in the modern Dunluce Centre, with a fake lighthouse sprouting from its roof (July-Aug daily 9:00-19:00; April-June and Sept Mon-Fri 9:00-17:00, Sat-Sun 12:00-17:00; March and Oct Sat-Sun 12:00-17:00, closed Mon-Fri; closed Nov-Feb; tel. 028/7082-3333). Get the Collins Northern Ireland road map (£4), the free *Visitor Attractions* brochure, and a free Belfast map if you're Belfast-bound.

Arrival in Portrush

The train tracks stop at the base of the tiny peninsula that Portrush fills (no baggage storage at station). The TI is three long blocks from the train station (follow signs down Eglinton Street and turn left at the fire station). All listed B&Bs are within a 10-minute walk of the train station. The bus stop is two blocks from the train station.

Helpful Hints

Phone Tips: To call the Republic of Ireland from Northern Ireland, dial 00-353, then the area code without its initial 0, then the local number. To call Northern Ireland from the Republic of Ireland, dial 048, then the local eight-digit number.

Internet Access: Ground Espresso Bar has coin-op machines with fast connections (daily June-Aug 8:30-22:00, Sept-May 8:30-18:00, 52 Main Street, tel. 028/7082-5979).

Laundry: Viking Launderette charges £9/load for full service (Mon-Tue & Thu-Fri 9:00-17:30 except closed 13:00-14:00 for lunch, Sat 9:00-13:00, closed Sun and Wed, 68 Causeway Street, tel. 028/7082-2060).

Portrush

1. Adelphi Guest House & Bistro
2. Beulah Guest House
3. Anvershiel B&B
4. Ardenlee B&B
5. Harbour Heights B&B
6. The Scullery Deli
7. Ground Espresso Bar & Internet Access
8. 55 North Rest. & 55 Down Under Café
9. Harbour Road Eateries & Waterworld
10. Spring Hill Pub
11. Launderette

Atlantic Ocean

200 Meters
200 Yards

RECREATION GROUNDS

LOWER LANDOWNE RD.
LANDOWNE CRESCENT
RAMORE AVE.
BATH TERR.
MAIN ST.
MARK ST.
KERR ST.

Harbor

POST

BARRY'S ARCADE

TRAIN STATION

West Strand

CAUSEWAY ST.

East Strand

EGLINTON ST.
SANDHILL DR.
DUNLUCE AVE.

DUNLUCE CENTRE

To Pitch-and-Putt Golf Course & Giant's Causeway

CROCKNAMAC

To Coleraine, Derry & Belfast

Sights in Portrush

Barry's Old Time Amusement Arcade—This is a fine chance to see Northern Ireland at play (open weekends and summer only). Located just below the train station on the harbor, it's filled with "candy floss" (cotton candy) and little kids learning the art of one-armed bandits, 10p at a time. Get £1 worth of 10p coins from the machine and go wild, or brave the roller coaster and bumper cars (July-mid-Sept daily 12:30-22:30; May-June Mon-Fri 10:00-18:00, Sat 12:30-22:30, Sun 12:30-21:30; closed mid-Sept-April).

Pitch-and-Putt at the Royal Portrush Golf Course—Irish courses, like those in Scotland, are highly sought after for their lush but dry greens in glorious settings. Serious golfers can get a tee time at the Royal Portrush, occasional home of the Senior British Open (greens fees Mon-Fri-£125, Sat-Sun-£140). Those on a budget can play the adjacent, slightly shorter Valley Course (greens fees Mon-Fri-£35, Sat-Sun-£40). Meanwhile, rookies can get a wee dose of this wonderful golf setting at the neighboring Skerry 9 Hole Links pitch-and-putt range. You get two clubs and balls for £6, and they don't care if you go around twice (daily 8:30-19:00, 10-minute walk from station, tel. 028/7082-2311).

Portrush Recreation Grounds—For some easygoing exercise right in town, this well-organized park offers lawn-bowling greens (£3.50/hour with gear), putting greens, tennis courts, a great kids' play park, and a snack bar. Tennis shoes, balls, and rackets can all be rented for a low price (mid-May-mid-Sept Mon-Sat 10:00-dusk, Sun 13:00-18:00, closed mid-Sept-mid-May, tel. 028/7082-4441).

More Fun—Consider **Dunluce Centre** (kid-oriented fun zone, in same building with TI) and **Waterworld** (£4.50, pool, waterslides, bowling; June-Aug daily 10:00-19:00; closed Sept-May; wedged between the Harbour Bistro and Ramore Wine Bar, tel. 028/7082-2001).

Sleeping in Portrush

Portrush has a range of hotels, from decent to ritzy. Some B&Bs can be well-worn. August and Saturday nights can be tight. Otherwise, it's a "you take half a loaf when you can get it" town. Rates vary with the view and season—probe for softness. Many listings face the sea, though sea views are worth paying for only if you get a bay window. Ask for a big room (some doubles can be very small; twins are bigger). Lounges are invariably grand and have bay-window views. All places listed have lots of stairs, but most are perfectly central and within a few minutes' walk of the train station. Parking is easy.

PORTRUSH

Sleep Code

(£1 = about $1.60, country code: 44, area code: 028)
To call Portrush from the Republic of Ireland, dial 048 before
the local 8-digit number.
S = Single, **D** = Double/Twin, **T** = Triple, **Q** = Quad, **b** = bathroom,
s = shower only. Breakfast is included and credit cards are
accepted unless otherwise noted.

   To help you easily sort through these listings, I've divided
the rooms into two categories, based on the price for a
standard double room with bath:

  $$ Higher Priced—Most rooms £80 or more.
  $ Lower Priced—Most rooms less than £80.

   Prices can change without notice; verify the hotel's
current rates online or by email. For other updates, see www
.ricksteves.com/update.

$$ Adelphi Guest House is a breath of fresh air, with 25 tastefully furnished modern rooms, friendly staff, and a hearty bistro downstairs (Sb-£55-105, Db-£65-115, Tb-£75-125, Qb-£105-155, 67-71 Main Street, Wi-Fi, tel. 028/7082-5544, www.adelphi portrush.com, stay@adelphiportrush.com).

$ Beulah Guest House is an old-fashioned, good-value place. It's centrally located and run by cheerful Rachel and Jimmy Anderson, with 11 prim and smoke-free rooms (Ss-£33, Sb-£45-60, Db-£60-75, Tb-£85-95, parking, 16 Causeway Street, tel. 028/7082-2413, www.beulahguesthouse.com, stay@beulahguest house.com).

$ Anvershiel B&B, with six non-smoking rooms, is a five-minute walk south of the train station. Jovial Victor Bow, who runs the show with his wife Erna, is in the know about local golf (Sb-£45, Db-£65, Tb-£95, Qb-£125, cash only, 5 percent discount on Db with 2-night stay, Wi-Fi, parking, 16 Coleraine Road, tel. 028/7082-3861, www.anvershiel.com, enquiries@anvershiel.com).

$ Ardenlee B&B offers six smartly refurbished rooms, some with fine views of the ocean (Sb-£35-50, Db-£60-90, Tb-£100, 19 Kerr Street, tel. 028/7082-2639, mobile 078-0725-9460, russell .rafferty@btconnect.com).

$ Harbour Heights B&B rents nine homey rooms, each named after a different town in County Antrim. It has an inviting guest lounge, DVD players, and a small DVD library (Sb-£40, Db-£70-80, family rooms, Wi-Fi, 17 Kerr Street, tel. 028/7082-2765, mobile 078-9586-6534, www.harbourheightsportrush.com, info@harbourheightsportrush.com, Sam and Tim Swart).

Eating in Portrush

Being a get-away-from-Belfast town and close to a university town (Coleraine), Portrush has more than enough chips joints. Eglinton Street is lined with cheap and cheery eateries.

Lunch Spots

The Scullery makes sandwiches and healthy wraps to take away and enjoy by the beach—or on an Antrim Coast picnic (daily 8:30-17:00, close to the train station at 4 Eglinton Lane, tel. 028/7082-1000).

Ground Espresso Bar makes fresh £4 sandwiches or paninis, soup, and excellent coffee (daily June-Aug 9:00-22:00, Sept-May 9:00-17:00, 52 Main Street, tel. 028/7082-5979). They also offer coin-op Internet access (see "Helpful Hints," earlier).

55 Down Under Café serves basic sandwiches with a great patio view (Wed-Sun 9:00-21:00, Mon-Tue 9:00-17:00, shorter hours off-season, 1 Causeway Street, underneath fancier 55 North restaurant run by same owners and listed below, tel. 028/7082-2811).

Fine Dining

55 North (named for the local latitude) has the best sea views in town, with windows on all sides. The classy pasta-and-fish plates are a joy (£9-17 plates, daily 12:30-14:00 & 17:00-21:00 except closed Mon Sept-June, 1 Causeway Street, tel. 028/7082-2811).

Adelphi Bistro is a good bet for its relaxed family-friendly atmosphere and hearty meals (daily 12:00-15:00 & 17:00-21:00, 67-71 Main Street, tel. 028/7082-5544).

Harbour Road Eateries

The following four restaurants are located within 50 yards of each other (all under the same ownership and overlooking the harbor on Harbour Road), offering some of the best food values in town.

Ramore Wine Bar—salty, modern, and much-loved—bursts with happy eaters. They have the most inviting menu that I've seen in Ireland, featuring huge meals ranging from steaks to vegetarian food. Share a piece of the decadent banoffee (banana toffee) pie with a friend (£9-15 plates, daily 12:15-14:15 & 17:00-21:30, Sun until 21:00, tel. 028/7082-4313).

Downstairs, sharing the same building as the Ramore Wine Bar, is the energetic **Coast Italiano,** with (no surprise) great Italian dishes. Come early for a table or sit at the bar (Mon-Fri 17:00-21:30, Sat 16:30-22:00, Sun 15:00-21:00, Sept-June closed Mon-Tue, tel. 028/7082-3311).

The Harbour Bistro offers a more subdued, darker bistro ambience than the previous two eateries, with meals for a few pounds more (£9-16 dinners, daily 17:00-21:30, tel. 028/7082-2430).

Ramore Oriental sits at the high end of the bunch, farthest from the water, and serves the best Asian cuisine in town (£10-15 dinners, Wed-Sat 18:30-22:00, Sun 17:30-21:00, closed Mon-Tue, tel. 028/7082-4313).

Pubs

The **Harbour Bar** (next to the Harbour Bistro) has an old-fashioned pub downstairs and a plush, overstuffed, dark lounge upstairs. Or try the **Spring Hill Pub** (Causeway Street), with a friendly vibe and occasional music session nights.

Portrush Connections

Consider a £16.50 Zone 3 iLink smartcard, good for all-day train and bus use in Northern Ireland year-round (£15 top-up for each additional day; for more on iLink cards, see page 329). Useful updated schedules and prices for both trains and buses in Northern Ireland can be obtained from Translink (tel. 028/9066-6630, www .translink.co.uk).

From Portrush by Train to: Coleraine (hourly, 12 minutes, sparse on Sun morning), **Belfast** (11/day, 5/day Sun, 2 hours, transfer in Coleraine), **Dublin** (7/day, 2/day Sun, 5 hours, transfer in Coleraine or Belfast).

By Bus to: Belfast (12/day, 2 hours; scenic coastal route, 2.5 hours), **Dublin** (4/day, 5.5 hours).

Antrim Coast

The craggy 20-mile stretch of the Antrim Coast, extending eastward from Portrush to Ballycastle, rates second only to the tip of the Dingle Peninsula as the prettiest chunk of coastal Ireland. From your base in Portrush, you have a varied grab bag of sightseeing choices: the Giant's Causeway, Old Bushmills Distillery, Dunluce Castle, Carrick-a-Rede Rope Bridge, and Rathlin Island.

It's easy to weave these sights together by car, but connections are patchy by public transportation. Bus

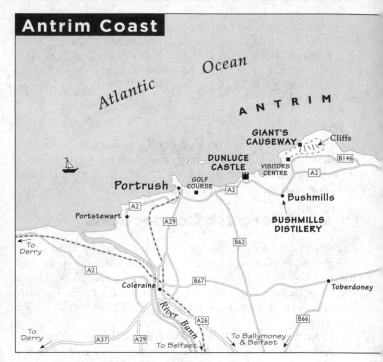

Antrim Coast

Ocean

Atlantic

A N T R I M

GIANT'S CAUSEWAY · Cliffs

B146

DUNLUCE CASTLE

VISITORS CENTRE

A2

Portrush

GOLF COURSE

A2

· Bushmills

Portstewart ·

A2

A29

BUSHMILLS DISTILLERY

To Derry

A2

B62

Coleraine

B67

· Toberdoney

River Bann

A26

B66

To Derry

A37

A29

To Belfast

To Ballymoney & Belfast

service is viable only in summer, and taxi fares are reasonable only for the sights closest to Portrush (Dunluce Castle and the Old Bushmills Distillery). For more on your transportation options, see "Getting Around the Antrim Coast," earlier.

Planning Your Time

With a car, you can do the Giant's Causeway, Old Bushmills Distillery, Dunluce Castle, and Carrick-a-Rede Rope Bridge in one busy day. Call ahead to reserve the Old Bushmills Distillery tour, and get an early start. Arrive at the Giant's Causeway by 9:00 when crowds are sparse. Park your car in the causeway lot and pay as you exit (after the visitors center opens). Although the Causeway's visitors center doesn't open (and the shuttle bus doesn't run) until 10:00, the trails are free and always open. Spend an hour and a half scrambling over Ireland's most unique alligator-skin geology.

Then catch a late-morning tour of the Old Bushmills Distillery, a 400-year-old whiskey distillery. Grab a cheap lunch in the hospitality room afterwards. A 20-minute drive east brings you to Carrick-a-Rede, where you can enjoy a scenic cliff-top trail hike all the way to the lofty rope bridge (one hour round-trip, 1.5 hours if you cross the rope bridge and explore the sea stack). Hop in your car and double back west all the way to dramatically cliff-perched Dunluce Castle for a late-afternoon tour. From here, you're only a five-minute drive away from Portrush.

Those with extra time, a car, and a hankering to seek out dramatic coastal cliff scenery may want to spend a half-day boating out to Rathlin Island, Northern Ireland's only inhabited island.

Sights on the Antrim Coast

▲Dunluce Castle

These romantic ruins, perched dramatically on the edge of a rocky headland, are a testimony to this region's turbulent past. During

the Middle Ages, the castle resisted several sieges. But on a stormy night in 1639, dinner was interrupted as half of the kitchen fell into the sea and took the servants with it. That was the last straw for the lady of the castle. The countess of Antrim packed up and moved inland, and the castle "began its slow submission to the forces of nature." While it's one of the largest castles in Northern Ireland and is beautifully situated, there's precious little left to see among its broken walls.

The 16th-century expansion of the castle was financed by the salvaging of a shipwreck. In 1588, the Spanish Armada's *Girona*—laden with sailors and the valuables of three abandoned sister ships—sank on her way home after the aborted mission against England. More than 1,300 drowned, and only 5 survivors washed ashore. The shipwreck was excavated in 1967, and a bounty of golden odds and silver ends wound up in Belfast's Ulster Museum.

Castle admission includes an impromptu guided tour of the ruins given by a small stable of dedicated guides. Before you leave, poke your head into the building opposite the gift shop and check out the large castle model, which shows the joint in its fully roofed heyday.

Cost and Hours: £2, daily April-Sept 10:00-18:00, Oct-March 10:00-16:30, last entry 30 minutes before closing, tel. 028/2073-1938.

▲▲Giant's Causeway

This four-mile-long stretch of coastline, a World Heritage Site, is famous for its bizarre basalt columns. The shore is covered with

largely hexagonal pillars that stick up at various heights. It's as if the earth were offering God his choice of 37,000 six-sided cigarettes.

Geologists claim the Giant's Causeway was formed by volcanic eruptions more than 60 million years ago. As the surface of the lava flow quickly cooled, it contracted and crystallized into hexagonal columns. As the rock (which looked like alligator skin) later settled and eroded, the columns broke off into many stair-like steps.

Of course, in actuality, the Giant's Causeway was made by a giant Ulster warrior named Finn MacCool who wanted to reach his love on the Scottish island of Staffa. Way back then, the causeway stretched to Scotland, connecting the two lands. Today, while the foundation has settled, the formation still extends undersea to Staffa, just off the Scottish coast. Finn's causeway was ruined (into today's "remnant of chaos") by a rival giant. As the rival fled from ferocious Finn back to his Scottish homeland, he ripped up the causeway so Finn couldn't chase him.

Visitors Centre—For cute variations on the Finn story, as well as details on the ridiculous theories of modern geologists, start out in the visitors center (free entry but £6 to park, daily 9:30-18:00,

The Scottish Connection

The Romans called the Irish the "Scoti" (meaning pirates). When the Scoti crossed the narrow Irish Sea and invaded the land of the Picts 1,500 years ago, that region became known as Scoti-land. Ireland and Scotland were never conquered by the Romans, and they retained similar clannish Celtic traits. Both share the same Gaelic branch of the linguistic tree.

On clear summer days from Carrick-a-Rede, the island of Mull in Scotland—only 17 miles away—is visible. Much closer on the horizon is the boomerang-shaped Rathlin Island, part of Northern Ireland. Rathlin is where Scottish leader Robert the Bruce (a compatriot of William "Braveheart" Wallace) retreated in 1307 after defeat at the hands of the English. Legend has it that he hid in a cave on the island, where he observed a spider patiently rebuilding its web each time a breeze knocked it down. Inspired by the spider's perseverance, Robert gathered his Scottish forces once more and finally defeated the English at the decisive battle of Bannockburn.

Flush with confidence from his victory, Robert the Bruce decided to open a second front against the English... in Ireland. In 1315, he sent his brother Edward over to enlist their Celtic Irish cousins in an effort to thwart the English. After securing Ireland, Edward hoped to move on and enlist the Welsh, thus cornering England with their pan-Celtic nation. But Edward's timing was bad—Ireland was in the midst of famine. His Scottish troops had to live off the land and began to take food and supplies from the starving Irish. He might also have been trying to destroy Ireland's crops to keep them from being used as a colonial "breadbasket" to feed English troops. The Scots quickly wore out their welcome, and Edward the Bruce was eventually killed in battle near Dundalk in 1318.

This was the first time in history that Ireland was used as a pawn by England's enemies. Ireland was seen as the English Achilles' heel by Spain and France, who later attempted Irish invasions. The English Tudor and Stuart royalty countered these threats in the 16th and 17th centuries by starting the "plantation" of loyal subjects in Ireland. The only successful long-term settlement by the English was here in Northern Ireland, which remains part of the United Kingdom today.

It's interesting to speculate how things would be different today if Ireland and Scotland had been permanently welded together as a nation 700 years ago. You'll notice the strong Scottish influence in this part of Ireland when you ask a local a question and he answers, "Aye, a wee bit." The Irish joke that the Scots are just Irish people who couldn't swim home.

July-Aug until 19:00, tel. 028/2073-1855, www.nationaltrust.org
.uk). A 12-minute video gives a worthwhile history of the Giant's
Causeway, with a regional overview (£1, 4/hour). A gift shop and
cafeteria are standing by.

Visiting the Causeway—The causeway itself—the highlight of
the entire coast—is free and always open. From the visitors center,
you have several options for visiting the causeway:

By Minibus: A minibus (4/hour, £1 each way) zips tired tourists a half-mile directly from the visitors center to the causeway.

By Foot: For a better dose of the causeway, follow the high
cliff-top trail uphill from the visitors center 10 minutes to a great
precipice viewpoint, then walk 15 minutes farther to reach the
Shepherd's Stairway. Zigzag down the stairs and switchbacks to
the coast; at the T junction, go 100 yards right, to the towering
pipes of "the Organ." Then retrace your steps and continue left
down to the tidal zone, where the "Giant's Boot" (on the right)
provides some photo fun. Another 100 yards farther you'll find the
dramatic point where the stairs step into the sea. Just beyond that,
at the asphalt turnaround, you'll see the bus stop for a lift back to
the visitors center.

You could also walk the trail that runs along the entire
five-mile-long Causeway Coast, though rock falls and slides
occasionally close the trail. The £1 hiking guide points out the
highlights named by 18th-century guides (Camel's Back, Giant's
Eye, and so on).

By Tourist Train: In summer, a quaint, narrow-gauge steam
locomotive connects the causeway to the town of Bushmills with a
two-mile, 15-minute journey (£5 one-way, £6.50 round-trip, daily
July-Aug, only on weekends June and Sept, tel. 028/2073-2844,
www.freewebs.com/giantscausewayrailway). The train runs hourly,
departing the causeway's station at the top of the hour (11:00-
17:00) and leaving Bushmills station on the half-hour (11:30-17:30,
on Ballaghmore Road, a 15-minute walk from distillery).

▲▲Old Bushmills Distillery

Bushmills claims to be the world's oldest distillery. Though King
James I (of Bible fame) only granted its license to distill "Aqua
Vitae" in 1608, whiskey has been made here since the 13th century. Distillery tours waft you through the process, making it
clear that Irish whiskey is triple distilled—and therefore smoother
than Scotch whisky (distilled merely twice and minus the "e").
The 45-minute tour starts with the mash pit, which is filled with
a porridge that eventually becomes whiskey. (The leftovers of that
porridge are fed to the county's particularly happy cows.) You'll see
thousands of oak casks—the kind used for Spanish sherry—filled
with aging whiskey.

The finale, of course, is the opportunity for a sip in the 1608 Bar—the former malt barn. Visitors get a single glass of their choice. Hot-drink enthusiasts might enjoy a cinnamon-and-cloves hot toddy.

To see the distillery at its lively best, visit when the 100 workers are staffing the machinery—Monday morning through Friday noon (weekend tours see a still still). Tours are limited to 35 people and book up. In summer, call before you go to put in your name and get a tour time. After the tour, you can get a decent lunch in the tasting room.

Cost and Hours: £6.50; April-Oct tours on the half-hour Mon-Sat from 9:30, Sun from 12:00, last tour at 16:00; Nov-March tours Mon-Sat at 10:00, 11:00, 12:00, 13:30, 14:30, and 15:30, Sun from 12:00. To find Bushmills, look for the distillery sign a quarter-mile from Bushmills town center. Tel. 028/2073-3218, www.bushmills.com.

▲▲Carrick-a-Rede Rope Bridge

For 200 years, fishermen have hung a narrow, 90-foot-high bridge (planks strung between wires) across a 65-foot-wide chasm

 between the mainland and a tiny island. Today, the bridge (while not the original version) still gives access to the salmon nets that are set during the summer months to catch the fish turning the coast's corner. (The complicated system is described at the gateway.) A pleasant, 30-minute one-mile walk from the parking lot takes you to the rope bridge. Cross to the island for fine views and great seabird-watching, especially during nesting season (£4.90 trail and bridge fee, pay at hut beside parking lot, coffee shop and WCs near parking lot, March-Oct daily 10:00-18:00, July-Aug until 19:00, closed Nov-Feb, tel. 028/2076-9839, www.nationaltrust.org.uk).

If you have a car and a picnic lunch, don't miss the terrific coastal **viewpoint** rest area one mile steeply uphill and east of Carrick-a-Rede (on B-15 road to Ballycastle). This grassy area offers one of the best picnic views in Northern Ireland (picnic tables but no WCs). Feast on bird's-eye views of the rope bridge, nearby Rathlin Island, and the not-so-distant Island of Mull in Scotland.

Rathlin Island

The only inhabited island off the coast of Northern Ireland, Rathlin is a quiet haven for hikers, bird-watchers, and seal spotters. Less

than seven miles from end to
end, this "L"-shaped island is
reachable by ferry from the town
of Ballycastle (see "Getting
There," later).

Its population of 75 islanders cluster around the ferry dock
at Church Bay. Here you'll find
the Rathlin Manor House, offering the island's most convenient
lodging, a restaurant, and a pub (tel. 028/2076-3964, www.rathlin
manorhouse.co.uk). The **Rathlin Boathouse Visitor Centre** operates as the island's TI (May-Aug daily 10:30-13:30 & 14:00-16:00,
on the bay 100 yards east of the ferry dock, tel. 028/2076-2225).

In summer, the Puffin shuttle bus (£5 round-trip, seats 25)
meets arriving ferries and drives visitors to the **Rathlin Island
Seabird Centre** at the west end of the island. Here a lighthouse
extends down the cliff with its beacon at the bottom. It's upside
down because the coast guard wants the light visible only from
a certain distance out to sea. The bird observation terrace at the
Centre (next to the lighthouse) overlooks one of the most dramatic
coastal views in Ireland—a sheer drop of more than 300 feet to
craggy sea stacks just offshore, draped in thousands of sea birds.
Photographers will want to bring their most powerful zoom lens.

For such a snoozy island, Rathlin has seen its fair share of
history. Flint axe-heads were quarried here in Neolithic times. The
island was one of the first in Ireland to be raided by Vikings, in
795. Robert the Bruce hid out from English pursuers on Rathlin
in the early 1300s (see sidebar on page 365). In the late 1500s, local
warlord Sorely Boy MacDonnell stashed his extended family on
Rathlin and waited on the mainland at Dunluce Castle to face his
English enemies...only to watch in horror as they headed for the
island instead to massacre his loved ones. And in 1917, a WWI
U-boat sank the British cruiser HMS *Drake* in Church Bay. (The
wreck is now a popular scuba-dive destination.)

Getting There: The Rathlin Island ferry departs from
Ballycastle, just east of Carrick-a-Rede. It does nine crossings
per day in summer. Five are fast 20-minute trips on passenger
boats, and four are slower 45-minute trips on car ferries (£10.80
round-trip per passenger on either type of boat, reserve ahead, tel.
028/2076-9299, www.rathlinballycastleferry.com).

Travelers with rental cars will have no problem reaching
Ballycastle. A taxi from Portrush to Ballycastle runs £20 one-way.
Bus service from Portrush to Ballycastle is spotty (check with the
TI in Portrush, or contact Translink—tel. 028/9066-6630, www
.translink.co.uk).

▲Antrim Mountains and Glens

Not particularly high (never more than 1,500 feet), the Antrim Mountains are cut by a series of large glens running northeast to the sea. Glenariff, with its waterfalls (especially the Mare's Tail), is the most beautiful of the nine glens. Travelers going by car can take a pleasant drive from Portrush to Belfast, sticking to the A-2 road that takes in parts of all of the Glens of Antrim. The two best stops en route are Cushendall (nice beach for a picnic) and the castle at Carrickfergus (see page 341).

DERRY
and COUNTY DONEGAL

The town of Derry (or Londonderry to Unionists) is the mecca of Ulster Unionism. When Ireland was being divvied up, the River Foyle was the logical border between the North and the Republic. But, for sentimental and economic reasons, the North kept Derry, which is on the Republic's side of the river. Consequently, this predominantly Catholic city has been much contested throughout the Troubles.

Even its name is disputed. While most of its population and its city council call it "Derry," some maps, road signs, and train schedules in the UK use "Londonderry," the name on its 1662 royal charter and the one favored by Unionists.

Still, the conflict is only one dimension of Derry; this pivotal city has a more diverse history and a prettier setting than Belfast. Derry was a vibrant city back when Belfast was just a mudflat. And with a quarter of the population (84,000), Derry feels more manageable to visitors.

County Donegal, to the west of Derry, is about as far-flung as Ireland gets. A forgotten economic backwater (part of the Republic but riding piggyback on the North), it lacks blockbuster museums or sights. But a visit here is more about the journey, and adventurous drivers—a car is a must—will be rewarded with a time-capsule peek into old Irish ways and uncompromisingly beautiful scenery.

Planning Your Time

Travelers heading north from Westport or Galway should get an early start. Donegal town makes a good lunch stop, with lots of choices surrounding its triangular town square, and then it's on to Derry, where you can spend a couple of hours seeing the essentials.

Visit the Tower Museum and catch some views from the town wall before continuing on to Portrush for the night.

With more time, spend a night in Derry, so you can see the powerful Bogside murals and take a walking tour around the town walls—you'll appreciate this underrated city. With two nights in Derry, consider crossing the border into the Republic for a scenic driving loop through part of remote County Donegal.

Derry

No city in Ireland connects the kaleidoscope of historical dots more colorfully than Derry. From a leafy monastic hamlet to a Viking-pillaged port, from a cannonball-battered siege survivor to an Industrial Revolution sweatshop, from an essential WWII naval base to a wrenching flashpoint of sectarian Troubles...Derry has seen it all.

But the past few years have brought some refreshing changes. Manned British Army surveillance towers were taken down in 2006, and British troops themselves finally departed in mid-2007, after 38 years in Northern Ireland. In early 2011, a new pedestrian bridge across the River Foyle should be complete, linking the predominantly Protestant Waterside (east bank) with the predominantly Catholic Cityside (west bank). Today, you can feel comfortable wandering the streets and enjoying this unique Irish city.

Orientation to Derry

(area code: 028)
The River Foyle flows north, slicing Derry into eastern and western chunks. The old town walls and worthwhile sights are all on the west side. Waterloo Place and the adjacent Guildhall Square, just outside the north corner of the old city walls, are the pedestrian hubs of city activity. The Strand Road area extending north from Waterloo Place makes a comfortable home base, with the majority of lodging and restaurant suggestions within a block or two on either side. The Diamond and its War Memorial statue mark the heart of the old city within the walls.

Tourist Information
The TI sits on the riverfront and offers a room-finding service, rents bikes, books bus and walking tours (see "Tours in Derry," later), and gives out free city maps (July-Sept Mon-Fri 9:00-19:00, Sat 10:00-18:00, Sun 10:00-16:00; Oct-June Mon-Fri 9:00-17:00,

DERRY

Derry

To County Donegal via A-2

100 Meters
100 Yards

River Foyle

ST. EUGENE'S CATHEDRAL

ASYLUM RD.
NORTHLAND RD.
CLARENDON ST.
STRAND RD.
PRINCES ST.
QUEEN ST.
QUEENS QUAY
GREAT JAMES ST.
PATRICK ST.
FRANCIS ST.

QUAYSIDE SHOPPING CENTRE

See Bogside Murals map

LITTLE DIAMOND
WILLIAM ST.
FREDERICK ST.
ABBEY ST.
ROSSVILLE ST.
FAHAN ST.
LISFANNON PK.
WESTLAND ST.

THE PEOPLE'S GALLERY

BLOODY SUNDAY MONUMENT

BOGSIDE

"H" BLOCK MONUMENT

FREE DERRY CORNER

ROYAL BASTION

MAGAZINE GATE

Waterloo Place

POST

GUILD HALL

Guildhall Square

SHIPQUAY GATE

PEDESTRIAN BRIDGE
To Waterside & Train Station

Ulsterbus Station

CHAMBERLAIN ST.
HIGH ST.
WATERLOO ST.
CASTLE GATE
BUTCHER GATE
FAHAN ST.
MAGAZINE ST.

TOWER MUSEUM

NERVE CENTRE

CRAFT VILLAGE

MILLENNIUM FORUM

WATER ST.
EMBANKMENT
FOYLE ST.

CITY WALLS

FOYLESIDE SHOPPING CENTRE

APPRENTICE BOYS MEMORIAL HALL

The Diamond

SOCIETY ST.
BISHOP ST.
PALACE ST.
WITHIN
LONDON ST.
PUMP ST.
FERRYQUAY ST.
LINENHALL ST.
ORCHARD ST.
MARKET ST.
ARTILLERY ST.
BRIDGE ST.

ST. AUGUSTINE CHAPEL

VERBAL ARTS CENTRE

WAR MEMORIAL

ST. COLUMB'S CATHEDRAL

FERRYQUAY GATE

NEW GATE

LONG TOWER CHURCH

DOUBLE BASTION

BISHOP'S GATE

JAIL TOWER

LONG TOWER ST.

BISHOP ST. WITHOUT

THE FOUNTAIN

FOUNTAIN

PEACE WALL

CITY WALLS

CARLISLE RD.
HAWKIN ST.
JOHN ST.
FOYLE RD.

HANDS ACROSS THE DIVIDE STATUES

BARRACK ST.
SUNBEAM TERRACE
BELLVUE AVE.
FERGUSON ST.
MAUREEN AVE.
IVY TERRACE
UPR BENNETT ST.
HARDING ST.
AUBREY ST.
WAPPING LN.
ABERCORN RD.
LOWER BENNETT ST.
FOYLE RD.

FORMER SHIRT FACTORY SITE

CRAIGAVON BRIDGE

To County Donegal (Republic of Ireland) via A-40

To Train Station, Portrush via A2 & Belfast via A6

1. Tower Hotel
2. Travelodge
3. Merchant's House
4. Saddler's House
5. Paddy's Palace Hostel
6. Mandarin Palace Rest.
7. Exchange Restaurant & Wine Bar
8. Fitzroy's Restaurant
9. Bay Leaf Restaurant
10. Austins Department Store Café
11. Peadar O'Donnell's Pub
12. Tesco Supermarket
13. SuperValu Supermarket
14. Internet Café
15. Laundry
16. Playhouse Theatre

Sat 10:00-17:00, closed Sun; 44 Foyle Street, tel. 028/7126-7284, www.derryvisitor.com).

Arrival in Derry

Next to the river on the east side of town, Derry's little end-of-the-line train station (no storage lockers) has service to Portrush, Belfast, and Dublin. Free shuttle buses to Ulsterbus station (on the west side of town, a couple of minutes' walk south of Guildhall Square on Foyle Street) await each arriving train. Otherwise, it's a 15-minute walk across Craigavon Bridge to the TI or a £5 taxi ride to Guildhall Square. The same free shuttle service leaves Ulsterbus station 15 minutes before each departing train.

Derry is compact enough to see on foot; drivers stopping for a few hours can park at the Foyleside parking garage across from the TI (£1/hour, £2.50/4 hours, Mon-Tue 8:00-19:00, Wed-Fri 8:00-22:00, Sat 8:00-20:00, Sun 12:00-19:00, tel. 028/7137-7575). Drivers staying overnight can ask about parking at their B&B or try the Quayside parking garage behind the Travelodge (£0.80/hour, £3/4 hours, Mon-Thu 7:30-21:00, Fri-Sat open 24 hours, Sun 12:30-18:00).

Helpful Hints

Phone Tips: To call the Republic of Ireland from Northern Ireland, dial 00-353, then the area code without its initial 0, then the local number. To call Northern Ireland from the Republic of Ireland, dial 048, then the local eight-digit number.

Money: Northern Bank is on Guildhall Square, and the **Bank of Ireland** is on Strand Road (both open Mon-Fri 9:30-16:30, Sat 9:30-12:30, closed Sun).

Internet Access: Located inside the walls, **Claudes Café** is just north of the Diamond on Shipquay Street (£3/30 minutes, daily 9:00-17:30, tel. 028/7127-9379).

Post Office: The main post office is just off Waterloo Place (Mon-Fri 9:00-17:30, Sat 9:00-12:30, closed Sun, Custom House Street).

Laundry: Smooth Operators can do a load of laundry for £8.50 (drop off in morning to pick up later that day, Mon-Fri 8:30-18:00, Sat 8:30-17:30, closed Sun, 8 Sackville Street, tel. 028/7136-0529).

Taxi: Try **Derry Taxis** (tel. 028/7126-0247) or **Foyle Delta Cabs** (tel. 028/7127-9999).

Car Rental: Enterprise is a handy place to rent a car (tel. 028/7186-1699, 70 Clooney Road, www.enterprise.com).

Tours in Derry

Walking Tours—The **Bogside Artists** explain the impassioned inspiration behind their famous murals on walks departing from their studio, The People's Gallery, at the corner of Rossville and William streets. These walks provide a rare opportunity to discuss this community's tragic history with guides who lived through it (£4; daily at 11:00, 14:00, and 16:00; call to confirm schedule, tel. 028/7137-3842, www.bogsideartists.com).

Martin McCrossan and his staff lead insightful hour-long tours of the city, departing from 11 Carlisle Road just below Ferryquay Gate (£4; daily at 10:00, 12:00, and 14:00; call to confirm schedule, also offers private tours, tel. 028/7127-1996, mobile 077-1293-7997, www.irishtourguides.com).

Stephen McPhilemy leads private tours of his hometown, Belfast, and the North Coast—when he's not on the road guiding Rick Steves tours several months a year (tel. 028/7130-9051, mobile 078-0101-1027, www.irishexperience.ie, steve@irishexperience.ie). Stephen also runs the recommended Paddy's Palace Hostel.

Free Derry Tours depart daily at 10:00 and 14:00 from the Museum of Free Derry. Tours focus on the surrounding Bogside neighborhood's history as the flashpoint that ignited the modern Troubles (£6, tel. 028/7126-2812, mobile 077-9328-5972, www.freederry.net, freederrytours@gmail.com).

Bus Tours—**Top Tours'** double-decker buses are a good option on a rainy day. You'll be driven around the city in a one-hour loop that covers both sides of the river, including Guild Hall, the old city walls, political wall murals (Nationalist as well as Unionist), cathedrals, and former shirt factories. Your ticket is good for one lap around the loop, and you stay on the bus for the duration (£8, pay driver, April-Sept daily on the hour 10:00-16:00, departs from in front of TI and beside the Guild Hall, mobile 077-9116-4431, www.derryvisitor.com, info@toptoursireland.com).

Top Tours also offers trips from Derry to the Giant's Causeway and Carrick-a-Rede Rope Bridge in County Antrim (£20, runs daily May-Sept, depart TI at 11:00, return at 18:00). Starting in 2011, they plan to offer tours to Glenveagh National Park in County Donegal. All of their tours can be booked through the Derry TI.

Self-Guided Walks

Though calm today, Derry is marked by years of tumultuous conflict. These two walks (each taking less than an hour) will increase your understanding of the town's history. The first walk, starting on the old city walls and ending at the Anglican Cathedral, focuses on Derry's early days. The second walking tour helps you easily find the city's compelling murals, which document the time of the Troubles. These tours can be done separately or linked, depending on your time.

▲▲Walk the Walls

Squatting determinedly in the city center, the old city walls of Derry (built 1613-1618 and still intact, except for wider gates to handle modern vehicles) hold an almost mythic place in Irish history.

It was here in 1688 that a group of brave apprentice boys, many of whom had been shipped to Derry as orphans after the great fire of London in 1666, made their stand. They slammed the city gates shut in the face of the approaching Catholic forces of deposed King James II. With this act, the boys galvanized the city's indecisive Protestant defenders inside the walls.

Months of negotiations and a grinding 105-day siege followed, during which a third of the 20,000 refugees and defenders crammed into the city perished.

The siege was finally broken in 1689, when supply ships broke through a boom stretched across the River Foyle. The sacrifice and defiant survival of the city turned the tide in favor of newly crowned Protestant King William of Orange, who arrived in Ireland soon after and defeated James at the pivotal Battle of the Boyne.

To fully appreciate the walls, take a walk on top of them (free and open from dawn to dusk). Almost 20 feet high and at least as thick, the walls form a mile-long oval loop that you can cover in less than an hour. But the most interesting section is the half-circuit facing away from the river, starting at Magazine Gate (stairs face the Tower Museum Derry inside the walls) and finishing at Bishop's Gate.

• *Enter the walls at Magazine Gate and find the stairs opposite the Tower Museum. Once atop the walls, head left.*

Walk the wall as it heads uphill, snaking along the earth's contours like a mini-Great Wall of China. In the row of buildings on the left (just before crossing over Castle Gate), you'll see an arch entry into the **Craft Village,** an alley lined with a cluster of cute shops that showcase the recent economic rejuvenation of Derry (Mon-Sat 9:30-17:30, closed Sun).

• *After crossing over Butcher Gate, stop at the corner of Society Street (on the left) to view the...*

Apprentice Boys Memorial Hall: Built in 1873, it houses the private lodge and meeting rooms of an all-male Protestant

DERRY

Derry's History

Once an island in the River Foyle, Derry (from *daire,* Irish for "oak grove") was chosen by St. Colmcille (St. Columba in English) circa A.D. 546 for a monastic settlement. He later banished himself to the island of Iona in Scotland out of remorse for sparking a bloody battle over the rights to a holy manuscript that he had secretly copied.

A thousand years later, the English defeated the last Ulster-based Gaelic chieftains in the battle of Kinsale (1601). With victory at hand, the English took advantage of the power vacuum. They began the "plantation" of Ulster with loyal Protestant subjects imported from Scotland and England. The native Irish were displaced to less desirable rocky or boggy lands, sowing the seeds of resentment that fueled the modern-day Troubles.

A dozen wealthy London guilds (grocers, haberdashers, tailors, and others) took on Derry as an investment and changed its name to "Londonderry." They built the last great walled city in Ireland to protect their investment from the surrounding—and hostile—Irish locals. The walls proved their worth in 1688-1689, when the town's Protestant defenders, loyal to King William of Orange, withstood a prolonged siege by the forces of Catholic King James II. "No surrender" is still a passionate rallying cry among Ulster Unionists determined to remain part of the United Kingdom.

The town became a major port of emigration to the New World in the early 1800s. Then, when the Industrial Revolution provided a steam-powered sewing factory, the city developed a thriving shirt-making industry. The factories here employed mostly Catholic women who had honed their skills in rural County Donegal. Although Belfast grew larger and wealthier, Unionists tightened their grip on "Londonderry" and the walls that they regarded with almost holy reverence. In 1921, they insisted that the city be included in Northern Ireland when the province was partitioned from the new Irish Free State (later to become the

organization. The group is dedicated to the memory of the original 13 apprentice boys who saved the day during the 1688 siege. Each year, on the Saturday closest to the August 12 anniversary date, the modern-day Apprentice Boys Society celebrates the end of the siege with a controversial march atop the walls. These walls are considered sacred ground for devout Unionists, who claim that many who died during the famous siege were buried within the battered walls because of lack of space.

Next, you'll pass a large, square pedestal on the right atop Royal Bastion. It once supported a column in honor of Governor George Walker, the commander of the defenders during the famous siege. In 1973, the IRA blew up the column, which had

Republic of Ireland). A bit of gerrymandering (with three lightly populated Unionist districts outvoting two densely populated Nationalist districts) ensured that the Protestant minority maintained control of the city, despite its Catholic majority.

Derry was a key escort base for US convoys headed for Britain during World War II, and 60 surviving German U-boats were instructed to surrender here at the end of the war. After the war, poor Catholics—unable to find housing—took over the abandoned military barracks, with multiple families living in each dwelling. Only homeowners were allowed to vote, and the Unionist minority, which controlled city government, was not eager to build more housing that would tip the vot-

ing balance away from them. Over the years, sectarian pressures gradually built—until they reached the boiling point. The ugly events of Bloody Sunday on January 30, 1972, brought worldwide attention to the Troubles (for more details, see "Bogside Murals Walk").

Today, life has stabilized in Derry, and the population has increased by 25 percent in the last 30 years, to about 84,000. The modern Foyleside Shopping Centre, bankrolled by investors from Boston, opened in 1995. The 1998 Good Friday Peace Accord has provided two-steps-forward, one-step-back progress toward peace, and the British Army withdrew 90 percent of its troops in mid-2007. With a population that is 70 percent Catholic, the city has agreed to alternate Nationalist and Unionist mayors. There is a feeling of cautious optimism as Derry—the epicenter of bombs and bloody conflicts in the 1960s and 1970s—now boasts a history museum that airs all viewpoints.

105 steps to the top (one for each day of the siege). The governor's statue survived the blast and can be seen behind the Apprentice Boys Hall, down Society Street and behind a protective fence.

• *Opposite the empty pedestal is the small Anglican...*

St. Augustine Chapel: Set in a pretty graveyard, it's where some believe the original sixth-century monastery of St. Columba (St. Colmcille in Irish) stood. In Victorian times, this stretch of the walls was a fashionable promenade walk.

As you walk, you'll pass a wall (on the left)—all that's left of a British Army **surveillance tower** that stood here until 2006. Soldiers built it here for its bird's-eye view of the once-turbulent Catholic Bogside district below. The tower's dismantlement—as well as the removal of most of the British Army from Northern Ireland—is another positive sign in cautiously optimistic Derry. The walls of this former army base now contain a parking lot.

Stop at the Double Bastion **fortified platform** that occupies this corner of the city walls. The old cannon is nicknamed "Roaring Meg" for the fury of its firing during the siege.

From here, you can see across the Bogside to the not-so-far-away hills of County Donegal in the Republic. Derry was once an island, but as the River Foyle gradually changed its course, the area you see below the wall began to drain. Over time, and especially after the Great Potato Famine (1845-1849), Catholic peasants from rural Donegal began to move into Derry to find work during the Industrial Revolution. They settled on this least desirable land...on the soggy bog side of the city.

Directly below and to the right are Free Derry Corner and Rossville Street, where the tragic events of Bloody Sunday took place in 1972 (described later, under "Bogside Murals Walk"). Down on the left is the 18th-century Long Tower Catholic church, named after the monk-built round tower that once stood in the area (see page 387).

• *Head to the grand brick building behind you. This is the...*

Verbal Arts Centre: A former Presbyterian school, this center promotes the development of local literary arts in the form of poetry, drama, writing, and storytelling. Drop in for a cup of coffee in their coffeehouse and see what performances might be on during your visit (Mon-Thu 9:00-17:30, Fri 9:00-16:00, closed Sat-Sun, tel. 028/7126-6946, www.verbalartscentre.co.uk).

• *Continuing another 50 yards, go left around the corner to reach...*

Bishop's Gate: From here, look up Bishop Street Within (inside the walls). This was the site of another British Army sur-veillance tower. Placed just inside the town walls, it overlooked the neighborhood until 2006. Now look in the other direction to see Bishop Street Without (outside the walls). You'll spot a modern wall topped by a high mesh fence, running along the left side of Bishop Street Without. This is a **peace wall,** built to ensure the security of the Protestant enclave living behind it in Derry's Fountain neighborhood. When the Troubles reignited more than 40 years ago, 20,000 Protestants lived on this side of the river. Sadly, this small housing develop-ment of 1,000 people is all that remains of that proud community today. The rest have chosen to move across the river to the mostly Protestant Waterside district. The stone tower halfway down the peace wall was part of the old jail that briefly held doomed rebel Wolfe Tone after the 1798 revolt against the British.

• *From Bishop's Gate, those short on time can descend from the walls and walk 15 minutes directly back through the heart of the old city, along Bishop Street Within and Shipquay Street to Guildhall Square. With more time, consider visiting St. Columb's Cathedral, the Long Tower Church, and the murals of the Bogside.*

▲▲Bogside Murals Walk

The Catholic Bogside area was the tinderbox of the modern Troubles in Northern Ireland. A terrible confrontation more than 40 years ago sparked a sectarian inferno, and the ashes have not yet fully cooled. Today, the murals of the Bogside give visitors an accessible glimpse of this community's passionate perception of those events.

Inspired by civil rights marches in America in the mid-1960s, and the Prague Spring uprising and Paris student strikes of 1968, civil rights groups began to protest in Northern Ireland. Initially, their goals were to gain better housing, secure fair voting rights, and end employment discrimination for Catholics in the North. Tensions mounted, and clashes with the predominantly Protestant Royal Ulster Constabulary police force became frequent. Eventually, the British Army was called in to keep the peace. On January 30, 1972, a group protesting internment without trial held an illegal march through the Bogside neighborhood. They were fired upon by members of a British regiment, who claimed that snipers had fired on them first. The tragic clash, now remembered as **Bloody Sunday,** led to the death of 14 civilians and a flood of fresh IRA volunteers.

The events are memorialized in 12 **murals** painted on the ends of residential flats along a 300-yard stretch of Rossville Street and Lecky Road, where the march took place. You can reach them from Waterloo Place via William Street, from the old city walls at Butcher Gate via the long set of stairs extending below Fahan Street on the grassy hillside, or by the stairs leading down from the Long Tower Church. These days, this neighborhood is gritty but quiet and safe.

Two brothers and their childhood friend became known as the Bogside Artists. They grew up in the Bogside and witnessed the tragic events that took place there, which led them to begin painting the murals in 1994. One of the brothers, Tom Kelly, gained a reputation as a "heritage mural" painter, specializing in scenes of life in the old days. In a surprising and hopeful development, Kelly was invited into Derry's Protestant Fountain neighborhood to work with a youth club there on three proud heritage murals that were painted over paramilitary graffiti.

DERRY

Bogside Murals Walk

1 Peace
2 The Hunger Strikers
3 John Hume
4 The Saturday Matinee
5 Civil Rights
6 The Runners
7 Operation Motorman
8 Bloody Sunday
9 Bernadette
10 Petrol Bomber
11 The Death of Innocence
12 Bloody Sunday Commemoration

WILLIAM ST.

WALK BEGINS

THE PEOPLE'S GALLERY

To Waterloo Place

50 Meters
50 Yards

ABBEY ST.

CHAMBERLAIN

BOGSIDE

LISFANNON PK.

MUSEUM OF FREE DERRY

FAHAN ST.

ROSSVILLE ST.

BLOODY SUNDAY MONUMENT

BUTCHER GATE

"H" BLOCK MONUMENT

WESTLAND ST.

FAHAN ST.

LECKY RD.

FAHAN ST.

FREE DERRY CORNER

CITY WALLS

APPRENTICE BOYS MEMORIAL HALL

WESTLAND ST.

WALK ENDS

SOCIETY ST.

PALACE ST.

ROYAL BASTION

ST. AUGUSTINE CHAPEL

LECKY RD.

WALLED CITY

Start out at **The People's Gallery,** the Bogside Artists' studio, to gain an understanding of the inspiration that led to their memorable works. Ask to watch the illuminating 20-minute interview with the artists that aired on Irish TV (free entry, daily 10:00-18:00, corner of Rossville and William Streets, tel. 028/7137-3842, www.bogsideartists.com). Then take one of their walking tours (described earlier under "Tours in Derry") to learn about the murals from the artists themselves. If they're unavailable, take the following walk.

The Bogside murals face different directions (and some are

partially hidden by buildings), so they're not all visible from a single viewpoint. Plan on walking three long blocks along Rossville Street (which becomes Lecky Road) to see them all. Residents are used to visitors and don't mind if you photograph the murals.

The best place to start is from William Street (opposite The People's Gallery), walking south along the right side of Rossville Street toward Free Derry Corner. The murals will all be on your right.

The first mural you'll walk past is the colorful ❶ *Peace,* showing the silhouette of a dove in flight (left side of mural) and an oak leaf (right side of mural), both created from a single ribbon. A peace campaign asked Derry city schoolchildren to write suggestions for positive peacetime images; their words inspired this artwork. The dove is a traditional symbol of peace, and the oak leaf is a traditional symbol of Derry—recognized by both communities. The dove flies from the sad blue of the past toward the warm yellow of the future.

Next, ❷ *The Hunger Strikers* features two long-haired figures wearing blankets. This mural represents the IRA prisoners who refused to wear the uniforms of common criminal inmates—an attempt to force the British to treat them instead as legitimate political prisoners (who were allowed to wear their own clothes). The giant red letter *H* looms behind them, a symbol of the H-block layout of Maze Prison near Belfast.

Smaller and easy to miss (above a ramp with banisters) is ❸ *John Hume.* It's actually a collection of four faces (clockwise from upper left): Nationalist leader John Hume, Martin Luther King Jr., Nelson Mandela, and Mother Teresa. The Brooklyn Bridge in

the middle symbolizes the long-term bridges of understanding that the work of these four Nobel Peace Prize-winning activists created. Born in the Bogside, Hume still maintains a home here.

Now look for ❹ *The Saturday Matinee,* which depicts an outgunned but undaunted local youth behind a screen shield. He holds a stone, ready to throw, while a British armored vehicle approaches (echoing the famous Tiananmen Square photo of the lone Chinese man facing the tank). Why *Saturday Matinee?* It's because the weekend was the best time for

Political Murals

The dramatic and emotional murals you'll encounter in Northern Ireland will likely be one of the enduring travel memories that you'll take home with you. During the 19th century, Protestant neighborhoods hung flags and streamers each July to commemorate the victory of King William III at the Battle of the Boyne in 1690. Modern murals evolved from these colorful annual displays. With the advent of industrial paints, temporary seasonal displays became permanent territorial statements.

Unionist murals were created during the extended political debate that eventually led to the partitioning of the island in 1921 and the creation of Northern Ireland. Murals that expressed opposing views in Nationalist Catholic neighborhoods were outlawed. The ban remained until the eruption of the modern Troubles, when staunchly Nationalist Catholic communities isolated themselves behind barricades, eluding state control and gaining freedom to express their pent-up passions. In Derry, this form of symbolic, cultural, and ideological resistance first appeared in 1969 with the simple "You are now entering Free Derry" message that you'll still see painted on the surviving gable wall at Free Derry Corner.

Found mostly in working-class neighborhoods of Belfast and Derry, today's political murals have become a dynamic form of popular culture. They blur the line between art and propaganda, giving visitors a striking glimpse of each community's history, identity, and values.

locals to "have a go at" the army; people were off work and youths were out of school.

Nearby is ❺ *Civil Rights,* showing a marching Derry crowd carrying an antisectarian banner. It dates from the days when Martin Luther King Jr.'s successful nonviolent marches were being seen worldwide on TV, creating a dramatic, global ripple effect. Civil rights marches, inspired by King and using the same methods to combat a similar set of grievances, gave this long-suffering community a powerful new voice.

In the building behind this mural, you'll find the small but intense **Museum of Free Derry** (£3, Mon-Fri 9:30-16:30 year-round, April-Sept Sat 13:00-16:00, July-Sept Sun 13:00-16:00, 55 Glenfada Park, tel. 028/7136-0880, www.museumoffreederry.org). Photos, shirts with bullet holes, and a 45-minute video documentary convey the painful experience of the people of the Bogside during the worst of the Troubles. Walking tours of the neighborhood depart from here daily at 10:00 and 14:00 (see "Tours in Derry," earlier).

Cross over to the other side of Rossville Street to see the **Bloody Sunday Monument.** This small, fenced-off stone obelisk lists the names of those who died that day, most within 50 yards of this spot. Take a look at the map pedestal by the monument, which shows how a rubble barricade was erected to block the street. A 10-story housing project called Rossville Flats stood here in those days. After peaceful protests failed (with Bloody Sunday being the watershed event), Nationalist youths became more aggressive. British troops were wary of being hit by Molotov cocktails thrown from the rooftop of the housing project.

Cross back again, this time over to the grassy median strip that runs down the middle of Rossville Street. At this end stands a granite letter *H* inscribed with the names of the 10 IRA hunger strikers who died in the H-block of Maze Prison in 1981. The prison was closed after the release of all prisoners (both Unionist and Nationalist) in 2000.

From here, as you look across at the corner of Fahan Street, you get a good view of two murals. In ❻ *The Runners* (right), three rioting youths flee tear gas from canisters used by the British Army to disperse hostile crowds. More than 1,000 canisters were used during the Battle of the Bogside; "nonlethal" rubber bullets killed 17 people over the course of the Troubles. Meanwhile, in ❼ *Operation Motorman* (left), a soldier wields a sledgehammer to break through a house door, depicting the massive push by the British Army to open up the Bogside's barricaded "no-go" areas

that the IRA had controlled for three years (1969-1972).

Walk down to the other end of the median strip where the white wall of **Free Derry Corner** announces "You are now entering Free Derry" (imitating a similarly defiant slogan of the time in once-isolated West Berlin). This was the gabled end of a string of houses that stood here almost 40 years ago. During the Troubles, it became a traditional meeting place for speakers to address crowds.

Cross back to the right side of the street (now Lecky Road) to see ❽ *Bloody Sunday,* in which a small group of men carry a body from that ill-fated march. It's based on a famous photo of Father Edward Daly that was taken that terrible day. Hunched over, he waves a white handkerchief to request safe passage in order to evacuate a mortally wounded protester. The blood-stained civil rights banner was inserted under the soldier's feet for extra emphasis. After Bloody Sunday, the previously marginal IRA suddenly found itself swamped with bitterly determined young recruits.

Near it is a mural called ❾ *Bernadette.* The woman with the megaphone is Bernadette Devlin McAliskey, an outspoken civil rights leader, who at age 21 became the youngest elected member of Parliament. Behind her kneels a female supporter, banging a trash-can lid against the street in a traditional expression of protest in Nationalist neighborhoods. Trash-can lids were also used to warn neighbors of the approach of British patrols.

❿ *Petrol Bomber,* showing a teen wearing an army-surplus gas mask, captures the Battle of the Bogside, when locals barricaded their community, effectively shutting out British rule. Though the main figure's face is obscured by the mask, his body clearly communicates the resolve of an oppressed people. In the background, the long-gone Rossville Flats still looms, with an Irish tricolor flag flying from its top.

In ⓫ *The Death of Innocence,* a young girl stands in front of bomb wreckage. She is Annette McGavigan, a 14-year-old who

was killed on this corner by crossfire in 1971. She was the 100th fatality of the Troubles, which eventually took more than 3,000 lives (and she's also a cousin of one of the artists). The broken gun beside her points to the ground, signifying that it's no longer being wielded. The large butterfly above her shoulder symbolizes the hope for peace. For years, the artists left the butterfly an empty silhouette until they felt confident that the peace process had succeeded. They finally filled in the butterfly with optimistic colors in the summer of 2006.

Finally, around the corner, you'll see a circle of male faces. This mural, painted in 1997 to observe the 25th anniversary of the tragedy, is called ⓬ *Bloody Sunday Commemoration* and shows the 14 victims. They are surrounded by a ring of 14 oak leaves—the symbol of Derry. When relatives of the dead learned that the three Bogside Artists were beginning to paint this mural, many came forward to loan the artists precious photos of their loved ones, so they could be more accurately depicted.

Sectarian violence eventually gave way to negotiations and a tenuous settlement. In 2010, a 12-year investigation sponsored by the British government (the Saville Report) provided further healing. It determined that the Bloody Sunday civil-rights protesters were innocent and called the deaths of 14 protesters, shot by British soldiers, "unjustified." Nationalist leader John Hume (who shared the 1998 Nobel Peace Prize with Unionist leader David Trimble) once borrowed a quote from Gandhi to explain his nonviolent approach to the peace process: "An eye for an eye leaves everyone blind."

Sights in Derry

▲▲**Tower Museum Derry**—Housed in a modern reconstruction of a fortified medieval tower house that belonged to the local O'Doherty clan, this well-organized museum provides an excellent introduction to the city. Combining modern audiovisuals with historical artifacts, the displays tell the story of the city from a skillfully unbiased viewpoint, sorting out some of the tangled historical roots of Northern Ireland's Troubles. The museum is divided into two sections: the Story of Derry (on the ground floor) and the Spanish Armada (on the four floors of the tower).

Start with the Story of Derry, which explains the city's monastic origins 1,500 years ago. It moves through pivotal events, such as the 1688-1689 siege, as well as unexpected blips, like Amelia Earhart's emergency landing. Catch the thought-provoking 15-minute film in the small theater—it offers an evenhanded local perspective on the tragic events of the modern sectarian conflict, giving you a better handle on what makes this unique city tick. Scan the displays of paramilitary paraphernalia in the hallway lined with colored curbstones—red, white, and blue Union Jack colors for Unionists; and green, white, and orange Irish tricolor for Nationalists.

The tower section holds the Spanish Armada exhibits, filled with items taken from the wreck of *La Trinidad Valencera*. It sank in fierce storms nicknamed the "Protestant Winds" off the coast of Donegal in 1588.

Cost and Hours: £4; July-Aug Mon-Sat 10:00-17:00, Sun 12:00-16:00; Sept-June Tue-Sat 10:00-17:00, closed Sun-Mon;

Union Hall Place, tel. 028/7137-2411.

Guild Hall—This Neo-Gothic building, complete with clock tower, is the ceremonial seat of city government. It first opened

in 1890 on reclaimed lands that were once the mudflats of the River Foyle. Destroyed by fire and rebuilt in 1913, it was massively damaged by IRA bombs in 1972. In an ironic twist, Gerry Doherty, one of those convicted of the bombings, was elected as a member of the Derry City Council a dozen years later. In November 1995, US President Bill Clinton spoke to thousands who packed into Guildhall Square. Inside the hall are the Council Chamber, party offices,

and an assembly hall featuring stained-glass windows showing scenes from Derry history. Take an informational pamphlet from the front window and explore, if civic and cultural events are not taking place inside (Mon-Fri 9:00-17:30, closed Sat-Sun, tel. 028/7137-7335).

Hands Across the Divide—Designed by local teacher Maurice Harron after the fall of the Iron Curtain, this powerful metal sculpture of two figures extending their hands to each other was inspired by the growing hope for peace and reconciliation in Northern Ireland (located in a roundabout at the west end of Craigavon Bridge).

Until recently, the Tillie and Henderson's shirt factory (opened in 1857 and burned down in 2003) stood on the banks of the river beside the bridge, looming over the figures. In its heyday, Derry's shirt industry employed more than 15,000 workers (90 percent of whom were women) in sweathouses typical of the human toll of the Industrial Revolution. Karl Marx mentioned this factory in *Das Kapital* as an example of women's transition from domestic to industrial work lives.

St. Columb's Cathedral—Marked by the tall spire inside the walls, this Anglican cathedral was built from 1628 to 1633 in a style called "Planter's Gothic." Its construction was financed by the same London companies that backed the Protestant plantation of Londonderry. It was the first Protestant cathedral built in Britain after the Reformation, and the cathedral played an important part in the defense of the city during the siege. During that time, cannons were mounted on its roof, and the original spire was scavenged for lead to melt into cannon shot. Before you enter, walk over to the "Heroes' Mound" at the end of the churchyard closest to the town wall. Underneath this grassy dome is a mass grave of some of those who died during the 1689 siege.

In the cathedral entryway, you'll find a hollow cannonball that was lobbed into the city, containing the besiegers' surrender terms. Inside, along the nave, hangs a musty collection of battle flags and Union Jacks that once inspired troops during the siege, the Crimean War, and World War II. The American flag hangs among them, from the time when the first GIs to enter the European theater in World War II were based in Northern Ireland. Check out the small chapter-house museum in the back of the church to see the original locks of the gates of Derry and more relics of the siege.

Cost and Hours: £2 donation, Mon-Sat 9:00-17:00, closed Sun, tel. 028/7126-7313, www.stcolumbscathedral.org.

Long Tower Church—Built below the walls on the hillside above the Bogside, this modest-looking church is worth a visit for its stunning high altar. The name comes from a stone monastic round tower that stood here for centuries but was dismantled and used for building materials in the 1600s. The oldest Catholic church in Derry, it was finished in 1786, during a time of enlightened relations between the city's two religious communities. Protestant Bishop Hervey gave a generous-for-the-time £200 donation and had the four Corinthian columns shipped in from Naples to frame the Neo-Renaissance altar (free, usually open Mon-Sat 7:30-20:30, Sun 7:30-19:00—depending on available staff and church functions, tel. 028/7126-2301).

Hidden outside, behind the church and facing the Bogside, is a simple shrine beneath a hawthorn tree. It marks the spot where outlawed Masses were secretly held before this church was built, during the infamous Penal Law period of the early 1700s. Through the Penal Laws, the English attempted to weaken Catholicism's influence by banishing priests and forbidding Catholics from buying land, attending school, voting, and holding office.

Nightlife in Derry

The **Millennium Forum** is a modern venue that reflects the city's revived investment in local culture, concerts, and plays (box office open Mon-Sat 9:30-17:30, inside city walls on Newmarket Street near Ferryquay Gate, tel. 028/7126-4455, www.millenniumforum .co.uk, boxoffice@millenniumforum.co.uk).

The **Nerve Centre** shows a wide variety of art-house films and live concerts (inside city walls at 7-8 Magazine Street, near Butcher Gate, tel. 028/7126-0562, www.nerve-centre.org.uk).

The **Playhouse Theatre** is an intimate venue for plays (inside the walls on Artillery Street, between New Gate and Ferryquay Gate, tel. 028/7126-8027, www.derryplayhouse.co.uk).

If you want to get away from tourists and mingle with Derry residents, try **Peadar O'Donnell's** pub on Waterloo Street for Derry's best nightly traditional-music sessions (53 Waterloo Street, tel. 028/7137-2318).

Sleeping in Derry

$$$ Tower Hotel is the only hotel actually inside Derry's historic walls. It's a real splurge, with 93 modern and immaculate rooms, a classy bistro restaurant, and private basement parking (Sb-£57-99, Db-£64-110, online deals, Butcher Street, tel. 028/7137-1000, fax 028/7137-1234, www.towerhotelderry.com, reservations@thd.ie).

$$ Travelodge has 44 comfortable rooms, a great location, and a handy adjacent parking garage (Db-£50 Sun-Thu, Db-£60-85 Fri-Sat, significant online discounts if you book ahead, continental breakfast-£6, 22-24 Strand Road, tel. 028/7127-1271, fax 028/7127-1277, www.travelodge.ie).

$$ Merchant's House, on a quiet street a 10-minute stroll from Waterloo Place, is a fine Georgian townhouse with a grand, colorful drawing room and nine rooms sporting marble fireplaces and ornate plasterwork (Sb-£40-45, Db-£60-65, closed Jan-Feb, Wi-Fi, 16 Queen Street, tel. 028/7126-9691, www.thesaddlers house.com, saddlershouse@btinternet.com, Joan and Peter Pyne also run the Saddler's House, next). Ask the Pynes about their three self-catering townhouse rentals inside the walls.

Sleep Code

(£1 = about $1.60, country code: 44, area code: 028)
S = Single, **D** = Double/Twin, **T** = Triple, **Q** = Quad, **b** = bathroom, **s** = shower only. Breakfast is included and credit cards are accepted unless otherwise noted.

To help you easily sort through these listings, I've divided the rooms into three categories, based on the price for a standard double room with bath:

$$$ Higher Priced—Most rooms £80 or more.
$$ Moderately Priced—Most rooms between £40-80.
$ Lower Priced—Most rooms £40 or less.

Prices can change without notice; verify the hotel's current rates online or by email. For other updates, see www.ricksteves.com/update.

$$ Saddler's House, run by the owners of Merchant's House, is a charming Victorian townhouse with seven rooms located a couple of blocks closer to the old town walls (Sb-£40-45, Db-£60-65, closed Jan-Feb, Wi-Fi, 36 Great James Street, tel. 028/7126-9691, www.thesaddlershouse.com, saddlershouse@btinternet.com).

$ Paddy's Palace Hostel, located in the city center, rents 40 decent beds for £12 a night with breakfast. Look for the green-and-yellow building, and pause to read the great Mark Twain quote above the front door (4-6 beds/room, family rooms with private bathroom for up to four-£50, Internet access, laundry facilities, kitchen, 1 Woodleigh Terrace, Asylum Road, tel. 028/7130-9051, www.paddyspalace.com, steve@irishexperience.ie, Stephen McPhilemy). Ask about their adjacent self-catering apartments. Stephen also offers walking tours (see "Tours in Derry," earlier).

Eating in Derry

The **Mandarin Palace** dishes up good £10-15 Chinese dinners in a crisp dining room facing the river (open Mon-Sat 16:30-23:00, Sun 13:00-22:00, buffet lunch Mon-Fri 12:00-14:00, £10 early-bird two-course deals 16:30-19:00, Queens Quay at Lower Clarendon Street, tel. 028/7137-3656).

The hip, trendy **Exchange Restaurant and Wine Bar** offers £7-10 lunches and quality £12-16 dinners with flair, in a central location near the river behind Waterloo Place (Mon-Sat 12:00-14:30 & 17:30-22:00, Sun 16:00-21:00, Queen's Quay, tel. 028/7127-3990).

Easygoing **Fitzroy's,** tucked below Ferryquay Gate, serves good £7-10 lunches and £9-15 dinners (Mon-Sat 12:00-22:00, Sun 13:00-20:00, 2-4 Bridge Street, tel. 028/7126-6211).

The **Bay Leaf,** a local hangout close to my recommended hotels, has basic but hearty lunch and dinner options (Tue-Fri 12:00-14:30 & 17:30-21:45, Sat 17:30-21:45, Sun 16:00-21:00, closed Mon, 2 Clarendon Street, tel. 028/7126-0987).

Austins Department Store, right on the Diamond in the center of the old city, is Ireland's oldest department store (1830). It predates Harrods in London by 15 years and Macy's in New York by 25 years. Its basic top-floor café comes with lofty views and £5 lunch specials (Mon-Sat 9:30-17:30, Sun 13:00-17:00, 2-6 The Diamond, tel. 028/7126-1817).

Supermarkets: **Tesco** has everything for picnics and road munchies (Mon-Fri 8:00-21:00, Sat 8:00-20:00, Sun 13:00-18:00, corner of Strand Road and Clarendon Street). **SuperValu** meets the same needs (Mon-Wed 8:30-18:30, Thu-Fri until 20:00, Sat until 18:00, closed Sun, Waterloo Place).

Derry Connections

From Derry, it's an hour's drive to Portrush. If you're using public transportation, consider getting a £16.50 iLink smartcard (£15 top-up for each additional day), good for all-day train and bus use in Northern Ireland (see page 329). Useful updated schedules and prices for both trains and buses in Northern Ireland can be obtained from Translink (tel. 028/9066-6630, www.translink.co.uk). Keep in mind that some bus and train schedules, road signs, and maps may say "Londonderry" or "L'Derry" instead of "Derry."

From Derry by Train to: Portrush (9/day, 1.5 hours, change in Coleraine), **Belfast** (9/day, 2.5 hours), **Dublin** (7/day, 5 hours).

By Bus to: Galway (4/day, 6 hours), **Portrush** (5/day, 1.25 hours), **Belfast** (20/day, 1.75 hours), **Dublin** (5/day, 4.5 hours).

Between Derry and Galway

If you're driving into Northern Ireland from Galway, Westport, or Strokestown and don't have time to explore Donegal, consider these two interesting stops in the interior.

Belleek Pottery Visitors Centre—Just over the Northern Ireland border (30 miles northeast of Sligo) is the cute town of

Belleek, famous for its pottery. The Belleek Parian China factory welcomes visitors with a small gallery and museum (Mon-Fri 9:00-17:30, Sat 10:00-17:30, Sun 12:00-17:30, shorter hours off-season), a 20-minute video, a cheery cafeteria, and fascinating 30-minute tours of its working factory (£4, open April-June and Sept Mon-Fri 9:00-17:30, Sat 10:00-17:30, Sun 14:00-18:00; longer hours July-Aug, shorter hours Oct-March, closed Sun Nov-March; no tours Sat-Sun; call to confirm schedule and reserve a spot, tel. 028/6865-8501, www.belleek.ie). Crazed shoppers who forget to fill out a VAT refund form will find their financial situation looking Belleek.

▲Ulster American Folk Park—North of Omagh (five miles on A-5), this combination museum and folk park commemorates the many Irish who left their homeland during the hard times of the 19th century. Exhibits show life before emigration, on the boat, and in America. You'll gain insight into the origins of the tough Scotch-Irish stock—think Davy Crockett (his folk were from Derry) and Andrew Jackson (Carrickfergus roots)—who later shaped America's westward migration (£6; March-Sept Tue-Sun

10:00-17:00, closed Mon; Oct-Feb Tue-Fri 10:00-16:00, Sat-Sun 11:00-16:00, closed Mon; cafeteria, tel. 028/8224-3292, www .nmni.com).

The adjacent **Centre for Migration Studies** is handy for genealogy searches (Mon-Fri 11:00-16:00, closed Sat-Sun, tel. 028/8225-6315, www.qub.ac.uk/cms).

County Donegal

Donegal is the most remote (and perhaps the most ruggedly beautiful) county in Ireland. It's not on the way to anywhere, and it wears this isolation well. With more native Irish speakers than in any other county, the old ways are better preserved here. The northernmost part of Ireland, Donegal remains connected to the Republic by a slim, five-mile-wide umbilical cord of land on its southern coast. It's also Ireland's second-biggest county, with a wide-open "big sky" interior and a shattered-glass, 200-mile, jagged coastline of islands and inlets.

This is the home turf of St. Colmcille (St. Columba in English; means "dove of the church" in Irish), who was born here in 521. In the hierarchy of revered Irish saints, he's second only to St. Patrick. A proud Gaelic culture held out in Donegal to the bitter end, when its two famous clans (the O'Donnells and the O'Dohertys) were finally defeated by the English in the early 1600s. After their defeat, the region became known as Dun na nGall ("the fort of the foreigner"), which was eventually anglicized to Donegal.

As the English moved in, four friars (certain that Gaelic ways would be lost forever) painstakingly wrote down Irish history from Noah's Ark to their present. This labor of love became known as the Annals of the Four Masters, and without it, much of our knowledge of early Irish history and myth would have been lost. An obelisk stands in their honor in the main square of Donegal town.

The hardy people of County Donegal were famous for their quality tweed weaving, a cottage industry that has given way to modern industrial production in far-off cities. An energetic fishing fleet still churns offshore. The traditional Irish musicians of Donegal play a driving style of music with a distinctively fast and choppy rhythm. Meanwhile, Enya (local Gweedore gal made good) has crafted languid, ethereal tunes that glide from mood to mood. Both *Dancing at Lughnasa* and *The Secret of Roan Inish* were filmed in County Donegal. Today, emigration has taken its toll, and the region relies on a trickle of tourism spilling over from Northern Ireland.

County Donegal Loop Trip

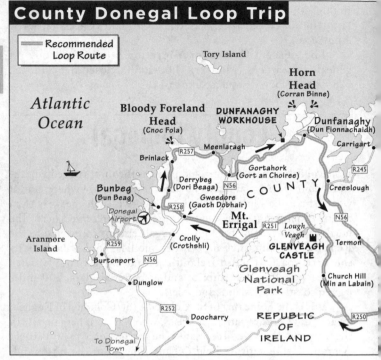

Recommended
Loop Route

Tory Island

Atlantic
Ocean

Horn
Head
(Corran Binne)

Bloody Foreland
Head
(Cnoc Fola)

DUNFANAGHY
WORKHOUSE

Dunfanaghy
(Dun Fionnachaidh)

Carrigart

R257   Meenlaragh

Brinlack

Gortahork
(Gort an Choiree)

R245

Creeslough

Derrybeg
(Dori Beaga)

N56

Bunbeg
(Bun Beag)

Gweedore
(Gaoth Dobhair)

C O U N T Y

Donegal
Airport

R258

Mt.
Errigal

R251

Lough
Veagh

N56

Termon

Aranmore
Island

R259

Crolly
(Crothshli)

GLENVEAGH
CASTLE

Burtonport

N56

Glenveagh
National
Park

Church Hill
(Min an Labain)

Dunglow

R252

Doocharry

REPUBLIC
OF
IRELAND

R250

To Donegal
Town

Self-Guided Driving Tour

Donegal Loop Trip

Here's my choice for a scenic mix of Donegal highlands and coastal views, organized as a daylong circuit (150 miles) for drivers based across the border in Derry. If you're coming north from Galway or Westport, you could incorporate parts of this drive into your itinerary.

Route Summary: Drive west out of Derry (direction: Letterkenny) on Buncrana Road, which becomes A-2 (and then N-13 across the border in the Republic). Follow the signs into Letterkenny, and take R-250 out the other (west) end of town. Veer right (north) onto R-251, and stay on it through Church Hill, all the way across the highlands, until you link up with N-56 approaching Bunbeg. After a couple of miles on N-56, take R-258 from Gweedore; it's another four miles into Bunbeg. Depart Bunbeg going north on R-257, around Bloody Foreland, and rejoin N-56 near Gortahork. Take N-56 through Dunfanaghy (possible Horn Head mini-loop option here) and then south, back into Letterkenny. Retrace your route from Letterkenny via N-13 and A-2 back into Derry.

Helpful Hints: An early start and an Ordnance Survey map are essential. It's cheapest to top off your gas tank in Letterkenny. Consider bringing along a picnic lunch to enjoy from a scenic roadside pullout along the Bloody Foreland R-257 road, or out on the Horn Head loop. Bring your camera and remember—not all who wander are lost.

Once you cross into the Republic of Ireland, all currency is in euros, not pounds. For B&B rates, entry fees, and all other costs in Donegal, keep this exchange rate in mind: €1 = about $1.25.

The sights along this route are well-marked. Don't underestimate the time it takes to get around here, as the narrow roads are full of curves and bumps. Dogs, bred to herd sheep, dart from side lanes to practice their bluffing techniques on the reflection in your hubcaps. If you average 30 miles per hour over the course of the day, you've got a very good suspension system. Folks wanting to linger at more than a couple of sights will need to slow down and consider an overnight stop in Bunbeg or Dunfanaghy.

The Tour Begins

• *Leave Derry on A-2, which becomes N-13 near the town of Bridge End. You'll see a sign for the Grianan Aileach Ring Fort posted on*

N-13, not far from the junction with R-239. Turn up the steep hill at the modern church with the round roof, and follow signs two miles (3 km) to find...

▲ Grianan Aileach Ring Fort

This dramatic, ancient ring fort perches on an 800-foot hill just inside the Republic, a stone's throw from Derry. It's an Iron Age fortification, built about the time of Christ, and was once the royal stronghold of the O'Neill clan, which dominated Ulster for centuries. Its stout, drystone walls (no mortar) are 12 feet thick and 18 feet high, creating an interior sanctuary 80 feet in diameter (entry is free and unattended).

Once inside, you can scramble up the stairs, built into the walls, to enjoy panoramic views in all directions. Murtagh O'Brien, King of Desmond, destroyed the fort in 1101 (the same year he gave the Rock of Cashel to the Church). He had each of his soldiers carry away one stone to make it tougher for the O'Neill clan to find the raw materials to rebuild. What you see today is mostly a reconstruction from the 1870s.

• *Return to N-13 and head to and through Letterkenny, continuing out the other (west) end of town on R-250. Five miles west of Letterkenny on this road, you'll reach the...*

Newmills Corn and Flax Mills

Come here for a glimpse of the 150-year-old Industrial Revolution, shown high-tech Ulster style. Linen, which comes from flax, was

king in this region. The 15-minute film does a nifty job of explaining the process, showing how the common flax plant ends up as cloth. Working conditions in a mill were noisy, unhealthy, and exhausting. Veteran mill workers often braved respiratory disease, deafness, lost fingers, and extreme fire danger. For their trouble, they usually got to keep about 10 percent of what they milled.

The corn mill is still in working condition but requires a skilled miller to operate it. This mill ground oats—"corn" means oats in Ireland. (What we call corn, they call maize.) The huge waterwheel, powered by the River Swilly, made five revolutions

Donegal or Bust

Part of western County Donegal is in the Gaeltacht, where locals speak the Irish (Gaelic) language. In the spring of 2005, a controversial law was passed that erased all English place names from local road signs in Gaeltacht areas. Signs now only have the Irish-language equivalent, an attempt to protect the region from the further (and inevitable) encroachment by the English language.

Here's a cheat sheet to help you decipher the signs as you drive the Donegal loop (parts of which are in the Gaeltacht). There's also a complete translation of all Irish place names in the recommended *Complete Road Atlas of Ireland* by Ordnance Survey (€13), in the Gazetteer section in the back.

Gaelic Name	Pronounced	English Name
Leitir Ceanainn	*LET-ir CAN-ning*	Letterkenny
Min an Labain	*MEEN on law-BAWN*	Churchill
Loch Ghleann	*LOCKH thown*	Lough (Lake)
Bheatha	*eh-VEH-heh*	Veagh
An Earagail	*on AIR-i-gul*	Mt. Errigal
Gaoth Dobhair	*GWEE door*	Gweedore
Crothshli	*CROTH-lee*	Crolly
Bun Beag	*bun bee-OWG*	Bunbeg
Dori Beaga	*DOR-uh bee-OWG-uh*	Derrybeg
Cnoc Fola	*NOK FAW-luh*	Bloody Foreland
Gort an Choirce	*gurt on HER-kuh*	Gortahork
Dun Fionnachaidh	*doon on-AH-keh*	Dunfanaghy
Corran Binne	*COR-on BIN-eh*	Horn Head

per minute and generated eight horsepower.

The entire operation could be handled by one miller, who knew every cog, lever, and flume in the joint. Call ahead to see when working mill demonstrations are scheduled; otherwise, tours last 20 minutes and are available on request.

Cost and Hours: Free, June-Sept daily 10:00-17:00, last entry 15 minutes before closing, closed off-season, Churchill Road, Letterkenny, tel. 074/912-5115.

• *Continue on R-250, staying right at Driminaught as the road becomes R-251. Watch for signs to Glenveagh Castle and National Park, and park in the visitors center lot.*

▲▲Glenveagh Castle and National Park

One of Ireland's six national parks, Glenveagh's jewel is pristine Lough Veagh (Loch Ghleann Bheatha in Gaelic). The lake is three miles long, occupying a U-shaped valley scoured out of the Derryveagh mountains by powerful glaciers during the last ice age.

In the 1850s, this scenic area attracted the wealthy land speculator John George Adair, who bought the valley in 1857. Right away, Adair clashed with local tenants, whom he accused of stealing his sheep. After his managing agent was found murdered, he evicted all 244 of his bitter tenants to great controversy, and set about to create a hunting estate in grand Victorian style.

His pride and joy was his country mansion, Glenveagh Castle, finished in 1873 on the shore of Lough Veagh. After his death, his widow added to the castle and introduced rhododendrons and rare red deer to the estate. After her death, Harvard art professor Kingsley Porter bought the estate and promptly disappeared on the Donegal coast. (He's thought to have drowned.) The last owner was Philadelphia millionaire Henry McIlhenny, who filled the mansion with fine art and furniture while perfecting the lush surrounding gardens. He donated the castle to the Irish nation in 1981.

The Glenveagh National Park **visitors center** explains the region's natural history. Hiking trails in the park are tempting, but beware of tiny midges that seem to want to nest in your nostrils.

The **castle** is only accessible by a 10-minute shuttle-bus ride (€3 round-trip, 4/hour, depart from visitors center, last shuttle at 17:00). Take the 45-minute castle tour, letting your Jane Austen and Agatha Christie fantasies go wild. Antlers abound on walls, in chandeliers, and in paintings by Victorian hunting artists. A table crafted from rare bog oak (from ancient trees hundreds of years old, found buried in the muck) stands at attention in one room, while Venetian glass chandeliers illuminate a bathroom. A round pink bedroom at the top of a tower is decorated in Oriental style, with inlaid mother-of-pearl furnishings. The library, which displays paintings by George Russell, has the castle's best lake views.

Afterward, stroll through the gardens and enjoy the lovely setting. A lakeside swimming pool had boilers underneath it to keep it heated. It's no wonder that Greta Garbo was an occasional guest, coming to visit whenever she "vanted" to be alone.

Cost and Hours: It's free to enter the national park. The castle can be visited with a guided tour (€5, mid-March-early Nov daily 9:00-18:00, last entry one hour before closing, early Nov-mid-March Sat-Sun only). Tel. 074/913-7090, www.glenveagh nationalpark.ie. Without a car, you can reach Glenveagh Castle

DONEGAL

and National Park by bus tour from Derry (see "Tours in Derry").
• *Leave the national park and follow R-251 west, watching for the Mount Errigal trailhead. It's southeast of the mountain, and starts at the small parking lot beside R-251 on the mountain's lower slope (easy to spot, with a low surrounding stone wall in the middle of open bog land).*

Mount Errigal (An Earagail)

The mountain (2,400 feet) dominates the horizon for miles around. Rising from the relatively flat interior bog land, it looks taller from

a distance than it is. Beautifully cone-shaped (but not a volcano), it offers a hearty nontechnical climb with panoramic views (4 hours round-trip, covering 5 miles). Hikers should get a weather report before setting out (frequent mists squat on the summit).

• *Continue on R-251 as it merges into N-56 headed west; at Gweedore, stay west on R-258. After four miles (6 km), you'll reach R-257 and...*

Bunbeg (Bun Beag)

This modest town offers a fine sandy beach. But take the trouble to seek out the quaint, hidden fishing harbor at the rocky south end of town. The harbor-access road is directly in front of you as you approach the town from the east on R-258 and pull up to the stop sign where R-258 meets R-257. At the dead end of the half-mile access road is a cute, watercolor-worthy harbor, with an old stone warehouse and a great guesthouse.

There's an ATM at the AIB bank (on the left, going north on R-257, 100 yards past Seaview Hotel). The post office is in the back of the tiny Macaire Clocair market (Mon-Fri 9:00-17:30, Sat 9:00-13:00, closed Sun).

Turasmara operates a limited ferry service from Bunbeg harbor. It's a 1.5-hour voyage to the ultra-remote and rugged Tory Island (€25 round-trip, runs daily June-Sept—weather permitting, departs at 9:00 and returns at 18:00, call to confirm schedule, tel. 074/953-1340). Active travelers will enjoy the invigorating and scenic Rib Boat Excursions, which depart from Bunbeg House on the shore of cozy Bunbeg harbor and weave among the nearby islands (€20, 45 minutes, daily mid-June-Aug, 10 people per boat, call for schedule, tel. 074/953-1305, www.bunbeghouse.com).

Sleeping in Bunbeg: **$$ Bunbeg House,** overlooking the snug and charming Bunbeg fishing harbor, has 12 simple, spacious rooms and a tiny, inviting pub downstairs. Andy and Jean Carr know about fun rib-boat sightseeing excursions, too (Sb-€45-50, Db-€75-80, Tb-€95-110, parking, tel. 074/953-1305, fax 074/953-1420, www.bunbeghouse.com, bunbeghouse@eircom.net).

$$ Teach Anraoi B&B is a comfortable home with five clean, economical, unpretentious rooms (Sb-€30, Db-€55, cash only, non-smoking; on R-257 in the middle of Bunbeg, 100 yards past the bank, down a steep driveway; tel. 074/953-1092, Roisin Gallagher).

Eating in Bunbeg: Try the **Seaview Hotel Bistro,** which specializes in fish dishes (€20-25 meals, June-Sept daily 18:30-21:00, Oct-May Fri-Sat only 18:30-21:00, on R-257, tel. 074/953-1159). You'll find a fine pub dinner, plus late-evening traditional-music sessions nightly, at **Leo's Tavern,** run by Enya's dad. To get there from Bunbeg, hop on N-56 going south through the nearby hamlet of Crolly. Take a right onto R-259 (sign says *Aerphort*), and go a half-mile, following signs to Leo's, which will bring you to a jack-knife—turn right and the pub is 100 yards up on the left (Mon-Sat 13:00-20:30, Sun 13:00-15:30, tel. 074/954-8143). Groceries are sold at the **Spar Market** in nearby Derrybeg (Mon-Sat 9:00-19:30, Sun 9:00-13:30).

• *The five miles of road heading north—as Bunbeg blends into Derrybeg (Dori Beage) and a bit beyond—are some of the most densely populated sections of this loop tour. Modern holiday cottages pepper the landscape in what the Irish have come to call "Bungalow Bliss" (or "Bungalow Blight" to nature-lovers). Next you'll come to the...*

Bloody Foreland (Cnoc Fola)

Named for the shade of red that backlit heather turns at sunset, this scenic headland is laced with rock walls and forgotten cottage ruins. Pull off at one of the lofty roadside viewpoints and savor a picnic lunch and rugged coastal views.

• *Continue on R-257, meeting N-56 near Gortahork. Stay on N-56 to the Dunfanaghy Workhouse, a half-mile south of Dunfanaghy town.*

Dunfanaghy Workhouse

Opened in 1845, this structure was part of an extensive workhouse compound (separating families by gender and age)—a dreaded last resort for the utterly destitute of coastal Donegal. There were once many identical compounds built across Ireland, a rigid Victorian solution to the spiraling riddle of Ireland's rapidly multiplying poor. But the system was unable to cope with the starving, homeless multitudes who were victims of the famine.

The harsh workhouse experience is told through the true-life narrative of Wee Hannah Herrity, a wandering orphan and former resident of this workhouse. She survived the famine by taking refuge here, dying at age 90 in 1926. You'll visit three upstairs rooms where hokey papier-mâché figures relate the powerful episodes in her life.

Cost and Hours: €4.50; April-Sept Mon-Sat 10:00-16:00, closed Sun; Oct-March Sat-Sun only, call to confirm winter hours, good bookstore and coffee shop, tel. 074/913-6540, www.dunfanaghyworkhouse.ie.

• *Now continue into the town of...*

Dunfanaghy (Dun Fionnachaidh)

This planned town, founded by the English in the early 1600s for local markets and fairs, has a prim and proper appearance. In Dunfanaghy (dun-FAN-ah-hee), you can grab a pub lunch or some picnic fixings from the town market. Enjoy them from a scenic viewpoint on the nearby Horn Head loop drive (described later).

The post office is at the southern end of town (Mon-Fri 9:00-17:30, Sat 9:00-13:00, closed Sun). Basic groceries are sold in **Ramsay's Store** (daily 7:30-21:30) on the pier opposite the Muck & Muffin.

Sleeping in Dunfanaghy: **$$$ The Mill Restaurant and Accommodation** is a diamond in the Donegal rough. Susan Alcorn nurtures six wonderful rooms with classy decor, while her husband Derek is the chef in their fine restaurant downstairs (Sb-€75, Db-€100-105, Tb-€135, non-smoking, parking, tel. & fax 074/913-6985, www.themillrestaurant.com, info@themillrestaurant.com).

$$ The Whins B&B has tastefully exotic furnishings in its four prim rooms (Sb-€35-45, Db-€70-75, Tb-€90-105, non-smoking, Wi-Fi, parking, 10-minute walk north of town, tel. 074/913-6481, www.thewhins.com, annemarie@thewhins.com, Anne-Marie Moore).

Eating in Dunfanaghy: **The Mill Restaurant and Accommodation** is gourmet all the way, specializing in memorable lamb or lobster dinners worth booking days ahead of time (€45, Tue-Sun 19:00-21:00, closed Mon, tel. 074/913-6985). **Muck & Muffin** is a simple sandwich café, great for quick, cheap lunches. It's above the pottery shop in the stone warehouse on the town square (Mon-Sat 9:30-17:00, mid-June-mid-Sept until 21:00; Sun 11:00-17:00; tel. 074/913-6780).

• *From Dunfanaghy, you can head back to Derry via Letterkenny, but first consider a detour to Horn Head.*

Horn Head Loop (Corran Binne)

If you have extra time, take an hour to embark on a lost-world plateau drive. This heaving headland with few trees has gripping coastal views. Consult your map and get off N-56, following the Horn Head signs all the way around the eastern lobe of the peninsula. There are fewer than eight miles of narrow, single-lane road out here, with very little traffic. But be alert and willing to pull over at wide spots to cooperate with other cars.

This stone-studded peninsula was once an island. Then, shortly after the last ice age ended, ocean currents deposited a sandy spit in the calm water behind the island. A hundred years ago, locals harvested its stabilizing dune grass, using it for roof thatching and sending it abroad to Flanders for soldiers to create beds for horses during World War I. However, with the grass gone, the sandy spit was free to migrate again. It promptly silted up the harbor, created a true peninsula, and ruined Dunfanaghy as a port town.

A short spur road leads to the summit of the headland, where you can park your car and walk another 50 yards up to the abandoned lookout shelter. The views from here are dramatic, looking west toward Tory Island and south to Mount Errigal. Some may choose to hike an additional 30 minutes across the heather, to the ruins of the distant signal tower (not a castle), clearly visible near the cliffs. The trails are not maintained, but it's easy bushwhacking, offering rewarding cliff views. Navigate back to your car, using the lookout shelter on the summit as a landmark.

IRELAND: PAST AND PRESENT

Ireland is rich with history, art, and language. And the country continues to transform and grow today, learning from its experience with the Celtic Tiger economy (now slumbering), searching for peace, and reexamining some of its long-held social customs.

Irish History

Hunters, Farmers, and Mysterious Mounds (Prehistory)

Ireland became an island when rising seas covered the last land bridge (7000 B.C.), a separation from Britain that the Irish would fight to maintain for the next 9,000 years. By 6000 B.C., Stone Age hunter-fishers had settled on the east coast, followed by Neolithic farmers (from the island of Britain). These early inhabitants left behind impressive but mysterious funeral mounds (passage graves) and large Stonehenge-type stone circles.

The Celts: Language and Legends (500 B.C.-A.D. 450)

Perhaps more an invasion of ideas than of armies, the Celtic culture from Central Europe (particularly that of the most influential tribe, called the **Gaels**) settled in Ireland, where it would dominate for a thousand years. A warrior people with more than a hundred petty kings, they feuded constantly with rival clans and gathered in ring forts for protection. There were more than 300 *tuatha* (clans) in Ireland, each with its own *rí* (king), who would've happily chopped the legs off anyone who called him "petty." The island was nominally ruled by a single *Ard Rí* (high king) at the **Hill of Tara** (north of Dublin), though there was no centralized nation.

Druid priests conducted pagan, solar-calendar rituals among

the megalithic stones erected by earlier inhabitants. The Celtic people peppered the countryside with thousands of Iron Age monuments. While most of what you'll see will be little more than rock piles that take a vigorous imagination to reconstruct (ring forts, wedge tombs, standing stones, and so on), just standing next to a megalith that predates the pharaohs is stirring.

The Celtic world lives on today in the Gaelic language and in legends of Celtic warriors such as **Finn McCool**—the "Gaelic King Arthur"—who led a merry band of heroes in battle and in play. Tourists marvel at large ritual stones decorated with ogham (rhymes with "poem") script, the peculiar Celtic-Latin alphabet that used lines as letters. The **Tara Brooch** and elaborately inscribed, jewel-encrusted daggers in Dublin's National Museum attest to the sophistication of this warrior society.

In 55 B.C., the Romans conquered the Celts in England, but Ireland and Scotland remained independent, their history forever skewed in a different direction—Gaelic, not Latin. The Romans called Ireland **Hibernia,** or Land of Winter; it was apparently too cold and bleak to merit an attempt at colonization. The biggest non-event in Irish history is that the Romans never invaded. While the mix of Celtic and Roman is part of what makes the French French and the English English, the Irish are purely Celtic. Hurling, the wild Irish national pastime, goes back more than 2,000 years to Celtic days, when it was played almost as a substitute for warfare. Perhaps best described as something like airborne hockey with no injury time-outs, hurling is as central to the Irish culture as cricket is to the English, or *boules* to the French.

Christianity: The Age of Saints and Scholars (A.D. 450-800)

When Ancient Rome fell and took the Continent with it, Gaelic Ireland remained. There was no Dark Age here, and the island was a beacon of culture for the rest of Europe. Ireland (population c. 750,000) was still a land of many feuding kings, but the culture was stable.

Christianity and Latin culture arrived first as a trickle from trading contacts with Christian Gaul (France), then more emphatically in A.D. 432 with **St. Patrick,** who persuasively converted the sun-and-nature-worshipping Celts. (Perhaps St. Patrick had an easy time converting the locals because they had so little sun to worship.) Patrick (c. 389-461), a Latin-speaking Christian from Roman Britain, was kidnapped as a teenager and carried off into slavery for six years in

What's a Celt?

The Irish are a Celtic people. The Celts, who came from Central Europe, began migrating west in about 1500 B.C. Over time, many settled in the British Isles and western France. When the Angles and Saxons came later, grabbing the best land in the British Isles (which became Angle-land...or England), the Celts survived in Brittany, Cornwall, Wales, Scotland, and Ireland. Today, this "Celtic Crescent" still nearly encircles England. The word "Celtic" (pronounced with a hard *C*) comes from the Greek "Keltoi," meaning barbarian.

From about 700 B.C. on, various Celtic tribes mixed, mingled, and fought in Ireland. The last and most powerful of the Celtic tribes to enter the fray were the Gaels, who probably entered Ireland from Scotland. The Irish and Scottish language, Gaelic, is named for them.

Celtic society revolved around warrior kings, who gathered groups of families into regional kingdoms. These small kingdoms combined to make the five large provincial kingdoms of ancient Ireland (whose names survive on maps today): Leinster, Munster, Connacht, Ulster, and the Middle Kingdom (now County Meath).

For defensive purposes, these early Irish lived in small thatched huts built on manmade islands or on high ground surrounded by ditches and a stone or earthen wall. A strictly observed hierarchy governed Celtic societies: the king on top, followed by poets, druids (priests), doctors, legal men, skilled craftsmen, freemen, and slaves. Rarely did a high king rule the entire island. Loyalty to one's clan came first, and alliances between clans were often temporary, lasting only until a more advantageous alliance could be struck with a rival clan. This fluid system of alliances ebbing and flowing across the Celtic-warrior cultural landscape meant that the Celts would never unite as a single nation. It also meant that an invading army could not destroy one main capital or kill one king to bring the entire island to its knees. Celtic culture was a multi-headed monster...tough to slay.

Unlike the Celtic tribes living in Western Europe and England, the Celts in Ireland were never conquered by the Romans. This gives Ireland a cultural continuity and unique-ness rare in Europe. Their culture—which evolved apart from Europe—remained strong and independent for centuries. Then, in the 12th century, English dominance led to suppression of the Gaelic language and Celtic traditions. But with Irish independence—won only in the 20th century—Irish ways are no longer threatened. The most traditional areas (generally along the west coast, such as the Dingle Peninsula) are protected as a Gaeltacht. The Gaeltacht (literally, places where the Gaelic language is spoken) is a kind of national park for the traditional culture. If much of Ireland's charm can be credited to its Celtic roots, that charm is most vivid in the Gaeltacht.

Stone Circles: The Riddle of the Rocks

Ireland is home to more than 200 evocative stone circles. These jaggedly sparse boulder rings are rudimentary in comparison to Britain's more famous Stonehenge. But their misty, mossy settings provide curious travelers with an intimate and accessible glimpse of the mysterious people who lived in Ireland before the arrival of the Celts.

Bronze Age Ireland (2000-600 B.C.) was populated by farming folk who had mastered the craft of smelting heated tin and copper together to produce bronze, which was used to produce more durable tools and weapons. Late in the Bronze Age, many of these primitive clannish communities also chose to put considerable time and effort into gathering huge rocks and arranging them into ceremonial circles for use in rituals with long-forgotten meanings. Many scholars believe that these circles may have been used as solar observatories, to calculate solstices and equinoxes, and to plan life-sustaining seasonal crop-planting cycles. Archaeologists have discovered a few ancient remains in the center of some circles, but their primary use seems to have been ceremonial rather than funerary. And without any written records, we can only make educated guesses as to their exact purpose.

In the Middle Ages, superstitious people believed that the stones had been arranged by an earlier race of giants. Later, Puritans thought that at least one circle was made up of petrified partiers who had dared to dance on the Sabbath. A nearby

Ireland. He escaped back to Britain, then traveled to Gaul to study for a life in the clergy. Inspired by a dream, he eventually returned to Ireland, determined to convert the pagan, often hostile, Celtic

inhabitants. Legends say he drove Ireland's snakes (symbolic of pagan beliefs) into the sea and explained the Trinity with a shamrock—three leaves on one stem.

Later monks (such as **St. Columba,** 521-597) continued Christianizing the island, and foreign monks flocked to isolated Ireland. They withdrew to scattered, isolated monasteries, living in Celtic-style beehive huts, translating and illustrating (illuminating) manuscripts. Perhaps the greatest works of art of Dark Age Europe are these manuscripts, particularly the standing stone was supposed to be the frozen figure of the piper who had been playing the dance tunes.

Irish stone circles are concentrated in two main regional clusters consisting of more than a hundred circles each: central Ulster, in the North (radiocarbon-dated 1500-700 B.C.); and Counties Cork and Kerry, in the south (radiocarbon-dated 1000-700 B.C.). The remaining dozen circles are scattered across central Ireland. Some circles have only recently been rediscovered after having been buried by rapidly accumulating bog growth over the centuries.

Dedicated travelers seeking stone circles will find them marked in the Ordnance Survey atlas and signposted along rural Irish roads. Ask a local farmer for directions—and savor the experience (wear shoes impervious to grass dew and sheep doo).

Here are my five favorite Irish stone circles, all within a druid's dance of other destinations mentioned in this book:

Kenmare's is in County Kerry, on the western fringe of Kenmare town. It's the most easily accessible of the circles listed here.

Drombeg is in County Cork, 35 miles southwest of Kinsale, up a narrow winding lane just south of the R-597 coastal road.

Glebe is in County Mayo, two miles east of Cong, and 100 yards south of the R-345 road to Neale (across a minefield of sheep droppings).

Beltany is in County Donegal, 10 miles southeast of Letterkenny, straight south of Raphoe.

Beaghmore is in County Tyrone, 20 miles east of Omagh, north off A-505 (Cookstown Road).

ninth-century **Book of Kells,** which you'll see at Dublin's Trinity College. Irish monks—heads shaved cross-wise from ear to ear, like the former Druids—were known throughout Europe as ascetic scholars.

St. Columbanus (c. 600; different from St. Columba) was one of several traveling missionary monks who helped to bring Christianity back to Western Europe, which had reverted to paganism and barbarism after the fall of the Roman Empire. The monks established monastic centers of learning that produced great Christian teachers and community builders. One of the monks, **St. Brendan,** may have sailed to America.

By 800, **Charlemagne** was importing Irish monks to help run his Frankish kingdom. Meanwhile, Ireland remained a relatively cohesive society based on monastic settlements rather than cities. Impressive round towers from those settlements still dot the Irish landscape—silent reminders of this exalted age.

Typical Castle Architecture

Castles were fortified residences for medieval nobles. Castles come in all shapes and sizes, but knowing a few general terms will help you understand them.

The Keep (or Donjon): A high, strong stone tower in the center of the castle complex that was the lord's home and refuge of last resort.

Great Hall: The largest room in the castle, serving as throne room, conference center, and dining hall.

The Yard (or Bailey or Ward): An open courtyard inside the castle walls.

Loopholes: Narrow slits in the walls (also called embrasures, arrow slits, or arrow loops) through which soldiers could

Viking Invasion and Defeat (800-1100)

In 795, Viking pirates from Norway invaded, first testing isolated island monasteries, then boldly sailing up Irish rivers into the interior. The many raids immediately wreaked havoc on the monasteries, and continued to shake Irish civilization for two chaotic centuries. The Vikings raped, pillaged, and burned Christian churches, making off with prized monastic booty such as gold chalices, silver candlestick holders, and the jeweled book covers of sacred illuminated manuscripts. Monks stood guard from their round towers to spy approaching marauders, ring the warning bells, and protect the citizens. In 841, a conquering Viking band decided to winter in Ireland, eventually building the island's first permanent walled cities, Dublin and Waterford. Viking raiders slowly evolved into Viking traders. They were the first to introduce urban life and commerce to Ireland.

Finally, **High King Brian Ború** led a Gaelic revival at the Battle of Clontarf (1014), near Dublin. Though he defeated a mershoot arrows at the enemy.

Towers: Tall structures serving as lookouts, chapels, living quarters, or the dungeon. Towers could be square or round, with either crenellated tops or conical roofs.

Turret: A small lookout tower projecting up from the top of the wall.

Moat: A ditch encircling the wall, often filled with water.

Wall Walk (or Allure): A pathway atop the wall where guards could patrol and where soldiers stood to fire at the enemy.

Parapet: Outer railing of the wall walk.

Crenellation: A gap-toothed pattern of stones atop the parapet.

Hoardings (or Gallery or Brattice): Wooden huts built onto the upper parts of the stone walls. They served as watch towers, living quarters, and fighting platforms.

Machicolation: A stone ledge jutting out from the wall, fitted with holes in the bottom. If the enemy was scaling the walls, soldiers could drop rocks or boiling oil down through the holes and onto the enemy below.

Barbican: A fortified gatehouse, sometimes a stand-alone building located outside the main walls.

Drawbridge: A bridge that could be raised or lowered, using counterweights or a chain-and-winch.

Portcullis: A heavy iron grille that could be lowered across the entrance.

Postern Gate: A small, unfortified side or rear entrance used during peacetime. In wartime, it could become a "sally-port" used to launch surprise attacks, or as an escape route.

cenary Viking army, which had allied with rebellious clans,Ború and most of his sons died in the battle, and his unified kingdom quickly fell apart. Over the centuries, Viking settlers married Gaelic gals and slowly blended in.

Anglo-Norman Arrival (1100-1500)

The Normans were Ireland's next aggressive guests. In 1169, a small army of well-armed and fearless soldiers of fortune invaded Ireland under the pretense of helping a deposed Irish king regain his lands. With the blessing of the only English pope in history (Adrian IV and his papal bull), a Welsh conquistador named **Strongbow** (c. 1130-1176) took Dublin and Waterford, married the local king's daughter, then succeeded his father-in-law as king of Leinster. This was the spearhead of a century-long invasion by the so-called Anglo-Normans—the French-speaking rulers of England, descended from William the Conqueror and his troops, who had invaded and conquered England a hundred years earlier at the Battle of Hastings (1066).

King Henry II of England soon followed (1171) to remind Strongbow who was boss, proclaiming the entire island under English (Anglo-Norman) rule. By 1250, the Anglo-Normans occupied two-thirds of the island, controlling the best land while clustered in walled cities surrounded by hostile Gaels. These invaders, who were big-time administrators, ushered in a new age in which society (government, cities, and religious organizations) was organized on a grander scale. They imposed feudalism and scoffed at the old Gaelic clan system that they intended to replace. Riding on the coattails of the Normans, monastic orders (Franciscans, Augustinians, Benedictines, and Cistercians) came over from the Continent and eclipsed Ireland's individual monastic settlements, once the foundation of Irish society, back in the Age of Saints and Scholars.

But English rule was weak and distant. Preoccupied with the Hundred Years' War with France and its own internal Wars of the Roses, England "ruled" through deputized locals such as the earls of Kildare. Many landowners actually resided in England, a pattern of absentee-landlordism that would persist for centuries. England's laws were fully enforced only in a 50-mile foothold around Dublin (**the Pale**—from the Norman-French word for a defensive ditch). A couple of centuries after invading, the Anglo-Normans saw their area of control shrink to only the Pale (perhaps 20 percent of the island)—with the rest of the island "beyond the Pale."

Even as their power eroded, the English kings considered Ireland theirs. To keep their small islands of English culture undiluted by Irish heathen ways, they passed the **Statutes of Kilkenny** (1366). These laws prohibited the settlers from going native and being seduced by Gaelic ways...or people. Intermarriage between Irish locals and English settlers, adoption of Irish dress, and the speaking of the Gaelic language were all outlawed. In practice, the statutes were rarely enforced.

The End of Gaelic Rule (1500s)

As European powers raced west to establish profitable colonies in North and South America, Ireland's location on the western edge of Europe became more strategic. England's naval power grew to threaten Spain's monopoly on New World riches. Meanwhile, Spain viewed Ireland as England's vulnerable back door—the best place to attack. (Think of how the USSR used Cuba to threaten the US in the early 1960s.) Martin Luther's **Reformation** split the

Christian churches into Catholic and Protestant, making Catholic Ireland an even hotter potato for newly Protestant England to handle. Catholic Spain and, later, France would use their shared Catholicism with Ireland as divine justification for alliances against heretic England.

In 1534, angered by **Henry VIII** and his break with Catholicism (and taking advantage of England's Reformation chaos), the **Earls of Kildare** (father, then son) led a rebellion. Henry crushed the revolt, executed the earls, and confiscated their land. Henry's daughter, **Queen Elizabeth I,** gave the land to colonists ("planters"), mainly English Protestants. The next four centuries would see a series of rebellions by Catholic, Gaelic-speaking Irish farmers fighting to free themselves from rule by Protestant, English-speaking landowners.

Hugh O'Neill (1540-1616), a Gaelic chieftain educated in Queen Elizabeth's court, was angered by planters and English abuses. He soon led a Gaelic revolt, in 1595. The rebels were supported by the Spanish, who were fellow Catholics and England's archrival on the high seas. At the Battle of Yellow Ford (1598), guerrilla tactics brought about an initial Irish victory.

But the **Battle of Kinsale** (1601) ended the revolt. The exhausted Irish, who had marched the length of Ireland in winter, arrived to help Spanish troops, who were pinned down inside the town. Though the Irish were skilled at guerrilla warfare on their own turf, they were no match for the English on open and unfamiliar ground, and were quickly crushed before they could join the Spanish. The Spanish soon surrendered, and O'Neill knelt before the conquering general, ceding half a million acres to England. Then he and other proud, Gaelic, Ulster-based nobles unexpectedly abandoned their remaining land and sailed to the Continent (the Flight of the Earls, 1607). They searched for further support on the Continent, but died before they could enlist additional armies to bring back to Ireland. Their flight signaled the end of Gaelic Irish rule.

English Colonization and Irish Rebellions (1600s)

King James I took advantage of the Gaelic power vacuum and sent 25,000 Protestant English and Scottish planters into the confiscated land (1610-1641), making Ulster (in the northeast) the most English area of the island. The Irish responded with two major rebellions.

In 1642, while England was embroiled in a civil war between a divine-right monarch (who answered only to God) and a power-hungry Parliament, Irish rebels capitalized on the instability. Tensions were already high, as tenant farmers had recently

PAST AND PRESENT

Typical Church Architecture

History comes to life when you visit a centuries-old church. Even if you wouldn't know your apse from a hole in the ground, learning a few simple terms will enrich your experience. Note that not every church has every feature, and a "cathedral" isn't a type of church architecture, but rather a designation for a church that's a governing center for a local bishop.

Aisles: The long, generally low-ceilinged arcades that flank the nave.

Altar: The raised area with a ceremonial table (often adorned with candles or a crucifix), where the priest prepares and serves the bread and wine for Communion.

Apse: The space beyond the altar, often bordered with small chapels.

Choir: A cozy area, often screened off, located within the church nave and near the high altar where services are sung in a more intimate setting.

Cloister: A square-shaped series of hallways surrounding an open-air courtyard, traditionally where monks and nuns got fresh air.

Facade: The outer wall of the church's main (west) entrance, viewable from outside and usually highly decorated.

Groin Vault: An arched ceiling formed where two equal barrel vaults meet at right angles. Less common usage: term for a medieval jock strap.

Narthex: The area (portico or foyer) between the main entry and the nave.

Nave: The long, central section of the church (running west to east, from the entrance to the altar) where the congregation stood through the service.

Transept: The north-south part of the church, which crosses (perpendicularly) the east-west nave. In a traditional Latin cross-shaped floor plan, the transept forms the "arms" of the cross.

West Portal: The main entry to the church (on the west end, opposite the main altar).

taken up pitchforks against their English landlords, slaughtering 4,000 in the **Massacre of the Planters** (1641). The landless, Irish-speaking rebels hadn't attacked the middle tier of Irish society—the English-speaking, but still Irish, landed gentry (descendants of the first Anglo-Norman invaders, they were called, rather confusingly, "Old English"). Like the peasant rebels, the "Old English" were Catholic, and they wanted more autonomy for Ireland. Both groups feared the rise of Protestant power in England, and together they formed a pro-Royalist confederation in opposition to the new Protestant Parliament of **Oliver Cromwell.** (This meant, oddly enough, that the Irish now found themselves on the side of the English monarchy.)

Once Cromwell had pulled off his *coup d'état* and executed King Charles I, he invaded Ireland with 20,000 men (1649-1650). Out to obliterate the last Royalist forces and to exact retaliation for the Massacre of the Planters, and armed with Puritanical, anti-Catholic religious zeal, he conquered the country—brutally. Thousands were slaughtered, priests were tortured, villages were pillaged, and rebels were sold into slavery. Most Catholic Irish landowners were forced into exile, having been given the choice of "to hell or to Connaught"—that is, they were forced on threat of death to give up their lands and move to the rocky countryside west of the River Shannon. Cromwell confiscated 11 million acres of Catholic land to give to English Protestants. (In 1641, Catholics owned 59 percent of Ireland—by 1714 they owned 7 percent.) Cromwell's scorched-earth invasion was so harsh (the "curse of Cromwell"), it still raises hackles in Ireland.

In 1688-1689, rebels again took advantage of England's political chaos. They rallied around Catholic **King James II,** who had been deposed by the English Parliament in the "Glorious Revolution" of 1688 and then had fled to France. He wound up in Ireland, where he formed an army to retake the crown. In the **Siege of Londonderry,** James' Catholic army surrounded the city, the last loyal Protestant power base. But some local apprentice boys locked them out, and after months of negotiations and a 105-day siege, James went away empty-handed.

The showdown came at the massive **Battle of the Boyne** (1690), north of Dublin. Catholic James II and his 25,000 men were defeated by the 36,000 troops of Protestant **King William III** of Orange. From this point on, the color orange became a symbol in Ireland for pro-English, pro-Protestant forces.

As the 17th century came to a close, Protestant England had successfully put down every rebellion. To counter Irish feistiness, the ruling English out-and-out attacked the indigenous Gaelic culture through a body of legislation called the **Penal Laws.** Catholics couldn't vote, hold office, buy land, join the army, play the harp, or even own a horse worth more than £5. Catholic education was banned and priests were outlawed. But the Penal Laws were difficult to enforce, and many Catholics were taught at hidden outdoor "hedge schools," and worshipped in private or at secluded "Mass rocks" in the countryside.

Protestant Rule (1700s)

During the 18th century, urban Ireland thrived economically, and even culturally, under the English. Dublin in the 1700s (pop. 50,000) was Britain's second city, one of Europe's wealthiest and most sophisticated. It's still decorated in Georgian (Neoclassical) style, named for the English kings of the time (consecutive kings George I, II, III, and IV, who ruled for more than a century).

But beyond the Pale surrounding Dublin, rebellion continued to brew. Over time, greed on the top and dissent on the bottom led to more repressive colonial policies. The Enlightenment provided ideas of freedom, and the Revolutionary Age emboldened the Irish masses. Irish nationalists were inspired by budding democratic revolutions in America (1776) and France (1789). The Irish say, "The Tree of Liberty sprouted in America, blossomed in France, and dropped seeds in Ireland." Increasingly, the issue of Irish independence was less a religious question than a political one, as poor, disenfranchised colonists demanded a political voice.

In Dublin, **Jonathan Swift** (1667-1745), the dean of St. Patrick's Cathedral, published his satirical *Gulliver's Travels* with veiled references to English colonialism. He anonymously wrote pamphlets advising, "Burn all that's British, except its coal."

The **Irish Parliament** was an exclusive club, and only Protestant, male landowners could be elected to a seat (1 percent of the population qualified). In 1782, led by **Henry Grattan** (1746-1820), the Parliament negotiated limited autonomy from England (while remaining loyal to the king) and fairer treatment of the Catholics. England, chastened by the American Revolution (and soon preoccupied with the French Revolution), tolerated a more-or-less independent Irish Parliament for two decades.

Then, in 1798, came the bloodiest Irish Rebellion. Inspired by the American and French revolutionary successes and buoyed by an "if they can do it, so can we" attitude, a band of Irish idealists rose up and rebelled. The **United Irishmen** (whose goals included introducing the term "Irishman" for all Irish, rather than labeling people as either Protestant or Catholic) revolted against Britain, led by **Wolfe Tone** (1763-1798), a Protestant Dublin lawyer. Tone, trained in the French Revolution, had gained French aid for the Irish cause. (Though a French naval invasion in 1796 already had failed after a freakish "Protestant wind" blew the ships away from Ireland's shores.) The Rebellion was marked by bitter fighting—30,000 died over six weeks—before British troops crushed the revolt.

England tried to solve the Irish problem politically by forcing Ireland into a "Union" with England as part of a "United

Kingdom" (**Act of Union,** 1801). The 500-year-old Irish Parliament was dissolved, with its members becoming part of England's Parliament in London. Catholics were not allowed in Parliament. From then on, "Unionists" have been those who oppose Irish independence, wanting to preserve the country's union with England.

Votes, Violence, and the Famine (1800s)

Irish politicians lobbied in the British Parliament for Catholic rights, reform of absentee-landlordism, and for **Home Rule**—i.e., independence. Meanwhile, secret societies of revolutionaries pursued justice through violence.

Daniel O'Connell (1775-1847), known as The Liberator, campaigned for Catholic equality and for repeal of the Act of Union (independence). Having personally witnessed the violence of the French Revolution in 1789 and the 1798 United Irishman Rebellion, O'Connell chose peaceful, legal means. He was a charismatic speaker, drawing half a million people to one of his "monster meeting" demonstrations at the Hill of Tara (1843). But any hope of an Irish revival was soon snuffed out by the biggest catastrophe in Irish history: the Great Potato Famine.

The **Great Potato Famine** (1845-1849) was caused by a fungus *(Phytophthora infestans)* that destroyed Ireland's main food crop. Roughly a million people starved to death or died of related diseases (estimates range between 500,000 and 1.1 million). Another one to two million emigrated—most to America and others to Canada and Australia.

The poorest were hardest hit. Potatoes were their main food source, because other crops—grown by tenant farmers on their landlords' land—went

to pay the rent and were destined for export.

Britain—then the richest nation on earth, with an empire stretching around the globe—could seemingly do nothing to help its starving citizens. A toxic combination of laissez-faire economic policies, racial bigotry, and religious self-righteousness conspired to blind the English to the plight of the Irish. While the English tend to blame the famine on overpopulation (Ireland's population had doubled in the 40 years leading up to the famine), many Irish say there actually was no famine, per se—just a calculated attempt to starve down the local population. For this reason, devout Irish Nationalists do not refer to this period as "the famine" (implying a lack of food) but rather as "An Gort Mór" (The Great Hunger... imposed by British colonial policies). Over the course of five long years, Ireland was ruined. To this day, Irish weather reports include mention of potential potato-blight conditions.

The island's population was suddenly cut by almost a third (from 8.4 million to 6 million). Many of their best and brightest had fled, and the island's economy—and spirit—took generations to recover. The Irish language, spoken by the majority of the population before the famine, became a badge of ignorance, and was considered useless to those hoping to emigrate. By 1900, emigration had further cut the island's population to just over 4 million (half of what it had been just before the famine).

Ireland, which remained one of Europe's poorest countries for more than a century, was slow to forget England's indifference. Ireland's population has only recently begun to grow again. Irish Nationalists point out that Britain's population, on the other hand, has grown from 12 million in 1845 to about 60 million today.

Before the famine, land was subdivided—each son got a piece of the family estate (which grew smaller with each generation). After the famine, the oldest son got the estate, and the younger siblings—with fewer options for making a living in Ireland (primarily joining the priesthood)—emigrated to Britain, Australia, Canada, or the US. Because of the huge emigration to the US (today there are 50 million Irish Americans), US influence increased. (As negotiations between Northern Ireland and the Irish Republic continue, US involvement in the talks is welcomed and considered essential by nearly all parties.)

Occasional violence demonstrated the fury of Irish nationalism, with the tragedy of the famine inflaming the movement. In 1848, the **Young Irelander** armed uprising was easily squelched. In 1858, the **Irish Republican Brotherhood** was formed (the forerunner of the IRA). Also called the **Fenians,** they launched a campaign for independence by planting terrorist bombs. Irish Americans sent money to help finance these revolutionaries. Uprising after uprising made it clear that Ireland was ready to close this 800-year chapter of invasions and colonialism.

Home Rule Party leader **Charles Stuart Parnell** (1846-1891), an Irishman educated in England, made "the Irish problem" the focus of London's Parliament. Parnell lobbied for independence and for the rights of poor tenant farmers living under absentee landlords, pioneering the first boycott tactics. Then, in 1890, at the peak of his power and about to achieve Home Rule for Ireland, he was drummed out of politics by a scandal involving his mistress, scuttling the Home Rule issue for another 20 years.

Culturally, the old Gaelic, rural Ireland was being crushed under the Industrial Revolution and the political control wielded by Protestant England. The **Gaelic Athletic Association** was founded in 1884 to resurrect pride in ancient Irish sports such as hurling. Soon after, in 1893, writers and educators formed the **Gaelic League** to preserve the traditional language, music, and poetry. Building on the tradition of old Celtic bards, Ireland turned out a series of influential writers: **W. B. Yeats, Oscar Wilde, George Bernard Shaw,** and **James Joyce** (see "Irish Literature," later).

Easter Uprising, War of Independence, Partition, and Civil War (1900-1950)

As the century turned, Ireland prepared for the inevitable show-down with Britain.

The **Sinn Fein** party (meaning "Ourselves") lobbied politi-cally for independence. The **Irish Volunteers** were more Catholic and more militant. Also on the scene was the **Irish Citizens Army,** with a socialist agenda to protect labor unions and clean up Dublin's hideous tenements, where 15 percent of the children died before the age of one.

Of course, many Irish were Protestant and pro-British. The **Ulster Volunteers** (Unionists, and mostly Orangemen) feared that Home Rule would result in a Catholic-dominated state that would oppress the Protestant minority.

Meanwhile, Britain was preoccupied with World War I, where it was "fighting to protect the rights of small nations" (except Ireland's), and so delayed granting Irish independence. The increasingly militant Irish rebels, believing that England's misfortune was Ireland's opportunity, decided to rise up and take independence while the time was ripe.

On Easter Monday, April 24, 1916, 1,500 Irish Volunteers, along with members of the Irish Citizens Army, marched on Dublin, occupied the General Post Office (and six other key build-ings across town), and raised a green, white, and orange flag. The teacher and poet **Patrick Pearse** stood in front of the post office and proclaimed Ireland an independent republic.

British troops struck back—in a week of street fighting and intense shelling, some 300 died. By Saturday, the greatly outnumbered rebels had been killed or arrested. The small-scale uprising—which failed to go national and was never popular even in Dublin—was apparently over.

However, the British government overreacted by swiftly executing the 16 ringleaders, including Pearse. Ireland was outraged, no longer seeing the rebels as troublemakers but as martyrs. From this point on, Ireland was resolved to win its independence at all costs. A poem by W. B. Yeats, "Easter, 1916," captured the struggle with his words: "All changed, changed utterly: A terrible beauty is born."

In the 1918 elections, the Sinn Fein party won big, but the new Members of Parliament refused to go to London, instead forming their own independent Irish Parliament in Dublin. Then Irish rebels began ambushing policemen—seen as the eyes and ears of British control—sparking two years of confrontations called the **War of Independence.** The fledgling Irish Republican Army faced 40,000 British troops, including the notorious "Black and Tans" (named for the color of their clothes: black for police and tan for army-surplus uniforms). A thousand people died in this war of street fighting, sniper fire, jailhouse beatings, terrorist bombs, and reprisals (for a more detailed timeline of the war and events leading up to it, see the sidebar on page 72).

Finally, Britain, tired of extended war after the slaughterhouse of World War I, agreed to Irish independence. But Ireland itself was a divided nation—the southern three-quarters of the island was mostly Catholic, Gaelic, rural, and for Home Rule; the northern quarter was Protestant, English, industrial, and Unionist. The solution? In 1920, in the **Government of Ireland Act,** the British Parliament partitioned the island into two independent, self-governing countries within the British Commonwealth: **Northern Ireland** and the **Irish Free State.** While the northern 6 counties (the only ones without a Catholic majority) chose to stay with Britain as Northern Ireland, the remaining 26 counties became the Irish Free State. (For a review of the ongoing Troubles between the North and the Republic, see the Northern Ireland chapter.)

Ireland's various political factions wrestled with this compromise solution, and the island plunged into a yearlong **Civil War** (1922-1923). The hard-line IRA opposed the partition, unwilling to accept a divided island, an oath of loyalty to the crown, or the remaining British Navy bases on Irish soil. They waged a street war on the armies of the Irish Free State, whose leaders supported the political settlement. Dublin and the southeast were ravaged in a year of bitter fighting before the Irish Free State, led by the charismatic young Nationalist **Michael Collins,** emerged victorious. The IRA went underground, moving its fight north and trying for the rest of the century to topple the government of Northern Ireland.

In 1937, the Irish Free State severed more ties with the British Commonwealth, writing up a new national constitution and taking an old name—**Éire** (pronounced AIR-uh—a Gaelic word possibly derived from the early Greeks' name for the island, Ierne). Ireland called World War II "The Emergency" and remained neutral. In 1949, the separation was completed, as the Irish Free State officially became the **Republic of Ireland.**

Celtic Tiger in the South, Troubles in the North (1950-2000)

Beginning in the 1960s, the Republic of Ireland—formerly a poor, rural region—was transformed into a modern, economic power, thanks to foreign investors and, in 1973, membership in the European Union. At the same time, reforms to Ireland's antiquated education system created a new generation of young people prepared for more than life on the farm.

The big social changes in the Republic were reflected in the 1990 election of Mary Robinson (a feminist lawyer who was outspoken on issues of divorce, contraception, and abortion) as the first female president of a once ultraconservative Ireland. Her much-respected tenure has been followed by the equally graceful presidency of Mary McAleese (elected in 1997 and re-elected in 2004), born in the North, and another example of the shrinking divide between the two political states that occupy the island.

Through the late 1990s, the Republic's booming, globalized economy grew a whopping 40 percent, and Dublin's property values tripled (between 1995 and 2007), earning the Republic's economy the nickname "The Celtic Tiger." (Like elsewhere, the global recession hit hard here in 2008—bursting the property bubble, plummeting home values, and driving up unemployment.)

Meanwhile, as the Republic moved toward prosperity, Northern Ireland—with a slight Protestant majority and a large, disaffected Catholic minority—was plagued by the **Troubles.** In 1967, the Northern Ireland Civil Rights Movement, inspired by the African American civil rights movement in the US, organized marches and demonstrations demanding equal treatment for Catholics (better housing, job opportunities, and voting rights). But they didn't have a Martin Luther King or a Bishop Desmond Tutu to advocate for them from a position of moral authority. Protestant **Unionist Orangemen** countered by continuing their marches through Catholic neighborhoods, flaunting their politically dominant position in the name of tradition, and thus provoking riots. In 1969, Britain sent troops to help Northern Ireland keep the peace, and met resistance from the IRA, which saw them as an occupying army supporting the Protestant pro-British majority.

From the 1970s to the 1990s, the North was a low-level battlefield, with the IRA using terrorist tactics to achieve their political ends. The Troubles, which claimed some 3,000 lives, continued with bombings, marches, hunger strikes, rock-throwing, and riots (notably Derry's **Bloody Sunday** in 1972), interrupted by cease-fires, broken cease-fires, and a string of peace agreements.

Then came the 1998 watershed settlement known as the **Good Friday Peace Accord** (to pro-Irish Nationalists) or the **Belfast Agreement** (to pro-British Unionists).

Global Nations (2000 and Beyond)

After years of negotiation, in 2005 the IRA formally announced an end to its armed campaign, promising to pursue peaceful, democratic means to achieve its goals. In 2006, I was stunned to discover that the British Army surveillance towers in Derry—disturbing fixtures since my very first visit—had been torn down. In the spring of 2007, the unthinkable happened when **Gerry Adams,** leader of the ultra-Nationalist Sinn Fein party, sat down across a table from **Reverend Ian Paisley,** head of the ultra-Unionist DUP party. It was their first face-to-face meeting. Also in 2007, London returned control of Northern Ireland to the popularly elected Northern Ireland Assembly. Perhaps most important of all, after almost 40 years, the British Army withdrew 90 percent of its forces from Northern Ireland that summer. The most recent signs of further healing came in 2010, when the long-awaited Saville Report—the result of a 12-year investigation by the UK government—found that the Bloody Sunday shootings were unjustified, and the victims legally innocent.

Now it's up to Northern Ireland to keep the peace. The 1998 peace accord gives Northern Ireland the freedom to leave the UK if ever the majority of the population approves a referendum to do so. At the same time, the Republic of Ireland withdrew its constitutional claim to the entire island of Ireland. Northern Ireland now has limited autonomy from London, with its own democratically elected, power-sharing government. It will be up to this body to untie this stubborn Gordian knot.

Today, both Northern Ireland and the Republic of Ireland have reason to be optimistic about the future. In spite of the recent recession, their economic growth through the 1990s and 2000s was impressive, and the political and cultural Troubles have lessened.

The formerly isolated island is welcoming tourists with open arms and reaching out to the rest of the globe. In 1999, the number of tourists visiting Ireland topped the 6 million mark, exceeding for the first time the native population on the island.

Visitors returning to Ireland are amazed at the country's transformation. Although there are still some tense areas in the North—as there are in all big cities—the peace process is grinding forward.

During its Celtic Tiger economic boom, the Irish imported labor and surpassed the English in per-capita income—both for the first time ever. Starting in 1980, when Apple set up its European headquarters here, streams of multinational and US corporations opened offices in Ireland. Ireland has one of the youngest populations in Europe. And those young Irish, beneficiaries of one of Europe's best educational systems, provide these corporations with a highly skilled workforce. Ireland's pharmaceutical, chemical, and software industries are well-established—this little country is second only to the US in the exportation of software.

By 2003, the rising economic tide had lifted Ireland to float beside Finland as one of the two most expensive countries in the European Union. Of course, rapid growth caused some problems. Urban sprawl, big-city traffic snarls, rising housing prices, water and air pollution, and the homogenizing effects of globalization have left their mark. Per-capita consumption of alcohol has tripled since 1970.

With the island's close business ties to its American partners, its economy is highly dependent on US market fluctuations. The Irish say, "When America sneezes, we get pneumonia." The global recession has been a cold shower on Ireland's long period of economic good times. Today's Irish parents (who remember 20 percent unemployment in the early 1980s) worry that their affluent young adult children will have to rein in their spending and learn to tighten their belts. Still, the Celtic Tiger economy, although tamed by the recession, taught the formerly downtrodden Irish that their luck can change for the better. The Irish—now business-savvy—are primed and ready for the recovery.

Meanwhile, the challenges of immigration (new arrivals into

Irish Brogue with a Polish Accent

As you walk down the street in an Irish city these days, you might be perplexed when you overhear an unfamiliar language being spoken by groups of enthusiastic young adults. It's Polish, and it may soon be to Ireland what Spanish is to the US: a good language to know if you want to communicate with a huge immigrant population. Polish food sections are popping up in grocery stores.

Bilingual English-Polish menus have made an appearance in some restaurants. And ask that chambermaid or waiter with the unusual accent where they're from. Chances are good that they'll say Warsaw or Kraków.

When 10 mostly Eastern European nations joined the EU in 2004, Sweden, Britain, and Ireland immediately removed major barriers for employment of these new EU nationals. Ireland's booming economy at that time needed a cheap labor force to fill the growing number of minimum-wage jobs. Hardworking, ambitious young Poles headed west to the land of opportunity. Ireland was their first choice because of its Catholicism, stronger economy, and opportunity to learn English (the international language of business). Now many of my favorite Irish B&B owners purr about their newly hired Polish chambermaids as if they were the latest innovation in household appliances, saying, "I don't know how I got along before without one!"

Granted, the Poles are not the only Eastern Europeans learning about capitalism, Irish-style. But the numbers of arriving Poles dwarf the number of Slovaks, Latvians, Estonians, and other Eastern Europeans headed to the Emerald Isle. Many Irish have taken to calling them all "Poles," just as many Americans might mistake a Guatemalan or Venezuelan for a "Mexican."

The healthy influx of new blood has added ethnic diversity to Ireland not seen since Spanish Armada sailors washed ashore 400 years ago. The Catholic Church has been re-energized with Poles attending Mass. And intermarriage is creating fun new combinations of names like Bridgit Jaruzelski or Colleen Kraszewski.

Irish-Polish ties continue to evolve. As the recession hit Ireland in 2008, Dell computer decided to close its big plant in Limerick. Where to move this facility? Production is now being handled by cheaper labor in a brand new Dell factory in Łódź, Poland.

Ireland) have replaced problems associated with the generations of emigration (young people leaving Ireland). Until recently, Ireland had the most liberal citizenship laws in the European Union, granting Irish citizenship to anyone born on Irish soil (even if neither parent had an Irish passport). This led to a flood of pregnant immigrant women arriving from Eastern Europe and Africa to give birth in Ireland so their children would gain EU citizenship. Families with a child born in an EU country faced fewer border restrictions, increasing their chances of moving into one of the 27 EU nations. In 2004, the Irish people closed that legal loophole in a referendum vote.

While the Irish are embracing the new economies and industries of the 21st century, many still see their island as an oasis of morality and traditional values when it comes to sex and marriage (homosexuality was decriminalized only 20 years ago). The Catholic Church continues to exert influence on Irish society. But since the Church no longer controls the legislature, the Irish government—driven by the popular demands of the youngest population in Europe—will undoubtedly push for some changes on the following issues.

Birth Control: People in the US take for granted that birth control is readily available. But Ireland only began allowing the widespread sale of condoms in 1993.

Abortion: Abortion is still illegal in Ireland. Women who choose to terminate their pregnancies must go to England for help—and counseling Irish women to go to England for abortions has only been legal since 1993. This was a big issue in 2001, when the Dutch anchored their "abortion ship" in Dublin's harbor, and again in 2002, when a referendum legalizing abortion was narrowly defeated. Watch for more referendums proposing the legalization of abortion. Many Irish refer to this as their next civil war.

Divorce: Ireland voted to legalize divorce in 1995—but only on very strict conditions. After the divorce papers are signed, it takes a four-year waiting period before the divorce is considered official, and little compensation is offered to Irish women who work as homemakers.

Irish Art

Megalithic tombs, ancient gold- and metalwork, illuminated manuscripts, high crosses carved in stone, paintings of rural Ireland, and provocative political murals—Ireland comes with some fascinating art. To best appreciate this art in your travels, kick off your tour in Ireland's two top museums, both in Dublin: the **National Museum: Archaeology and History** and the **National Gallery.** Each provides a good context to help you enjoy Irish art and architecture—from ancient to modern and both rural and urban. Here's a quick survey.

Megalithic Period: During the Stone Age 5,000 years ago, farmers living in the **Valley of the Boyne,** north of Dublin, built a "cemetery" of approximately 40 **burial mounds.** The most famous of these mound tombs is the passage tomb at Newgrange (part of Brú na Bóinne). More than 300 feet in diameter and composed of 200,000 tons of loose stone, Newgrange was constructed so that the light from the winter solstice sunrise (Dec 21) would pass through the eastern entrance to the tomb, travel down a 60-foot passage, and illuminate the inner burial chamber (not bad engineering for Stone Age architects). The effect is now re-created daily, so visitors can experience this ancient ritual of renewal and rebirth any time of year (see the Near Dublin chapter).

Some of Europe's best examples of megalithic (big rock) art are also at Newgrange. Carved on the tomb's stones are zigzags, chevrons, parallel arcs, and concentric spirals. Scholars think these designs symbolize a belief in the eternal cycle of life and the continuation of the life force, or that they pay homage to the elements in nature on which these ancient peoples depended for their existence.

Exploring these burial mounds (only Newgrange and Knowth are open to the public), you begin to understand the reverence that these people had for nature, and the need they felt to bury their dead in these great mound tombs, returning their kin to the womb of Mother Earth.

Bronze Age: As ancient Irish cultures developed from 2000 B.C., so did their metalworking skills. Gold and bronze were used to create **tools, jewelry,** and **religious objects.** (The National Museum: Archaeology and History in Dublin houses the most dazzling of these works.) Gold neck rings worn by both men and women, cufflink-like dress fasteners, bracelets, and lock rings (to hold hair in place) are just a few of the personal adornments fashioned by the ancient Irish.

Most of these objects were deliberately buried, often in bogs, as votive offerings to their gods or to prevent warring tribes from stealing them. Like the earlier megaliths, they're decorated with geometric and organic motifs.

Iron Age: The Celts, a warrior society from Central Europe, arrived in Ireland perhaps as early as the seventh century B.C. With their metalworking skills and superior iron weaponry, they soon overwhelmed the native population. And, though the Celts may have been fierce warriors, they wreaked havoc with a flair for the aesthetic. **Shields, swords,** and **scabbards** were embellished with delicate patterns, often enhanced with vivid colors. The dynamic energy of these decorations must have reflected the ferocious power of the Celts.

The Age of Saints and Scholars: Christianity grew in Ireland from St. Patrick's first efforts in the fifth century A.D. In the sixth and seventh centuries, its many great saints (such as St. Columba) established monastic settlements throughout Ireland, Britain, and the Continent, where learning, literature, and the arts flourished. During this "Golden Age" of Irish civilization, monks, along with metalworkers and stonemasons, created imaginative designs and distinctive stylistic motifs for **manuscripts, metal objects,** and **crosses.**

Monks wrote out and richly decorated manuscripts of the Gospels. These manuscripts—which preserved the written word in Latin, Greek, and Irish—eventually had more power than the oral tales of the ancient pagan heroes.

The most beautiful and imaginative of these illuminated manuscripts is the **Book of Kells** (c. A.D. 800), on display in the Old Library at Trinity College in Dublin. Crafted by Irish monks at a monastery on the Scottish island of Iona, the book was brought to Ireland for safekeeping from rampaging Vikings. The skins of 150 calves were used to make the vellum, which is painted with rich pigments from plants and minerals. The entire manuscript is colorfully decorated with flat, stylized human or angelic forms and intricate, interlacing animal and knot patterns. Full-page illustrations depict the life of Christ, and many pages are given over to highly complex yet symmetrical designs that resemble an Eastern carpet. Many consider this book the finest piece of art from Europe's Dark Ages.

The most renowned metalwork of this period is the **Ardagh Chalice,** made sometime in the eighth century. Now on display at the National Museum in Dublin, the silver and bronze gilt chalice is as impressive as the Book of Kells. Ribbons of gold wrap around the chalice stem, while intricate knot patterns ring the cup. A magnificent gold ring and a large glass stone on the chalice bottom reflect the desire to please God. (He would see this side of

the chalice when the priest drank during the Mass.)

The monks used Irish high crosses to celebrate the triumph of Christianity and to provide a means of educating the illiterate masses through simple stone carvings. The **Cross of Murdock** (Muiredach's Cross, A.D. 923) is

18 feet tall, towering over the remains of the monastic settlement at Monasterboice. It is but one of many monumental crosses that you'll come across throughout Ireland. Typically, stone carvers depicted Bible stories and surrounded these with the same intricate patterns seen in the Book of Kells and the Ardagh Chalice.

Early Irish art focused on organic, geometric, and linear designs. Unlike Mediterranean art, Irish art of this early period was not preoccupied with a naturalistic representation of people, animals, or the landscape. Instead, it reflects Irish society's rituals and the elements and rhythms of nature.

The Suppression of Native Irish Art: After invading Ireland in 1169, the English suppressed Celtic Irish culture. English traditions in architecture, painting, and literature replaced native styles until the late 19th century, when revivals in Irish language, folklore, music, and art began to surface.

Painters in the late 19th and early 20th centuries went to the west of Ireland, which was untouched by English dominance and influence, in search of traditional Irish subject matter.

Jack B. Yeats (1871-1957, brother of the poet W. B. Yeats), Belfast-born painter **Paul Henry** (1876-1958), and **Sean Keating** (1889-1977) all looked to the west for inspiration. The National Gallery in Dublin holds many of these artists' greatest works, with an entire gallery dedicated to Jack Yeats. Many of his early paintings illustrate scenes of his beloved Sligo. His later paintings are more expressionistic in style and patriotic in subject matter.

Henry's paintings depict the rugged beauty of the Connemara region and its people, with scenes of rustic cottages, mountains, and boglands. Keating, the most political of the three painters, featured stirring scenes from Ireland's struggle against the English for independence.

Contemporary Irish art is often linked to the social, political, and environmental issues that face Ireland today. Themes include the position of the Church in the daily lives of the modern Irish, the effects of development on the countryside, the changing roles of women in Ireland, and the Troubles. Look for this provocative art at the Irish Museum of Modern Art in Dublin (on Military Road, www.imma.ie) and at city galleries.

Today's Irish respect the artistic process, so much so that a provision in the tax system in the Republic of Ireland allows income from art sales to go untaxed. This is one reason many artists immigrate to Ireland.

In Northern Ireland, murals in sectarian neighborhoods (e.g., the Shankill and Falls

Roads in Belfast and the Bogside in Derry) are stirring public testaments to the martyrs and heroes of the recent Troubles.

Irish Literature

Since the Book of Kells, Ireland's greatest contributions to the world of art have been through words. As there was no Irish Gaelic written language, the inhabitants of Ireland were illiterate until Christianity came in the fourth century. Far from ignorant, Celtic society maintained a complex set of laws and historical records and legends...verbally. The druidic priests and bards who passed this rich oral tradition down from generation to generation were the most respected members of the clan, next to the king. After Christianity transformed Ireland into a refuge of literacy (while the rest of Europe crumbled into the Dark Ages), Charlemagne's imported Irish monks invented "minuscule," which became the basis of the lowercase letters we use in our alphabet today. The cultural importance placed on the word (spoken, and for the past 1,500 years, written) is today reflected in the rich output of modern Irish writers.

Three hundred years ago, Dublin native **Jonathan Swift** created his masterpiece, *Gulliver's Travels,* as an acidic satire of British colonialism. It pokes fun at religious hard-liners and the pompous bureaucrats in London who shaped England's misguided Irish policies, and ironically has survived as a children's classic.

William Butler Yeats, also born and raised in Dublin, dedicated his early writings in the 1880s to the "Celtic Twilight" rebirth of pride in mythic Irish heroes and heroines. His early poems and plays are filled with fairies and idyllic rural innocence, while his later poems reflect Ireland's painful transition to independence. Yeats' Nobel Prize for literature (1923) was eventually matched by three later, Nobel-winning Irish authors: **George Bernard Shaw** (1925), **Samuel Beckett** (1969), and **Seamus Heaney** (1995).

Oscar Wilde, born in Dublin and a graduate of Trinity College, wowed London with his quick wit, outrageous clothes, and flamboyant personality. Wilde wrote the darkly fascinating novel *The Picture of Dorian Gray* (1890)

and skewered upper-class Victorian society in witty comedic plays (e.g., *The Importance of Being Earnest*, 1895), with characters who speak very elegantly about the trivial concerns of the idle rich. He was the toast of London in the 1890s—before the scandal of his homosexuality turned Victorian society against him.

Meanwhile, **Bram Stoker** was conjuring up a Gothic thriller called *Dracula* (1897). Most inventive of all, perhaps, was **James Joyce,** who broke new ground and captured literary lightning in a bottle when he focused on Dublin's seedier side in a modern, stream-of-consciousness style. His famous novel *Ulysses,* set on a single day (June 16, 1904), follows Dubliners on an odyssey through the city's pubs, hospitals, libraries, churches, and brothels.

The **Abbey Theatre** (championed by Yeats) was the world's first national theater, built to house plays intended to give a voice to Ireland's flowering playwrights. When **J. M. Synge** staged *The Playboy of the Western World* there in 1907, his unflattering comic portrayal of Irish peasant life (and mention of women's underwear) caused riots. Twenty years later, **Sean O'Casey** provoked more riots at the Abbey when his *Plough and the Stars* production depicted the 1916 Uprising in a way that was at odds with the audience's cherished views of their heroes.

In recent decades, the bittersweet Irish literary parade has been inhabited by tragically volcanic characters like **Brendan Behan,** who exclaimed, "I'm not a writer with a drinking problem...I'm a drinker with a writing problem." Bleak poverty experienced in childhood was the catalyst for **Frank McCourt**'s memorable *Angela's Ashes.* Among the most celebrated of today's Irish writers is **Roddy Doyle,** whose feel for working-class Dublin resonates in his novels of contemporary life (e.g., *The Commitments*) as well as in historical slices of life (e.g., *A Star Called Henry*). **Seamus Heaney,** a poet who has won the Nobel and Pulitzer prizes, published a new translation in 1999 of the Old English epic *Beowulf*—wedding the old with the new.

Irish Language

The Irish have a rich oral tradition that goes back to their ancient fireside storytelling days. Part of the fun of traveling here is getting an ear for the way locals express themselves.

Irish Gaelic is one of four surviving Celtic languages, along with Scottish Gaelic, Welsh, and Breton (spoken in parts of French Brittany). A couple of centuries ago, there were seven surviving Celtic languages. But Cornish (spoken in Cornwall) is on life support, and two others have died out: Manx (from the Isle of Man) and Gallaic (spoken in Northern Spain). Some proud Irish choose to call their native tongue "Irish" instead of "Gaelic" to ensure that there is no confusion with what is spoken in parts of Scotland.

Only 165 years ago, the majority of the Irish population spoke Irish Gaelic. But most of the speakers were of the poor laborer class that either died or emigrated during the famine. After the famine, Irish Gaelic was seen as a badge of backwardness. Parents and teachers understood that English was the language that would serve children best when they emigrated to better lives in the US, Canada, Australia, or England. Children in schools wore a tally stick around their necks, and a notch was cut by teachers each time a child was caught speaking Irish. At the end of the day, the child received a whack for each notch in the stick. It wasn't until the resurgence of cultural pride, brought on by the Gaelic League in 1884, that an attempt was made to promote use of the language again.

These days, less than 5 percent of the Irish population is fluent in their native tongue. However, it's taken seriously enough that all national laws passed must first be written in Irish, then translated into English. Irish Gaelic can be heard most often in the western counties of Kerry, Galway, Mayo, and Donegal. Each of these counties has a slightly different dialect. You'll know you're entering an Irish Gaelic-speaking area when you see a sign saying *Gaeltacht* (GAIL-tekt).

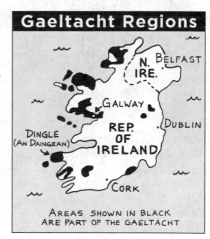

Irish Gaelic doesn't use the letters *j, k, q, x,* or *z*. And there's no "th" sound—which you can hear today when an Irish person says something like "turdy-tree" (33). There is also no equivalent of the simple words "yes" or "no." Instead, answers are given in the affirmative or negative rephrasing of the question. For example, a question like "Did you mail the letter today?" would be answered with "I did (mail the letter)," rather than a simple "yes." Or "It's a nice day today, isn't it?" would be answered with "It is," or "'Tis."

Irish Place Names

Here are a few words that appear in Irish place names. You'll see these on road signs or at tourist sights.

Irish	Phonetics	English
Alt	ahlt	cliff
An Lár	ahn lar	city center
Ard	ard	high, height, hillock
Baile	BALL-yah	town, town land
Beag	beg	little
Bearna	bar-na	gap
Boireann	burr-en	large rock, rocky area
Bóthar	boh-er	road
Bun	bun	end, bottom
Caiseal	CASH-el	circular stone fort
Caislean	cash-LOIN	castle
Cathair	caht-HAR	circular stone fort, city
Cill	kill	church
Cloch	clockh	stone
Doire	dih-ruh	oak
Droichead	DROCKH-ed	bridge
Drumlin	DRUM-lin	small hill
Dun	doon	fort
Fionn	fin	white, fair-haired person
Gaeltacht	GAIL-tekt	Irish language district
Gall	gaul	foreigner
Garda	gar-dah	police
Gort	gort	field
Inis	in-ish	island
Mileac	mee-luch	low marshy ground
Mór	mor	large
Muck	muck	pig
Oifig an Phoist	UFF-ig un fwisht	post office
Poll	poll	hole, cave
Rath	rath	ancient earthen fort
Ross	ross	peninsula
Sí	shee	fairy mound, bewitching
Slí	slee	route, way
Sliabh	sleeve	mountain
Sraid	shrawd	street
Teach	chockh	house
Trá	traw	beach, strand
Tur	toor	tower

Irish Pleasantries

When you reach the more remote western fringe of Ireland, you're likely to hear folks speaking Irish. Although locals in these areas can readily converse with you in English, it's fascinating to hear their ancient Celtic language spoken. Here are some basic Irish phrases:

Irish	Phonetics	English
Fáilte	FAHLT-shuh	Welcome
Conas ta tu?	CONN-us A-thaw too	How are you?
Go raibh maith agat	guh rov mah UG-ut	Thank you
Slán	slawn	Bye

Irish Pub and Music Words

The Irish love to socialize. Pubs are like public living rooms, where friends gather in a corner to play tunes and anyone is a welcome guest. Here are some useful pub and music words:

Irish	Phonetics	English
Poitín	po-CHEEN	moonshine, homemade liquor
Craic	crack	fun atmosphere, good conversation
Bodhrán	BO-run	traditional drum
Uilleann	ILL-in	elbow (uilleann pipes are elbow bagpipes)
Trad	trad	traditional Irish music
Ceilidh	KAY-lee	Irish dance gathering
Fleadh	flah	music festival
Slainte	SLAWN-chuh	cheers, to your health
Táim súgach!	taw im SOO-gakh	I'm tipsy!
Lei thras	LEH-hrass	toilets
Mná	min-AW	women's room
Fír	fear	men's room

Irish Politics

Politics is a popular topic of conversation in Ireland. Whether you pick up a local newspaper or turn on your car radio, you're likely to encounter these Irish political terms in the media:

Irish	Phonetics	English
Taoiseach	TEE-shock	Prime minister of Irish Republic
Seanad	SHAN-ud	Irish Senate
Dáil	DOY-ill	Irish House of Representatives
Teachta Dála (TD)	TALK-tah DOLL-ah	Member of Irish Parliament

Irish-Yankee Vocabulary

If some of these words seem more British than Irish, those are ones you're likely to hear more often in Northern Ireland (part of the UK).

advert—advertisement
anticlockwise—counterclockwise
aubergine—eggplant
banger—sausage
bang on—correct
banjaxed—messed up
bank holiday—legal holiday
beer mat—coaster
bespoke—custom
billion—a thousand of our billions (a trillion)
biro—ballpoint pen
biscuit—cookie
Black Mariah—police van
black pudding—sausage made from pig's blood
blather—rambling, empty talk
bloody—damn (from medieval blasphemy: "Christ's blood")
blow off—fart
boffin—nerd
bog—slang for toilet
bolshy—argumentative
bonnet—car hood
boot—car trunk
braces—suspenders
bridle way—path for walkers, bikers, and horse riders
brilliant—cool
bum—bottom or "backside"
busker—street musician
cacks—trousers, underpants
candy floss—cotton candy
caravan—trailer
car boot sale—temporary flea market, often for charity
car park—parking lot
carry on—nonsense
casualty—emergency room
cat's eyes—road reflectors
ceilidh—dance, party
champ—mashed potatoes and onions
chemist—pharmacist
chicory—endive
chippy—fish-and-chips shop

chips—french fries
chock-a-block—jam-packed
chuffed—pleased
cider—alcoholic apple cider
clearway—road where you can't stop
coach—long-distance bus
concession—discounted admission
cos—romaine lettuce
cotton buds—cotton swabs
courgette—zucchini
craic (pronounced "crack")—fun, good conversation
crisps—potato chips
crusties—New Age hippies
culchie—hick, country yokel
cuppa—cup of tea
Da—father
deadly—really good
dear—expensive
digestives—round graham crackers
dinner—lunch or dinner
diversion—detour
dodgy—iffy, risky
done and dusted—completed
donkey's years—until the cows come home, forever
draughts (pronounced "drafts")—checkers
draw—marijuana
dual carriageway—divided highway (four lanes)
Dubs—people from Dublin
eejit—moron
en suite—bathroom attached to room
face flannel—washcloth
fair play (to you)—well done, good job
fanny—vagina
fell—hill or high plain
fiddler's fart—worthless thing
first floor—second floor (one floor above ground)
fiver—five-euro note
flat—apartment
fluthered—drunk
flutter—a bet
football—Gaelic football
fortnight—two weeks
full monty—the whole shebang, everything
GAA—Gaelic Athletic Association
gallery—balcony
gammon—ham

gangway—aisle

gaol—jail (same pronunciation)

Garda—police

gargle—to have an alcoholic drink

gasman—the life of the party

give way—yield

giving out—chewing out, yelling at

glen—valley

gob—mouth

gobsmacked—astounded

goods wagon—freight truck

grand—good, well ("How are you?" "I'm grand, thanks")

guards—police (Garda)

gurrier—hooligan

half eight—8:30 (not 7:30)

hen night—bachelorette party

holiday—vacation

homely—likable or cozy

hooley—party or informal shindig

hoover—vacuum cleaner

hurling—Irish field hockey

iced lolly—popsicle

interval—intermission

ironmonger—hardware store

jacket potato—baked potato

jacks—toilet

jars—drinks (alcohol)

jelly—Jell-O

jumble—sale, rummage sale

jumper—sweater

just a tick—just a second

kipper—smoked herring

knackered—exhausted

knickers—ladies' panties

knocking shop—brothel

knock up—wake up or visit

ladybird—ladybug

lash—a try ("give it a lash")

left luggage—baggage check

let—rent

lift—elevator

listed—protected historic building

lorry—truck

Ma, Mam, Mammy—mother

mac—mackintosh (trench) coat

mangetout—snow peas

mate—buddy (boy or girl)
mean—stingy
mental—crazy
minced meat—hamburger
minerals—soft drinks
mobile (MOH-bile)—cell phone
mod cons—modern conveniences (not convicts in bell-bottoms)
naff—dorky, tacky
nappy—diaper
natter—talk and talk
"Norn Iron" (pronounced)—Northern Ireland
nought—zero
noughts & crosses—tic-tac-toe
OAP—old-age pensioner (qualified for senior discounts)
off-license—liquor store
Oirish—exaggerated Irish accent
on offer—for sale
paddywhackery—exaggerated Irish accent
paralytic—passed-out drunk
pasty—(PASS-tee) crusted savory (usually meat) pie
pavement—sidewalk
pear-shaped—messed up, gone wrong
petrol—gas
**pissed (rude), paralytic, bevvied, wellied, popped up, ratted,
     pissed as a newt**—drunk
pitch—playing field
plaster—Band-Aid
publican—pub manager
pull—to attract romantic attention
punter—partygoer, customer
put a sock in it—shut up
quay (pronounced "key")—waterside street, ship offloading area
queue—line
queue up—line up
quick smart—immediately
quid—pound (money in Northern Ireland, worth about $1.60)
ramps—speed bumps
randy—horny
redundant, made—laid off
return ticket—round-trip
ride—have sex with
ring up—call (telephone)
roundabout—traffic circle
RTE—Irish Republic's broadcast network
rubber—eraser
sanitary towel—sanitary pad**

sausage roll—sausage wrapped in a flaky pastry (like a pig in a blanket)
scarlet—embarrassed
Scotch egg—hard-boiled egg wrapped in sausage meat
self-catering—apartment with kitchen
sellotape—Scotch tape
serviette—napkin
session—musical evening
shag—have sex with
shag all—hardly any
shebeen—illegal drinking hole
single ticket—one-way ticket
skint—broke, poor
skip—Dumpster
slag—to ridicule, tease
smalls—underwear
snogging—kissing, making out
solicitor—lawyer
sort out—figure out, organize
spanner—wrench
spend a penny—urinate
stag night—bachelor party
starkers—buck naked
starters—appetizers
stick—criticism
stone—14 pounds (weight)
strand—beach
stroppy—bad-tempered
subway—underground pedestrian passageway
sultanas—golden raisins
surgical spirit—rubbing alcohol
swede—rutabaga
take the mickey—tease
tatty—worn out or tacky
taxi rank—taxi stand
tenner—10-euro note
theatre—live stage
tick—a check mark
tight as a Scotsman (derogatory)—cheapskate
tights—panty hose
tip—public dump
tipper lorry—dump truck
tin—can
to let—for rent
top up—refill a drink or your mobile-phone credit
torch—flashlight

towpath—path along a river
trad—traditional music
Travellers—itinerants, once known as Tinkers
turf accountant—bookie
twee—corny, too cute
twitcher—bird-watcher
underground—subway
verge—grassy edge of road
victualler—butcher
wain—small child
way out—exit
wee (v.)—urinate
wee (n.)—tiny (in the North)
Wellingtons, wellies—rubber boots
whacked—exhausted
whinge (rhymes with hinge)—whine
witter on—gab and gab
woolies—warm clothes
your man—that guy, this guy
zebra crossing—crosswalk
zed—the letter z

APPENDIX

Contents

Tourist Information

Tourist Offices

Ireland's national tourist office **in the US**—called **Tourism Ireland**—offers a wealth of information on both the Republic of Ireland and Northern Ireland. Before your trip, scan their website (www.discoverireland.com) and download brochures and maps. You can ask questions and request that information be mailed to you (such as the free vacation planning packet, regional and city maps, walking routes, and festival schedules) by using the website's "live chat," emailing info.us@tourismireland.com, or calling 800-SHAMROC (US tel. 800-742-6762).

In Ireland, your best first stop in every town is generally the tourist information office—abbreviated **TI** in this book. A TI is a great place to get a city map, advice on public transportation (including bus and train schedules), walking-tour information, information on special events, and recommendations for nightlife. For all the help TIs offer, steer clear of their room-finding services (bloated prices, booking fee up to €5, no opinions, and they take a

10 percent cut from your B&B host). Many TIs have information on the entire country or at least the region, so try to pick up maps for destinations you'll be visiting later in your trip. If you're arriving in town after the TI closes, call ahead or pick up a map in a neighboring town.

In **Dublin,** try to get everything you'll need for Ireland in one stop at the TI in the old church on Suffolk Street (see page 47). The general nationwide tourist-information phone number for travelers calling from within Ireland is 1-850-230-330 (and their nationwide room-booking phone number is 1-800-363-626; office open Mon-Sat 9:00-20:00, closed Sun).

Communicating

Telephones
Smart travelers use the telephone to reserve or reconfirm rooms, get tourist information, reserve restaurants, confirm tour times, or phone home. Generally the easiest, cheapest way to call home is to use an international phone card purchased in Ireland. This section covers dialing instructions, phone cards, and types of phones (for more in-depth information, see www.ricksteves.com /phoning).

How to Dial
Calling from the US to Ireland, or vice versa, is simple—once you break the code. The European calling chart in this chapter will walk you through it.

Dialing Domestically Within Ireland
Ireland, like much of the US, uses an area-code dialing system. To make domestic calls, if you're dialing within an area code, you just dial the local number to be connected; but if you're calling outside your area code, you have to dial both the area code (which starts with a 0) and the local number.

Area codes are listed in this book, and are available from directory assistance (dial 11811 in the Republic, 192 in Northern Ireland).

The Republic of Ireland has a special way to call Northern Ireland: dial 048, then the local number without the area code. For instructions on how to call the Republic of Ireland from Northern Ireland, see next page.

Dialing Internationally to or from Ireland
If you want to make an international call, follow these steps:
1. Dial the international access code (00 if you're calling from Europe, 011 from the US or Canada).

2. Dial the country code of the country you're calling (353 for the Republic of Ireland, 44 for Northern Ireland, or 1 for the US or Canada).

3. Dial the area code (Dublin's area code is 01) and the local number, keeping in mind that if you're calling Ireland, drop the initial zero of the area code (the European calling chart lists specifics per country).

Calling from the US to the Republic of Ireland: To call a recommended Dublin hotel from the US, dial 011 (the US international access code), 353 (the Republic of Ireland's country code), 1 (Dublin's area code without its initial 0), then 679-6500 (the hotel's number).

From any European country—including Northern Ireland—to the Republic of Ireland: Dial 00-353, then the area code without its initial 0, then the local number.

From the US or Canada to Northern Ireland: Dial 011-44-28 (44 is the country code for the United Kingdom; 28 is Northern Ireland's area code without its initial 0), then the local number.

From the Republic of Ireland to Northern Ireland: Dial 048, then the local number. (In this case, Northern Ireland's area code, 028, is omitted entirely.)

From any European Country (except the Republic of Ireland) to Northern Ireland: Dial 00-44-28 (Northern Ireland's area code without its initial 0), then the local number.

From anywhere in Ireland (Republic and Northern Ireland) to the US: To call from Ireland to my office in Edmonds, Washington, I dial 00 (Ireland's international access code), 1 (the US country code), 425 (Edmonds' area code), and 771-8303.

Note: You might see a + in front of a European number. When dialing the number, replace the + with the international access code of the country you're calling from (00 from Europe, 011 from the US or Canada).

Public Phones and Hotel Room Phones

To make calls from public phones, you'll need a prepaid phone card. There are two types: insertable and international. International calling cards work only within the country of purchase, with the exception of some brands of cards that are usable in both the Republic of Ireland and the UK. But confirm before buying a card by checking for both an 1800 access number (used in the Republic of Ireland) and an 0800 access number (for the UK—don't use the 0845, 0870, or 0871 numbers, which cost about 10p per minute). If you have a live card at the end of your trip, give it to another traveler to use up.

Don't expect to have a vast array of spiffy public phone booths at your service. Given the proliferation of mobile phones, quite a

European Calling Chart

Just smile and dial, using this key:
AC = Area Code, LN = Local Number.

European Country	Calling long distance within…	Calling from the US or Canada to…	Calling from a European country to…
Austria	AC + LN	011 + 43 + AC (without the initial zero) + LN	00 + 43 + AC (without the initial zero) + LN
Belgium	LN	011 + 32 + LN (without initial zero)	00 + 32 + LN (without initial zero)
Bosnia-Herzegovina	AC + LN	011 + 387 + AC (without initial zero) + LN	00 + 387 + AC (without initial zero) + LN
Britain	AC + LN	011 + 44 + AC (without initial zero) + LN	00 + 44 + AC (without initial zero) + LN
Croatia	AC + LN	011 + 385 + AC (without initial zero) + LN	00 + 385 + AC (without initial zero) + LN
Czech Republic	LN	011 + 420 + LN	00 + 420 + LN
Denmark	LN	011 + 45 + LN	00 + 45 + LN
Estonia	LN	011 + 372 + LN	00 + 372 + LN
Finland	AC + LN	011 + 358 + AC (without initial zero) + LN	999 (or other 900 number) + 358 + AC (without initial zero) + LN
France	LN	011 + 33 + LN (without initial zero)	00 + 33 + LN (without initial zero)
Germany	AC + LN	011 + 49 + AC (without initial zero) + LN	00 + 49 + AC (without initial zero) + LN
Gibraltar	LN	011 + 350 + LN	00 + 350 + LN
Greece	LN	011 + 30 + LN	00 + 30 + LN
Hungary	06 + AC + LN	011 + 36 + AC + LN	00 + 36 + AC + LN
Ireland	AC + LN	011 + 353 + AC (without initial zero) + LN	00 + 353 + AC (without initial zero) + LN

European Country	Calling long distance within ...	Calling from the US or Canada to ...	Calling from a European country to ...
Italy	LN	011 + 39 + LN	00 + 39 + LN
Montenegro	AC + LN	011 + 382 + AC (without initial zero) + LN	00 + 382 + AC (without initial zero) + LN
Morocco	LN	011 + 212 + LN (without initial zero)	00 + 212 + LN (without initial zero)
Netherlands	AC + LN	011 + 31 + AC (without initial zero) + LN	00 + 31 + AC (without initial zero) + LN
Norway	LN	011 + 47 + LN	00 + 47 + LN
Poland	LN	011 + 48 + LN (without initial zero)	00 + 48 + LN (without initial zero)
Portugal	LN	011 + 351 + LN	00 + 351 + LN
Slovakia	AC + LN	011 + 421 + AC (without initial zero) + LN	00 + 421 + AC (without initial zero) + LN
Slovenia	AC + LN	011 + 386 + AC (without initial zero) + LN	00 + 386 + AC (without initial zero) + LN
Spain	LN	011 + 34 + LN	00 + 34 + LN
Sweden	AC + LN	011 + 46 + AC (without initial zero) + LN	00 + 46 + AC (without initial zero) + LN
Switzerland	LN	011 + 41 + LN (without initial zero)	00 + 41 + LN (without initial zero)
Turkey	AC (if there's no initial zero, add one) + LN	011 + 90 + AC (without initial zero) + LN	00 + 90 + AC (without initial zero) + LN

- The instructions above apply whether you're calling a land line or mobile phone.
- The international access codes (the first numbers you dial when making an international call) are 011 if you're calling from the US or Canada, or 00 if you're calling from virtually anywhere in Europe (except Finland, where it's 999 or another 900 number, depending on the phone service you're using).
- To call the US or Canada from Europe, dial 00, then 1 (the country code for the US and Canada), then the area code and number. In short, 00 + 1 + AC + LN = Hi, Mom!

few phone booths have been neglected, targeted by vandals, and fallen into disrepair.

Insertable Phone Cards: This type of card can be used only at Irish pay phones. It's handy and affordable for local and domestic calls, but more expensive for international calls. Telecom Éireann phone cards are sold for €5, €10, or €20 at newsstands, TIs, and post offices. To use the card, physically insert it into a slot in the pay phone.

International Phone Cards: These are the cheapest way to make international calls from Europe—with the best cards, it costs literally pennies a minute. They also work for local calls.

You can use international phone cards from any type of phone, even the one in your hotel rooms (but ask at the front desk if there are any fees for toll-free calls). The cards are sold at many post offices, newsstands, mini-marts, and exchange bureaus. Ask the clerk which of the various brands has the best rates for calls to America. Because cards are occasionally duds, avoid the high denominations. Some cards are rechargeable (you can call up the number on the card, give your credit-card number, and buy more time). Some shops also sell cardless codes, printed right on the receipt.

To use the card, scratch to reveal your code, then dial the free access number. The message tells you to enter your code. Dial the number you're calling, usually followed by either the pound (#) or star (*) key; you don't have to listen through the entire sales pitch. When using an international calling card, the area code must be dialed even if you're calling across the street.

Remember that you don't need the actual card to use a card account, so it's shareable. You can write down the access number and code in your notebook and share it with friends.

Hotel Room Phones: Calling from your room can be cheap for local calls (ask for the rates at the front desk first), but is often a rip-off for long-distance calls, unless you use an international phone card (explained above). Incoming calls are free, making this a cheap way for friends and family to stay in touch (provided they have a good long-distance plan for calls to Europe—and a list of your hotels' phone numbers). In-room phones are rare in B&Bs.

US Calling Cards: These cards, such as the ones offered by AT&T, Verizon, or Sprint, are the worst option. You'll nearly always save a lot of money by using a locally purchased phone card instead.

Mobile Phones

Many travelers enjoy the convenience of traveling with a mobile phone.

Using Your Mobile Phone: Your US mobile phone works in

Europe if it's GSM-enabled, tri-band or quad-band, and on a calling plan that includes international calls. Phones from T-Mobile and AT&T, which use the same GSM technology that Europe does, are more likely to work overseas than Verizon or Sprint phones (if you're not sure, ask your service provider). Most US providers charge $1.29 per minute while roaming internationally to make or receive calls, and 20-50 cents to send or receive text messages.

You'll pay cheaper rates if your phone is electronically "unlocked" (ask your provider about this); then in Europe, you can simply buy a tiny **SIM card,** which gives you a European phone number. SIM cards are sold at mobile-phone stores and some newsstand kiosks for about $5-10, and generally include several minutes' worth of prepaid domestic calling time. When you buy a SIM card, you may need to show ID, such as your passport. Insert the SIM card in your phone (usually in a slot behind the battery), and it'll work like a European mobile phone. When buying a SIM card, always ask about fees for domestic and international calls, roaming charges, and how to check your credit balance and buy more time.

Many **smartphones,** such as the iPhone or BlackBerry, work in Europe—but beware of sky-high fees, especially for data downloading (checking email, browsing the Internet, watching videos, and so on). Ask your provider in advance how to avoid unwittingly roaming your way to a huge bill. Some applications allow for cheap or free smartphone calls over a Wi-Fi connection (described under "Calling over the Internet," below).

Using a European Mobile Phone: Mobile-phone shops all over Europe sell basic phones. Phones that are "locked" to work with a single provider start around $20; "unlocked" phones (which allow you to switch out SIM cards to use your choice of provider) start around $60. You'll also need to buy a SIM card (explained earlier) and prepaid credit for making calls. When you're in the phone's home country, domestic calls are reasonable, and incoming calls are free. You'll pay more if roaming in another country.

Calling over the Internet

Some things that seem too good to be true...actually are true. If you're traveling with a laptop, you can make calls using VoIP (Voice over Internet Protocol). With VoIP, two computers act as the phones, and the Internet-based calls are free (or you can pay a few cents to call from your computer to a telephone). If both computers have webcams, you can even see each other while you chat. The major providers are Skype (www.skype.com) and Google Talk (www.google.com/talk).

Useful Phone Numbers

Note that calls beginning with 1800 are free throughout Ireland, but 1850 calls cost the same as local calls.

Emergencies and Directory Assistance

In the Republic of Ireland

Emergency (police and ambulance): tel. 999

Operator Assistance: tel. 10 for Ireland, tel. 114 to call outside Ireland

Directory Assistance Within Ireland: tel. 11811 (free from phone booth)

International Info: tel. 11818 (free from phone booth)

In Northern Ireland

Emergency (police and ambulance): tel. 999

Operator Assistance: tel. 100 for Britain, tel. 155 to call outside Britain

Directory Assistance Within Britain: tel. 192 (20p from phone booth, otherwise £1.50)

International Info: tel. 153 (20p from phone booth, otherwise £1.50)

US Embassies

In the Republic of Ireland: 42 Elgin Road, Dublin, Mon-Tue and Thu-Fri 8:30-11:30, closed Wed and Sat-Sun, tel. 01/668-7122 or 01/668-8777, http://dublin.usembassy.gov

In Northern Ireland: Danesfort House, 223 Stranmillis Road, Belfast, tel. 028/9038-6100, www.usembassy.org.uk/nireland

Canadian Embassies

In the Republic of Ireland: 7-8 Wilton Terrace, Dublin, Mon-Fri 9:00-13:00 & 14:00-16:30, consular and passport services open Mon-Fri 9:00-12:00, closed Sat-Sun, tel. 01/234-4000, www.canada.ie

In Northern Ireland: 9 Cromac Avenue, Belfast, tel. 028/9127-2060

Travel Advisories

US Department of State: tel. 202/647-5225, www.travel.state.gov

Canadian Department of Foreign Affairs: Canadian tel. 800-267-6788, www.dfait-maeci.gc.ca

US Centers for Disease Control and Prevention: tel. 800-CDC-INFO (800-232-4636), www.cdc.gov/travel

Airlines

These are phone numbers for the Republic of Ireland. (To call the special 1800 numbers from the US, dial 011-353, then the 800 number without the initial 1).

Aer Arann: tel. 081-821-0210 (www.aerarann.com)
Aer Lingus: tel. 081-836-5000 (www.aerlingus.com)
American: tel. 01/602-0550 (www.aa.com)
bmi: tel. 01/407-3036 (www.flybmi.com)
British Airways: tel. 1/890-626-747 (www.ba.com)
Continental Airlines: tel. 01/672-7070 (www.continental.com)
Delta: tel. 01/407-3165 (www.delta.com)
Lufthansa: tel. 01/844-5544 (www.lufthansa.com)
Ryanair (cheap fares): tel. 081-830-3030 (www.ryanair.com)
Scandinavian Airlines System (SAS): tel. 01/844-5440 (www .flysas.com)

Dublin Car-Rental Agencies
Avis: 35-39 Old Kilmainham Road, tel. 021/428-1111, airport tel. 01/605-7500, www.avis.ie
Hertz: 151 South Circular Road, tel. 01/676-7476, airport tel. 01/844-5466, www.hertz.ie
Budget: 151 Lower Drumcondra Road, tel. 01/837-9611, central reservations tel. 09066/27711, airport tel. 01/844-5150, www.budget.ie
Europcar: 2 Haddington Road, tel. 01/614-2888, airport tel. 01/812-0410, www.europcar.ie

Internet Access
It's useful to get online periodically as you travel—to confirm trip plans, check train or bus schedules, get weather forecasts, catch up

on email, blog or post photos from your trip, or call folks back home (explained earlier, under "Calling over the Internet").

Many hotels offer a computer in the lobby with Internet access for guests. Smaller B&Bs may sometimes let you sit at their desk for a few minutes just to check your email, if you ask politely. If your hotel doesn't have access, ask your hotelier to direct you to the nearest place to get online. Most of the towns where I've listed accommodations in this book also have Internet cafés. Many libraries offer free access, but they also tend to have limited opening hours, restrict your online time to 30 minutes, and may require reservations.

Traveling with a Laptop: With a laptop or netbook, it's easy to get online if your hotel has Wi-Fi (wireless Internet access) or a port in your room for plugging in a cable. Some hotels offer Wi-Fi for free; others charge by the minute or hour. You'll find plenty of coffee shops that offer Wi-Fi to travelers with laptop computers. A cellular modem—which lets your laptop access the Internet over a mobile phone network—provides more extensive coverage, but is much more expensive than Wi-Fi.

Mail

Get stamps at the neighborhood post office, newsstands within fancy hotels, and some mini-marts and card shops. Don't use stamps from the Republic of Ireland on postcards mailed in Northern Ireland (part of the UK), and vice versa.

You can arrange for mail delivery to your hotel (allow 10 days for a letter to arrive), but phoning and emailing are so easy that I've dispensed with mail stops altogether.

Transportation

By Car or Public Transportation?

To see all of Ireland, especially the sights with far-flung rural charm, I prefer the freedom of a rental car. Connemara, the Ring of Kerry, the Antrim Coast, County Donegal, County Wexford, and the Valley of the Boyne are really only worth it if you have wheels.

Cars are best for three or more traveling together (especially families with small kids), those packing heavy, and those scouring the countryside. Trains and buses are best for solo travelers, blitz tourists, and city-to-city travelers. Travelers who don't want (or can't afford) to drive a rental car find that they still enjoy their travels using public transportation. Ireland has a good train-and-bus system, though departures are not as frequent as the European norm. Most rail lines spoke outward from Dublin, so you'll need to mix in bus transportation to bridge the gaps. Buses pick you up when the trains let you down.

I've included a sample itinerary for drivers (with tips and tweaks for those using public transportation) to help you explore Ireland smoothly; you'll find it on page 10.

Rails, Wheels, and Wings

Schedules: The best overall source of schedules for public transportation in the Republic as well as Northern Ireland—including rail, cross-country and city buses, and Dublin's DART and LUAS transit—is the Tourism Ireland website: www.discoverireland.com (select "Plan Your Visit," then "Getting Around").

Trains: Ireland's various passes offer a better value than BritRail's pricey "BritRail plus Ireland" pass (see chart on page 450). Irish railpasses can be purchased easily and cheaply in Ireland at major stations (Dublin info tel. 01/836-6222). For a free sum-

Another One Rides the Bus

Travelers from North America are understandably hesitant when they consider driving in Ireland (although careful drivers—with the patient support of an alert navigator—usually get the hang of it by the end of the first day). If you opt for public transportation, you'll probably spend more time on Irish buses than Irish trains.

Be aware: Public transportation (especially cross-country Irish buses) will likely put your travels into slow motion. For example, driving across County Kerry from Kenmare to Dingle takes two hours. If you go by bus, the same trip takes four hours—twice as long. The trip by bus necessitates two transfers (in Killarney and Tralee, each involving a wait for the next bus), and the buses take a rural milk-run route, making multiple stops along the way.

Not every Irish coach trip will involve this kind of delay. But if you opt to go by coach, be realistic about your itinerary and study the schedules ahead of time (www.buseireann.ie).

Before you board the coach, you'll be asked to stow your bag in the large compartment beneath the passenger cabin. Try to get a window seat on the side of the coach where the luggage is unloaded, and be alert whenever the bus stops to take on or let off passengers. Otherwise, someone may—likely accidentally—take your bag. Many bags look alike; decorate yours distinctively.

mary of railpass deals and the latest prices, check my Guide to Eurail Passes at www.ricksteves.com/rail.

Most tourists don't travel enough in Ireland to make a rail or bus pass pay off. Chances are that you'll save money by buying point-to-point tickets as you go. Fares are often higher for peak travel on Fridays and Sundays. To avoid long station lines in Dublin, you can book train tickets in advance online (often with a hefty discount on the fare). Otherwise, you can book by phone with your credit card or in person at the Iarnrod Éireann Travel Centre (Mon-Fri 9:00-17:00, closed Sat-Sun, 35 Lower Abbey Street, tel. 01/703-4070).

Research options in advance by studying Irish train schedules at www.irishrail.ie (Republic of Ireland) or www.translink.co.uk (Northern Ireland) or listening to a recorded timetable at 01/805-4222.

Students are eligible for an **Irish Rail Student Travelcard** (which offers varying discounts per ride), but you have to plan a couple months ahead: Go to www.studenttravelcard.ie, print the application form, get it stamped at your university student-travel office, and mail it to Ireland (include two passport photos and €12,

Ireland Public Transportation

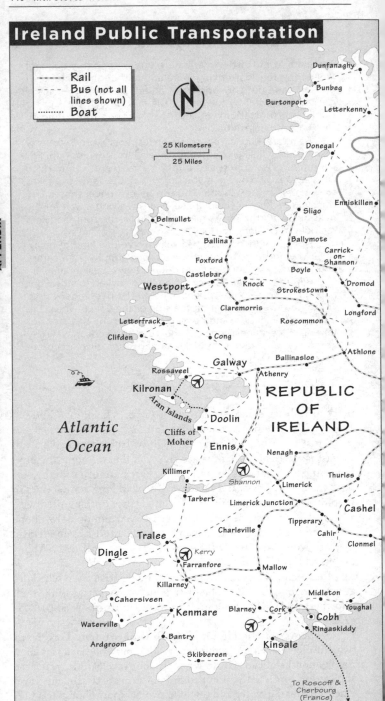

Rail
Bus (not all lines shown)
Boat

N

25 Kilometers
25 Miles

Dunfanaghy
Bunbeg
Burtonport
Letterkenny

Donegal

Enniskillen

Belmullet
Sligo

Ballina
Ballymote

Foxford
Carrick-on-Shannon

Castlebar
Boyle

Westport
Knock
Dromod

Strokestown

Claremorris
Longford

Letterfrack
Roscommon

Clifden
Cong

Galway
Ballinasloe
Athlone

Rossaveel
Athenry

Kilronan
REPUBLIC

Aran Islands
OF

Doolin
IRELAND

Cliffs of Moher

Atlantic
Ocean
Ennis
Nenagh

Killimer
Thurles

Shannon
Limerick

Tarbert
Limerick Junction
Cashel

Charleville
Tipperary

Tralee
Cahir

Dingle
Clonmel

Kerry

Farranfore
Mallow

Killarney

Midleton

Cahersiveen
Blarney
Cork
Youghal

Kenmare
Cobh

Waterville
Ringaskiddy

Bantry

Ardgroom
Kinsale

Skibbereen

To Roscoff &
Cherbourg
(France)

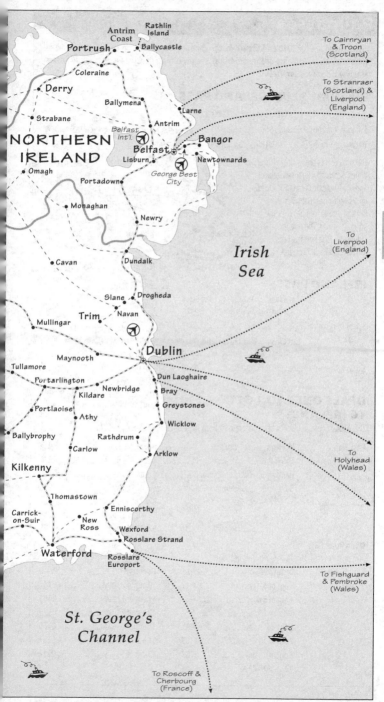

Railpasses

Prices listed are for 2010 and are subject to change. For the latest prices, details, and train schedules (and easy online ordering), see my comprehensive *Guide to Eurail Passes* at www.ricksteves.com/rail.

BRITRAIL PLUS IRELAND PASS

	1st Class	2nd Class
5 days in 1 month	$665	$469
10 days in 1 month	1,185	839

This pass covers the entire British Isles (England, Wales, Scotland, Northern Ireland, and the Republic of Ireland). Does not cover ferries. Consider the BritRail passes (online) over the 10-day version. The fare for kiddies 5–15 is half the fare. Kids under age 5 travel free.

IRELAND PASS

	1st Class Adult	1st Class Senior	1st Class Youth
5 days in 1 month	$366	$275	$311

	2nd Class Adult	2nd Class Senior	2nd Class Youth
5 days in 1 month	$293	$220	$250

Map key:
Approximate point-to-point one-way second-class fares in US dollars by rail (solid line), bus (dashed line), and ferry (dotted line). First class costs 50 percent more. Add up fares for your itinerary to see whether a rail and/or bus pass will save you money.

DEALS ONCE YOU GET TO IRELAND:

These local specials are sold at major train stations in Ireland. €1 = about $1.25 US.

Pass Name	Version	Area	Duration	Price
Irish Explorer	Rail & Bus	Republic only	8 out of 15 days	€220
	Rail only	Republic only	5 out of 15 days	€180
Irish Rover	Bus only	Republic & North	3 out of 8 days	€76
			8 out of 15 days	€172
			15 out of 30 days	€255
	Rail only	Republic & North	5 out of 15 days	€145

Open Road Pass
This pass covers buses in the Republic of Ireland.

Duration	Price	Duration	Price
3 out of 6 days	€49	10 out of 20 days	€147
4 out of 8 days	€63	11 out of 22 days	€161
5 out of 10 days	€77	12 out of 24 days	€175
6 out of 12 days	€91	13 out of 26 days	€189
7 out of 14 days	€105	14 out of 28 days	€203
8 out of 16 days	€133	15 out of 30 days	€217
9 out of 18 days	€147		

Ferry Information

INTERNATIONAL FERRY CONNECTIONS

Ireland has good ferry connections with Britain and France, thanks to various ferry companies. Check the websites listed per route below for specifics on price, frequency, and length of journey.

Republic of Ireland

Irish Port	To...	Web Site
Dublin	Liverpool (England)	www.poirishsea.com and www.steam-packet.com
Dublin	Birkenhead (near Liverpool)	www.norfolkline-ferries.co.uk
Dublin	Holyhead (Wales)	www.irishferries.com
Dun Laoghaire (near Dublin)	Holyhead (Wales)	www.stenaline.com
Rosslare	Fishguard (Wales)	www.stenaline.com
Rosslare	Pembroke (Wales)	www.irishferries.com
Rosslare	Cherbourg (France)	www.irishferries.com and www.aferry.to/celtic-link-ferries.htm
Rosslare	Roscoff (France)	www.irishferries.com
Ringaskiddy (near Cork)	Roscoff (France)	www.brittanyferries.ie

Northern Ireland

Belfast	Stranraer (Scotland)	www.stenaline.com
Belfast	Liverpool (England)	www.steam-packet.com
Belfast	Birkenhead (near Liverpool)	www.norfolkline-ferries.co.uk
Larne (near Belfast)	Troon (Scotland)	www.poirishsea.com
Larne	Cairnryan (Scotland)	www.poirishsea.com
Larne	Fleetwood (near Blackpool, England)	www.stenaline.com

payable by credit card; they'll mail you the card in 4-6 weeks).

Buses: Buses are about a third slower than trains, but they're also much cheaper. Round-trip bus tickets usually cost less than two one-way fares (e.g., Tralee to Dingle is €11 one-way and €17 round-trip). The Irish distinguish between "buses" (for in-city travel with lots of stops) and "coaches" (long-distance cross-country runs). On some Irish buses, sports games are piped throughout the bus; have earplugs handy if you prefer silence.

Some trips must be done partly by train. For instance, if you're going from Dublin to Dingle without a car, you'll need to take a train to Tralee and catch a bus from there. Similarly, to go from Dublin to Kinsale without a car, take a train to Cork and then a bus; and from Dublin to Doolin, take a train to Galway and then a bus.

If you're traveling up and down Ireland's west coast, buses are best (or a combination of buses and trains); relying on rail-only here is too time-consuming. Note that some rural coach stops are by "request only." This means the coach will drive right on by unless you flag it down by extending your arm straight out, with your palm open.

Bus stations are normally at or near train stations. The Bus Éireann Expressway Bus Timetable comes in handy (free, available at some bus stations or online at www.buseireann.ie, bus info tel. 01/836-6111).

Some companies offer **backpacker's bus circuits.** These hop-on, hop-off bus circuits take mostly youth hostelers around the country cheaply and easily, with the assumption that they'll be sleeping in hostels along the way. For example, Paddy Wagon cuts Ireland in half and offers three- to six-day "tours" of each half (north and south) that can be combined into one whole tour connecting Dublin, Cork, Killarney, Dingle, Galway, Westport, Donegal, Derry, and Belfast (May-Oct, 3 days/£139, 6 days/£289, 5 Beresford Palace, Dublin, tel. 01/823-0822, toll-free from UK tel. 0800-783-4191, www.paddywagontours.com). They also offer day tours to the Giant's Causeway, Belfast, Cliffs of Moher, Glendalough, or Kilkenny (£25-65).

Students can use their ISIC (student card, www.isic.org) to get discounts on cross-country coaches (up to 50 percent). Children 5-15 pay half-price on trains, and wee ones under age 5 go free.

Renting a Car

To rent a car in Ireland, you must be at least 21 years old and have held your license for two years. An International Driving Permit is recommended, but not required, if your driver's license has been renewed within the last year ($15 through your local AAA, plus two passport photos, www.aaa.com); I've frequently rented cars in Ireland and traveled problem-free with just my US license.

Drivers under the age of 26 may incur a young-driver surcharge (if that describes you, try STA Travel, which seeks young renters; www.statravel.com, tel. 800-781-

STOP AND LEARN THESE ROAD SIGNS

Speed Limit (km/hr) · Yield · No Passing · End of No Passing Zone

One Way · No Stopping · Roundabout Ahead · Freeway

Road Narrows · No Entry · No Entry for cars · All Vehicles Prohibited

Parking · No Parking · Customs · Peace

Driving in Ireland

m = miles
h = hours
...... = ferry

Note: Your times may vary based on traffic, construction, and sheep on road.

4040). In the Republic of Ireland, you generally can't rent a car if you're 75 or over, and you'll pay extra if you're 70-74. Some companies in Northern Ireland won't rent to anyone over 69.

Research car rentals before you go. It's cheaper to arrange most car rentals from the US. Call several companies and look online to compare rates, or arrange a rental through your home-town travel agent.

Most of the major US rental agencies (such as Alamo/National, Avis, Budget, Dollar, Hertz, and Thrifty) have offices in Ireland. It can be cheaper to use a consolidator, such as Auto Europe (www.autoeurope.com) or Europe by Car (www.ebctravel.com), but by using a middleman, you risk trading customer service for lower prices; if you have a problem with the rental company, you can't count on the consolidator to intervene on your behalf.

For the best rental deal, rent by the week with unlimited mileage. (Note that you can't lease a car in Ireland; you can only rent.) If you want to save money on gas, ask for a diesel car.

Tips on Driving

Driving gives you access to the most rural sights and is my favorite mode of transportation in Ireland. Here's what I've learned in the school of hard brakes and adrenaline rushes:

- *The Complete Road Atlas of Ireland* by Ordnance Survey (€13, handy ring-binder style, 1:210,000 scale) is the best Irish road map, and includes translations of Irish place names on the last pages. It covers every road your car can wedge onto. Flipping to the next page of an atlas is easier to manage in a cramped front seat than wrestling with a large, ungainly folding map. Buy the atlas at the first TI or gas station you come to.

- Study your map before taking off. Know the areas you'll be lacing together, as road numbers are inconsistent.

- Road signs can be confusing, too little, and too late. There are three main kinds of signs: (1) Those with white lettering on a green background are found on major routes and give distances in kilometers. (2) Signs with black lettering on a white background are older and trickier: Distances shown with a "km" following the numbers are in kilometers, while distances with nothing following the numbers are in miles (and are slowly being phased out). (3) Brown signs with white lettering alert drivers to sights, lodging, and tourist offices.

- Figure out your lights, wipers, and radio before you're on the road.

- Adjust your side-view mirrors and get in the habit of using them. Many are spring-loaded to snap back into place (a pragmatic solution on narrow roads). Get comfortable with the sound of vegetation whisking the side of your car (it rarely scratches).

- Drive with your lights on to make your vehicle more visible.

- Get used to shifting with your left hand. Find reverse...before you need it. (I love the smell of burnt clutch in the morning.)

- The most common mistake is getting a late start, which causes you to rush, which makes you miss turns, which causes you stress, which decreases your enjoyment, which makes it feel less like a vacation.

- Car travel in Ireland isn't fast. Plan your itinerary estimating an average speed of 40 mph (1 km per minute). Give your itinerary a reality check by finding distances and driving times between towns on the driving map (see the chart in this chapter) or online (www.viamichelin.com).

- The shortest distance between any two points is usually the motorway (highway). Miss a motorway exit and you can lose 30 minutes.
- Avoid driving in big cities if possible; use ring roads to skirt the congestion. Dublin is clogged with traffic—you'll find sightseeing easier on foot, by bus (particularly the hop-on, hop-off tours), or by taxi. Spare yourself the traffic stress and parking expense (€3/hr) of trying to drive in Dublin.
- When it comes to narrow rural roads, adjust your percep-tions of personal space. It's not "my side of the road" or "your side of the road." It's just "the road"—and it's shared as a cooperative adventure. Locals are usually courteous, pulling over against a hedgerow and blinking their head-lights for you to pass while they wait. Return the favor when you are closer to a wide spot in the road than they are. Pull over frequently—to let faster locals pass and to check the map.
- Watch the road ahead and expect a slow tractor, a flock of sheep, a one-lane bridge, and a baby stroller to lurk around the next turn. Honk when approaching blind corners to alert approaching drivers.
- On narrow rural roads, buses always have the right of way, so you'll need to back up to give way.
- Tune in RTE One, the national radio station (89 FM), for long drives. Its interviews and music are an education in Irish cul-ture. The same goes for BBC Ulster (94.5 FM) in Northern Ireland.
- Make your road trip fun. Establish a cardboard-box pantry of munchies. Keep a rack of liter boxes of juice in the trunk. Buy some Windex and a roll of paper towels for cleaner sightseeing.
- Don't drink and drive. The Gardí (police) set up random checkpoints. If you've had more than one pint, you're legally drunk in Ireland.
- If you're driving between the Republic and Northern Ireland, keep these basic differences in mind: In the Republic, the speed limit is in kilometers per hour, unleaded costs about €1.30 per liter ($6.15 per gallon), and the roads can be bumpy, narrow, and winding. In Northern Ireland, the speed limit is in miles per hour, unleaded costs about £1.15 per liter (about $7 per gallon), and roads are better maintained.
- Travelers who want to use designated disabled parking spaces in Ireland can bring their Disabled Persons Parking Card from the US (even though the Irish have a different card that they set on their dashboard). For more information, call the Irish Wheelchair Association at tel. 045/893-094 (from the US, dial 011-353-45-893-094).

I normally rent the least-expensive model with a stick shift. Almost all rentals are manual by default, so if you need an automatic, you must request one in advance; beware that these cars are usually larger models. Roads and parking spaces are narrow in Ireland, so you'll do yourself a favor by renting the smallest car that meets your needs and feels safe. An automatic adds about 50 percent to the car-rental cost over a manual transmission. But weigh this against the fact that in Ireland you'll be sitting on the right side of the car, and shifting with your left hand...while driving on the left side of the road. The floor pedals are in the same locations as in the US, and the gears are still found in the same basic "H" pattern as at home (i.e., first gear, second, etc.).

Expect to pay about $400 per week ($600 for an automatic), including gas and insurance, for a basic rental. The Ford 1.3-liter Escort-category car costs about $75 more per week than the smallest cars, but feels better on the motorways and safer on the small roads. Minibuses are a great budget way to go for five to nine people.

Big companies have offices in most cities (ask to be picked up at your hotel). Small local rental companies can be cheaper but aren't as flexible. Some companies such as Auto Europe (www.autoeurope.com) or Dan Dooley (www.dan-dooley.ie) will do longer-term rentals at a slight discount.

Compare pickup costs (downtown can be cheaper than the airport), and explore drop-off options. Returning a car at a big-city train station can be tricky; get precise details on the car drop-off location and hours.

If your trip covers both Ireland and Great Britain (Scotland, England, and Wales), you're better off with two separate car rentals, rather than paying for your car to ride the ferry between the two islands. On an all-Ireland trip, you can drive your rental car from the Republic of Ireland into Northern Ireland, but be aware of drop-off charges ($75-150) if you drop it off in the North. You'll pay a smaller drop-off charge ($25-50) for picking up the car at one place and dropping it off at another within the same country (even picking up in downtown Dublin and dropping off at Dublin Airport). If you pick up the car in a smaller city, you'll more likely survive your first day on the Irish roads. If you drop the car off early or keep it longer, you'll be credited or charged at a fair, pro-rated price.

When you pick up the car, check it thoroughly and make sure any damage is noted on your rental agreement. Find out how your car's lights, turn signals, wipers, and gas cap function. Ask what type of fuel your car takes before you fill up. When you return the car, make sure the agent verifies its condition with you.

Car Insurance Options

In recent years, Ireland has run neck-and-neck with Portugal for the most traffic accidents in Western Europe. When you rent a car, you're liable for a very high deductible, sometimes equal to the entire value of the car. Limit your financial risk by choosing one of these two options: Buy Collision Damage Waiver (CDW) coverage from the car-rental company, or get coverage through your credit card (free, but more complicated).

CDW includes a very high deductible (typically $1,000-1,500). Though each rental company has its own variation, basic **CDW** costs $15-25 a day (figure roughly 25 percent extra) and reduces your liability, but does not eliminate it. When you pick up the car, you'll be offered the chance to "buy down" the deductible to zero (for an additional $15-30/day; this is sometimes called "super CDW").

If you opt for **credit-card coverage** (and your credit card is one of the few accepted for this type of coverage in Ireland), there's a catch. You'll technically have to decline all coverage offered by the car-rental company, which means they can place a hold on your card (which can be up to the full value of the car). In case of damage, it can be time-consuming to resolve the charges with your credit-card company. Before you decide on this option, quiz your credit-card company about how it works.

For more on car-rental insurance, see www.ricksteves.com/cdw.

Driving in Ireland

Remember to bring your driver's license. Seat belts are mandatory for all, and kids under age four must ride in a child-safety seat. An Irish Automobile Association membership comes with most rentals (www.aaireland.ie). Understand its towing and emergency road-service benefits.

Your US credit and debit cards are unlikely to work at self-service gas pumps and automated parking garages. The easiest solution is carrying sufficient cash in euros (pounds in the North).

Driving in Ireland is basically wonderful—once you remember to stay on the left and after you've mastered the roundabouts. Don't let a roundabout spook you. After all, you routinely merge into much faster traffic on American highways back home. The traffic in a roundabout has the right-of-way; entering traffic yields (look to your right as you merge). It helps to remember that the driver is always in the center of the road.

But be warned: Every year I get a few emails from traveling readers advising me that, for them, trying to drive Ireland was a nerve-racking and regrettable mistake. If you want to get a little slack on the roads, drop by a gas station or auto shop and buy a

How to Navigate a Roundabout

NOTE:

- TRAFFIC IN ROUNDABOUTS FLOWS IN A CLOCKWISE DIRECTION.

- WHITE CARS ARE ENTERING THE ROUNDABOUT, GRAY CARS ARE EXITING

- VEHICLES ENTERING A ROUNDABOUT MUST YIELD TO VEHICLES IN THE ROUNDABOUT.

- LOOK TO YOUR RIGHT AS YOU MERGE! ☺

red *L* (new driver with license) sign to put in your back window. Wait to use it until you get away from Dublin, as Irish "Learners" are not allowed to drive on the motorways that cluster around the city.

Speed Limits: Speed limits are 50 kilometers per hour (roughly 30 miles per hour) in towns, 80 kph (approximately 50 mph) on rural roads (such as R-257, R-600, etc.), 100 kph (about 60 mph) on national roads (N-8, N-30, etc.), and 120 kph (roughly 75 mph) on motorways (M-1, M-50, etc.). Note that road-surveillance cameras strictly enforce speed limits. Any driver (including foreigners renting cars) photographed speeding will get a nasty bill in the mail. (Cameras—you'll see the foreboding gray boxes—flash on your rear license plate in order not to invade the privacy of anyone sharing the front seat with someone they shouldn't be with.)

Tolls: The M-50 ring road surrounding Dublin carries a €3 toll, paid electronically with an E-flow pass. Get details from your rental-car company at Dublin Airport (see sidebar on page 50, more details at www.eflow.ie).

Parking: Parking is confusing. One yellow line marked on the pavement means no parking Monday through Saturday during business hours. Double yellow lines mean no parking at any time. Broken yellow lines mean short stops are OK, but you should always look for explicit signs or ask a passerby.

Even in small towns, rather than fight it, I just pull into the most central "disk" or "pay-and-display" parking lot I can find. Disks can be bought at nearby shops. You buy one disk for each hour you want to stay. Scratch off the time you arrived on the disk and put it on your dashboard. I keep a bag of coins in the ashtray for meter/voucher machines (no change given for large coins). These modern pay-and-display machines are solar-powered and placed regularly along the street (about six feet tall, look for blue circle with white letter *P*). Signs along the street will state whether parking disk or pay-and-display laws are in effect for that area.

Cheap Flights

If you're visiting other countries in Europe, consider intra-European airlines.

One of the best websites for comparing inexpensive flights is www.skyscanner.net. Other comparison search engines include www.wegolo.com and www.which budget.com.

Airlines offering inexpensive flights from Ireland include Ryanair (Irish tel. 081-830-3030, www.ryanair.com), Aer Lingus (Irish tel. 081-836-5000, www.aerlingus.com), bmi (Irish tel. 01/407-3036, US tel. 800-788-0555, www.flybmi.com), and easyJet (flies in and out of Belfast only, Irish tel. 1-890-923-922, British tel. 0871-244-2366, www.easyjet.com).

Be aware of the potential drawbacks of flying on the cheap:

nonrefundable and nonchangeable tickets, minimal or nonexistent customer service, additional charges for everything (with Ryanair being the worst offender), treks to airports far outside town, and pricey baggage fees. To avoid unpleasant surprises, read the small print—especially baggage policies—before you book.

Airports and Intra-Ireland Airlines

All direct flights from the US land in either Dublin, Shannon, or Belfast. Cork has become a handy arrival point as well (via connecting flights from London). Dublin's booming population has outgrown the Dublin Airport, where construction is under way on a second terminal. If you're offered a choice and have no interest in sightseeing in Dublin, you'll find Shannon Airport to be a far less stressful entry or exit point into or out of Ireland. Drivers will especially appreciate getting used to the "other side of the road" around rural Shannon, as compared to urban Dublin. Be aware that smaller regional airports may have fewer car-rental offices.

For flights within Ireland, try Aer Arann (Irish tel. 081-821-0210, British tel. 0800-587-2324, if calling from the US dial 011-353-61-704-428, www.aerarann.com).

Resources

Resources from Rick Steves

Rick Steves' Ireland 2011 is one of many books in my series on European travel, which includes country guidebooks (such as

Rick Steves' Great Britain, which covers nearby Wales, Scotland, and England), city and regional guidebooks, Snapshot guides (excerpted chapters from my country guides), Pocket guides (full-color little books on big cities), and my budget-travel skills handbook, *Rick Steves' Europe Through the Back Door*. My phrase books—for French, Italian, German, Spanish, and Portuguese—are practical and budget-oriented. My other books include *Europe 101* (a crash course on art and history) and *Travel as a Political Act* (a travelogue sprinkled with tips for bringing home a global perspective). For a list of my books, see the inside of the last page of this book.

Video: My public television series, *Rick Steves' Europe*, covers European destinations in 100 shows, with four episodes on Ireland. To watch episodes, visit www.hulu.com/rick-steves-europe; for scripts and other details, see www.ricksteves.com/tv.

Begin Your Trip at www.ricksteves.com

At our travel website, you'll find a wealth of free information on European destinations, including fresh monthly news and helpful tips from thousands of fellow travelers. You'll also find my latest guidebook updates (www.ricksteves.com/update) and my travel blog.

Our **online Travel Store** offers travel bags and accessories specially designed by Rick Steves to help you travel smarter and lighter. These include my popular carry-on bags (roll-aboard and rucksack versions), money belts, totes, toiletries kits, adapters, other accessories, and a wide selection of guidebooks, planning maps, and DVDs.

Choosing the right **railpass** for your trip—amidst hundreds of options—can drive you nutty. We'll help you choose the best pass for your needs, plus give you a bunch of free extras.

Rick Steves' Europe Through the Back Door travel company offers **tours** with more than three dozen itineraries and about 400 departures reaching the best destinations in this book...and beyond. We offer a 14-day Ireland tour, as well as multiple tours in nearby England, Wales, and Scotland. You'll enjoy great guides, a fun bunch of travel partners (with small groups of generally about 28), and plenty of room to spread out in a big, comfy bus. You'll find European adventures to fit every vacation length. For all the details, and to get our Tour Catalog and a free Rick Steves Tour Experience DVD (filmed on location during an actual tour), visit www.ricksteves.com or call the Tour Department at 425/608-4217.

Audio: My weekly public radio show, *Travel with Rick Steves*, features interviews with travel experts from around the world. I've also produced free self-guided audio tours of the top sights and neighborhoods in London, Paris, Florence, Venice, and Rome. All of this audio content is available for free at Rick Steves Audio Europe, an extensive online library organized by destination. Choose whatever interests you, and download it for free to your iPod, smartphone, or computer at www.ricksteves.com or iTunes.

Maps

The black-and-white maps in this book, designed by my well-traveled staff, are concise and simple. The maps are intended to help you locate recommended places and get to local TIs, where you can pick up more in-depth maps of towns or regions (usually free). Better maps are sold at newsstands and bookstores. Before you buy a map, look at it to be sure it has the level of detail you want.

Train travelers do fine with a simple rail map (available as part of the free Intercity Timetable found at Irish train stations) and city maps from the TI offices. (You can get free maps of Dublin and Ireland from Tourism Ireland before you go; see "Tourist Offices" at the beginning of this chapter.) If you're driving, get a road atlas that covers all of Ireland. Ordnance Survey maps are best and available only once you reach Ireland (about €13 in TIs, gas stations, and bookstores). Drivers, hikers, and cyclists may want more detailed maps for Dingle, Connemara, Donegal, Wexford, the Antrim Coast, the Ring of Kerry, and the Valley of the Boyne (easy to buy locally at TIs).

Other Guidebooks

If you're like most travelers, this book is all you need. But if you're heading beyond my recommended destinations, $40 for extra maps and books can be money well spent.

Racks of fine guidebooks are sold at bookstores throughout Ireland and in the US, and each place you will visit has plenty of great little guidebooks to fill you in on local history. Especially for several people traveling by car, the extra weight and expense are negligible. Note that none of the following guidebooks are updated annually; check the publication date before you buy.

For cultural and sightseeing background in bigger chunks, Michelin and Cadogan guides to Ireland are good. The Lonely Planet and Let's Go books on Ireland are fine budget-travel guides—Lonely Planet's guidebook is more thorough and informative; *Let's Go Ireland* is youth-oriented, with good coverage of nightlife, hostels, and cheap transportation deals. Also consider *Culture Shock: Ireland* and *Living Abroad in Ireland*, especially if you'll be in the Emerald Isle for an extended stay.

Recommended Books and Movies

To learn more about Ireland past and present, check out a few of these books or films:

Nonfiction

For a quick overview, Richard Killeen's *A Short History of Ireland* is a well-illustrated walk through key events. *Ireland: A Concise History* (Máire and Conor Cruise O'Brien) is just that, while *How the Irish Saved Civilization* (Thomas Cahill) shows how this "island of saints and scholars" changed the course of world history. In *Traveller's History of Ireland,* Peter Neville leads readers on a tour through Ireland's complicated history.

Frank McCourt's autobiography, *Angela's Ashes,* recounts his impoverished childhood in 1930s Limerick. *Are You Somebody? The Accidental Memoir of a Dublin Woman* (Nuala O'Faolain) and *To School Through the Fields* (Alice Taylor) are well-written memoirs. Two New Yorkers move to a tiny Irish village in *O Come Ye Back to Ireland* (first in a series of four books by Niall Williams and Christine Breen). For a humorous jaunt through the Irish countryside, read *Round Ireland with a Fridge* (Tony Hawks) or *The Back of Beyond: A Search for the Soul of Ireland* (James Charles Roy).

Fiction

Ireland is the home to its share of great writers, among them masters such as James Joyce (try his *Dubliners* for a look at Irish life in the 1900s), Oscar Wilde, Jonathan Swift, W. B. Yeats, George Bernard Shaw, and Samuel Beckett. Other classic Irish authors include Brendan Behan, Oliver Goldsmith, Thomas Kinsella, and Seamus Heaney.

Edward Rutherfurd's thick, two-part *Dublin Saga* traces key events in Irish history from A.D. 430 to the fight for independence. Other historical epics include *Trinity* (Leon Uris), *The Last Prince of Ireland* (Morgan Llywelyn), and *Ireland* (Frank Delaney).

The Bódhran Makers (John B. Keane) is a heartwarming look at poor families in 1950s Ireland. Roddy Doyle's gritty novels, such as *The Barrytown Trilogy* and *A Star Called Henry,* capture the day-to-day life of working-class Dubliners. Also set in Dublin, *Finbar's Hotel* and *Ladies' Night at the Finbar's Hotel* (Dermot Bolger) were written collaboratively, with each chapter penned by a different modern Irish author. Consider also any of Maeve Binchy's soapy novels such as *Circle of Friends.*

Films

The Quiet Man (1952), starring John Wayne as a disgraced boxer, remains a sentimental favorite. David Lean's epic WWI love story *Ryan's Daughter* (1970) was filmed near Dingle. For hard-hitting drama, see *The Field* (1991, an Irish farmer fights to keep his land) or *Angela's Ashes* (1999, based on the Frank McCourt memoir). In *Evelyn* (2002), single-dad Pierce Brosnan goes to court to keep his kids, and unwed mothers struggle to survive a 1960s nunnery in *The Magdalene Sisters* (2003).

For insight into the struggle for independence from Britain, see *Michael Collins* (1996, Liam Neeson), a biopic about the Irish Free State revolutionary, and *The Wind That Shakes the Barley* (2006), told through the story of two brothers. *Odd Man Out* (1947) is a film noir about the early IRA, with a great scene filmed in Belfast's Crown Bar. The Troubles haunt a widow and her lover in *Cal* (1984). *In the Name of the Father* (1993, Daniel Day-Lewis) is a biopic of accused bomber Gerry Conlon. The families of IRA hunger strikers are the focus of *Some Mother's Son* (1996), while the documentary-like *Omagh* (2004) recounts a deadly 1998 IRA bombing. In *Fifty Dead Men Walking* (2008), an IRA informer navigates the brutal world of the Troubles.

Equally bleak but worthwhile films include *My Left Foot* (1989), which garnered an Academy Award for Daniel Day-Lewis, and *Veronica Guerin* (2003), in which Cate Blanchett fights corruption as a journalist.

For a fun, throwaway romance, try *Far and Away* (1992), with Tom Cruise and Nicole Kidman as penniless Irish immigrants. For a comedic break, watch at least one of the films adapted from books by Roddy Doyle: *The Commitments* (1991), *The Snapper* (1993), or *The Van* (1996). In *Waking Ned Devine* (1998), a deceased villager wins the lottery (it's funnier than it sounds). Children bring Irish folk tales to life in *Into the West* (1993) and *The Secret of Roan Inish* (1995). *Leap Year* (2009), with Amy Adams, was filmed on Inishmore.

Holidays and Festivals

This list includes many—but not all—major festivals, plus national holidays observed throughout Ireland. Some dates have yet to be set. Before planning a trip around a festival, make sure you verify the festival dates by checking the festival's website or contacting the Ireland TI (listed at the beginning of the appendix).

Here is a sampling of events and holidays in 2011:

Jan 1	New Year's Day (banks closed)
Jan 26-30	Temple Bar Trad—Irish Music and Culture Festival, Dublin (www.templebartrad.com)

2011

JANUARY
S	M	T	W	T	F	S
						1
2	3	4	5	6	7	8
9	10	11	12	13	14	15
16	17	18	19	20	21	22
23/30	24/31	25	26	27	28	29

FEBRUARY
S	M	T	W	T	F	S
		1	2	3	4	5
6	7	8	9	10	11	12
13	14	15	16	17	18	19
20	21	22	23	24	25	26
27	28					

MARCH
S	M	T	W	T	F	S
		1	2	3	4	5
6	7	8	9	10	11	12
13	14	15	16	17	18	19
20	21	22	23	24	25	26
27	28	29	30	31		

APRIL
S	M	T	W	T	F	S
					1	2
3	4	5	6	7	8	9
10	11	12	13	14	15	16
17	18	19	20	21	22	23
24	25	26	27	28	29	30

MAY
S	M	T	W	T	F	S
1	2	3	4	5	6	7
8	9	10	11	12	13	14
15	16	17	18	19	20	21
22	23	24	25	26	27	28
29	30	31				

JUNE
S	M	T	W	T	F	S
			1	2	3	4
5	6	7	8	9	10	11
12	13	14	15	16	17	18
19	20	21	22	23	24	25
26	27	28	29	30		

JULY
S	M	T	W	T	F	S
					1	2
3	4	5	6	7	8	9
10	11	12	13	14	15	16
17	18	19	20	21	22	23
24/31	25	26	27	28	29	30

AUGUST
S	M	T	W	T	F	S
	1	2	3	4	5	6
7	8	9	10	11	12	13
14	15	16	17	18	19	20
21	22	23	24	25	26	27
28	29	30	31			

SEPTEMBER
S	M	T	W	T	F	S
				1	2	3
4	5	6	7	8	9	10
11	12	13	14	15	16	17
18	19	20	21	22	23	24
25	26	27	28	29	30	

OCTOBER
S	M	T	W	T	F	S
						1
2	3	4	5	6	7	8
9	10	11	12	13	14	15
16	17	18	19	20	21	22
23/30	24/31	25	26	27	28	29

NOVEMBER
S	M	T	W	T	F	S
		1	2	3	4	5
6	7	8	9	10	11	12
13	14	15	16	17	18	19
20	21	22	23	24	25	26
27	28	29	30			

DECEMBER
S	M	T	W	T	F	S
				1	2	3
4	5	6	7	8	9	10
11	12	13	14	15	16	17
18	19	20	21	22	23	24
25	26	27	28	29	30	31

APPENDIX

March 17-20	St. Patrick's Day celebration throughout Ireland (parades, drunkenness, 4-day festival in Dublin, www.stpatricks day.ie)
April 2	Good Friday (banks closed)
April 24-25	Easter Sunday and Monday
April 26-May 1	Pan Celtic International Festival, Dingle (festival rotates locations every year, www.panceltic.ie)
May 2	Early May Bank Holiday, Ireland and UK (banks closed)
May 30	Spring Bank Holiday, UK only (banks closed)
June 6	June Holiday, Ireland (banks closed)
June 16-19	Bloomsday, Dublin (James Joyce festival, www.jamesjoyce.ie)

July 12	Battle of the Boyne anniversary, Northern Ireland (Protestant marches, protests)
July 11-24	Galway Arts Festival, Galway (www.galwayartsfestival.com)
July 25-31	Galway Races, Galway (www.galwayraces.com)
July 30-Aug 8	Féile an Phobail, West Belfast Irish cultural festival, Northern Ireland (www.feilebelfast.com)
Aug 1	August Bank Holiday, Ireland (banks closed)
Mid-Aug	Kenmare Fair, Kenmare (www.kenmare.com)
Second weekend in Aug	Dingle Races, Dingle (boat races)
Aug 10-12	Puck Fair, Killorglin, Kerry ("Ireland's Oldest Fair" and drink-fest, www.puckfair.ie)
Third weekend in Aug	Dingle Regatta, Dingle
Late Aug	Rose of Tralee International Festival, Tralee (http://roseoftralee.ie)
Aug 29	Late Summer Bank Holiday, UK only (banks closed)
Late Aug– early Sept	Blessing of the Boats, Dingle (maritime festival)
Mid-Sept	Galway Races, Galway (www.galwayraces.com)
Sept 22-25	Galway Oyster Festival, Galway (4 days, www.galwayoysterfest.com)
Late Oct	Galway Races, Galway (www.galwayraces.com)
Oct 14-29	Belfast Queens Festival, Belfast (www.belfastfestival.com)
Oct 31	October Bank Holiday, Ireland (banks closed)
Dec 25	Christmas holiday, Ireland and UK
Dec 26	St. Stephen's Day, Ireland (religious festival); Boxing Day, UK
Dec 31	New Year's Eve

Conversions and Climate

Numbers and Stumblers

- Some Europeans write a few of their numbers differently than we do: 1 = 1, 4 = 4, 7 = 7.
- In Europe, dates appear as day/month/year, so Christmas is 25/12/11.
- Commas are decimal points and decimals commas. A dollar and a half is 1,50, and there are 5.280 feet in a mile.
- When pointing, use your whole hand, palm down.
- When counting with fingers, start with your thumb. If you hold up your first finger to request one item, you'll probably get two.
- What Americans call the second floor of a building is the first floor in Europe.
- On escalators and moving sidewalks, Europeans keep the left "lane" open for passing. Keep to the right.

Metric Conversions (Approximate)

Both the Republic of Ireland and Northern Ireland use the metric system for everything but driving measurements. Weight and volume are typically calculated in metric: A kilogram is 2.2 pounds, and a liter is about a quart. The weight of a person is measured by "stone" (one stone equals 14 pounds). Temperatures are generally given in both Celsius and Fahrenheit.

On the road, the Republic of Ireland is still converting from miles to kilometers, and you'll likely see signs in both (especially in rural destinations). Northern Ireland uses miles and posts speed limits in miles per hour.

1 foot = 0.3 meter	1 square yard = 0.8 square meter
1 yard = 0.9 meter	1 square mile = 2.6 square kilometers
1 mile = 1.6 kilometers	1 ounce = 28 grams
1 centimeter = 0.4 inch	1 quart = 0.95 liter
1 meter = 39.4 inches	1 kilogram = 2.2 pounds
1 kilometer = 0.62 mile	32°F = 0°C

Clothing Sizes

When shopping for clothing, use these US-to-Ireland comparisons as general guidelines (but note that no conversion is perfect).

- Women's dresses and blouses: Add 4
  (US women's size 10 = Ireland size 14)
- Men's suits and jackets: US and Ireland use the same sizing
- Men's shirts: US and Ireland use the same sizing
- Women's shoes: Subtract 2½
  (US size 8 = Ireland size 5½)

- Men's shoes: Subtract about ½
  (US size 9 = Ireland size 8½)

Climate

First line, average daily high; second line, average daily low; third line, average days without rain. For more detailed weather statistics for destinations in this book (as well as the rest of the world), check www.worldclimate.com.

J	F	M	A	M	J	J	A	S	O	N	D
Dublin											
46°	47°	51°	55°	60°	65°	67°	67°	63°	57°	51°	47°
34°	35°	37°	39°	43°	48°	52°	51°	48°	43°	39°	37°
18	18	21	19	21	19	18	19	18	20	18	17

Temperature Conversion: Fahrenheit and Celsius

FOR WEATHER   FOR HEALTH

Ireland uses both Celsius and Fahrenheit to take its temperature. For a rough conversion from Celsius to Fahrenheit, double the number and add 30. For weather, remember that 28°C is 82°F—perfect. For health, 37°C is just right.

APPENDIX

Essential Packing Checklist

Whether you're traveling for five days or five weeks, here's
what you'll need to bring. Remember to pack light to enjoy
the sweet freedom of true mobility. Happy travels!

- ❏   5 shirts
- ❏   1 sweater or lightweight fleece jacket
- ❏   2 pairs pants
- ❏   1 pair shorts
- ❏   1 swimsuit (women only—men can use shorts)
- ❏   5 pairs underwear and socks
- ❏   1 pair shoes
- ❏   1 rain-proof jacket
- ❏   Tie or scarf
- ❏   Money belt
- ❏   Money—your mix of:
  - ❏   Debit card for ATM withdrawals
  - ❏   Credit card
  - ❏   Hard cash in US dollars ($20 bills)
- ❏   Documents (and back-up photocopies):
  - ❏   Passport
  - ❏   Printout of airline e-ticket
  - ❏   Driver's license
  - ❏   Student ID and hostel card
  - ❏   Railpass/car rental voucher
  - ❏   Insurance details
- ❏   Daypack
- ❏   Sealable plastic baggies
- ❏   Camera and related gear
- ❏   Empty water bottle
- ❏   Wristwatch and alarm clock
- ❏   Earplugs
- ❏   First-aid kit
- ❏   Medicine (labeled)
- ❏   Extra glasses/contacts and prescriptions
- ❏   Sunscreen and sunglasses
- ❏   Toiletries kit
- ❏   Soap
- ❏   Laundry soap
- ❏   Clothesline
- ❏   Small towel
- ❏   Sewing kit
- ❏   Travel information
- ❏   Necessary map(s)
- ❏   Address list (email and mailing addresses)
- ❏   Postcards and photos from home
- ❏   Notepad and pen
- ❏   Journal

*If you plan to carry on your luggage, note that all liquids must be in
three-ounce or smaller containers and fit within a single quart-size
baggie. For details, see www.tsa.gov/travelers.*

Hotel Reservation

To: _____   _____
               hotel   *email or fax*

From: _____   _____
               name   *email or fax*

Today's date: _____ /_____ /_____
                    day   *month*   *year*

Dear Hotel _____ ,
Please make this reservation for me:

Name: _____

Total # of people: _____   # of rooms: _____   # of nights: _____

Arriving: _____ /_____/_____   My time of arrival (24-hr clock): _____
             day *month* *year*   (I will telephone if I will be late)

Departing: ____ /____ /____
              day *month* *year*

Room(s): Single____   Double ____   Twin ____   Triple ____   Quad____

With: Toilet _____   Shower____   Bath ____   Sink only____

Special needs: View____ Quiet____ Cheapest ____ Ground Floor____

Please email or fax confirmation of my reservation, along with the type of
room reserved and the price. Please also inform me of your cancellation
policy. After I hear from you, I will quickly send my credit-card information
as a deposit to hold the room. Thank you.

_____
Name

_____
Address

_____
City   *State*   *Zip Code*   *Country*

*Before hoteliers can make your reservation, they want to know the informa-
tion listed above. You can use this form as the basis for your email, or you can
photocopy this page, fill in the information, and send it as a fax (also available
online at www.ricksteves.com/reservation).*

INDEX

INDEX

INDEX

INDEX

MAP INDEX

Audio Europe

Free mobile app (and podcast)

With the **Rick Steves Audio Europe** app, your iPhone or smartphone becomes a powerful travel tool.

This exciting app organizes Rick's entire audio library by country—giving you a playlist of all his audio walking tours, radio interviews, and travel tips for wherever you're going in Europe.

Let the experts Rick interviews enrich your understanding. Let Rick's self-guided tours amplify you guidebook. With Rick in your ear, Europe gets even better.

Thanks Facebook fans for submitting photos while on location! From top: John Kuijper in Florence, Brenda Mamer with her mother in Rome, Angel Capobianco in London, and Alyssa Passey with her friend in Paris.

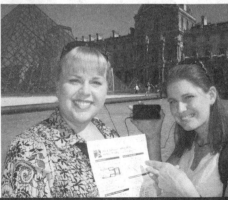

Find out more at ricksteves.com/audioeurope

Start your trip a

Free information and great gear t

▸ Plan Your Trip

Browse thousands of articles and
a wealth of money-saving tips for
planning your dream trip. You'll
find up-to-date information on
Europe's best destinations, packing
smart, getting around, finding
rooms, staying healthy, avoiding
scams and more.

▸ Eurail Passes

Find out, step-by-step, if a railpass
makes sense for your trip—and
how to avoid buying more than yo
need. Get a bunch of free extras!

▸ Graffiti Wall & Travelers' Helpline

Learn, ask, share—our online
community of savvy travelers is
a great resource for first-time
travelers to Europe, as well as
seasoned pros.

Rick Steves' Europe Through the Back Door, Inc.

Rick Steves.

www.ricksteves.com

EUROPE GUIDES

Best of Europe
Eastern Europe
Europe Through the Back Door

COUNTRY GUIDES

Croatia & Slovenia
England
France
Germany
Great Britain
Ireland
Italy
Portugal
Scandinavia
Spain
Switzerland

CITY & REGIONAL GUIDES

Amsterdam, Bruges & Brussels
Athens & the Peloponnese
Budapest
Florence & Tuscany
Istanbul
London
Paris
Prague & the Czech Republic
Provence & the French Riviera
Rome
Venice
Vienna, Salzburg & Tirol

SNAPSHOT GUIDES

Barcelona
Berlin
Bruges & Brussels
Copenhagen & the Best of
    Denmark
Dublin
Dubrovnik
Hill Towns of Central Italy
Italy's Cinque Terre
Krakow, Warsaw & Gdansk
Lisbon
Madrid & Toledo
Munich, Bavaria & Salzburg
Naples & the Amalfi Coast
Northern Ireland
Norway
Scotland
Sevilla, Granada & Southern Spain
Stockholm

TRAVEL CULTURE

Europe 101
European Christmas
Postcards from Europe
Travel as a Political Act

Rick Steves guidebooks are published by Avalon Travel,
a member of the Perseus Books Group.

NOW AVAILABLE: eBOOKS, APPS, DVDS, & BLU-RAY

eBOOKS

Most guides available as eBooks
from Amazon, Barnes & Noble,
Borders, Apple iBook and Sony
eReader, beginning January 2011

RICK STEVES' EUROPE DVDs

Austria & the Alps
Eastern Europe, Israel & Egypt
England & Wales
European Travel Skills & Specials
France
Germany, Benelux & More
Greece & Turkey
Iran
Ireland & Scotland
Italy's Cities
Italy's Countryside
Rick Steves' European Christmas
Scandinavia
Spain & Portugal

BLU-RAY

Celtic Charms
Eastern Europe Favorites
European Christmas
Italy Through the Back Door
Surprising Cities of Europe

PHRASE BOOKS & DICTIONARIES

French
French, Italian & German
German
Italian
Portuguese
Spanish

JOURNALS

Rick Steves' Pocket Travel Journal
Rick Steves' Travel Journal

APPS

Rick Steves' Ancient Rome Tour
Rick Steves' Historic Paris Walk
Rick Steves' Louvre Tour
Rick Steves' Orsay Museum Tour
Rick Steves' St. Peter's Basilica Tour
Rick Steves' Versailles

PLANNING MAPS

Britain, Ireland & London
Europe
France & Paris
Germany, Austria & Switzerland
Ireland
Italy
Spain & Portugal

Rick Steves books and DVDs are available at bookstores
and through online booksellers.

Credits

Contributor
Gene Openshaw

Gene is the co-author of seven Rick Steves books. For this book, he wrote material on Ireland's art, history, and contemporary culture. When not traveling, Gene enjoys composing music, recovering from his 1973 trip to Europe with Rick, and living everyday life with his daughter.

Acknowledgments

Thanks to Rozanne Stringer for her writing on the Celts, Celtic Tiger, St. Brendan, and Irish art. Thanks also to Mike Kelly for his help.

Images

Location	Photographer
Republic of Ireland (full page):	
Cliffs of Moher, near Galway	Pat O'Connor
Dublin: Ha' Penny Bridge	Pat O'Connor
Near Dublin: Newgrange, in	
Valley of the Boyne	Pat O'Connor
Kilkenny and Cashel: Rock of Cashel	Pat O'Connor
Waterford and County Wexford:	
Waterford's Waterfront	Pat O'Connor
Kinsale and Cobh:	
Kinsale's Summer Cove Area	Pat O'Connor
Kenmare and Ring of Kerry: Ring of Kerry	Pat O'Connor
Dingle Peninsula: Great Blasket Island	Pat O'Connor
County Clare and the Burren:	
Poulnabrone Dolmen, The Burren	Pat O'Connor
Galway: High Street	Pat O'Connor
The Aran Islands: The Aran Islands	Pat O'Connor
Connemara and County Mayo:	
Lough Corrib, Connemara	Pat O'Connor
Northern Ireland (full page):	
Giant's Causeway, Antrim Coast	Pat O'Connor
Belfast: Donegall Square and City Hall	Pat O'Connor
Portrush and Antrim Coast:	
Portrush Harbor	Pat O'Connor
Derry and County Donegal: Derry's Walls	David C. Hoerlein

Rick Steves' Guidebook Series

Country Guides

Rick Steves' Best of Europe
Rick Steves' Croatia &
  Slovenia
Rick Steves' Eastern Europe
Rick Steves' England
Rick Steves' France
Rick Steves' Germany

Rick Steves' Great Britain
Rick Steves' Ireland
Rick Steves' Italy
Rick Steves' Portugal
Rick Steves' Scandinavia
Rick Steves' Spain
Rick Steves' Switzerland

City and Regional Guides

Rick Steves' Amsterdam,
  Bruges & Brussels
Rick Steves' Athens &
  the Peloponnese
Rick Steves' Budapest
Rick Steves' Florence &
  Tuscany
Rick Steves' Istanbul
Rick Steves' London

Rick Steves' Paris
Rick Steves' Prague &
  the Czech Republic
Rick Steves' Provence &
  the French Riviera
Rick Steves' Rome
Rick Steves' Venice
Rick Steves' Vienna,
  Salzburg & Tirol

Rick Steves' Phrase Books

French
French/Italian/German
German
Italian
Portuguese
Spanish

Snapshot Guides

Excerpted chapters from country guides, such as *Rick Steves'
Snapshot Barcelona, Rick Steves' Snapshot Scotland,* and
Rick Steves' Snapshot Hill Towns of Central Italy.

Pocket Guides (new in 2011)

Condensed, pocket-size, full-color guides to Europe's top
cities: Paris, London, and Rome.

Other Books

Rick Steves' Europe 101: History and Art for the Traveler
Rick Steves' Europe Through the Back Door
Rick Steves' European Christmas
Rick Steves' Postcards from Europe
Rick Steves' Travel as a Political Act

Avalon Travel
a member of the Perseus Books Group
1700 Fourth Street
Berkeley, CA 94710

Text © 2011 by Rick Steves.
Maps © 2011 by Europe Through the Back Door.
Printed in the United States of America by Worzalla.
Second printing March 2011.

ISBN 978-1-59880-664-9
ISSN 1538-1587

For the latest on Rick's lectures, guidebooks, tours, public radio show, and public television
series, contact Europe Through the Back Door, Box 2009, Edmonds, WA 98020, tel.
425/771-8303, fax 425/771-0833, www.ricksteves.com, rick@ricksteves.com.

Europe Through the Back Door Reviewing Editors: Cameron Hewitt, Jennifer Madison
  Davis
ETBD Editors: Gretchen Strauch, Tom Griffin, Cathy Lu, Sarah McCormic
ETBD Managing Editor: Risa Laib
Avalon Travel Senior Editor and Series Manager: Madhu Prasher
Avalon Travel Project Editor: Kelly Lydick
Copy Editor: Judith Brown
Proofreader: Ellie Winters
Indexer: Stephen Callahan
Production & Typesetting: McGuire Barber Design
Cover Design: Kimberly Glyder Design
Graphic Content Director: Laura VanDeventer
Maps & Graphics: David C. Hoerlein, Brice Ticen, Laura VanDeventer, Lauren Mills,
  Barb Geisler, Mike Morgenfeld
Front Matter Color Photos: p. i and p. viii, © Pat O'Connor
Cover Photo: Great Blasket Island © Pat O'Connor
Photography: Pat O'Connor, Rick Steves, David C. Hoerlein

Foldout Color Map ▶

The foldout map on the opposite page includes:
- **A map of Ireland on one side**
- **City maps of Dublin, Galway, Belfast, Derry, and
  Dingle on the other side**